><calbizcentral®
presented by **CalChamber**

2009
California
Labor Law Digest

A Comprehensive Reference of California and Federal
Employment Laws, Regulations and Court Rulings

Published by
The California Chamber of Commerce
P.O. Box 1736
Sacramento, CA 95812-1736

ISBN 1-57997-228-4   2-Volume Set

5 4 3 2 1

The information compiled in this handbook is being provided by the California Chamber of Commerce as a service to the business community. Although every effort has been made to ensure the accuracy and completeness of this information, the California Chamber of Commerce and the contributors and reviewers of this publication cannot be responsible for any errors and omissions, nor any agency's interpretations, applications and changes of regulations described herein.

This publication is designed to provide accurate and authoritative information in a highly summarized manner with regard to the subject matter covered. It is sold with the understanding that the publisher and others associated with this publication are not engaged in rendering legal, technical or other professional service. If legal and other expert assistance is required, the services of competent professionals should be sought.

This publication is available from:

CalBizCentral, by the California Chamber of Commerce
P.O. Box 1736
Sacramento, CA 95812-1736
(916) 444-6670
http://www.calbizcentral.com

Table of Contents

Chapter 4

Chapter 5

Chapter 6

Chapter 7

Chapter 8

Chapter 9

Chapter 10

Chapter 11

Chapter 12

Chapter 13

Hours of Work and Recording
Time Worked

Chapter 14

Overtime

Chapter 15

Alternative Workweek Scheduling

Volume 2

Chapter 26

Chapter 27

Chapter 30

Chapter 31

Chapter 32

Chapter 33

Here's What's New in 2009

Following is a list of new laws, regulations, court cases, interpretations, and resources:

General

- Employment laws unique to the city and county of San Francisco are now compiled into one section. See "San Francisco Employers" in Chapter 3, page 35;

- The Family Medical Leave chapter is revised for further clarity and to reflect the federal regulations released in November of 2008 . See Chapter 21, "Family/Medical and Sick Leaves;

- With the help of Dennis A. Davis, a nationally recognized expert in the area of violence in the workplace, we have revised the Violence in the Workplace chapter to reflect the latest figures and best practices. See Chapter 25, "Violence in the Workplace; and

- With the help of David Warren Peters, a reknown ADA attorney, we have added a chapter on providing access to persons with disabilities. See Chapter 30, "Providing Access.

Hiring

- On January 1, 2009, the San Francisco minimum wage increased to $9.79 per hour. See "San Francisco Minimum Wage" in Chapter 3, page 35;

- Effective January 9, 2008, the Health Care Security Ordinance (HCSO) requires covered employers to make health-care expenditures for their covered employees and mandates the Department of Public Health (DPH) to create the Health Access Plan (HAP), now called Healthy San Francisco. See "San Francisco Health Care Security Ordinance" in Chapter 3, page 36; and

- San Francisco employers with 20 or more employees are required to provide commuter benefits to employees who work at least 10 hours per workweek within the geographic boundaries of San Francisco. See "San Francisco Commuter Benefits" in Chapter 3, page 37.

Verifying Eligibility to Work

- The Department of Homeland Security (DHS) issued a new I-9 Form reflecting the list of most up-to-date documents acceptable for purposes of employment verification; See "New I-9 Form for 2009" in Chapter 4, page 62; and

- The Department of State and Homeland Security now issues "passport cards" which may be used for employment verification as a List A document on the I-9 form. See "Passport Cards Issued" in Chapter 4, page 62.

Employee Handbooks

- Since July 1, 2008, drivers have been required to use a hands-free device while talking on a cell phone and driving. Starting January 1, 2009, text-based communication while driving is prohibited as well, with the same penalties — $20 for the first offense and $50 for subsequent offenses. See "Cell Phones and PDAs" in Chapter 6, page 121.

Privacy

- The Ninth U.S. Circuit Court of Appeals held that employees have a right to privacy over information held on third-party servers, as opposed to company owned and controlled servers. See "Privacy and Third-Party Servers" in Chapter 8, page 170; and

- The California Supreme Court confirmed that noncompetition agreements are unenforceable in California. See "Court Rules Against Agreements" in Chapter 8, page 176.

Drugs, Alcohol and Smoking In the Workplace

- The California Supreme Court held that employers have the right to enforce a drug-free policy in their workforce, even though medical marijuana use is permitted under state law. See ""Legal" Marijuana User Not Protected" in Chapter 9, page 212.

Arbitration

- Disputes under arbitration agreements requiring all disputes relating to the agreement to be arbitrated must be heard by an arbitrator, regardless of any state law requiring another form of dispute resolution. See "Arbitration Agreements and State Administrative Hearings" in Chapter 10, page 229.

Wage and Hour Law

- Wages for employees of temporary services employers must be paid weekly, or daily if an employee is assigned to a client on a day-to-day basis, or to a client engaged in a trade dispute. See "Employees of Temporary Agencies" in Chapter 11, page 243.

Wages, Salaries and Other Compensation

- Effective January 1, 2009, the standard IRS mileage rate is 55 cents per mile. See "Expense Reimbursements" in Chapter 12, page 287;

- Wages for employees of temporary services employers must be paid weekly, or daily if an employee is assigned to a client on a day-to-day basis, or to a client engaged in a trade dispute. See "Temporary Employees" in Chapter 12, page 291;

- The DLSE issued two opinion letters stating that, with some exceptions, the use of payroll debit cards and money network checks does not violate the Labor Code. See "Form of Payment of Wages" in Chapter 12, page 291; and

- The governor signed a bill amending Labor Code 206.5 which makes null and void the execution of any release on account of wages due. See "Execution of Release" in Chapter 12, page 293.

Hours of Work and Recording Time Worked

- The issue of whether employers must "ensure," or simply "provide" meal and rest breaks remains in flux. See "Meal and Rest Compliance Unresolved" in Chapter 13, page 324.

Exempt and Nonexempt

- A California company avoided costly penalties of alleged unpaid overtime and meal and rest breaks after a California Court of Appeal upheld an administrative exemption for a high-level IT position. See "Administrative Exemption Upheld" in Chapter 16, page 395.

- A licensed physician or surgeon primarily engaged in performing duties that require a license is exempt from overtime if paid $69.13 per hour or more. See "Exemption for Physicians Paid on Hourly Basis" in Chapter 16, page 398; and

- Effective January 1, 2009, Labor Code 515.5 was amended to allow payment to computer professionals as a monthly or annual salary. Additionally, the minimum hourly rate for exempt computer professionals in 2009 is $37.94 per hour. See "Computer Professional Exemption" in Chapter 16, page 399.

Family and Medical Leave

- For purposes of the FMLA, when two or more employers exercise some control over the working conditions of employees, the businesses may be joint employers, even if they are separate and distinct entities. See "Joint Employers Under the FMLA" in Chapter 21, page 528;

- There are now significant differences between the FMLA regulations and the CFRA regulations. See "New FMLA Regulations Create Additional Differences between Federal and State Law" in Chapter 21, page 529;

- Eligible employees under the FMLA, but not the CFRA, are entitled to up to 12 weeks of leave because of "any qualifying exigency" arising because the spouse, son, daughter or parent of the employee is on active duty, or has been notified of an impending call to active duty status, in support of a contingency operation. See "Qualifying Exigency" in Chapter 21, page 531;

- An employee who is the spouse, son, daughter, parent or next of kin of a covered service member is entitled to a total of 26 workweeks of leave during a 12-month period to care for the service member. If the employee does not take the entire 26 weeks of leave entitlement within the 12-month period, the remaining amount of leave available is forfeited. See "Caring for Ill or Injured Servicemember" in Chapter 21, page 531;

- An employee does not need to meet the eligibility tests again to requalify for additional leave within the 12-month period if the additional leave is requested for the same reason as the first leave. See "Employee Eligibility for Leave" in Chapter 21, page 532;

- New FMLA regulations clarify what is not "treatment," "continuing treatment" or a "serious health condition." See "Examples That Do Not Qualify for Family Leave" in Chapter 21, page 534;

- FMLA regulations require employers to notify an employee within five business days whether the employee is eligible for leave and if not, state at least one reason why. See ""Family Leave" Designation" in Chapter 21, page 535;

- For leave to care for an ill or injured servicemember, an employee may take up to 26 workweeks of family leave in a 12-month period. See "Duration and Timing of Leave" in Chapter 21, page 535;

- FMLA regulations effective January 16, 2009, specify that "others capable of providing health care services" include only podiatrists, dentists, clinical psychologists, optometrists, and chiropractor treatment consisting of manual manipulation of the spine. See "Medical Certification" in Chapter 21, page 539;

- FMLA regulations effective January 16, 2009, authorize employers to get second and third medical opinions regarding the serious health condition of a family member. See "Validity of the Certification" in Chapter 21, page 540;

- Under federal FMLA regulations effective January 16, 2009, employees on FMLA who receive pay under a disability benefit plan may not be required by the employer to use accrued benefits such as sick, vacation or paid time off (PTO) during the leave. See "Pay and Benefits" in Chapter 21, page 545;

- Under FMLA regulations effective January 16, 2009, an employee who fraudulently obtains FMLA leave from an employer is not protected by FMLA's job restoration or maintenance of health benefit provisions. See "Refusing Reinstatement Entirely" in Chapter 21, page 549;

- An employer may choose not to use a dispute-resolution mechanism contained in the CFRA to settle a question of an employee's serious health condition. See "Second and Third Opinion as Dispute Resolution" in Chapter 21, page 551;

- An employer who willfully violates the FMLA posting requirements may be fined $110 for each separate offense. See "Penalties" in Chapter 21, page 552; and

- Under FMLA regulations effective January 16, 2009, employees cannot waive prospective rights under FMLA. See "FMLA Waivers" in Chapter 21, page 552.

Workers Compensation

- Labor Code section 6409.1 was amended to change the reporting of work related injuries and illnesses. See "Workers' Comp Injury Reporting" in Chapter 26, page 723.

Employment Discrimination

- The California Department of Public Health, on or after January 1, 2009, must allow and create forms to authorize either party to a marriage to change their middle and/or last names. See "Name Change, Domestic Partnership and Marriage License" in Chapter 27, page 750;

- Employers meet the burden of providing reasonable accommodation of an employee's religion when it makes all reasonable attempts to work with the employee, but the employee's request cannot be accommodated. See "What's "Reasonable"?" in Chapter 27, page 754; and

- Employees who voluntarily use employer internal remedies before filing a complaint under the California Fair Employment and Housing Act (FEHA) do not risk missing the filing deadline with the Department of Fair Employment and Housing (DFEH). See "Employee Filing Deadlines under FEHA" in Chapter 27, page 775.

Sexual Harassment

- An employer's antiharassment policy helped protect against a lawsuit. See "Affirmative Defenses under Federal Law" in Chapter 28, page 801;

- A supervisor who "leered" at an employee's breasts consistently over a period of years, and his employer, which demoted the employee after complaining, were found liable for hostile work environment sexual harassment and retaliation. See ""Leering" Boss, Employer Liable for Hostile Environment Sexual Harassment" in Chapter 28, page 809;

- A supervisor who was not the harasser is not personally liable for not stopping known sexual harassment. See "Supervisor Not Liable for Not Stopping Harassment by Others" in Chapter 28, page 816;

- As with discrimination, supervisors cannot be held personally liable for retaliation under the FEHA. See "Supervisor Not Liable for Retaliation" in Chapter 28, page 816; and

- The 2008 case of *Steele v. Youthful Offender Parole Board* illustrates how an employer conducted an improper investigation into allegations of sexual harassment. See "Investigation – Example of Improper Investigation" in Chapter 28, page 822.

Disabilities in the Workplace

- A California Court of Appeal found that an employee must show that his or her employer knew of a protected disability — before the employer makes an adverse employment decision — to establish discrimination under the California FEHA. See "No Liability if Employer Is Unaware of Disability" in Chapter 29, page 865;

- President Bush signed HR 493 — the Genetic Information Nondiscrimination Act of 2008 — into law. See "Genetic Testing Prohibited" in Chapter 29, page 871; and

- Employers must follow progressive discipline consistently, particularly among similarly situated employees. See "Association Provision" in Chapter 29, page 876.

Labor Relations in Private Employment

- The National Labor Relations Act (NLRA) applies to a California Indian casino that employs both members and nonmembers of its tribe and derives much of its business from people outside the reservation. See "Engaged in Interstate Commerce" in Chapter 33, page 932.

CalBizCentral Resources

CalBizCentral offers several publications to help employers comply with employment laws and Cal/OSHA regulations. These include:

- *2009 Required Notices Kit;*
- *2009 HR Handbook for California Employers;*
- *2009 Employee Handbook Software;* and
- *2009 Labor Law Administration.*

We also provide several online products:

- *HRCalifornia Extra,* a free e-mail service designed to give you employment law updates as they happen. Register at ***http://www.calbizcentral.com/Store/Pages/FreeNewslettersSignup.aspx***;

- *HRCalifornia,* a comprehensive website designed to help California human resource managers deal with issues that come up every day. It's easy to navigate, great for powerful searches, and contains dozens of user-friendly, time-saving HR features. Visit us at ***www.hrcalifornia.com***; and

- Preferred and Executive Members of the California Chamber of Commerce (CalChamber) can also access our *Labor Law Helpline,* staffed by highly qualified labor law professionals with years of experience helping California employers. For more information, visit us at ***www.hrcalifornia.com***.

Forms Available Online

Throughout this book, you'll find references to many forms and checklists. As regulations can change throughout the year, accessing your forms online ensures that you will always have the most current version of each form.

Be sure to check **www.calbizcentral.com/support** occasionally for updates to forms, as well as descriptions of important mid-year regulatory changes.

Accessing Your Forms

To download all of the forms mentioned in this book:

1. Go to **www.calbizcentral.com/support**.

2. From the list of product titles, select "Labor Law Digest."

3. Enter your product security code in the input field and select "Continue."

Labor Law Digest Forms

Please enter the product code found in the back of your book in the box below and click Continue. Remember, codes are case-sensitive.

[   ] [Continue]

 You'll find the product security code on the inside covers of this book.

 To find the form you need easily after downloading, open _ViewFormsListingFirst.htm. This page provides links to all downloaded forms, as well as helpful descriptions of each.

Chapter 1

Which Laws Apply to You

This chapter is designed to help you quickly identify which employment laws affect you. Use the following chart to determine which labor laws apply to you based on the number of employees you have.

Since employee count determines which laws are applicable to you, this chapter also discusses factors used by law enforcement agencies to determine who qualifies as an employee.

Law/Requirement	All employers	2 or more	4 or more	5 or more	15 or more	20 or more	25 or more	50 or more	75 or more	100 or more
Affirmative Action								✓	✓	✓
Alcohol/Drug Rehabilitation							✓	✓	✓	✓
Americans with Disabilities Act (ADA)					✓	✓	✓	✓	✓	✓
Cal-COBRA (health insurance continuation)		✓	✓	✓	✓	✓	✓	✓	✓	✓
Child Labor	✓									
COBRA (health insurance continuation)						✓	✓	✓	✓	✓
Disability Insurance	✓									
Discrimination and Foreign Workers			✓	✓	✓	✓	✓	✓	✓	✓
Discrimination Laws (State)				✓	✓	✓	✓	✓	✓	✓
Discrimination Laws (Federal)					✓	✓	✓	✓	✓	✓
Domestic Violence							✓	✓	✓	✓
Employee Safety	✓									
Equal Employment Opportunity (EEO)Reporting*										✓
Family and Medical Leave (FMLA & CFRA)								✓	✓	✓
Fair Employment and Housing Act (FEHA)	✓									
Illiteracy							✓			
Immigration Reform and Control Act (IRCA)	✓									

Law/Requirement	All employers	2 or more	4 or more	5 or more	15 or more	20 or more	25 or more	50 or more	75 or more	100 or more
Independent Contractors	✓									
Mandatory Supervisor Sexual Harassment Training								✓	✓	✓
Military Leave (USERRA)	✓									
Military Spouse Leave							✓	✓	✓	✓
New Employee Reporting	✓									
Paid Family Leave	✓									
Posters and Notices	✓									
Pregnancy Disability Laws				✓	✓	✓	✓	✓	✓	✓
Privacy	✓									
School Activities							✓	✓	✓	✓
Sexual Harassment Training	✓									
Smoking in the Workplace	✓									
Time Off	✓									
Unemployment Insurance	✓									
Volunteer Firefighters								✓	✓	✓
Wages and Hours	✓									
WARN Act (plant closings)									✓	✓
Workers' Compensation	✓									

*EEO reporting also applies to employers subject to Title VII who have fewer than 100 employees if the company is owned or affiliated with another company, or there is centralized ownership, control or management (such as central control of personnel policies and labor relations) so that the group legally constitutes a single enterprise, and the entire enterprise employs a total of 100 or more employees.

Who is an Employee?

You can often answer the question of whether you are covered by a federal or state employment law by counting your employees. For example, a company must comply with the federal Americans with Disabilities Act (ADA) if it has 15 or more employees.

Shareholders

The United States Supreme Court said that enforcement agencies and courts could examine the relationship between a company and its shareholders to determine whether they should be considered employees.

Four doctors were shareholders and made up the board of directors of a medical practice group. A former employee sued, claiming disability discrimination in violation of the ADA. The company's first defense was that its four shareholders were not employees and therefore it did not have the 15 or more employees subjecting it to coverage by the ADA.

The Supreme Court said that an individual's right to control the business determines whether he or she is an employee. It relied on six factors created by the Equal Employment Opportunity Commission (EEOC) as among those to be considered:

- Can the organization hire or fire the individual or set the rules and regulations for his/her work?

- What is the extent to which the organization supervises his/her work?

- Does he/she report to someone higher in the organization?

- How much influence is he/she able to exert over the organization?

- What relationship is intended, as expressed in oral or written agreements?

- Does he/she share in the profits, losses, and liabilities of the organization?

While not exhaustive, the list illustrates the factors that enforcement agencies and courts may use to determine whether shareholders, directors, officers, or partners in a small business are to be treated as employees for law enforcement purposes.[1]

1.*Clackamas Gastroenterology Associates, P.C. v. Wells*, 123 S. Ct. 1673 (2003)

Posting and Notice Requirements

State and federal laws require employers to conspicuously display a variety of posters in all workplaces where they can be easily read by employees and job applicants. Additionally, employers must distribute notices or pamphlets to their employees either when they are hired or in connection with certain events. Failure to comply with these requirements can be punishable by a fine, imprisonment or both.

This chapter discusses how to comply with these requirements by indicating which posters you are required to display, how to display them, which other notices or pamphlets you are required to distribute, and when.

 Download forms referenced in this chapter at **www.calbizcentral.com/support**. Be sure to have your access code from the inside covers of this book ready to enter into the forms download area. Your access code for the forms in the online Formspack is on the inside covers of this book. See "Forms Available Online" on page xix for more information.

Posters

The chart, *Required Posters for the Workplace*, available in your online Formspack, shows postings required for California employers, including:

- Poster title and number;

- Which employers are covered by each posting law or regulation;

- The government agency (source) that makes the poster available to employers; and

- The current poster date.

Obtaining Posters

You can purchase the *2009 California and Federal Employment Poster*, consisting of the posters required for most California employers, from CalBizCentral. The posters are updated when there are changes, and can be purchasedin English or Spanish versions. Federal and state family leave posters (required for employers with 50 or more employees), a pregnancy disability poster, and a summary of additional posters, which might be required for some employers, are included with CalBizCentral's *2009 California and Federal Employment Notices Poster*. For more information, or to order an *Employer Poster*, call (800) 331-8877, or visit our online store at **www.calbizcentral.com**. Alternatively, you can obtain the individual posters by calling or writing the government agency responsible for its distribution. Some also are available for download from the agencies' Web sites.

Penalties

It is a misdemeanor, punishable by fines and/or imprisonment, if you fail to comply with posting requirements.

Special Rules and Information

In addition to providing required posters, you must comply with the following rules.

State and Federal Minimum Wage

Although you must pay the state minimum wage (because it is higher than the federal rate), you must display both the state and federal minimum wage posters.

Wage Orders

California law requires you to post your Industrial Welfare Commission (IWC) Wage Order(s) in the workplace. The law also requires you to post a *Summary* of the revisions to the Wage Orders published by the IWC.

Go to ***https://www.calbizcentral.com/HRC/LawLibrary/Posters/Pages/Default.aspx*** for more information about which Wage Order to post and to ensure that you have the most current version. If you are unsure which Wage Order applies to your business, CalChamber members can use the "Wage Order Wizard" at ***https://www.calbizcentral.com/HRC/Tools/Pages/WageOrderWizardSplash.aspx***.

The "Beck" Poster

An existingExecutive Order requires certain federal contractors and subcontractors to display a poster advising employees of their legal right to withhold part of their union dues in all places where notices to employees are customarily posted. The "Beck" poster informs nonunion employees who are required by a union contract to pay dues that they can refuse to pay any dues that do not support collective bargaining, contract administration or grievance adjustment. The requirement stems from a U.S. Supreme Court decision (*CWA v. Beck*), which held that nonunion employees are not required to pay dues to support activities such as lobbying and political events.[1]

If you entered into a contract with the federal government on or after April 18, 2001, you must display the "Beck" poster. Contracts entered into before that date are exempt from the requirement, as are contracts for less than $100,000. Even if you have no union employees, you must post the notice.

Federal contractors and subcontractors also must include a clause regarding display of the Beck poster in all federally connected subcontracts and purchase orders.

You can download the Beck poster at ***www.calbizcentral.com/HRC/LawLibrary/Posters/Pages/Default.aspx***. For more information, visit the U.S. Department of Labor's Web site at ***www.dol.gov/esa/whd/index.htm***.

1.*Communications Workers v. Beck*, 487 U.S. 735 (1988)

Unemployment/Disability Insurance

If you are subject to the unemployment insurance (UI), state disability insurance (SDI) and Paid Family Leave (PFL) benefit programs, the law requires you to post a notice informing employees of their rights under those programs (Form DE 1857A). However, some employers are subject to only one of the programs, and should not post the notice informing employees of their rights under the other programs. If you are subject to UI only, use Form DE 1857D.[2]

If you are subject to SDI only, use Form DE 1858. The *Employer Poster,* available from CalBizCentral, contains the Form DE 1857A (explaining both UI and SDI rights). Employers not subject to both programs should cover Form DE 1857A with either the DE 1857D or DE 1858.

All three forms/posters are available from the Employment Development Department (EDD).

Pamphlets and Notices

Various state and federal laws and regulations require you to distribute notices and informational pamphlets to their employees. Some notices are distributed at the time of hiring or termination, while other notice requirements are triggered by events such as disability leave.

California's EDD requires you to distribute the following pamphlets, available free of charge from EDD.

Unemployment/Disability Insurance

You must distribute the pamphlet *For Your Benefit* (DE 2320), explaining California's UI and SDI programs, when you discharge or lay off an employee or place an employee on a leave of absence. It must be distributed no later than the effective date of the discharge or layoff, or the beginning of the leave of absence.[3] Copies of this pamphlet, updated to reflect increased UI benefits as well as other changes to the UI system, are available from the state's EDD or CalBizCentral.

You must distribute the *State Disability Insurance Provisions* (DE 2515) pamphlet, explaining an employee's disability insurance rights to all new hires, within five days of hire. You must give another copy of the pamphlet to any employee who is unable to work because he/she is ill, injured or hospitalized due to causes not related to work, or is disabled due to pregnancy, childbirth or related medical conditions.[4] This pamphlet is available from the EDD or CalBizCentral.

The poster and employee pamphlet for California Paid Family Leave are available from CalBizCentral at *www.calbizcentral.com.*

Workers' Compensation

You must give all new employees a workers' compensation pamphlet to inform them of their rights and obligations regarding workers' compensation.[5] This pamphlet is an addition to the

---

2.22 CCR sec. 1089-1(b)(1)
3.22 CCR secs. 1089-1(b)(3), 1089-1(d)(1)
4.*California Employers' Guide*, Employment Development Department

required poster. Most workers' compensation carriers provide these informational pamphlets to covered workers, or you may obtain suitable pamphlets in English or Spanish for a small fee from CalBizCentral. For more information, you may also order online at **www.calbizcentral.com**.

Sexual Harassment

Every California employee must receive a sexual harassment information sheet from his/her employer.[6] This information sheet is in addition to any posting or employee handbook policy. You may design an information sheet that complies with the law, or obtain preprinted information sheets in English or Spanish from CalBizCentral at **www.calbizcentral.com** or the Department of Fair Employment and Housing (DFEH) at **www.dfeh.ca.gov**.

Discharge, Layoff and Leaves of Absence

Unemployment Insurance Code section 1089 requires you to give immediate **written notice** to an employee of his/her discharge, layoff or leave of absence. This notice must contain, at a minimum:

- The name of the employer;
- The name of the employee;
- The Social Security number of the employee;
- The type of action (discharge, layoff, leave of absence or a change in status from employee to independent contractor); and
- The date of the action.[7]

Though there is no required format for this notice, a sample is provided in your online Formspack: *Notice to Employee as to Change in Relationship* .

Health Insurance

If you have 20 or more employees, and you provide them health insurance, under certain conditions you must notify employees being terminated or voluntarily resigning of the availability of continued health insurance coverage at the state's expense.[8] This notice is in addition to any Consolidated Omnibus Budget Reconciliation Act (COBRA) notice requirements under federal law. Sample Health Insurance Premium Payment (HIPP) notices (in English and Spanish) are provided: *HIPP Notice - English* and *HIPP Notice - Spanish* .

Deferred Compensation Plans

You must provide employees to whom you offer an employer-managed deferred compensation plan with a notice regarding the plan prior to enrollment and quarterly notices thereafter.[9]

5. Lab. Code sec. 3551
6. Gov't Code sec. 12950
7. 22 CCR sec. 1089-1(d)(2)
8. Lab. Code sec. 2807
9. Lab. Code sec. 2809

The written notice that you give to the employee prior to enrollment must include the following:

- The reasonably foreseeable financial risks accompanying participation in the plan;

- Any historical information to date as to the performance of the investments or funds available under the plan; and

- An annual balance sheet, annual audit or similar document that describes the employer's financial condition as of a date no earlier than the immediately preceding year.

If you directly manage the investments of a deferred compensation plan, you must provide a written report to all employees enrolled in the plan within 30 days after the end of each calendar quarter.

This report should contain:

- A summary of your current financial condition;

- A summary of the financial performance during the preceding quarter for each investment or fund available under the plan; and

- A description of the actual performance of the employee's funds that were invested in each investment or fund in the plan.

You may delegate these obligations to a plan manager, who may contract with an investment manager for that purpose.

The law does not require any of these notices if the employee is enrolled in a deferred compensation plan that is self-directed through a financial institution.

Further Information

At the CalBizCentral Posters and Notices Web page (***www.calbizcentral.com/HRC/LawLibrary/ Posters/Pages/Default.aspx***), you may verify at any time that you have the most up-to-date employer posters that California and federal law require. This is a free Web site and does not require CalChamber membership.

The *Poster Checklist* has been included to help ensure legal compliance with all posting requirements.

Chapter 2 Forms

This chapter contains samples of forms associated with this topic. *The forms in this section are for visual reference only; download the most up-to-date forms and checklists in their entirety from CalBizCentral.*

To download either individual forms or your entire Formspack containing all the forms referenced in this book:

1. Visit **www.calbizcentral.com/support** and select "Labor Law Digest" from the list of product titles.

2. Have this copy of Labor Law Digest handy — you will need to enter the access code featured on the inside covers of this book.

3. Enter the access code, select the documents you want to download to your computer, then follow the on-screen instructions.

For more detailed instructions, see "Forms Available Online" on page xix.

Required Posters for the Workplace

The following is a chart of current required posters for California employers. You have the most current posters if you have a CalBizCentral *2007 Employer Poster*.

Required posters must be displayed at each work site and must be in an area accessible to all employees. Generally speaking, the most current version of each poster must be displayed. State and federal agencies periodically make changes to required posters. To find out about poster updates after the date of this printing go to *http://www.hrcalifornia.com/poster.*

Poster Title	Who Must Post?	Source	Version/Date
Veterans Benefits (USERRA Notice)	All employers	Federal Department of Labor www.dol.gov	January 2006
Emergency Phone Numbers	All employers	Department of Industrial Relations www.dir.ca.gov	S-500 March 1990
Pay Day Notice	All employers	Department of Industrial Relations www.dir.ca.gov	No version number No date
Safety and Health Protection on the Job	All employers	Department of Industrial Relations, Division of Occupational Safety & Health www.dir.ca.gov/dosh	No version number February 2006
Notice to Employees - Injuries Caused by Work	All employers	Department of Workers' Compensation www.dir.ca.gov/dwc	DWC Form 7 (8/1/04)
Discrimination or Harassment in Employment is Prohibited by Law	All employers	Department of Fair Employment & Housing www.dfeh.ca.gov	DFEH-162 (05/06) DFEH-162S (07/06)
California Minimum Wage*	All employers	Industrial Welfare Commission www.dir.ca.gov/IWC	MW-2007
Federal Minimum Wage*	All employers	Federal Department of Labor www.dol.gov	WH Pub 1088 Revised October 1996
Pregnancy Disability Leave (5-49 employees)	Employers of five to 49 employees	Department of Fair Employment & Housing www.dfeh.ca.gov	DFEH 100-20 (01/00)
Family Care and Medical Leave (CFRA Leave) and Pregnancy Disability Leave	Employers of 50 or more employees and all "public agencies"	Department of Fair Employment & Housing www.dfeh.ca.gov	DFEH 100-21 (01/00)
Your Rights Under the Federal Family and Medical Leave Act of 1993	Employers of 50 or more employees and all "public agencies"	Federal Department of Labor www.dol.gov	WH Pub. 1420 Revised August 2001
Equal Employment Opportunity is the Law	All employers	Equal Employment Opportunity Commission www.eeoc.gov	EEOC-P/E-1 (Revised 9/02)
Time Off for Voting	All employers. Must be posted for 10 days preceding statewide election.	California Secretary of State www.ss.ca.gov	No version number No date
Notice Employee Polygraph Protection Act	All employers	Federal Department of Labor www.dol.gov	WH Pub. 1462 June 2003

Required Posters for the Workplace (Page 1 of 2)

Required Posters for the Workplace

Poster Title	Who Must Post?	Source	Version/Date
Notice to Employees - Unemployment Insurance	Most employers	Employment Development Department www.edd.ca.gov	DE 2320 Rev. 54 (11/06)
State Disability Insurance	Most employers	Employment Development Department www.edd.ca.gov	DE 2515 Rev. 55 (8/06)
Paid Family Leave	Most employers	Employment Development Department www.edd.ca.gov	DE 2511 Rev. 4 (1/07)
Protection for Employee Whistleblowers	All employers	Office of the California Attorney General	No version number (01/1/04)
Log of Work-Related Injuries and Illnesses (Log 300)	High hazard employers of 10 or more employees.	Department of Industrial Relations, Division of Occupational Safety & Health www.dir.ca.gov/dosh	Form 300, Revised 4/2004
Wage Orders (17)	All employers must post the industry-specific. Wage Order for their business	Department of Industrial Relations www.dir.ca.gov www.hrcalifornia.com/wageorders	There are 17 Wage Orders, with various version dates, with required changes for 2007.
Log of Work-Related Injuries and Illnesses (Log 300A)	High hazard employers of 10 or more employees.	Department of Industrial Relations, Division of Occupational Safety & Health www.dir.ca.gov/dosh	Form 300A, Revised 4/2004

Other Required Postings

IWC Wage Orders — All employers must post the industry-specific Wage Order appropriate to their business. Visit *http://www.hrcalifornia.com/wageorders* to download the wage orders.

Log 300 — Not every employer must comply with Cal/OSHA's Log 300 record keeping requirements.
- Find out whether your company is required to record workplace injuries and illnesses using the Exempt Wizard at *http://www.hrcalifornia.com/log300*
- Download the Log 300 forms from *http://www.hrcalifornia.com/log300* if you are not exempt.

Other — Unique posters and notices may be required depending on certain circumstances such as heavy equipment or forklifts, chemical use and government contracts. See *http://www.calchamber.com/HRC/BusinessResources/Posters/uniquepostersandnotices.htm*

* Both the state and federal minimum wage posters must be posted, even though California's minimum wage is currently higher than the federal minimum wage.

Required Posters for the Workplace (Page 2 of 2)

CalBizCentral

Standard Industrial Classification (SIC) Codes

Agriculture, Forestries & Fisheries
01 Agricultural Products - Crops
02 Agricultural Products - Livestock
07 Agricultural Services
08 Forestry
09 Fishing, Hunting & Trapping

Mining
10 Metal Mining
11 Anthracite Mining
12 Bituminous Coal, Lignite Mining
13 Oil/Gas Extraction
14 Nonmetallic Minerals/No Fuels

Contract Construction
15 General Building Contractors
16 Heavy Construction Contractors
17 Special Trade Contractors

Manufacturing
20 Food & Kindred Products
21 Tobacco Manufacturers
22 Textile Mill Products
23 Apparel/Other Textile Products
24 Lumber/Wood Products
25 Furniture & Fixtures
26 Paper/Allied Products
27 Printing/Publishing
28 Chemicals/Allied Products
29 Petroleum/Coal Products
30 Rubber/Misc. Plastic Products
31 Leather/Leather Products
32 Stone/Clay/Glass Products
33 Primary Metal Industries
34 Fabricated Metal Products
35 Machinery, Except Electrical
36 Electric/Electronic Equipment
37 Transportation Equipment
38 Instruments/Related Products
39 Misc. Manufacturing Industries

Transportation, Communications & Public Utilities
40 Railroad Transportation
41 Local/Suburban Passenger Trains
42 Trucking & Warehousing
43 U.S. Postal Service
44 Water Transportation
45 Transportation by Air
46 Pipe Lines, Except Natural Gas
47 Transportation Services
48 Communication
49 Electric/Gas/Sanitary Services

Wholesale Trade
50 Wholesale Trade - Durable
51 Wholesale Trade - Non-durable

Retail Trade
52 Building Materials/Garden Supplies
53 General Merchandise Stores
54 Food Stores
55 Auto Dealers/Service Stations
56 Apparel/Accessory Stores
57 Furniture/Home Furnishing Stores
58 Eating/Drinking Places
59 Miscellaneous Retail

Finance, Insurance & Real Estate
60 Banking
61 Credit Agencies Except Banks
62 Security, Comm. Brokers/Services
63 Insurance Carriers
64 Insurance Agents/Brokers/Services
65 Real Estate
66 Combined Real Estate/Insurance
67 Holding/Other Investment Offices

Business Services
70 Hotels/Other Lodging Places
72 Personal Services
73 Business Services
75 Auto Repair/Service & Garages
76 Misc. Repair Services
78 Motion Pictures, except 781-Production
79 Amusement/Recreation Services

Professional Services
80 Health Services
81 Legal Services
82 Educational Services
83 Social Services
84 Museums/Art Galleries
86 Membership Organizations
87 Engineering/Accounting/ Research/Mgmt & Related Services
88 Private Households
89 Misc. Services

Public Administration
91 General Government Except Finance
92 Justice/Public Order/Safety
93 Finance/Taxes/Monetary
94 Administration/Human Resources
95 Environmental Quality/Housing
96 Administration/Economic Programs
97 National Security/International Affairs

Poster Tips

If you are using CalBizCentral's *Employer Poster*, follow these instructions before you post.

Step 1
Fill in the Blanks
Fill in the information for the "Injuries on the Job" (Workers' Compensation), "Pay Day Notice" and "Emergency" notices.

Step 2
Family Leave Posters
Your poster contains a section with three family leave posters. You must check the box next to the family leave notice(s) that apply to your organization. Which one(s) you check depends upon the number of employees you have.
• One to four employees: Check none.
• Five to forty nine employees: Check Notice A (Pregnancy and Disability Leave)
• Fifty plus employees: Check Notice B (Family Care and Medical Leave and Pregnancy Disability) and Notice C (Your Rights Under the Federal Family and Medical Leave Act of 1993).

Step 3
Display the Poster
The poster must be placed conspicuously where all employees and applicants can see it. Typical locations are the lunchroom, a predominant hallway or outside restrooms.

Step 4
Industrial Welfare Commission Wage Order
You must post one of the IWC Wage Orders based upon the "main purpose" of your business. You can obtain your Wage Orders from *http://www.calbizcentral.com/wageorders* using the Wage Order Wizard tool to help you select the correct wage order for your business.

Step 5
Unique Postings and Notices
A few employers are required to have other posters. Go to *http://www.calbizcentral.com/HRCLawLibrary/Posters/Pages/uniquepostersandnotices.aspx* to determine whether any of these postings apply to your business.

Step 6
Do You Have Employees in Other Locations?
You need additional posters for other buildings and in remote facilities if those employees do not frequent the "main" facility.

Step 7
Do You Need Posters in a Language Other Than English?
• Minimum Wage – If any of your employees speak and read only Spanish, you must post in Spanish.
• Workers' Compensation Notice of Carrier – If the primary language of any of your employees is Spanish, you must post in Spanish.
• Department of Fair Employment and Housing – If 10% or more of your employees speak a language other than English, you must post in that language.
• Federal Family/Medical Leave – If your workforce is comprised of a significant portion of workers who are not literate in English, you must provide the notice in a language in which the employees are literate.
• California Family/Medical and Pregnancy Disability – If the primary language of 10% or more of your workers is a language other than English, you must post in that language.
• In defending against a lawsuit such as a sexual harassment suit, citing a poster shows you have communicated the employee's rights and protections in his or her own language and may reduce your liability.

Step 8
Other Required Notices Available from CalBizCentral:
• *Sexual Harassment Information Sheets* – Every employer must give a "Sexual Harassment Information Sheet" to each employee (annually is a good reminder) and to each new employee. It is also good practice to provide a copy to each vendor/independent contractor associated with your company.
• *UI Pamphlets* – This is required for terminating employees.

v092306

Hiring and Training

Recruiting and training new employees is a difficult task involving some legal risk. When done improperly, employers can easily create discrimination liability and jeopardize the at-will employment relationship.

This chapter explains how to properly recruit, interview and hire a competent and trustworthy workforce; reduce your liability; protect your at-will employment relationship; and reduce your odds of hiring negligent employees.

This chapter also provides samples of the most commonly used forms in hiring, such as employment applications, background checks, at-will acknowledgement, hiring checklists, and state and federal forms.

 Download forms referenced in this chapter at **www.calbizcentral.com/support**. Be sure to have your access code from the inside covers of this book ready to enter into the forms download area. Your access code for the forms in the online Formspack is on the inside covers of this book. See "Forms Available Online" on page xix for more information.

Advertising Positions

When advertising a position, consider two important aspects of any proposed advertisement:

- Does it imply a contract that would contradict an at-will employment relationship?

- Does it comply with all state and federal discrimination laws?

Employment Types and Duration

California's Labor Code specifies that an employment relationship with no specified duration is presumed to be employment at-will.[1] This means, at least in theory, that the employer or employee may terminate the employment relationship at any time, with or without cause.

However, a number of court decisions have seriously eroded California's at-will presumption. Even where you make no written or oral contract specifying the duration of employment, various factors, including employment advertisements and applications, could create an "implied" contract.

For example, courts may find an implied contract if an employment advertisement describes a "secure position" or asks for candidates willing to make a "long-term commitment to the company." Avoid advertisements indicating your company is "like one big happy family" or "looking for someone who can grow with the company." For more information about at-will employment, see "At-Will Employment Defined" in Chapter 31, page 889.

1.Lab. Code sec. 2922

When adding to your workforce, you may also want to consider relationships other than regular, direct employment. Such arrangements may involve personnel provided by employee leasing companies or temporary agencies, or independent contractors. Create these relationships carefully; otherwise, unanticipated liabilities and penalties may arise when the worker is found to have employee status rather than the desired nonemployee status. For more information, see Chapter 5, "Alternative Employment and Independent Contractors."

Developing Your Advertisement

Always consider discrimination laws when placing a job advertisement. See Chapter 27, "Employment Discrimination for more information about discrimination laws.

The words you use in a job advertisement or internal job posting can be used against you by a member of a protected class who is not selected for the position. Since everyone is a member of some protected class, it is important to avoid using any terms that might imply a preference for or prejudice against anyone unless there is a bona fide occupational qualification (BFOQ) inherent in the job.

Using Appropriate Language

When drafting a help-wanted advertisement, avoid language indicating limitations or exclusions on the basis of race, color, national origin, religion, sex, pregnancy, age, marital status, veteran status, sexual orientation or disability. Avoid words or phrases such as "young and energetic salesman," "waitress," "repairman" and "perfect for a single person willing to travel." Replace them with "enthusiastic salesperson," "food server," "repair person" and "travel required."

 You may use terms such as "mature" or "experienced," as these do not discriminate against those protected by age discrimination laws.

Considering Bona Fide Occupational Qualifications

While *extremely rare,* courts will not find discrimination if you use otherwise prohibited language to identify a "bona fide occupational qualification." For example, an advertising agency may specify a "male model" and include only photographs of men for the purpose of finding a model for an advertisement for men's suits. Being male is a BFOQ for this job.

A California law passed in 2003 raises doubts about the validity of gender-related BFOQs. AB 196 added "gender" to the definition of sex discrimination under the California Fair Employment and Housing Act (FEHA), and in particular, provides protection for transgender employees who come to work dressed according to his/her "gender identity," so long as they meet reasonable appearance standards. Thus, being male may no longer be a BFOQ for modeling men's clothing if a female who maintains a male gender identity and dresses appropriately as a male seeks employment to model men's suits or other clothing.

Selecting Illustrations

If pictures or drawings of people will be part of an advertisement, be sure to include minorities, women and people with disabilities.

Most California employers are not required to have affirmative action programs, but for those who are, the use of illustrations depicting a diverse workforce helps increase minority applicant flow. For more information about affirmative action programs, see "Affirmative Action" in Chapter 27, page 789.

Placing Your Advertisement

Running an advertisement solely in publications geared toward one sex, religion race or any other protected class could be evidence of your intent to discriminate, unless you have an obligation to do so under an affirmative action plan. Instead, place job advertisements in general interest publications, or in a wide range of special interest publications.

In addition to newspaper classifieds, the use of Internet job boards and company Web sites significantly expands the exposure of your employment needs. Some job boards, particularly those operated by professional organizations, can focus your advertising dollars on a particular segment of job seekers.

Many companies have policies or union contracts that require an initial period of exclusive notification to the company's existing employees. Adherence to these policies or union contract provisions is important to avoid legal liability for improperly awarding a position.

Applications for Employment

Employment applications are a simple method for evaluating a potential employee's experience, skills, training and limitations. Though resumes are helpful tools, they often do not contain the range of information that may be revealed by completion of a standardized employment application, such as the two contained in this *Digest.*

You may not require individuals to pay to apply for a job. This includes any form of payment to:

- Apply orally or in writing;

- Receive, obtain, complete or submit an employment application; or

- Provide, accept or process an employment application.

A violation of this law is a misdemeanor.[2]

Employers are no longer required to file a sample copy of their employment application forms with the Division of Labor Standards Enforcement. Labor Code section 431 was repealed in SB 1809 in 2004.

Gathering Appropriate Candidate Information

The sample employment applications, *Employment Application - Long Form*, and *Employment Application - Short Form*, allow you to gather a great deal of pertinent information without creating liability for discrimination.

---

2. Lab. Code sec. 450

The *Guide for Pre-Employment Inquiries* contains 19 categories of potentially discriminatory questions, as well as examples of what is prohibited and what is acceptable. Note that this list applies to all pre-employment inquiries, whether on an application, in an interview or even during an informal lunch with an applicant.

Look carefully at any application you currently are using and compare it with the *Guide for Pre-Employment Inquiries* and the sample applications contained in this *Digest*. Does your employment application contain prohibited questions?

Employers are discouraged from asking for Social Security numbers on applications. This information is not required until you reach the point of seeking the applicant's background information or until he/she is actually hired. At either of those points, other forms can be used to obtain the SSN.

Excluding Discriminatory Questions

California's discrimination laws often are more stringent than those in other states. Avoid using applications that are drafted and printed in another state (for example, where your company is headquartered) unless you review them with extra caution for compliance with California laws.

When reviewing your application, be sure to consider the impact of federal and state disability discrimination laws, which require reasonable accommodations for all persons with disabilities. Many "generic" applications contain inquiries prohibited under these laws, such as "Do you have any health condition that may prevent you from performing the job for which you are applying?" For more detailed information, see "When Medical Exams and Inquiries Are Permitted" in Chapter 29, page 866.

Application Provisions That Protect You

The sample applications in this *Digest* contain several "damage control" provisions. For maximum legal protection, be aware that upon hiring an applicant, each of these provisions should ideally become part of independent agreements between you and your new employee.

The sample applications include the following important provisions:

- An *authorization to check all references* listed by the applicant. Since you may be liable for "negligent hiring" if you fail to check an applicant's references, this damage-control provision will help protect you from a claim that the applicant's privacy was invaded. It will also be easier to gain information from former employers if they are aware that their former employee has authorized disclosure to you. Be aware, however, that this release cannot protect you against claims of intentional misconduct or employment discrimination, such as deliberately asking a former employer for protected information, like medical history or marital status. Keep in mind, the employee's authorization for you to check references applies only to the employment application and cannot be used after hire;

- A *statement that all answers given by the applicant are true,* and any omissions or false information are grounds for rejection of the application or termination. Recent court decisions allow you to use an applicant's placement of false information on a job application as evidence in your defense against a wrongful termination lawsuit, even if you did not discover the information was false until after the employee left; and

- An initial statement that any future *employment will be on an at-will basis.* This clause helps to preserve the presumption that employment is at-will, and states that any contrary representations must be contained in a signed agreement to become binding.

Have the applicant initial each of the provisions in the application separately in a space provided in the margin. By drawing attention to these important provisions, you will make it less likely that an applicant will later be able to claim successfully that he/she was not made aware of what he/she was signing. Though not foolproof, such provisions may keep you out of court or tip the balance of evidence in your favor.

Making Notes on Applications

If you talk to an applicant at the time he/she gives you his/her completed application, you may be tempted to jot down a few things in the margins. Resist that temptation unless your notes meet the tough test of being completely legible and not open to any misinterpretation and do not touch upon any of the discriminatory categories.

Notations in the margin of an application may seem insignificant at first. However, consider the following real-life scenario: an employer made a notation on the application of a candidate for a position at the jewelry counter of a large department store. While he intended the notation to mean "no experience selling jewelry," the words "no jew" resulted in the applicant filing religious discrimination charges against the store.

If you feel you must make some notes, be sure they are brief, clear and legible. Do not use a coded rating system that could be interpreted wrongly in the future.

Retaining Applications

Retention requirements vary among each of the laws pertaining to them. See *Records Retention Requirements* outlining these requirements. A good rule of thumb is simply to keep all job applications of those who are not hired for at least two years. Keep applications from those who are hired for the duration of employment plus two years.

You are not required to keep unsolicited resumes or applications. Some employers simply send them back to the applicant along with a note explaining that there currently are no openings for the position sought. On the other hand, you may decide to keep unsolicited applications and resumes in a separate folder as a pool of potential employees who wanted to work for you strongly enough to send resumes even though they did not know of a job opening.

Federal Contractors and Internet Applicants

The federal Office of Federal Contract Compliance Programs (OFCCP) issued new regulations amending federal contractors' recordkeeping requirements for Internet-based job applications and for defining "Internet applicant." These new regulations took effect on February 6, 2006.

The definition of "Internet applicant" is important because it determines the size of applicant pools used for adverse impact analysis in connection with affirmative action programs and responsibilities. Therefore, how and when a contractor identifies a person as an "applicant" is significant. The larger the applicant pool, the greater the potential liability.

The new regulations define "Internet Applicants" as those who:

- Submit an "expression of interest" in employment, through the Internet or related technology (i.e., email, resume database, job bank, electronic scanning technology, applicant tracking systems, applicant screening services);

- Are considered by the contractor for employment in a particular position;

- Submit an expression of interest indicating that they possess the "basic qualifications" for the position; and

- Do not remove themselves from further consideration, or otherwise indicate that they are no longer interested in the position at any point in the selection process.

Defining an "Expression of Interest in Employment"

An "expression of interest," made through the Internet or related electronic data technologies, may be received in a variety of ways. The regulations contain these examples:

- A contractor posts an opening for a mechanical engineering position on its ebsite, encouraging potential applicants to complete an online profile, and also advises potential applicants that they can send a hard copy resume to the HR manager with a cover letter identifying the position oth individuals who complete the online profile and those who send a paper resume and cover letter meet this part of the definition of an Internet Applicant for this position.

- A contractor posts an opening for an Accountant II position on its ebsite encouraging interested potential applicants to complete an online profile. The contractor also receives a large number of unsolicited paper resumes in the mail each year and stores them in an internal resume database which also includes all the online profiles that individuals have completed throughout the year for various jobs (including possibly for the Accountant II position). The scan reveals individuals who have the basic qualifications for the Accountant II position. Because the contractor considers both Internet and traditional expressions of interest in the Accountant II position, both the individuals who completed a personal profile and those who sent a paper resume to the employer meet this part of the definition of an Internet Applicant for this position.

- A contractor advertises for mechanics in a local newspaper, and instructs interested candidates to mail their resumes to the employer's address. Walk-in applications are also permitted. Because the contractor considers only paper resumes and application forms for the mechanic position, no individual meets this part of the definition of an Internet Applicant for this position.

Setting "Basic Qualifications" for the Position

The "basic qualifications" for the position are either:

- Those that the contractor advertises or posts on its ebsite to potential applicants; or

- Those that the contractor establishes criteria in advance, by making and maintaining a record of basic qualifications for the position prior to considering any expression of interest.

If the contractor does not advertise, and instead uses an alternative tool (such as an external resume database) to find individuals for consideration, the qualifications must be:

- Non-comparative (for example, having three years of experience requirement would be acceptable, but requiring that the individual be one of the top five individuals in terms of experience would not);

- Objective, not dependent on the contractor's subjective judgment (e.g., a requirement of a college degree in a related field would be acceptable, but requiring a degree from a "good school" would not); and

- Relevant to the performance of the particular position.

Required Record Keeping

For internal databases, you must retain the following:

- Each resume added to the database;

- The date each resume was added to the database;

- The position for which each search of the database was made;

- The substance of search criteria used for all searches; and

- The date of all searches.

For external databases, you must retain the following:

- The position for which each search of the database was made;

- The substance of search criteria used for all searches;

- The date of all searches; and

- The resumes of job seekers who met the basic qualifications of the particular position who are considered by the contractor.

These records must be maintained regardless of whether the individual qualifies as an Internet Applicant. Because the OFCCP can review company efforts to provide equal employment opportunity, you must retain and be able to produce applications and resumes for Internet Applicants even if they do not possess minimum qualifications to be included in applicant flow and adverse impact analysis.

Contractors are required to solicit race, gender and ethnicity data from all individuals who meet the definition of Internet Applicant. Regulations do not specify when during the employment process such information must be solicited. The OFCCP encourages applicant self-identification, using tear-off sheets or similar techniques. Recording visual observation by a recruiter is permitted when the applicant appears in person and declines to self-identify.

Covered contractors can meet the regulation's requirements, and minimize their burden by the manner in which they structure and conduct internal or external database job searches. Setting "basic qualifications" clearly and narrowly as possible can reduce the number of "expressions of interest." Data management techniques that are facially neutral, and do not produce disparate impact based on race, gender or ethnicity, are effective when dealing with a large number of expressions of interest received via the Internet. These techniques can include random sampling, or limiting the number of applicants that you will consider. For more information, see "EEO-1 Reporting" in Chapter 27, page 785.

Record Retention

For contractors employing more than 150 employees and government contracts of at least $150,000, records must be retained for a period of not less than two years from the date of the making of the record or the personnel action involved, whichever occurs later. For contractors with fewer than 150 employees and government contracts of at least $150,000, the minimum record retention period is one year from the date of the making of the record or the personnel action involved, whichever occurs later.

These new regulations do not change required practices relating to traditional applicants, meaning those who are minimally qualified for the opening at issue, have made an expression of interest in the opening through non-electronic media and were considered for the opening.

Interviewing Applicants

The most important thing to keep in mind when interviewing is that any question prohibited on a job application is similarly prohibited in an interview. However, while an application is in writing and relatively easy to limit to acceptable questions, interviews are verbal and often quite different from one another. It is easy, as one question leads to another during the course of the interview, to inquire about subjects that are prohibited in the employment context.

Avoid Overpromising in Interviews

You must train managers and supervisors who participate in the interview process not to exaggerate the employment opportunity no matter how anxious they may be to recruit the applicant. For example, an interviewing supervisor who misrepresented that the applicant would earn substantially more as his employee than at the applicant's current job created a significant loss for the supervisor's employer. The applicant accepted the new job, but after several months of complaining that his earnings were lower than represented, he was fired. Unable to return to his former job or find other work matching his former income, the disappointed employee sued and was awarded over a million dollars that included future lost income plus punitive damages. Such damages are recoverable, said the court, against an employer who induces an applicant to leave secure employment by knowingly making false promises regarding the terms of his future employment.[3]

---

3. *Helmer v. Bingham Toyota Isuzu*, 129 Cal. App. 4th 1121 (Cal. App., 5th Dist., 2005)

Conducting Consistent Interviews

To ensure that the interviews you conduct do not expose you to lawsuits, create a list of acceptable questions and stick to them. You may choose to ask all of the questions on your list or only those you feel pertain to a particular job. Be sure all questions are strictly job-related, non-discriminatory and not an invasion of the applicant's privacy.

Before the interview, review your entire list and clearly mark those questions you believe are most related to the position for which you are interviewing. Then, ask each candidate only those questions you have marked. If more than one person is interviewing candidates, be sure each interviewer has the same list of questions. Instruct each interviewer not to deviate from the pre-selected questions.

Asking Appropriate Questions

Do not ask questions about marital status or children. For example, you may not ask an applicant if she is pregnant, has children or is planning to have them. If you know an applicant has children, you may not ask whether he/she has made provisions for child care. Similarly, if you would not ask a question of a man, do not ask it of a woman (for example, "If you became pregnant, how much time would you need away from work?").

Be careful when asking about hobbies or outside activities. It is discriminatory to ask about clubs, societies, lodges or organizations to which the applicant belongs that might indicate race, religion, national origin, sex, age, etc. Become familiar with the *Guide for Pre-Employment Inquiries*, which outlines discriminatory and acceptable interview topics.

Don't ask what language an applicant knows unless the job requires the applicant to speak and/ or write a particular language fluently.

Rarely is it appropriate to ask an applicant's age, although there are a few exceptions noted in the *Guide for Pre-Employment Inquiries*. If required for the job, you may ask if the applicant is over a particular age (for example, a bartender or cocktail server).

Be aware that some questions about an applicant's education may be interpreted as seeking information about age. Though it is fine to ask where an applicant went to school, asking what year he/she graduated from high school or college, or inquiring if he/she is a "recent graduate" may be deemed discriminatory.

Due to potential liability under the Americans with Disabilities Act (ADA) and California's Fair Employment and Housing Act (FEHA), it is wise to familiarize yourself with the basic requirements of those laws before interviewing. Though it may seem only natural to ask certain questions of an interviewee whose physical disability is obvious to you, you may discover that many of those questions are strictly prohibited. For more information about disability discrimination, see Chapter 29, "Disabilities In the Workplace.

Taking Notes During Interviews

It is important to ensure that you are recording interview information in a manner that will not come back to haunt you in a court of law. Take brief, clear and legible notes that pertain to the candidate's answers. Don't use abbreviations or a coded rating system that could be incorrectly interpreted at a later date.

Keep objective records of why an applicant was or was not hired to avoid any inference of discriminatory motives:

- For an alarm installer: "Did not have experience with necessary equipment" rather than "not impressed;" or

- For a retail clothing store: "Unwilling to work weekends" rather than "wasn't right for the job."

In addition, be sure your notes evaluate criteria actually necessary to perform the job. For instance, when interviewing for a telemarketer, your notes should reflect items such as "good interpersonal skills, types 75 wpm," rather than "handsome, blue suit."

Testing Applicants

You may wish to administer a variety of tests to all or selected candidates for employment. The permissible timing of such tests varies based on the attribute being tested. You must also be concerned with the validity of the tests that you administer. The tests must be job related and accurate predictors of success in the job for which the candidate is being considered. For more information see "Testing Applicants and Employees" in Chapter 8, page 159, and "When Medical Exams and Inquiries Are Permitted" in Chapter 29, page 866. Labor Code section 450 prohibits employers from charging applicants for any costs related to applying for a position. Employers must absorb the cost of all such testing.

Checking References and Background

Though no specific law exists requiring that you check a potential employee's references, courts have held employers liable for negligent hiring for certain acts of their employees, which the employer should have known might occur. For example, by initially checking the references of an employee who later assaults someone in your workplace, you could have discovered that the employee had a record of similar assaults. Your actual ignorance of the employee's record is unlikely to be a good defense, because with a few simple telephone calls, you could have become aware of the previous assaults. Even if the applicant's former employer refuses to give you any information, documenting that you have attempted to check the applicant's prior work history may fulfill your obligation to avoid negligent hiring.

View the sample *Reference Check for Employment*.

Use of credit agencies and investigative consumer reporting agencies to check the backgrounds of applicants and employees is regulated by both federal and state law. See "Investigating Applicants" in Chapter 8, page 161, for details.

Signing Waivers

If you intend to check an applicant's references, you should require the applicant to sign a waiver allowing you to investigate all information he/she submits on a job application. This *Digest* includes a basic waiver (allowing you to check past employment, personal references and education) as part of the sample employment applications. You can see a more extensive *Employee Information Release* in your online Formspack.

If relevant to the potential job (for a bank teller, accounts receivable post or other position handling large sums of cash), you may choose to include in the waiver a release to investigate the applicant's credit record. However, to investigate the applicant's credit record, you also must comply with all aspects of the Fair Credit Reporting Act (FCRA) and state law. Both require specific disclosures in a specific format, in addition to any waiver that might be on an application, before checking the applicant's credit. The requirements are discussed in detail in "Investigating Applicants" in Chapter 8, page 161.

Contacting References

When contacting references, the key to gaining the maximum relevant information about an applicant without creating liability for invasion of privacy is sticking to questions related directly to job performance. Use the *Guide for Pre-Employment Inquiries* to determine whether a question to a reference is acceptable. Inquiring about the applicant's past attendance record is fine, but questions about the type of illness that kept the employee on sick leave for three weeks is not.

Personal references generally are not helpful in the reference checking process, as they are often close friends of the applicant and therefore more than likely to give a biased report. You can improve your chances of obtaining relevant information if you request personal references with knowledge of the applicant's work performance, such as past supervisors, subordinates or clients.

Responding to Reference Requests

Many employers are concerned about the potential liabilities involved in giving out information about former employees. Within the limits shown on the *Guide for Pre-Employment Inquiries*, the law protects employers who give truthful and relevant information about former employees.

A communication indicating whether you would rehire a current or former employee is protected under California law. In all cases, make such communications in a non-malicious way to avoid liability.[4]

Additional protection is afforded by the waiver of rights contained in the sample employment applications in this *Digest* and the sample *Employee Information Release*.

Good Selection Practices

In view of the increase in negligent employment claims and the unique aspects of liability to the employer that may result from off-duty activities unrelated to the job, it is strongly advised that you examine your selection, evaluation, retention and training procedures, with the goal of exercising reasonable care in determining an applicant's fitness for employment and continuation of employment. At the same time, it is crucial to be informed about federal, state and local discrimination laws, to understand which questions may or may not be asked legally during an interview or on a job application. For further information on this subject, see the *Guide for Pre-Employment Inquiries*.

4.Civ. Code sec. 47(c)

With the background of state and federal discrimination law in mind, carefully review potential questions and consider the following checklist as a guide in lessening liability for negligent hiring, retention and training:

- Identify potential liability factors such as high stress, handling negotiable instruments, driving vehicles, working with children and access to private property;

- Identify the traits related to the potential risk for each of those factors, such as poor driving records, criminal records, credit records, etc.;

- Question the applicant about any gaps in employment. If he/she refuses to answer, ask why. You may not wish to further consider any applicant who refuses to answer;

- Contact each previous employer to verify not only dates of employment and positions held, but also information concerning such things as the employee's reliability, tendency to engage in violent conduct, if any, and any instances of insubordination, dishonesty or other potential problems. Though many employers follow a policy limiting the amount of such information given to prospective employers, carefully document the fact that you attempted to obtain the additional information but were unsuccessful, and document all information received from prior employers and references;

- Obtain a release protecting you and the persons you contact regarding references from invasion of privacy or defamation claims;

- If an applicant has a criminal history, determine the job-relatedness of the applicant's criminal background, analyzing such factors as the job and its duties, the timing, nature, number and circumstances of convictions; the relationship of the conviction to the job; and the applicant's employment background before and after the conviction to see the extent of rehabilitation. For more information, see "Criminal Records" in Chapter 8, page 151;

- Where necessary for the job, require applicants to provide certified copies of driver records, insurance, credentials, licenses, transcripts or other documents that you may require for employment; and

- Revise employment applications to advise applicants that omissions, misrepresentations, or falsifications of information will result in rejection of the applicant or termination of employment.

Many other factors necessary to lessen liability in the area of negligent retention are set forth in Chapter 31, "Disciplining and Terminating At-will Employees," which addresses elements to consider in discipline and discharge decisions. In addition, an established performance appraisal program also is important in limiting liability. Supervisors should document any noteworthy incidents concerning the employee's ability or inability to perform a job, and give special attention to personality traits that demonstrate a quick temper, frequent frustrations or violent reactions. If a trend becomes apparent with regard to behavioral patterns or propensities inconsistent with job requirements, immediate disciplinary action may be necessary up to and including discharge. Fully investigate and document any alleged incidents of serious misconduct, including interviews with potential witnesses and with the charged employee. Advise employees that such an investigation should remain confidential.

Preventing Negligence in Hiring

As discussed in Chapter 8, "Personnel Records and Privacy," employees in California have a constitutional right to privacy, and employers are restricted in inquiries into many areas of the private lives of both employees and applicants, including some which have an impact upon the job. At the same time, employers are coming under increased scrutiny for "negligently" hiring and/or retaining employees whose criminal records, history of drug or alcohol abuse, or related problems involve an unreasonable risk of harm to others. This is so particularly with employees whose work actions may affect the health and safety of both coworkers and the public, such as employees who deal regularly with customers in their homes or those operating motor vehicles.

Before the recent upswing in negligent hiring/retention cases, employers generally were held liable only for negligent and intentional acts of employees done in the course and scope of employment when such acts injured others, under the doctrine of *respondeat superior*. Under that doctrine, injured third parties generally could not recover against employers if the wrongful acts occurred outside the scope of the employee's employment or were not in furtherance of the employer's business.[5]

Under the negligent hiring/retention doctrine, however, injured third parties have, in certain situations, successfully sued employers for negligent hiring/retention of employees who engage in criminal or violent acts that occur after working hours or outside the scope of employment. Negligent hiring/retention, therefore, enables plaintiffs to recover in situations where the employer previously was protected from liability.

The origin of the doctrine making the employer liable for negligent hiring and retention arose out of the common law fellow-servant rule, which imposed the duty on employers to select employees who would not endanger fellow employees by their presence on the job. It also now includes the duty to "exercise reasonable care for the safety of members of the general public," and provides that a person conducting an activity through employees or other agents is subject to liability "(a) for harm resulting in his conduct if he is negligent or reckless; and (b) in the employment of improper persons or instrumentalities in work involving risk or harm to others."[6]

Liability is predicated on the negligence of an employer in placing persons with known propensities (or propensities that should have been discovered by reasonable investigation) in an employment position where, because of the circumstances of the employment, it should have been foreseeable that the individual posed a threat of injury to others.[7]

For example, you may be found negligent in selecting an applicant for employment when you neglect to contact the applicant's former employers, verify any necessary licenses or certificates, or check references where such investigation would have demonstrated that the applicant had a violent or criminal background, or was otherwise unfit for the job. Current law emphasizes the importance of a thorough investigation into an employee's background, especially in sensitive positions or those with public contact. Where the employer knew or should have known of, or failed to use reasonable care to discover, the employee's unfitness for a position before hiring him/her, employers generally have been held liable. Circumstances where plaintiffs have prevailed in such matters include situations where:

- A pastor sexually molested one of his adolescent parishioners, where there was evidence that he had sexually molested young males in the past;[8]

- A cab driver, apparently unhappy with the amount of the tip he received from a passenger, jumped out of the cab, beat the passenger with an iron bar, pulled off the passenger's trousers and drove off with the trousers and their contents;[9]

---

5. *See e.g., DiCosala v. Kay,* 450 A.2d 508, 513 (N.J., 1982)
6. Restatement (Second) of Agency, sec. 213 (1958)
7. *Ponticas v. K.M.S. Investments,* 331 N.W.2d 907, 910 (1983)
8. *Hughson v. United Methodist Church,* 8 Cal. App. 4th 828 (1992)
9. *Burch v. A & G Associates, Inc.,* 333 N.W.2d 140 (Mich. Ct. of App. 1983)

- A teacher, hired by a boarding school, kidnapped and assaulted several children. The teacher had admitted on his employment application that he had been arrested and charged with violating a public indecency statute and that he had a bench warrant outstanding against him. The school failed to investigate this incident and hired him anyway;[10] and

- A liquor store clerk argued with, and ultimately shot, a bottling company employee making delivery to the store. In that case, the court of appeals found that, though an employer could be liable under the doctrine of *respondeat superior* for the wrongful acts of the employee, it also could be independently liable for failing to exercise due care in selecting the employee for employment.[11]

Liabilities and Penalties

To recover damages against you for negligently hiring or retaining an employee who causes the plaintiff's injury, the plaintiff generally must establish:

- The existence of the employment relationship;

- The incompetence of the employee who caused the specific negligent act on which the legal action is based;

- The employer's actual or constructive knowledge of the employee's incompetence;

- The employer's legal duty to select fit and competent employees;

- That the employee's act or omission caused the plaintiff's injury; and

- That the employer's negligence in hiring and/or retaining the employee resulted in harm to the third party.

In addition, a plaintiff may recover punitive damages under the negligent hiring or retention theory if it is shown that the employer recklessly or intentionally hired or continued the employment of the employee who caused the injury. Under California law, you must have:

- Advance knowledge of the unfitness of the employee with a conscious disregard of the rights or safety of others;

- Authorized or ratified the wrongful conduct for which the damages are awarded; or

- Been personally guilty of repression, fraud or malice.[12]

The plaintiff must prove these factors by clear and convincing evidence, not merely by a preponderance of the evidence.[13]

Offering Employment

Though not required by law, you can avoid misunderstandings as to the job being offered and the conditions of employment by being clear as to who has the authority to make an offer of employment and/or through the use of employment offer letters. During the hiring process, ask each interviewer to make clear to applicants how the company makes offers of employment. If your

---

10. *Bennett v. United States*, 803 F.2d 1502 (9th Cir. 1986)
11. *Underwriters Insurance Company v. Purdie*, 145 Cal. App. 3d 57 (1983)
12. Civ. Code sec. 3294(b)
13. Civ. Code sec. 3294(a)

company uses employment offer letters, stipulate that an offer letter is the only way an offer can be communicated.

Offer letters should, at a minimum, contain:

- Job title;

- Exempt or nonexempt status;

- Starting salary or wage;

- Work schedule;

- Full-time or part-time classification for benefits;

- Reporting date;

- Any conditions to which the offer is subject, such as:

  - Post-offer medical exam;

  - Post-offer drug test; and

  - Reference and/or background check.

- A statement of the at-will basis of employment; and

- A deadline by which you expect an acceptance of the position by way of return of a signed copy of the offer letter.

Once an offer has been made and an applicant relies on it to give notice to his current employer, you can be held liable for losses suffered by the applicant should you subsequently withdraw the offer. Damages may include loss of earnings that would have been received at the applicant's previous job through retirement.[14]

Care should be taken in preparing an accurate offer letter. You may be responsible for promises made about the scope, compensation, security and working conditions even though the employment relationship is on an at-will basis.[15]

An incomplete description of at-will status in an offer letter resulted in litigation all the way to the state Supreme Court. The offer letter stated "As with all our company employees, your employment is at will. This means that the company has the right to terminate your employment at any time just as you have the right to terminate your employment with the company at any time." The employee tried to convince the court that because the employer's definition failed to say he could be terminated for any reason, the employer had to prove just cause for termination. Although the employer ultimately prevailed in the litigation, it was an expensive error.[16]

You may wish to prepare a separate letter for employees hired on a temporary basis that clearly describes the limited duration of their employment in terms of either a specific time or a specific assignment. Do not fail to include at-will language in this letter, or your description of the temporary assignment may be misunderstood to be a contract for a specified period of time or until the completion of the assignment.

Though not a requirement, you may wish to send a letter to applicants not hired so they know they are no longer under consideration. There is no need and it is not advisable to state a reason

14. *Toscano v. Greene Music* 124 Cal. App. 4th 685 (2004)
15. *Agosta v. Arthur Astor, et. al.* 120 Cal. App. 4th 596 (2004)
16. *Dore v. Arnold Worldwide, Inc.* 39 Cal. 4th 384 (2006)

for passing them over or describing the qualities of the person selected. A simple letter thanking them for their interest and wishing them well in their future employment is sufficient.

New Employee Orientation

Every time a new employee begins work with your company, follow a routine to get him or her off on the right track. Use the *Hiring Checklist* to assist you to do just that.

Most of the items on the checklist require little explanation. The following items are required for each new employee:

- *I9 - Employment Eligibility Verification (Employment Eligibility Verification)* (see Chapter 4, "Verifying Eligibility to Work");

- *Pamphlet: Rights to Workers' Compensation Benefits* (see Chapter 26, "Workers' Compensation");

- *Personal Chiropractor or Acupuncturist Designation Form* (see Chapter 26, "Workers' Compensation");

- *Pamphlet: State Disability Insurance Provisions (DE 2515)* (see Chapter 29, "Disabilities In the Workplace");

- *General Notice of COBRA Continuation Coverage Rights - California Employees* or *General Notice of COBRA Continuation Coverage Rights - Outside California* (see Chapter 20, "Health and Retirement Benefits");

- *Sexual Harassment Information Sheet* (see Chapter 28, "Sexual Harassment");

- *W-4 - Employees Withholding Allowance Certificate* and *DE 4 - California Employees Withholding Certificate* (state tax withholding — not required unless employee wishes different withholding arrangements for state taxes).

  Under California law only, registered domestic partners are permitted to file income tax returns jointly or separately on terms similar to those governing spouses. The earned income of registered domestic partners is recognized as community property. Registered domestic partners who file separate income tax returns each report one half of the combined income earned by both domestic partners just as spouses do, rather than their respective individual incomes for the taxable year. As a result, a registered domestic partner may wish to file a DE 4 form to have payroll tax deductions determined as a married individual; and

- *Permit to Employ and Work - Form B1-4* (for minors) (see "Work Permits" in Chapter 7, page 133.)

An individual New Employee Orientation Checklist is required by law in certain industries, such as health care, and optional in others. It is advisable to create and use such a form to record initial training of employees on such matters as:

- Safety training;

- Policies and work rules;

- Benefits availability and eligibility;

- Emergency procedures;

- Sexual harassment training;

- At-will employment acknowledgement;

- Confidentiality;

- Internet, e-mail and cell phone usage;

- Receipt of employee handbook; and

- Employer property and equipment.

Finally, federal law requires all employers to report information on newly hired employees who work in California to the Employment Development Department (EDD)'s "New Employee Registry" no later than 20 days after the start-of-work date. The start-of-work date is the first day services were performed for wages. All employees must be reported regardless of age or projected wages; even those who work less than a full day, are part-time employees, are seasonal employees or discontinue their employment before the 20th day of employment. A rehire occurs when the employment relationship ends and the returning individual is required to submit a Form W-4.

If you operate in multiple states, you may elect to report, via magnetic media, all newly hired employees to one state in which you have employees. If you choose to report via electronic or magnetic media, you must submit two monthly transmissions, not fewer than 12 nor more than 16 days apart.

The following employee information must be reported to EDD:

- First name, middle initial and last name;

- SSN;

- Home address; and

- Start-of-work date.

Include the following information about your company when you report employee information to EDD:

- Business name and address;

- California Employer Account Number;

- Federal Employer Identification Number (FEIN); and

- Contact person's name and telephone number.

You may elect to use any of the following to report information to EDD:

- Report of New Employee(s), Form DE 34;

- Copy of the employee(s) Form W-4;

- Alternate equivalent form; and

- Magnetic media.

Copies of Form DE 34 may be printed from EDD's Web site at **www.edd.ca.gov**, or call EDD at (888) 745-3886.

You must send your reports to:

    Employment Development Department
    P.O. Box 997016, MIC 23
    West Sacramento, CA 95799-7016
    Fax: (916) 653-5214

Or contact the EDD Magnetic Media Unit at (916) 651-6945.

Verifying Social Security Numbers

The Social Security Administration (SSA) created an online program called the Social Security Number Verification System (SSNVS). The only purpose of the SSNVS is to verify that Social Security numbers and names that employers have been provided match and are correct for purposes of completing W-2 forms. An employer can verify up to 10 names and Social Security numbers and receive immediate results. Additionally, an employer can upload up to 250,000 names and Social Security numbers into the SSA database and receive results the next business day.

The registration and use of the SSNVS is free, and employers can register through SSA's Business Services Online at *www.socialsecurity.gov/bso/bsowelcome.htm*. The use of SSNVS only requires Internet access, a browser with cookies enabled and Adobe Acrobat Reader.

The use of this service should be implemented and utilized in a nondiscriminatory manner. Employers should specify, through policy, what classifications of employees will be submitted to the SSNVS system. The SSA emphasizes that such verifications can only occur after an employee has been hired and that the use of SSNVS is applied to employees consistently.

If an employee's name and Social Security number do not match, provide the employee with a reasonable amount of time to correct the error, either by demonstrating that there was typographical or similar error or by providing additional documentation proving they are eligible to work. Do not allow the employee to start performing work until you have established he/she is legally eligible to work in the United States.

Handling "No Match" Letters From the Social Security Administration

On June 15, 2006, the Department of Homeland Security (DHS) issued proposed regulations describing how to react to a "no match" letter from the SSA or the DHS. Receipt of a "no-match" letter may indicate innocent clerical errors and name changes, or can expose submission of false information by an alien not authorized to work in the United States. The proposed regulations also describe procedures to avoid being charged with "knowledge" that the employee was not authorized to work in the United States. The final rule was published on October 28th, 2008. However, there is continuing litigation over the enforceability of this rule, and as of the date of this book, a preliminary injunction is still in effect.

If you have concerns about the status of these requirements, consult with legal counsel.

Employers need to be aware of some important particulars:

- No document containing the SSN or alien number referred to in the no-match letter may be used to establish employment authorization or identity or both;

- No receipt for an application for a replacement of such a document may be used to establish employment authorization, identity or both;

- A discrepancy will be considered resolved only if the employer verifies with SSA or DHS that the employee's name matches a number assigned to that name in the SSA's records, and the number is valid for work in the United States; and

- The procedure to re-verify the employee's identity and work authorization described in the proposed rule would involve the employer and employee completing a new Form I-9, using the same procedures as if the employee were newly hired.

An employer who attempts to resolve the no-match following the process specified in these regulations will likely avoid liability for hiring an unauthorized worker. The regulations provide a maximum of 63 days to resolve the discrepancy. An employer unable to verify an employee's eligibility to work within the 63 days is faced with the choice of a possible penalty for employing an illegal alien, or terminating the individual's employment and being hit with a discrimination or unlawful termination claim.

Training New Hires

The introductory period for any new employee is often challenging for both employee and supervisor. Often the attention given to the task of training at this time will set the employee on the road to success or allow the supervisor to identify and deal with bad hiring decisions. Do not refer to the introductory period of employment as a "probationary period," because the completion of a probationary period implies a commitment to employ the person as a permanent employee, which overrides the at-will nature of employment.

You may want to develop a training checklist that documents the essential functions of the job as found in your job description and use it to record the date the new employee demonstrated competence in performing each function. This assures that each employee is given the training needed to be successful, and that every employee receives the same attention to training.

Conduct periodic training to ensure that the employee's skills are maintained, and document the content and identity of employees who participated in all training and education programs. Monitor employees' work performance, and provide regular feedback regarding employees' on-the-job performance. Finally, document incidents of the employee's inability to perform the job properly and effectively, and take corrective action. See Chapter 27, "Employment Discrimination."

Mandatory Heat Illness Training

All employees working in outdoor places of employment when environmental risk factors for heat illness are present must be trained on the risks and prevention of heat illness, including how to recognize symptoms and respond when they appear.[17] The training must include:

- The environmental and personal risk factors for heat illness;

- The employer's procedures for identifying, evaluating and controlling exposures to the environmental and personal risk factors for heat illness;

- The importance of frequent consumption of small quantities of water, up to four cups per hour under extreme conditions of work and heat;

- The importance of acclimatization;

- The different types of heat illness and the common signs and symptoms of heat illness;

---

17. Title 8 CCR sec. 3395

- The importance of immediately reporting to the employer, directly or through the employee's supervisor, symptoms or signs of heat illness in themselves or observed in co-workers;

- The employer's procedures for responding to symptoms of possible heat illness, including how emergency medical services will be provided should they become necessary;

- Procedures for contacting emergency medical services and, if necessary, for transporting employees to a point where they can be reached by an emergency medical service provider; and

- How to provide clear and precise directions to the work site.

New Supervisor Training

California law mandates that employees receive two hours of sexual harassment training within six months of being hired or promoted into a supervisory position. For more information on this requirement, see "Mandatory Supervisor Training" in Chapter 28, page 804.

Additionally a 2005 Cal/OSHA regulation[18] specifies that all supervisory employees must receive training on the risks and prevention of heat illness, including how to recognize symptoms and respond when they appear. In addition to the training provided to all affected employees, see "Mandatory Heat Illness Training" on page 33, supervisors must be trained in the following before supervising employees exposed to outdoor work in the heat:

- The procedures the supervisor is to follow to implement the applicable heat exposure regulations; and

- The procedures the supervisor is to follow when an employee exhibits symptoms consistent with possible heat illness, including emergency response procedures.

Preventing Negligence in Training

Liability for negligent training may occur if you fail to train, or improperly train, an employee. Negligent training can include cases such as:

- Failing to provide an employee who is responsible for securing your facility or guarding the safety of your patrons with the proper training/education to perform the job safely and effectively; or

- Failing to provide an employee who is responsible for using a dangerous tool or instrument with the knowledge/training necessary to perform the job safely.

Examples of Negligence in Training

Examples of cases in which plaintiffs have prevailed on the theory of negligent training include situations where:

- A woman was assaulted and raped in a parking garage. Testimony showed that if security agents hired to provide security for the parking garage received proper training, the assault could have been prevented;[19]

18. Title 8 CCR sec 3395

19. *Erickson v. Curtis Investment Co.*, 432 N.W.2d 199 (Minn. Ct. App. 1988), Aff'd 447 N.W.2d 165 (Minn. 1989)

- A 16-year-old employee of a rental car agency, driving a rental car without authorization, collided with another automobile, killing two of its occupants and seriously injuring two others. The rental franchise was found negligent in hiring youngsters as employees, failing to properly train them and leaving them unsupervised and in sole control of the premises;[20] and

- Several plaintiffs were beaten and placed under arrest by police officers and the police department had a policy of issuing blackjacks without adequate supervision or training in the use of such weapons.[21]

San Francisco Employers

 San Francisco has numerous laws and ordinances the are unique to the city, and do not apply to the rest of the state.

These include:

- A higher minimum wage than California law prescribes;

- Mandatory sick leave;

- A health care ordinance; and

- Required commuter benefits.

San Francisco Minimum Wage

 Voters in San Francisco approved Proposition L in 2004, which established a city minimum wage. On January 1, 2009, the city minimum wage increased to $9.79 per hour. Every January 1, the San Francisco minimum wage increases by an amount matching the prior year's increase. These year-by-year indexes are based on increases, if any, in the Consumer Price Index (CPI) for urban wage earners in the San Francisco-Oakland-San Jose metropolitan statistical area. The city minimum wage applies to employees who work within the San Francisco's boundaries of San Francisco.

The ordinance requires a new poster that must be displayed in each workplace in English, Spanish, Chinese and any other language spoken by at least 5 percent of the workforce. The poster is updated annually by the San Francisco Office of Labor Standards Enforcement (*http://www.sfgov.org/site/olse_index.asp?id=27605*).

The ordinance further provides that a notice containing the employer's name, address and telephone number must also be given to every employee at the time of hire, which contains the employer's name, address and telephone number.

Violators, including corporate officers and executives, could face penalties through legal actions brought by the enforcing city agency, aggrieved employees or other interested parties. This includes responsibility for "leased" employees.

---

20. *O'Boyle v. Avis Rent A Car, Inc.*, 435 N.Y.S.2d 296 (1981)
21. *Hardeman v. Clark*, 593 F. Supp. 1285 (D.D.C. 1984)

San Francisco Mandatory Sick Leave

An ordinance requiring employers to provide paid sick leave for all employees who work within San Francisco County went into effect on February 6, 2007. One hour of paid sick leave must accrue for every 30 hours worked, with a 72-hour cap (40 hours for small employers with fewer than 10 employees). Part-time and temporary employees are included in the number of total employees.

Paid sick leave begins to accrue for current employees as of the effective date. Employees hired after this date will accrue paid sick leave after 90 days of employment. This leave must be available for an employee's own illness or to provide care for a sick child, parent, sibling, grandparent, grandchild, spouse registered domestic partner or other "designated person." If an employee has no spouse or registered domestic partner, the employee may designate, within 10 days from the date of hire, one person for whom the employee may use paid sick leave to provide aid or care. The assignment may be changed on an annual basis.

Employers may require reasonable notification for use of paid sick leave, but cannot require employees to find replacement workers to cover the hours they are absent from work. Employees are protected from retaliation for exercising their rights under this program.

Accrued unused paid sick leave under this ordinance carries over from year to year, subject to the applicable cap, but does not get paid out at termination. Employers with a paid time off policy that meets or exceeds the requirements of the ordinance are not required to provide additional sick leave.

Employers must post a notice published by the San Francisco Office of Labor Standards Enforcement advising employees of this benefit. The notice must be posted in English, Spanish, Chinese and any other language spoken by at least five percent of the employees in the workplace. Employers face significant penalties for noncompliance with this ordinance and the posting requirement.

San Francisco Health Care Security Ordinance

 Effective January 9, 2008, the Health Care Security Ordinance (HCSO) requires covered employers to make health-care expenditures for their covered employees and mandates the Department of Public Health (DPH) to create the Health Access Plan (HAP), now called Healthy San Francisco. Healthy San Francisco is only one option by which a covered employer can satisfy its obligation to make the required health-care expenditure (HCE). Covered employers may also purchase health insurance coverage for their covered Employees, make payments to the city for the benefit of their covered employees or make the required HCE in a variety of other manners.

In November of 2006, the Golden Gate Restaurant Association (GGRA) filed a lawsuit challenging the HCSO's "Employer Spending Requirement" (ESR). The hearing before the Ninth Circuit Court of Appeals was held on April 17, 2008, and the decision was issued on September 30, 2008.

The decision upholds the ESR, which was effective on January 9, 2008, for employers with 50 or more employees, and April 1, 2008, for-profit employers with 20-49 employees.

 This case will likely be appealed again, possibly to the U.S. Supreme Court, but the exact status of the case is unknown as of the date of publication. Nonetheless, while the case travels through the courts, the law is in effect.

Covered employers are for-profit businesses with 20 or more employees and nonprofit businesses with 50 or more employees. All employees, regardless of where they live or work, must be counted for purposes of determining employer coverage. All members of a controlled group of corporations are considered one employer.

Covered employees include individuals who have been employed by their employer for at least 90 calendar days and perform at least 10 hours of work per week within the geographic boundaries of the city and county of San Francisco.

The health-care expenditure rates for 2008 and 2009 are as follows:

* Non-profits with less than 50 employees are exempt from the spending requirement.

Employer Health Care Expenditure Rate Schedule			
Business Size	**January 9, 2008**	**April 1, 2008**	**January 1, 2009**
100+ employees	$1.76/hr		$1.85/hr
50-99 employees	$1.17/hr		$1.23/hr
20-49 employees	Not Applicable	$1.17/hr	
1-19 employees	Not Applicable		

For more information on this ordinance, visit ***http://www.healthysanfrancisco.org/***.

San Francisco Commuter Benefits

San Francisco employers with 20 or more employees are required to provide commuter benefits to employees who work at least 10 hours per workweek within the geographic boundaries of San Francisco. This includes offering employees at least one of the following transportation benefits:

• A pre-tax election of a maximum of $120 per month, consistent with current federal law;

• An employer-provided transportation pass (or reimbursement for pass not provided by the employer) equal in value to $45 (or more) per month; or

• Employer provided transportation at no cost to employees.

Additional rules and regulations will follow. Failure to comply with this program will result in an "infraction" of monetary fines against your company. Consult with legal counsel immediately if you have employees working in San Francisco so your company can prepare to comply. Read the new requirements at ***http://www.sfport.com/site/uploadedfiles/bdsupvrs/ordinances08/o0199-08.pdf***.

Further Information

Helpful guidance on recruitment and hiring is available for your managers and supervisors in the CalBizCentral publication, ***HR Handbook for California Employers***, a product geared for beginners in the field of labor law. Visit ***www.calbizcentral.com*** for more information.

Employers may verify a SSN with SSA by telephoning toll-free 1-800-772-6270, weekdays from 7 a.m. to 7 p.m. EST. See *www.ssa.gov/employer/ssnvadditional.htm* or *www.socialsecurity.gov/bso/ bsowelcome.htm.*

Chapter 3 Forms

This chapter contains samples of forms associated with this topic. *The forms in this section are for visual reference only; download the most up-to-date forms and checklists in their entirety from CalBizCentral.*

To download either individual forms or your entire Formspack containing all the forms referenced in this book:

1. Visit **www.calbizcentral.com/support** and select "Labor Law Digest" from the list of product titles.

2. Have this copy of Labor Law Digest handy — you will need to enter the access code featured on the inside covers of this book.

3. Enter the access code, select the documents you want to download to your computer, then follow the on-screen instructions.

For more detailed instructions, see "Forms Available Online" on page xix.

Hiring Checklist

Employee Name: _____ Date of Hire: _____ Company Name: _____

Need to Use?	Form Description	Date Given	Date Rec'd	Date Filed/Sent
☐	Employment Application			
☐	Credit and Background Checking Forms*			
☐	Employment Interview Checklist			
☐	Employment Offer Letter			
☐	Letter to Temporary Employees		N/A	N/A
☐	**W-4 Form: Employee Withholding**			
☐	**I-9 Form: Employment Eligibility Verification**			
☐	**Workers' Compensation Brochure, with:**		N/A	N/A
☐	Personal Chiropractor or Acupuncturist Designation Form, and	N/A		N/A
☐	Personal Physician Designation Form	N/A		N/A
	(Brochure must be provided in Spanish if employee's primary language is Spanish)			
☐	General Notice of COBRA Continuation Coverage Rights	N/A	N/A	N/A
☐	**Form DE 2511: Paid Family Leave Pamphlet**	N/A	N/A	N/A
☐	**Form DE 2515: Disability Insurance Pamphlet**	N/A	N/A	N/A
☐	**Work Permit (if employee is a minor)**			
☐	HIPAA Questionnaire	N/A	N/A	N/A
☐	**New Employee(s) Report: Form DE-34**	N/A	N/A	N/A
☐	**Sexual Harassment Information Sheet**		N/A	N/A
☐	Initial Safety Training			
☐	Emergency Information			
☐	Employee Handbook Receipt			
☐	Code of Conduct/Ethics Policy (if separate from Handbook)			
☐	Health Insurance and Benefits Information			
☐	Property Return Agreement			
☐	Form DE-4: California Employee Withholding			
☐	Independent Contractors Report - DE542			
☐	Absence Request Forms			
☐	Appropriate Exempt Analysis Worksheet		N/A	N/A
☐	List of Holidays for Current Year		N/A	N/A

* Required if you do a credit or background check.
Note: Forms in bold are legally required for all California employers.

calbizcentral™

© CalChamber Page 1 of 1

Hiring Checklist

Guide for Pre-Employment Inquiries

Category	It is discriminatory to inquire about:	Examples of acceptable inquiries:
1. **Name**	a. The fact of a change of name or the original name of an applicant whose name has been legally changed. b. Maiden name.	a. Information relative to change of name, use of an assumed name or nickname necessary to enable a check on applicant's work records.
2. **Birthplace and Residence**	a. Birthplace of applicant or spouse. b. Birthplace of applicant's parents. c. Requirement that the applicant submit birth certificate, naturalization or baptismal record (see citizenship item).	a. Applicant's place of residence. b. Length of applicant's residence in city where the employer is located.
3. **Creed and Religion**	a. Applicant's religious affiliation. b. Church, parish or religious holidays observed by applicant, and whether religious beliefs prevent applicant from working on those days.	a. None; however, an employer may state the regular work days, hours and shifts to be worked, as well as religious days on which operations are closed.
4. **Race or Color**	a. Applicant's race. b. Color of applicant's skin, eyes, hair, etc.	a. None
5. **Photographs and Finger-prints**	a. Photographs with application. b. Photographs after interview, but before hiring.	a. Statement that photograph and/or fingerprints may be required after employment.
6. **Age**	a. Date of birth or age of an applicant except when such information is needed for or to: 1. Maintain apprenticeship requirements based upon a reasonable minimum age. 2. Satisfy the provisions of either state or federal minimum age statutes. 3. Avoid interference with the operation of the terms and conditions and administration of any bona fide retirement pension employee benefit program. 4. Verify that applicant is above the minimum legal age but without asking for a birth certificate.	a. Statement that applicant's hire is subject to verification that he/she meets legal age requirements. b. If hired, can you furnish proof of age? c. Are you over 18 years of age? d. If under 18, can you submit a work permit after employment?
7. **Education**	a. Specific years of attendance or graduation. b. Who paid for educational expenses while in school. c. Whether applicant still owes on loans taken out while in school.	a. Academic, vocational or professional education and the public and private schools attended.

Guide for Pre-Employment Inquires (Page 1 of 3)

Guide for Pre-Employment Inquiries

Category	It is discriminatory to inquire about:	Examples of acceptable inquiries:
8. Citizenship	a. Any inquiry into whether applicant is or intends to become a citizen of the United States. b. Any requirement that applicants produce naturalization or alien registration prior to employment. c. Requirement of production of naturalization or alien registration prior to employment.	a. Can you, after employment, submit verification of your legal right to work in the United States?
9. National Origin and Ancestry	a. Applicant's lineage, ancestry, national origin, descent, parentage or nationality. b. Language commonly used by applicant. c. How applicant acquired the ability to read, write or speak a foreign language.	a. What language the applicant speaks, writes, reads or understands (may be asked only if language other than English is relevant to the job being applied for).
10. Language	a. Applicant's mother tongue. b. Language commonly used by applicant at applicant's home. c. How the applicant acquired ability to read, write or speak a foreign language.	a. Languages applicant speaks and/or writes fluently.
11. Relatives	a. Name and/or address of any relative of applicant.	a. Names of relatives already employed by the company or by a competitor.
12. Military Experience	a. Applicant's military experience in other than U.S. Armed Forces. b. National Guard or Reserve Units of applicant. c. Draft classification or other eligibility for military service. d. Dates and conditions of discharge.	a. Military experience of applicant in the U.S. Armed Forces, including any relevant skills acquired. b. Whether separation from military service was for any reason other than an honorable discharge. c. Whether applicant has received any notice to report for duty in the Armed Forces.
13. Organization(s)	a. Clubs, societies, lodges or organizations to which the applicant belongs, which might indicate race, religion, etc. b. Names of any service organizations of which applicant is a member.	a. Applicant's membership in any professional or trade organization, unless they indicate applicant's race, religion, ancestry, sex or age.
14. References	a. The name of the applicant's pastor or religious leader. b. Any questions of applicant's former employers or acquaintances that elicit information concerning applicant's race, sex, color, religion, national origin, physical handicap, marital status, age, sexual orientation or medical condition.	a. Names of persons willing to provide professional and/or character references for applicant. b. Names of persons who suggested applicant apply for a position with the employer. c. Request of applicant for written consent to a former employer's giving of a narrative job reference.

Guide for Pre-Employment Inquiries

Category	It is discriminatory to inquire about:	Examples of acceptable inquiries:
15. Sex and Marital Status	a. Sex of applicant. b. Marital status of applicant. c. Dependents of applicant. d. Whether applicant has made provisions for child care. e. Whether applicant is pregnant, or uses birth control. f. With whom applicant resides. g. Whether applicant lives with his/her parents. h. Applicant's maiden name. i. Name of spouse or children. j. Child support obligations.	a. The name and address of applicant's parent or guardian (for minors only, if applicable to the job). b. Name and position of any relatives already employed by the company.
16. Arrest Record	a. The number and kinds of arrests of an applicant. b. Misdemeanor convictions for possession of marijuana that are more than two years old.	a. Number and kinds of convictions for criminal offenses (must be accompanied by a statement that a conviction will not necessarily disqualify an applicant for employment).
17. Height or Weight	a. Any inquiry into height or weight of applicant, except where it is a bona fide occupational requirement.	
18. Disability or Physical or Mental Condition	a. Inquiry into applicant's general medical condition, state of health or illness, physical or mental disabilities. b. Questions regarding receipt of workers' compensation.	a. Whether applicant is able to perform the essential functions of this job (if applicant voluntarily discloses a disability, can inquire whether applicant can perform the job notwithstanding the disability or with reasonable accommodation). b. Statement that employment offer may be made contingent to applicant passing a job-related physical exam.
19. Notice in Event of Emergency	a. Name and address of *relative* to be notified in case of accident or emergency.	a. Name and address of *person* to be notified in case of accident or emergency.

Employment Application – Short Form

An Equal Opportunity Employer

Please Print

Date _____

Present Address

Last Name _____   **First Name** _____   **Middle** _____

No. & Street _____   City _____   State _____   Zip _____

Permanent Address (if different from present address)

No. & Street _____   City _____   State _____   Zip _____

Business Phone (___) ___-___   Home Phone (___) ___-___

Employment Desired

Position applying for: _____

Personal Information

Have you ever applied to or worked for _____   before? ☐ Yes ☐ No

If yes, when? _____

Do you have any friends or relatives working for _____ ? ☐ Yes ☐ No
If yes, state name(s) and relationship:

Name _____   Relationship _____

Name _____   Relationship _____

Why are you applying for work at _____ ?

If hired, would you have a reliable means of transportation to and from work? .... ☐ Yes ☐ No

Are you at least 18 years old? (If under 18, hire is subject to verification that you are of minimum legal age.) .... ☐ Yes ☐ No

If hired, can you present evidence of your U.S. citizenship or proof of your legal right to live and work in this country? .... ☐ Yes ☐ No

Are you able to perform the essential functions of the job for which you are applying, either with or without reasonable accommodation? .... ☐ Yes ☐ No
If no, describe the functions that cannot be performed.
_____

(Note: We comply with the ADA and consider reasonable accommodation measures that may be necessary for eligible applicants/employees to perform essential functions. Hire may be subject to passing a medical examination, and to skill and agility tests.)

Employment Application — Short Form
(Page 1 of 4)

Employment Application – Short Form

Have you ever been convicted of a criminal offense (felony or serious misdemeanor)? (Convictions for marijuana-related offenses that are more than two years old need not be listed.).............. ☐ Yes ☐ No
If yes, state nature of the crime(s), when and where convicted, and disposition of the case.
_____

(Note: No applicant will be denied employment solely on the grounds of conviction of a criminal offense. The nature of the offense, the date of the offense, the surrounding circumstances and the relevance of the offense to the position(s) applied for may, however, be considered.)

Education, Training, and Experience

		No. of Years Completed	Did you Graduate?	Degree or Diploma
High School	Name _____	_____	☐ Yes ☐ No	_____
	Address _____			
	City _____ State _____ Zip _____			
College/ University	Name _____	_____	☐ Yes ☐ No	_____
	Address _____			
	City _____ State _____ Zip _____			
Vocational/ Business	Name _____	_____	☐ Yes ☐ No	_____
	Address _____			
	City _____ State _____ Zip _____			
Health Care Training	Name _____	_____	☐ Yes ☐ No	_____
	Address _____			
	City _____ State _____ Zip _____			

Employment Application — Short Form
(Page 2 of 4)

Employment Application – Short Form

Employment History

List below all present and past employment starting with your most recent employer (last five years is sufficient). Account for all periods of unemployment. You must complete this section even if attaching a resume.

Name of Employer

Telephone No. (   ) -

Type of Business

Your Supervisor's Name

Address & Street

City   State   Zip -

Dates of Employment: From   To   Weekly Pay: Starting   Ending

Your Position and Duties

Reason for Leaving

May we contact this employer for a reference? .... ☐ Yes ☐ No

Name of Employer

Telephone No. (   ) -

Type of Business

Your Supervisor's Name

Address & Street

City   State   Zip -

Dates of Employment: From   To   Weekly Pay: Starting   Ending

Your Position and Duties

Reason for Leaving

May we contact this employer for a reference? .... ☐ Yes ☐ No

Note: Attach additional page(s) if necessary.

References

List below three persons not related to you who have knowledge of your work performance within the last three years.

First Name   Last Name

Telephone No. (   ) -

Address & Street

City   State   Zip -

Occupation   No. of Years Acquired

Employment Application – Short Form

References, continued

First Name   Last Name

Telephone No. (   ) -

Address & Street

City   State   Zip -

Occupation   No. of Years Acquired

First Name   Last Name

Telephone No. (   ) -

Address & Street

City   State   Zip -

Occupation   No. of Years Acquired

Please Read Carefully, Initial Each Paragraph and Sign Below

Initials ___ I hereby certify that I have not knowingly withheld any information that might adversely affect my chances for employment and that the answers given by me are true and correct to the best of my knowledge. I further certify that I, the undersigned applicant, have personally completed this application. I understand that any omission or misstatement of material fact on this application or on any document used to secure employment shall be grounds for rejection of this application or for immediate discharge if I am employed, regardless of the time elapsed before discovery.

Initials ___ I hereby authorize _____ to thoroughly investigate my references, work record, education and other matters related to my suitability for employment and, further, authorize the references I have listed to disclose to the company any and all letters, reports and other information related to my work records, without giving me prior notice of such disclosure. In addition, I hereby release the Company, my former employers and all other persons, corporations, partnerships and associations from any and all claims, demands or liabilities arising out of or in any way related to such investigation or disclosure.

Initials ___ I understand that nothing contained in the application, or conveyed during any interview which may be granted or during my employment, if hired, is intended to create an employment contract between me and the Company. In addition, I understand and agree that if I am employed, my employment is for no definite or determinable period and may be terminated at any time, with or without prior notice, at the option of either myself or the Company, and that no promises or representations contrary to the foregoing are binding on the company unless made in writing and signed by me and the Company's designated representative.

☐ Should a search of public records (including records documenting an arrest, indictment, conviction, civil judicial action, tax lien or outstanding judgment) be conducted by internal personnel employed by the Company, I am entitled to copies of any such public records obtained by the Company unless I mark the check box below. If I am not hired as a result of such information, I am entitled to a copy of any such records even though I have checked the box below.

☐ I waive receipt of a copy of any public record described in the paragraph above.

Date _____   Applicant's Signature _____

Employment Application – Long Form

An Equal Opportunity Employer

Please Print

Date _____

Present Address

Last Name	First Name	Middle

No. & Street _____ City _____ State _____ Zip _____

Permanent Address (if different from present address)

No. & Street _____ City _____ State _____ Zip _____

Business Phone (___) ___ - ___   Home Phone (___) ___ - ___

Employment Desired

Position applying for: _____

Are you applying for:

Regular full-time work? .... ☐ Yes ☐ No
Regular part-time work? .... ☐ Yes ☐ No
Temporary work, e.g., summer or holiday work? .... ☐ Yes ☐ No

What days and hours are you available for work? _____

If applying for temporary work, during what period of time will you be available?

From: _____ To: _____

Are you available for work on weekends? .... ☐ Yes ☐ No
Would you be available to work overtime, if necessary? .... ☐ Yes ☐ No

If hired, on what date can you start work? _____

Salary desired: _____

Employment Application — Long Form
(Page 1 of 7)

Employment Application – Long Form

Personal Information

Have you ever applied to or worked for _____ before? ☐ Yes ☐ No

If yes, when? _____

Do you have any friends or relatives working for _____ ☐ Yes ☐ No

If yes, state name(s) and relationship:

Name	Relationship
Name	Relationship

Why are you applying for work at _____ ?

If hired, would you have a reliable means of transportation to and from work? .... ☐ Yes ☐ No

Are you at least 18 years old? (If under 18, hire is subject to verification that you are of minimum legal age.) .... ☐ Yes ☐ No

If hired, can you present evidence of your U.S. citizenship or proof of your legal right to live and work in this country? .... ☐ Yes ☐ No

Are you able to perform the essential functions of the job for which you are applying, either with or without reasonable accommodation? .... ☐ Yes ☐ No

If no, describe the functions that cannot be performed. _____

(Note: We comply with the ADA and consider reasonable accommodation measures that may be necessary for eligible applicants/employees to perform essential functions. Hire may be subject to passing a medical examination, and to skill and agility tests.)

Have you ever been convicted of a criminal offense (felony or serious misdemeanor)? (Convictions for marijuana-related offenses that are more than two years old need not be listed.) .... ☐ Yes ☐ No

If yes, state nature of the crime(s), when and where convicted, and disposition of the case.

(Note: No applicant will be denied employment solely on the grounds of conviction of a criminal offense. The nature of the offense, the date of the offense, the surrounding circumstances and the relevance of the offense to the position(s) applied for may, however, be considered.)

Are you currently employed? .... ☐ Yes ☐ No

If so, may we contact your current employer? .... ☐ Yes ☐ No

Employment Application — Long Form
(Page 2 of 7)

Employment Application – Long Form

Education, Training, and Experience

		No. of Years Completed	Did you Graduate?	Degree or Diploma
School	Name and Address			

High School
Name
Address
City · State · Zip ☐ Yes ☐ No

College/University
Name
Address
City · State · Zip ☐ Yes ☐ No

Vocational/Business
Name
Address
City · State · Zip ☐ Yes ☐ No

Health Care Training
Name
Address
City · State · Zip ☐ Yes ☐ No

Many of our customers (clients) do not speak English. Do you speak, write or understand any foreign languages? .... ☐ Yes ☐ No

If yes, which language(s)?

Do you have any other experience, training, qualifications, or skills that you feel make you especially suited for work at _____? ☐ Yes ☐ No

If so, please explain:

Employment Application – Long Form

Answer the following questions if you are applying for a professional position:

Are you licensed/certified for the job applied for? .... ☐ Yes ☐ No

Name of license/certification:

License/certification number: _____ Issuing state: ____

Has your license/certification ever been revoked or suspended? .... ☐ Yes ☐ No
If yes, state reason(s), date of revocation or suspension, and date of reinstatement.

Employment History

List below all present and past employment starting with your most recent employer (last five years is sufficient). Account for all periods of unemployment. You must complete this section even if attaching a resume.

Name of Employer — Telephone No. ( ) -
Type of Business — Your Supervisor's Name
Address & Street — City · State · Zip
Dates of Employment: From ____ To ____ — Weekly Pay: Starting ____ Ending ____
Your Position and Duties
Reason for Leaving
May we contact this employer for a reference? .... ☐ Yes ☐ No

Name of Employer — Telephone No. ( ) -
Type of Business — Your Supervisor's Name
Address & Street — City · State · Zip
Dates of Employment: From ____ To ____ — Weekly Pay: Starting ____ Ending ____
Your Position and Duties
Reason for Leaving
May we contact this employer for a reference? .... ☐ Yes ☐ No

Employment Application – Long Form

Employment History, continued

Name of Employer _____ Telephone No. ( ) ___ – ___

Type of Business _____ Your Supervisor's Name _____

Address & Street _____ City _____ State ___ Zip ___

Dates of Employment: From _____ To _____ Weekly Pay: Starting _____ Ending _____

Your Position and Duties _____

Reason for Leaving _____

May we contact this employer for a reference? .... ☐ Yes ☐ No

Name of Employer _____ Telephone No. ( ) ___ – ___

Type of Business _____ Your Supervisor's Name _____

Address & Street _____ City _____ State ___ Zip ___

Dates of Employment: From _____ To _____ Weekly Pay: Starting _____ Ending _____

Your Position and Duties _____

Reason for Leaving _____

May we contact this employer for a reference? .... ☐ Yes ☐ No

Name of Employer _____ Telephone No. ( ) ___ – ___

Type of Business _____ Your Supervisor's Name _____

Address & Street _____ City _____ State ___ Zip ___

Dates of Employment: From _____ To _____ Weekly Pay: Starting _____ Ending _____

Your Position and Duties _____

Reason for Leaving _____

May we contact this employer for a reference? .... ☐ Yes ☐ No

Note: Attach additional page(s) if necessary.

Employment Application — Long Form
(Page 5 of 7)

Employment Application – Long Form

Military Service

Have you obtained any special skills or abilities as the result of service in the military?   ☐ Yes ☐ No

If so, describe: _____

_____

_____

References

List below three persons not related to you who have knowledge of your work performance within the last three years.

First Name _____ Last Name _____ Telephone No. ( ) ___ – ___

Occupation _____ No. of Years Acquainted _____

Address & Street _____ City _____ State ___ Zip ___

First Name _____ Last Name _____ Telephone No. ( ) ___ – ___

Occupation _____ No. of Years Acquainted _____

Address & Street _____ City _____ State ___ Zip ___

First Name _____ Last Name _____ Telephone No. ( ) ___ – ___

Occupation _____ No. of Years Acquainted _____

Address & Street _____ City _____ State ___ Zip ___

Employment Application — Long Form
(Page 6 of 7)

Employment Application — Long Form

Please Read Carefully, Initial Each Paragraph and Sign Below

Initials _____

I hereby certify that I have not knowingly withheld any information that might adversely affect my chances for employment and that the answers given by me are true and correct to the best of my knowledge. I further certify that I, the undersigned applicant, have personally completed this application. I understand that any omission or misstatement of material fact on this application or on any document used to secure employment shall be grounds for rejection of this application or for immediate discharge if I am employed, regardless of the time elapsed before discovery.

I hereby authorize _____ to thoroughly investigate my references, work record, education and other matters related to my suitability for employment and, further, authorize the references I have listed to disclose to the company any and all letters, reports and other information related to my work records, without giving me prior notice of such disclosure. In addition, I hereby release the Company, my former employers and all other persons, corporations, partnerships and associations from any and all claims, demands or liabilities arising out of or in any way related to such investigation or disclosure.

Initials _____

I understand that nothing contained in the application, or conveyed during any interview which may be granted or during my employment, if hired, is intended to create an employment contract between me and the Company. In addition, I understand and agree that if I am employed, my employment is for no definite or determinable period and may be terminated at any time, with or without prior notice, at the option of either myself or the Company, and that no promises or representations contrary to the foregoing are binding on the company unless made in writing and signed by me and the Company's designated representative.

Initials _____

Should a search of public records (including records documenting an arrest, indictment, conviction, civil judicial action, tax lien or outstanding judgment) be conducted by internal personnel employed by the Company, I am entitled to copies of any such public records obtained by the Company unless I mark the check box below. If I am not hired as a result of such information, I am entitled to a copy of any such records even though I have checked the box below.

☐ I waive receipt of a copy of any public record described in the paragraph above.

_____
Applicant's Signature

_____
Date

Employer Property Policy

Lockers, desks, computers, vehicles and _____ (list other company-owned items) are _____ (the Company) property and must be maintained according to Company rules and regulations. They must be kept clean and are to be used only for work-related purposes. The Company reserves the right to inspect all Company property to ensure compliance with its rules and regulations, without notice to the employee and at any time, not necessarily in the employee's presence.

Company voice mail and/or electronic mail (e-mail) are to be used for business purposes only. The Company reserves the right to monitor voice mail messages and e-mail messages to ensure compliance with this rule, without notice to the employee and at any time, not necessarily in the employee's presence.

No personal locks may be used on Company-provided lockers unless the employee furnishes a copy of the key or the combination to the lock. Unauthorized use of a personal lock by an employee may result in losing the right to use a Company locker.

The Company may periodically need to assign and/or change "passwords" and personal codes for _____ (e.g., list voice mail, e-mail, computer, etc.) These communication technologies and related storage media and databases are to be used only for Company business and they remain the property of the Company. The Company reserves the right to keep a record of all passwords and codes used and/or may be able to override any such password system.

Prior authorization must be obtained before any Company property may be removed from the premises.

For security reasons, employees should not leave personal belongings of value in the workplace. Personal items are subject to inspection and search, with or without notice, with or without the employee's prior consent.

Terminated employees should remove any personal items at the time they leave the Company. Personal items left in the workplace are subject to disposal if not claimed at the time of an employee's termination.

Employment Application — Long Form

Employer Property Policy

Reference Check for Employment

Applicant: _____

SSN: _____

To:

Representative _____

Company Name _____

Address _____

City _____ State _____ Zip _____

Telephone ( ) ___ - ___ Fax ( ) ___ - ___

From:

Representative _____

Company Name _____

Address _____

City _____ State _____ Zip _____

Telephone ( ) ___ - ___ Fax ( ) ___ - ___

We are considering _____ for a position with _____. This applicant has provided us with written authorization to thoroughly investigate all references listed on his/her application for employment. You therefore are authorized to disclose to us all letters, reports, and other information related to his/her work records. A copy of that authorization will be faxed or mailed to you at your request.

The California Civil Code, Section 47(c) protects you in furnishing us with information concerning the job performance or qualifications of this applicant based on credible evidence and without malicious intent.

We thank you in advance for your cooperation in returning this form as soon as possible at the address or fax number noted above.

Reference Check for Employment (Page 1 of 2)

Reference Check for Employment

Name of Applicant _____

Dates of Employment _____

Positions Held _____

Duties _____

Starting Salary _____ Ending Salary _____

☐ Would Retire ☐ Would Not Retire (Response to this question is protected by California Civil Code, Section 47(c).)

Voluntary or Involuntary Termination _____

Reason for Terminating Employment _____

Number of Employees Supervised _____

Attendance (check one): ☐ excellent ☐ satisfactory ☐ poor

Overall performance (check one): ☐ excellent ☐ satisfactory ☐ poor

Additional comments _____

All information provided herein is true and accurate, and provided solely in response to inquiries that are of legitimate business interest to all parties.

Name of Person Completing this Reference Check _____

Signature _____ Date _____

(Employer seeking information should complete this portion if reference check is completed by telephone)

The information contained in this reference check is an accurate reflection of the information provided to me by _____, and was procured for legitimate business purposes.

Name of Telephone Interviewer _____

Signature of Telephone Interviewer _____

Reference Check for Employment (Page 2 of 2)

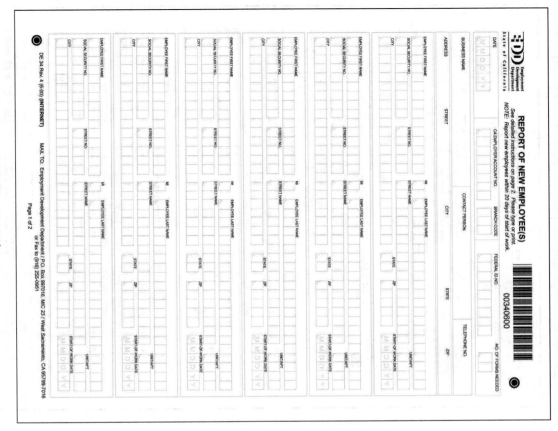

Employment Development Department
State of California

REPORT OF NEW EMPLOYEE(S)
PRINTING SPECIFICATIONS
COMPUTER OR LASER GENERATED ALTERNATE DE 34 FORMS

The Employment Development Department (EDD) provides DE 34 forms suitable for laser printers at no cost to our customers.

However, if you prefer to create your own Report of New Employee(s) forms, these specifications will assist you in creating an alternate DE 34 form that we can process on our optical character readers. The DE 34 form is the correct template to use to verify that the data on your alternate format is correct. Please use the print and line positions provided in these specifications to create your alternate form. Place the DE 34 over or under your alternate format and visually verify that the data on your alternate format is printing within the corresponding boxes on the DE 34. If this is the case, the alternate format has been designed to meet our specifications.

TEST FORMS MUST BE SUBMITTED FOR APPROVAL BEFORE USE

Please submit a sample deck for testing and approval. The test deck should include 25 original documents - no photocopies. You may use dummy data and you may repeat the data on all the pages.

The test deck should be mailed to the following address:

Alternate Forms Coordinator
Information Management Group/MIC 96
Employment Development Department
P O Box 826880
Sacramento, CA 94280-0001

TEST SAMPLES MUST MEET A 95% OR BETTER READ RATE TO BE APPROVED.

Our address for express mail is 9815 C Goethe Road, Sacramento, CA 95827, Attn: Alternate Forms Coordinator, MIC 96. Be sure to include my telephone number, (916) 255-0649, on the airbill.

GENERAL REQUIREMENTS

Non-scannable file copies: If you provide your customers with copies that are not OCR compatible, please advise them **not** to send their file copies to EDD. We have found that the warning **DO NOT SEND THIS COPY TO EDD** is effective when printed on file copy.

User codes: If you print code numbers or letters on your forms, please position them above the title "**SERVICE-RECIPIENT**" field on lines 6 or 7 and print positions 7 thru 40.

EDD Approval Number: This number will be assigned once EDD has tested and approved the forms.

Paper: Use 8 1/2" by 11" white, 20 pound bond paper. NCR or recycled paper will not feed into the scanners and is not acceptable.

Printer: Do not use a dot matrix printer. Dot matrix printing will not meet the 95% read rate.

Ink: Use black ink only. If possible, use non-ferric ink contains metal, which interferes with our automated mail sorting equipment.

Font type: Please use 10 or 12 point Courier, Helvetica or OCR A font to print the data to be captured. **DO NOT PRINT YOUR ALTERNATE FORMAT IN BOLD TYPE UNLESS SPECIFIED.**

Alignment: The top edge of the form is zero, the bottom of the form is line 66, the left edge is print position zero, and the right edge is print position 85.

DE 34 Print Specifications Rev. 4 (6-00) (INTERNET)

Page 1 of 5   2

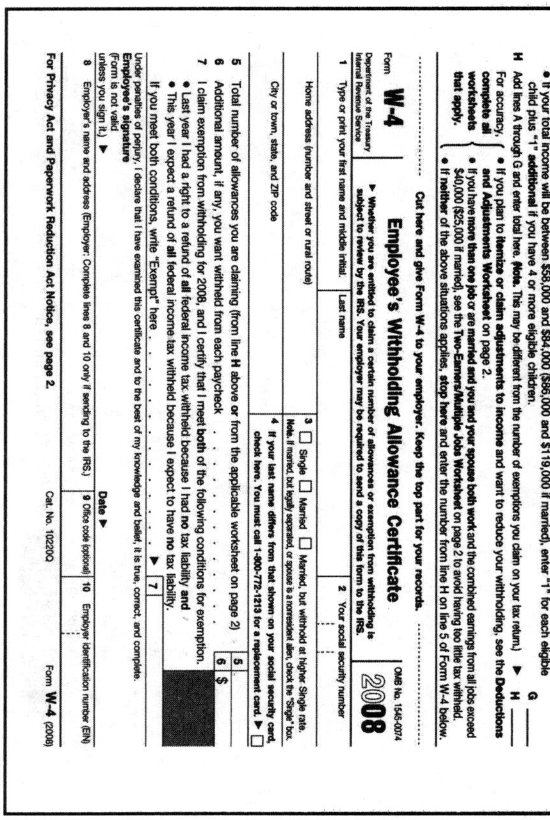

W-4 Form – Employee's Withholding Allowance Certificate (2008) (Page 1 of 2)

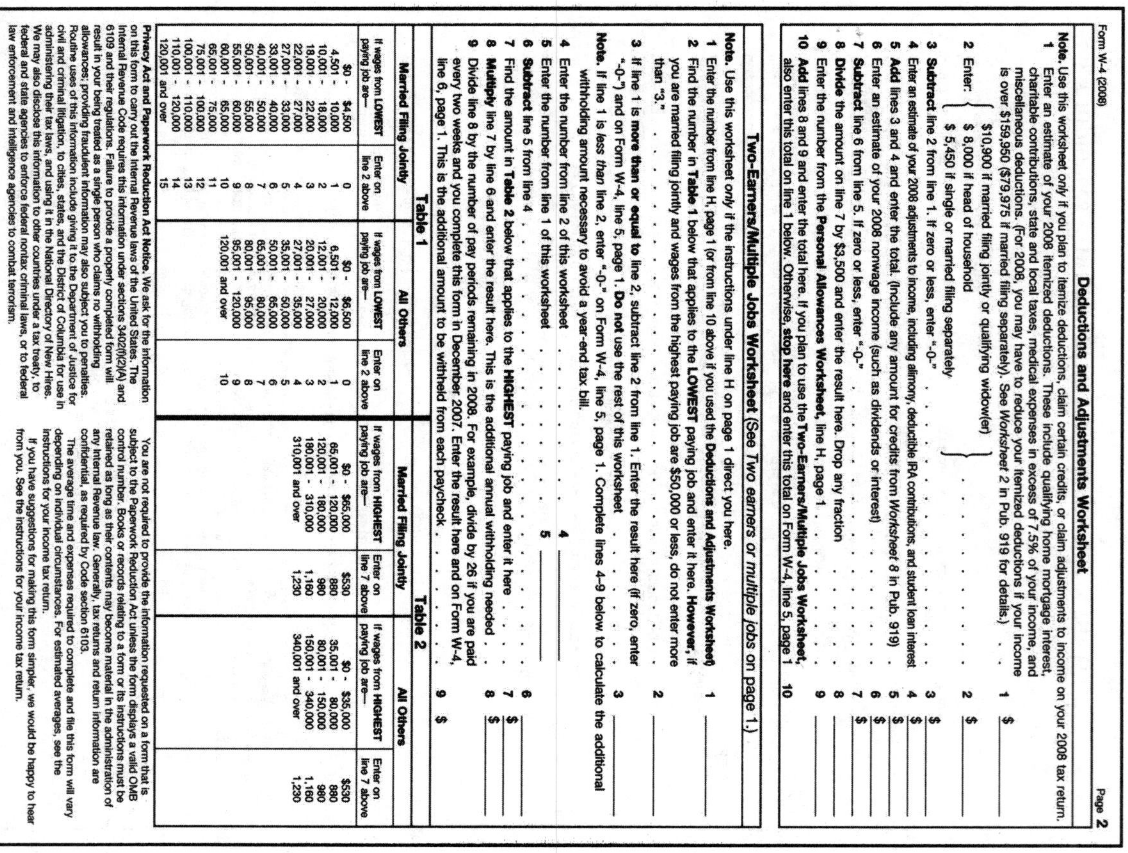

Form W-4 (2008)

Purpose. Complete Form W-4 so that your employer can withhold the correct federal income tax from your pay. Consider completing a new Form W-4 each year and when your personal or financial situation changes.

Exemption from withholding. If you are exempt, complete only lines 1, 2, 3, 4, and 7 and sign the form to validate it. Your exemption for 2008 expires February 16, 2009. See Pub. 505, Tax Withholding and Estimated Tax.

Note. You cannot claim exemption from withholding if (a) your income exceeds $900 and includes more than $300 of unearned income (for example, interest and dividends) and (b) another person can claim you as a dependent on their tax return.

Basic instructions. If you are not exempt, complete the Personal Allowances Worksheet below. The worksheets on page 2 adjust your withholding allowances based on itemized deductions, certain credits,

adjustments to income, or two-earner/multiple job situations. Complete all worksheets that apply. However, you may claim fewer (or zero) allowances.

Head of household. Generally, you may claim head of household filing status on your tax return only if you are unmarried and pay more than 50% of the costs of keeping up a home for yourself and your dependent(s) or other qualifying individuals. See Pub. 501.

Tax credits. You can take projected tax credits into account in figuring your allowable number of withholding allowances. Credits for child or dependent care expenses and the child tax credit may be claimed using the Personal Allowances Worksheet below. See Pub. 919, How Do I Adjust My Tax Withholding, for information on converting your other credits into withholding allowances.

Nonwage income. If you have a large amount of nonwage income, such as interest or dividends, consider making estimated tax

payments using Form 1040-ES, Estimated Tax for Individuals. Otherwise, you may owe additional tax. If you have pension or annuity income, see Pub. 919 to find out if you should adjust your withholding on Form W-4 or W-4P.

Two earners or multiple jobs. If you have a working spouse or more than one job, figure the total number of allowances you are entitled to claim on all jobs using worksheets from only one Form W-4. Your withholding usually will be most accurate when all allowances are claimed on the Form W-4 for the highest paying job and zero allowances are claimed on the others. See Pub. 919 for details.

Nonresident alien. If you are a nonresident alien, see the Instructions for Form 8233 before completing this Form W-4.

Check your withholding. After your Form W-4 takes effect, use Pub. 919 to see how the dollar amount you are having withheld compares to your projected total tax for 2008. See Pub. 919, especially if your earnings exceed $130,000 (Single) or $180,000 (Married).

Personal Allowances Worksheet (Keep for your records.)

A	Enter "1" for **yourself** if no one else can claim you as a dependent	A ___
B	Enter "1" if: { • You are single and have only one job; or • You are married, have only one job, and your spouse does not work; or • Your wages from a second job or your spouse's wages (or the total of both) are $1,500 or less. }	B ___
C	Enter "1" for your **spouse**. But, you may choose to enter "-0-" if you are married and have either a working spouse or more than one job. (Entering "-0-" may help you avoid having too little tax withheld.)	C ___
D	Enter number of **dependents** (other than your spouse or yourself) you will claim on your tax return	D ___
E	Enter "1" if you will file as **head of household** on your tax return (see conditions under Head of household above)	E ___
F	Enter "1" if you have at least $1,500 of **child or dependent care expenses** for which you plan to claim a credit	F ___
	(**Note.** Do not include child support payments. See Pub. 503, Child and Dependent Care Expenses, for details.)	
G	**Child Tax Credit** (including additional child tax credit). See Pub. 972, Child Tax Credit, for more information. • If your total income will be less than $58,000 ($86,000 if married), enter "2" for each eligible child plus "1" additional if you have 4 or more eligible children. • If your total income will be between $58,000 and $84,000 ($86,000 and $119,000 if married), enter "1" for each eligible child	G ___
H	**Add lines A through G and enter total here.** Note. This may be different from the number of exemptions you claim on your tax return.	H ___

For accuracy, complete all worksheets that apply. { • If you plan to **itemize or claim adjustments to income** and want to reduce your withholding, see the **Deductions and Adjustments Worksheet** on page 2. • If you are **single** and have more than one job or are **married** and you and your spouse both work and the combined earnings from all jobs exceed $40,000 ($25,000 if married), see the **Two-Earners/Multiple Jobs Worksheet** on page 2 to avoid having too little tax withheld. • If **neither** of the above situations applies, **stop here** and enter the number from line H on line 5 of Form W-4 below. }

-------- Cut here and give Form W-4 to your employer. Keep the top part for your records. --------

Form W-4
Department of the Treasury
Internal Revenue Service

Employee's Withholding Allowance Certificate

▶ Whether you are entitled to claim a certain number of allowances or exemption from withholding is subject to review by the IRS. Your employer may be required to send a copy of this form to the IRS.

OMB No. 1545-0074
2008

1 Type or print your first name and middle initial.	Last name		2 Your social security number
Home address (number and street or rural route)		3 ☐ Single ☐ Married ☐ Married, but withhold at higher Single rate. Note. If married, but legally separated, or spouse is a nonresident alien, check the "Single" box.	
City or town, state, and ZIP code		4 If your last name differs from that shown on your social security card, check here. You must call 1-800-772-1213 for a replacement card. ▶ ☐	

5	Total number of allowances you are claiming (from line H above or from the applicable worksheet on page 2)	5	
6	Additional amount, if any, you want withheld from each paycheck	6	$
7	I claim exemption from withholding for 2008, and I certify that I meet **both** of the following conditions for exemption. • Last year I had a right to a refund of **all** federal income tax withheld because I had **no** tax liability **and** • This year I expect a refund of **all** federal income tax withheld because I expect to have **no** tax liability. If you meet both conditions, write "Exempt" here ▶	7	

Under penalties of perjury, I declare that I have examined this certificate and to the best of my knowledge and belief, it is true, correct, and complete.

Employee's signature
(Form is not valid unless you sign it.) ▶ _____ Date ▶ _____

8 Employer's name and address (Employer: Complete lines 8 and 10 only if sending to the IRS.)	9 Office code (optional)	10 Employer identification number (EIN)

For Privacy Act and Paperwork Reduction Act Notice, see page 2.   Cat. No. 10220Q   Form **W-4** (2008)

W-4 Form – Employee's Withholding Allowance Certificate – 2008 (Page 2 of 2)

Form W-4 (2008)   Page **2**

Deductions and Adjustments Worksheet

Note. Use this worksheet *only* if you plan to itemize deductions, claim certain credits, or claim adjustments to income on your 2008 tax return.

1	Enter an estimate of your 2008 itemized deductions. These include qualifying home mortgage interest, charitable contributions, state and local taxes, medical expenses in excess of 7.5% of your income, and miscellaneous deductions. (For 2008, you may have to reduce your itemized deductions if your income is over $159,950 ($79,975 if married filing separately). See Worksheet 2 in Pub. 919 for details.)	1	$
2	Enter: { $10,900 if married filing jointly or qualifying widow(er) / $8,000 if head of household / $5,450 if single or married filing separately }	2	$
3	Subtract line 2 from line 1. If zero or less, enter "-0-"	3	$
4	Enter an estimate of your 2008 adjustments to income, including alimony, deductible IRA contributions, and student loan interest	4	$
5	Add lines 3 and 4 and enter the total. (Include any amount for credits from Worksheet 8 in Pub. 919)	5	$
6	Enter an estimate of your 2008 nonwage income (such as dividends or interest)	6	$
7	Subtract line 6 from line 5. If zero or less, enter "-0-"	7	$
8	Divide the amount on line 7 by $3,500 and enter the result here. Drop any fraction	8	
9	Enter the number from the Personal Allowances Worksheet, line H, page 1	9	
10	Add lines 8 and 9 and enter the total here. If you plan to use the **Two-Earners/Multiple Jobs Worksheet**, also enter this total on line 1 below. Otherwise, **stop here** and enter this total on Form W-4, line 5, page 1	10	

Two-Earners/Multiple Jobs Worksheet (See Two earners or multiple jobs on page 1.)

Note. Use this worksheet *only* if the instructions under line H on page 1 direct you here.

1	Enter the number from line H, page 1 (or from line 10 above if you used the **Deductions and Adjustments Worksheet**)	1	
2	Find the number in **Table 1** below that applies to the **LOWEST** paying job and enter it here. **However, if** you are married filing jointly and wages from the highest paying job are $50,000 or less, do not enter more than "3."	2	
3	If line 1 is **more than or equal to** line 2, subtract line 2 from line 1. Enter the result here (if zero, enter "-0-") and on Form W-4, line 5, page 1. **Do not use the rest of this worksheet**	3	

Note. If line 1 is less than line 2, enter "-0-" on Form W-4, line 5, page 1. Complete lines 4–9 below to calculate the additional withholding amount necessary to avoid a year-end tax bill.

4	Enter the number from line 2 of this worksheet	4	
5	Enter the number from line 1 of this worksheet	5	
6	Subtract line 5 from line 4	6	
7	Find the amount in **Table 2** below that applies to the **HIGHEST** paying job and enter it here	7	$
8	Multiply line 7 by line 6 and enter the result here. This is the additional annual withholding needed	8	$
9	Divide line 8 by the number of pay periods remaining in 2008. For example, divide by 26 if you are paid every two weeks and you complete this form in December 2007. Enter the result here and on Form W-4, line 6, page 1. This is the additional amount to be withheld from each paycheck	9	$

Table 1

Married Filing Jointly		All Others	
If wages from **LOWEST** paying job are—	Enter on line 2 above	If wages from **LOWEST** paying job are—	Enter on line 2 above
$0 - $4,500	0	$0 - $6,500	0
4,501 - 10,000	1	6,501 - 12,000	1
10,001 - 18,000	2	12,001 - 20,000	2
18,001 - 22,000	3	20,001 - 27,000	3
22,001 - 27,000	4	27,001 - 35,000	4
27,001 - 33,000	5	35,001 - 50,000	5
33,001 - 40,000	6	50,001 - 65,000	6
40,001 - 50,000	7	65,001 - 80,000	7
50,001 - 55,000	8	80,001 - 95,000	8
55,001 - 60,000	9	95,001 - 120,000	9
60,001 - 65,000	10	120,001 and over	10
65,001 - 75,000	11		
75,001 - 95,000	12		
95,001 - 110,000	13		
110,001 - 120,000	14		
120,001 and over	15		

Table 2

Married Filing Jointly		All Others	
If wages from **HIGHEST** paying job are—	Enter on line 7 above	If wages from **HIGHEST** paying job are—	Enter on line 7 above
$0 - $65,000	$530	$0 - $35,000	$530
65,001 - 120,000	880	35,001 - 80,000	880
120,001 - 180,000	980	80,001 - 150,000	980
180,001 - 310,000	1,160	150,001 - 340,000	1,160
310,001 and over	1,230	340,001 and over	1,230

Privacy Act and Paperwork Reduction Act Notice. We ask for the information on this form to carry out the Internal Revenue laws of the United States. The Internal Revenue Code requires this information under sections 3402(f)(2)(A) and 6109 and their regulations. Failure to provide a properly completed form will result in your being treated as a single person who claims no withholding allowances; providing fraudulent information may also subject you to penalties. Routine uses of this information include giving it to the Department of Justice for civil and criminal litigation, to cities, states, and the District of Columbia for use in administering their tax laws, and using it in the National Directory of New Hires. We may also disclose this information to other countries under a tax treaty, to federal and state agencies to enforce federal nontax criminal laws, or to federal law enforcement and intelligence agencies to combat terrorism.

You are not required to provide the information requested on a form that is subject to the Paperwork Reduction Act unless the form displays a valid OMB control number. Books or records relating to a form or its instructions must be retained as long as their contents may become material in the administration of any Internal Revenue law. Generally, tax returns and return information are confidential, as required by Code section 6103.

The average time and expenses required to complete and file this form will vary depending on individual circumstances. For estimated averages, see the instructions for your income tax return.

If you have suggestions for making this form simpler, we would be happy to hear from you. See the instructions for your income tax return.

Confidentiality Agreement

v042507

I, the undersigned employee, understand that in the course of my employment with _____ (the Company). I may have access to and become acquainted with information of a confidential, proprietary or secret nature which is or may be either applicable or related to the present or future business of the Company, its research and development, or the business of its customers. Such trade secret information includes, but is not limited to, devices, inventions, processes, compilations of information, records, specifications and information concerning customers and/or vendors.

I agree that I will not disclose any of the above mentioned trade secrets, directly or indirectly, or use them in any way, either during the term of my employment or at any time thereafter, except as required in the course of my employment with the Company.

I further understand that I am an at-will employee of this Company and that this agreement is not to be construed as constituting a promise of continued employment.

Name of Employee

Signature of Employee _____ Date _____

Confidentiality Agreement

Confirmation of Receipt Policy

I have received my copy of the employee handbook for _____ (the Company). I understand and agree that it is my responsibility to read and familiarize myself with the policies and procedures contained in the handbook.

I understand that except for employment at-will status, any and all policies or practices can be changed at any time by the Company. The Company reserves the right to change my hours, wages, and working conditions at any time. I understand and agree that other than the president of the Company, no manager, supervisor, or representative of the Company has authority to enter into any agreement, express or implied, for employment for any specific period of time, or to make any agreement for employment other than at-will; only the president has the authority to make any such agreement and then only in writing signed by the president.

I understand and agree that nothing in the employee handbook creates or is intended to create a promise or representation of continued employment and that employment at the Company is employment at-will; employment may be terminated at the will of either the Company or myself. My signature certifies that I understand that the foregoing agreement on at-will status is the sole and entire agreement between the company and myself concerning the duration of my employment and the circumstances under which my employment may be terminated. It supersedes all prior agreements, understandings and representations concerning my employment with the Company.

Employee's Signature _____ Date _____

✕ calbizcentral™

© CalChamber   Page 1 of 1

Confirmation of Receipt Policy

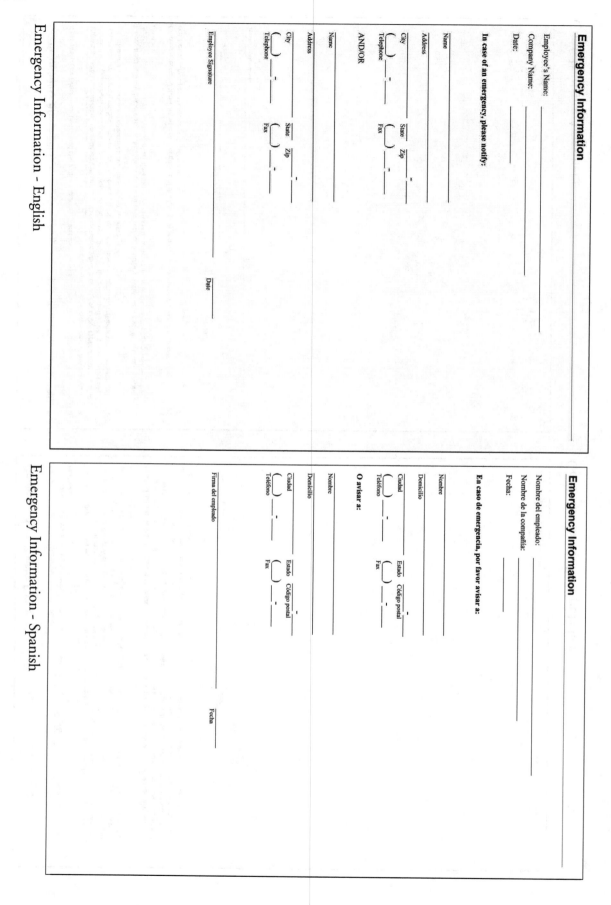

Emergency Information

Emergency Information - English

Employee's Name: _____

Company Name: _____

Date: _____

In case of an emergency, please notify:

Name _____

Address _____

City _____ State _____ Zip _____

Telephone (___) ___ - _____ Fax (___) ___ - _____

AND/OR

Name _____

Address _____

City _____ State _____ Zip _____

Telephone (___) ___ - _____ Fax (___) ___ - _____

Employee Signature _____ Date _____

Emergency Information

Emergency Information - Spanish

Nombre del empleado: _____

Nombre de la compañía: _____

Fecha: _____

En caso de emergencia, por favor avisar a:

Nombre _____

Domicilio _____

Ciudad _____ Estado _____ Código postal _____

Teléfono (___) ___ - _____ Fax (___) ___ - _____

O avisar a:

Nombre _____

Domicilio _____

Ciudad _____ Estado _____ Código postal _____

Teléfono (___) ___ - _____ Fax (___) ___ - _____

Firma del empleado _____ Fecha _____

Recruiting Checklist

Use this checklist to guide you through the recruiting process for new and existing positions. The recommended steps are outlined in chronological order; however, individual situations may differ. Skip steps 6 and 7 if your Company policy does not require you to post openings internally before you advertise to outside applicants.

Position Title: _____

Position Type: ☐ New ☐ Existing

Classification: ☐ Exempt ☐ Non-exempt

Department: _____

Reports to: _____

Task	Date Completed
1. Verify recruiting need List supervisor/manager and all others required to signoff on the hire, along with verification dates.	
2. Obtain management approval to post the job opening List management personnel and approval dates.	
3. Determine the hiring criteria Identify the key job qualifications, traits, characteristics, training and experience needed. If filling a vacancy, reassess the position's needs and requirements carefully. Avoid limiting the needs to the characteristics of the prior incumbent. Ensure that criteria are stated in neutral terms and do not violate any fair employment laws, e.g., "able to lift 50lbs." is more objective than "physically fit."	
4. Develop or review the job description Involve key management players and particularly the person to whom the position will report when creating or modifying the description. If this is an existing position, review the most recent job description in light of current business needs and skill-set requirements and update as needed. Review to whom the position will report, possible compensation range and opportunities for advancement. Also specify any skill, physical or education requirements. Review with managers and supervisors all essential functions of the position as well as qualifications that would be preferred, but may not be necessary (such as foreign language or certain computer skills).	
5. Determine a salary (exempt) or hourly rate (non-exempt) range Take into account the required qualifications, job description and market conditions in your geographic area. List final ranges and quantify requirements necessary at each level.	

Recruiting Checklist (Page 1 of 3)

Recruiting Checklist

Task	Date Completed
6. Post the position internally for a specified time (Optional) If you have a policy of allowing employees the first chance at newly opened positions, then post all new openings on your Company's intranet and/or a hiring bulletin board for a minimum period of time (2 weeks to one month is typical) before advertising the job to outside applicants. Note minimum period.	
7. Interview and evaluate internal candidates (Optional) If a suitable internal applicant comes forward and accepts your promotion offer, restart the recruiting process to fill the promoted candidate's position. Note outcome of internal interviews.	
8. Identify external job posting venues Identify the external venues where you are likely to find candidates with the right qualifications and from the right geographic area (websites, newspapers, industry journals, etc.).	
9. Post the job in the appropriate external locations Keep detailed records of the job posting locations and note when each posting expires.	
10. Consider offering a referral bonus to reach staff contacts (Optional) A referral bonus system gives your staff an incentive to get the word out to their personal networks, and it may help you find a great candidate who is not actively job-hunting. Note referral bonus details, if implemented.	
11. Accept applications and track venue performance To track which recruiting venues work best for you, include a question on your application form that asks the applicant how he/she learned of the opening. Note performance outcomes.	
12. Acknowledge application receipt Acknowledge application receipt through an email and/or postcard system. To cut down on administrative time, consider adding a statement to your acknowledgment that only those candidates chosen to interview will be contacted again.	

Recruiting Checklist (Page 2 of 3)

Recruiting Checklist

Task	Date Completed
13. Keep a list of accepted applications and actions taken Note candidate name and action taken. Use additional sheets as necessary.	
14. Screen resumes Use objective, consistent, non-discriminatory criteria. Note criteria.	
15. Conduct telephone interviews to narrow the candidate pool (Optional) Note telephone interview dates and outcomes.	
16. Conduct in-person interviews Find detailed information on interview strategies, as well as interview checklists and forms, on HRCalifornia.com.	
17. Evaluate candidates Use objective, consistent, non-discriminatory criteria. Note criteria.	
18. Select candidate and extend offer Note candidate selected, offer extended, and acceptance/rejection.	

Recruiting Checklist (Page 3 of 3)

Individual Employee Training Documentation - Initial Safety Training

Name of Trainer _____

Company Name _____

Training Subject _____

Training Materials Used _____

Name of Employee _____ Date of Hire/Assignment _____

I, the undersigned employee, hereby certify that I received training in the following areas:

- ☐ The potential occupational hazards in general in the work area and associated with my job assignment.
- ☐ The Codes of Safe Practices which indicate the safe work conditions, safe work practices and personal protective equipment required for my work.
- ☐ The hazards of any chemicals to which I may be exposed and my right to information contained on material safety data sheets for those chemicals, and how to understand this information.
- ☐ My right to ask any questions, or provide any information to the employer on safety either directly or anonymously without any fear of reprisal.
- ☐ Disciplinary procedures the employer will use to enforce compliance with Codes of Safe Practices.

I understand this training and agree to comply with the Code of Safe Practices for my work area.

Employee Signature _____ Date _____

Individual Employee Training Documentation - Initial Safety Training

Pre-Hire Checklist

Employment Advertisement
- ☐ Is the language of the advertisement nondiscriminatory?
- ☐ Is the advertisement placed in a general interest publication?
- ☐ Does the language of the advertisement promise something other than employment at will?

Employee v. Independent Contractor
- ☐ Will the individual be an employee or an independent contractor?
- ☐ Review the various tests under state and federal law to ensure you do not misclassify an employee as an independent contractor.

Affirmative Action
- ☐ Is this position one which requires compliance with an affirmative action program (most often due to government contracts)?

EDD's Job Match Service
- ☐ Is this the type of position for which EDD might be able to provide you with qualified applicants?

Job Training Partnership Act
- ☐ Consider the benefits of tax credits for hiring JTPA participants.
- ☐ Reimbursement of training costs is available through JTPA.
- ☐ Might a customized training package be of help?

Employment Applications
- ☐ Determine whether a long or short form application is the most appropriate for the position.
- ☐ Be sure the required posters are placed where job applicants can easily see them. Posters necessary for applicants include: Employee Polygraph Protection Act (WH 1462); Equal Employment Opportunity is the Law (EEOC P/E-1), and; Harassment or Discrimination in Employment (DFEH 162).

EEO Data
- ☐ Are you an employer of 15 or more employees who must keep records of EEO compliance?
- ☐ Is the EEO data kept private, and separate from the job application once completed?

Interview
- ☐ Are all interviewers trained to avoid illegal discrimination in the interviewing process?
- ☐ Have all interviewers been given a pre-approved list of questions?

Background Check
- ☐ Has the applicant signed a release allowing you to check his/her references and other background information?
- ☐ Have you made reasonable efforts to check the applicant's previous employment and references, to avoid negligent hiring?
- ☐ Have you sent all appropriate notices as required by state and federal law?

Pre-Hire Checklist

Credit Check
- ☐ Will a credit check be necessary for this position?
- ☐ Have you certified your compliance with the Fair Credit Reporting Act (FCRA) to the credit reporting agency?
- ☐ Have you provided the employee with a separate notification that his/her credit will be checked?
- ☐ Has the employee signed a release allowing for a credit check?
- ☐ If adverse action will be taken based on the applicant's credit history, has the applicant been provided with a pre-adverse action notice?
- ☐ Once adverse action is taken, was the applicant provided with an adverse action notice, and the required information under the FCRA?

Drug Testing
- ☐ Will drug testing be required for this position?
- ☐ Has the applicant signed a release allowing a drug test?
- ☐ Is the drug test performed as part of a physical exam? If so, the physical exam must be done after a job offer has been made, in compliance with the Americans with Disabilities Act.
- ☐ Even if the drug test is not part of a physical exam, remember that drug testing of applicants is extremely limited. Be sure the applicant successfully passes the drug screen before you put him/her to work.

Exempt or Non-exempt Status
- ☐ Review the information in this publication to determine whether this will be an exempt or nonexempt position. Note that the required minimum salary for exempt status increased January 1, 2002. The minimum salary level now required for exempt white collar employees is no less than two times the state minimum wage for full time employment. This translates to a minimum of $2,340 per month based on the current minimum wage of $6.75 per hour ($6.75 x 2,080 = $14,040, times two = $28,080, divided by 12 months = $2,340).
- ☐ Complete the worksheets provided for further help determining exempt or nonexempt status.
- ☐ If exempt, be certain the applicant is offered a salary rather than hourly compensation.

Work Permits for Minors
- ☐ Is the individual being hired under the age of 18?
- ☐ Will the spread of hours required for this position be in conflict with the legal limitations on the spread of hours that can be worked by a minor?
- ☐ Remember that minors are generally limited to no more than eight hours of work per day.
- ☐ Is the job to be performed on the list of prohibited occupations for a minor? Prohibited occupations vary depending on the age of the minor.
- ☐ Has a work permit been obtained?
- ☐ Will the employee be required to drive as part of the job? A minor may not drive a motor vehicle on public highways or streets as part of his/her employment, even with a valid drivers' license.

Injury and Illness Prevention Program
(Page 1 of 5)

Injury and Illness Prevention Program

The following document is the Injury and Illness Prevention Program to meet the written program requirements of Cal/OSHA standard (8 CCR§3203) for the employer described below.

Employer's Name: _____

Address: _____

Telephone Number: ( ) _____

1. Management Approval and Persons Responsible

Adoption: This Injury and Illness Prevention Program is hereby approved and supersedes any previous program that has been in effect since July 1, 1991.

Signature of Management Official _____ Date _____

Printed Name _____ Title _____

Person responsible for implementing this injury and illness prevention program:

Name _____ Title _____

Other persons may assist the above-named person as designated by management or the responsible person.

2. Safety Policy Statement

It is the policy of our company to provide a safe and healthful workplace. Every employee is responsible for the safety of himself/herself as well as others in the workplace. To achieve our goal of maintaining a safe workplace, everyone must be safety conscious at all times. In compliance with California law, and to promote the concept of a safe workplace, the company maintains an injury and illness prevention program. The injury and illness prevention program is available for review by employees and/or employee representatives in the general manager's office.

3. System to Identify and Prevent Safety and Health Hazards

Identification of Hazards: This IIPP's system to identify safety and health hazards includes using information from Cal/OSHA standards and other relevant material in this program to discover any potential hazards in the workplace. In addition, potential hazards may be identified by reviewing causes of injury and illness (*OSHA Log 300 and Workers' Compensation Employer's Report of Occupational Injury or Illness*, also known as the "Employer's First Report"), periodic scheduled inspections, investigating injuries, illnesses and accidents, and considering information provided by employees.

Prevention of Hazards: Compliance with any applicable Cal/OSHA standard will be assured to address hazards covered by such standards. In addition, any unsafe or unhealthy condition or work practice that is discovered will be corrected in a timely manner based on the following:

- If the hazard discovered may cause a serious injury or illness, it shall be corrected immediately or employees removed from the area, source of exposure or unsafe piece of equipment.
- If the hazard is one that is easily abated, it shall be corrected immediately.
- Other hazards shall be corrected in a timely manner.

Documentation used in discovering the hazard will be used to confirm abatement (for example, noting the correction on a new *Hazard Prevention Data Sheet*, inspection checklist or an injury and illness investigation form).

Injury and Illness Prevention Program
(Page 2 of 5)

Injury and Illness Prevention Program

4. Elements Included in Employer's IIPP

This IIPP includes all of the following elements consistent with 8 CCR §3203 and other applicable Cal/OSHA standards:

Injury and Illness Prevention Program Requirements: This IIPP includes all of the following minimum elements consistent with the injury and illness prevention standard:

- A system to identify and prevent safety and health hazards.
- Periodic scheduled inspections.
- Investigation of injuries, illnesses and accidents.
- Employee safety training.
- Communication with employees regarding safety and enforcement of safety rules.
- Recordkeeping consistent with applicable requirements.

Other Mandatory Cal/OSHA standards: This IIPP includes information that addresses certain standards that apply to all employees:

- Emergency action planning, including medical emergencies.
- Fire prevention and fire emergency planning.
- Work surface and work space safety.
- Office and commercial establishment safety, including ergonomics (repetitive motion 1 injuries) and office chemical safety.

Additional Regulated Activities: The employer has reviewed additional regulated activities and safety requirements. Those checked apply to this workplace and are covered within this IIPP:

- ☐ Personal protective equipment use by employees.
- ☐ Ergonomics safety, including prevention of repetitive motion injuries and back and joint injuries.
- ☐ Hazardous substance handling.
- ☐ Machine guarding and maintenance.
- ☐ Power tools and ladders.
- ☐ Vehicle operation.
- ☐ Forklifts, battery charging and material handling.
- ☐ Pressure vessels (air compressors) and LPG tanks.
- ☐ Construction activities.
- ☐ Security and violence prevention.

5. Periodic Scheduled Inspection

Responsibility and Frequency of Inspections: Periodic scheduled inspections are conducted by, or under the direction of, the person responsible for implementing IIPP at the following frequency:

Office Areas: _____

Injury and Illness Prevention Program

Other Areas (indicate area and frequency):

Area	Inspection

In addition, whenever information indicates that a previously unrecognized hazard may be present, the area in which the suspected hazard is present will be inspected promptly.

Documentation of Inspections: Inspection forms will be completed by the inspector for each inspection, noting the area inspected, person or persons conducting the inspection, findings and any deficiencies noted. Correction of deficiencies shall be accomplished according to Paragraph 4, Other Mandatory Cal/OSHA standards, and indicated on the inspection checklist.

6. Investigating Injuries, Illnesses and Accidents

Policy and Responsibility: Any injuries, illnesses or accidents will be investigated to determine if any preventable safety or health hazard contributed to the occurrence. The person responsible for implementing the IIPP will conduct the investigation within a timely manner after being advised of the incident. If a reportable serious injury or death results, the responsible person will assure that a report is made to Cal/OSHA within eight hours. Any hazardous condition or work practices that contributed to the injury, illness or accident will be abated according to the policy stated at Paragraph 4, Other Mandatory Cal/OSHA standards.

Documentation of Investigation: Each investigation of an injury, illness or accident will be documented to indicate information about the incident, the investigation's finding, whether a workplace hazard contributed to the incident, how the hazard will be abated and the investigator. The investigation can be documented by using workers compensation form *Employer's First Report* or the *Supplemental Injury, Illness and Accident Investigation.*

7. Safety Training for Employees

Policy and Responsibility: Employees have been provided training in safe work practices and prevention of injuries and illnesses when the IIPP was first established and whenever a new hazard is identified or an employee is reassigned or newly hired prior to exposure to any potential hazards.

The person responsible for implementing the IIPP is responsible for assuring the employee training is provided and documented. Supervisors and other designated employees may be designated to assist in providing training.

Documentation of Training: Training is documented in the following manner:

- Each employee's personnel records contain a form that indicates the status of the employee's training. The form indicates that IIPP training was provided and when additional training was received for new hazards, new assignments or to meet refresher training requirements.
- Training sessions will be documented with a sign-up sheet that indicates the date, subject of training, trainer and attendees. This form will be used to update individual employee training records.

8. Communicating with Employees about Safety and Enforcement of Safety Work Practices

Policy and Responsibility: A system to communicate with employees about safety and to assure compliance with safe work practices is in effect. Communications are implemented through safety meetings, anonymous notification procedures, one-on-one counseling and disciplinary procedures.

Injury and Illness Prevention Program

The person responsible for the IIPP shall assure that effective employee communications are maintained through the following methods:

- Explanation of the IIPP and its procedures.
- Description of any new hazards that have been introduced or identified through inspection or investigation of injuries, illnesses or accidents.
- Consideration of employee safety suggestions and questions (including anonymous ones) and a response provided.

Employee Compliance: Employees are required to comply with safe work practices. If non-compliance is observed, the following disciplinary measures will be used as appropriate to assure future compliance. The method used should be selected based on the gravity of the violation and the frequency of such violation and be administered according to progressive discipline employee relations policies:

- Private counseling by the person responsible for implementing the IIPP or the employee's supervisor;
- Loss of incentives, negative effect on performance evaluation and similar personnel actions;
- A written warning or warnings; and
- Suspension or termination.

Documentation of Safety Communications and Enforcement: Each instance of employee communication is documented. The documentation includes the following:

- Safety meetings are documented through a sign-in sheet.
- Written employee safety suggestions or questions are maintained on file along with the response, including information on how the response was provided to employees.
- Actions taken to enforce compliance with safe work practices in cases that exceeds verbal counseling will be documented in the employee's personnel record by the person responsible for the IIPP.

9. Recordkeeping and Posting Requirements

Policy and Responsibility for IIPP Recordkeeping: Records that document implementation of the IIPP will be maintained by the person responsible for the program. The following records will be maintained for the period indicated, at a minimum:

- The Written IIPP ....Indefinitely
- OSHA Log 300 Forms ....5 years
- Inspection Forms ....1 year
- Investigation Forms ....1 year (if a Log 200 injury, 5 years)
- Employee Training Forms:
  - ‣ Personnel Records ....Duration of Employment
  - ‣ Training Sign-up Sheets ....1 year
- Records Relating to Employee Communication and Enforcement
  - ‣ Safety Meeting Sign-up Sheets ....3 years
  - ‣ Employee Suggestion/Question and Responses ....3 years
  - ‣ Disciplinary Actions ....3 years
- All Other Safety Records other than
  Those Subject to the Access Standard ....3 years
- Employee Exposure Records (Subject to §3204) ....30 years
- Medical Records (Subject to §3204) ....Duration of Employment Plus 30 years

Injury and Illness Prevention Program

Poster Policy: It is the policy of this employer that all posters required by federal and state occupational safety and health and labor laws and regulations will be posted in the workplace.

10. Maintaining the Injury and Illness Prevention Program

Reviewing and Updating the IIPP: This IIPP will be periodically reviewed by the person responsible for implementing it. This person shall verify effective implementation of each element of the program, make any changes needed and communicate program status and changes made to management and to affected employees.

New Employees: Each new employee hired will be subject to the IIPP. Each employee transferred to a new job will be trained in the safety aspects of the new assignment. The person responsible for implementation will assure that each new employee is included in the IIPP and will provide training on any provisions applicable to the new or any transferring employee's position.

Injury and Illness Prevention Program
(Page 5 of 5)

Training Requirements

Note: Initial/Annual training is indicated per mandatory requirements of respective standards. It is the employer's obligation to determine when refresher training is necessary to meet the periodic training requirements, e.g. upon discovery of new hazards, observed unsafe operations, post accident, changes to equipment or workplace, or upon changes to the *Injury and Illness Prevention Program (IIPP)*.

Standard	Trainees and Nature of Training	Initial	Annual	Periodic
Accident Investigation	*Supervisors/Accident Investigators:* • How to conduct investigations • Proper documentation procedures	✓		
Agricultural Equipment & Tractors	*Involved employees and operators:* • Safe operating procedures	✓		
Bloodborne Pathogens (BBP)	*Employees who render emergency medical care or who may be exposed to infectious materials:* • Employer's Exposure Control Program • Exposure prevention measures • Hazards of BBP	✓	✓	
Chemical Protective Standards	*Employees who are exposed to the presence of, or in excess of, action levels for a regulated substance (depending on the standard):* • Employer's program • Hazards of the substance • Exposure prevention	✓	✓	✓
Confined Space Entry (Permit Required)	*Any confined space entrants or rescue personnel:* • How to safely execute entries under permit or alternative safety procedures • Rescue procedures	Entrants: ✓ Rescuers:	✓	✓ ✓
Emergency Action	*All employees:* • Safe practices and evacuation in an emergency	✓		✓
Ergonomics	*Employees in affected job classifications (identical jobs) when standard is triggered:* • Injury prevention	✓		✓
Explosives	*Assigned employees:* • Safe handling methods and practices • Exposure prevention	✓		✓
Fall Protection	*Affected employees:* • Safety procedures	✓		✓
Fire Prevention	*All employees:* • Safety procedures and evacuation in a fire emergency • How to carry out fire prevention and response duties, if assigned			✓

Training Requirements
(Page 1 of 3)

Training Requirements

Standard	Trainees and Nature of Training	Frequency		
		Initial	Annual	Periodic
Hazard Communication	Employees who work with hazardous substances or may be exposed in an emergency: • Employer's Hazard Communication Program • Hazards of chemicals • Safe work practices during ordinary use and in emergencies	✓		
Hazardous Exposure to Substances in Laboratories	Employees who work with chemicals in laboratories: • Employer's Chemical Hygiene Program • Hazards of chemicals • Exposure controls	✓		
Hazardous Waste Operation & Emergency Response (HAZWOPER)	Employees engaged in emergency response activities described as: • First Responders Awareness Level (sufficient training on hazard recognition and procedures) • First Responders Operations Level (8 hours of emergency response-spill containment) • Incident Commanders, Specialists and Technicians (24 hours of aggressive emergency response)	✓	✓	
Heat Stress	Outdoor employees: • Illness prevention • Emergency procedures	✓		
Industrial/Lift Trucks (Forklifts), Tractors & Material Handling	Forklift and industrial truck operators: • Proficiency and safe operation rules	✓		✓
Injury and Illness Prevention Program (IIPP)	All employees: • Hazards and safe work practices and the employer's IIPP • Supervisor hazard prevention	✓	✓	✓
Lockout/Tagout & Machinery Guarding	Employees who operate and service machinery: • Lockout/tagout procedures to eliminate hazardous energization	✓	✓	✓
Medical Service & First Aid	Emergency medical responders: • First aid/CPR certified by qualified training service (American Red Cross)	✓	✓	
Noise Exposure (Occupational)	Any employee exposed over 85dBA: • Hearing conservation practices and noise hazard information	✓	✓	

Training Requirements

Standard	Trainees and Nature of Training	Frequency		
		Initial	Annual	Periodic
Personal Protective Equipment (PPE)	Employees required to wear PPE: • Hazard the PPE addresses • Basis for its selection • Use, care and maintenance	✓		
Respiratory Protective	Any respirator user: • Employer's respirator program • Hazards and proper respirator fitting and use	✓	✓	

DE - 4 Employee's Witholding Allowance Certificate (-

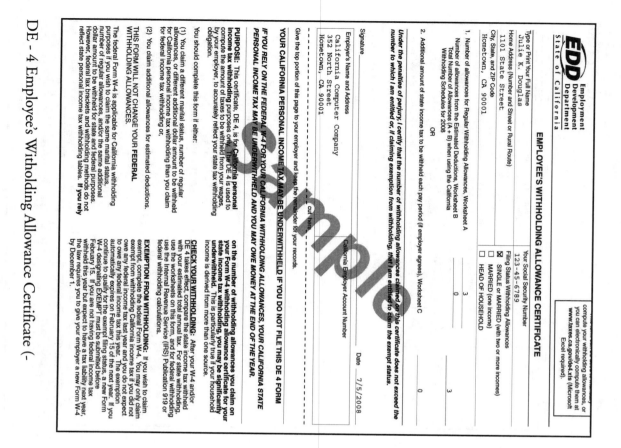

Verifying Eligibility to Work

Federal immigration and naturalization laws impose complex compliance requirements on every employer, regardless of size. Among other things, these laws require employers to institute procedures for verifying that an individual is authorized to work in the United States. They also establish civil and criminal penalties for knowingly hiring, referring, recruiting or retaining in employment unauthorized workers when they are identified.

This chapter explains how to comply with immigration and naturalization laws and how to avoid related liabilities, such as discrimination and harassment claims. This chapter also provides instruction on completing Form I-9 (Employment Eligibility Verification), complying with document verification requirements, retaining records, and working with the United States Citizenship and Immigration Services (USCIS).

 Download forms referenced in this chapter at **www.calbizcentral.com/support**. Be sure to have your access code from the inside covers of this book ready to enter into the forms download area. Your access code for the forms in the online Formspack is on the inside covers of this book. See "Forms Available Online" on page xix for more information.

Verifying Eligibility for Employment/Establishing Identity

It is illegal for a person or other entity to hire, recruit or refer for employment (for a fee):

- A worker unauthorized to work in the U.S.; or

- Any individual without complying with the employment verification procedures of the Immigration Reform and Control Act (IRCA).[1]

You must verify that every new hire is either a U.S. citizen or authorized to work in the United States. You make this verification by examining documents that provide evidence of the person's identity and employment eligibility.

If you comply with the verification requirements when hiring the individual, but later discover the employee is an unauthorized worker, you may not continue to employ that person. Similarly, it is unlawful to contract for worker labor if you know that the worker is unauthorized.[2]

You may not require additional or alternate identity and work authorization documents other than those specified by the USCIS, and you must honor documents that appear valid on their face.[3]

---

1. IRCA sec. 101
2. IRCA sec. 101
3. 8 U.S.C. 1324 b(a)(6)

Form I-9 Not Required

Form I-9 is not required for:

- Employees hired prior to November 6, 1986, and continuously employed by the same employer;

- Casual employees performing irregular domestic service in a private home;

- Independent contractors; or

- Workers provided by contract services, such as temporary agencies.

 It is illegal to contract for labor for which you know the worker is not authorized. This may subject you to civil and criminal penalties.

New I-9 Form for 2009

 The list of acceptable documents for the I-9 Form was revised in 2007. This form had a revision date on it (lower right hand corner of the form) that read "Form I-9 (Rev. 06/05/07)N." On or about June 16, 2008, the Department of Homeland Security (DHS) issued a "revised" I-9 Form with an expiration date of June 30, 2009, and a revision date on it that read "Form I-9 (Rev. 06/16/08)N. "About a week after issuing this "revised I-9 Form", the DHS issued a "re-revised" form that had the same expiration date (June 30, 2009), but the revision date was changed back to the 06/05/07 date. The new form reflects the list of most up-to-date documents acceptable for purposes of employment verification.The Unexpired Employment Authorization Document (I-766) document was added to List A of the List of Acceptable Documents.

All unexpiredEmployment Authorization Documents with photographs have been consolidated as one item on List A:

I-766, I-688, I-688A, I-688B

Instructions for Section 1 of the *I-9 Form* now indicate that the employee is not obliged to provide his or her Social Security number in Section 1 of the I-9, unless he or she is employed by an employer who participates in E-Verify.

 E-Verify is an Internet-based system operated by the DHS, in partnership with the Social Security Administration. It allows employers to electronically verify the employment eligibility of newly hired employees. To find out more, visit this DHS Website: ***www.dhs.gov/ximgtn/programs/ gc_1185221678150.shtm***.

Passport Cards Issued

 The Department of State and Homeland Security now issues "passport cards" which may be used for employment verification as a List A document on the I-9 form.

The "passport card" is more limited in its uses for international travel (e.g., it may not be used for international air travel), but it is a valid passport that attests to the U.S. citizenship and identity of the bearer. Accordingly, the car may be used for the Form I-9 process and can also be accepted by employers participating in the E-Verify program.

The passport card is considered a "List A" document that may be presented by newly hired employees during the employment eligibility verification process to show work authorized status. "List A" documents are those used by employees to prove both identity and work authorization when completing the Form I-9.

Employers may now sign and retain Forms I-9 electronically. See "Electronic I-9" below.

Do not file Form I-9 with U.S. Immigrations and Customs Enforcement (ICE) or USCIS. You must keep the I-9 for either:

- Three years after the date of hire; or

- One year after employment is terminated, whichever is later. The form must be available for inspection by authorized U.S. Government officials (e.g., ICE, Department of Labor).

 The Spanish version of *Form I-9* may be filled out by employers and employees in Puerto Rico ONLY. Spanish-speaking employers and employees in the 50 states and other U.S. territories may print this for their reference, but may only complete the form in English to meet employment eligibility verification requirements. Any documents used for I-9 purposes that must be "unexpired" will require you to reconfirm the employee's ability to work in the United States once the document expires. You should note the document's expiration date, and several months prior to that date, remind your employee that he/she will need to provide new I-9 documentation. The employee does not have to provide the same document again. He/she may provide any document from List A or C that establishes the employee's right to work in the United States.

Electronic I-9

Employers have the option of filling out and storing I-9 forms electronically.

In the past, the forms could only be filled out manually and retained as either paper, microfilm or microfiche. This made it difficult, particularly for large employers, to store and retrieve forms for audit purposes. Though the retention period is unchanged, existing forms, whether kept as paper, microfilm or microfiche, can be transferred to electronic format.

Employers may also use electronic signatures by the employee and employer, permitting the documentation of employment verification to be accomplished directly on a computer. Presumably the DHS will issue regulations establishing standards for electronic signatures that are not specified in the law. Employers must still view original documents presented by the employee to prove identity and work authorization, making verification from a remote location unavailable.

CalBizCentral will monitor the regulatory process and provide updated information on ***www.hrcalifornia.com*** as it becomes available. For the most recent guidelines, see "Temporary Guidance for Electronic Form I-9" on page 66.

Validity of Documents

You comply with the verification requirements for document examination if the documents reasonably appear on their face to be genuine and relate to the individual who presents it. You are not required to further investigate the authenticity of documents that meet that criterion.

You are liable for accepting documents if you know or have reason to know that the documents are false. USCIS regulations define "knowing" as:

> ...including not only actual knowledge, but also constructive knowledge... knowledge which may fairly be inferred through notice of certain facts and certain circumstances which would lend a person, through the exercise of reasonable care, to know about certain conditions.

In summary, if you knew or should have known, because of the availability of certain information, that the applicant worker held an unauthorized status and had no right to work, you will be held liable.

Use of Receipts for Missing Documents

If an individual's document has been lost, stolen, or damaged, then he/she can present a receipt for the application for a replacement document. The replacement document must be presented to the employer within 90 days of hire or, in the case of re-verification, the date employment authorization expires. If the employee fails to provide the actual document within that time limit, he/she must be laid off or terminated until the actual document can be produced.

The arrival portion of a Form I-94, Arrival-Departure Record, is an acceptable receipt, provided it contains an unexpired temporary I-551 stamp and a photograph of the individual. This document, indicating temporary evidence of permanent resident status, satisfies the I-9 documentation requirement until the expiration date on the Form I-94. If no expiration date is indicated, you may accept the receipt for one year from the issue date of the I-94 Form.

Form I-94, with a refugee admission stamp on the departure portion, is acceptable as a receipt for 90 days, within which time the employee must present an unrestricted Social Security card together with a "List B" identity document, or an Employment Authorization Document (Form I-688B or I-766). To indicate refugee status, the stamp may include a reference to section 207 of the Immigration and Nationality Act rather than use the word "refugee."

A receipt is never valid for employment of less than three working days.

Discovering an Unauthorized Worker

If you discover that an employee has been working without authorization, you should re-verify work authorization by allowing the employee another opportunity to present acceptable documentation and complete a new I-9. Suspend the employee for three days pending production of acceptable documentation. If the employee is unable to produce acceptable documentation, you must terminate employment to avoid penalties for "knowingly continuing to employ" an unauthorized worker.

California employers cannot immediately terminate employees when their visas expire unless it is clear and undisputed that their status cannot be remedied. Individuals who have the opportunity to transfer their expired visas to some other form of legal work authorization should be given the opportunity to do so. In certain circumstances, a reasonable unpaid leave of absence may be required. An employee's immigrant status does not affect the requirement in California that "good cause" employment terminations must be lawful.

Giancarlo Incalza, a citizen of Italy, after assurances that his employment was secure, took a sales position in Fendi's New York City store. Fendi helped him secure an E-1 visa and renewed it several times over the next 10 years, and gave Incalza additional assurances regarding his job security. He eventually was promoted to store manager in Fendi's Beverly Hills store, where he worked for two years with positive performance reviews. However, his supervisor did not like him and wanted to replace him.

When Fendi was sold to a French company, it was advised that the E-1 visas issued to Incalza and one other employee were no longer valid, but H1-B visas were probably available for these employees. Fendi could get a determination within 15 days as to whether the two employees would qualify. Fendi did so for the one other employee, whose employment was not interrupted, but refused to do so for Incalza and terminated him, explaining, "Nothing could be done to remedy his visa problems." Incalza requested an unpaid leave of absence because he was planning on getting married to an American citizen within the next couple of months, which would resolve the visa issue. Fendi refused.

Incalza sued, claiming he was wrongfully terminated in violation of an implied contract that he would only be fired for cause. Incalza showed that Fendi had a policy of termination only for good cause and he was given oral assurances of continued employment. California law requires an employer to have fair and honest reasons, and good faith without pretext, prior to terminating an employee for cause. Fendi said it had good cause because the IRCA required it to terminate Incalza when it discovered Incalza's E-1 visa was no longer valid. IRCA makes continued employment of an unauthorized worker illegal. Incalza claimed that Fendi's reason for his termination was pretext and he was unlawfully terminated. The court agreed.

The court clarified that an employer cannot continue the employment of unauthorized workers, but IRCA does not restrict an employer from suspending or placing an employee on an unpaid leave for a reasonable period of time to remedy his immigration status. According to the IRCA, an individual is "employed" only if he is performing work and getting paid. The IRCA's intent is to ensure unauthorized immigrants are not getting paid wages, but also to protect legal immigrants from immediate termination without further inquiry or opportunity to remedy their status. Fendi could have assisted Incalza and obtained an H1-B visa within 15 days (as it did for a similarly situated employee), or provided an unpaid leave of absence until Incalza got married – both reasonable alternatives to immediate dismissal. Thus, Incalza's visa status was not good cause for termination.

Employees should have an opportunity to gather documents or otherwise prove their immigration status without losing their job. According to the court, placing employees on unpaid leave for a reasonable period furthers the intent of IRCA by ensuring unauthorized workers are not getting paid. At the same time, it protects legal immigrants from being terminated without an opportunity to remedy their status.[4]

Re-Verification

You must re-verify employment eligibility when an employee's documentation expires. You may also re-verify employment authorization, in lieu of completing a new I-9 Form, when an employee is rehired within three years of the date that the I-9 Form was originally completed and the employee's work authorization or evidence of work authorization expires.

You must re-verify employment authorization on Section 3 of the I-9, or by completing a new I-9 Form to be attached to the original I-9 Form, no later than the expiration date of prior authorization. To re-verify expired status (I-9, Section 1) and/or expired work authorization document(s) (I-9, Section 2), an employee may present any currently valid "List A" or "List C" document.

Employees are not required to present, for re-verification purposes, a new version of the same document that was previously presented to satisfy Section 2. Any document, or combination of documents, that would be acceptable to demonstrate work eligibility/authorization is acceptable.

---

4. *Incalza v. Fendi North America* 479 F.3d 1005 (9th Cir., 2007)

Receipts showing that the employee has applied for an extension of an expired employment authorization document are not acceptable.

The re-verification requirement does not apply to the U.S. passport or "green card" (Form I-551) issued to lawful permanent residents. Temporary evidence of permanent resident status, in the form of an unexpired foreign passport containing a temporary I-551 Alien Documentation Identification and Telecommunication System (ADIT) stamp, is subject to the re-verification requirement.

"List B" documents need not be re-verified when they expire. In fact, "List B" documents are acceptable when initially shown, even when expired.

You may wish to create a "tickler" system that reminds you when an employee's authorization document will expire. Advance warning is important so the employee can apply for, and receive, replacement documents in time to maintain uninterrupted employment.

Retention of Records

You must retain these records for at least three years from the date of hire or one year from the date of termination, whichever is longer. The *I-9 Employment Eligibility Verification* and supporting documents should be kept in a location separate from the employee's personnel file and be made available for USCIS inspection within three days of a request for lawful inspection. You face civil penalties for violating these recordkeeping requirements, ranging from $100 to $1,000 for each infraction.

Acquiring a Business

If you acquire a business as a result of a corporate reorganization, merger or sale of stock or assets and you retain the predecessor's employees, you are not required to complete new I-9s for those employees. You may rely on the I-9s completed by the previous employer if the employees continue in employment, and they have a reasonable expectation of employment at all times. However, you will be held responsible if the predecessor's I-9s are deficient or defective. Therefore, a review of the predecessor's I-9 Form file and procedures should be part of your standard operating procedure.

Penalties

The IRCA provides for progressive monetary penalties and cease and desist orders for any person who knowingly hires, recruits, or refers for a fee, unauthorized workers. Fines range from $250 to $2,000 for the first offense for each unauthorized worker. You may have to pay as much as $10,000 for the third offense for each unauthorized worker. Repeat violators are subject to up to six months in jail for each violation.

Temporary Guidance for Electronic Form I-9

The DHS adopted an interim rule establishing standards for electronic signatures and the electronic retention of the Form I-9.

This interim rule permits employers to sign and store I-9 Forms electronically, as long as employers met certain performance standards set forth in the interim rule for the electronic filing system. The interim rule provides a reasonable set of standards for creating a trustworthy system for Form I-9 completion and storage. The standards are technology neutral, and allow businesses the flexibility to keep records in a manner consistent with other business processes. They also provide DHS investigators with a framework for inspecting the records and assessing their trustworthiness.

The interim rule sets standards for electronic retention of Form I-9. The rule does not limit employers to using one system for the storage of Form I-9 electronically, nor does it identify one method for acceptable electronic signatures. Electronic signatures can be accomplished using various technologies including, but not limited to:

- Electronic signature pads;

- Personal Identification Numbers (PIN);

- Biometrics; and

- "Click to accept" dialog boxes.

The DHS determined that "off- the shelf" computer programs and commercial automated data processing systems in use comply with the standards required by this rule.

An employer complying with the current recordkeeping and retention requirements is not required to take any additional or different action to comply with the revised rules. The revised rules simply offer an additional option.

 Whether filled out manually or electronically, an employer representative must still physically examine required identification and work eligibility documentation.

These interim guidelines also address how employers should handle "no match" letters from DHS or the SSA. For more information, see "Handling "No Match" Letters From the Social Security Administration" in Chapter 3, page 32.

Staying Out of Trouble

It is unlawful to discriminate against or harass employees because of their ethnic background or national origin, or to exclude applicants lawfully entitled to work in the United States for similar reasons. These prohibitions are contained in numerous overlapping statutes at the federal and state levels.

Discrimination

If you employ four or more people, you may not discriminate against any individual (other than an unauthorized worker) on the basis of national origin or citizenship status.[5] You cannot refuse to hire a legal worker on the basis of the prospective employee's physical, cultural or linguistic characteristics or national origin because of a presumed higher risk that immigration-related problems may occur. Workers protected under the amnesty provisions of the IRCA as temporary residents also enjoy protection from employment discrimination.[6] These anti-discrimination provisions apply to all employers with more than three employees.

The full force and effect of *Title VII* of the federal Civil Rights Act remains in force in the hiring, employment and termination of all workers covered by the IRCA. Specifically, Title VII bans all

---

5. IRCA sec. 102
6. 8 U.S.C. 1324b

employment practices that subject individuals to different or unequal treatment because of their national origin (see Chapter 27, "Title VII of the Civil Rights Act of 1964").

 California law limits your ability to adopt or enforce an "English-only" policy.[7] See "English-only Policies" in Chapter 27, page 771, for more information about this new law.

Citizenship Requirements

Citizenship, as a condition of employment, may be unlawful if it has the effect of discriminating against individuals because of their national origin. Though the IRCA prohibits discrimination on the basis of citizenship, the act specifically states that to prefer a citizen over a worker, where both are equally qualified, is not a violation of federal law.[8]

Harassment

Harassment of employees on the basis of their national origin in the form of ethnic slurs or other verbal or physical conduct constitutes unlawful harassment when such conduct:

- Has the effect of creating an intimidating, hostile or offensive work environment;

- Has the effect of unreasonable interference with the individual's work performance; or

- Otherwise interferes with an employee's employment opportunities.

Award of Damages to Undocumented Workers

The U.S. Supreme Court ruled that undocumented workers are not entitled to back pay for lost wages resulting from an unlawful termination. The court rejected an award of back pay by the National Labor Relations Board (NLRB) to an employee who was laid off for supporting a union organizing effort. The court found that an award of back pay would conflict with federal immigration policy, as expressed by Congress in the IRCA. That policy prohibited the NLRB from awarding back pay to an undocumented worker who has never been legally authorized to work in the United States.[9]

Under California law, all individuals who applied for employment, or who are or have been employed in the state are entitled to all protections, rights and remedies available under state law, except any reinstatement remedy prohibited by federal law, regardless of immigration status. The law further provides that for the purposes of enforcing state labor, employment, civil rights, and employee housing laws, a person's immigration status is irrelevant to the issue of liability. No inquiry is permitted into a person's immigration status except when necessary by clear and convincing evidence to comply with federal immigration law.[10]

Employees' undocumented status is not a defense for an employer that fails to pay the legal wage, according to a California court of appeal. Regardless of employees' immigrant status, they must be paid at least the prevailing, or minimum, wage for all time worked.

Employees for Van Elk performed welding-related work on a public works project. Employees on public works projects must be paid the prevailing wage, or the general prevailing rate for the particular skill or

7. Gov't Code sec. 12951
8. USC 1324b(4)
9. *Hoffman Plastic Compounds, Inc. v. National Labor Relations Board* 122 S. Ct. 1275 (2002)
10. Civ. Code sec. 3339, Lab. Code sec. 1171.5, Health and Safety Code sec. 24000, Gov't Code sec. 7285

job involved. Prevailing wage laws are minimum wage laws mandated by statute. They give employees property rights to the money earned while working under the public contract. The court emphasized that employees have an unconditional right to all prevailing wages they earned for work performed.

Van Elk claimed that the employees were undocumented, and, therefore, the IRCA prevents them from suing to recover any wages. The court disagreed because there is no stated limit of remedies under the IRCA for unpaid wages, and federal and state wage and hour laws do not provide an exception for payment of wages for undocumented workers. If the IRCA did have such an exemption, then employers would have an incentive to hire these workers and pay them subminimum wages – directly in conflict with the purpose of prevailing wage laws. Indeed, prevailing wage laws only refer to "workers" and do not restrict their application to citizens. There is significant precedent supporting the position that employers who hire undocumented workers must also bear the burden of complying with wage, hour and workers' compensation laws.

Although wages for work performed must be paid regardless of employees' immigrant status, the U.S. Supreme Court has ruled that there is no such requirement or authorization for a court to require payment of loss of future wages or unearned "back pay." Allowing employers to hire undocumented workers and pay them less than the prevailing wage subverts immigration policy by condoning and encouraging employers to continue to hire undocumented workers. In contrast, the court noted, awarding workers for wages they have already earned makes it clear to employers that they cannot profit from hiring and exploiting these workers.[11]

California employers must comply with all wage and hour laws — paying employees, paying them on time and so forth — even if the employee is not legally eligible to work in the United States. If you hire illegal workers, not only can you be subject to fines and penalties for doing so, you still must pay the workers. First and foremost, you should not have had the person performing any work until you verified eligibility to work in the same manner as you would for all other employees — such as using the Social Security Administration's online verification service. For more information, see "Verifying Social Security Numbers" in Chapter 3, page 32. Nonetheless, you must still pay him or her for all hours worked.

Wages cannot be run through payroll without a valid Social Security number. However, payroll can run the person's wages and give you the calculation of how much money should be paid to the employee and the amount of each required withholding. You may have to issue a check or cash through accounts payable to ensure the person is paid and set aside the required withholdings.

Working With the USCIS

The USCIS has a well-deserved reputation for being slow-moving and bureaucratic when it comes to processing employment eligibility matters. For this reason, consider consulting a specialist in immigration law when seeking to qualify a foreign worker for employment.

Temporary Resident Alien Status

Applicants who qualify for citizenship under IRCA may apply for temporary resident alien status and must meet most current citizenship requirements, including registration under the Military Selective Service Act. In addition, any criminal record on the applicant's part must include no more than two misdemeanor convictions and must be clear of any felony convictions. Applicants meeting

---

11. *Reyes v. Van Elk* 148 Cal. App. 4th 604 (2007)

these qualifications will be given the status of temporary resident alien for employment purposes. After the 18 months of temporary status under the act, applicants may have their status adjusted for full permanent residence.

Premium Processing Service

The USCIS offers employers a Premium Processing Service for certain immigration applications. Premium Processing Service allows you to pay a $1,000 fee in exchange for 15-calendar day processing of your immigration related petitions and applications.

The USCIS guarantees that within 15 days it will issue either an approval notice, a notice of intent to deny, a request for evidence, or a notice of investigation for fraud or misrepresentation. If the USCIS fails to process the petition within 15 days, it will refund your $1,000 and continue to process the petition as part of the Premium Processing Service.

In addition to expedited processing, participating in the program allows you to use a dedicated phone number and e-mail address to check on the status of your petition or ask any other questions you may have concerning your petition.

More information about the USCIS Premium Processing Service is available at **http://www.uscis.gov**. Or call the USCIS National Customer Service Center at (800) 375-5283.

Further Information

The USCIS offers several toll-free numbers from which additional information can be obtained. You can also find valuable information for employers at **http://www.uscis.gov/portal/site/uscis**.

The Employer Business Investor and School Services Hotline (EBISS), formerly the Office of Business Liaison, also has a toll-free information number at (800) 357-2099, or 1-800-767-1833 for the hearing impaired. It is generally available from 8:00 A.M. to 6:00 P.M EST, Monday through Friday (Federal holidays excluded). This office will send out limited quantities of the Form I-9, Employment Eligibility Verification, and the Form M-274, Handbook for Employers, and provide copies of any of our series of Employer Information Bulletins. These bulletins present information on complex immigration matters and procedures of frequent concern to employers, in plain language format. They can also be downloaded from **http://www.uscis.gov/portal/site/uscis**.

The SSA offers several ways in which you can verify Social Security numbers. To verify up to five names and SSNs, you may call (800) 772-6270 on weekdays from 7:00 A.M. to 7:00 P.M. EST. You will be asked for your company name and Employer Identification Number (EIN). Then you will be asked to provide the following information for each name/SSN you want to verify:

1. SSN;

2. Last name;

3. First name;

4. Middle initial (if applicable);

5. Date of birth; and

6. Gender.

An Internet-based system for verification services is being pilot tested, which will provide immediate or next business day response to name/SSN verification requests.

For further information about the verification process, and how to verify more than five SSNs at one time, go to ***www.socialsecurity.gov/employer/ssnv.htm***.

Chapter 4 Forms

This chapter contains samples of forms associated with this topic. *The forms in this section are for visual reference only; download the most up-to-date forms and checklists in their entirety from CalBizCentral.*

To download either individual forms or your entire Formspack containing all the forms referenced in this book:

1. Visit **www.calbizcentral.com/support** and select "Labor Law Digest" from the list of product titles.

2. Have this copy of Labor Law Digest handy — you will need to enter the access code featured on the inside covers of this book.

3. Enter the access code, select the documents you want to download to your computer, then follow the on-screen instructions.

For more detailed instructions, see "Forms Available Online" on page xix.

Questions and Answers about Immigration Law

Q. *Is an employer subject to penalties if a legal alien is hired who later becomes illegal, if, for example, he/she remains in the United States beyond the authorized time?*

A. Yes, when an employer knows the alien has become illegal. The penalties would not apply, however, if the alien was hired before the legislation was signed into law.

Q. *What is the employer's responsibility?*

A. An employer must ask all job applicants for documents required by law to verify that the job applicant is either a U.S. citizen or an alien authorized to work in the United States.

Q. *Does the employer have to investigate the authenticity of the documents?*

A. No. An employer fulfills his/her responsibility if he/she examines the documents and each document "reasonably appears, on its face, to be genuine."

Q. *Do U.S. citizens have to show these documents?*

A. Yes. The immigration act affects each new hire and imposes new paperwork requirements.

Q. *Is there any penalty for an employer who fails to ask job applicants for identification documents?*

A. Yes. The employer is subject to a civil penalty of $100 to $1,000 each time he/she fails to verify the status of the job applicant. Increased civil penalties may be assessed for subsequent violations. Criminal penalties may be applied to situations showing a pattern or practice of knowingly hiring, or continuing to employ, unauthorized workers.

Q. *Is the employer subject to such penalties even if the person he/she hires is a U.S. citizen?*

A. Yes.

Q. *How will the government know if an employer has complied with the requirements of IRCA?*

A. Employers must sign INS Form I-9 certifying that they have examined the required documents. In addition, each person hired must certify, on the same form, that he/she is a U.S. citizen or an alien authorized to work in the United States. The employer must retain all required forms for at least three years and may not dispose of them until one year after the individual's employment ends.

Q. *Does an employer have to keep the paperwork for people not hired?*

A. The act does not require this of the employer. However, some employers may voluntarily retain the records to show they were not discriminating.

Q. *What happens if an employer simply refuses to hire people who, in his/her eyes, appear to be foreigners, and he/she doesn't want the hassle of bureaucratic requirements?*

A. It is illegal for an employer to discriminate on the basis of national origin under the Civil Rights Act of 1964. The Equal Employment Opportunity Commission (EEOC) will continue to investigate complaints of discrimination. IRCA also makes it illegal for employers to discriminate against legal aliens because of their citizenship status. A special counsel's office has been established in the Justice Department to investigate complaints of such discrimination. If appropriate, this office will issue complaints and prosecute the case before an administrative law judge. If there is a finding of discrimination, the government could impose a civil penalty of $1,000 and could order the employer to hire the complainant with back pay.

Questions and Answers about Immigration Law
(Page 1 of 3)

I-9 Employment Eligibility Verification

OMB No. 1615-0047; Expires 06/30/09

Department of Homeland Security
U.S. Citizenship and Immigration Services

Form I-9, Employment Eligibility Verification

Instructions

Please read all instructions carefully before completing this form.

Anti-Discrimination Notice. It is illegal to discriminate against any individual (other than an alien not authorized to work in the U.S.), in hiring, discharging, or recruiting or referring for a fee because of that individual's national origin or citizenship status. It is illegal to discriminate against work eligible individuals. Employers **CANNOT** specify which document(s) they will accept from an employee. The refusal to hire an individual because the documents presented have a future expiration date may also constitute illegal discrimination.

What Is the Purpose of This Form?

The purpose of this form is to document that each new employee (both citizen and non-citizen) hired after November 6, 1986 is authorized to work in the United States.

When Should the Form I-9 Be Used?

All employees, citizens and noncitizens, hired after November 6, 1986 and working in the United States must complete a Form I-9.

Filling Out the Form I-9

Section 1, Employee: This part of the form must be completed at the time of hire, which is the actual beginning of employment. Providing the Social Security number is voluntary, except for employees hired by employers participating in the USCIS Electronic Employment Eligibility Verification Program (E-Verify). **The employer is responsible for ensuring that Section 1 is timely and properly completed.**

Preparer/Translator Certification. The Preparer/Translator Certification must be completed if **Section 1** is prepared by a person other than the employee. A preparer/translator may be used only when the employee is unable to complete **Section 1** on his/her own. However, the employee must still sign **Section 1** personally.

Section 2, Employer: For the purpose of completing this form, the term "employer" means all employers including those recruiters and referrers for a fee who are agricultural associations, agricultural employers or farm labor contractors. Employers must complete **Section 2** by examining evidence of identity and employment eligibility within three (3) business days of the date employment begins. If employees are authorized to work, but are unable to present the required

---

documents(s) within three business days, they must present a receipt for the application of the document(s) within three business days and the actual document(s) within ninety (90) days. However, if employers hire individuals for a duration of less than three business days, **Section 2** must be completed at the time employment begins. **Employers must record:**

1. Document title;
2. Issuing authority;
3. Document number;
4. Expiration date, if any; and
5. The date employment begins.

Employers must sign and date the certification. Employees must present original documents. Employers may, but are not required to, photocopy the document(s) presented. These photocopies may only be used for the verification process and must be retained with the Form I-9. However, employers are still responsible for completing and retaining the Form I-9.

Section 3, Updating and Reverification: Employers must complete **Section 3** when updating and/or reverifying the Form I-9. Employers must reverify employment eligibility of their employees on or before the expiration date recorded in **Section 1**. Employers **CANNOT** specify which document(s) they will accept from an employee.

1. If an employee's name has changed at the time this form is being updated/reverified, complete Block A.

2. If an employee is rehired within three (3) years of the date this form was originally completed and the employee is still eligible to be employed on the same basis as previously indicated on this form (updating), complete Block B and the signature block.

3. If an employee is rehired within three (3) years of the date this form was originally completed and the employee's work authorization has expired or if a current employee's work authorization is about to expire (reverification), complete Block B and:

   1. Examine any document that reflects that the employee is authorized to work in the U.S. (see List A **or** C);

   2. Record the document title, document number and expiration date (if any) in Block C; and

   3. Complete the signature block.

Form I-9 (Rev. 06/05/07) N

What Is the Filing Fee?

There is no associated filing fee for completing the Form I-9. This form is not filed with USCIS or any government agency. The Form I-9 must be retained by the employer and made available for inspection by U.S. Government officials as specified in the Privacy Act Notice below.

USCIS Forms and Information

To order USCIS forms, call our toll-free number at **1-800-870-3676.** Individuals can also get USCIS forms and information on immigration laws, regulations and procedures by telephoning our National Customer Service Center at **1-800-375-5283** or visiting our internet website at **www.uscis.gov.**

Photocopying and Retaining the Form I-9

A blank Form I-9 may be reproduced, provided both sides are copied. The Instructions must be available to all employees completing this form. Employers must retain completed Forms I-9 for three (3) years after the date of hire or one (1) year after the date employment ends, whichever is later.

The Form I-9 may be signed and retained electronically, as authorized in Department of Homeland Security regulations at 8 CFR § 274a.2.

Privacy Act Notice

The authority for collecting this information is the Immigration Reform and Control Act of 1986, Pub. L. 99-603 (8 USC 1324a).

This information is for employers to verify the eligibility of individuals for employment to preclude the unlawful hiring, or recruiting or referring for a fee, of aliens who are not authorized to work in the United States.

This information will be used by employers as a record of their basis for determining eligibility of an employee to work in the United States. The form will be kept by the employer and made available for inspection by officials of U.S. Immigration and Customs Enforcement, Department of Labor and Office of Special Counsel for Immigration Related Unfair Employment Practices.

Submission of the information required in this form is voluntary. However, an individual may not begin employment unless this form is completed, since employers are subject to civil or criminal penalties if they do not comply with the Immigration Reform and Control Act of 1986.

Paperwork Reduction Act

We try to create forms and instructions that are accurate, can be easily understood and which impose the least possible burden on you to provide us with information. Often this is difficult because some immigration laws are very complex. Accordingly, the reporting burden for this collection of information is computed as follows: **1)** learning about this form, and completing the form, 9 minutes; **2)** assembling and filing (recordkeeping) the form, 3 minutes, for an average of 12 minutes per response. If you have comments regarding the accuracy of this burden estimate, or suggestions for making this form simpler, you can write to: U.S. Citizenship and Immigration Services, Regulatory Management Division, 111 Massachusetts Avenue, N.W., 3rd Floor, Suite 3008, Washington, DC 20529. OMB No. 1615-0047.

EMPLOYERS MUST RETAIN COMPLETED FORM I-9
PLEASE DO NOT MAIL COMPLETED FORM I-9 TO ICE OR USCIS

Form I-9 (Rev. 06/05/07) N Page 2

Department of Homeland Security
U.S. Citizenship and Immigration Services

OMB No. 1615-0047; Expires 06/30/09
Form I-9, Employment
Eligibility Verification

Please read instructions carefully before completing this form. The instructions must be available during completion of this form.

ANTI-DISCRIMINATION NOTICE: It is illegal to discriminate against work eligible individuals. Employers CANNOT specify which document(s) they will accept from an employee. The refusal to hire an individual because the documents have a future expiration date may also constitute illegal discrimination.

Section 1. Employee Information and Verification. To be completed and signed by employee at the time employment begins.

Print Name: Last	First	Middle Initial	Maiden Name

Address (Street Name and Number)	Apt. #	Date of Birth (month/day/year)

City	State	Zip Code	Social Security #

I am aware that federal law provides for imprisonment and/or fines for false statements or use of false documents in connection with the completion of this form.

I attest, under penalty of perjury, that I am (check one of the following):

☐ A citizen or national of the United States
☐ A lawful permanent resident (Alien #) A _____
☐ An alien authorized to work until _____
(Alien # or Admission #) _____

Employee's Signature	Date (month/day/year)

Preparer and/or Translator Certification. (To be completed and signed if Section 1 is prepared by a person other than the employee.) I attest, under penalty of perjury, that I have assisted in the completion of this form and that to the best of my knowledge the information is true and correct.

Preparer's/Translator's Signature	Print Name

Address (Street Name and Number, City, State, Zip Code)	Date (month/day/year)

Section 2. Employer Review and Verification. To be completed and signed by employer. Examine one document from List A OR examine one document from List B and one from List C, as listed on the reverse of this form, and record the title, number and expiration date, if any, of the document(s).

List A	OR	List B	AND	List C

Document title: _____

Issuing authority: _____

Document #: _____

Expiration Date (if any): _____

Document #: _____

Expiration Date (if any): _____

CERTIFICATION - I attest, under penalty of perjury, that I have examined the document(s) presented by the above-named employee, that the above-listed document(s) appear to be genuine and to relate to the employee named, that the employee began employment on (month/day/year) _____ **and that to the best of my knowledge the employee is eligible to work in the United States.** (State employment agencies may omit the date the employee began employment.)

Signature of Employer or Authorized Representative	Print Name	Title

Business or Organization Name and Address (Street Name and Number, City, State, Zip Code)	Date (month/day/year)

Section 3. Updating and Reverification. To be completed and signed by employer.

A. New Name (if applicable)	B. Date of Rehire (month/day/year) (if applicable)

C. If employee's previous grant of work authorization has expired, provide the information below for the document that establishes current employment eligibility.

Document Title:	Document #:	Expiration Date (if any):

I attest, under penalty of perjury, that to the best of my knowledge, this employee is eligible to work in the United States, and if the employee presented document(s), the document(s) I have examined appear to be genuine and to relate to the individual.

Signature of Employer or Authorized Representative	Date (month/day/year)

Form I-9 (Rev. 06/05/07) N

Alternative Employment and Independent Contractors

Established labor law provides few answers to the multitude of issues you face regarding variations of the traditional workforce — telecommuters, contingent workers and independent contractors. The courts are just beginning to grapple with liability issues created by workplace variations. Until the rules become established, you must educate yourself about the issues that are likely to arise in the evolving workplace so you may make informed decisions and policy.

This chapter provides a thorough explanation and discussion of the many issues you are likely to face. The subject of telecommuting is covered through a comprehensive compilation of topics such as supervision, computer issues, wage and hour issues, workers' compensation and even safety and health concerns.

The distinction between direct employment and indirect employment (temporary workers, leased employees and independent contractors) is often blurred by the details of the arrangements and laws or court decisions designed to protect the interests of workers. This chapter also explains how to make those distinctions and the implications of failing to do so.

In this chapter, you will also learn about related requirements such as reporting obligations, wages/hours and workers' compensation. Health-care staffing, benefits and union issues are also discussed.

 Download forms referenced in this chapter at **www.calbizcentral.com/support**. Be sure to have your access code from the inside covers of this book ready to enter into the forms download area. Your access code for the forms in the online Formspack is on the inside covers of this book. See "Forms Available Online" on page xix for more information.

Telecommuters

The United States General Accountability Office issued a report in 2001 estimating that telecommuting has grown about 20 percent per year over a 10-year period. An estimated 16.5 million employees telecommute at least once a month, with 9.3 million employees telecommuting at least once a week.[1]

The majority of those who telecommute do so from home. Whether working at the kitchen table or in a bedroom converted to an office, these individuals arrive at work via technology rather than the freeways. However, the very technology that allows the flexibility to work from home creates questions which must be answered if the employment relationship is to run smoothly and litigation is to be avoided.

---

1. *Telecommuting: Overview of Potential Barriers Facing Employers*, GAO-01-926, (July 11, 2001)

Selection

Before an employee begins telecommuting, consider the following important issues. Where the law has given some direction on a particular issue, comments appear in italics after the issue is raised.

- Who will decide which employees telecommute?

- If you decide an employee should work from home, does he/she have the choice to refuse and remain in the main office?

- If the employee requests telecommuting, on what basis do you decide to allow or disallow it? *Adopt a systematic approach to telecommuting requests, perhaps by creating a standard request form which you can use to track any inequities in the decision-making process. It might be wise to stay out of the issue of **why** the employee wants to telecommute altogether, to avoid having to make a value judgment about whether one employee's new baby is more important than another employee's plans to go to law school at night.*

- If the employee's request to work from home is a suggested reasonable accommodation for a disability under the Americans with Disabilities Act (ADA), must you allow it? *The federal courts are split as to whether an employer must grant an employee's request to work at home as a reasonable accommodation.[2] See Chapter 29, "Disabilities In the Workplace" for more information.*

- If the employee works from home as a reasonable accommodation under the ADA, do you have an obligation to make reasonable accommodations in the employee's home office (for example, providing a desk to accommodate a wheelchair, a special telephone for hearing impairment)? *If the request to work from home is granted as a reasonable accommodation for a disability, you probably have the same obligation to make reasonable accommodations for the employee's home office as you would for the employee's on-site office. However, it would probably not be reasonable to require you to make major structural modifications to the employee's home, such as wheelchair ramps and accessible restrooms.*

Location

- Will the telecommuter work from home each day, or come in to the main office for part of the week?

- How often will he/she be required to report to the main office?

- Will there be a place in the main office that the employee can work?

- Is there a place for the telecommuter to park when he/she comes into the main office? Who will be responsible for parking costs? *The California Labor Code requires an employer to reimburse an employee for all the costs the employee necessarily expends or loses in direct consequence to the performance of his/her duties.[3] The employee who normally telecommutes and incurs no parking costs may argue that you must reimburse him/her for those costs when you require the employee to come to the main office.*

---

2. *Anzalone v. Allstate Insurance Co.*, 74 F.3d 1236 (5th Cir.1995); *Vande Zande v. Wisconsin Dept. of Administration*, 44 F.3d 538 (7th Cir. 1995)
3. Lab. Code sec. 2802

Support Staff

- Will the telecommuter have support staff, such as a secretary or assistant? If so, where will the support staff work? If the support staff is in the main office, how will communication between the two be set up?

- How will work get back and forth between the employee and support staff?

Meetings

- Will you require the employee to report to the main office for meetings?

- Can the employee attend some or all of these meetings by teleconference?

- If so, is there a mechanism for getting materials that will be distributed at the meetings to the telecommuter so that he/she can participate fully?

Communicating With Customers/Clients

- When a customer/client calls the employee at the main office number, will there be a way to transfer the call to the employee's home? If so, does a toll or long distance charge apply to the transferred call? If not, how will the message be forwarded to the employee?

- Will you give the employee's home or home office number to customers/clients?

- Will more calls from the employee's home to the company's customers/clients be long distance than they would from the main office?

- Will the cost of long distance calls be higher from the employee's home than from the main office, which may have a discount long distance rate due to the high volume of calls?

Turning In Work/Picking Up Projects

- Who will bear responsibility for getting projects from the main office to the employee's home office and back again?

- Will the employee's work deadlines be adjusted in any way to accommodate the time necessary to transport work between the two locations?

Supervision and Evaluation

- How will you monitor the employee's production/performance?

- Will you measure criteria found on most performance evaluations, such as "interaction with coworkers?"

Company Policies

- Will your policies change for telecommuters? For example, will an employee working at home still be required to comply with your dress code specifying "professional attire?"

- How will you monitor employees for complying with policies, such as those relating to drug and alcohol use on the job?

Employee Family Interaction

- What will your policy be relating to the employee's children or elderly parents needing home care while the employee is working? Though an employee obviously cannot be productive while supervising a three-year-old at home, would a teenager coming home from school and doing homework or other activities interfere with the employee's work? What about an elderly parent whose need for care may interfere every few hours with the employee's work?

- Will you have a policy regarding the employee's children helping out by, for example, stuffing envelopes or answering the telephone used for business calls when the employee is momentarily away from it? *Be aware that courts could construe this as a violation of child labor laws.*

Office Equipment and Supplies

- Who will decide what office equipment and supplies the employee needs at home? Will you supply the same type of equipment the employee would have access to in the main office, or supply less expensive/smaller equipment? If the equipment you provide for home is slower, a laptop computer versus a powerful desktop computer, will that be considered when evaluating the employee's productivity?

- Who will be responsible for shopping for, transporting and paying for equipment required for a home office? Will the employee be expected to provide items such as a computer, printer, fax, copier, telephone, desk, chair and filing cabinet? If the employee already uses a personal computer or related items at home, will you require him/her to use those items rather than company- provided equipment?

- Who will be responsible for shopping for, transporting and paying for office supplies such as paper, staples and tape?

- If you purchase office supplies, how will the employee get them to his/her home? Will you deliver the supplies? Will the employee be required to drive to the main office to pick them up?

- If the employee purchases supplies, how and when will you reimburse him/her? *Note that it may be more costly to have employees purchase small quantities of supplies rather than purchasing in bulk.*

- Will the employee be paid his/her regular rate of pay for time spent shopping for office supplies? *Remember that this will be work time for which wages are due, including overtime if applicable.*

Maintenance

- Who will pay for maintaining and repairing home office equipment? If the high-speed Internet access equipment for an employee's computer breaks while he/she is using the computer after hours for personal use, who will be responsible for the repair?

- If the employee is responsible for the repair and cannot afford it for some time, what will you do to restore e-mail communication with the employee?

Computer Issues

- Will the employee be allowed to use a computer, which you have provided, for personal use during non-work time?

- Will other members of the household be allowed to use the computer you provide?

- Is the employee's computer secured by a password or other device?

- Will other members of the household have access to confidential documents?

- How are drafts of confidential documents discarded (for example, shredded or simply added to the household trash)?

- Are attacks by computer viruses more likely, as computer disks are traded between home and main office?

- Could your company files accidentally be wiped out by a member of the employee's household using the computer for personal use?

Telephone/Fax/Modem

- Who will decide what type of telephone equipment the employee needs at home?

- Will you supply the same type of telephone equipment the employee would have access to in the main office? *Note that many office telephone systems are not compatible with home telephone jacks.*

- How many lines will the employee need to work from home?

- Will the employee use his/her personal household telephone for work, as well as personal calls? Or will a line dedicated to business be required? If so, will one line that can be switched between telephone to fax be sufficient, or will multiple lines be required?

- Will the employee be able to install a sufficient number of lines in his/her house? *The employee may need to check with his/her local telephone company for the answer to these questions.*

- Who will be responsible for shopping, transporting and paying for telephone equipment required for a home office?

- Will the employee be expected to provide a telephone and/or answering machine?

- If the employee already has a second telephone line at home (perhaps for an outside business), will you require him/her to use that line rather than provide another?

- Who will pay for maintaining and repairing telephone equipment?

- Who will pay for telephone, fax and modem service charges?

- If the employee uses any of the business lines for personal communication during non-working hours, how will you divide the monthly service charges? Because the employee will be home all day, will the employee be reimbursed for the increased heating and cooling costs for his/her home? Will there be any reimbursement for the employee's increased cost for the electricity required to run his/her computer, monitor, fax, printer, copier and lights in the home office? *The California Labor Code requires an employer to reimburse an employee for all money the employee necessarily expends or loses in direct consequence to the performance of his/her duties.*[4]

Miscellaneous Laws

- Will you require the employee working at home to **post** the posters and notices which state and federal law require to be posted in the workplace? *Laws requiring an employer to display a poster contain no exemption for home offices. An employee working at home technically should post all the required workplace posters in his/her home office.*

- If an employee works outside the state where the employer's main office is located, how will you monitor and comply with that state's employment laws? *The law in the state in which the employee works is the law that applies to him/her. An employee in Nevada working at home for an employer headquartered in California will be governed by Nevada employment laws.*

- Similarly, for employees outside the city or county where the main office is located, how will you monitor and comply with local ordinances affecting employment (for example, San Francisco's discrimination ordinances) in the employee's location?

- Will the employee need a license or permit to perform industrial homework? *California's Labor Code and the Fair Labor Standards Act (FLSA) regulate certain types of work performed in the home. Though most of these laws target manufacturing, they may be construed broadly enough to include much of the work done utilizing home technology. If industrial homework laws apply, permits are required and you have a number of legal responsibilities as an employer of an industrial homeworker.*

City/County Taxes and Licenses

- Cities and counties may not impose business taxes and related licensing requirements on an employee working at home.[5] For purposes of this law, "employee" means a common law employee as reflected in rulings or guidelines used by either the Internal Revenue Service or the California Franchise Tax Board.

- Individuals who work at home operating as independent contractors remain subject to city and county taxes and licensing requirements. See "Independent Contractors" on page 93 for more information about the difference between employees and independent contractors.

Wage and Hour Issues

- How will you monitor a nonexempt employee's work hours? Will the employee call the main office to record his/her starting and ending times each day? Will the employee log on to his/her computer, which transmits starting and ending times via a modem to the main office? Will the employee keep a record on paper of hours worked? *Note that the law does require a record of the hours a nonexempt employee works, including a record of when meal breaks are taken.*[6]

---

4. Lab. Code sec. 2802
5. Bus. & Prof. Code sec. 16300
6. Lab. Code sec. 1174

- How will overtime be tracked? How will you control the employee's overtime hours? *You must pay overtime for all overtime hours worked, regardless of whether the employee was authorized to do so, if you knew or had reason to know the overtime was being worked.[7] You could argue that you had no knowledge or reason to know an employee was working overtime at home. However, a sudden increase in work completed or an employee's comment that he/she "simply can't get it all done in eight hours (or 40 hours)" could be construed as reason for you to know that the employee was working overtime.*

- How will you know the employee is taking the required meal and break periods?

- How will you know how much meal and break time the employee is taking?

- Will the employee be on an alternative workweek schedule?

- Is the employee a part of the rest of his/her "identifiable work unit" working at the main office, or a separate identifiable work unit altogether? *This is important for determining who must participate in the process required to implement an alternative workweek schedule. An identifiable work unit is defined as a "division, department, job classification, shift, separate physical location or a recognized subdivision of any work unit."[8] An employee working from home could arguably be an identifiable, individual work unit based on his/her separate physical location, allowing him/her to work a different alternative schedule than the employees in the main office. See "Alternative Workweek Scheduling" in Chapter 15, page 363.*

- When is the telecommuting employee's on-call time compensable? *If the employee is free to do whatever he/she chooses at home while waiting for the employer's call to begin work, wages probably are not required for that time. See "On-Call/Standby Pay" in Chapter 12, page 277, for more information regarding on-call time.*

- If the employee keeps a written record of hours worked, how will the employee transmit that record to your payroll department?

- When and where will the employee receive his/her paycheck? *California's Labor Code requires employers to post a notice informing employees of the regular time and place of wage payment.[9] However, a telecommuting employee who would rather receive his/her paycheck by mail probably could sign an enforceable agreement to that effect.*

- If the employee who normally works at home and has no regular commute must drive to the main office, will the travel time be compensable? *Normally, an employee's regular commute to the workplace is not compensable time. However, since a telecommuting employee does not have a regular commute, he/she could make a plausible argument to the Labor Commissioner that he/she should be compensated for commute time when you require him/her to report to the main office.*

- Will you reimburse the employee for mileage? *The California Labor Code requires an employer to reimburse an employee for all the employee necessarily expends or loses in direct consequence to the performance of his/her duties.[10] The employee who normally telecommutes and incurs no commuting costs may have an argument that you must reimburse him/her for mileage when you require the employee to come to the main office.*

- Will the answer to the two previous questions be affected by whether the employer has requested that the employee come to the main office, or whether the choice to come in was the employee's?

---

7. IWC Orders sec. 3
8. IWC Orders sec. 3
9. Lab. Code sec. 207
10. Lab. Code sec. 2802

- Will you pay an exempt employee on a day where he/she calls in to the office to check messages or logs onto the computer for a few minutes to answer an e-mail message from the main office? *Remember, you must pay exempt employees their full salary for any day in which they perform* **any** *work.*[11]

Workers' Compensation

- How will you determine whether an injury occurred in the course and scope of employment? For example, if the employee injures his/her back while taking out a bag of trash containing discarded items from both the home office and the kitchen, was the employee acting within the course of employment?

- Can you effectively fight fraudulent claims when there rarely will be witnesses to an injury?

- Will the employee's inability to physically get away from the work on his/her desk during non-working hours become too stressful? Will the isolation and monotony of being home so much lead to a stress claim?

Safety and Health

- How will you fulfill your duty to provide the employee with a safe and healthy workplace? The U.S. Department of Labor issued a policy statement in February of 2000 stating that the agency will not hold companies responsible for the safety of telecommuting employees' home offices. The directive says the government:

  - Will not inspect employees' home offices, expect employers to inspect them or hold companies liable for the offices' safety conditions;

  - May pass complaints received from workers about home office safety to employers but will not follow-up; and

  - Can hold companies responsible for safety problems with at-home jobs other than office work. That could include things such as manufacturing piecework involving materials, equipment or work processes which the employer provides or requires to be used in an employee's home. However, even those risky at-home work sites will be inspected only if the government receives complaints.

- The above directive does not affect your liability under workers' compensation laws for on the job injuries in home offices. The directive is available on the U.S. Department of Labor's Web site at:
  www.osha.gov/pls/oshaweb/owadisp.show_document?p_table=DIRECTIVES&p_id=2254.

- How will you know if the employee is using safety equipment you provide (glare screens for computers, wrist rests for keyboards or equipment cord covers)?

- Do you have the right to inspect the employee's home for unsafe conditions? *This question pits the employer's duty to provide a safe workplace directly against the employee's constitutional right to privacy. To date, no court has squarely addressed this issue.*

- If conditions in the home need adjustments to meet safety standards, who will make and pay for the adjustments?

- Will your Injury and Illness Prevention Plan (IIPP) (required by law) include items relating to the home office?

---

11. 29 CFR 541.602(a)

- How will you conduct legally required safety training?

- How will you ensure that the home is a secure place to work? Will you require the employee to keep doors locked and windows closed during working hours? If so, how will you enforce this?

- What is your liability for an incident of violence that occurs in the home during working hours? Will that determination be affected by whether the perpetrator is another member of the household or a stranger?

Relocation

- If the employee moves to a new residence, who will pay the charges to set up new telephone, fax and modem lines?

- Who will pay the cost of moving office equipment and supplies?

Termination

- When the employee quits or is terminated, what provisions have you made for return of equipment, supplies, and files?

- How will you transfer work-related computer files from the employee's computer to the main office?

- How will outstanding bills (for example, telephone/fax/modem line) be apportioned?

- If the employee is terminated, will you go to the employee's home to deliver the final wages? *When an employee is terminated, California law specifies that all unpaid wages and accrued but unused vacation are due and payable immediately.*[12]

Industrial Homeworkers

Industrial homework is the manufacture of materials or articles in a home for an employer, when such articles or materials are not for the personal use of the employer or a member of his or her family. This includes activity to make, process, prepare, alter, repair or finish in whole or in part, or to assemble, inspect, wrap or package any articles or materials.

The Labor Code establishes restrictions on such activities in any room, house, apartment or other premises used in whole or in part as a place of dwelling, including outbuildings, such as garages, under the control of the person dwelling on such premises.

---

12. Lab. Code sec. 201

Licenses and Permits

You are required to have a valid industrial homework license from the Division of Labor Standards Enforcement (DLSE) to employ an industrial homeworker in any industry. This applies to any person who engages or permits any person to do industrial homework, or to tolerate or permit articles or materials under one's custody or control to be manufactured in a home by industrial homework.

Each industrial homeworker must pay a fee of $100 for a license, which is valid for a period of one year from the date of issuance unless revoked or suspended. The division may revoke or suspend the license for violation of the law or regulations.

An industrial homeworker must have a valid homeworker's permit issued by the California Division of Labor Standards Enforcement (DLSE). The permit fee is $25, and the permit is valid for industrial homework performed for the particular licensed employer for a period of one year, unless revoked or suspended sooner. The permit applies only to the particular applicant in his own home. The DLSE may waive the fee when the applicant can establish financial hardship. The DLSE will not issue a homeworker's permit to any person:

- Who is under 16 years of age;

- Who suffers from an infectious, contagious or communicable disease; or

- Who is living in a home that is not clean, sanitary and free from infectious, contagious or communicable disease.

Prohibited Products

Certain items may not be produced by industrial homework. This includes:

- Articles of food or drink;

- Articles for use in connection with the serving of food or drink;

- Articles of wearing apparel;

- Toys and dolls;

- Tobacco, drugs and poisons;

- Bandages and other sanitary goods;

- Explosives, fireworks and articles of like character; and

- Other articles as prohibited by regulation.

Identification of Products

Articles manufactured by industrial homework must have a label or other mark of identification conspicuously affixed to each article or material. This label must bear the employer's name and address — printed or written legibly in English. If this is impossible, the label must be displayed on the package or other container in which such goods are kept.

Violations

Negligent failure to prevent articles or materials under your custody or control from being taken to a home for manufacture by industrial homework is a misdemeanor.

Unlicensed employment or use of an industrial homeworker, or advertisement for industrial homework performance that is not permitted, is a misdemeanor, punishable for the first offense by:

- A fine of not more than $1,000;
- Imprisonment in the county jail for not more than 30 days; or
- Both fine and imprisonment.

A second conviction is punishable by:

- A fine of not more $5,000;
- Imprisonment in the county jail for not more than six months; or
- Both.

A third or subsequent conviction is punishable by:

- A fine of not more than $30,000;
- Imprisonment in the county jail for not more than one year; or
- Both.

Upon a third conviction, in addition to any penalties or fines imposed, the business license of the manufacturer or owner of the goods, garments or products manufactured by unlawful industrial homework is suspended for a period not to exceed three years. The court may suspend all or a part of any penalty imposed by this section on condition that the defendant refrains from any future or other violation of this part.

A person who does industrial homework without a valid permit is guilty of a misdemeanor, which is punishable for the first offense by a fine of not more than $50 and for the second offense by a fine of not more than $100. The court may suspend this fine on the condition that the industrial homeworker cooperates with the division in the lawful prosecution of persons violating this part, and to secure compliance with this part, or on condition the defendant refrains from any future violation of this part.

The DLSE is empowered to investigate and remedy violations of the industrial homework law and rules. Effective January 1, 2004, any article or material being manufactured in a home in violation of any provision may be confiscated by the DLSE. Articles or materials confiscated pursuant to this section shall be placed in the custody of the DLSE, which is responsible for destroying or disposing of them pursuant to regulations. The articles or material must not be permitted to enter the mainstream of commerce and can't be offered for sale.

The DLSE must give notice by certified mail of the confiscation and the procedure for appealing the confiscation to the person whose name and address are affixed to the article or material as provided in this part. The notice shall state that failure to file a written notice of appeal with the Labor Commissioner within 15 days after service of the notice of confiscation will result in the destruction or disposition of the confiscated article or material. Within 30 days after the timely filing of a notice of appeal, the Labor Commissioner will hold a hearing on the appeal. The Labor Commissioner may affirm, modify or dismiss the confiscation within 15 days of the conclusion of the hearing and may order the return of the confiscated articles or material, under terms that the Labor Commissioner may specify. Judicial review may be requested within 45 days of service of the decision.

Records

Employers of industrial homeworkers must keep and make available for inspection the following records:

- Full name and home address of each industrial homeworker that he/she employs;

- Amount and description of materials delivered to each industrial homeworker that he/she employs, with date of delivery and rate of compensation;

- Gross amount of compensation paid to each industrial homeworker that he/she employs, and date of payment;

- Names and addresses of all agents or independent contractors who received materials or articles for manufacture by industrial homework together with quantity, description of materials and date of delivery; and

- Names and addresses of all manufacturers or independent contractors from whom he/she received articles or materials for industrial homework together with quantity, description of materials and date of receipt.

Contingent Workers

The term "contingent workforce" refers to the nearly one-quarter of this country's workforce that are part-time, temporary or, seasonal, or secured through "temp agencies" or under employee leasing arrangements. The distinction between direct employment (temporary, seasonal and part-time employees) and non-employee (temp agency, leased employees and independent contractors) is often blurred by the details of the arrangements and the laws or court decisions designed to protect the interests of the workers.

Temporary/Seasonal and Part-Time Employees

Short-term employees, such as temporary, seasonal and specialized employees, all are employed for a limited period of time or an identified project. The law does not specify a duration of time after which he/she becomes a regular employee.

Specialized employees are those who are brought in for a short time due to their expertise in a particular area. They may be hired on a short-term basis to handle a project outside the employer's normal realm, such as setting up a computer system or heading up an employer's efforts to rezone a piece of property on which it wants to build a new plant.

Short-term employment creates a number of issues that you should consider before hiring these employees:

- Will the short-term employee work enough hours to be entitled to participate in your retirement plan? *Consult with your retirement plan administrator to determine employee eligibility.*

- The short-term employee will count toward the threshold number of employees for purposes of the federal plant closing law — the Worker Adjustment and Retraining Notification Act

(WARN), or its California equivalent. *WARN counts short-term employees toward the threshold. The California law covers employers of 75 or more "persons" and so would include temporary and seasonal employees for the purpose of determining applicability of the law.*

- In a union workplace, is a short-term employee within the scope of a collective bargaining unit? In a non-union workplace, could short-term employees cause or participate in organizational activity? *Short-term employees may be included. See "Health-Care Staffing" on page 91.*

- Can you provide different benefits to short-term and regular employees, or no benefits at all to short-term employees? *You may provide different benefit levels to different employees as long as the benefit is not withheld on an illegally discriminatory basis. Differentiating between short-term and regular employees is not illegal discrimination. You need only provide short-term employees with the benefits required by law, such as workers' compensation coverage. However, if you provide a short-term employee with health benefits, he/she may be entitled to rights under COBRA. See "COBRA" in Chapter 20, page 472, for more information.*

- Though a short-term employee is clearly entitled to the protections of anti-discrimination laws, will he/she count toward the minimum employee threshold determining whether a particular anti-discrimination law applies to the employer? *Some anti-discrimination laws, such as the Age Discrimination in Employment Act (ADEA), do not clearly define whether a short-term employee is counted toward the threshold number. Conflicting answers on this and other laws have come from various courts and policy-making bodies, such as the Equal Employment Opportunity Commission (EEOC).*

Part-time employees are those who do not work enough hours to meet the employer's definition of full-time. There are generally no legal definitions of full time or part time, so you may set the threshold number of hours at any level you want. (See "Full-Time and Part-Time" in Chapter 12, page 264, and "Affected Employees" in Chapter 32, page 920, for two important exceptions.) Employees who "job share" voluntarily split the hours and duties of a single job, prorating its wages and benefits. Job sharing raises many of the same questions as part-time employment.

Some important issues to consider:

- Does the part-time employee work enough hours to be entitled to participate in your retirement plan?

- If a full-time employee reduces his/her hours to part-time, does that create eligibility for continuing health benefits under COBRA or the California Continuation Benefits Replacement Act (Cal-COBRA)? *See "COBRA" in Chapter 20, page 472, for more information on these two requirements.*

- Can you provide different benefits to part-time and full-time employees, or no benefits at all to part-time employees? *You may provide different benefit levels to different employees as long as the benefit is not withheld on an illegally discriminatory basis. Differentiating between part-time and full-time employees is not illegal discrimination. You need only provide part-time employees with the benefits required by law, such as workers' compensation coverage.*

- Will an exempt employee who works only part time meet the required wage threshold to remain exempt? *See "Minimum Salary Level Increased in 2008" in Chapter 16, page 388.*

- In a union workplace, is the part-time employee within the scope of a collective bargaining unit? *Normally, part-time employees are included.*

- Though a part-time employee is clearly entitled to the protections of anti-discrimination laws, will he/she count toward the minimum employee threshold determining whether a particular anti-discrimination law applies to you? *Some anti-discrimination laws, such as the Family and Medical Leave Act (FMLA), make clear that part-time employees count toward the threshold. However, many other laws do not, and conflicting answers have come from various courts and policy-making bodies, such as the EEOC.*

Leased Workers

Employee leasing firms handle much of the responsibility the law imposes on an employer, allowing you to spend more time on the business itself. On the other hand, an employer who leases employees may lose much of the control necessary to avoid employment-related litigation. Courts have often found joint-employer status between the leasing firm and the company leasing an employee. Joint-employment status destroys the benefit of being relieved of employment law responsibilities, and creates liability where there often is little control. If you lease an employee, you may be found jointly liable where the leasing company did not adequately address the issue of sexual harassment by failing to provide a sexual harassment policy or inadequately responding to an allegation of harassment.

Some issues to consider when deciding whether to lease employees, and from whom to lease them:

- Is the leasing company well-versed in the payroll and personnel record keeping requirements under California and federal law? Request a sample personnel file and a description of the leasing company's payroll process. Have your counsel review this information to ensure it meets with legal requirements.

- How does the leasing company screen employees in the hiring process? You may be responsible for negligent hiring if the leasing company fails to properly screen applicants before hiring them. Inquire as to how thoroughly the leasing company checks references, and what type of background checks are available.

- Does the leasing company provide and administer employee benefits for the leased employees? Consider how these benefits compare with those provided to its "regular" employees to avoid the morale problems that could be created if there is great disparity between the two. On the other hand, leasing companies may self-insure or be entitled to low group-rate premiums, meaning lower costs for providing benefits.

- What type of indemnification is provided for liability arising from the violation of employment laws? Request proof of bonding or insurance and written assurance of indemnification, then review the leasing company's assets to ensure it is a solid company apt to remain in business.

- Who will provide workers' compensation coverage for the leased employees? You may enter into a written agreement with the leasing company regarding who will provide coverage.[13] For more information, see Chapter 26, "Workers' Compensation" (See *Agreement to Secure Payment of Workers Compensation* for a sample agreement). Note that you may not enter into such an agreement to avoid the appropriate experience rating. Also consider that you risk losing the "exclusive remedy" defense of the workers' compensation system when faced with certain employment-related legal claims. For more information, see "What is Workers' Compensation?" in Chapter 26, page 691.

- Who will be responsible for workplace-safety issues, such as training? Existing case law indicates that an employer cannot divest itself of its duties under the occupational safety and health laws.

- Will employees receive different pay for the same work depending on whether you or the leasing company employs them? Be aware that this could violate the *Equal Pay Act*, which

---

13.Lab. Code sec. 3602(d)

prohibits gender discrimination in wage rates and requires equal pay for work requiring equal skill, effort and responsibility performed under similar working conditions.

- Will the leased employees count toward the minimum employee threshold for purposes of various employment laws? Leased employees may count toward these thresholds, especially if a joint-employment relationship is found. Leased employees appear not to count toward the threshold for purposes of the federal WARN Act, which relates to plant closing.

- If your current employees will be hired by a leasing company and then leased back to you, what are the ramifications? You should formally terminate your employees, including all normal termination procedures (final wages, payment for accrued vacation and required notices). The leasing company should then comply with all normal hiring procedures (compliance with immigration laws, required notices and completion of withholding forms). Note that certain employee benefit rights could arise as a result.

Health-Care Staffing

Employment agencies that provide temporary certified nurse assistants (CNAs) or licensed nursing staff for long-term health-care facilities are subject to special requirements. Prior to referring CNAs or licensed nursing staff, an employment agency must:

- Conduct a personal interview with each individual;

- Verify the individual's experience, training, references and licensing/certification; and

- Verify that the individual has successfully secured a criminal record clearance.[14]

In addition, employment agencies referring CNAs or licensed nursing staff for employment must:

- Adopt policies and procedures regarding prevention of resident abuse;

- Provide written verification that referred CNAs or licensed nursing staff do not have unresolved allegations against them involving the mistreatment, abuse or neglect of a patient; and

- Provide a list of temporary employees who have been referred to a specific facility during a labor action, if requested by the state Department of Health Care Services.[15]

Posted daily staffing levels in long-term health-care facilities must identify temporary staff in accordance with federal regulations.[16]

Verification for Certified Nurse Assistants

An employment agency that refers temporary CNAs to a long-term health-care facility must give the facility written verification that each CNA:

- Is in good standing with state certification requirements;

- Has had at least six months of experience working in a long-term care facility;

- Meets health and training requirements; and

---

14. Civ. Code sec. 1812.509(e)
15. Civ. Code sec. 1812.543
16. Civ. Code sec. 1812.543(e)

- Will participate in the facility's orientation program and any in-service training programs at the facility's request.[17]

The employment agency also must provide each CNA's professional certification number and the date his/her certification expires.[18]

Verification for Licensed Nursing Staff

An employment agency that refers temporary licensed nursing staff to a long-term health-care facility must provide the facility with written verification that the individual:

- Is in good standing with state certification requirements; and
- Meets health requirements.[19]

Benefits

Two recent court decisions have indicated that without careful planning on your part, temporary and leased employees may become eligible for employee benefits.

The Ninth U.S. Circuit Court of Appeals found that temporary or leased employees may be "common law" employees entitled to participate in certain employee benefit plans.[20] In this case, individuals were leased to PG&E through a series of employment agencies for more than a decade. They used PG&E's equipment, including computers, telephones, and email. They were sent to the same training classes as PG&E employees, used PG&E business cards and letterhead, and drove PG&E cars. Although they were paid by the employment agencies, travel expenses were reimbursed by PG&E.

The court held that unless all contingent workers specifically are excluded from an employee benefit plan, they may become entitled to benefits under the theory that they are "common law" employees. The court sent the case back to the trial court to determine whether the particular individuals involved met the test of being common law employees. The Ninth Circuit found that if the individuals were determined to be common law employees by the trial court, they should be retroactively eligible for medical, pension and retirement plan benefits, which they had been denied throughout their tenure with PG&E.

In a second important decision, a Ninth U.S. Circuit Court panel held that current and former temporary employees of Microsoft Corporation should be entitled to the same benefits as were the misclassified independent contractors in the case of *Vizcaino v. Microsoft*.[21] See "Benefits" on page 104 for more information about this case.

Given the potential impact of these cases on employers who use contingent workers, employee handbooks and benefit plans should clearly define which individuals are eligible for participation in company benefit plans. Contingent workers should not be treated in the same manner as regular employees, and should not be kept on contingent status for more than a year without consulting legal counsel.

---

17. Civ. Code sec. 1812.541
18. Civ. Code sec. 1812.541(a)
19. Civ. Code sec. 1812.541(c)
20. *Burrey v. Pacific Gas & Electric Co.*, 159 F.3d 388, (9th Cir. 1998)
21. *Vizcaino v. Microsoft*, 173 F. 3d 713, (9th Cir. 1999)

Unions

According to the National Labor Relations Board (NLRB), temporary employees have the right to join unions.[22] See Chapter 33, "Labor Relations in Private Employment," for details.

The ruling arose from an NLRB regional director's earlier decision allowing an employer to exclude temporary employees from a bargaining unit of the company's employees. The regional director held that because employees supplied by a staffing agency were jointly employed by both companies, they could not join with the regular employees to bargain without the consent of the staffing agency.

On appeal, the NLRB found the temporary employees worked side-by-side with regular employees, performed the same work, kept the same hours and were subject to the same supervision. The NLRB found the temporary and regular employees shared a "sufficient community of interest to constitute an appropriate unit." See "Appropriateness of the Bargaining Unit" in Chapter 33, page 941, for details.

As a result of the ruling, temporary employees are considered employees of a temporary agency's client for bargaining purposes. When the temporary employee is jointly employed by both the agency and the client, the temporary employee, without the consent of the agency or client, can:

- Enter into collective bargaining agreements;

- Vote in a union organizing campaign; and

- Join an existing union.

Independent Contractors

This section explains the difference between an independent contractor and an employee, and details the many factors the courts and various government agencies use to determine independent contractor status. Simply calling someone an independent contractor does not make him/her one in the legal sense, and creates potential liability for employment taxes and penalties, and liability for failure to fulfill the many legal obligations owed to an employee. It is wise to ensure that a person working as an independent contractor truly meets the difficult tests required by law.

Using a true independent contractor can relieve you of the many burdens placed upon you by state and federal employment laws. For instance, independent contractors:

- Need not be covered by workers' compensation;

- Do not have employment taxes deducted from their earnings by an employer;

- Have no rights to employee benefits;

- Are not employees subject to the Immigration Reform and Control Act (IRCA) of 1986;

- Are not covered by many state and federal antidiscrimination laws;

- Do not subject you to vicarious liability for their acts;

- Are not included under Cal/OSHA and federal OSHA regulations in an employer's duty to provide a safe and healthy work environment;

---

22. *M.B. Sturgis, Jeffboat Division, et al.*, 331 NLRB No. 173 (2000)

- Are not covered by state and federal wage and hour laws;

- Are not entitled to unemployment insurance benefits from your account;

- Are excluded from coverage under the National Labor Relations Act (NLRA) (unions); and

- Do not count for purposes of the WARN Act (plant closure law).

On the other hand, because they are not covered by workers' compensation, an independent contractor (or his/her employee) can sue you for personal injury sustained on your premises. This litigation can be far more costly than a workers' compensation claim.

Defining Independent Contractor Generally

California labor law defines an independent contractor as "any person who renders service for a specified recompense for a specified result, under the control of his principal as to the result of his work only and not as to the means by which such result is accomplished."[23]

The true principal/independent contractor relationship offers significant advantages both to the contractor and to the principal. Contractors enjoy freedom, flexible working conditions, certain tax advantages and the financial and personal rewards of self-employment. Principals are not required to provide certain statutory employment benefits, such as workers' compensation coverage, unemployment benefits, overtime payments or minimum wage obligations, nor withhold income taxes from payments for services.

California administrative agencies and the Internal Revenue Service (IRS) closely scrutinize alleged principal/independent contractor relationships to assure that those relationships are not, in reality, employer/employee relationships. Challenges to the legitimacy of an existing independent contractor/principal relationship can arise in many forms, including:

- Filings for unemployment insurance (UI) benefits;

- Claims for unpaid wages;

- Claims for workers' compensation;

- Charges of employment discrimination; and

- Investigations by the IRS and Employment Development Department (EDD) to audit wage payments, workers' compensation coverage, and Unemployment Insurance Fund contributions.

Simply put, many alleged independent contractor relationships fail when closely examined under both traditional legal criteria and more rigorous tests adopted by the California Supreme Court, as discussed in this chapter and presented by *How Six Agencies Determine Independent Contractor-Employee Relationships* .

The consequences for misclassifying an employee as an independent contractor can include significant tax, wage, and benefits liabilities, as well as massive fines that may be imposed by the IRS and the EDD. You can find extensive information on federal requirements for independent contractor status on the IRS Web site at ***www.irs.gov.*** You can find information on state requirements, which vary from federal requirements, on EDD's Web site at ***www.edd.ca.gov.***

---

23. Lab. Code sec. 3353

Common Misconceptions

Many employers operate on the misconception that they will be safe from the significant penalties of misclassification if their relationship meets any of the conditions listed below. This simply is not the case. It is a myth that hiring firms are safe from these concerns just because the worker:

- Wanted to be treated as an independent contractor;

- Signed a written contract;

- Does assignments sporadically, inconsistently or on call;

- Is paid commission only;

- Has no supervision; or

- Performs assignments for more than one company.

The California Common-Law Test

California courts and administrative agencies generally apply common-law principles to determine independent contractor status, since the law does not specify criteria for such determinations. The most important factor in that determination involves the independent contractor's right to control the manner and means of accomplishing the desired result, even if the contractor did not exercise that right with respect to all details.

Factors examined within that right to control include:

- Whether you had the right to discharge at-will without cause;

- Whether the person performing services is engaged in a distinct occupational business;

- Whether the work is usually performed under close direction or by a specialist without supervision;

- The skills required in the particular occupation;

- Whether you or the worker supplied the instruments, tools and place for performing the work;

- The length of time for which the services are to be performed;

- The method of payment, whether by time or by job;

- Whether the work is part of your regular business; and

- Whether the parties believe they are creating the relationship of employer/employee.[24]

Under the common-law test, no one factor is decisive, but the right to control the manner and means of employment is clearly the most important factor.[25]

---

24. *Empire Star Mines Co. v. California Employment Commission,* 28 Cal. 2d 33, 43 (1946)
25. *Barton v. Studebaker Corp. of America,* 46 Cal. App. 707 (1920)

Defining Independent Contractors for Workers' Compensation

The California Supreme Court discarded the common-law test of independent contractor status as the exclusive means of determining the application of workers' compensation coverage, and broadened the test to include other factors balanced against the purposes of the workers' compensation laws. After discussing the broad definition of employment and purposes of the Workers' Compensation Act, the court declared that a "balance" must be struck when deciding whether a worker is an employee or an independent contractor for purposes of the Workers' Compensation Act. Though not entirely discarding the common law test, the court approved six factors federal authorities used in addition to the right-to-control factor:

- The alleged employee's opportunity for profit or loss depending upon his/her managerial skills;

- The alleged employee's investment in equipment or materials required for his/her task;

- The alleged employee's employment of helpers;

- Whether the services rendered required a specific skill;

- The degree of permanence of the working relationship; and

- Whether the service rendered is an integral part of the alleged employer's business.[26]

The court noted that the Workers' Compensation Act is one of many laws intended to protect employees, and mentioned a number of legal protections offered by other laws. It is apparent that this decision affects independent contractor status not only for workers' compensation purposes but for many other purposes as well, and has resulted in a decrease in the number of independent contractor relationships upheld by the courts and administrative agencies. Subsequent decisions significantly narrowed the definition of independent contractor in using this balancing test.[27]

If you have misclassified an individual as an independent contractor and have not provided him/her with workers' compensation coverage, you can be held liable for civil tort liability not only to the individual,[28] but also to third parties who are injured as a result of negligent acts by the misclassified individual during the course of employment. In addition, if you fail to secure workers' compensation insurance for your employees, you are subject to the following potential liabilities:

- Workers' compensation claims and lawsuits filed by injured employees;

- A penalty of up to $10,000 payable to the state;[29]

- An additional penalty of 10 percent of any workers' compensation benefits recoverable by the injured employee;[30] and

- Attorneys' fees.[31]

Liability for Injuries to an Independent Contractor's Employee

The employee of an independent contractor who is injured by the subcontractor's negligence cannot sue the party who hired the independent contractor. The California Supreme Court held

---

26. *S.G. Borello & Sons, Inc. v. Department of Industrial Relations*, 48 Cal. 3d 341 (1989)
27. *Rinaldi v. Workers' Compensation Appeals Board*, 227 Cal. App. 3d 756 (1991); *Yellow Cab Cooperative Inc. v. Workers' Compensation Appeals Board*, 226 Cal. App. 3d 1288 (1991)
28. Lab. Code sec. 3706
29. Lab. Code sec. 3710.2
30. Lab. Code sec. 4554
31. Lab. Code sec. 4555

that it's unfair to subject the hiring party to civil litigation when the independent contractor, who had control over the work, can't be subjected to civil litigation because of the rule of workers' compensation exclusivity.[32]

Similarly, a dairy was not liable for injuries to a trucking company's employee on the theory that the dairy negligently hired the trucking company. The court found the dairy had exercised no control over the work performed by employees of the trucking company whose liability is limited by workers' compensation law.[33]

Liability for injuries to a contractor's employee outside workers' compensation may be assessed against a hiring party where that party provides faulty equipment that causes injury to the contractor's employee[34] or where the hiring company retains control of safety procedures in the work environment and is negligent in exercising that control.[35]

Defining Independent Contractor for Unemployment/Disability Insurance

For unemployment and disability insurance, the general statutory definition of an employee is an individual who, under usual common-law rules, has a status of an employee.[36]

If individuals classified as independent contractors are found to be employees, you will be assessed for amounts due for unemployment insurance contributions, disability insurance contributions and state income tax withholding amounts. In addition, if you, without good cause, fail to pay required contributions for unemployment or disability insurance benefits, you are liable for a penalty of 10 percent of the amount of the contributions (plus interest) on any unpaid contributions.[37]

Defining Independent Contractor for Federal Tax Purposes

The IRS is the federal taxing authority that determines whether an employment relationship exists between a worker and employer that requires payment of federal employment taxes, including Social Security taxes, payment under the Federal Unemployment Tax Act and withholding of worker-owed employment taxes.

Misclassification of bona fide employees as independent contractors resulted in the federal government collecting significant financial penalties from employers and the IRS aggressively auditing companies to expose abuses. It is estimated that as much as $1.5 billion in income, Social Security withholdings and unemployment tax revenue is lost annually due to misclassification of as many as 3.5 million workers as independent contractors. Companies judged by the IRS to have misclassified employees as independent contractors face not only large government fines but also payment of employment taxes (including 100 percent of the employer's Social Security contributions), federal income taxes not withheld and an employment insurance tax equal to 6.2 percent of the compensation paid to the worker. The company is not entitled to collect these amounts from the alleged independent contractor.

---

32. *Toland v. Sunland Housing Group, Inc.*, 18 Cal. 4th 253 (1998)
33. *Camargo v. Tjaarda Dairy* 25 Cal. 4th 1235 (2001)
34. *McKown v. Wal-Mart Stores* 27 Cal. 4th 219 (2002)
35. *Hooker v. Department of Transportation*, 27 Cal. 4th 198 (2002)
36. UI Code sec. 621(b)
37. UI Code secs. 1112, 1113

Independent Contractor (Self-Employed) or Employee

The IRS provides the following guidance in determining if a worker is an independent contractor or an employee:

It is critical that you, the employer, correctly determine whether the individuals providing services are employees or independent contractors. Generally, you must withhold income taxes, withhold and pay Social Security and Medicare taxes, and pay unemployment tax on wages paid to an employee. You do not generally have to withhold or pay any taxes on payments to independent contractors.

Before you can determine how to treat payments you make for services, you must first know the business relationship that exists between you and the person performing the services. The person performing the services may be -

An independent contractor

An employee (common-law employee)

A statutory employee

A statutory nonemployee

In determining whether the person providing service is an employee or an independent contractor, all information that provides evidence of the degree of control and independence must be considered.

Common Law Rules

Facts that provide evidence of the degree of control and independence fall into three categories:

Behavioral: Does the company control or have the right to control what the worker does and how the worker does his or her job?

Financial: Are the business aspects of the worker's job controlled by the payer? (these include things like how worker is paid, whether expenses are reimbursed, who provides tools/supplies, etc.)

Type of Relationship: Are there written contracts or employee type benefits (i.e. pension plan, insurance, vacation pay, etc.)? Will the relationship continue and is the work performed a key aspect of the business?

Businesses must weigh all these factors when determining whether a worker is an employee or independent contractor. Some factors may indicate that the worker is an employee, while other factors indicate that the worker is an independent contractor. There is no "magic" or set number of factors that "makes" the worker an employee or an independent contractor, and no one factor stands alone in making this determination. Also, factors which are relevant in one situation may not be relevant in another.

The keys are to look at the entire relationship, consider the degree or extent of the right to direct and control, and finally, to document each of the factors used in coming up with the determination.

Form SS-8

If, after reviewing the three categories of evidence, it is still unclear whether a worker is an employee or an independent contractor, Form SS-8, Determination of Worker Status for Purposes of Federal Employment Taxes and Income Tax Withholding (which can be obtained form the IRS Web site at *http://www.irs.gov/pub/irs-pdf/fss8.pdf*) can be filed with the IRS. The form may be filed by either the business or the worker. The IRS will review the facts and circumstances and officially determine the worker's status.

Be aware that it can take at least six months to get a determination, but a business that continually hires the same types of workers to perform particular services may want to consider filing the Form SS-8.

Employment Tax Obligations

Once a determination is made (whether by the business or by the IRS), the next step is filing the appropriate forms and paying the associated taxes.

Consequences of Treating an Employee as an Independent Contractor

If you classify an employee as an independent contractor and you have no reasonable basis for doing so, you may be held liable for employment taxes for that worker (the relief provisions, discussed below, will not apply). See Internal Revenue Code section 3509 for more information.

Relief Provisions

If you have a reasonable basis for not treating a worker as an employee, you may be relieved from having to pay employment taxes for that worker. To get this relief, you must file all required federal information returns on a basis consistent with your treatment of the worker.

Misclassified Workers Can File Social Security Tax Form

Workers who believe they have been improperly classified as independent contractors by an employer can use Form 8919, Uncollected Social Security and Medicare Tax on Wages (which can be obtained form the IRS Web site at **http://ftp.irs.gov/pub/irs-pdf/f8919.pdf**) to figure and report the employee's share of uncollected Social Security and Medicare taxes due on their compensation.

The primary source for this above information is at **http://www.irs.gov/businesses/small/ article/0,,id=99921,00.html**.

Defining Independent Contractors — Help From the IRS and EDD

Both the IRS and the EDD will provide a written determination as to whether a worker is an employee or an independent contractor for tax withholding purposes. The IRS provides Form SS-8 to be filled out when you request a determination for federal tax purposes. The EDD provides Form DE 1870 when you request a determination for state tax purposes, but also will accept the IRS's Form SS-8. Contact your local IRS or EDD office for copies of these forms.

 Though forms SS-8 and DE 1870 can be helpful for a self-audit, it is not recommended that you use them to seek a written determination from the IRS or EDD. Not only will the agencies likely find an employment relationship exists, but you may become subject to an audit as a result of requesting a written determination.

Consider simply using the Form SS-8 as an internal tool to determine what factors the IRS and EDD consider in evaluating whether a worker is an employee or an independent contractor.

Another alternative is to use EDD's Form DE 38(1-97), a fairly simple worksheet designed for the proprietor of a business to use while conducting a self-audit.

An employer's complaint against the EDD for recovery of unemployment taxes paid — for what the employer claimed were independent contractors — backfired as a California court of appeal found that the individuals were actually employees. The simplicity of the work involved (package delivery) made detailed supervision and control unnecessary. The drivers worked regular schedules, were not involved in a separate profession or operating their own business and did not make major investments in materials or equipment. Additionally, the job they performed was an integral and entirely essential aspect of the business.[38]

Air Couriers International filed a complaint for a refund of more than $600,000 in taxes paid to the EDD for its delivery drivers. Air Couriers claimed that the drivers were independent contractors because they worked flexible schedules; determined their own breaks and time off; worked with other companies; were paid by the job; drove their own vehicles; provided their own business cards; and only wore the company uniform to expedite airport or other security access. Almost every driver signed an independent contractor agreement that clearly outlined the responsibilities of the company and the driver in an independent contractor — not an employee/employer — relationship.

After the EDD audited 17 independent contractors, 16 were found to be employees because the drivers only worked for Air Couriers and not other employers; none of the drivers invested in a vehicle for the purpose of deliveries; none owned a business license; and no independent contractor agreements were found. The one driver that qualified as an independent contractor during this audit made a substantial investment in a large, long-haul truck. The court agreed with EDD's finding because the company provided the drivers all necessary forms, delivery routes, uniforms, identification badges and vehicle placards with the company name on them. The customers were those of the company, which set the rates charged, billed the customers and collected payment, thereby retaining all necessary control over the drivers. Most of the drivers work with the company for a long period of time, and had not worked with any other company. Finally, Air Couriers could not exist without its drivers – a clear indication the drivers were employees and not independent contractors.

The financial impact of this case on the company is unclear, except that Air Couriers will not be getting a refund from the EDD. It may, however, trigger audits from the California Franchise Tax Board, the IRS and the Industrial Welfare Commission's Division of Workers' Compensation, which will expose the company to additional penalties if they agree that the drivers were indeed employees.

Reporting Obligations

All businesses and government entities who hire independent contractors must file reports with the EDD. This independent contractor reporting program is designed to locate parents who are delinquent in their child-support obligations.[39]

Specific information must be reported within 20 days of entering into a contract for (or making payments of) $600 in any calendar year to an independent contractor. EDD matches the reports against child-support records to locate parents delinquent in payments.

When hiring an independent contractor, the law requires a report from anyone who is:

- Doing business in California;

- Deriving trade or business income from sources within California; or

- Otherwise subject to California law.

---

38. *Air Couriers International et al v. Employment Development Department* (2007) 150 Cal. App. 4th 923
39. UI Code sec. 1088.8

This means that businesses operating outside California are subject to this law. For example, an independent contractor who works in California for a business based in Texas must be reported to California's EDD.

Hiring entities subject to the law include:

- Individuals;

- Corporations;

- Associations;

- Partnerships;

- Agents of any of the above;

- California or any of its political subdivisions;

- Charter cities; and

- Any political body that is not a subdivision or agency of the state.

Hiring entities who have no employees and, therefore, are not registered with EDD, are not required to register and receive a California employer account number solely for purposes of reporting independent contractor service-providers. Unregistered hiring entities complete the *Independent Contractors Report - DE542* using a Social Security number or Federal Employer Identification Number (FEIN).

Both Contractor and Employee

You may have a worker classified as an employee who also performs work as an independent contractor. For example, a sales clerk (employee) might own a small janitorial firm that is hired to clean the store each evening (independent contractor). Report the individual under both the New Employee Registry program, *New Employees Report - Form DE34* and under the Independent Contractor Reporting program, *Independent Contractors Report - DE542*.

Report Content

The independent contractor reporting requirements apply if an independent contractor is hired and:

- You are required to file a Form 099-MISC for the services performed by the independent contractor;

- You pay the independent contractor $600 or more, or enter into a contract for $600 or more (if the cost of parts and materials is included in the contract or payments, this cost must be included in determining whether the independent contractor has been paid $600 or more); and

- The independent contractor is an individual or sole proprietorship.

If all three of the above statements apply, you must report the independent contractor to EDD. No reporting is required for independent contractors that are corporations, general partnerships, limited liability partnerships and limited liability companies.

If you are a California business or government entity, you must report all independent contractors who meet the minimum dollar requirements regardless of where they live or work.

For example, a California business hires an independent contractor who lives and works in New York. This independent contractor must be reported to the EDD.

If the independent contractor works in California, you must report to EDD even if you are based in another state. A business based in New York must report to EDD if it hires an independent contractor who lives and works in California.

The EDD requires a report of all of the following:

- The hiring entity's:
  - FEIN;
  - California employer account number;
  - Social Security account number (if applicable); and
  - Business name, address and telephone number.
- The independent contractor's:
  - First name, middle initial and last name;
  - SSN; and
  - Address.
- The start date of contract; and
- The contract expiration date (unless it is an ongoing contract).

Independent contractors may have FEINs and business names, making it difficult to determine whether they are a sole proprietor whom you must report. Unfortunately, reporting a FEIN does not meet the legal requirement of reporting the independent contractor's SSN. By statute, you must obtain and report the first name, last name and SSN of any independent contractors that are sole proprietors. The IRS's Form W-9 was revised in December 2000 to require sole proprietors to list their first and last names. You may wish to ask independent contractors to complete new Form W-9s. If you still don't know the SSN after reviewing the Form W-9, you may ask the independent contractor for the SSN. If the independent contractor does not provide it, fill in the SSN box on the *Independent Contractors Report - DE542* with zeroes (000000000). Form W-9 is available on the IRS Web site at ***www.irs.gov/***.

Forms

A copy of the form is included in the *Independent Contractors Report - DE542*. You can also find the form online at ***www.edd.ca.gov/pdf_pub_ctr/de542.pdf***. Mail or fax the completed report to:

Employment Development Department
P.O. Box 997350 MIC 99
Sacramento, CA 95899-7350
Fax: (916) 255-3211

When hiring a large number of independent contractors, you may send the information via magnetic media. For details, contact the EDD's Magnetic Media Unit at (916) 651-6945.

Filing Deadlines

Send the report to EDD within 20 days of entering into a contract for $600 or more in any calendar year with an independent contractor, or within 20 days of making payments totaling $600 in any calendar year to an independent contractor, whichever is earlier. The contract may be written or verbal. If you are unable to determine when total payments issued equal or exceed $600, estimate the dollar amount of the contract and check the box on the *Independent Contractors Report - DE542* that indicates "ongoing."

If you hire an independent contractor on more than one occasion during a year, report the independent contractor at whatever point the $600 threshold is met, even if it is not during the first period of work. Once the report is made for a calendar year, there is no need to file further reports that year simply because the same independent contractor receives another $600.

Penalties

There is a penalty of $24 for each instance of late filing or failure to file the report, unless there is good cause. The penalty increases to $490 if conspiracy exists between the hiring entity and the independent contractor not to supply the required report or to supply a false or incomplete report.

Other Issues

Though retaining true independent contractors may allow you to avoid many employment obligations, the following concerns require your attention.

Harassment

California's Fair Employment and Housing Act (FEHA) protects independent contractors from harassment.[40] The FEHA makes it illegal to harass an independent contractor, defined as any "person providing services pursuant to a contract," on the basis of race, religious creed, national origin, ancestry, physical disability, mental disability, medical condition, marital status, sex, age or sexual orientation.

 Though the law extends protection from harassment to independent contractors, it does not extend protection from discrimination to independent contractors.

Wages and Hours

Since the state wage/hours regulations apply only to employees, the state Labor Commissioner has no jurisdiction to order wage payments to independent contractors.[41] Therefore, the true nature of the relationship between a wage claimant and a purported employer is addressed by the state Labor Commissioner when the issue of independent contractor status is raised in a wage claim or audit proceeding. Traditional common-law principles have been used by the state Labor Commissioner's hearing officers and auditors in making such determinations.

---

40. Gov't. Code sec. 12940 (h)(1)
41. *Resnik v. Anderson & Miles*, 109 Cal. App. 3d 569 (1980)

The consequences of misclassifying an employee as an independent contractor in a wage/hour context include, but are not limited to, liability for unpaid wages for a period of up to three years, including potential overtime pay. If employee status is found, the failure to pay all wages due every pay period may result in penalties of $100 to $200 per employee per pay period, and up to 25 percent of the wages not paid to each employee for each pay period.[42] Moreover, employers making lump sum payments to individuals improperly classified as independent contractors may violate the statutory obligation to provide itemized wage statements to employees each pay period, and become subject to additional civil penalties of $250 per employee for the first violation and $1,000 per employee for each subsequent violation.[43]

In addition, failing to pay a terminated employee improperly classified as an independent contractor all wages due and owed in a timely fashion can subject you to penalties of up to 30 times the employee's daily wage without regard to the actual amounts of unpaid wages.[44]

Benefits

Independent contractors typically are ineligible for benefits offered to employees, such as health insurance, vacations and retirement plans. However, an employee misclassified as an independent contractor now could retroactively be entitled to those benefits under a Ninth U.S. Circuit Court of Appeals decision.[45] In that case, the IRS conducted an audit of "freelancers" hired as independent contractors by Microsoft Corporation and found them to be employees. These employees brought suit and were found to be eligible for Microsoft's retirement and stock option plans for the period they were misclassified. The court reached this decision despite the fact that the freelancers:

- Signed contracts expressly agreeing to work as independent contractors;

- Received higher wages than regular employees in lieu of fringe benefits; and

- Were paid through the accounts receivable department after submitting invoices.

Further Information

For further information on these types of workers, examine the following sources.

Discrimination and Contingent Workers

The EEOC Web site offers information about how federal antidiscrimination statutes apply to temporary, contract and other contingent employees. The EEOC prepared a document called *Enforcement Guidance: Application of EEO Laws to Contingent Workers Placed by Temporary Employment Agencies and Other Staffing Firms*. The Web site address is ***www.eeoc.gov/policy/docs/conting.html***.

---

42. Lab. Code sec. 210
43. Lab. Code sec. 226.3
44. Lab. Code sec. 203
45. *Vizcaino v. Microsoft Corp.*, 97 F.3d 1187 (9th Cir. 1996)

Labor Laws and Independent Contractors

In addition to the assistance provided by this publication, the IRS offers both publications and small business workshops concerning tax responsibilities in this area. To obtain IRS publication 1976, *Independent Contractor or Employee,* call the IRS at (800) 829-3676. This and other IRS publications are available on the IRS Web site at ***www.irs.gov***. For small business workshops, contact your local IRS office for dates and locations of workshops in your area.

Independent Contractor Reporting

You can find more information about independent contractor reporting requirement on the EDD Web site at ***www.edd.cahwnet.gov/pdf_pub_ctr/de542faq.pdf***, or by calling the EDD's hotline number at (916) 657-0529, Monday through Friday, from 8:00 a.m. to 5:00 p.m. (PST).

Chapter 5 Forms

This chapter contains samples of forms associated with this topic. *The forms in this section are for visual reference only; download the most up-to-date forms and checklists in their entirety from CalBizCentral.*

To download either individual forms or your entire Formspack containing all the forms referenced in this book:

1. Visit **www.calbizcentral.com/support** and select "Labor Law Digest" from the list of product titles.

2. Have this copy of Labor Law Digest handy — you will need to enter the access code featured on the inside covers of this book.

3. Enter the access code, select the documents you want to download to your computer, then follow the on-screen instructions.

For more detailed instructions, see "Forms Available Online" on page xix.

EDD Employment Development Department
State of California

EMPLOYMENT DETERMINATION GUIDE

Purpose:

This worksheet is to be used by the proprietor of a business to determine whether a worker is most likely an employee or an independent contractor.

General Information:

Generally speaking, whether a worker is an employee or an independent contractor depends on the application of the factors contained in the California common law of employment and statutory provisions of the California Unemployment Insurance Code.

If a worker is an employee under the common law of employment, the business by which the worker is employed must report the worker's earnings to the Employment Development Department (EDD) and must pay employment taxes on those wages. If the worker is an independent contractor, reporting to EDD is not required. However, if the business pays $600 or more in payments to an independent contractor, the business must file a Form 1099-Misc with the Internal Revenue Service (IRS) and must file a Report of Independent Contractor(s) (DE 542) with the EDD within 20 days of either making payments totaling $600 or more, or entering into a contract for $600 or more with an independent contractor in any calendar year. For more detailed information regarding your Independent Contractor reporting requirements, obtain the latest revision of the California Employer's Guide (DE 44).

The basic test for determining whether a worker is an independent contractor or an employee is whether the principal has the right to direct and control the manner and means by which the work is performed. When the principal has the "right of control," the worker will be an employee even if the principal never actually exercises the control. If the principal does not have the right of direction and control, the worker will generally be an independent contractor.

If it is not clear from the face of the relationship whether the worker or the principal has the "right of control," reference is made to a list of secondary factors that are evidence of the existence or nonexistence of the right of control.

If use of the attached worksheet clearly demonstrates that a worker is an employee, you should contact EDD and arrange to report the worker and pay the relevant taxes. You may also want to contact the IRS and your workers' compensation insurance carrier to ensure that you are in compliance with federal tax laws and with state workers' compensation statutes.

If after completing the worksheet you are not sure whether the worker is an independent contractor or employee, you may also contact the Taxpayer Education and Assistance (TEA) for consultation and advice by calling (888) 745-3886 or request a written ruling by completing a Determination of Employment Work Status, DE 1870. The DE 1870 is designed to analyze a working relationship in detail and serves as the basis for a written determination from EDD on employment status.

DE 38 Rev. 1 (3-05) **(INTERNET)** Page 1 of 7 CU

Employment Determination Guide (Form DE 38)
(Page 1 of 7)

WORKSHEET ON EMPLOYMENT STATUS

Questions 1 – 3 are significant questions. If the answer to any of them is "Yes," it is a strong indication that the worker is an employee, and you have a high probability of risk if you classify the worker as an independent contractor.

1. Do you instruct or supervise the person while he or she is working? Yes ___ No ___

   Independent contractors are free to do jobs in their own way, using specific methods they choose. A person or firm engages an independent contractor for the job's end result. When a worker is required to follow company procedure manuals and/or is given specific instructions on how to perform the work, the worker is normally an employee.

2. Can the worker quit or be discharged (fired) at any time? Yes ___ No ___

   If you have the right to fire the worker without notice, it indicates that you have the right to control the worker.

   Independent contractors are engaged to do specific jobs and cannot be fired before the job is complete unless they violate the terms of the contract. They are not free to quit and walk away until the job is complete. For example, if a shoe store owner hires an attorney to review his or her lease, the attorney would get paid only after satisfactory completion of the job.

3. Is the work being performed part of your regular business? Yes ___ No ___

   Work which is a necessary part of the regular trade or business is normally done by employees. For example, a sales clerk is selling shoes in a shoe store. A shoe store owner could not operate without sales clerks to sell shoes. On the other hand, a plumber engaged to fix the pipes in the bathroom of the store is performing a service on a one-time or occasional basis that is not an essential part of the purpose of the business enterprise. A certified public accountant engaged to prepare tax returns and financial statements for the business would also be an example of an independent contractor.

DE 38 Rev. 1 (3-05) **(INTERNET)** Page 2 of 7 CU

Employment Determination Guide (Form DE 38)
(Page 2 of 7)

CalBizCentral

A "No" answer to questions 4 – 6 indicates that the individual is not in a business for himself or herself and would therefore normally be an employee.

4. Does the worker have a separately established business?

When individuals hold themselves out to the general public as available to perform services similar to those performed for you, it is evidence that the individuals are operating separately established businesses and would normally be independent contractors. Independent contractors are free to hire employees and assign the work to others in any way they choose. Independent contractors have the authority to fire their employees without your knowledge or consent. Independent contractors can normally advertise their services in newspapers and/or publications, yellow page listings, and/or seek new customers through the use of business cards.

Yes ___ No ___

5. Is the worker free to make business decisions which affect his or her ability to profit from the work?

An individual is normally an independent contractor when he or she is free to make business decisions which impact his or her ability to profit or suffer a loss. This involves real economic risk, not just the risk of not getting paid. These decisions would normally involve the acquisition, use, and/or disposition of equipment, facilities, and stock in trade which are under his or her control. Further examples of the ability to make economic business decisions include the amount and type of advertising for the business, the priority in which assignments are worked, and selection of the types and amounts of insurance coverage for the business.

Yes ___ No ___

6. Does the individual have a substantial investment which would subject him or her to a financial risk of loss?

Independent contractors furnish the tools, equipment, and supplies needed to perform the work. Independent contractors normally have an investment in the items needed to complete their tasks. To the extent necessary for the specific type of business, independent contractors provide their own business facility.

Yes ___ No ___

Employment Determination Guide (Form DE 38)
(Page 3 of 7)

Questions 7 – 13 are additional factors that should be considered. A "Yes" answer to any of the questions is an indication the worker may be an employee, but no one factor by itself is deciding. All factors must be considered and weighed together to determine which type of relationship exists. However, the greater the number of "Yes" answers to questions 7 – 13 the greater the likelihood the worker is performing services as an employee.

7. Do you have employees who do the same type of work?

If the work being done is basically the same as work that is normally done by your employees, it indicates that the worker is an employee. This applies even if the work is being done on a one-time basis. For instance, to handle an extra workload or replace an employee who is on vacation, a worker is hired to fill in on a temporary basis. This worker is a temporary employee, not an independent contractor.

(Note: If you contract with a temporary agency to provide you with a worker, the worker is normally an employee but may be an employee of the temporary agency. You may wish to request EDD's DE 231F, Information Sheet: Temporary Services and Employee Leasing Industries, on the subject of temporary service and leasing employers.)

Yes ___ No ___

8. Do you furnish the tools, equipment, or supplies used to perform the work?

Independent business people furnish the tools, equipment, and supplies needed to perform the work. Independent contractors normally have an investment in the items needed to complete their tasks.

Yes ___ No ___

9. Is the work considered unskilled or semi-skilled labor?

The courts and the California Unemployment Insurance Appeals Board have held that workers who are considered unskilled or semi-skilled are the type of workers the law is meant to protect and are generally employees.

Yes ___ No ___

10. Do you provide training for the worker?

In skilled or semi-skilled work, independent contractors usually do not need training. If training is required to do the task, it is an indication that the worker is an employee.

Yes ___ No ___

Employment Determination Guide (Form DE 38)
(Page 4 of 7)

Helping California Business Do Business

109

11. Is the worker paid a fixed salary, an hourly wage, or based on a piece rate basis?   Yes _____ No _____

Independent contractors agree to do a job and bill for the service performed. Payments to independent contractors for labor or services are made upon the completion of the project or completion of the performance of specific portions of the project.

12. Did the worker previously perform the same or similar services for you as an employee?   Yes _____ No _____

If the worker previously performed the same or similar services for you as an employee, it is an indication that the individual is still an employee.

13. Does the worker believe that he or she is an employee?   Yes _____ No _____

Although belief of the parties is not controlling, intent of the parties is a factor to consider when making an employment or independent contractor determination. When both the worker and principal believe the worker is an independent contractor, an argument exists to support an independent contractor relationship between the parties.

Employment Determination Guide (Form DE 38)
(Page 5 of 7)

Interpretations of Answers

Depending on the services being performed and the type of occupation, this questionnaire may produce a variety of results. There may be some factors which lean toward employment and some which lean toward independence. The answers to questions 1 – 6 provide a strong indication of the presence or absence of direction and control. The answers to questions 7 – 13 when joined with other evidence may carry greater weight when indicating the presence or absence of direction and control.

1. If all of the answers to questions 1 – 3 are "No" and all of the answers to questions 4 – 6 are "Yes," there is an indication of independence. When this is the case, there are likely to be a number of "No" answers to questions 7 – 13 which add to the support of the determination.

2. If all of the answers to questions 1 – 3 are "Yes" and all of the answers to questions 4 – 6 are "No," it is very strong indication that the worker in question is an employee. When this is the case, there are likely to be a number of "Yes" answers to questions 7 – 13 which add to the support of the determination.

3. If the answer to question 1 or 2 is "Yes" or the answer to any one of questions 4 – 6 is "No," there is a likelihood of employment. At the very least, this pattern of answers makes the determination more difficult since the responses to questions 7 – 13 will probably be mixed. In such situations, the business owner would be well advised to complete a DE 1870, giving all of the facts of the working relationship and requesting a ruling from EDD.

4. If the answer to question 3 is "Yes" and the answer to question 4 is "No," there is a likelihood of employment. Given this pattern of answers, it is probable that the answers to questions 5 and 6 will also be "No." When this happens you may also see more "Yes" answers to the last group of questions (7 – 13). This scenario would support an employment determination.

These four scenarios illustrate only a few combinations of answers that could result from the use of this Employment Determination Guide, depending on the working relationship a principal may have with a worker and the type of occupation. The more the pattern of answers vary from the above four situations, the more difficult it is to interpret them. In situations 1 and 2, there is a greater chance that the interpretation will be accurate, and they present the least risk to the business owner of misclassifying the worker. With other combinations of answers, EDD recommends that business owners complete a DE 1870, giving a complete description of the working relationship and requesting a ruling from the Department.

NOTE: Some agent or commission drivers, traveling or city salespeople, homeworkers, artists, authors, and workers in the construction industry are employees by law even if they would otherwise be considered independent contractors under common law. If you are dealing with workers in any of these fields, request the DE 231SE, Information Sheet: Statutory Employees, from the Employment Tax Customer Service Office.

Employment Determination Guide (Form DE 38)
(Page 6 of 7)

SOME EXAMPLES OF INDEPENDENT CONTRACTORS AND COMMON LAW EMPLOYEES

Independent Contractors

An attorney or accountant who has his or her own office, advertises in the yellow pages of the phone book under "Attorneys" or "Accountants," bills clients by the hour, is engaged by the job or paid an annual retainer, and can hire a substitute to do the work is an example of an independent contractor.

An auto mechanic who has a station license, a resale license, buys the parts necessary for the repairs, sets his or her own prices, collects from the customer, sets his or her own hours and days of work, and owns or rents the shop from a third party is an example of an independent contractor.

Dance instructors who select their own dance routines to teach, locate and rent their own facilities, provide their own sound systems, music and clothing, collect fees from customers, and are free to hire assistants are examples of independent contractors.

A repairperson who owns or rents a shop, advertises the services to the public, furnishes all of the tools, equipment, and supplies necessary to make repairs, sets the price for services, and collects from the customers is an example of an independent contractor.

NOTE: Payroll tax audits conducted by EDD have disclosed misclassified workers in virtually every type and size of business. However, certain industries seem more prone to have a higher number of misclassified workers than others. Historically, industries at higher risk of having misclassified workers include businesses that use:

- Construction workers
- Seasonal workers
- Short-term or "casual" workers
- Outside salespersons

Employees

An attorney or accountant who is employed by a firm to handle their legal affairs or financial records, works in an office at the firm's place of business, attends meetings as needed, and the firm bills the clients and pays the attorney or accountant on a regular basis is an example of an employee.

An auto mechanic working in someone's shop who is paid a percentage of the work billed to the customer, where the owner of the shop sets the prices, hours, and days the shop is open, schedules the work, and collects from the customers is an example of an employee.

Dance instructors working in a health club where the club sets hours of work, the routines to be taught and pays the instructors from fees collected from the customers are examples of employees.

A repairperson working in a shop where the owner sets the prices, the hours and days the shop is open, and the repairperson is paid a percentage of the work done is an example of an employee.

Employment Determination Guide (Form DE 38)
(Page 7 of 7)

Telecommuting Request

Employee Name _____   Date of Request _____

Job Title _____

1. Reason for request: _____

2. How will telecommuting benefit the Company? _____

3. What days do you propose to telecommute? _____

4. Are you proposing a change in work schedule/hours? ☐ Yes ☐ No   If yes, please describe. _____

5. What hours will you be available for contact? _____

6. What tasks will you handle from home? _____

7. How will working from home change your current work practices? _____

8. How will you communicate with your supervisor and ensure projects are delivered in a timely manner? _____

9. Please describe the proposed workspace in your home: _____

10. What equipment will you need in order to effectively telecommute? _____

11. Are you requesting equipment from the Company? ☐ Yes ☐ No   If yes, please describe. _____

Telecommuting Request

Report of Independent Contractors - Form DE542
(Page 1 of 2)

EDD Employment Development Department State of California

REPORT OF INDEPENDENT CONTRACTOR(S)

05420101

See detailed instructions on page 2. Please type or print.

SERVICE-RECIPIENT (BUSINESS OR GOVERNMENT ENTITY):

DATE

FEDERAL ID NO.   CA EMPLOYER ACCOUNT NO   SOCIAL SECURITY NO.

SERVICE-RECIPIENT NAME / BUSINESS NAME   CONTACT PERSON

ADDRESS   TELEPHONE NO.

CITY   STATE   ZIP

SERVICE-PROVIDER (INDEPENDENT CONTRACTOR):

FIRST NAME   MI   LAST NAME

SOCIAL SECURITY NO.   STREET NO.   STREET NAME   UNIT/APT.

CITY   STATE   ZIP

START DATE OF CONTRACT   AMOUNT OF CONTRACT   CONTRACT EXPIRATION DATE   CHECK HERE IF CONTRACT IS ONGOING
M M D D Y Y   M M D D Y Y

FIRST NAME   MI   LAST NAME

SOCIAL SECURITY NO.   STREET NO.   STREET NAME   UNIT/APT.

CITY   STATE   ZIP

START DATE OF CONTRACT   AMOUNT OF CONTRACT   CONTRACT EXPIRATION DATE   CHECK HERE IF CONTRACT IS ONGOING
M M D D Y Y   M M D D Y Y

FIRST NAME   MI   LAST NAME

SOCIAL SECURITY NO.   STREET NO.   STREET NAME   UNIT/APT.

CITY   STATE   ZIP

START DATE OF CONTRACT   AMOUNT OF CONTRACT   CONTRACT EXPIRATION DATE   CHECK HERE IF CONTRACT IS ONGOING
M M D D Y Y   M M D D Y Y

DE 542 Rev. 3 (3-05) (INTERNET)   MAIL TO: Employment Development Department • P.O. Box 997350, MIC 96 • Sacramento, CA 95899-7350
or Fax to (916) 319-4410.
Page 1 of 2

Report of Independent Contractors - Form DE542
(Page 2 of 2)

INSTRUCTIONS FOR COMPLETING THE REPORT OF INDEPENDENT CONTRACTOR(S)

WHO MUST REPORT:

Any business or government entity (defined as a "Service-Recipient") that is required to file a Federal Form 1099-MISC for service performed by an independent contractor (defined as a "Service-Provider") must report. You must report to the Employment Development Department within twenty (20) days of EITHER making payments of $600 or more OR entering into a contract for $600 or more with an independent contractor in any calendar year, whichever is earlier. This information is used to assist state and county agencies in locating parents who are delinquent in their child support obligations.

An independent contractor is further defined as an individual who is not an employee of the business or government entity for California purposes and who receives compensation or executes a contract for services performed for that business or government entity either in or outside of California. For further clarification, request *Information Sheet: Employment Work Status Determination* (DE 231ES). See below for additional information on how to obtain forms.

YOU ARE REQUIRED TO PROVIDE THE FOLLOWING INFORMATION THAT APPLIES:

Service-Recipient (Business or Government Entity):
- Federal employer identification number
- California employer account number
- Social security number
- Service-recipient name/business name, address, and telephone number

Service-Provider (Independent Contractor):
- First name, middle initial, and last name
- Social security number
- Address
- Start date of contract (if no contract, date payments equal $600 or more)
- Amount of contract including cents (if applicable)
- Contract expiration date (if applicable)
- Ongoing contract (check box if applicable)

HOW TO COMPLETE THIS FORM:

If you use a typewriter or printer, ignore the boxes and type in UPPER CASE as shown. Do not use commas or periods.

If you handwrite this form, print each letter or number in a separate box as shown. Do not use commas or periods.

FIRST NAME   MI   LAST NAME
I M O G E N E   A   S A M P L E

SOCIAL SECURITY NO.   STREET NO.   STREET NAME   UNIT/APT.
1 2 3 4 5 6 7 8 9   1 2 3 4 5   M A I N   S T R E E T   3 0 1

FIRST NAME   MI   LAST NAME
IMOGENE   A   SAMPLE

SOCIAL SECURITY NO.   STREET NO.   STREET NAME   UNIT/APT.
123456789   12345   MAIN STREET   301

GENERAL INFORMATION:

If you have any questions concerning this reporting requirement, please call (916) 657-0529. You may also contact your local Employment Tax Customer Service Office listed in your telephone directory in the State Government section under "Employment Development Department." Or you may access our Internet site at www.edd.ca.gov.

To obtain additional DE 542 forms:
- Visit our Internet site at www.edd.ca.gov; or
- For 25 or more forms, telephone (916) 322-2835.
- For less than 25 forms, telephone (916) 657-0529.

To obtain information for submitting *Report of Independent Contractors* on magnetic media, call (916) 651-6945.

HOW TO REPORT:

Please record the information in the spaces provided and mail to the following address or fax to (916) 319-4410.

EMPLOYMENT DEVELOPMENT DEPARTMENT
P.O. Box 997350, Document Management Group, MIC 96
Sacramento, CA 95899-7350

DE 542 Rev. 3 (3-05) (INTERNET)   Page 2 of 2

Telecommuting Policy

Telecommuting provides employees with an opportunity to work from an alternative work environment instead of in the primary location of the Company. Telecommuting must be pre-approved by an employee's supervisor and cannot be initiated without a *Telecommuting Agreement*.

_____ (the Company) retains the right in its sole discretion to designate positions that are appropriate for telecommuting and approve employees for telecommuting. Telecommuting must be approved by an employee's supervisor. Telecommuting does not change the conditions of employment or required compliance with all Company policies and procedures. The Company reserves the right to change or terminate the *Telecommuting Agreement* at any time, without cause or advance notice. An employee's ability to work under a *Telecommuting Agreement* rests in the sole discretion of the Company. Telecommuting is a privilege and may not be appropriate for all employees. If an employee wishes to request a *Telecommuting Agreement*, s/he should contact his or her supervisor and ask for a *Telecommuting Request* form.

Telecommuting Safety

The Telecommuter is solely responsible for ensuring the safety of his or her alternative work environment. However, because the Company is legally obligated to provide its employees with a workplace that is free from hazards that might cause serious harm or injury, the Company reserves the right to periodically inspect the Telecommuter's home work space. Any such inspection will be preceded by advance notice and an appointment will be scheduled. Telecommuters are protected by the Company's workers' compensation insurance. As such, Telecommuters are required to immediately report any injuries that occur while working.

The Telecommuter shall be liable for any injuries that occur to third parties at or around the Telecommuter's alternative work environment.

Telecommuting Plan

All Telecommuters will be required to sign a *Telecommuting Agreement* with their supervisor that outlines the days and work hours (as applicable) of the Telecommuter; equipment the Telecommuter will need; how the Telecommuter will communicate with the Company; use of support or secretarial staff; and other appropriate information.

Hours of Work

Unless otherwise agreed in the *Telecommuting Agreement*, hours and days of work will not change. Employees agree to apply themselves during work hours. Telecommuting is not intended as a substitute for child care or care for another adult. If a child or adult needs care during work time, another responsible individual is expected to be present.

Attendance at Meetings

Telecommuters are expected to attend all required meetings.

Costs Associated with Telecommuting

The Company shall not incur additional costs due to a *Telecommuting Agreement*. The *Telecommuting Agreement* will specify any costs the Company will cover. All other expenses are the responsibility of the Telecommuter.

How Six Agencies Determine Independent Contractor-Employee Relationships

	IRS	EDD/FTB	INS	Workers' Comp	US Dept of Labor	CA Labor Comm
No right to control worker		◆	◆	◆		◆
No instructions	■			■		
No training	■					
Assistants can do work	■	◆				
Work not hiring firm's primary business	■					
No set work hours	■					
Not a continuing relationship	■	●		■		
Control assistants	■					
Time to work for others	■					
Determine job location	●					
Set order of work	■					
No interim reports	■					
Paid by job	■		■	■	■	
Work for many companies			■	■		■
Pay own expenses				■	■	■
Have own tools			■	■		■
Made significant investment	■	■	■	■		■
Offer services to public	■		■		■	
Can make profit or loss			■			■
Can't be fired at will	■	◆	■	■		■
Aren't paid for partial work	■	■		■		■
Distinct occupation or operate separate business		■				■
Part of industry practice						
Skill required		■	■	■		■
Work typically non-supervised		■				■
Parties believe worker is independent contractor				■	■	■
Who hired the worker						
Amount of initiative or judgment needed to succeed					■	

Legend: ◆ Most important factor ■ Important factor ● Lesser factor

---

Telecommuting Agreement

Use this sample agreement once a telecommuting relationship has been approved to describe the expectations your company has of employees who telecommute. This document may need to be customized to reflect the agreement between you and a telecommuting employee and your company's policy. By signing this agreement, employees affirm that they have reviewed and understand your *Telecommuting Policy* and this *Telecommuting Agreement*.

This agreement is part of CalBizCentral's *Telecommuter Toolkit*, which includes the following forms: *Telecommuting Policy*, *Telecommuting Agreement*, *Telecommuting Request*, *Telecommuting Request Checklist* and *Telecommuting Safety Checklist*.

Telecommuting Agreement (Page 1 of 3)

Telecommuting Agreement

I have read and understand the attached *Telecommuting Policy*, and agree to the duties, obligations, responsibilities and conditions for telecommuters described in that document. I understand that I remain subject to all confidentiality, sexual harassment and workplace safety.

_____ (the Company) policies including, but not limited to, use of technology,

I agree that, among other things, I am responsible for establishing specific telecommuting work hours, furnishing and maintaining my remote work space in a safe manner, employing appropriate telecommuting security measures and protecting company assets, information, trade secrets and systems.

I understand that telecommuting is voluntary and I may stop telecommuting at any time. I also understand that the Company may at any time change any or all of the conditions under which I am permitted to telecommute, or withdraw permission to telecommute.

Work Schedule

I will be telecommuting on the following days: (check all that apply)

☐ Monday ☐ Tuesday ☐ Wednesday ☐ Thursday ☐ Friday ☐ Saturday ☐ Sunday

I will be telecommuting during the following hours. I understand that I must report to my supervisor when I check in for the day, when I leave for the day, and at all mandatory breaks so my hours will be properly recorded:

☐ I am a non-exempt employee and will be telecommuting during the following hours.

☐ I am an exempt employee.

Company Equipment

The Company has supplied me with the following equipment. I understand that I am responsible for immediately reporting any malfunctions. I further understand that I am solely responsible for any damages that may occur to this equipment. At the termination of this Agreement, or upon request of the Company, I agree to immediately return this equipment or reimburse the Company for the value of this equipment. I will only use the equipment for work related activities:

Item	Date Issued	Identification# (Serial #)	Date Returned	Condition	
				Acceptable	Not Acceptable

Telecommuting Agreement (Page 2 of 3)

Telecommuting Agreement

Contact Information

While working, I will be available by: (check all that apply and fill in appropriate contact information)

☐ Telephone _____
☐ Email _____
☐ Fax _____
☐ Cellular phone _____

Staff Assistance and Communication

While telecommuting, I will require regular assistance of the following staff:

_____

I intend to communicate with staff in the following manner:

_____

I intend to communicate with my supervisor in the following manner:

_____

Company Covered Costs

The Company will cover the following costs. I understand that all other expenses related to telecommuting are my responsibility.

_____

_____

My signature below affirms that I have reviewed the *Telecommuting Agreement* and the contents of this *Telecommuting Policy* with my supervisor and understand their contents. I understand that this *Agreement* may be altered or terminated at any time.

_____   _____
Employee Signature   Date

_____   _____
Supervisor Signature   Date

Telecommuting Agreement (Page 3 of 3)

Telecommuting Request Checklist

Employee Name _____   Date of Request _____

Job Title* _____   Date of Hire _____

	Yes	No
1. Is Employee self-motivated?	☐	☐
2. Is Employee able to work productively on his or her own?	☐	☐
3. Can Employee work with little or no supervision?	☐	☐
4. Is Employee well organized?	☐	☐
5. Does Employee have a high level of knowledge of his or her job?	☐	☐
6. Has Employee received above average evaluations?	☐	☐
7. Does Employee meet deadlines?	☐	☐
8. Is Employee dependable and trustworthy?	☐	☐
9. Does Employee have a low need for social interaction?	☐	☐
10. Does Employee's position require face-to-face contact?	☐	☐
11. Does Employee have above average communication skills?	☐	☐
12. Does Employee have an appropriate work site?	☐	☐

* Attach job description to this form before filing.

Telecommuting Request Checklist

Telecommuting Safety Checklist

Employee Name _____

Supervisor Name _____

Location _____

Telephone (___) ___ - _____

The following checklist is designed to assess the overall safety of the alternate work location. Each participant should read and complete the self-certification safety checklist. Upon completion, the participating employee and his or her immediate supervisor should sign and date this checklist.

The alternate work location is located (check one): ☐ in home   ☐ not in home

Describe the designated work area:

_____

_____

_____

To the best of one's knowledge:

		Yes	No
1.	Is the space free of asbestos-containing materials?	☐	☐
2.	If asbestos-containing material is present, is it undamaged and in good condition?	☐	☐
3.	Is the space free of indoor air quality problems?	☐	☐
4.	Is there adequate ventilation for the desired occupancy?	☐	☐
5.	Is the space free of noise hazards (noises in excess of 85 decibels)?	☐	☐
6.	Is there a potable (drinkable) water supply?	☐	☐
7.	Are lavatories available with hot and cold running water?	☐	☐
8.	Are all stairs with four or more steps equipped with handrails?	☐	☐
9.	Are all circuit breakers and/or fuses in the electrical panel labeled as to intended service?	☐	☐
10.	Do circuit breakers clearly indicate if they are in the open or closed position?	☐	☐
11.	Is all electrical equipment free of recognized hazards that would cause physical harm (frayed wires, bare conductors, loose wires, flexible wires running through walls, exposed wires fixed to the ceiling)?	☐	☐
12.	Will the building's electrical system permit the grounding of electrical equipment?	☐	☐
13.	Are aisles, doorways and corners free of obstructions to permit visibility and movement?	☐	☐
14.	Are file cabinets and storage closets arranged so drawers and doors do not open into walkways?	☐	☐

Telecommuting Safety Checklist (Page 1 of 2)

Telecommuting Safety Checklist

		Yes	No
15.	Do chairs have any loose casters (wheels)? Are the rungs and legs of chairs sturdy?	☐	☐
16.	Is the work area overly furnished in such a way that it prevents safe entry/exit in case of emergency?	☐	☐
17.	Are the phone lines, electrical cords and extension wires secured under a desk or alongside a baseboard?	☐	☐
18.	Is the office space neat, clean and free of excessive amounts of combustibles?	☐	☐
19.	Are floor surfaces clean, dry, level and free of worn or frayed seams?	☐	☐
20.	Are carpets well-secured to the floor and free of frayed or worn seams?	☐	☐

Items in Need of Repair	Repair(s) Necessary

Employee Signature _____ Date _____

Supervisor Signature _____ Date _____

Telecommuting Safety Checklist (Page 2 of 2)

Chapter 6

Employee Handbooks

There is no legal requirement for you to prepare and distribute an employee handbook or policy manual. However, the absence of a formal handbook or policy manual or a poorly drafted one puts you at a disadvantage to defend yourself should you face a lawsuit based on your policies, procedures or accusations of discrimination or sexual harassment. Should you decide to develop an employee handbook or policy manual, be aware that numerous federal, state and even local laws affect the content of policies and procedures included in such publications.

This chapter explains how to develop a quality employee handbook or policy manual that provides employees and supervisors with a clear understanding of the performance and behaviors you expect of them and what they can expect of the company in return. This common understanding of goals and expectations enhances productivity and reduces the opportunity for conflict. This chapter explains what laws affect your manual contents and how to preserve your employment-at-will relationship, including:

- Whom the handbook will cover;

- What topics to include;

- How to review and include existing policies;

- How to implement the handbook; and

- The relevance of creating supervisors' manuals.

Preserving Employment-at-Will

A carefully drafted statement of your at-will employment policy should be contained in your handbook and repeated wherever there is any possibility that other subject matter may be read as creating a more permanent employment relationship. Examples of such other policies include:

- Hiring;

- Introductory period;

- Introductory statement;

- Discipline and termination;

- Benefits; and

- Training.

Language in employee handbooks and policy statements has been an issue in numerous cases concerning the nature of the employment relationship and whether "cause" is required for employee termination. Case law indicates that you may create detrimental ambiguities in the employment-at-will relationship by promising fairness or equity in termination decisions, or by setting forth discipline or termination policies or procedures that conflict with at-will employment. Explicit promises in a handbook can create contractual liabilities for you if you fail to follow your policies.

Conversely, appropriate language in a handbook can help protect and preserve the employment-at-will relationship. Without an employee handbook, you create significant vulnerability to a variety of wrongful termination lawsuits.

To the extent that statements of at-will employment in the employee handbook are consistent with other policies and statements in employment applications, employment contracts and other materials, the nature of the employment relationship will not be based upon the handbook language alone. Collect and review all such materials during the preparation phase of the handbook to ensure consistency in preserving the at-will relationship.

Defining Who Is Covered by a Handbook

The first step in preparing an employee handbook or manual is to determine which employees the policies will cover. Consider workforce size, your geographic scope of operations, and employee job duties. If you employ a significant number of employees in widely varying functions at different physical locations, you may find that setting forth policies in separate publications addressed to particular groups prevents confusion, misinterpretation or misapplication of the policies. Variations in laws between states in which you have work locations may necessitate separate handbooks covering each of those operations. Whatever the decision in this area, all handbooks should contain a clear statement of who is and is not covered by its policies.

Determining which employees are covered by the handbook will affect which topics you should include. Hiring policies and pre-employment matters may be required knowledge for managers and supervisors, but likely not appropriate for handbooks governing rank-and-file employees. Some policies are included in handbooks affecting both employees and supervisors, but with varying emphasis and approach. Though while a supervisor's handbook might require the supervisor to refer all employee reference inquiries to a centralized source, such as the human resources director, the handbook for employees might simply state the employer's policy to limit release of employment information to outside parties only to dates of employment and positions held.

Including Relevant Topics

There is no one policy or collection of policies that is appropriate in all employment settings, and policies appropriate for inclusion in employee handbooks may vary. You can use the checklist, *Policies - Mandatory and Recommended*, to help you determine what to include. Of the thousands of calls CalChamber's *Labor Law Helpline* staff take from employers each year, a significant percentage deals with the following personnel policies. Your obligations and rights under these policies are outlined in alphabetical order for ease of reference.

Acknowledgment and Receipt

An *Confirmation of Receipt Policy*, which employees must sign and return, records their receipt of, understanding of, and agreement to abide by provisions of the handbook. Such forms help establish that employees had notice of your policies, expectations, and prohibitions. They are critical to defending against wrongful termination actions by demonstrating the employee's knowledge and acceptance of the at-will employment relationship.

Arbitration

Do not include agreements to arbitrate employment termination or other disputes in your employee handbook. An arbitration agreement should be a separately executed document. See Chapter 10, "Arbitrating Employment Claims," for further information on arbitration.

Benefits

A benefits section sets forth vacations, holidays, sick leave, "kin care" rights, leaves of absence, insurance coverage, pension plans and other benefits available to employees. Pregnancy disability and family leave policies are required by law for some employers. Clearly set forth eligibility requirements and conditions for receipt of benefits, and include brief statements of state and federally mandated benefits, such as Social Security, unemployment insurance, workers' compensation insurance, etc.

Camera-phones

The use of cell phones with built-in cameras (camera-phones) presents several areas of concern for employers.

First, allowing employees to use personal cell phones in the workplace, and those cell phones have cameras, creates privacy issues. Employees expect privacy in certain areas of the workplace, including:

- Restrooms;
- Changing rooms;
- Locker rooms;
- Break rooms;
- Lunch rooms; and
- Areas designated as private, solely for use of women to express breast milk.

You should draft a policy prohibiting the use of camera phones in such areas, and in other areas where employees expect privacy.

Second, for some employers, protection of trade secrets or other issues of workplace security is a significant concern. You should create a policy prohibiting the use of camera phones completely, or in specified areas.

Confidentiality

An employee handbook that includes a broad confidentiality policy or restricts reasonable employee speech violates both state and federal law.

California law prohibits employers from publishing or enforcing policies that limit the employee's right to discuss wages and working conditions.[1]

The National Labor Relations Board (NLRB) rejected a policy that included "violating a confidence or unauthorized release of confidential information" as among behaviors that could result in disciplinary action. The NLRB ruled that the handbook content violated federal labor law because employees could reasonably understand it to restrict discussion of wages and other terms and conditions of employment with fellow employees and with the union.[2]

This follows an earlier NLRB decision rejecting rules prohibiting employees from complaining to customers about the terms and conditions of their employment while wearing the company's uniform.[3]

Discipline

Make clear to all employees that you expect certain work performance standards, that certain personal conduct is required in the workplace and that you will not tolerate other conduct. These are conditions of employment. Examples include requiring employees to arrive at work on time, prohibiting drinking or being drunk in the workplace, etc. The policy should indicate that violating such rules or expectations will trigger discipline or immediate termination of the employee. See Chapter 31, "Disciplining and Terminating At-will Employees" for further information on discipline and termination procedures.

Equal Employment Opportunity — Prohibition of Discrimination

An equal employment opportunity policy sets forth the company's commitment to equal employment opportunity (and affirmative action, if applicable). A specific enumeration of the factors the company does not consider in making employment decisions (race, sex, age, national origin, disabilities, etc.) is useful both as a matter of information to employees and in defending against allegations of unlawful discrimination. The policy should, at a minimum, state that you do not discriminate against employees on any basis prohibited by law and that you forbid sexual or other harassment. California law concerning sexual harassment requires a separate handbook policy section on this subject. Your handbook should also identify a process for bringing complaints of discrimination or harassment to the attention of management.

Family/Medical Leave and Pregnancy Disability Leave

All employee handbooks published or revised after August 12, 1995, must contain a policy regarding family leave and/or pregnancy disability leave if the handbook describes other types of personal or disability leaves available to employees. Of course, include these policies only if you are subject to the family leave and/or pregnancy disability leave laws. See Chapter 22, "Pregnancy Disability Leave," and Chapter 21, "Family/Medical and Sick Leaves" for more information. Review your family leave policy to be sure the policy is clear as to what method is used to calculate the 12-month period in which an employee is eligible for 12 weeks of leave. According to a 2001 decision of the Ninth U.S. Circuit Court of Appeals, employees who do not receive clear notice of the calculation method an employer uses can choose whichever method provides them the most family leave time. See "Calculation Method Notification" in Chapter 21, page 538, for more information about this case.

1.Lab. Code selections 232, 232.5
2.Cints Corp., 344 NLRB No. 118 (June 30, 2005)
3.Guardsmark, LLC, 344 NLRB No. 97 (June 7, 2005)

State your policies regarding the Paid Family Leave Law, including coordination with vacation pay, and your requirements for notice of absences. See Chapter 18, "Unemployment Insurance."

Health Insurance Benefits

Health insurance benefits for employees are not required by law. If you offer such benefits, you may choose to pay all, part or none of the costs. You may have a standard plan for all employees or may offer each employee the same amount of dollar benefits and permit him or her to select desired benefits from a menu of options offered by the insuring company. You may offer different insurance plans to different groups of employees, such as production versus managerial employees, as long as that distinction is not based on any "protected class" considerations (see "Protected Classes" in Chapter 27, page 742). You may also establish a weekly work hour threshold concerning eligibility for such benefits.

Hours of Work

An "hours of work" section describes work schedules; breaks; meal periods; the seven-day workweek; the 24-hour workday established for calculating overtime pay; methods used by employees in recording worktime and overtime work requirements. The language of such sections should clearly specify the categories of employees eligible for overtime pay and specifically exclude exempt employees from that eligibility. Because you are legally required to pay for all hours of work performed by non exempt employees, include the requirement that any overtime work requires previous authorization. The policy should indicate that the requirement will be enforced through disciplinary procedures, and may not include a threat of non payment for non authorized overtime.

Internet and Other Electronic Media

For employees who have access to the Internet through their employers, it may be necessary to implement a policy for its appropriate use. Such a policy may provide guidance to employees who may have access to the Internet during working hours, clarify disciplinary procedures for personal use of the Internet at work and detail proper and improper use of your Web pages.

Include additional language telling employees that they should have no expectation of privacy regarding communications sent and received through the company's e-mail and/or intranet system and access to the Internet. Many employers also include a policy concerning the safe use of company cell phones and limitations on their use for personal business. See the *Cell Phone Policy*.

Cell Phones and PDAs

NEW for 2009 Since July 1, 2008, drivers have been required to use a hands-free device while talking on a cell phone and driving. Starting January 1, 2009, text-based communication while driving is prohibited as well, with the same penalties — $20 for the first offense and $50 for subsequent offenses. Specifically, the law prohibits writing, sending or reading text-based communication including text messaging, instant messaging and e-mail, on a wireless device or cell phone while driving. Until July 1, 2011, this prohibition does not apply to a person driving a motor truck or truck tractor, an agricultural vehicle, tow truck or a commercial vehicle when using a digital two-way radio service using a wireless telephone that operates by depressing a push-to-talk feature as long as it does not require immediate proximity to the user's ear.

The law does not apply to a person driving a school bus or transit vehicle that is subject to certain existing wireless telephone usage restrictions, or to a person while driving a motor vehicle on private property.

Introductory Period

When you hire an employee, you can provide the new employee with an introductory or trial period. This period is literally a get-acquainted period of time designed to test the character and qualifications of the new employee. It is a period of trial and examination during which employer and employee judge how the employment arrangement is working out. Introductory periods can create contractual rights to employment after the period is successfully completed, so it is important that such a policy clearly state that it is not meant to alter the at-will employment relationship.[4] Most introductory periods last three months, though the period can be of any length depending upon the employer's policy. If your policy disallows accrual of benefits during any introductory period, you should explicitly state it in the employee handbook. Otherwise, claims for vacation and other benefits are allowed by the Labor Commissioner upon complaint by the employee.

Introductory Statement

An introduction describes the purpose of the handbook, the employees to whom it applies, sources of additional information, a description of the employment-at-will relationship and a statement that the policies in the handbook replace any previously existing policies and practices.

Job Abandonment

Neither California nor federal law regulates the amount of time you must hold a job for an employee who neither appears for work nor calls in to explain his/her absence. Your actions in this area are controlled only by your policy. Clearly set forth the consequences of "no-call, no-show" behavior, indicate that the employee will be considered to have quit his/her employment if "no-call, no-show" occurs for the designated number of scheduled work days, and indicate exceptions may be made for emergencies. Require employees to read and acknowledge the company policy in this area.

Job Requirements

You have complete control over the work requirements for jobs offered by your company. Periodically review job descriptions to fulfill changing company needs. You may use oral and/or written examinations in the selection process, and you can require a physical examination (post-offer, pre-employment) under certain conditions. For more information, see Chapter 29, "Disabilities In the Workplace."

---

4. *Walker v. Northern San Diego County Hosp. Dist.,* 135 Cal. App. 3d 896 (1982)

Job Termination

Either party may terminate an employment relationship having no specific term on notice to the other. Remember that a union contract or a verbal agreement normally constitutes an enforceable agreement between employer and employee, and that any termination of an employee must be conducted according to that agreement.

It is imperative that you document all events concerning the termination process. Because this has become a very sensitive legal problem, consult Chapter 31, "Disciplining and Terminating At-will Employees," and/or an experienced labor law attorney before terminating an employee, particularly if extenuating circumstances exist, or the employee is a member of a protected class.

Part-Time Employment

You may define part-time employment as any number of hours. No legal definition of "part-time exists." The part-time designation may or may not identify employees who are not entitled to company benefits, at your discretion.

California's Labor Code sets 40 hours as the legal requirement for full-time employment, but only for the purpose of calculating the overtime rate for a "full-time salaried employee."[5] (See "Salaried Nonexempt Employees" in Chapter 14, page 345.) This 40-hour requirement does not apply to any other aspect of law. You are otherwise free to set your own minimum number of hours for full-time employment.

Pay

You control what you will pay each employee for each job in your company. You are limited only by the minimum wage and the marketplace. You must pay men and women the same wage for the same job or substantially equivalent jobs, making exceptions only for job experience that may place one employee above another within the same pay range.

Safety

Include work safety and/or conduct rules informing employees of your expectations for workplace behavior. However, avoid defining punishments for particular acts to prevent wrongful termination claims.

Severance Pay

The law does not require you to provide severance pay. It can be the result of a settlement of an unhappy employer-employee relationship, a reward for many years of satisfactory service to an employee who is moving on, or a reduction in workforce affecting many employees. It represents dollars paid to the employee at the termination of the employee's service and is usually based upon the weekly earnings of the employee and length of service. Be aware that

---

5.Lab. Code sec. 515(c)

severance pay given to one employee may establish a precedent when, at a later date, you face a similar situation involving another employee.

If severance pay involves continuation of an employee's pay for a certain period, that employee may not be eligible to receive unemployment compensation during the time he/she receives the severance pay.

Temporary Employment

No law defines temporary employment. Although a temporary employee may work full-time, such arrangements should be for a fixed period, and that fixed period should be outlined to the employee in advance. Employees cannot be classified as temporary indefinitely.

Time Between Shifts

With the exception of certain employees in the airline, railroad, trucking and health-care industries, no federal or state statutory restrictions exist upon the number of hours an employee must be off duty between workdays or shifts. Safety considerations may make it advisable in certain hazardous occupations to provide a minimum time between work shifts in company policy, with exceptions only in emergencies.

Vacation Pay

You can offer vacation pay, but it is not required by law. If you do provide vacation pay, legally the pay belongs to the employee. The employee's accrued vacation days can never be lost. If an introductory period is explicitly excluded from vacation accrual by company policy, the vacation pay does not begin to accrue until the employee successfully completes the introductory period. You must pay accrued but unused vacation if the employee's services terminate, regardless of the cause for termination. See "Vacations" in Chapter 17, page 413, for further information on vacation pay treatment.

Workplace

You may determine the place the employee will work, and make working in that location a condition of employment. You must comply with certain state regulations, such as providing restroom facilities for men and women, and clean water to drink. The workplace also must be made a safe place in which to work. Workplace safety considerations include exposure to chemicals, clean air, the safety of mechanical devices used in the workplace and a company policy on a drug-free workplace. See Chapter 9, "Drugs, Alcohol and Smoking In the Workplace" for further information regarding a drug-free workplace.

Work Rules

You can establish and enforce work rules in the workplace as long as these rules do not conflict with the law. These rules may include employee conduct, procedures for accomplishing work, cleanliness, safety, accounting for work hours, etc.

Additional Policies

It often is desirable to include additional policies in employee handbooks for non supervisory personnel, such as:

- Attendance and punctuality;

- Bonus programs and incentive pay;

- Bulletin board use;

- Confidentiality requirements;

- Conflicts of interest and business ethics;

- Dress codes;

- Drug/alcohol use;

- Educational benefits;

- Employment classifications;

- Jury duty;

- Performance evaluations;

- Personnel records access;

- Solicitation/distribution rules; and

- Trade secrets.

For a checklist, see *Policies - Mandatory and Recommended.*

Reviewing Existing Policy Information

Collect and review existing policy and procedure statements, including employment applications, personnel action forms, vacation leave request forms, etc., to serve as the basis for your handbook. Include all established policies reflecting current practice, and manuals or management memoranda that accurately depict your personnel policy, meet applicable requirements and function to the satisfaction of supervisors and employees. Sample policies from resource books on personnel policies and handbooks from other employers in similar industries or geographical areas are also useful. However, all policies should be specifically tailored to the employment setting in which they will apply.

Drafting Handbook Language

Clarity and legal compliance are the most important elements in drafting employee handbook language. Eliminate ambiguous language that can be confused and disputed. The handbook must avoid statements and promises inconsistent with the employment-at-will relationship, particularly those that could be interpreted as promising "just cause" for termination.

Clearly denote provisions applying only to certain employees in the language contained in the handbook. If, for example, you have commission-only outside salespersons statutorily exempt from overtime pay, or employee benefits accrue only to employees working a certain number of hours per week, clearly state in the handbook the classifications to which such provisions apply.

When preparing employee handbooks or manuals, take special care not to invade the privacy rights of employees. Avoid unnecessary or unjustified attempts to regulate employee conduct outside the workplace. For example, replace a blanket prohibition on "moonlighting" with a requirement that employees must avoid actual, potential or the appearance of conflicts of interest.

In addition, nonunion employers must avoid infringing on the rights of employees to organize. The National Labor Relations Act (NLRA) protects the rights of employees to engage in concerted activities for the purpose of collective bargaining or other mutual aid or protection. Employer policies that interfere with, restrain or coerce employees in the exercise of these rights constitute unfair labor practices. See Chapter 33, "Labor Relations in Private Employment."

To avoid the risk of liability, carefully consider the job-relatedness of requirements, such as dress codes or personal appearance, before including them in the handbook.

Drafting consistent, understandable and legally permissible employment policies is a difficult task. However, your expended effort and resources can result in significant long-term benefit.

Reviewing the Handbook

Upon completion of the initial draft of an employee handbook or policy manual, submit it to company managers for review. Their input can be extremely helpful in providing another perspective to the draft and in uncovering omissions or inconsistencies. In addition, early consultation regarding employment policies makes managers and supervisors more likely to be supportive when these policies are implemented.

Due to the potential for employer liability for policy statements violating employment laws and regulations upon completion of all these steps, submit the draft handbook to experienced labor counsel for review.

Implementing New or Revised Handbook Policies

Distribute the employee handbook to employees before the date that new policies will be implemented. This allows employees and supervisors to review the new information and raise any issues requiring clarification. Advanced distribution also prevents any implication of a forfeiture of benefits or compensation earned before the effective date of the new policies. Forfeiture of any benefits that have been "vested" before implementing the new policies is unlawful.

Consistency in applying policy is fundamental to good personnel relations and critical to favorable resolution of allegations of unlawful discrimination and other claims. Orientation and training of supervisors and managers before implementing new or revised policies is critical. Before distributing the materials and discussing them with nonsupervisory personnel, make sure that supervisors understand the policies in the areas of application, content and any required administrative procedures.

Questions may arise as to the meaning of the employment-at-will relationship and your intent in making the policy known. Warn supervisors or managers against responding to such inquiries with assurances of job security or other promises contrary to the employment-at-will relationship. Instead, emphasize the employee's right to leave at any time, and your desire to avoid extensive litigation.

Carefully document the distribution of new or revised employee handbooks, and record the dates of distribution and the names of employees to whom you give materials. Collecting and retaining receipt forms from employees for a new or revised handbook or manual play an essential part of the implementation process. If an employee refuses to sign the acknowledgment form, inform the employee that the policies contained therein will be implemented as of the effective date of the handbook, and that his/her continuation of work for and receipt of wages will be considered acceptance of the terms of the handbook. If reluctance continues, inform the employee again, in writing, and retain a copy of that notification.

Your actions in implementing new or revised handbooks or manuals can clearly affect employee acceptance of such materials. Where policies are carefully explained, employee questions are reasonably answered and sufficient time for discussion and questions is allowed, the process is likely to proceed smoothly.

After initial implementation, you and your labor counsel should periodically review your handbook to ensure continued consistency of the policy manual with legal requirements.

Creating Supervisors' Manuals

Manuals for supervisory employees often contain information not relevant to current non-supervisory employees. Such manuals may include information on hiring policies, appropriate pre-employment inquiries, drug testing, physical examinations, U.S. Citizenship and Immigration Service (USCIS) regulations, etc. You may also include information on day-to-day procedural matters, such as vacation or leave requests, or information that addresses on-the-job injuries, performance evaluations, disciplinary procedures, etc.

In addition, include supervisors' proper methods of response to employee complaints of discrimination, harassment in violation of company policy and other types of employee grievances in supervisory manuals to help ensure company policies are consistently administered and that supervisors know what is expected of them.

Changing or Terminating a Handbook Policy

In the wake of a court ruling, California employers may unilaterally change or terminate policies contained in their employee handbooks without having to be concerned about violating an implied contract of employment.[6]

The court ruled that a policy may be terminated or changed as long as the employer:

- Makes the change after the policy has been in place for a reasonable time;

- Gives employees reasonable notice; and

- Does not interfere with employees' vested benefits.

This decision resulted from a company's cancellation of a policy which had promised job security to management employees if no change materially affected Pacific Bell's business plan achievement. By continuing to work for Pacific Bell after the job security policy was cancelled, management employees indicated acceptance of the terms of the new layoff policy.

6.*Asmus v. Pacific Bell*, 23 Cal.4th 1 (2000)

In its opinion, the court also stressed that once an employer creates a policy, the employer must follow the policy until actually terminating or modifying it after giving reasonable notice to employees.

The Family and Medical Leave Act (FMLA) does not interfere with the right of an employer to make changes in its sick leave policies, provided the requirements of FMLA remain satisfied.[7]

Further Information

CalBizCentral's interactive software wizard, *Employee Handbook Software*, will walk you through the entire process of developing your own employee handbook. This software uses a simple interview process to provide policies tailored to your company's situation. For more information, call (800) 331-8877, or visit our online store at ***www.calbizcentral.com***.

7.*Funkhouser et. al. v. Wells Fargo Bank*, 289 F.3d 1137 (9th Cir., 2002)

Employing Minors

Employment of minors is regulated under numerous authorities such as the California Labor Code, the Education Code, the federal Fair Labor Standards Act (FLSA) and others. This chapter addresses the pertinent laws regarding the employment of minors, explaining them in plain language. It explains exceptions and restrictions, and discusses work permits, record keeping, wages and possible penalties when codes or laws are violated.

Download forms referenced in this chapter at **www.calbizcentral.com/support**. Be sure to have your access code from the inside covers of this book ready to enter into the forms download area. Your access code for the forms in the online Formspack is on the inside covers of this book. See "Forms Available Online" on page xix for more information.

Child Labor Law Coverage

Almost all workers under the age of 18 are subject to California's child labor protections. Under the California Labor Code, "minor" means any person under the age of 18 years required to attend school under the provisions of the Education Code, and includes all minors under the age of six.

The California Labor Code entirely excludes any high-school graduate under the age of 18, and not subject to the compulsory education laws, permit requirements, work hour restrictions and all occupational prohibitions. However, under federal regulation, high-school graduates under 18 may not be employed in an occupation prohibited to minors under 18 unless they also have completed a bona fide course of training in that occupation.[1]

"Dropouts" are still subject to California's compulsory education laws, and thus are subject to all state child labor requirements. Emancipated minors are subject to all California's child labor laws, except that they may apply for a work permit without their parents' permission.[2]

Exceptions for Parents and Guardians

Generally, when parents or guardians employ their minor children they must meet all the child labor requirements imposed upon other employers. Parent/guardians who employ their minor children in "manufacturing, mercantile, or similar commercial enterprises" must obtain work permits.[3] The phrase is broadly construed to mean any business in which parent/guardians employ their children.

The only parent/guardian employers who are exempt from California child labor laws are those that employ their minor children in agriculture, horticulture, viticulture or domestic labor on or in connection with premises that the parent/guardian owns, operates or controls.[4] These

---

1. 29 CFR 570.50
2. Family Code sec. 7050
3. Educ. Code sec. 49141

parent/guardian employers are uniquely exempt from work permit requirements, most work hour restrictions and hazardous occupation prohibitions. Minors may not be employed by their parent/guardians in these exempted occupations during school hours, even if the minor is under school age.[5] Under federal law, minors employed on a farm owned or operated by his/her parent or person standing in place of the parent are exempt from the FLSA's child labor provisions, including hazardous occupations, but they may not be employed in any mining or manufacturing occupation on the farm.[6]

The "domestic labor" exemption should not be construed to mean the employment of a minor in the parent/guardian's home in an occupation otherwise prohibited. Domestic labor refers to the type of duties performed — that is, household duties — not the location where labor is performed. Minors may not be freely employed to manufacture goods in their parents' home; they must be at least 16 and possess a home worker permit issued by the Labor Commissioner in addition to possessing a work permit issued by the minor's school.[7]

Similarly, under federal law, parents do not have carte blanche when they employ their own children. Parent/guardians may not employ their minor children under 16 in mining or manufacturing, nor may they employ their children in the occupations declared hazardous for persons under 18[8] in federal regulation. Under federal law, parent/guardians may employ their children under 16 in any other occupation. However, where state law imposes a more protective occupational standard, that standard applies to parent employers. State law does not permit parent/guardians to employ their underage children in prohibited occupations, except in agriculture on premises the parent/guardian owns, operates or controls.[9]

Parent/guardian employers in these particular industries are entirely exempt from both state and federal minimum wage and overtime pay requirements. Indeed, parent/guardians need not pay their employee children any wages at all.[10]

Finally, parent/guardians have special liability for violations of certain child labor laws even when they are not the employer.[11]

Record Keeping

You must keep all Permit to Employ and Work forms on file. (See *Permit to Employ and Work - Form B1-4.*) Keep records open at all times for inspection by school authorities and officers of the Division of Labor Standards Enforcement (DLSE).[12] Failure to produce Permits to Work or to Employ is evidence of the illegal employment of minors and subjects you to a $500 fine on the first offense.[13]

You must keep a record showing the names, ages (dates of birth) and addresses of all minors employed, and time and payroll records required by the applicable Industrial Welfare Commission (IWC) Wage Order for three years. You must furnish this information when requested.[14]

4. Lab. Code sec. 1394
5. Lab. Code sec. 1394
6. 29 U.S.C 213(c)(1) and (2); 29 CFR 570 Subpart E
7. Lab. Code secs. 2659, 2661
8. 29 U.S.C. 20391)(1) and (2); 29 CFR 570 Subpart E
9. Lab. Code sec. 1394
10. IWC Orders sec. 1; 29 U.S.C. 203(s)(2)
11. Lab. Code secs.1308,1308.5
12. Lab. Code sec. 1299; Educ. Code secs. 49161, 49164, 49181
13. Lab. Code secs. 1304, 1288; Educ. Code sec. 49181
14. Lab. Code secs. 1174, 1175

If you employ student-learners, you must keep a copy of the written agreement with the minor's other employment records.[15]

You must furnish each of your employees, at the time you pay wages, a separate or detachable itemized statement of deductions.[16]

Farm Employer Postings

In addition to posters required of all employers (see "Posters" in Chapter 2, page 5), as an owner, tenant or operator of a farm employing parents having minor children in their immediate care and custody, you must post at a conspicuous place on the property or place of employment, where it may be easily read, a notice stating that minor children are not allowed to work unless legally permitted and unless the proper work permits have been secured. You must furnish your own notice, which must be printed in both English and Spanish.[17]

Door-To-Door Sales Registration

If you employ minors under 16 engaged in door-to-door sales more than 10 miles from the minor's residence, you must register with the Labor Commissioner. Among other requirements, you must identify the company, company officers, employer identification (ID) number and all individuals employed to transport or in any way supervise, accompany, recruit, solicit, hire, furnish, employ, pay or otherwise direct or measure the work of the minors. The Labor Commissioner issues registration cards that the minor must carry at all times. The initial fee is $350; the annual renewal fee is $200.[18]

Transporters and supervisors must register separately and individually. Registration cards are issued and must be carried at all times. The initial fee is $100; the annual renewal fee is $50.[19]

Among other requirements, all applicants — whether employer, transporter or supervisor — must submit two sworn affidavits of character, a personal record and a set of fingerprint cards. All applicants must describe the method and level of adult supervision, the merchandise to be sold or distributed and promotional statements the minor will deliver. You must describe how the sales operation will be presented to the public. All applicants must identify all vehicles used to transport minors and present proof of liability insurance.[20]

You are bound by these registration requirements for minors' door-to-door sales if you employ minors to deliver newspapers to consumers.[21] Any violation of the laws protecting minors is grounds for suspension, revocation or refusal to renew any registration.[22]

All applications for registration are subject to investigation. All statements on an application are subject to a penalty for perjury. Any false statement on an application is grounds for non-issuance, suspension or revocation of a registration and a felony.[23]

---

15. Lab. Code sec. 1295
16. Lab. Code sec. 226
17. Educ. Code sec. 49140
18. Lab. Code sec. 1308.3
19. Lab. Code sec. 1308.2
20. Lab. Code secs. 1308.2, 1308.3
21. Lab. Code sec. 1286(e)
22. Lab. Code sec. 1308.4
23. Lab. Code secs. 1308.2, 1308.3, 1308.4

Exceptions

You are not bound by these registration requirements if you are:

- The parent or guardian of the minor;

- A person acting on behalf of a bona fide trustee of charitable assets or on behalf of a charitable organization;

- Part of a government agency (including schools);

- Part of any religious corporation or organization that holds property for religious purposes or any officer, director or trustee who holds property for like purposes;

- Part of a bona fide cemetery corporation;

- Part of a bona fide political committee; or

- Part of a bona fide charitable corporation organized and operated primarily as a religious organization, educational institution, hospital or a licensed health-care service plan.[24]

Employment Restrictions

Employment in certain industries, such as entertainment and agriculture, is subject to different requirements than most other industries. This *Digest* contains requirements for these industries in the *Basic Provisions and Regulations - Child Labor Laws*.

Employing Minors under 14

The FLSA prohibits employment of minors under the age of 14 except in certain limited occupations. These include certain agricultural firms, the entertainment industry, newspaper delivery, home workers in the making of certain wreaths and employment on a farm owned or operated by a parent or guardian.

Working in Hazardous Occupations

Both state and federal law prohibit minors from working in certain hazardous occupations. These occupations are detailed in the *Basic Provisions and Regulations - Child Labor Laws*.

Driving on Public Highways and Streets

It is important to remember that you may not employ minors for the purpose of driving a motor vehicle on public highways and streets.[25] This includes delivering any type of goods from a motor vehicle.[26]

---

24. Lab. Code sec. 1308.2(f)0; Gov't. Code secs. 12582, 12582.1, 12583
25. Vehicle Code sec. 12515
26. 29 CFR 570.52(b)(6)

Work Permits

With certain limited exceptions, you must acquire the required work permits before employing a minor. Permits are required year-round, even when school is not in session.[27] The California Department of Education revised the statement of intent and work permit forms in 2001. See samples of the most recent versions of the forms *Permit to Employ and Work - Form B1-4* and *Statement of Intent to Employ Minor and Request for Work Permit - Form B1-1*.

Issuing Permits

The superintendent of each school district has the authority for issuing work permits.[28] This responsibility is often delegated to other school district officials who take into consideration a minor's health, education and welfare before issuing a permit. Neither school nor labor officials may waive any established minimum labor standard for minors. The issuing authority may revoke a work permit if he/she determines that the employment is impairing the health or education of the minor.[29]

Special Circumstances

A minor employed in the entertainment industry must have an Entertainment Work Permit issued by the DLSE.[30] You must have a Permit to Employ Minors in the Entertainment Industry, which the DLSE also issues.[31] You can find the procedures for obtaining an Entertainment Work Permit on the DLSE Web site at ***www.dir.ca.gov/DLSE/Form-EntertainmentWorkPermit.pdf.***

Minors visiting from another state (or country, if eligible to work in the United States) who wish to work in California must have a work permit.[32] The local school district in which the minor resides while visiting issues these permits.[33]

Expiration Dates

Permits issued in one school year expire five days after a new school year begins.[34]

Exceptions for Requiring Permits

Permits are not required for:

- Any minor who is a high school graduate or who has been awarded a Certificate of Proficiency;[35]

- Minors who irregularly work at odd jobs, such as yard work and babysitting in private homes where the minor is not otherwise regularly employed;[36]

---

27. Educ. Code sec. 49160; Lab. Code sec. 1299; 29 CFR 510.9
28. Educ. Code sec. 49110
29. Lab. Code sec. 1300; Educ. Code secs. 49164, 49116
30. Lab. Code sec. 1308.5, CCR sec. 11753
31. CCR sec. 11752
32. Lab. Code secs. 1286 and 1299; Educ. Code secs. 49160 and 49164
33. Educ. Code sec. 49110
34. Educ. Code sec. 49118
35. Educ. Code sec. 49162

- Minors who are at least 14 years of age and employed to deliver newspapers to consumers;[37]

- Minors who work for a parent or guardian in agriculture, horticulture, viticulture or domestic labor on or in connection with property the parent or guardian owns, operates or controls;[38] note that these minors may not be employed during school hours, even when they are under school age;[39]

- Minors of any age who participate in any horseback riding exhibition, contest or event, whether they receive payment for services or prize money;[40]

- Self-employed minors; or

- Minors directly employed by state and local agencies, unless expressly included in the state's Labor Code. The FLSA covers state and local agencies, and these agencies must meet all its requirements.[41]

Accessing Permits on File

You must have a *Statement of Intent to Employ Minor and Request for Work Permit - Form B1-1* on file with the school district of attendance for each minor required to attend school.[42] Every employer must have a *Permit to Employ and Work - Form B1-4* on file in the workplace for each minor.[43] Keep these records open at all times for inspection by school authorities and DLSE officers.[44]

Completing Permit Forms

A Statement of Intent to Employ Minor and Request for Work Permit - Form B1-1 should be completed by the minor and signed by you and the parent or guardian of the minor.[45] Once the student files a *Statement of Intent to Employ Minor and Request for Work Permit - Form B1-1* with the school district, the district may issue a work permit, which will specify the maximum number of hours of work per day when school is in session, other limitations and the expiration date of the permit.

Minors requesting work permits must have the names of your workers' compensation carrier on their *Statement of Intent to Employ Minor and Request for Work Permit - Form B1-1*. If minors enrolled in work experience education programs receive pay for their work, you must carry workers' compensation insurance for them. In the case of minors not paid for their work in work experience education programs, workers' compensation insurance must be carried by the school district.[46]

Requesting Forms

You or the minor must obtain the necessary forms before employing a minor. Contact the Office of the Superintendent of the school district in which the minor attends school to request the *Statement*

36. 18 Ops. Cal Atty. Gen. 114, Aug 31, 1951
37. Educ. Code sec. 49112(d)
38. Lab. Code sec. 1394
39. Lab. Code sec. 1394
40. Educ. Code secs. 49119 and 49165; Labor Code 1308(b)(3)
41. 29 U.S.C. 203(s)(1)
42. Educ. Code sec. 49101
43. Lab. Code sec. 1299; Educ. Code sec. 49161
44. Educ. Code sec. 49164
45. Educ. Code sec. 49163
46. Educ. Code sec. 51769; Lab. Code sec. 3368

of Intent to Employ Minor and Request for Work Permit - Form B1-1 and the *Permit to Employ and Work - Form B1-4.*

Working Hours

The total number of hours a minor may work, and the permitted spread of hours, varies depending on the age of a minor and the time of year in which work will be performed. With specific exceptions, it is a misdemeanor to require any minor to work more than eight hours a day.[47]

The chart *Basic Provisions and Regulations - Child Labor Laws* was taken from the Child Labor Law Pamphlet issued by the DLSE, a division of California's Department of Industrial Relations (DIR). Note that wherever state and federal standards overlap or appear to contradict, the more protective standard always applies.

It is important to note that if a minor works two jobs, both jobs together may not total more than the legal number of hours for the minor's age group and circumstance.

Extended Working Hours

Minors working in certain industries may work extended hours under permits issued by the Labor Commissioner. Contact the DLSE to obtain an application.

Professional Baseball Games

Minors ages 14 and 15 may work providing sports-attending services at professional games until 12:30 a.m. during any evening preceding a non-school day, and until 10:00 p.m. any evening preceding a school day. When school is in session, 14- and 15-year-olds may work a maximum of five hours per day and 18 hours per week as professional baseball "sports attendants." When school is not in session, they may work a maximum of 40 hours per week.[48]

School authorities who issue the minor's work permit must monitor the academic achievement of the minor to ensure that his/her educational progress is being maintained or improved during the period of employment.[49]

Agricultural Packing Plants

Sixteen- and 17-year-olds employed in agricultural packing plants during the peak harvest season may work up to 10 hours on any day school is not in session. Before you schedule a minor for a shift of more than eight hours, you must obtain a special permit from the Labor Commissioner. This permit will be granted only if it does not materially affect the safety and welfare of minor employees and will prevent you undue hardship. The Labor Commissioner may require an inspection of a packing plant prior to granting the permit. A permit may be revoked after reasonable notice is given in writing, or immediately if any of its terms or conditions are violated. The Labor Commissioner provides applications for such permits, and a

---

47. Lab. Code sec. 1392
48. Lab. Code sec. 1295.5
49. Lab. Code sec. 1295.5

copy of the completed application must be posted at the place of employment at the time the application is submitted.[50]

Lake County Exemption

Sixteen- and seventeen-year-olds who work in agricultural packing plants in Lake County, Calif., are exempted from the normal working hours limitations. These minors, if enrolled in public or private school in Lake County, may work between 48 and 60 hours per week under an exemption issued by the state Labor Commissioner with prior written approval of the Lake County Board of Education.[51] This exemption is set to be repealed on January 1, 2012.

As a condition of receiving an exemption or a renewal of an exemption, you must, on or before March 1 of each year, file a written report to the Labor Commissioner containing the following information regarding the prior year's payroll:

- The number of minors employed; and

- A list of the age and hours worked on a weekly basis of each minor employed.

Prior to issuing or renewing an exemption, the Labor Commissioner must inspect the agricultural packing plant.

Wages

You may not pay minors who have graduated from high school or have a Certificate of Proficiency less than adult employees in the same establishment for the same quantity and quality of work. However, differences in pay may be based on seniority, length of service, ability, skills, difference in duties or services performed, difference in the shift or time of day worked, hours of work or other reasonable differentiation exercised in good faith.[52]

You may, in limited circumstances, pay minors less than the minimum wage. Both state and federal law regulate these subminimum wages. The federal Opportunity Wage now allows employers to pay a subminimum rate to individuals under the age of 20 for the first 90 consecutive days of employment with an employer. State law allows you to pay "learners" 85 percent of the minimum wage rounded to the nearest nickel, but not less than $6.38. Unfortunately, the overlapping of the state and federal standards severely limits the payment of subminimum wages in California. See "Subminimum Wages" in Chapter 12, page 266, for a thorough discussion of the subminimum wages which may be paid to minors by California employers. You should always check with legal counsel before paying subminimum rates.

Apprentices

You may pay apprentices at subminimum rates, but only in accordance with federal standards.[53]

---

50. Lab. Code sec. 1393
51. Lab. Code sec. 1393.5
52. Lab. Code sec. 1391.2
53. IWC Orders sec. 4; 29 U.S.C. 214; 29 CFR 521.5

Organized Camps

You may pay organized camp student employees, camp counselors or program counselors, regardless of age, a weekly salary amounting to 85percent of the minimum wage for a 40-hour week, regardless of the number of hours worked per week.[54] If individuals employed in these occupations work fewer than 40 hours per week, you must pay them at least 85percent of the minimum wage for each hour worked.

State law defines an "organized camp" as a site with program facilities established for the primary purposes of providing an outdoor group living experience with social, spiritual, educational or recreational objectives for five days or more during one or more seasons of the year. The term does not include a motel, tourist camp, trailer park, resort, hunting camp, auto court, labor camp, penal or correctional camp, child-care institution, home-finding agency or any charitable or recreational organization operating a special (for example, temporary) occupancy trailer park.[55] The organized camp must meet the standards established by the American Camping Association.

The federal FLSA also exempts employees of organized camps (and amusement or recreational establishments and religious or nonprofit educational conference centers) from minimum wage and overtime requirements if the facility does not operate for more than seven months in any calendar year, or if its average receipts for any six months of the preceding year do not exceed 33.3 percent of the receipts for the remaining six months of the preceding year. However, private entities providing services or facilities in a national park, national forest or national wildlife refuge are not exempt from federal wage requirements, unless the services or facilities relate to skiing.[56]

Penalties

If you employ or permit underage minors to work in the prohibited occupation or hazardous duty — no matter how voluntary the act is on the part of the minor— you are liable for Class A penalties (see "Civil Penalties" on page 138). Even minors regarding themselves as self-employed may not engage in these prohibited activities. Also, a client who permits such a minor to engage in the prohibited activity is liable for Class A penalties. This type of liability also extends to underage employment in any of the federally regulated occupations adopted by California. For example, minors under 16 may not be employed or permitted to work in occupations involving mining, manufacturing or processing, or perform any duties in related workrooms.[57] Minors under 14, may not be employed or permitted to work in clerical or food service occupations since a minor must be at least 14 to engage in these activities.[58]

Owners of real property who knowingly benefit from child-labor violations are subject to all applicable civil penalties, regardless of whether the person is the minor's employer.[59]

The Labor Commissioner may require garment manufacturers who, within a two-year period, commit a second violation involving child labor, minimum wage or maximum hours of labor and in any combination of violations, to post a surety bond. Upon a third or subsequent

---

54. Lab. Code sec. 1182.4
55. Health and Safety Code secs. 18897
56. 29 U.S.C. 213(a)(3)
57. Lab. Code secs. 1294.1, 1290
58. Lab. Code sec. 1294.3
59. Lab. Code sec. 1301

violation within a two-year period, the Labor Commissioner may suspend a garment manufacturer's registration for up to one year and confiscate any partially or fully assembled garments.[60]

Civil Penalties

California law provides two types of civil penalties for violations of child labor laws: Class A and Class B.[61]

Class A Violations

The more severe violations, Class A, generally involve underage employment in hazardous occupations. Class A violations include violations of laws relating to:

- Manufacturing and underage employment;[62]
- Hazardous occupations;[63]
- Door-to-door sales;[64]
- Eight-hour days;[65]
- Hazardous activities;[66] and
- Any other violations that the DIR's director determines present an imminent danger to minor employees or a substantial probability that death or serious physical harm would result.[67]

The violation of work hour limitations[68] for the third or subsequent occasion also constitutes a Class A violation.[69]

Class A violations incur penalties of not less than $5,000 and up to $10,000 for each and every violation.[70]

Class B Violations

Class B violations include violations of laws relating to:

- Work permits;[71]
- The entertainment industry;[72] and

60. Lab. Code sec. 2679(b)
61. Lab. Code sec. 1288
62. Lab. Code sec. 1290
63. Lab. Code secs. 1292, 1293, 1293.1, 1294, 1294.1, 1294.5, 1308
64. Lab. Code sec. 1308.1; 8 CCR sec. 11706
65. Lab. Code sec. 1392
66. 8 CCR secs. 11701, 11703, 11707
67. Lab. Code sec. 1288; 8 CCR 11780
68. Lab. Code sec. 1391
69. Lab. Code sec. 1288
70. Lab. Code sec. 1288; 8 CCR secs. 11779, 11779.1
71. Lab. Code sec. 1299
72. Lab. Code sec. 1308.5

- Other violations that the DIR's director determines have a direct or immediate relationship to the health, safety, or security of minor employees other than Class A violations.[73]

The violation of work hour limitations[74] is a $500 Class B violation upon the first violation and a $1,000 Class B violation on the second violation.[75]

Class B violations carry civil penalties of not less than $500 and up to $1,000 for each and every violation.[76]

In addition, you may be liable for civil penalties for failure to:

- Pay the applicable minimum wage;[77]

- Carry workers' compensation insurance;[78] and

- Provide a written deduction statement.[79]

Criminal Penalties

Criminal violations of child labor laws are misdemeanors punishable by fines ranging up to $10,000 or by confinement in the county jail for periods of up to six months, or by both fine and imprisonment.[80]

Further Information

The Internet offers many resources on the topics in this chapter:

- A summary of child labor laws in California, called *Child Labor Laws Pamphlet 2000,* is available on the DIR Web site at ***www.dir.ca.gov/DLSE/ChildLaborPamphlet2000.html***;

- For more information on work permits, see *Work Permit Frequently Asked Questions*, a pamphlet prepared by the California Department of Education. The pamphlet can be found on the California Department of Education's Web site at ***www.cde.ca.gov/ci/ct/we/wpfaq.asp***; and

- More information about door-to-door child labor regulations is available on the DIR Web site at ***www.dir.ca.gov/DLSE/DoortoDoorRegs.html***.

---

73. Lab. Code sec. 1288; 8 CCR sec. 11782
74. Lab. Code sec. 1391
75. Lab. Code sec. 1288
76. Lab. Code sec. 1288(b); 8 CCR secs. 11781, 11781.1
77. Lab. Code sec. 1197.1
78. Lab. Code sec. 3722
79. Lab. Code sec. 226
80. Lab. Code secs. 1175, 1199, 1303, 1308, 1308.2, 1308.3, 1308.5, 1391, 1392, 1308.7, 1309, 1309.5; Educ. Code secs. 48454, 49182, 49183

Chapter 7 Forms

This chapter contains samples of forms associated with this topic. *The forms in this section are for visual reference only; download the most up-to-date forms and checklists in their entirety from CalBizCentral.*

To download either individual forms or your entire Formspack containing all the forms referenced in this book:

1. Visit **www.calbizcentral.com/support** and select "Labor Law Digest" from the list of product titles.

2. Have this copy of Labor Law Digest handy — you will need to enter the access code featured on the inside covers of this book.

3. Enter the access code, select the documents you want to download to your computer, then follow the on-screen instructions.

For more detailed instructions, see "Forms Available Online" on page xix.

Basic Provisions and Regulations — Child Labor Laws

MINORS UNDER AGE 12

	California Law	Federal Law
School Attendance	Must attend school full-time.	State law applies.
Permits to Work and to Employ	Not permitted to work, except in the entertainment industry on permits issued by the Labor Commissioner.	Certificate of age required. (State permit suffices.)
Hours of Work		May not be employed in firms subject to the Fair Labor Standards Act, except certain agricultural firms.
Maximum Hours: Daily: 8 hours; Weekly: 40 hours		
Spread of Hours: 7:00 a.m. to 7:00 p.m. (Labor Day – May 31); 7:00 a.m. to 9:00 p.m. (June 1 – Labor Day)		
See text and separate table for entertainment industry employment.		
Wages	Must be paid at least wage rates required by the Industrial Welfare Commission.	Must be paid at least the wage rates required by the FLSA.
	Exceptions: Parents are exempt from minimum wage and overtime requirements.	**Exceptions:** Casual babysitting (under 20 hours per week) and companionship services. Subminimum rates available only under a special federal certificate and must comply with state child labor standards.

Employing Minors Checklist

Name of Minor _____

v081208

☐ The proper work permits have been obtained and are on file.

☐ Employer has a valid Form B1-1 (*Statement of Intent to Employ Minor and Request for Work Permit*) for the current school year and it is on file with the school district.*

☐ The student's parent or guardian signed the Form B1-1 (*Statement of Intent to Employ Minor and Request for Work Permit*), if the minor is not emancipated.

☐ The school district has issued a work permit, Form B1-4 (*Permit to Employ and Work*) for the current school year and the employer has it on file in the workplace.*

☐ The minor's work schedule complies with the hours that the minor is permitted by law to work and the number of hours that the minor is permitted to work.

☐ The employer has notified the workers' compensation carrier of the employment of a minor.

☐ The minor is paid minimum wage and overtime if applicable. (Minors typically are not allowed to work more than eight hours in a day.)

☐ The minor employee will not drive a motor vehicle on public highways or streets.

* *The school year in California begins each July 1 and ends each June 30. If the student attends a Charter school, the work permit must still be obtained from the local school district office.*

PERMIT TO EMPLOY AND WORK

EXPIRES:
(No later than five days after beginning of the next school year.)

Type:
Regular _____ Work Experience Education _____
Vacation _____ Other (specify) _____
Year-Round _____ (specify schedule under "Remarks")

School in Session

(Any week in which public school is scheduled for at least one day.)

Maximum Work Hours

School Not In Session

(Any week in which public school is not scheduled for at least one day.)

Mon. - Thurs.*	**Friday***	**Sat.** 8	**Sun.** 8		**Monday through Sunday:** 8	

Weekly Maximum _____ **Spread of Hours:** _____ | **Weekly Maximum** _____ **Spread of Hours:** _____

* And any schoolday that immediately precedes a non-schoolday, e.g., a school holiday.

** Ages 14/15: May not work before 7:00 a.m. nor later than 7:00 p.m., except June 1 through Labor Day may work until 9:00 p.m.
May not work when public schools are in session unless enrolled in Work Experience Education or career exploration programs.
(EC 49116; LC 1391)
** Ages 16/17: May not work before 5:00 a.m. nor later than 10:00 p.m., except when a schoolday does not follow. School may be exempt from the 10:00 p.m. limit with specified written permission. (EC 49116; LC 1391/1391)

Spread of hours minor must be in school _____ (required for "Regular" and "Year-Round" permits only)

Remarks

- May not be employed in or around hazardous occupations as specified in the Fair Labor Standards Act, U.S. Department of Labor Bulletins 101 and 102, California Labor Code and California Code of Regulations, Title 8.
- Work Permit does not verify citizenship.
- Under 18 years, may not drive a vehicle on public streets as a condition of employment [VC: 12515; L.C. 1294.1(b)]
- Other remarks/limitations: _____

Valid only at _____
Name of Business _____

Minor's Name (last name first)	Social Security Number	Date of Birth	Age at Issuance
Street Address	City	ZIP Code	Home Telephone
School Name	City	ZIP Code	School Telephone

Signature of Minor _____ Signature of Issuing Authority _____ Date _____

California Department of Education Form No. B1-4 (revised 06/01) **IMPORTANT: See reverse side for additional information**

General Summary of Minors' Work Regulations

- **If federal laws, state laws and school district policies conflict, the more restrictive law (that which is most protective of the employee) prevails.**
- Generally, minors must attend school until age 18 unless they are 16 years or older and have graduated from high school or received a state Certificate of Proficiency.
- Employers of minors required to attend school must complete a "Statement of Intent to Employ Minor and Request for Work Permit" (form B1-1) for the school district of attendance for each such minor.
- Employers must retain a "Permit to Employ and Work" (form B1-4) for each such minor.
- A work permit (B1-4) must be retained for three years and open at all times for inspection by sanctioned authorities.
- A work permit (B1-4) must be revoked whenever the issuing authority determines the employment is illegal or is impairing the health or education of the minor.

Minors under the age of 18 may not work in occupations declared hazardous for young workers as listed below:

1. Explosives	10. Power-driven meat slicing/processing
2. Motor vehicle driving/outside helper	11. Power baking machines
3. Coal mining	12. Power-driven paper products/paper bailing
4. Logging and sawmilling	13. Manufacturing brick, tile products
5. Power-driven woodworking machines	14. Power-driven shears
6. Radiation exposure	15. Power-driven demolition
7. Power-driven metal forming, punching, and shearing machines	16. Roofing
8. [illegible]	Excavation.
9. Other mining	

For more complete information about hazardous occupations, contact the U.S. Department of Labor (Child Labor Bulletins 101 and 102) and the California Department of Industrial Relations, Division of Labor Standards Enforcement. Regional offices are located in several California cities. They are listed in the "Government Listings" sections under "phone directories.

- Minors younger than 16 years are allowed to work only in limited specific occupations which exclude baking, manufacturing, processing, construction, warehouse, and transportation occupations.
- In addition to safety regulations, labor laws applicable to minor employees are also generally applicable to minor employees, including workers' compensation insurance requirements.
- Child labor laws do not generally apply to minors who deliver newspapers or work at odd jobs, such as yard work and baby-sitting, or in private homes where the minor is not regularly employed.
- A day of rest from work is required if the total hours worked exceed 30 or if more than 6 hours are worked on any one day during the week.

Hours of Work

16–17 When school is in session, any maximum 4 hours, Monday through Thursday. May work up to 8 hours on any nonschool day or on any day that precedes a non-schoolday. May be permitted to work up to 48 hours per week. Students in Work Experience Education or cooperative vocational education programs may be permitted to work a maximum of 8 hours on a schoolday. When school not in session: May [illegible] to 48 hours per week but no more than 8 hours in any one day.

14–15 When school is in session: On schooldays daily maximum 3 hours. On non-schooldays may work 8 hours. Weekly maximum 18 hours. Students in Work Experience Education and career exploration programs may work up to 23 hours per week. Work must be performed no earlier than 5:00 a.m. nor later than 10:00 p.m., except that work may extend to 12:30 a.m. on nights preceding non-school days. Students in Work Experience Education or cooperative vocational education programs may be authorized to work until 12:30 a.m. on nights preceding school days with specified written permission.

When school is not in session: Daily maximum 8 hours and weekly maximum 40 hours.

Younger than 14: May not work during public school hours except students in Work Experience Education and career exploration programs. Work must be performed no earlier than 7:00 a.m. nor later than 7:00 p.m. any day of the week. From June 1 to Labor Day work hours may be extended to 9:00 p.m.

Labor laws generally prohibit nonfarm employment of children younger than 14. Special rules apply to agricultural work, domestic work and the entertainment industry.

Statement of Intent to Employ Minor and Request for Work Permit

NOT A WORK PERMIT – PRINT ALL INFORMATION EXCEPT SIGNATURES

For Minor to Complete – Sec. 1

Minor's Name (Print last name first)

Social Security Number | Date of Birth | Age | Grade

Street Address | City | ZIP Code

School Name | Address | City | ZIP Code

Home Phone | School Phone

For Employer to Complete – Sec. 2

(Please review rules for employment of minors on reverse)

Business Name | Street Address | City | ZIP Code

Business Phone | Minor's Work Duties | Hourly Wage

Maximum number of hours of employment when school is in session:

Mon. ___ Tue. ___ Wed. ___ Thurs. ___ Fri. ___ Sat. ___ Sun. ___ Weekly = ___

In compliance with California labor laws, this employee is covered by Workers' Compensation Insurance. This business does not discriminate unlawfully on the basis of race, ethnic background, religion, sex, color, national origin, ancestry, age, physical handicap, or medical condition. I hereby certify that, to the best of my knowledge, the information herein is correct and true.

Supervisor's Signature | Supervisor's Name (print or type)

For Parent to Complete – Sec. 3

This minor is being employed at the place of work described with my full knowledge and consent. I hereby certify that, to the best of my knowledge, the information herein is correct and true. I request that a work permit be issued.

In addition to this employer, my child is working for:

Signature of Parent or Legal Guardian

Name | Date

For School to Complete

TYPE: Regular ☐ Year-Round ☐

Evidence of Minor's Age: Vacation ☐ Other (Specify) ☐

Work Experience Education ☐

Signature of Verifying Authority

California Department of Education Form No. B1-1 (Revised 06/05)

Application – Front Page | See back for further information

General Summary of Minors' Work Regulations

- **If federal laws, state laws and school district policies conflict, the more restrictive law (that which is most protective of the employee) prevails.**
- Generally, minors must attend school until age 18 unless they are 16 years or older and have graduated from high school or received a state Certificate of Proficiency.
- Employers of minors required to attend school must complete a "Statement of Intent to Employ Minor and Request for Work Permit" (form B1-1) for the school district of attendance for each such minor.
- Employers must retain a "Permit to Employ and Work" (form B1-4) for each such minor.
- Work permits (B1-4) must be retained for three years and open at all times for inspection by sanctioned authorities.
- A work permit (B1-4) must be revoked whenever the issuing authority determines the employment is illegal or is impairing the health or education of the minor.

Minors under the age of 18 may not work in occupations declared hazardous for young workers as listed below:

1. Explosives
2. Motor vehicle driving/outside helper
3. Coal mining
4. Logging and sawmilling
5. Power-driven woodworking machines
6. Radiation exposure
7. Power-driven hoists/forklifts
8. Power-driven metal forming, punching, and shearing machines
9. Other mining
10. Power-driven meat slicing/processing
11. Power baking machines
12. Power-driven paper products/paper bailing
13. Manufacturing brick, tile products
14. Power saws and shears
15. Wrecking, demolition
16. Roofing
17. Excavation operation.

For more complete information about hazardous occupations, contact the U.S. Department of Labor (Child Labor Bulletins 101 and 102) and the California Department of Industrial Relations, Division of Labor Standards Enforcement. Regional offices are located in several California cities. They are listed in the "Government Listings" sections of telephone directories.

Hours of Work

- Minors younger than 16 years are allowed to work only in limited, specified occupations which exclude baking, manufacturing, processing, construction, warehouse, and transportation occupations.
- In addition to safety regulations, labor laws applicable to adult employees are also generally applicable to minor employees, including workers' compensation insurance requirements.
- Child labor laws do not generally apply to minors who deliver newspapers or work at odd jobs, such as yard work and baby-sitting, or in private homes where the minor is not regularly employed.
- A day of rest from work is required if the total hours worked per week exceed 30 or if more than 6 hours are worked on any one day during the week.

16–17 When school is in session: Daily maximum 4 hours, Monday through Thursday. May work up to 8 hours on any nonschool day or on any day that precedes a nonschool day. May be permitted to work up to 48 hours per week.
Students in Work Experience Education or cooperative vocational education programs may be permitted to work a maximum of 8 hours on a schoolday.
When school not in session: May work up to 48 hours per week but no more than 8 hours in any one day.
Work must be performed no earlier than 5:00 a.m. nor later than 10:00 p.m. except that work may extend to 12:30 a.m. on nights preceding non-school days. Students in Work Experience Education or cooperative vocational education programs may be authorized to work until 12:30 a.m. on nights preceding school days with specified written permission.

14–15 When school is in session: On schooldays daily maximum 3 hours. On non-schooldays may work 8 hours. Weekly maximum 18 hours. Students in Work Experience Education and career exploration programs may work up to 23 hours per week.
When school is not in session: Daily maximum 8 hours and weekly maximum 40 hours.

May not work during public school hours except students in Work Experience Education or career exploration programs. Work must be performed no earlier than 7:00 a.m. nor later than 7:00 p.m. any day of the week. From June 1 to Labor Day work hours may be extended to 9:00 p.m.

Younger than 14: Labor laws generally prohibit nonfarm employment of children younger than 14. Special rules apply to agricultural work, domestic work and the entertainment industry.

For more information on Minors' Work Regulations please visit www.ca.gov.

Application – Back Page

Statement of Intent to Employ Minor and Request for Work Permit (Page 1 of 2)

Statement of Intent to Employ Minor and Request for Work Permit (Page 2 of 2)

Personnel Records and Privacy

Workplace privacy is an important and growing concern for business. Unfortunately, it is often difficult to sort through and understand privacy issues, considering the multitude of federal and state constitutional guarantees, limitations imposed by federal and state statutes, and case law. In addition, new technology expands both employer and employee concerns about privacy rights.

This chapter sorts the law for you and gives you the information you need to understand the issues at hand and make sound, informed decisions respecting the rights of your employees while understanding your own rights. This knowledge will allow you to operate your business more effectively. This chapter thoroughly discusses all aspects of workplace privacy:

- Constitutional law — the basis for the right to privacy;

- Keeping employee information private — your obligations to your employees to protect their privacy;

- Employee access to personnel records — employee rights to view, copy or receive information about themselves from your files;

- Types of employment testing, such as drug and polygraph tests, and whether you can require applicants or employees to take such tests;

- Credit reports and background investigations — the legal restrictions and procedures you must follow when gathering information on applicants and employees;

- Employee monitoring (video, phone or e-mail) — the extent of your right to know what goes on in your workplace;

- Medical records including Health Insurance Portability and Accountability Act (HIPAA) requirements and other federal and state safeguards for employee health information; and

- Records retention — the type of records you must keep and how long you must keep them.

 Download forms referenced in this chapter at **www.calbizcentral.com/support**. Be sure to have your access code from the inside covers of this book ready to enter into the forms download area. Your access code for the forms in the online Formspack is on the inside covers of this book. See "Forms Available Online" on page xix for more information.

Constitutional and Common Law Privacy Protections

The right to privacy is not specifically enumerated in the U.S. Constitution. However, the U.S. Supreme Court has ruled that a right to privacy was explicit in the Bill of Rights, which prohibits various types of unreasonable government intrusion upon personal freedom.[1]

Since these cases specifically relate to government intrusion upon personal freedom, private employers are not covered by federal constitutional restrictions. However, California is one of

---

1. *Griswald v. Connecticut*, 381 U.S. 479 (1965)

seven states that provide a constitutional right to privacy. Article 1, Section 1, of the California Constitution provides that:

> All people are by nature free and independent and have inalienable rights. Among these are enjoying and defending life and liberty, acquiring, possessing, and protecting property, and pursuing and obtaining safety, happiness and privacy.

The California Supreme Court stated that this privacy provision is directed at the overly broad assemblage and retention of unnecessary personnel information by government and business, the improper use of information obtained for a specific purpose and the lack of a reasonable check on the accuracy of existing records.[2]

Common Law Privacy Claims

In addition to statutory claims, employees may bring common-law claims for invasion of privacy against you. You could be subject to claims of having placed the employee in a "false light" or giving unreasonable publicity to that employee's personal life if you disseminate information obtained through voice-mail or e-mail access.

Common-law causes of action involving intrusion into the personal privacy rights of individuals include:

- Appropriation of the name and likeness of another;
- Unreasonable publicity given to another's private life;
- Unreasonable intrusion upon the seclusion of another; and
- Publicity that unreasonably places a person in a false light before the public.

Each of these privacy violations can arise in the workplace. Using photographs or names of employees in your advertising or marketing, particularly former employees without their permission, can result in a claim for appropriation. Engaging in surveillance of an employee during a background check of an employee applying for a sensitive position can lead to claims for unreasonable intrusion into the employee's seclusion. You can place an employee in a false light by publicizing sensitive facts about them; for example, telling a group of employees that another employee was fired for dishonesty when, in fact, the employee resigned with no proof of dishonesty. Unreasonable publication of private facts about an employee occurs if others are told that the employee was suffering from AIDS or recently had been divorced.

Keeping Employee Information Private

A variety of information is gathered about applicants for employment. Once employed, additional information accumulates regarding the employee's performance, health, family and other personal issues. Growing concern over the possession of this data contributed to states and the federal government developing laws governing the privacy of employer records.

---

2. *White v. Davis*, 13 Cal. 3d 757 (1975)

Personnel Records

The right to privacy guaranteed by the California Constitution protects employee personnel files from improper disclosure to third parties.[3] An employee may waive the privacy of his/her own personnel records by authorizing the release of personnel information to his/her union.[4] When a former employee sues you for wrongful discharge, failure to promote or a disciplinary action or other employment decision, the employee generally is held to have placed his/her employment history at issue, thereby waiving the right to privacy for his/her own personnel records for purposes of the lawsuit.

You have a number of potential liabilities for improperly releasing personnel information. For example, you may not make misrepresentations that prevent or attempt to prevent a former employee from obtaining employment.[5] You may make a truthful statement concerning the reason for a former employee's discharge or voluntary termination, but exercise caution. If your statement is not in response to a request, or is accompanied by marks or symbols which convey information contrary to the statement, that action is considered misrepresentation.[6] Even when your response to a prospective employee's appropriate request is truthful and accurate, liability still may arise if that response is adverse and in reprisal for the employee's exercise of the right to file a claim under employment laws.[7]

You may also be liable for inaccurate or misleading information about an employee on the basis of defamation or interference with prospective economic advantage. Defamation is an unlawful invasion of an individual's interest in maintaining a favorable reputation. It encompasses communications that have a tendency to injure a person in his/her occupation. Unlawful interference with prospective economic advantage may occur when a prospective employer decides not to hire an employee based on false statements or inappropriate facts disclosed by a former employer.[8]

See "Responding to Reference Checks" on page 172 before releasing personnel information.

Medical Information

California law mandates that you establish appropriate procedures to keep all employee medical records and information confidential and protect them from unauthorized use and disclosure. Failing to establish such procedures is a misdemeanor and allows an employee to collect monetary damages, attorney's fees and the costs of litigation.[9]

You may not use or disclose medical information pertaining to your employees without a written authorization from the affected employee.[10] This includes knowingly permitting an employee to use or disclose another employee's medical information. However, such information may be disclosed in limited circumstances:

- When compelled by a court of law or by a lawsuit filed by an employee;
- When used for administering and maintaining employee benefit plans; or

3. *Board of Trustees, Stanford University v. Superior Courts*, 119 Cal. App. 3d 516 (1981)
4. *New Jersey Bell Telephone Company v. NLRB*, 720 F.2d 789 (3rd Cir. 1983)
5. Lab. Code secs. 1050, 1052
6. Lab. Code sec. 1053
7. *Dunlap v. Carriage Carpet Co.*, 548 F.2d 139 (6th Cir. 1977)
8. *Buckaloo v. Johnson*, 14 Cal. 3d 815 (1975)
9. Civ. Code sec. 56.35
10. Civ. Code sec. 56.20(c)(1)

- In relation to a workers' compensation claim or request for medical leave.[11]

You are not liable for any unauthorized use of the medical information by the person or entity to which you disclosed the information if you have attempted, in good faith, to comply with these medical privacy laws.[12]

You may not discriminate against an employee who refuses to sign an authorization releasing medical records.[13] The law does not prohibit you from taking whatever action is necessary in the absence of medical information due to the employee's refusal to sign a medical release authorization.[14]

For example, if you are unable to ascertain an employee's physical ability to perform a job function due to the employee's refusal to sign an authorization, including a test to evaluate alcohol or drug usage based on reasonable suspicion, you have the right to discipline an employee based on the information available.

Authorization for an employer to disclose medical information is valid if:

- Handwritten by the employee/patient who signs it, or is in typeface no smaller than eight-point type;

- Clearly separate from any other language on the same page;

- Signed only to authorize release of medical information and for no other purpose; and

- Signed and dated by the employee/patient, or a legal representative if the employee/patient is a minor or the representative of a deceased employee/patient.[15]

An employee who signs an authorization to release medical information is entitled to a copy of the release at his/her request.[16] The release may be canceled or modified at any time, effective upon written notice to the employer.[17]

Establish a second file for each employee for information related to employee medical issues. Keep it separate from the regular personnel files and only grant access to those with a legitimate need to know the information. A supervisor who is considering a particular employee for a promotion to a clerical position in another department probably has no need to know information about that employee's pre-employment physical. But if the position to which the employee will be promoted requires heavy lifting, records from the pre-employment physical may be necessary to assess the individual's restrictions or necessary accommodations.

Files related to employee financial matters, such as wage assignments, garnishments, credit inquiries, etc., should be kept separately. They are usually included with payroll records available only to those who administer payroll matters.

Records protected under these laws encompass more than a physician's report or the lab results from a drug test. Medical records may include:

- Family and medical leave request forms if an employee voluntarily discloses the nature of his/her illness on such a form;

---

11. Civ. Code sec. 56.20(c)(2)
12. Civ. Code sec. 56.23
13. Civ. Code sec. 56.20(b)
14. Civ. Code sec. 56.20(b)
15. Civ. Code sec. 56.21
16. Civ. Code sec. 56.22
17. Civ. Code sec. 56.24

- Return to work releases;

- Workers' compensation records;

- Information about disabilities being accommodated under the federal Americans with Disabilities Act (ADA) or California's Fair Employment and Housing Act (FEHA); and

- Other records that relate in any way to an employee's medical history.

The ADA and FEHA also require that you maintain medical history information of an applicant or employee, which must be maintained on separate forms, treated as confidential and kept in separate files from the employee's general personnel information.[18] You may disclose such information only if:

- Supervisors or managers need information regarding necessary restrictions or accommodations for work duties;

- First aid personnel might require the information to administer emergency treatment; or

- Government officials, investigating ADA or FEHA compliance, request the information.[19]

Credit Information

California law restricts the dissemination of credit information to an employee's creditors who contact you.[20] Although you may verify employment dates and job duties, you should only respond to third parties concerning employment information if a written release explicitly identifies the information to be disclosed and authorizes you to disclose it. To prevent inappropriate disclosures, you should require that requests for such information be made in writing, and decline to answer questions relating to an employee's prospects for future or continued employment, citing company policy as the reason.

Consumer credit reporting agencies that furnish reports for employment purposes may not report information on the age, marital status, race or creed of any consumer.[21] If you request the report, you must provide written notice to the consumer before requesting that report, and send the consumer a free copy of the report if the consumer so requests.[22]

In addition, you may not discriminate against an employee or job applicant in employment solely because the individual has filed for bankruptcy.[23]

Your failure to comply with the Fair Credit Reporting Act (FCRA) can result in state or federal enforcement actions, as well as private lawsuits.[24] In addition, any person who knowingly and willfully obtains a consumer report under false pretenses may face criminal prosecution.[25]

The Fair Credit Reporting Act (FCRA) prohibits employers from taking adverse action based on information from a consumer credit report, unless the employer first gives notice to the consumer of what is in the report and its relationship to the adverse action. A knowing violation of this requirement could result in an award to the consumer, limited to actual

---

18. 42 U.S.C. 12112(c)(3)(B)
19. 29 U.S.C. 12112(c)3(B)
20. Civ. Code sec. 1785.20.5
21. Civ. Code sec. 1785.18(c)
22. Civ. Code secs. 1785.18, 1785.20.5
23. 11 U.S.C. 525
24. FCRA secs. 616, 617, 621
25. FCRA sec. 619

damages and no greater than $1,000. A willful violation, which must be committed knowingly and recklessly, triggers actual damages or $1,000 — whichever is greater — plus punitive damages and possible attorney's fees. Although a reasonable mistake will not be deemed a willful violation, employers who use the FCRA as a basis for adverse employment actions should ensure that the required notice is provided, unless legal counsel consults otherwise.[26]

Insurance companies using credit scores from consumer credit reports to determine an applicant's policy rate without sending notice to the applicant violate the FCRA if the applicant's rate is greater because of the credit score. One company only sent an adverse action notice if the applicant's costs would be greater with a worse credit score. However, the company did not send an adverse action if an applicant's costs could be less with a better score. Applicants sued through a class action, claiming willful violations of the FCRA because decisions on the cost of their coverage were influenced by the credit reports and the applicants were not notified, as is required under the FCRA.

The court found that if the credit report was reviewed and an insured's rate was affected to the disadvantage of the insured without the required notice under the FCRA, then the FCRA was violated. If a neutral standard affected the insured's rate without regard to the credit report, no such violation occurs. The court also determined that the FCRA does not differentiate between the applicant and current customer (or, translated for employment purposes, applicant or current employee) because the FCRA was created to protect the consumer.

Regarding negligent oversight vs. willful violations of the FCRA, the court stated that a company that has a reasonable belief that it was not obligated to send the notice does not willfully violate the FCRA. Specifically, "a company does not act in reckless disregard of the FCRA unless the action is not only a violation under a reasonable reading of the statute, but shows that the company ran a risk of violating the law substantially greater than the risk associated with a reading that was merely careless." In this case, the company's reading of the statute was merely careless and didn't rise to the level of "unjustifiably high risk."

 As a general rule, financial records are considered private records. Keep them confidential.

Personal Relationships

California law prohibits you from discriminating on the basis of marital status.[27] You do have the right when employing a married couple to refuse to place both spouses in the same department, division or facility if the work involves potential conflicts of interest or other hazards that are greater for married couples than for other persons.[28]

You should avoid intruding into, and basing employment decisions on, employees' non-marital personal relationships. As a general rule, avoid inquiry into an employee's off-duty activities in these areas, particularly in the absence of any showing of effect upon the employee's work performance.

You may not discriminate against employees on the basis of their sexual orientation.[29] Even before the enactment of this law, courts in California ruled that discharging an employee based on sexual orientation alone constitutes a violation of the employee's right to privacy.[30] See also "Lawful Conduct Discrimination" in Chapter 27, page 765.

---

26. *Safeco Ins. Co. v. Burr* (U.S. 2007) 127 S. Ct. 2201
27. Gov't. Code sec. 12940(a)
28. Gov't. Code sec. 12940(a)(3)
29. Gov't. Code sec. 12940

The Ninth U.S. Circuit Court of Appeals also ruled that under certain circumstances, harassing an employee because of sexual orientation violates Title VII of the federal Civil Rights Act.[31]

Accordingly, use caution in imposing discipline for an employee's off-duty conduct, at least where the discipline is based on the employee's romantic or social activities.[32]

Political Affiliation

You may not adopt or enforce any policy that tends to control or direct political activities or affiliations of employees, nor coerce or influence employees to follow or refrain from following any particular line of political activity by threatening a loss of employment.[33]

Illiteracy

If you have 25 or more employees, you must reasonably accommodate and assist any employee who reveals a problem of illiteracy and requests your assistance in enrolling in an adult literacy education program, unless this would cause you undue hardship.[34] Legally, your assistance includes, among other things, providing the employee with the locations of local literacy education programs or arranging for a literacy education provider to visit the jobsite. You must make reasonable efforts to safeguard the employee's privacy as to the fact that he/she has a problem with illiteracy. You don't need to provide time off with pay to allow the employee to enroll in and attend an adult literacy program, but you may not terminate an employee who discloses his/her illiteracy and who is satisfactorily performing his/her work.

Criminal Records

You may not ask job applicants to disclose information concerning an arrest or detention not resulting in conviction, or information relating to a referral to or participation in a criminal diversion program (a work or education program as part of probation). You may not seek the same information from any other source, nor use it as a factor in decisions related to hiring, promotion, training or termination. You may ask employees and applicants about any arrest for which the employee or applicant is out on bail or out on his/her own recognizance pending trial.[35] Certain exceptions exist for peace officers, health-care workers and persons with access to drugs and medication.[36] In addition, you may not inquire about convictions for most marijuana possession offenses more than two years old.[37]

Under federal and state law, you may inquire about criminal convictions of applicants and can deny employment upon establishing a legitimate business purpose. However, you should avoid a rule that automatically bars employment to any applicant who has a record of criminal conviction. Such a policy may violate California law if the conviction is not job-related and the policy has a disparate impact upon a protected class.

30. *Gay Law Students v. Pacific Telephone & Telegraph*, 24 Cal. 3d 458 (1979)

31. *Medina Rene v. MGM Grand Hotel, Inc.,* (Ninth Cir., September 24, 2002) No. 98-16924

32. *Rulon Miller v. IBM Corp.*, 162 Cal. App. 3d 241 (1984)

33. Lab. Code secs. 1101, 1102

34. Lab. Code secs. 1040-1044

35. Lab. Code sec. 432.7

36. Lab. Code sec. 432.7(b) et seq.

37. Lab. Code sec. 432.8

Fingerprints and Photographs

You may maintain photographs and fingerprints of employees and applicants, but only for your use. You generally may not require applicants or employees to provide fingerprints or photographs as a condition of employment if they will be:

- Provided to a third party; or

- Used to the applicant's or employee's detriment.[38]

However, some employers, such as certain financial institutions and the child-care industry, *must* obtain fingerprints before hiring. Consult legal counsel before fingerprinting any applicant or employee.

Requiring submission of photographs with employment applications may be deemed an inappropriate screening of applicants who belong to a protected class.

Electronic Information

As workplace technology use grows, so do legitimate employer fears of unauthorized access to confidential information and worries about new liability arising from employee technology use.

Your responsibility for keeping certain personnel information private is not excused simply because you keep the information electronically. You must closely guard access to computer files containing sensitive information, and you may be held liable for negligently failing to protect your system from unauthorized access. Carefully look at a computer's password system to see if the system is vulnerable to break-ins. In some situations, encryption technology may be necessary. Encryption scrambles data to make the information unreadable to anybody who does not have the "key" to unscramble (or decrypt) the data. But encryption technology also can allow the message sender to disguise the message's origin. As a result, it may be impossible to discover which employee is, for example, sending sexually suggestive messages in violation of your company's sexual harassment policy. Similarly, encryption technology may prevent you from accessing and monitoring e-mail messages between employees.

On July 1, 2003, a law was passed affecting all companies and state agencies that own or license computerized data that includes personal information. Personal information is defined as a person's first name (or first initial) and last name combined with any of the following:

- Social Security number (SSN);

- Driver's license or California Identification Card number; or

- Account number, credit- or debit-card number combined with any required security code, access code or password.

If a security breach involves any such unencrypted data, the company must notify all affected California residents of that breach. Employers must give notice by one of several approved methods and within specified time limits.

For purposes of this section, "notice" may be provided by one of the following methods:

- Written notice;

---

38. Lab. Code sec. 1051

- Electronic notice, if the notice provided is consistent with the provisions regarding electronic records and signatures set forth in Section 7001 of Title 15 of the United States Code;

- Substitute notice, if the agency demonstrates that the cost of providing notice would exceed two hundred fifty thousand dollars ($250,000), or that the affected class of subject persons to be notified exceeds 500,000, or the agency does not have sufficient contact information:

  - E-mail notice when the agency has an e-mail address for the subject persons;

  - Conspicuous posting of the notice on the agency's Web site page, if the agency maintains one; and

  - Notification to major statewide media.

Notwithstanding subdivision the above, an agency that maintains its own notification procedures as part of an information security policy for the treatment of personal information and is otherwise consistent with the timing requirements of this part shall be deemed to be in compliance with the notification requirements of this section if it notifies subject persons in accordance with its policies in the event of a breach of security of the system.

The law also requires any person or business that becomes aware of a security breach to notify the data's owner or licensee immediately. Allowances are made for delay in giving notice at the direction of a law enforcement agency.[39]

Social Security Numbers

California law on the use and publication of SSNs prohibits:[40]

- Posting or publicly displaying in any manner an individual's SSN. "Publicly posting" or "publicly displaying" means to intentionally communicate or otherwise make available to the general public;

- Printing an individual's SSN on any card required for the individual to access products or services. This may include your employee identification cards and badges;

- Requiring an individual to transmit his/her SSN over the Internet, unless the connection is secure or the SSN is encrypted;

- Requiring an individual to use his/her SSN to access a Web site, unless a password or unique PIN or other authentication device is also required to access the Web site. This may require a change in systems used to access or transmit personnel, business, human resources or payroll information over the Internet;

- Printing an individual's SSN on any materials mailed to the individual, unless state or federal law requires the SSN to be on the document. Applications and forms sent by mail may include SSNs;

- Printing a SSN on a postcard or other mailer not requiring an envelope or visible on the envelope or without the envelope being opened if the SSN may be mailed in an otherwise permissible manner; and

---

39. California Civ. Code secs. 1798.29 and 1798.82
40. California Civ. Code sec. 1798.85

- Encoding or embedding an SSN in or on a card or document, including, but not limited to, using a bar code, chip, magnetic strip or other technology, in place of removing the SSN, as required by law.

If you have used an individual's SSN in any of these ways prior to July 1, 2002, you may continue using that individual's SSN in that manner on or after July 1, 2002, if you meet the following conditions:

- You use the SSN continuously. If you stop using the SSN for any reason, you cannot resume its use; and

- You provide the individual with an annual disclosure, beginning immediately, that he or she has the right to make a written request to stop the use of his or her SSN in a prohibited manner. You must:

    - Implement the request within 30 days of receipt;

    - Not charge a fee for implementing the request; and

    - Not deny services to an individual because the individual makes such a request.

The new law does not prevent the collection, use or release of an SSN as required by state or federal law or the use of an SSN for internal verification or administrative purposes.

If you maintain computer personnel files (or customer files) that include names and SSNs, driver's license numbers or account numbers and security codes that permit access to financial information, you must maintain the security of those data files. If a breach of security results in unauthorized acquisition of unencrypted data, you must give timely notification of the breach to any affected California resident.[41]

You must give this notice as quickly as possible, delayed only by the reasonable time necessary to discover the scope of the breach and to allow steps to restore the integrity of the data, consistent with the needs of law enforcement to investigate the breach.

You must give notice in written form or by electronic means that comply with the law. In cases requiring notice to more than 50,000 people or where the expense of actual notice exceeds $250,000, you may use other authorized means of giving notice, including the use of e-mail, Web site postings and statewide media. You may maintain your own notification procedures as part of an overall information security policy provided it meets the timeliness requirements of the law. You must, of course, comply with your policies.

To ensure a uniform, statewide approach to this issue, this state law supersedes all local laws, rules and regulations.

All employers must print no more than the last four digits of an employee's Social Security number on check stubs or similar documents, or substitute some other identifying number.

Allowing Access to Employee Information

Employees and various government agencies have the right to access certain records in certain circumstances.

41.Civ. Code sec. 1798.82

Personnel Files

Every employee has the right to inspect the personnel records that you maintain relating to his/her performance or to any grievance concerning the employee.[42] You must make personnel records available to the employee upon request at reasonable intervals and at reasonable times. The law does not explain whether "reasonable intervals" means once per week, once per month or some other interval. Nor does it define whether "reasonable times" means during business hours only, any time the personnel office is open, only immediately before or after an employee's shift or some other time.

The law does permit the state Labor Commissioner to adopt regulations that determine the reasonable times and reasonable intervals for private employers. In the past, the Labor Commissioner took the position that reasonableness can only be determined on a case-by-case basis without arbitrary deadlines.[43]

Generally, you do not need to allow an employee to review his or her personnel records during his/her scheduled working time. However, there is an exception if the employee must view the personnel records at a corporate facility located someplace other than where he/she reports to work. In that instance you must allow the employee to view the personnel records during his/her scheduled working time without loss of pay.

---

42. Lab. Code sec. 1198.5
43. DLSE Opinion Letter 1998.08.27

Options for Access to Personnel Records

You have three options with regard to storing personnel records and allowing employees access to those records:

- Keep a copy of each employee's personnel records at the place where the employee reports to work;

- Make the employee's personnel records available at the place where the employee reports to work within a reasonable period of time following an employee's request; or

- Permit the employee to inspect the personnel records at the location where you store the personnel records, during the employee's working hours and with no loss of pay.

You have a right and responsibility to monitor the employee's inspection of a personnel file to ensure that nothing is removed, destroyed or altered, and to return the file to the proper place when the inspection is completed. For sample guidelines, see *Personnel File or Payroll Records Request*.

Exceptions

An employee's right to view his/her personnel file does not apply to:

- Records relating to the investigation of a possible criminal offense;

- Letters of reference;

- Ratings, reports or records that were:

  - Obtained prior to the employee's employment;

  - Prepared by identifiable examination committee members; or

  - Obtained in connection with a promotional examination.

- Employees who are subject to the Public Safety Officers Procedural Bill of Rights; and

- Employees of agencies subject to the Information Practices Act of 1977.

 Additional rules for the inspection of personnel records may be established as the result of agreements between you and a recognized employee organization.

Right to Copy Personnel Records

An employee does not have an absolute right to a copy of his/her entire personnel records. However, he/she does have a right to a copy of any document he/she has signed relating to obtaining or holding employment (subject to a reasonable fee for each copy).[44] This means any document related to getting the job or keeping the job, such as signed:

- Employment applications;

- Employment contracts;

- Warning notices; and

- Records of employee discipline.

---

44. Lab. Code sec. 432

Except for those documents listed under "Exceptions" on page 156, which you may temporarily remove from the file, employees have the right to take notes about the entire contents of the file.

Payroll Files

Either semi-monthly, or at time of payment, you must give a statement of deductions to the employee and the inclusive dates for which the employee is paid. You must maintain records regarding employees in English and in indelible ink or an equivalent form, properly dated.[45] For more information, see "Timekeeping and Recording Guidelines" in Chapter 13, page 326.

You must maintain comprehensive payroll records and make them available to the employee upon reasonable request.[46] California law requires you to comply with a written or oral request from a current or former employee to inspect or copy payroll records within 21 days. You may designate the person to whom the request for payroll records must be addressed. Impossibility of performance not caused by or not resulting from violation of the law (such as failure to maintain the records as required by law) is an affirmative defense for an employer charged with violating this requirement.[47]

Failure to comply entitles the current or former employee, or the Labor Commissioner, to recover a penalty of $750.00. An employee may also bring an action in court to require compliance with the request and, in any such action, is entitled to recover costs and reasonable attorneys' fees.[48]

Government Agencies

You must give the Industrial Welfare Commission (IWC) and duly authorized representatives of the Division of Labor Standards Enforcement (DLSE) access to records and workplaces to enforce provisions of IWC orders. The DLSE's agents must conduct any inspections or investigations in a reasonable manner and DLSE agents must comply with the same rules as others with regard to what the law permits you to reveal from an employee's personnel file.

Civil Action Subpoena of Records

In most civil actions, a subpoena for employment records must contain an affidavit stating that the employee received notice of the subpoena.[49] Anyone who subpoenas employment records must comply with these rules:

- The date the subpoena specifies for producing the employment records cannot be fewer than 15 days from the date the subpoena is issued;

- The party issuing the subpoena must provide notice of the subpoena to the employee whose records are being subpoenaed. The employee must receive a copy of the subpoena and a copy of the affidavit that supports the issuance of the subpoena;

---

45. All IWC Orders
46. Lab. Code sec. 1174
47. Lab. Code sec. 226(c)
48. Lab. Code sec. 226(f)-226(g)
49. Code of Civil Procedure sec. 1985.6

- Service to the employee can be made by mail to the employee's last known address, or to the employee's attorney of record;

- The witness (employer) must receive the subpoena and a copy of the affidavit that supports the issuance of the subpoena. Alternatively, the employer may accept a release for the records, signed by the employee; and

- Every copy of the subpoena and affidavit served on the employee or his/her attorney must be accompanied by a notice, in a typeface that calls attention to the notice, indicating that:

  - Employment records about the employee are being sought from the witness (employer) named on the subpoena;

  - The employment records may be protected by a right of privacy;

  - If the employee objects to the witness furnishing the records to the party seeking the records, the employee must file papers with the court before the date specified on the subpoena for producing the records; and

  - If the subpoenaing party does not agree in writing to cancel or limit the subpoena, an attorney should be consulted about the employee's interest in protecting his/her rights of privacy.

If you receive subpoenas for employment records that do not comply with the rules stated above, you should not respond to the subpoena until you have obtained advice from legal counsel as to the validity of the subpoena.

This law does not apply to certain state and local agencies, nor to certain Department of Industrial Relations (DIR) and workers' compensation proceedings.

District Attorney

You must cooperate with a written request from the district attorney for relevant employment and income information in connection with enforcement of child-support obligations.[50] The district attorney must provide you with its case file number when making the request, and at least three of the following items about the person who is the subject of the inquiry:

- First and last name and middle initial, if known;

- SSN;

- Driver's license number;

- Birth date;

- Last known address; and

- Spouse's name.

You incur no liability for providing this information. Failure to provide the information within 30 days of receiving the request subjects you to a penalty of up to $1,000, plus attorneys' fees and costs.[51]

You must provide relevant employment and income information including, but not limited to, the following:

---

50. Family Code sec. 5283
51. Family Code sec. 5283

- Whether you have or have not employed a named person;

- The full name of the employee, or the first and middle initial and last name of the employee;

- The employee's last known residence address;

- The employee's date of birth;

- The employee's SSN;

- The dates of employment;

- All earnings paid to the employee and reported as W-2 compensation in the prior tax year and the employee's current basic rate of pay; and

- Whether dependent health insurance coverage is available to the employee through employment.

Testing Applicants and Employees

As with other employee records, the results of the tests you administer to applicants and employees should remain confidential and available to those authorized to know the results.

Physical Examinations

You may require an employee to undergo a physical examination, at your expense, before beginning employment but after a job offer has been made. California law requires the examination to be job-related and consistent with business necessity, and requires that all entering employees in the same job classification are subject to the same examination.[52]

You may not require an employee or applicant to pay for the cost of any physical examination required as a condition of employment or required by any law or regulation of federal, state or local government. You may not make deductions from an employee's compensation to pay for such exams.[53] If you require an employee to have a driver's license as a condition of employment, you must pay the cost of any physical exam that may be required for the issuance of the driver's license unless the physical exam was prior to the time the employee applied for the job.[54]

The ADA and FEHA address several issues surrounding the right to require physical examinations, and impose strict limitations on the use of information obtained from such examinations and inquiries. For further information about the ADA and FEHA, see Chapter 29, "Disabilities In the Workplace".

Drug/Alcohol Tests

California courts have drawn a distinction between the rights of job applicants and the rights of employees in the area of drug testing. Although the California Supreme Court addressed the

---

52. Gov't. Code sec. 12940(e)
53. Lab. Code sec. 222.5
54. Lab. Code sec. 231

issue of drug testing, your right to test current employees for drugs and alcohol remains somewhat unclear.

In a 1997 case, the California Supreme Court refused to allow the city of Glendale to drug test current employees applying for promotions, but did allow testing of applicants. The case applied the law relating to public employers, analyzing whether the city violated the federal Fourth Amendment constitutional right against unreasonable search and seizure by the government. This analysis would not apply to a private employer wanting to drug test current employees. However, the court also considered the right to privacy under the state constitution in its decision, which would apply to private employers.[55]

In another California Supreme Court case, the court considered the privacy rights of college athletes being randomly tested for drugs by an intercollegiate athletic association.[56] In that case, the court emphasized the difference between the employment setting and the intercollegiate athletic setting, with its inherent emphasis on bodily conditions, physical training and extracurricular competition.

It would appear from the most recent cases that testing of job applicants generally will be upheld, and testing of current employees will be held to a much higher standard. If you regularly test current employees, be prepared to show that a legitimate business necessity justifies the invasion of privacy. You should consult with legal counsel before implementing a testing program. For more information, see also Chapter 9, "Drugs, Alcohol and Smoking In the Workplace."

Polygraphs and Lie Detectors

The Employee Polygraph Protection Act of 1988 places stringent regulations upon the employer's use of polygraphs, extremely limiting their usefulness. Federal law greatly restricts the use of lie-detector tests as pre-employment screening devices, and prohibits the great majority of employers from either requiring or suggesting that applicants undergo such tests or from using test results. Federal law also prohibits:

- Requiring, requesting, suggesting or causing, directly or indirectly, any employee or prospective employee to take or submit to a lie detector test;

- Basing employment decisions solely on the results of such a test; or

- Disciplining, discharging or discriminating against any employee or applicant for refusing to take a lie detector test.[57]

In addition to these protections under federal law, state law similarly prohibits retaliation against or discharge of an employee for refusing to submit to a polygraph, lie detector or similar test.[58]

The federal act contains severely limited exceptions to the general ban on polygraph testing. Under extremely limited circumstances, you can perform polygraph tests on:

- Prospective employees of security-guard firms;

- Employees involved in the manufacture, distribution or dispensation of controlled substances; or

- Current employees who are reasonably suspected of being involved in a workplace incident that resulted in an economic loss or injury to your business.[59]

55. *Loder v. City of Glendale*, 14 Cal. 4th 846 (1997)
56. *Hill v. NCAA*, 7 Cal. 4th 1 (1994)
57. 29 U.S.C. 2001-2009
58. Lab. Code sec. 432.2

Written Honesty Tests

Honesty tests may be viable alternatives to lie-detector tests, but you must administer them carefully due to current uncertainty as to how legislatures and courts will treat them. Written paper-and-pencil honesty examinations are intended to assess accurately the honesty of an applicant by quantifying the applicant's self-perceptions of honesty through a series of questions directed at attitudes toward theft and personal experience with dishonesty. The purpose of most of the questions is to isolate dishonest behavioral tendencies and attitudes of the test taker about dishonesty.

A profile of the test taker is compiled from his/her answers, generally in multiple choice, true/false or yes/no format. The individual's profile is then obtained by comparing his/her answers to the profiles of persons who have been independently judged as honest and dishonest. The results are used as a predictor of the applicant's on-the-job integrity.

The use of paper-and-pencil honesty tests is a relatively new phenomenon. It is unclear whether such honesty examinations would violate the Labor Code section 432.2 ban on polygraph "or similar" tests as a condition of employment.

Psychological Tests

You must justify psychological testing by a compelling interest. California courts also addressed the issue of psychological testing of job applicants in the context of the state's constitutional right to privacy. In contrast to the employee/applicant distinction relied upon in drug testing cases, a California Court of Appeal ruled that in psychological testing, no distinction should be made between the privacy rights of job applicants and employees. Accordingly, it held that any violation of an applicant's right to privacy must be justified by a compelling interest. The court found that the employer could not justify such an interest when including questions about religious beliefs and sexual orientation in the psychological test, because no relation exists between such questions and job performance.[60]

Investigating Applicants

Collection, dissemination and use of personal and credit information gathered by consumer credit reporting agencies is subject to both federal and state law. Most of these laws intend to ensure that the applicant or employee is aware that such information is being sought and provides the employee the opportunity to question and assure the information's accuracy.

Credit Reports

Both federal and state laws restrict the use of credit information in the hiring process.[61] A credit report in the employment context is any written, oral or other communication of any information by a consumer credit reporting agency (CRA) bearing on an individual's credit worthiness, credit standing or credit capacity, which is used as a factor in evaluating an applicant for employment, promotion, reassignment or retention.[62]

59. 29 U.S.C. 2006
60. *Soroka v. Dayton Hudson Corp.*, 18 Cal. App. 4th 1200 (1991)
61. Civ. Code sec. 1785.1 et seq.; 15 U.S.C. 1681-1681(u)

The FCRA places restrictions on your ability to use credit reports for employment purposes. This includes investigation of applicants and current employees, as well as other employment-related purposes.[63] If information from a credit report is used for employment purposes, you must:

- Make a clear and conspicuous written disclosure to the applicant before the report is obtained, in a document consisting solely of the disclosure, that a consumer report may be obtained;

- Obtain prior written authorization from the applicant. See *Authorization to Obtain Consumer Credit Report*;

- Certify to the CRA that you made the disclosure, obtained authorization and that you will not use the information in violation of any federal or state equal-opportunity law or regulation. You must also certify that if you take any adverse action based on the credit report, you will provide a copy of the report and a summary of the FCRA rights to the consumer. See *Certification to Consumer Credit Reporting Agency*; and

- Before taking adverse action based on the credit report, provide the person a copy of the *Pre-Adverse Action Disclosure*, a copy of the credit report and a summary of FCRA rights. Obtain this summary from the CRA.

You must notify the individual once you take any adverse action based at least in part on information contained in a credit report.[64] See the *Adverse Action Notice*. The notification must be done in writing and must include the following:

- Name, address and telephone number of the consumer reporting agency that provided the report (including a toll-free telephone number if it is a nationwide consumer reporting agency);

- A statement that the consumer reporting agency did not make the adverse decision and is not able to explain why the decision was made;

- A statement setting forth the person's right to obtain a free disclosure of his/her file from the consumer reporting agency if requested within 60 days; and

- A statement setting forth the person's right to dispute directly with the consumer reporting agency the accuracy or completeness of any information provided by the consumer reporting agency.

If you take an adverse action based on information of the type covered by the FCRA and you obtained this information from an entity affiliated with you by common ownership or control,[65] you must notify the individual of the adverse action. The notification must inform the individual that he/she may obtain a disclosure of the nature of the information relied upon by making a written request within 60 days of receiving the adverse action notice. If the individual makes such a request, you must disclose the nature of the information no later than 30 days after receiving the request.

If you take adverse action based on the report and the applicant requests a copy of the report from you, you must furnish a copy of the report and the summary of FCRA rights to the applicant within three business days from receipt of the request.

---

62. Civ. Code sec. 1785.3 (c)(f); 15 U.S.C. 1681a (d) and (h)
63. 15 U.S.C. 1681-1681(u)
64. FCRA sec. 615(a)
65. FCRA sec. 615(b)(2)

Investigative Consumer Reports

Investigative consumer reports go further than credit reports by supplying information regarding the character, general reputation, personal characteristics and mode of living of the subject of the report. This information is obtained through a more intensive investigation, which may include personal interviews with neighbors, friends, business associates, etc. The FCRA provides special rights regarding such reports, as does California law. This *Digest* provides the rules and forms that satisfy the requirements of both federal and state law. Failure to comply with these rules can result in significant penalties and costs.[66]

If you intend to obtain an investigative consumer report, you must disclose this intention to the individual being investigated, also stating the purpose of the report. You should also provide a "Summary of Rights" under the FCRA. Make your disclosure of intent, in a separate document consisting solely of the disclosure, any time before the report is requested or caused to be made. See the *Disclosure and Authorization to Obtain Investigative Consumer Report*.

The report must disclose to the individual:

- That an investigative consumer report will be made regarding his/her character, general reputation, personal characteristics and mode of living;

- The permissible purpose of the report;

- The name, address and telephone number of the investigative consumer reporting agency conducting the investigation; and

- The nature and scope of the investigation requested.[67]

The disclosure must also state that, under section 1786.22 of the California Civil Code, the consumer may view, during normal business hours, the file maintained by the consumer reporting agency. He/she may also obtain a copy of this file upon submitting proper identification and paying the costs of duplication services, by appearing at the consumer reporting agency in person or by mail. He/she may also receive a summary of the file by telephone. The agency is required to have personnel available to explain the file, and the agency must explain any coded information appearing in the file. If the individual appears in person, another person of his/her choice may come along, provided that this person furnishes proper identification.

You must obtain written authorization from the individual to obtain the report.[68] The authorization must provide, by means of a check box, a way for the individual to request a copy of any report that is prepared. If the individual wishes to receive a copy of the report, you must send a copy of the report within three business days of receipt. You may contract with any other entity, such as the consumer reporting agency, to send a copy to the individual. The notice to request the report may be contained on either the disclosure form or a separate consent form. The copy of the report furnished to the individual must contain the name, address and telephone number of the party that issued the report, and how to contact that party.[69]

You are required to certify to the consumer reporting agency that applicable disclosures have been made to the individual who is the subject of the report, including acceptance of the obligation to provide the individual with a copy of the report in a timely manner if such a request has been made. You must also advise the individual of the name and address of the

66.Civ. Code sec. 1786.50
67.Civ. Code sec. 1786.16 (a)(2)(B)
68.Civ. Code sec. 1786.16 (a)(2)(C)
69.Civ. Code sec. 1786.16(b)

consumer reporting agency in the event that adverse action is taken.[70] See the *Certification to Consumer Credit Reporting Agency*.

Before taking adverse action based on an investigative consumer report, provide the person with a copy of the *Pre-Adverse Action Disclosure*, a copy of the credit report and a *Summary of Your Rights Under the Fair Credit Reporting Act*.

If you deny employment after obtaining an investigative consumer report, before taking the action, advise the individual facing the adverse action and supply the name and address of the investigative consumer reporting agency making the report.[71] Use the *Adverse Action Notice*.

These rules do not apply to an investigative consumer report procured or caused to be prepared by an employer if the report is sought for employment purposes due to the employer's suspicion of wrongdoing or misconduct by the person that is the subject of the investigation.[72]

The FCRA prohibits consumer reporting agencies from providing consumer reports that contain medical information for employment purposes or in conjunction with credit or insurance transactions, without the specific prior consent of the individual who is the subject of the report. In the case of medical information being sought for employment purposes, the individual must explicitly consent to the release of the information in addition to generally authorizing the obtaining of a consumer report.

You should limit the scope of such investigations to job-related information, since investigative reports that are not job-related may violate federal and state civil rights laws if they have a disparate impact on minority job applicants.

Background Checks and Investigations by Employers

You may conduct an investigation, such as a background check into an individual's character, general reputation, personnel characteristics or mode of living for employment purposes without using the services of an investigative consumer reporting agency. Special rules apply[73] to any person who collects, assembles, evaluates, compiles, reports, transmits, transfers or communicates information or receives such information where the information is on matters of public record. Public records include records documenting an arrest, indictment, conviction, civil judicial action, tax lien or outstanding judgment.

Such persons must provide the investigated individual with a copy of the public record within seven days of receipt of the information, regardless of whether the information is received in written or oral form, unless the right to receive that information is waived in writing by the individual. You may secure a written waiver by a check box on an employment application or any other written form whereby the individual waives the right to receive a copy of the public record. If you take any adverse action, including denial of employment or any other action that adversely affects any current or prospective employee, as a result of receiving information contained in those public records, you must provide to the consumer a copy of the public record, regardless of whether the consumer waived his/her rights to receive a copy.

If you gather the information in connection with an investigation for suspicion of wrongdoing or misconduct by the subject of the investigation, you may withhold the public records until the

---

70. Civ. Code sec. 1786.16(a)(4)
71. Civ. Code sec. 1786.40
72. Civ. Code sec. 1786.16(c)
73. Civ. Code sec. 1786.53

investigation is completed. Where such information is gathered on employees who are not the subject of the investigation, the public records obtained on those individuals must also be provided unless waivers have been secured or adverse action is ultimately taken against those additional individuals.

Fingerprinting and Criminal Offender Records

For employers who must perform background checks that include criminal offender records, effective July 1, 2005, the California Department of Justice (DOJ) will only accept fingerprint images transmitted electronically. The state attorney general established a statewide communication network in conjunction with private service providers to facilitate this program. Exceptions may be made allowing the continued use of hard fingerprint cards based on regional unavailability of transmission sites.

Certain health related workers must submit electronic fingerprint images to the state DOJ and are responsible for any cost associated with transmitting the fingerprint images. The individuals affected are as follows:

- Certified nurse assistants and home health aides;

- Nursing home administrators;

- Administrators, program directors and fiscal officers of adult, day health-care centers; and

- An owner or owners, anyone having a 10 percent or greater interest in the corporation, partnership or association, and administrators of home health agencies and private duty nursing agencies.

Investigation of Wrongdoing

In 1999, an opinion letter issued by the Federal Trade Commission interpreted the FCRA as requiring third party investigations' strict compliance with notice and disclosure requirements of that Act. The letter opined that, once an employer turns to an outside organization for assistance in investigation of harassment claims, the assisting entity is a credit reporting agency as defined in the Act because it furnishes the equivalent of a consumer report or an investigative consumer report to a third party — in this case, the employer. The effect of the opinion was to require that an employer using an outside third party to conduct an investigation of employee wrongdoing must notify the subject of the investigation and provide the disclosures and notices required of investigative consumer reports. Moreover, if adverse action was to be taken as a result of the investigation, the subject of the investigation was entitled to a copy of the investigative report.

This interpretation was reversed in the 2003 Fair and Accurate Transactions Act, which became effective in March, 2004. Third-party workplace investigations are now permitted, as long as they "are not for the purpose of investigating employee credit." The requirements for advance notice and prior consent are abolished, and the employer no longer has to give a copy of the third-party investigator's report to the employee. If adverse action is taken in whole or in part based on the investigator's report, the employer must only provide the employee with a summary report that need not disclose the identity of the individuals interviewed or the sources that provided information used in the report.

Some limitations remain. The third-party investigations can relate only to:

- Suspected misconduct relating to employment;

- Compliance with federal, state or local laws and regulations, or rules of a self-regulatory organization; or

- Pre-existing written policies of the employer.

The report can only be provided to the employer or its agent, or federal, state or local agencies or a self-regulatory organization with jurisdiction over the employer. Other persons, presumably including labor unions, cannot be given the report. Employees against whom adverse actions are taken, following a third party's investigation, may still argue the employer must have had reasonable suspicion before engaging the third-party investigator, and/or that pre-existing or written employer policies were not in place when that investigation began.

Monitoring Employees

Concern over inventory loss, customer service, drug and alcohol abuse, misuse of company facilities and equipment and illegal activity on company premises spawned an increasing desire to conduct surveillance in the workplace. New technologies replaced the one-way mirror and the surveillance station of days past, but have also prompted new employee privacy concerns.

Shopping Investigations

You may hire "shopping investigators" to test the integrity of employees and review sales techniques and service. Before discharging or disciplining an employee on the basis of a shopping investigator's report, you must provide the employee with a copy of the report. During an interview that might result in the termination of an employee for dishonesty, you must hand the employee a copy of the latest investigation report on which the interview was based. You are excused from these requirements if the shopping investigator is employed exclusively and regularly by you and the entire investigation is conducted solely for you.[74]

Electronic Surveillance

Consult with counsel before using cameras to electronically monitor employee activities. At a minimum, you should notify employees that cameras have been installed, and obtain their consent to be monitored in writing. In addition, you should never place cameras in an area where employees legitimately expect privacy, such as restrooms or changing areas.

State Law Prohibitions

California law prohibits public and private employers (except the federal government) from making audio or video recordings of employees in rest rooms, locker rooms or rooms designated by the employer for changing clothes, unless authorized by a court order. You may not use recordings made in violation of this law for any purpose.[75]

---

74. Lab. Code sec. 2930
75. Lab. Code sec. 435

Union Employee Rights

The Ninth U.S. Circuit Court of Appeals held that, when an employer violates state privacy laws by secret surveillance, union employees may sue for invasion of privacy regardless of the terms of their collective bargaining agreement.

Consolidated Freightways, defending its installation of audio and video devices in employee restrooms to uncover drug abuse, argued that its collective bargaining agreement (CBA) prohibited the employees from bringing state law privacy claims because the CBA contained a provision allowing Consolidated to use video cameras to prove employee theft or dishonesty. The Ninth Circuit disagreed, finding the privacy claims were "not even arguably covered by the collective bargaining agreement." It determined that the provision in the CBA allowing video cameras had no bearing on "secret spying on Consolidated's employees in company restrooms — no matter how well-intentioned Consolidated's alleged purpose may have been in doing so."[76]

Union E-mail

Employers may restrict the use of company e-mail, even if such restriction includes a ban on the use of e-mail for "union business." Employees can be disciplined for using company e-mail to announce union rallies and other related union activities. Although the employer in this case allowed personal e-mails, so long as the employer prohibits solicitations on behalf of all third party organizations (unions, political groups, insurance salespersons, etc.) across the board, then the employer may prohibit union solicitation as well.[77]

Secret Videotaping in Open Workplace

The California Supreme Court held that a journalist secretly videotaping an employee in an open workspace constituted an invasion of privacy.[78] The secret videotaping in that case was done as a part of an undercover investigative report on "tele-psychics" by a television reporter in a workplace with low, open cubicles where conversations could easily be overheard by anyone in the room.

The Supreme Court concluded that the fact that a workplace interaction might be witnessed by others on the premises does not eliminate an employee's reasonable expectation of privacy. In an office or other workplace to which the general public does not have free access, employees enjoy a limited, but legitimate, expectation that their conversations and other interactions will not be secretly videotaped by undercover television reporters, even though those conversations may not have been completely private from the participants' co-workers.

Property Searches

California courts have not defined the extent of an employee's right to privacy in the area of employer-owned property used exclusively by the employee. Existing case law appears to suggest that the privacy provision is not intended to protect employees from searches of company-owned property such as lockers, desks and vehicles.

---

76. *Cramer v. Consolidated Freightways, Inc.,* 255 F3d 683 (Ninth Cir., 2001)
77. *The Guard Publishing Company v. NLRB,* Case No. 36-CA-08743-1 (December 16, 2007)
78. *Sanders v. American Broadcasting Companies,* 20 Cal. 4th 907 (1999)

Your search of employee property brought onto company premises more closely approaches invasion of a constitutional privacy interest. The scope of a potential privacy right in such circumstances turns upon an objective assessment of the employee's expectation of privacy. Nonetheless, the employee's privacy interests may be outweighed by your interest in the productivity and well-being of your workforce and security of your premises.[79]

California courts have not yet ruled on the applicability to private sector employees of the broadly interpreted "reasonable expectation of privacy" used in public employee search-and-seizure cases under the Fourth Amendment. If you wish to conduct searches, follow these precautions to minimize exposure to liability for inappropriate searches:

- Maintain keys or combinations to each desk, vehicle or locker used by employees on company property, and employees should be so notified;

- Disseminate written policies concerning your right to conduct searches of lockers, desks, vehicles, etc., to all employees, and obtain employees' acknowledgment of receiving and reading such policies;

- Provide notice to employees that pockets, purses, lunch boxes, tool kits, etc., may be searched, and employee consent should be obtained before any such search is conducted;

- Supply any lock used on company property, and forbid employees from using their own locks;

- Conduct searches in an even-handed and non discriminatory manner; and

- Do not proceed with the search if the employee credibly denies knowledge of your search policy.

Even if you take all of these precautions, litigation and liability still may arise from any search, particularly given the unsettled state of the law in this area. Check with a competent labor and employment law attorney before engaging in any search activities.

Telephone, Voice-Mail and E-mail Monitoring

The incredible expansion of information technology in the workplace over the last several years opened a Pandora's box of legal issues for employers. The typewriter with carbon paper and the telephone message pad have been almost totally replaced by computers, voice mail and e-mail. With these new modes of communication come questions about employee privacy and employer security.

The law in this area is still taking shape and remains largely undefined. This section will address the issues created by the new workplace technology and the current state of the law as it applies to these issues.

Civil Electronic Privacy Statutes

The Electronic Communications Privacy Act gives an employer who maintains e-mail and/or voice-mail systems the right to access those systems.[80] This right does not exist under the Act if the systems are provided by an outside entity. Certain unauthorized disclosures are prohibited by the act. Disclosure may be made only to:

- The addressee or intended recipient;

---

79. *O'Connor v. Ortega*, 480 U.S. 709 (1987)
80. 18 U.S.C. 2701

- An agent of the addressee or intended recipient; or

- Other persons, with the consent of the originator, addressee or intended recipient.

The Omnibus Control and Safe Streets Act regulates the interception of wire, electronic and oral communications.[81] It prohibits the intentional interception of any such communication through the use of any electronic, mechanical or other device. However, merely retrieving information after transmission has ceased probably would not be considered an interception of information.[82]

An employee may give consent, either explicitly or implied, to an otherwise impermissible monitoring of a communication. The courts are split on what constitutes an implied consent, and often will look to the way a company sets forth and applies its policies relating to privacy.[83] The court may find implied consent if a well-known monitoring/access policy exists and you consistently enforce the policy against use of your communication devices for personal reasons. On the other hand, courts might not find implied consent where an employee has consented to your policy of monitoring business calls but not personal calls.

The Act does not prohibit intercepting communications by telephone or related equipment being used in the ordinary course of business. This exception would allow you to monitor your employee's telephone calls for customer service or training purposes. Monitoring voice-mail messages would not likely be a prohibited interception, since voice-mail systems rely on telephone equipment, but monitoring e-mail messages probably would not fall under this exception. Be aware that the question of whether a particular message was monitored "in the ordinary course of business" will be determined on a case-by-case basis, and standards for making this determination vary among the courts.

Criminal Electronic Privacy Statutes

In addition to the federal civil statutes, California places criminal sanctions on persons who engage in wiretapping or various related activities. Activities prohibited include:

- Intentional wiretapping;

- Willfully attempting to learn the contents or meaning of a communication in transit over a wire;

- Attempting to use or publicize information obtained in either of the above ways;[84]

- Eavesdropping on/recording confidential communications;[85] and

- Disclosing the contents of a telegraph or telephone message by a person other than the addressee without permission of the addressee.[86]

In general, eavesdropping is prohibited under these statutes only if done while the message is in transit. Therefore, listening to voice-mail messages once recorded or reading e-mail messages once transmission is completed should limit exposure to criminal penalties.

Listening to or recording confidential communications is prohibited if either party to the conversation expects it to be private. Outgoing voice-mail messages should not indicate that

---

81. 18 U.S.C. 2510
82. *United States v. Meriwether,* 917 F.2d 955 (6th Cir. 1990)
83. *Simmons v. Southwestern Bell Tel. Co.,* 452 F. Supp. 392 (W.D. Okla. 1978)
84. Penal Code sec. 631; *Warden v. Kahn,* 160 Cal. Rptr. 471 (1979)
85. Penal Code sec. 632
86. Penal Code sec. 637

the caller may "leave a private message," and might even go so far as to state that incoming messages may be monitored by the company. You should warn all e-mail users in writing that you do not guarantee e-mail communications to be private, and that you may access them. Your best defense is to clearly inform employees and all others using your electronic communication systems that they should not expect communications to be private.

Computers and Privacy

In 2002, a California appellate court case offers some guidance on creation of policies governing use of business computers, e-mail systems and Internet access.

TBG Insurance Services Corporation terminated an employee for accessing pornographic Web sites on his computer at work. TBG requested a court order requiring the former employee to turn over a computer provided by the company for home use. The company wanted to discover whether the employee used the home computer for similar purposes. The employee agreed to return the computer, but wanted first to delete personal information he and family members placed on the hard drive, which he claimed was subject to the California Constitution's right to privacy.

The court rejected the employee's claim. The employee signed an agreement to be bound by the company's computer use policy that said computers were provided for business purposes and not for personal use unless explicitly approved. Company policy also prohibited computer use for obscene purposes and included a consent to company monitoring as needed. The court said the employee could not have had any reasonable expectation of privacy.[87]

It is unlawful for any elected state or local officer, including any state or local appointee, employee or consultant, to knowingly use a state-owned or state-leased computer to access, view, download or otherwise obtain obscene matter, as defined in the penal code. The law does not apply to accessing, viewing, downloading or otherwise obtaining obscene matter for use consistent with legitimate law enforcement purposes, to permit a state agency to conduct an administrative disciplinary investigation, or for legitimate medical, scientific, academic or legislative purposes, or for other legitimate state purposes.

Privacy and Third-Party Servers

NEW for 2009 The Ninth U.S. Circuit Court of Appeals held that employees have a right to privacy over information held on third-party servers, as opposed to company owned and controlled servers. Arch Wireless provided wireless text messaging services for the City of Ontario Police Department (OPD). In the case, Arch gave the OPD information about text messages that employees transmitted via the vendor's equipment. The Court said the vendor should not have released that information to the employer.[88]

OPD employees were given two-way pagers provided by Arch Wireless, but OPD did not provide an explicit policy regarding employee use of the pagers' text-messaging function. The only policy provided noted that each pager was allotted 25,000 characters, after which OPD would have to pay overage charges. OPD's general "Computer Usage, Internet and E-mail Policy" specified that OPD-owned computers and associated equipment, software, programs, networks, Internet e-mail and other systems operating on OPD computers is limited to work-related business. The policy also noted that there should be no expectation of privacy relating to the use of OPD equipment, all use will be monitored and inappropriate use will not be tolerated. All employees signed an acknowledgement they received and reviewed this policy.

---

87. *TBG Insurance Services Corporation v. Superior Court of Los Angeles,* 96 Cal. App. 4th 443 (2002)
88. *Quon v. Arch Wireless Operating Company,* 529 F.3d 892 (2008)

When an OPD employee exceeded the limit for the fourth time, OPD leadership requested the pager transcripts from Arch Wireless to determine if the messages were work related. An employee from Arch Wireless printed out the transcripts associated with OPD pager numbers, put the transcripts in a manila envelope and brought them to OPD. The OPD employee sued OPD for violating his 4th Amendment right from unlawful searches. A jury found in favor of the employee, but the Ninth Circuit disagreed and found Arch Wireless violated the employee's privacy by releasing the transcripts to the OPD.

The federal Stored Communications Act, part of the Electronic Communications Privacy Act, governed the Court's analysis in the case. Arch Wireless is considered an electronic communication service – defined as "any service which provides to users of the service the ability to send or receive wire or electronic communications" – that stored communication relating to the use of the pagers on its own servers. This is to be contrasted with remote communication service that provides computer data storage and processing services to the public. The Court analogized the use of an Internet service provider that stores e-mails after delivery to an e-mail recipient for purposes of back-up protection.

The messages were not stored on OPD's behalf or for its benefit. Arch Wireless served as a conduit for the transmission of messages between users and stored the messages as a "backup" for the user. The user in this case is the individual sending and receiving messages. Arch Wireless knowingly released the transcripts to OPD, which was a subscriber to OPD's service and not a user or addressee or intended recipient of such communication. As such, the messages and privacy belonged to the employee and not to OPD and Arch Wireless unlawfully released the transcripts to OPD.

Conducting Harassment Investigations

Workplace harassment investigations performed by independent contractors, such as human resources consultants, may trigger employer responsibilities under the federal FCRA, the state law on investigative consumer reports and California's Private Investigator Act.

Investigation of a sexual harassment complaint by an outside organization, such as a consultant or law firm, may subject you to the requirements of the FCRA[89] and state law.[90] According to the FTC, once you turn to an outside organization for assistance in investigating harassment claims, the assisting entity is a CRA because it furnishes "consumer reports" to a "third party" (you). For purposes of determining whether an entity is a CRA, the FCRA does not distinguish whether the information is obtained by that entity from your internal records or from outside your workplace. As long as the outside organization assembles or evaluates information about the consumer/employee, such information becomes an investigative consumer report. Thus, the employee who is the subject of the harassment investigation would be entitled to the forms and notices required by the FCRA.

State law contains a specific exclusion for the procurement of investigative credit reports where you suspect the subject of the report of misconduct or wrongdoing. However, if in the course of an investigation you make an investigative consumer report concerning other employees, you must provide them with the forms and notices required by law.

---

89. Federal Trade Commission Staff Advisory Letter, April 5, 1999
90. Civ. Code sec. 1786.16

Private Investigator Act

California's Department of Consumer Affairs (DCA) took the position that, under the Private Investigator Act, any nonattorney outside party hired to conduct an investigation of employee misconduct must be a licensed private investigator. Any unlicensed investigator who conducts such an investigation, or the entity that hires them as an outside party, is guilty of a misdemeanor punishable by a fine of five thousand dollars ($5,000) or by imprisonment in the county jail not to exceed one year, or by both fine and imprisonment.[91]

California law has always prevented outside third parties from being able to perform harassment investigations unless they are licensed attorneys or licensed private investigators. If you intend to engage an outside third party to perform investigations, ensure they are properly licensed. An HR consultant is not legally able to perform these investigations. Using an outside HR consultant (as opposed to your HR staff) will negatively impact the validity of any investigation results if a lawsuit should occur.

Responding to Reference Checks

The law makes it clear that you may communicate information about the job performance or qualifications of a current or former employee upon the request of a prospective employer. The law specifically provides protection from claims of libel or slander when you respond to an inquiry as to whether you would or would not rehire a current or former employee.[92] In addition to the protections offered by this law, you may lessen exposure to liability by establishing uniform procedures for responding to requests for information.

Some companies set a policy of not providing references at all. This is not a wise choice, as it could lead to liability if a former employee has been terminated for violence, or is known to be violent. If that employee is hired by another company and commits a violent act on the job, your company could be liable for failing to provide information that could have prevented the incident.

General Policy Guidelines

Follow these guidelines when developing your reference check policies:

- Always be consistent when providing employee references. Your policy should name certain individuals within the company who are authorized to provide references. Managers and supervisors should understand that all requests for references must be directed to those with authority to provide the information;

- Create a waiver for former employees to sign at the time employment ends if they wish information to be released to potential future employers;

- Do not provide automatic letters of reference to terminating employees. If you wish to provide a letter of reference, draft it to reflect the facts about the specific employee's performance;

- Verify the caller's identity before providing any references by telephone. You can do this by telephoning the caller's employer;

- Determine what information will be provided. Respond to the inquirer's questions if they fall within your policy guidelines. If the inquiry goes outside the information your company

---

91. Business and Professions Code sections 7520 et seq.
92. Civ. Code sec. 47(c)

decided to provide, inform the inquirer that your company policy prohibits giving out that information;

- Determine whether you will allow oral references or require all references to be in writing. Create a form marked "confidential" for written references. The form can be sent or faxed to anyone requesting information. When returning the form to the employer who requested the reference, mark the envelope confidential. Returning the form by fax compromises the privacy of the information;

- State that references will be provided only to those with a need to know the information, such as a prospective employer's personnel manager;

- Provide only truthful job-related information rather than personal data. It may be helpful to create a form for terminating employees that shows the type of information commonly requested in reference checks, such as dates of employment, positions held, rates of pay and eligibility for rehire. This will help ensure that the information provided was truthful, relevant and based on proper documentation; and

- Document each request for a reference, including the name, title, telephone number of the person requesting the information and the information provided.

Compelled Self-Publication

You may be held liable for defamation of character without ever having given out a single piece of information about a former employee. Liability has been found under an extremely creative claim called "defamation by compelled self-publication." This occurs when a job seeker is compelled to tell a prospective employer about negative information, allegedly untrue, in the job seeker's former employer's personnel file. The theory runs that if the job seeker does not tell the prospective employer about the negative information, the prospective employer will discover it upon calling the former employer and presume that the job seeker was trying to hide something. According to the theory, the job seeker has no choice but to defame himself to avoid this negative presumption.

One California case[93] provides guidance in protecting yourself against this type of claim. In this case, the appeals court refused to hold the employer liable for the former employee's alleged compelled defamatory self-publication. The company had a strict policy against giving out any information to prospective employers about former employees except their dates of employment. Because of this strict policy, the court held the former employee was not compelled to self-publish the reason for his discharge since the company would not have given out this information in any case.

As this decision shows, you should have a strict policy on providing references. This policy should be made known to employees, via a handbook or company memo, so employees will not have a reasonable belief that they are compelled to self-publish defamatory information.

Statements to a Police Department

An employer provided information to the Los Angeles Police Department (LAPD) about a former employee who was applying for a job as a police officer. The employer included information about a complaint filed against the employee regarding drinking on the job. The employee claimed the statements made by her former employer were false and misleading

93. *Davis v. Consolidated Freightways, Inc.*, 29 Cal. App. 4th 354 (1994)

negative information, and sued for defamation of character. A California Court of Appeal held that the employer did not defame the former employee because its statements to the LAPD were privileged under California Civil Code section 47(b), which protects communications to a police agency engaged in a background investigation.[94]

Retaining Records

Employers are often confused about which records to keep, how long to keep them and where to store them.

How Long to Retain Records

At least seven laws, both state and federal, mandate different lengths of time various employment records must be kept. See the *Records Retention Requirements* showing which records are covered by these laws and the length of time records must be kept under each law.

For the sake of practicality, many employers simply keep the bulk of an employee's personnel file and other records for the *duration of employment plus four years*. This covers nearly every law, with the exception of three types of records that must be removed from a file before it is disposed of and retained for a longer duration:

- Pension and welfare plan information (six years);[95]

- First-aid records of job injuries causing loss of work time (five years);[96] and

- Safety and toxic/chemical exposure records, including Material Safety Data Sheets (30 years).[97]

Electronic Records Retention

In an age when more and more records are stored on hard disks, network servers and backup tapes, careful attention must be paid to retention policies and practices to be sure they include records stored in such form.

Consideration should be given to segregating the electronic storage of business records, confidential data and privileged communications that are to be retained for extended periods of time, and records that have mandated retention periods, such as e-mails and other routine communications which should be destroyed after a reasonable period of time. Policies and schedules that describe routine records destruction upon completion of legal retention periods should include electronic versions as well a paper records. Routines should be established, communicated and enforced throughout your organization. These should include the computers of telecommuters who use company or personal computers for company business.

The goal should be to avoid the appearance of selective records destruction should your company need to defend a claim or lawsuit. Should a lawsuit occur, however, you must have a policy and be prepared for preservation of relevant electronic files and the production of such files as are required.

---

94. *Bardin v. Lockheed Aeronautical Sys. Co.*, 70 Cal. App. 4th 494 (1999)
95. 29 CFR 516.1 et seq.
96. 8 CCR 14300.7
97. 8 CCR 3204

Where to Retain Records

Keep employment records in individual personnel files; access to these files should be restricted. Because personnel files often contain sensitive and private information, keep them in a locked cabinet with access controlled by a single individual or department from whom authorization must be gained before others may view the files. The *Personnel File Checklist* describes the records to keep in a personnel file.

Though you can keep the majority of the documents together in a personnel file, certain types of documents must or should be kept separately.

Medical Records

California law mandates that you establish appropriate procedures to ensure all employee medical records and information will remain confidential and will be protected from unauthorized use and disclosure.[98] Failing to establish such procedures is a misdemeanor and allows an employee to collect damages and attorneys' fees.[99] For more information, see "Medical Information" on page 147.

Equal Employment Opportunity Classification Information

If you have 15 or more employees, you must maintain a record of the sex, race and national origin of applicants and employees apart from personnel files.[100] Maintain these records to demonstrate, if necessary, that you are attempting to recruit and develop a workforce reflective of the community's ethnic profile. Keep these Equal Employment Opportunity (EEO) records in a common file rather than in each employee's own personnel file.

Employment Eligibility Verifications (Form I-9)

Keep forms and information verifying the right of your employees to work in this country (Form I-9 and photocopies of verification documents) in a common file rather than in each employee's own personnel file. This ensures that you can access the information easily for an audit by immigration or labor officials. It also allows you to readily review all the forms on a regular basis to determine whether it is necessary to re-verify expiring documents.

Disposing of Records

Employment documents that contain personal information must be disposed of by shredding or burning them. The Fair and Accurate Credit Transactions (FACT) Act, passed in 2003, imposed this requirement, effective in 2005, on all employers — regardless of size. The purpose is to protect current, past and prospective employees' personal information such as Social Security numbers, addresses, telephone numbers and any other information reported to an employer by a consumer reporting agency.

Employers that use an outside party to dispose of records are expected to conduct due diligence in hiring a document destruction contractor. Due diligence could include:

---

98. Civ. Code sec. 56.20
99. Civ. Code secs. 56.35, 56.36
100. 42 U.S.C. 2000e-8(c)

- Reviewing an independent audit of a disposal company's operations and/or its compliance with this rule;

- Obtaining information about the disposal company from several references;

- Requiring that the disposal company be certified by a recognized trade association; and

- Reviewing and evaluating the disposal company's information security policies or procedures.

If such information is stored on computer disks or other recordable media, it must be destroyed before being discarded. If the data is stored on the hard drive of a computer that is being sold or donated to another party, the data must be removed in a way that makes it unrecoverable.

Employers also must restrict access to this information while being stored. Failure to comply with the new regulations could result in federal or state fines or civil liability in individual or class-action lawsuits.

Protecting Employer Information

Employers often must give certain employees access to confidential information so they may do their jobs. Concern naturally arises as to what the employee may do with that confidential information, particularly after the termination of employment. An ex-employee could use confidential client lists, trade secrets, formulas or techniques to compete with his/her former employer, making the ex-employee a formidable business competitor.

How can you protect yourself from an employee using confidential information that he/she gained during employment? The most common method is an agreement called a "covenant not to compete" or a "noncompetition agreement." The employee may sign this agreement at the time he/she begins work or any time thereafter. However, it is important to understand the limited protection afforded by a covenant not to compete under California law.

Noncompetition Agreements

California Business and Professions Code section 16600 provides that "every contract by which anyone is restrained from engaging in a lawful profession, trade, or business of any kind is to that extent void." Therefore, section 16600 invalidates provisions in employment contracts (or noncompetition agreements) that prohibit an employee from working for a competitor after completion of his/her employment or imposing a penalty for doing so, unless they are necessary to protect your trade secrets.[101] Noncompetition agreements are strictly construed against you and in favor of the employee.[102] This body of law was developed to ensure that employees would not be prevented from earning a livelihood if they chose to leave a particular job.

Court Rules Against Agreements

The California Supreme Court confirmed that The California Supreme Court confirmed that noncompetition agreements are unenforceable in California. agreements are unenforceable in California. Agreements that restrict an employee's ability to pursue similar employment after leaving a job are prohibited, even if narrowly written and leave a substantial portion of

---

101.*Muggill v. Rueben H. Donnelly Corp.*, 62 Cal. 2d 239 (1965)

102.*KGB, Inc. v. Giannoulas*, 104 Cal. App. 3d 844 (1980); *Campbell v. Board of Trustees*, 817 F.2d 499 (9th Cir. 1987)

the available employment market open to the employee. Unless a non-competition agreement clearly falls under one of the following exceptions, it will be unenforceable in California:

- Trade secrets protections, which can legally restrict an employee's ability to use confidential information or company-defined trade secrets;

- Sale of a business, which can legally restrict a seller's ability to compete with the buyer in the geographic location where the seller had carried on his or her business; and

- Dissolution of a partnership, which can legally define a geographic area within which one of the partners cannot conduct a similar business.

The Court reiterated the law in California that noncompetition agreements go against public policy because they restrict an individual's ability to earn a living. Further, the Court found that requiring a former employee to get a release of an invalid agreement constitutes unlawful interference with the employee's rights. In addition, a waiver of "any and all" claims is not an illegal waiver of employee indemnification rights unless the waiver specifies that indemnification is being waived.[103]

Trade Secrets

Whether you can prohibit an employee from using information gained from you in future employment is essentially dependent on whether that information may be classified as a "trade secret," a term that is somewhat misleading. The term implies a highly protected, extremely secretive method of production and conjures up images of "Secret Formula X" in a guarded vault. In fact, the definition is much more broad in relation to the area of employer confidentiality.

A trade secret is information, including a formula, pattern, program, customer list, device, technique or process that:

- Derives independent economic value, actual or potential, from not being generally known to the public or to persons who can obtain economic value from its disclosure or use; and

- Is the subject of reasonable efforts under the circumstances to maintain its secrecy.[104]

A showing of value, by itself, is not sufficient to satisfy the statutory definition of a trade secret. Other businesses must be unaware of the information and must be able to put that information, if it were known to them, to beneficial use.[105]

To be considered a trade secret, information must be:

- Closely guarded;

- An investment of considerable amount of time and expense by the employer; and

- Not readily available to the public.[106]

Some examples of trade secrets include:

---

103. *Edwards v. Arthur Andersen LLP* 44 Cal. 4th 937 (2008)
104. Civ. Code secs. 3426-3426.10; Code of Civil Procedure sec. 2019(d)
105. *Abba Rubber Co. v. Sequist*, 235 Cal. App. 3d 1 (1991)
106. *State Farm Mutual Auto Ins. Co. v. Dempster*, 174 Cal. App. 2d 418 (1959)

- Customer lists that you compiled with a significant investment of time and/or money. Such a list would be a trade secret if you refined a general customer list by noting particular product or other preferences of each customer;

- A particular method or sequence of manufacturing a product;

- A closely guarded product formula (the Coca-Cola® formula is a classic example);

- The identity of a source of raw material not generally known in the industry;

- Compensation and other financial data;

- Marketing strategies;

- Labor relations strategies;

- Research into new materials, processes, etc.; and

- Pending projects.

The sample agreement, *Agreement Not to Disclose or Use Trade Secrets Policy*, prohibits the use or disclosure of trade secrets and/or confidential information. It is not intended to constitute a comprehensive employment agreement, and you should have it reviewed by legal counsel before implementation.

Inevitable Disclosure

In many states, employers can block employees from going to work for a competitor under the doctrine of "inevitable disclosure." The theory behind this rule is that if an employee is exposed to trade secrets in one job, he/she will inevitably disclose those secrets to a new employer.

The California Supreme Court has made it clear that the inevitable disclosure doctrine does not apply in California.[107] Therefore, in California a former employee cannot be prevented from employment with one of the company's competitors simply because the former employee might inevitably disclose trade secrets of the first employer. See also, "Noncompetition Agreements" on page 176.

General Knowledge or Skills Not Protected

A person has a substantial interest in the unrestrained pursuit of his/her livelihood, and generally is allowed to change employers and compete with former employers.[108] As long as an employee does not use any of the former employer's trade secrets,[109] he/she may use the general knowledge, skill and experience acquired from prior employment and even solicit some of the same clients to better succeed when working for later employers.[110]

However, covenants not to compete are enforceable where the contracting party sells or disposes of stock, assets or other business interests and transfers goodwill,[111] and in agreements for dissolution of partnerships.[112]

107.*Electro Optical Industries Inc. v. White*, 76 Cal. App. 4th 653, depublished April 12, 2000
108.*KGB, Inc. v. Giannoulas*, 104 Cal. App. 3d 844 (1980)
109.*Matull & Associates v. Cloutier*, 194 Cal. App. 3d 1049 (1987)
110.*American Alloy Steel Corp. v. Ross*, 149 Cal. App. 2d. 215 (1957)
111.Business & Professions Code sec. 16601
112.Business & Professions Code sec. 16602

Soliciting Customers

·An employee may notify customers that he/she is severing his/her business relationship with you and engaging in business for himself/herself, even before the employee resigns.[113] However, an employee, during employment, owes you a duty of diligent and faithful service, and thus may not solicit customers before leaving employment.[114] With the exception of solicitation using a former employer's trade secrets, an employee generally is free to solicit customers of his/her former employer after he/she resigns, consistent with the above discussion.[115]

Unfair Competition

Unfair competition is a generalized term for business conduct that is contrary to honest practice in industrial or commercial matters.[116] Misappropriation of trade secrets is one form of unfair competition,[117] but the term encompasses a broader range of misconduct concerning confidential business information. Ultimately, the term has no fixed meaning, but depends instead on the facts of each case.[118]

The case law suggests several limited instances in which relief may be granted against a former employee now in competition with you:

- When an employee forms a competing business before resigning his/her employment;[119]

- In certain circumstances relating to soliciting customers; or

- By disparaging your products or services, secretly diverting business to a competitor or soliciting only your preferred or most profitable customers.[120]

Employee Inventions

If you have employees who conduct research and who may invent products or devices in the course of that research, you should put an agreement in place with those employees from the beginning of employment.

However, if you require or offer an employee to assign his/her invention rights to you, know that these rights do not apply to an invention if:

- The invention is developed entirely on the employee's own time;

- The equipment, supplies and facilities belong to the employee;

- The employee did not use any of your trade secrets;

- The invention does not relate to your business or to your actual research or development; and

- The invention does not result from any work performed by the employee for you.

113.*Aetna Building Maintenance Co. v. West*, 39 Cal. 2d 198 (1952)

114.Civ. Code sec. 2322; Lab. Code sec. 2859

115.*Continental Car-Na-Var Corp. v. Mosely*, 24 Cal. 2d 104 (1944)

116.*American Heritage Life Insurance Co. v. Heritage Life Insurance Co.*, 494 F.2d 3 (5th Cir. 1991)

117.*Klamath-Orleans Lumber, Inc. v. Miller*, 87 Cal. App. 3d 458 (1978)

118.*Grant v. California Bench Co.*, 76 Cal. App. 2d 706 (1946)

119.*Bancroft-Whitney Co. v. Glen*, 64 Cal. 2d 327 (1966)

120.*Scavengers Protective Association v. Serv U Garbage Co.*, 218 Cal. 568 (1933)

You cannot enforce any agreement that purports to apply to such inventions.[121]

An employment agreement in which the employee agrees to assign his/her rights and interests in inventions to you can simplify problems that may arise with employee inventions as long as that agreement is consistent with the above. The employment agreement may require the employee to assign or offer to assign the employee's rights to an invention if, when the invention is conceived or put into practice, the invention relates to your business or to your actual or demonstrably anticipated research.

Use of E-mail Systems

A company's effort to prevent a former employee from using the company's computer system to distribute e-mails critical of the company's policies to other employees was rejected by the California Supreme Court.

On six occasions over a period of approximately two years, an ex-employee sent e-mails to large numbers of former co-workers criticizing the company's personnel practices. There was no breach of any security barriers or damage to, or disruption of, systems. The sender complied with employee requests to be removed from his mailing list, but he rejected company requests that he stop his disruptive e-mails. The company sued, alleging trespass to the corporate computer network. The trial judge agreed and ordered the e-mails be stopped. That order was affirmed by the court of appeals.

The Supreme Court rejected the trespass theory, saying that the company failed to show that the e-mails damaged its computer systems or interfered with the property's use or possession. According to the Court, the loss of employee productivity resulting from the controversial content did not injure the company's interest in its computer systems.

The Supreme Court observed that its decision is not intended to grant senders any special immunity from liability for the message content, such as defamatory statements.[122]

The decision underlines the importance of taking all necessary steps to secure your electronic communication systems, data and address books. Publish policies that limit employee use of company computer systems to matters reasonably related to company business and forbid transmission of inappropriate messages that offend or harass others.

Advise employees that they should have no expectation of privacy with regard to messages sent through the company system and that you have the right to monitor messages to assure compliance with company policies.

---

121. Lab. Code sec. 2870
122. *Intel Corporation v. Hamidi*, 30 Cal. 4th 1342 (2003)

Balancing Privacy against Business Needs

The following four keys balance privacy against legitimate business needs to create the highest likelihood of avoiding litigation.

Provide Advance Notice

Provide advance notice of what employees can and cannot expect to remain private in the workplace. Reducing the expectation of privacy is your best defense against allegations of invasion of privacy. A written policy informing employees that their desks, lockers, voice mail, computers (including e-mail) and personal effects are subject to search by the company at any time reduces an employee's expectation that the contents of those items will remain private.

A sample *Voice-mail and E-mail Policy* provides advance notice to employees that any messages created, sent, received or stored on these systems are the property of the company and may be accessed by the company at any time.

Obtain Consent

In addition to providing advance notice, you should obtain consent from employees to search or access information stored in e-mail or voice mail.

Consent is best obtained in advance and in writing. Keep on file a written acknowledgment from each employee that he/she has received, read and understood the company's policy relating to its access to electronic information. You may include this in the general acknowledgment of receipt for employee handbooks containing such a policy, or create a separate document entirely.

In addition, it is best to obtain consent from an employee at the time you access electronic communications. Of course, this is not always possible because you may legitimately need to access information when the employee is not available to give consent, perhaps when the employee is on vacation or even on a lunch break.

Have a Legitimate Business Purpose

The U.S. Supreme Court's "reasonableness test" has been used to balance legitimate business needs against a public sector employee's expectation of privacy in his own office.[123] Though this case applies only to public sector employers, it is a good indication of the test that courts will likely apply with respect to you. The test focuses on whether:

- Reasonable grounds exist for suspecting that the search will reveal evidence of work-related misconduct; or

- The search is necessary for a noninvestigative, work-related purpose (looking in an employee's desk to find a work-related document on a day that employee is out sick); and

- The scope of the search was reasonably related to the objectives of the search and not excessively intrusive in light of the nature of the suspected misconduct.

---

123. *O'Connor v. Ortega*, 480 U.S. 709 (1987)

A federal court applied this test to workplace technology in 1993. In that case, a supervisor removed a computer disk from a public employee's desk while he was on leave. The supervisor then read the information on the disk to locate work-related documents and discovered it also contained personal documents. The court held that it was not unreasonable for a supervisor to enter an employee's office to retrieve important work-related materials while the employee was on leave. Review of the personal documents on the disk while searching for work-related material was not considered unreasonable.[124] Though this case dealt with a public employer, it is an excellent example of how the courts will balance competing rights and will likely become part of the precedent applied to private sector employers.

Seek Advice of Counsel

Most employees are well aware of the right to privacy guaranteed them by the California Constitution. When an employee feels that right has been violated, litigation often follows. You would be wise to consult counsel in any situation where privacy is an issue, such as when an employee is suspected of misconduct warranting an investigation. Also consult counsel when creating policy relating to employee privacy issues; the law in this area remains unsettled and constantly changes.

HIPAA Privacy Rule

The Health Insurance Portability and Accountability Act (HIPAA) privacy rule, which relates to the protection of medical records, went into effect on April 14, 2003. The rule was created to provide greater protection against involuntary disclosure of an individual's medical information, particularly as that information is stored and exchanged electronically among health-care providers, insurance companies and employers. Most of the burdens imposed by these rules fall on organizations known as "covered entities," typically a health-care provider, health insurance plan or third party administrator (TPA), or health-care clearinghouse that collects and maintains health-care records. Generally, you have few obligations under the privacy rules, unless you also fall into one of the categories of "covered entities" described below.

This section is not intended to be an exhaustive description of the HIPAA privacy rules, but rather to alert you to:

- The possibility that you might be a "covered entity" and the obligations that status entails; and

- Other impacts of HIPAA privacy rules on your status as an employer.

Organizations Covered

An employer may be a "covered entity" if its health plan is self-insured or if it administers health benefits internally. Also, employers that run on-site health clinics for their employees are referred to as "hybrid entities," and the HIPAA privacy rules cover the part of their operations involved in health care.

A "covered health plan" is a group health plan, defined as an employee welfare benefit plan under the Employment Retirement Security Act (ERISA) of 1974. Covered health plans include both

---

124. *Williams v. Philadelphia Housing Authority*, 826 F. Supp. 952 (E.D. Pa. 1993)

insured and self-insured plans, hospital and medical benefits plans, dental plans, vision plans, health flexible spending accounts (FSAs) and employee assistance plans.

An exception exists for self-administered plans with less than 50 participants. However, small plans that are administered by a TPA are covered by HIPAA.

A health FSA is considered a covered plan and, where self-funded, must comply with HIPAA privacy requirements.

Information Protected

Information subject to the privacy rule is referred to as "protected health information" (PHI). This is individually identifiable health information transmitted or maintained in any form or medium. This individually identifiable information includes a long list of health and personal information that either identifies or can be used to identify an individual and his/her related medical data.

Under HIPAA, a covered entity generally may not use or disclose PHI except:

- For treatment, payment or health-care operations (in compliance with HIPAA requirements);

- Upon the individual's agreement in certain limited situations (after an opportunity to agree or object);

- To the individual, subject to his or her rights under HIPAA;

- As permitted or required by HIPAA (for governmental or other purposes); or

- Pursuant to an authorization from an individual.

In addition, HIPAA grants certain rights to individuals, such as the right to access, amend and receive an accounting of disclosures of their protected health information. HIPAA also imposes certain administrative responsibilities on covered entities.

Employers and Self–Insured Health Plans

If your health plan is self-insured or if an employee administers your health plan, you are covered under HIPAA. Employers that self-insure or administer their group health plan will have further compliance obligations, including:

- Designating a privacy official;

- Developing procedures for handling protected information; and

- Maintaining training, compliance and documentation processes.

HIPAA does allow a health plan to release "summary health information" to the plan sponsor.

As a plan sponsor, you may not access a participant's medical data from the health plan except:

- As authorized by the participant;

- As needed for health plan administration; or

- In summary form for the purpose of evaluating plan design.

HIPAA requires you to have procedures that prevent the information from being used for employment-related functions or functions related to other employee benefit plans or other benefits provided by the plan sponsor. As the plan sponsor, you must use and disclose protected health information received from the health plan only for plan administrative functions, which must be specified in the plan documents.

You must:

- Amend plan documents to describe the permitted uses of the protected health information;

- Document limitations on the use of the information in plan documents; and

- Provide adequate firewalls between employees with access to the information and other employees and train such employees on the HIPAA privacy obligations.

Disclosure of "Protected Health Information" By a Health Plan

Generally, PHI may be used or disclosed by a health plan *only* as follows:

- To the individual;

- For "treatment," "payment" or "health-care operations;"

- To family members or close personal friends if the disclosure relates to the individual's health care or payment of health care, and, in most situations, if the individual has been given the advance opportunity to agree or object to the disclosure;

- With the individual's written authorization; or

- For public policy or legal reasons.

Health Plan Obligations

If you have a self-insured or self-administered health plan you must create policies and procedures to safeguard PHI, including:

- Creating and distributing a Notice of Privacy Practices and rules prohibiting intimidation or retaliation against persons asserting their protected rights and forbidding demand for waiver of rights to receive coverage or treatment;

- Establishing and maintaining, for at least six years, policies and procedures to safeguard PHI;

- Designating a Privacy Officer and contact persons;

- Training employees regarding privacy practices; and

- Establishing technical and physical PHI safeguards.

Employers and Insured Health Plans

The insured group health plan that receives PHI is subject to the basic requirements discussed above. But the insured group health plan can avoid some of the "infrastructure" requirements if it creates or receives only summary health information or enrollment information. The insured plan is still subject to the "No Intimidation," "No Waiver" and "Documentation" requirements. The health insurer is responsible for providing the Notice of Privacy Practices and creating necessary policies and procedures regarding PHI storage and disclosure.

If a fully-insured group health plan receives PHI beyond summary health information or enrollment information, it is subject to all the requirements discussed above.

Verify that *all* of your group health plans are fully insured, including FSAs, which are considered "group health plans" and usually self-funded. Determine if the health information that the group health plan currently receives will subject it to the requirements of a self-insured plan. If it will, consider whether the group health plan can avoid the requirements by receiving only summary health information and enrollment information. If this is not practical, work with your insurer and legal advise to determine the best manner to comply with the HIPAA privacy rules.

Small Employer Basic Compliance Issues

For many small employers, compliance obligations are minimal. Health information obtained in connection with general employment matters, as opposed to that obtained in connection with your role as a health plan sponsor, is not covered by HIPAA. This includes:

- Requests for sick leave;
- Family and Medical Leave Act requests;
- Workers' compensation claims;
- Disability claims; and
- Life insurance issues.

Other privacy laws require that you protect the privacy of this health information by segregating it from other human resources files and limiting access to a need-to-know basis. For more information, see "Medical Information" on page 147.

A fully insured group health plan under which no one at the company can access to employee health information is partially exempt from these rules under the "administrative exception." The administrative exception for fully insured plans may be lost when company personnel assist with employees to file or contest claims.

FSAs and similar plans are self-insured, and the administrative exception does not apply. This is true even if an outside party performs the plan's administrative functions.

Group health plans governed by the federal ERISA law are totally exempt if they have fewer than 50 eligible employees and are self-administered. The exemption is lost if administration is outsourced to a third party administrator (TPA).

Employers and Health-Care Providers

Any physical examination or testing performed by a physician, clinic or lab that collects individually identifiable health information as part of a job offer creates PHI. Because the use is not for treatment, payment or health-care operations, you or your health-care provider must obtain a HIPAA-compliant authorization before the physician can release the information to you. You may only use the information for the purposes explicitly stated in the authorization provided to the physician; that is, to confirm employability for the job that was offered.

This affects the release of drug and alcohol test results for job applicants and employees, and reports from Employee Assistance Programs (EAP) and substance-abuse rehabilitation programs to which employees may be referred under company substance abuse policies.

If you maintain an on-site medical clinic, you are a "hybrid entity" and must comply with HIPAA privacy rules.

Other Employer Issues

Though most employers are not "covered entities," many are plan sponsors subject to the obligations of a plan sponsor and/or plan administrator under HIPAA or ERISA. Plan sponsors likely have an obligation to ensure their plans comply with HIPAA. This creates a two-fold role for employers. First, the employer needs to ensure that any covered plans comply with the applicable HIPAA requirements; and employers should verify that any of its TPAs or insurance carriers comply with HIPAA requirements.

An employer that wants or needs access to its plan's PHI needs to comply with the plan sponsor requirements.

The HIPAA rules include special exemptions for medical information relating to workers' compensation cases, allowing disclosure of only such information as is authorized by, and necessary to comply with, relevant law. For more information, see "Privacy of Medical Records" in Chapter 26, page 712.

The rules have limited impact on compliance with family leave, pregnancy leave, sick leave and disability laws. In such situations, the medical information is voluntarily provided by the employee or by the treating physician with the employee's authorization.

Americans With Disabilities Act

Many employers seek medical information from health-care professionals to determine how to accommodate an individual's disability or to determine whether an individual can perform a job function. The medical information is not PHI and is not regulated by HIPAA when held by the employer. However, medical information generally is PHI and regulated by HIPAA when held by a health-care professional. HIPAA often prevents health-care professionals from disclosing PHI to the employer unless the employer or health-care professional obtains the individual's authorization to disclose the PHI. Review forms and ensure that they contain an authorization compliant with HIPAA and any applicable state law.

Generally, you are subject to the ADA's confidentiality rules even if you are not subject to the HIPAA Privacy Rules. The ADA confidentiality rules — like the HIPAA Privacy Rules — restrict how ADA-related medical information can be used or disclosed.

FMLA

Employers often receive medical certification forms under the FMLA. These forms are completed by a health-care provider and verify the existence of a "serious health condition" under the FMLA. These forms often contain medical information.

You are not subject to HIPAA simply because a completed FMLA form contains medical information. However, the health-care professional completing the form generally cannot disclose the PHI to the employer without the employee's authorization. HR professionals should review FMLA forms and ensure that they contain an authorization compliant with HIPAA and any applicable state law.

Workers' Compensation Laws

The HIPAA Privacy Rules contain special rules relating to workers' compensation laws. These rules allow a covered entity, such as a health-care provider, to disclose PHI if needed to "comply with" workers' compensation laws. This is a welcome relief for many employers, but raises a troubling question: When is a disclosure required to comply with workers' compensation laws? A health-care professional may require you to verify that the PHI is needed to comply with workers' compensation laws. You should verify that all uses and disclosures of the information are needed to comply with workers' compensation laws. If not, you may misrepresent how you use or disclose the PHI to the health-care professional. As an alternative, you can obtain an authorization from the individual allowing the health-care professional to disclose PHI to the employer.

Drug Testing

You may use a medical laboratory or clinic to assist with drug or other substance abuse testing. Like the disclosures discussed above, you should obtain an individual's authorization to allow the laboratory or clinic to disclose PHI to you. A medical laboratory or clinic can also disclose PHI to you if applicable state or federal law require such a disclosure.

Workplace Injuries

A health-care provider that is your employee (an employee of an on-site clinic) or who provides services at your request can disclose limited PHI to the employer related to workplace injuries or medical surveillance at the workplace if the disclosure is required by OSHA or similar state law. If the medical care is rendered at the workplace, you must post a conspicuous notice addressing the disclosure or provide the notice to the individual at the time the health care is administered.

Litigation Matters

HIPAA's Privacy Rules draw a sharp distinction between the employer and the employer's group health plan. The group health plan generally cannot disclose PHI to the employer. You may need to establish a "firewall" and clearly state which HR professionals are "employer representatives" and which are "health plan representatives."

You should examine whether a health plan representative discloses PHI to an employer representative. This is especially true in employment litigation, where this sharp distinction could raise difficulties for employers. For example, suppose an individual claims that he or she is disabled. The health plan representative may have information demonstrating that the individual is not disabled. The health plan representative cannot share this information with your representative because that sharing would be a prohibited disclosure of PHI to the plan sponsor. You may have difficulty defending certain employment litigation matters because the health plan representative cannot disclose relevant medical information to the employer representative. You should consult with counsel on this issue.

Further Information

For questions about consumer reporting agencies or creditors, contact:

Federal Trade Commission
Consumer Response Center - FCRA
Washington, D.C. 20580
(202) 326-3761

More information about the FCRA, written specifically for employers by the FTC, may be obtained on the FTC Web site at *www.ftc.gov/bcp/conline/pubs/buspubs/credempl.shtm.*

More information about the HIPAA Privacy Rule is available on the U.S. Department of Health and Human Services Web site at *http://hhs.gov/ocr/hipaa.*

Chapter 8 Forms

This chapter contains samples of forms associated with this topic. *The forms in this section are for visual reference only; download the most up-to-date forms and checklists in their entirety from CalBizCentral.*

To download either individual forms or your entire Formspack containing all the forms referenced in this book:

1. Visit **www.calbizcentral.com/support** and select "Labor Law Digest" from the list of product titles.

2. Have this copy of Labor Law Digest handy — you will need to enter the access code featured on the inside covers of this book.

3. Enter the access code, select the documents you want to download to your computer, then follow the on-screen instructions.

For more detailed instructions, see "Forms Available Online" on page xix.

Certification to Investigative Consumer Reporting Agency

This notice is to certify that _____ (the Company) is in compliance with the Fair Credit Reporting Act and California Civil Code Section 1786.16 and has received written authorization from _____ (applicant name).

Information received will be used for employment-related purposes. No information received by the Company from an investigative consumer reporting agency will be misused in violation of any federal or state law or equal employment opportunity law or regulation.

Before any adverse action is taken the subject of the report will receive timely notice, a copy of the report you provide and a summary of rights under the Fair Credit Reporting Act.

_____   _____
Signature of Company Representative   Date

Certification to Investigative Consumer Reporting Agency

Personal File Checklist

v031007

Step 1: Establish a policy for personnel files.
Include:

- ☐ A determination as to what types of information are to be kept in the file.
- ☐ Who is responsible for maintaining the file?
- ☐ Where the files are to be kept.
- ☐ Who will monitor the contents and maintenance of the files?
- ☐ How long information will be kept in the files.
- ☐ A procedure for keeping information current.
- ☐ A policy for review of files by only those with a need to know.
- ☐ A policy for review by the employee of his/her own file, including:
  - Whether a written request will be required.
  - When the file may be reviewed.
  - Where the file may be reviewed.
  - How often the file may be reviewed.

Step 2: Establish a system for purging the files after the required retention period. See the *Records Retention Requirements* Chart.

Step 3: Establish separate "Confidential" files for:

- ☐ Medical records - including:
  - Family/medical leave request forms if the employee has disclosed the nature of his/her illness.
  - Return to work releases.
  - Workers' compensation records.
  - Medical information about the employee related to reasonable accommodation under the Americans with Disabilities Act or Fair Employment and Housing Act.
  - Any other medical information.
- ☐ Equal Employment Opportunity records.
- ☐ I-9 Files (all I-9s should be kept in one common file rather than individual employee files)
- ☐ Other "Confidential" files such as investigative files for harassment, discrimination claims and background and reference checks.

Step 4: Establish a personnel file for each employee. Some of the items that may be included in each file are:

- ☐ Employment application and/or resume.
- ☐ Payroll authorization forms.
- ☐ Records reflecting a change in payroll rate, date of seniority and other changes such as name change, date of birth and correction of Social Security number.
- ☐ Notices of commendation, warning, discipline or termination.
- ☐ Notices of layoff, leave of absence and similar matters.
- ☐ Wage attachments or garnishment notices.
- ☐ Notices of union requirements and membership dues check-off.

Personal File Checklist

Personnel File or Payroll Records Request

Date: _____

Employee Name: _____

Company Name: _____

My signature below acknowledges my request to review my:

☐ personnel file

☐ payroll records — for payroll period from _____ to _____ (dates)

_____   _____
Employee Signature   Date

EMPLOYER RESPONSE TO REQUEST TO VIEW PERSONNEL FILE/PAYROLL RECORDS

Date: _____

Employee Name: _____

In response to your request to review your personnel file/payroll records:

☐ You are scheduled for an appointment with _____
                                                              Name

_____   _____   for the purpose of reviewing the items you requested.
Date   Time

Note that during your review, nothing may be removed from or added to your personnel file.

Your review of your file is limited to

Specific amount of time, specific time - i.e., one-half hour/9:00-9:30 a.m.

Your review of your file must be conducted in the presence of

_____
Name

OR

☐ Your request to review your personnel file has been denied. You last reviewed your personnel file on

_____.
Date

Summary of Your Rights Under the Fair Credit Reporting Act

Para informacion en espanol, visite www.ftc.gov/credit o escribe a la FTC Consumer Response Center, Room 130-A 600 Pennsylvania Ave. N.W., Washington, D.C. 20580

The federal Fair Credit Reporting Act (FCRA) promotes the accuracy, fairness, and privacy of information in the files of consumer reporting agencies. There are many types of consumer reporting agencies, including credit bureaus and specialty agencies (such as agencies that sell information about check writing histories, medical records, and rental history records). Here is a summary of your major rights under the FCRA. **For more information, including information about additional rights, go to www.ftc.gov/credit or write to: Consumer Response Center, Room 130-A, Federal Trade Commission, 600 Pennsylvania Ave. N.W., Washington, D.C. 20580.**

- **You must be told if information in your file has been used against you.** Anyone who uses a credit report or another type of consumer report to deny your application for credit, insurance, or employment – or to take another adverse action against you – must tell you, and must give you the name, address, and phone number of the agency that provided the information.

- **You have the right to know what is in your file.** You may request and obtain all the information about you in the files of a consumer reporting agency (your "file disclosure"). You will be required to provide proper identification, which may include your Social Security number. In many cases, the disclosure will be free. You are entitled to a free file disclosure if:
  - A person has taken adverse action against you because of information in your credit report;
  - You are the victim of identify theft and place a fraud alert in your file;
  - Your file contains inaccurate information as a result of fraud;
  - You are on public assistance;
  - You are unemployed but expect to apply for employment within 60 days.

  In addition, as of September 2005 all consumers are entitled to one free disclosure every 12 months upon request from each nationwide credit bureau and from nationwide specialty consumer reporting agencies. See www.ftc.gov/credit for additional information.

- You have the right to ask for a credit score. Credit scores are numerical summaries of your credit-worthiness based on information from credit bureaus. You may request a credit score from consumer reporting agencies that create scores or distribute scores used in residential real property loans, but you will have to pay for it. In some mortgage transactions, you will receive credit score information for free from the mortgage lender.

- You have the right to dispute incomplete or inaccurate information. If you identify information in your file that is incomplete or inaccurate, and report it to the consumer reporting agency, the agency must investigate unless your dispute is frivolous. See www.ftc.gov/credit for an explanation of dispute procedures.

- Consumer reporting agencies must correct or delete inaccurate, incomplete, or unverifiable information. Inaccurate, incomplete or unverifiable information must be removed or corrected, usually within 30 days. However, a consumer reporting agency may continue to report information it has verified as accurate.

- Consumer reporting agencies may not report outdated negative information. In most cases, a consumer reporting agency may not report negative information that is more than seven years old, or bankruptcies that are more than 10 years old.

- Access to your file is limited. A consumer reporting agency may provide information about you only to people with a valid need – usually to consider an application with a creditor, insurer, employer, landlord, or other business. The FCRA specifies those with a valid need for access.

- You must give your consent for reports to be provided to employers. A consumer reporting agency may not give out information about you to your employer, or a potential employer, without your written consent given to the employer. Written consent generally is not required in the trucking industry. For more information, go to www.ftc.gov/credit.

- You may limit "prescreened" offers of credit and insurance you get based on information in your credit report. Unsolicited "prescreened" offers for credit and insurance must include a toll-free phone number you can call if you choose to remove your name and address from the lists these offers are based on. You may opt-out with the nationwide credit bureaus at 1-888-567-8688.

Summary of Your Rights Under the Fair Credit Reporting Act

- You may seek damages from violators. If a consumer reporting agency, or, in some cases, a user of consumer reports or a furnisher of information to a consumer reporting agency violates the FCRA, you may be able to sue in state or federal court.

- Identify theft victims and active duty military personnel have additional rights. For more information, visit www.ftc.gov/credit

States may enforce the FCRA, and many states have their own consumer reporting laws. In some cases, you may have more rights under state law. For more information, contact your state or local consumer protection agency or your state Attorney General. Federal enforcers are:

Type of Business:	Contact:
Consumer reporting agencies, creditors and others not listed below	Federal Trade Commission Consumer Response Center - FCRA Washington, DC 20580 877-382-4357
National banks, federal branches/agencies of foreign banks (word "National" or initials "N.A." appear in or after bank's name)	Office of the Comptroller of the Currency Compliance Management, Mail Stop 6-6 Washington, DC 20219 800-613-6743
Federal Reserve System member banks (except national banks, and federal branches/agencies of foreign banks)	Federal Reserve Board Division of Consumer & Community Affairs Washington, DC 20551 202-452-3693
Savings associations and federally chartered savings banks (word "Federal" or initials "F.S.B." appear in federal institution's name)	Office of Thrift Supervision Consumer Complaints Washington, DC 20552 800-842-6929
Federal credit unions (words "Federal Credit Union" appear in institution's name)	National Credit Union Administration 1775 Duke Street Alexandria, VA 22314 703-519-4600
State-chartered banks that are not members of the Federal Reserve SystemRequired	Federal Deposit Insurance Corporation Consumer Response Center 2345 Grand Avenue, Suite 100 Kansas City, Missouri 64108-2638 877-275-3342
Air, surface, or rail common carriers regulated by former Civil Aeronautics Board or Interstate Commerce Commission	Department of Transportation Office of Financial Management Washington, DC 20590 202-366-1306
Activities subject to the Packers and Stockyards Act, 1921	Department of Agriculture Office of Deputy Administrator - GIPSA Washington, DC 20250 202-720-7051

Summary of Your Rights Under the Fair Credit Reporting Act (Page 2 of 2)

Authorization to Obtain Consumer Credit Report

To: _____

From: _____

Date: _____

Your consumer credit report will be obtained from a consumer reporting agency for employment related purposes.

Your signature below will indicate you authorize _____ (the Company) to obtain your consumer report from a Consumer Reporting Agency. If you wish us to provide you with a copy of the report, please include your address where indicated. This authorization is in accordance with the Fair Credit Reporting Act.

Signature _____ Date _____

Yes, I wish to receive a copy of my consumer report.
Please send it to:

Representative _____

Company Name _____

Address _____

City _____ State _____ Zip _____ - _____

Authorization to Obtain Consumer Credit Report

Certification to Consumer Credit Reporting Agency

This notice is to certify that _____ (the Company) is in compliance with the Fair Credit Reporting Act.

Authorization to receive a consumer report has been obtained in writing from

_____ .

Applicant Name

Information received will be used for employment related purposes. No information contained in any report received by the Company from a Consumer Reporting Agency will be misused in violation of federal or state equal employment opportunity laws or regulations.

Before adverse action is taken based on the report you provide, a copy of the report and a summary of rights under the Fair Credit Reporting Act will be provided to the subject of the report.

Signature of Company Representative _____ Date _____

Adverse Action Notice

To: _____

From: _____

Company Name: _____

Date: _____

Adverse action (i.e. denial of job application, reassignment, termination, denial of promotion)

This notice is provided to you in accordance with the Fair Credit Reporting Act and/or applicable state law. The following adverse employment action has been taken against you based at least in part on a consumer credit report, or investigative consumer report, received, with your prior authorization, from a Consumer Reporting Agency (CRA):

The report was supplied by:

Consumer Reporting Agency _____

Address of CRA _____

City _____ State _____ Zip _____

(____) ____ - _____
Telephone Number of CRA (toll-free number required if nationwide CRA)

The CRA that supplied the report did not make the decision to take the adverse action and cannot give specific reasons for it. You have a right to dispute directly with the CRA the accuracy or completeness of any information the agency furnished, as well as a right to free consumer report from the CRA upon request within 60 days from the date shown above.

Disclosure and Authorization to Obtain Investigative Consumer Report

In connection with my application for employment or promotion or other job change, I understand that

_____ (the Company) may obtain an INVESTIGATIVE CONSUMER REPORT that will include information as to my character, general reputation, personal characteristics and mode of living. This report may reveal information about work habits, including oral assessments of my job performance, experiences and abilities, along with reasons for termination of past employment. Such a report may be requested by the Company or on behalf of the Company. Further, I understand and agree that the Company may request information from various federal, state, and other agencies, including public and private sources which maintain records concerning my past activities relating to my driving record, credit history, criminal record, civil matters, previous employment, educational background and professional licensing if any.

Report will be ordered from:

Consumer Reporting Agency Name

Address

City _____ State ___ Zip _____

( ) ___ - ___
Telephone

You have the right, upon written request made within a reasonable period of time (not to exceed 30 days) after receipt of this notice to receive a written disclosure of the nature and scope of any investigation.

If a consumer investigative report is obtained and an adverse decision is made affecting your employment, the Company will provide to you, before making the adverse decision, a copy of the investigative consumer report and a description in writing of your rights under the Fair Credit Reporting Act.

****

NOTICE TO CALIFORNIA APPLICANTS

You have a right to obtain a copy of any investigative consumer report obtained by

_____ by checking the box provided below. The report will be provided to you within three business days after the report is provided to

I request to receive a free copy of this report by checking this box. ☐

Under section 1786.22 of the California Civil Code, you may view the file maintained on you by the consumer reporting agency named above during normal business hours. You may also obtain a copy of this file upon submitting proper identification and paying the costs of duplication services, by appearing at the Consumer Reporting Agency identified above in person or by mail. You may also receive a summary of the file by telephone. The agency is required to have personnel available to explain your file to you and the agency must explain to you any coded information appearing in your file. If you appear in person, a person of your choice may accompany you, provided that this person furnishes proper identification.

Disclosure and Authorization to Obtain Investigative Consumer Report (Page 1 of 2)

Disclosure and Authorization to Obtain Investigative Consumer Report

I acknowledge that a fax or copy of this Disclosure and Authorization bearing my signature shall be as valid as the original. This release is valid for all federal, state, county and local agencies and authorities. I acknowledge that I have received a copy of the Summary of Rights pursuant to the Fair Credit Reporting Act (FCRA).

Name

Address

City _____ State ___ Zip _____

( ) ___ - ___   SSN
Home Telephone

Date of Birth   Driver's License #

Applicant Signature   Date

Disclosure and Authorization to Obtain Investigative Consumer Report (Page 2 of 2)

Nondisclosure or Use of Trade Secrets Policy

During the term of employment with _____ (the Company), employees may have access to and become familiar with information of a confidential, proprietary, or secret nature, which is or may be either applicable or related to the present or future business of the Company, its research and development, or the business of its customers. For example, trade secret information includes, but is not limited to, devices, inventions, processes and compilations of information, records, specifications, and information concerning customers or vendors. Employees shall not disclose any of the above-mentioned trade secrets, directly or indirectly, or use them in any way, either during the term of their employment or at any time thereafter, except as required in the course of employment with the Company. The above agreement should not be construed as constituting a promise of continued employment for at-will employment purposes.

Customer Lists

The employee understands that customer lists of _____ (the Company), for which the employee has or will have access to during the employee's employment, are trade secrets and shall be solely the property of the employer.

The employee agrees that he/she shall neither directly nor indirectly solicit business as to products or services competitive with those of the Company based on information from the customer lists.

v020608

Voice-Mail and E-Mail Policy

Voice-Mail and E-mail Policy

Company-maintained systems: Voice-mail and electronic mail (e-mail) systems including texting, pagers, and mobile email are maintained by _____ (the Company) in order to facilitate Company business. Therefore, all messages sent, received, composed, and/or stored on these systems are property of the Company.

Personal use extremely limited: These systems are to be used by employees in conducting business and are not for employees' personal use. The Company understands that on occasion immediate family members may need to leave messages on the voice-mail system for an employee, and is willing to accommodate such personal use of the system to a limited degree. However, personal use of the voice-mail system which interferes with an employee's work performance will not be tolerated.

Privacy not guaranteed: The Company reserves the right to access an employee's voice-mail (outgoing and incoming) and e-mail messages at any time. Therefore, an employee's outgoing voice-mail message must not indicate to the caller that his/her incoming message will be confidential or private. The existence of a password on either system is not intended to indicate that messages will remain private, and passwords must be made known to the Company by all employees.

Erasure not reliable: Employees should be aware that even when a message has been erased, it still may be possible to retrieve it from a backup system. Therefore, employees should not rely on the erasure of messages to assume a message has remained private.

Message access: Messages on the voice-mail and e-mail systems are to be accessed only by the intended recipient and by others at the direct request of the intended recipient. However, the Company reserves the right to access messages on both systems at any time. Any attempt by persons other than the above to access messages on either system will constitute a serious violation of Company policy.

Harassment and discrimination: Messages on the Company voice-mail and e-mail systems are subject to the same policies regarding harassment and discrimination, as are any other workplace communications. Offensive, harassing or discriminatory content in such messages will not be tolerated.

Cell Phone Policy

Cell Phone Policy

v050006

(Choose the option that applies to your Company regarding prohibiting or allowing personal use of Company cell phones and delete the other. Note: *Prohibited Use of Company Cell Phone While Driving* and *Prohibited Use of Company Cell Phone While Driving for Employees Under 18* are required by law effective July 1, 2008 and should be included in your cell phone policy. The texting portion of the policy is a violation of law effective January 1, 2009.)

Prohibiting Personal Use of Company Cell Phone

Employees who are provided a Company cell phone may use the phone for personal reasons only in case of an emergency. Other personal use is prohibited.

Personal Use of Company Cell Phone

Employees who are provided a Company cell phone may use up to _____ (amount of time) for personal use. Employees are responsible for paying for additional time.

Employees are prohibited from using Company issued cell phones and other Company property to conduct personal business.

Prohibited Use of Company Cell Phone While Driving

In the interest of the safety of our employees and other drivers, _____ (the Company) employees are prohibited from using cell phones while driving on Company business and/or Company time.

If your job requires that you keep your cell phone turned on while you are driving, you must use a hands-free device. Under no circumstances should employees place phone calls while operating a motor vehicle while driving on Company business and/or Company time. The Company recommends preprogramming frequently used numbers into your phone rather than looking up numbers before dialing them. *Violating this policy is a violation of law beginning July 1, 2008 and a violation of Company rules.*

Writing, sending, or reading text-based communication – including text messaging, instant messaging, and e-mail – on a wireless device or cell phone while driving is also prohibited under this policy. *Violating this policy is a violation of law beginning January 1, 2009 and a violation Company rules.*

Prohibited Use of Company Cell Phone While Driving for Employees Under 18

Beginning July 1, 2008, a person under the age of 18 years is prohibited from driving a motor vehicle while using a wireless telephone, even if equipped with a hands-free device, or while using a mobile service device. The prohibition would not apply to such a person using a wireless telephone or a mobile service device for emergency purposes. *Violating this policy is a violation of law beginning July 1, 2008 and a violation of Company rules.*

Writing, sending, or reading text-based communication – including text messaging, instant messaging, and e-mail – on a wireless device or cell phone while driving is also prohibited under this policy. *Violating this policy is a violation of law beginning January 1, 2009 and a violation of Company rules.*

Option -
You must also safely pull off the road before conducting Company business.

Authorization to Release Personnel Records

I understand that the policy of _____ (company name) is to release the following information to potential employers:

• • • • •

_____
_____
_____

I hereby authorize _____ (company name) to release additional information regarding my employment with the company. The information to be released is denoted by my initials.

___ Eligibility for rehire
___ Reason for separation
___ Last salary

___ Copies of performance reviews
___ Job description for position last held
___ Other (please list in the space below)

_____
_____
_____
_____
_____

_____ (company name) is authorized to release the additional information initiated above to other potential employers upon their request for the following period of time: (Check and initial one)

___ Indefinitely
___ The next 90 days
___ Other (please define the time period) _____

___ The next 30 days
___ The next 12 months

Employee's signature: _____
Date: _____
Received by: _____
Title: _____
Date: _____

Authorization to Release Personnel Records

Pre-Adverse Action Disclosure

To: _____

From: _____

Company: _____

Date: _____

Adverse action (i.e. denial of job application, reassignment, termination, denial of promotion)

This disclosure is to inform you that the following adverse employment action may be taken against you, based at least in part on a consumer report received, with your prior authorization, from a Consumer Reporting Agency (CRA):

_____
_____
_____
_____
_____
_____

Enclosed is a copy of your consumer report and a "Summary of Your Rights Under the Fair Credit Reporting Act" from the Federal Trade Commission. This disclosure is provided to you in accordance with the Fair Credit Reporting Act.

Pre-Adverse Action Disclosure

Records Retention Requirements

Numerous federal and state laws have specific records retention periods for specific records made in, or collected in connection with, employment. Often the same records have different retention periods under different laws. Keep records for the longest period of time required by any applicable law or circumstance, as specified in the following chart.

Personnel Data Category	Longest Retention Period	Laws Requiring Retention
Recruitment, Hiring, and Job Placement Records • Job applications • Resumes • Other job inquiries sent to employer • Employment referral records • Applicant identification records • Help wanted ads • Opportunities for training, promotion or overtime • Job opening notices sent to employment agencies or labor unions • Employment testing results	2 years (Or the duration of any claim or litigation involving hiring practices)	Title VII FEHA ADA ADEA
Payroll Records • Name, employee number, address, age, sex, occupation • Individual wage records • Time and day work week begins • Regular hourly rate • Hours worked (daily and weekly) • Weekly overtime earnings • Daily or weekly straight time earnings • Deductions from or additions to wages • Wages paid each pay period • Payment dates and periods • Piece rates	4 years	FLSA Cal. Unemployment Insurance Code
Employee Wage Records • Time cards • Wage rate calculation tables for straight time and overtime • Shift schedules • Individual employees' hours and days • Piece rates • Records explaining wage differentials between sexes	3 years	FLSA Cal. Labor Code
Employment Eligibility Forms Verification (I-9 Forms)	The later of 3 years from hire date or 1 year after termination	Immigration Reform and Control Act
Child Labor Certificates and Notices	3 years	FSLA Cal. Labor Code

Records Retention Requirements (Page 1 of 2)

Records Retention Requirements

Personnel Data Category	Longest Retention Period	Laws Requiring Retention
Employee Personnel Files • Disciplinary notices • Promotions and demotions • Performance evaluations • Discharge, layoff, transfer, and recall files • Training and testing files • Physical files	2 years	Title VII ADEA FEHA ADA
Affirmative Action Programs and Documents	5 years (Discretionary, but recommended)	Title VII EO11246
Employee Health Records • First aid records for job injuries causing loss of work time • Drug and alcohol test records	5 years (Chemical safety and toxic exposure records must be kept for duration of employment, plus 30 years)	OSHA Cal-OSHA
Unlawful Employment Practices, Claims, Investigations and Legal Proceedings Records • Personnel and payroll records about complaining parties • Personnel and payroll records about all others holding or applying for similar positions	Until disposition of case	
Union and Employee Contracts	3 years	Title VII FEHA ADEA ADA NLRA FLSA
Employee Benefits Data	**6 years, but not less than 1 year following a plan termination** Documentation of benefits elections, beneficiary designations, eligibility determinations, COBRA Notices and summary plan descriptions and earnings. Records required to determine retirement benefits, including 401(k) and similar plans, must be kept indefinitely.	ERISA

Records Retention Requirements (Page 2 of 2)

Notice of Intent to Obtain Consumer Report

To: _____

From: _____

Company: _____

Date: _____

Your consumer report will be obtained from a Consumer Reporting Agency for employment related purposes.

A copy of the report will be provided to you, free of charge, if you wish. This notice is provided to you in accordance with the Fair Credit Reporting Act.

Notice of Intent to Obtain Consumer Report

Drugs, Alcohol and Smoking In the Workplace

Eliminating substance abuse in the workplace is good for business. It reduces health insurance costs, improves employee productivity and reduces the likelihood of accidents, which adversely affects workers' compensation costs. California has gone so far as to eliminate smoking from the workplace.

This chapter familiarizes you with the federal and California Drug-Free Workplace Acts, local ordinances and federal Department of Transportation (DOT) testing regulations. This chapter also provides detailed discussion about testing, privacy issues, disability discrimination and drug use, rehabilitation, smoking in the workplace and policy creation for your workplace.

Download forms referenced in this chapter at **www.calbizcentral.com/support**. Be sure to have your access code from the inside covers of this book ready to enter into the forms download area. Your access code for the forms in the online Formspack is on the inside covers of this book. See "Forms Available Online" on page xix for more information.

Federal Drug-Free Workplace Act of 1988

If you enter into a federal contract for the procurement of property or services valued at $100,000 or more or receive any federal grant, you must follow the regulations of the Drug-Free Workplace Act of 1988.[1] The Act requires you to certify to the federal agency issuing the contract that you will provide a drug-free workplace. This certification requires you to create a plan that provides for a drug-free workplace, and to file that plan with the federal government.

To do business with the federal government, you must:

- Certify to the government agency with whom you are doing business that you maintain a drug-free workplace. The government does not approve or disapprove drug testing of employees, but false certification is grounds for suspending or terminating the contract. Serious lack of drug enforcement in the workplace could result in being barred from obtaining any further contracts with the federal government;

- Publish, circulate and provide each employee a statement notifying him or her that it is unlawful for them to manufacture, distribute, dispense, possess or use a controlled substance in your workplace. The statement must specify the penalties for each violation;

- Establish a "Drug-Free Awareness Program" to inform your employees about:

  - The dangers of drug abuse in the workplace;

  - Your policy of maintaining a drug-free workplace;

  - The availability of any drug counseling, rehabilitation or employee assistance programs (EAPs); and

---

1.41 U.S.C. 701 et. seq.

- The penalties that may be imposed upon employees for drug abuse violations in the workplace.

- Notify all employees in a written statement that, as a condition of employment, employees must:

  - Abide by the terms of the program; and

  - Notify you of any criminal drug statute conviction for a violation occurring in the workplace no later than five days after such a conviction. You must report the violation to the government contracting office within 10 days of receiving notice of the conviction.

- Impose corrective measures on the employee convicted of drug abuse violations in the workplace within 30 days after receiving notice of his/her conviction, and:

  - Take action against the employee, up to and including termination; or

  - Require the employee to satisfactorily participate in a drug abuse assistance or rehabilitation program approved by federal, state or local health, law enforcement or other appropriate agency.

If you fail to follow the requirements of the Drug-Free Workplace Act, you may be subject to suspension of payments on a federal contract or grant, and even barred from receiving future contracts.

California's Constitutional Right to Privacy

Numerous states, including California, have drug testing laws. However, California is one of seven states whose constitutions also guarantee an individual's right to privacy.[2] This guarantee places additional restrictions on laws and regulations applying to alcohol and drug testing programs.

California's Drug-Free Workplace Act

California's Drug-Free Workplace Act of 1990 is almost identical to the federal act, but applies only to persons or businesses contracting with or receiving grants from California state government.[3] Each of these businesses must certify that it does or will provide a drug-free workplace before doing business with the state.

The state requires you to:

- Write and publish a statement notifying all employees that it is unlawful to manufacture, distribute, dispense, possess or use a controlled substance, and that such acts are prohibited in your workplace. If any violation of the policy occurs, advise the employee of what actions you will take against him/her for these violations;

- Establish a drug-free awareness program that informs all employees about:

  - The dangers of drug abuse in the workplace;

  - Your policy of maintaining a drug-free workplace;

  - The availability of drug counseling, rehabilitation and EAPs; and

  - The penalties that you may impose upon employees for drug abuse violations.

---

2. California Constitution, Article 1 sec. 1
3. Gov't. Code sec. 8350

- Give each employee engaged in the state contract a copy of your statement that, as a condition of employment on the state's contract or grant, the employee agrees to abide by the statement's terms.

As required by the federal government, the state also requires organizations awarded a state contract or grant to provide a drug-free workplace program or be subject to suspension of payments or termination of the contract or grant.

The state may suspend or terminate the contract if you:

- Have made false certifications of a drug-free workplace program; and/or

- Violate the certification by failing to carry out the requirements of its drug-free workplace program.

Local Drug Testing Ordinances

The cities of Berkeley and San Francisco have enacted local ordinances relating to drug testing. In those cities, you may wish to consult legal counsel before engaging in drug testing of any kind.

Berkeley's ordinance prohibits drug testing of public sector applicants and employees within city limits. The federal DOT drug testing regulations (discussed in this chapter) would likely take precedence over this ordinance.[4] (See "Transportation Industry Testing" on page 203.)

San Francisco's ordinance limits testing of employees, but places no restrictions on testing of applicants.

The ordinance requires that the following conditions exist:

- Reasonable grounds to drug test;

- A clear and present physical danger to the employee, another employee or members of the public; and

- The opportunity for the employee to retest the sample by another facility.[5]

Transportation Industry Testing

In 1994, the DOT issued drug and alcohol testing regulations covering about seven million employees in the transportation industry, pursuant to the Omnibus Transportation Employee Testing Act (OTETA).[6] The regulations, developed and administered by the DOT, apply to employees under the Federal Highway Administration (FHWA); the Federal Railroad Administration (FRA); the Federal Transit Administration (FTA); the Federal Aviation Administration (FAA); and the Research and Special Programs Administration (RSPA).

The OTETA regulations prohibit:

- Being on duty while having an alcohol concentration of 0.04 or greater;

- Possessing alcohol;

4.The City of Berkeley, Labor Bill of Rights, Res. No. 54, 533-N.S.

5.San Francisco, CA Municipal Code Pt. II, Police Code, Chapter VII sec. 3300A.1 et.seq (1985)

6.Pub. L. No. 102-143; 59 Fed Reg. 7301; 49 CFR 382

- Using alcohol on duty;

- Using alcohol before duty;

- Using alcohol after an accident;

- Refusing to submit to a required alcohol or controlled substances test;

- Reporting for or remaining on duty when using a controlled substance, except when used pursuant to a physician's instructions, and when the physician advised a driver that the substance does not adversely affect the ability to operate a commercial motor vehicle; and

- Any driver who has tested positive for controlled substances from remaining on duty or performing safety-sensitive functions.

The regulations allow you to require a driver to advise you of any therapeutic drug use.

The regulations also require you to:

- Maintain records related to:

  - The testing process;

  - Test results;

  - Substance abuse professional evaluations; and

  - Violations of the regulations.

- Maintain calendar-year summaries of results of alcohol and controlled substances testing programs using required management information system forms;

- Provide information when a driver applies for a position with a new employer;

- Obtain information on:

  - A prospective driver's alcohol tests with a 0.04 or greater concentration level;

  - Refusals to be tested; and

  - Positive controlled substances test results.

- Prohibit a driver from performing safety-sensitive functions for more than 14 days if the above information is not obtained;

- Provide specific educational materials to drivers and obtain a signed certificate of receipt for the materials; and

- Provide at least two hours of alcohol and controlled substance training to supervisors.

A driver who engages in conduct prohibited by the regulations must:

- Be removed from safety-sensitive functions;

- Be referred to a substance abuse professional for evaluation, unless:

  - The driver is an applicant; or

  - The positive test is for alcohol at a concentration of 0.02 or greater but less than 0.04.

- Obtain a negative result in a return-to-duty test;

- Properly follow a rehabilitation program if recommended; and

- Be subject to unannounced follow-up testing following a return to duty.

The DOT revised transportation employee drug and alcohol testing regulations in 2001. Highlights of the revised rules include:

- A requirement that you obtain drug and alcohol test results from applicants' previous employers from the past two years;

- Mandatory validity testing for all specimens;

- Options for temporarily removing employees from safety-sensitive duties before final verification of a positive, adulterated or substituted laboratory test result;

- Service agents (such as labs, technicians and medical review officers) who fail or refuse to comply with the rules may be temporarily barred from providing drug testing services to DOT-covered employers;

- Enhanced training requirements for collectors, technicians, medical review officers and substance abuse professionals;

- Changes in specimen collection procedures and laboratory processes;

- New forms;

- Education and/or treatment for all applicants who have positive test results or refuse to test;

- Greater use of electronic means to transmit and store data; and

- Specific requirements for releasing information to employees and third parties.

A summary of the revised rules (and a link to the published rules) is available on the U.S. DOT Web site at **www.dot.gov/ost/dapc/NEW_DOCS/part40.html?proc**.

Triple Damages For Injury

You may be liable for triple damages when one of your commercial vehicle drivers injures another person in the course of employment if:

- The driver of the commercial vehicle was under the influence of alcohol or a controlled substance at the time of the injury; and

- You willfully failed at the time of the injury to comply with DOT testing requirements.[7]

Pre-Employment Requirements

An applicant for employment as a commercial driver or as an owner-operator may not be placed on duty until receiving a negative test result for all required DOT testing.[8] In addition, you must complete a full investigation of the driver's employment history as required by federal law. You must, whether making or receiving inquiries concerning a driver's history, document all steps you take to comply with this requirement.[9]

7.Civ. Code sec. 3333.7
8.Vehicle Code sec. 34520(e)
9.Vehicle Code sec. 34520(f)

Pre-employment Screening Services

You may use a pre-employment screening service to review applications if the screening services provided satisfy the requirements of state and federal law. You must abide by any of the screening service's findings that disqualify an applicant from operating a commercial vehicle.[10]

Penalties

Violation of these new laws is a misdemeanor punishable by six months in jail and/or a fine of up to $5,000.[11]

The California Highway Patrol (CHP) may suspend your motor carrier permit for up to a year for failure to comply with the DOT testing regulations, or failure to make copies of test results and other records available for inspection by the CHP.[12]

Termination Not Justified Despite Two Positive Drug Tests

The U.S. Supreme Court ruled that an employer may be required to reinstate a truck driver to his job even though the driver was fired for two positive drug tests.

The driver, James Smith, worked for Eastern Associated Coal Corporation in West Virginia for 17 years. Since his job required driving heavy vehicles on public highways, Smith was subject to federal DOT random drug testing requirements. After he tested positive for marijuana in 1996, Smith was disciplined and required to undergo random drug tests for five years. A year later he again tested positive for marijuana and Eastern discharged him.

Smith's union went to arbitration, and an arbitrator concluded that Smith's use of marijuana did not amount to "just cause" for discharge. The arbitrator ordered that Smith be reinstated after a three-month suspension, subject to further random testing and substance abuse treatment. Smith also was ordered to pay arbitration costs and provide a signed, undated resignation letter, to take effect if he again tested positive within the next five years.

Eastern brought suit in federal court, arguing the award contravened public policy against the operation of dangerous machinery by workers who test positive for drugs. Though recognizing there is a strong public policy against drug use by workers in safety-sensitive jobs, the U.S. Supreme Court unanimously held that Smith's conditional reinstatement did not violate that policy. It found that DOT's drug testing regulations do not mandate the discharge of a worker who twice tests positive for drugs, and instead favors rehabilitation of employees who use drugs.[13]

Employer Not Responsible for Lab Error

A federal appeals court refused to hold an employer liable for the acts of a drug testing facility. In that case, a driver subject to DOT-mandated testing was terminated for a positive drug test result. The driver claimed the testing facility was negligent in its collection procedure, resulting in a false

---

10. Vehicle Code sec. 34520(g)
11. Vehicle Code sec. 34520(h)
12. Vehicle Code sec. 34623(c)
13. *Eastern Associated Coal Corp. v. United Mine Workers of America*, 531 US 57 (2000)

positive result. The court held that even if the employer thought the test was inaccurate, it was prohibited by law from employing a driver who tested positive, since DOT regulations do not permit drivers who test positive to remain "on duty."[14]

Circumstances In Which You May Require Drug Testing

In essence, there are five typical circumstances in which an employer may want to drug test:

- Pre-employment screening;
- As part of a physical examination;
- "Reasonable suspicion;"
- Post-accident testing; and
- Random testing.

The following is a discussion of each of these circumstances, and the legal restrictions placed upon each type of testing.

Screening of Applicants or Employees Seeking Promotion

Drug testing in pre-employment physicals has become a generally accepted practice. Most employers can require an applicant, as a condition of hiring, to successfully pass a pre-employment drug screen.[15]

The federal Americans with Disabilities Act (ADA) and California's Fair Employment and Housing Act (FEHA) place restrictions on the timing of any pre-employment medical examination. You can only require a medical examination after you make an offer of employment and before the beginning of the applicant's duties. However, a test to determine whether an applicant is illegally using drugs is *not* considered a medical examination. Therefore, if you wish to conduct a drug test even before making a conditional offer of employment to an applicant, that test must be designed to accurately identify illegal drugs and should not be performed in conjunction with any pre-employment physical examination.

The California Supreme Court has addressed the issue of drug testing current employees seeking promotions. In that case, applicants for employment as well as current employees seeking promotions were required to undergo urinalysis testing for drugs and alcohol. The court upheld the portion of the drug testing program requiring applicants to undergo testing, but found the requirement that current employees be tested was unconstitutional.[16]

Suspicionless Drug Test Immediately After Employment

Though suspicionless drug testing must take place before the beginning of employment, a California Court of Appeal recently held that post-employment suspicionless testing may be permitted in limited circumstances. The case involved an applicant who was offered a job on the condition that he pass a drug test. Due to the complications of relocating his family for the

---

14.*Carroll v. Federal Express Corporation*, 113 F.3d 163 (Ninth Cir. 1997), cert. denied, 118 S. Ct. 852 (1998)

15.*Wilkenson v. Times Mirror Corp.*, 215 Cal. App. 3d 1034 (1989)

16.*Loder v. City of Glendale*, 14 Cal. Fourth 846 (1997)

new job, the future employee on two separate occasions requested and was granted a delay in the date for which the test was scheduled. The employee was placed on payroll, spent a few hours filling out hiring paperwork, and then took four days off to find a new home. When the employee finally took the drug test and tested positive for marijuana, the employer withdrew the offer of employment.

The employee sued, claiming that since he had been placed on the payroll he no longer was an applicant, and therefore could not be subjected to a suspicionless drug test. The Court of Appeals held that:[17]

> ... a job applicant, who requests and receives a delay in submitting to the pre-employment drug test... until after the start of employment, may not evade the employer's testing requirement post-employment on the ground the applicant thereby became an "employee" and is, consequently, immune from such testing. In such circumstances, and for purposes of suspicionless drug testing, the job applicant who caused the drug testing delay must submit to such testing after the employment date. If the "employee" fails the test given in the brief period between employment and administration of the test, that employment, conditioned on passing the test which the "employee" delayed, may be terminated.

Routine Testing in Annual or Periodic Physical Examinations

Although the issue is not yet determined in California, federal courts and some state courts approved testing as part of annual or periodic physical examinations, particularly in union employment relationships governed by collective bargaining agreements.[18] However, under the ADA and FEHA, the physical examination must be either part of a voluntary employee health program or job-related and consistent with business necessity.

If you choose this type of testing program, you should notify employees that drug and alcohol tests will be administered as part of the physical examination and advise employees that you may take disciplinary action if they refuse to consent to a test. However, an employee's refusal to consent to the release of purely medical information obtained from the test cannot be the basis for discipline under the California Confidentiality of Medical Information Act.[19] Accordingly, inquire only of a doctor's opinion concerning whether the employee is able to satisfactorily perform his/her job duties.

Random Drug Testing

"Random" drug testing programs are those in which an employer informs employees that they may have to submit to drug testing at any time during their employment for any reason or for no reason at all. Although these may be the most effective programs to detect and deter drug or alcohol use, their legality, particularly in California, is extremely limited.

Cases upholding random drug testing are limited to those involving employees in specific, narrowly defined job classifications or professions that may be categorized as part of a pervasively regulated industry (where the employee has less expectation of privacy given the nature of employment) or where positions are critical to public safety or the protection of life, property or national security. For example, random testing has been upheld for truck drivers under the FHWA regulations,[20] certain

---

17. *Pilkington Barnes Hind v. Superior Court,* 66 Cal. App. 4th 28 (1998)

18. See e.g., *International Brotherhood of Teamsters v. Department of Transportation,* 932 F.2d 1292 (9th Cir. 1991); *Amalgated Transit Union Division 1279 v. Cambria County Transit Authority,* 691 F. Supp. 898 (W. D. Pa. 1988)

19. Civ. Code sec. 56.20(b)

pipeline workers,[21] aviation personnel[22] and correctional officers having contact with prisoners.[23]

Further, according to the American Professional Captain's Association, a random test program is required for all licensed officers on vessels that require a license to operate. It also includes all crew members working on those boats requiring a licensed officer. Because the pre-employment test is given with notice, it does not replace the need for a random program to exist. However, a random program, if already in place, may be used in lieu of a pre- employment test."

With these exceptions, random drug testing is not allowed in California. In a case involving the type of justification needed to test employees, the court held that any intrusion into an individual's privacy "must be justified by a compelling interest." The court found that the employer's concern in that case about deterrence, efficiency, competency, a drug-free environment, rule enforcement and ensuring public confidence in the railway system were not compelling interests. Moreover, the court held that safety was not a compelling reason for testing the employee involved — a computer operator for a railroad in a nonsafety sensitive position — and that her discharge for refusing to consent to the test breached the covenant of good faith and fair dealing.[24]

Reasonable Suspicion Testing

"Reasonable suspicion" has been defined by one court as something less than probable cause but more than mere suspicion. It is suspicion that requires further investigation and which has some factual foundation in the surrounding circumstances observed in light of the observer's knowledge.[25] Specific objective facts and rational inferences drawn from those facts must justify reasonable suspicion. Evidence sufficient to justify reasonable suspicion does not need to rise to the level of full probable cause. This may include alcohol on the breath, lapses in performance, inability to appropriately respond to questions and physical symptoms of alcohol or drug influence.[26]

The constitutionality of a drug test under the California Constitution is evaluated by balancing the employee's reasonable expectation of privacy against the employer's legitimate interests in imposing the test. If a drug test is not triggered by a reasonable belief the employee is intoxicated, the employee may have a stronger reason to expect to maintain his or her privacy and the employer may have less need to demand the test.

In one case, an employer lost its motion for summary judgment after the employee, a former secretary, demonstrated there was a factual dispute over whether her employer had reason to believe she was impaired, and that the supervisors who requested the test bore her some personal animosity that could have affected the decision. Nonetheless, the court found the existence of reasonable cause was relevant to determining the constitutionality of defendant's drug test demand. Without requiring an employer to exhibit reasonable cause for imposing the test, an employer with a valid drug testing policy would have free license to conduct random testing at any time.

20. *International Brotherhood of Teamsters v. Department of Transportation,* 932 F.2d 1292 (9th Cir. 1991)
21. *International Brotherhood of Electrical Workers v. Skinner,* 913 F.2d 1454 (9th Cir. 1990)
22. *Bluestein v. Skinner,* 908 F.2d 454 (9th Cir. 1990)
23. *Taylor v. O'Grady,* 888 F.2d 1189, 1199 (7th Cir. 1989)
24. *Luck v. Southern Pacific Transportation Co.,* 218 Cal. App. 3d 1 (1990), cert. denied, 111 S.Ct. 344 (1990)
25. *City of Palm Bay v. Bauman,* 475 So. 2d 1322 (Fla. Dist. Ct. of App. 1985)
26. *Assoc. of Western Pulp and Paperworkers v. Boise Cascade Corp.,* 644 F. Supp. 183, 186 (D. Or. 1986)

The employee's declarations that she never used drugs, that she did not appear intoxicated and the suggestion that the employer wanted to fire the employee created a factual issue as whether the employer had reasonable cause to give plaintiff a drug test. The employee did not consent to a random drug test, and plaintiff's submission to a pre-employment drug test did not eliminate her reasonable expectations of privacy in relation to a random drug test.[27]

Post-accident Testing

Courts have generally upheld post-accident testing where an employer has reasonable suspicion that an employee involved in the accident was under the influence of drugs and/or alcohol, or if the accident was a serious one.[28] Consistent with that concept, the Supreme Court upheld the FRA's post-accident drug testing regulations even though the regulations did not require individual suspicion of drug use.

Employee Privacy and Drug Testing

Although the courts have addressed the issue of drug testing, the right of private employers to test current employees for drugs and alcohol remains somewhat unsettled.

In a 1997 case, the California Supreme Court refused to allow Glendale, California., to drug test current employees applying for promotions, but did allow testing of applicants. The case applied the law relating to public employers, analyzing whether the city violated the federal Fourth Amendment constitutional right against unreasonable search and seizure by the government. This analysis would not apply to a private employer wanting to drug test current employees. However, the court also considered the right to privacy under the state constitution in its decision, which would apply to private employers.[29]

In a 1994 California Supreme Court case, the court considered the privacy rights of college athletes being randomly tested for drugs by an intercollegiate athletic association. In a statement that sheds some light on the right of private employers to randomly drug test, the Court stated:

> We intimate no views about the legality of blanket or random drug testing conducted by employers, whether of current employees or applicants for employment, or by other kinds of entities. Employment settings are diverse, complex, and very different from intercollegiate athletic competition. Reasonable expectations of privacy in those settings are generally not diminished by the emphasis on bodily conditions, physical training, and extracurricular competition inherent in athletics.[30]

Based on this case, it is extremely risky to randomly drug test except in the fairly unique circumstance, as with college athletes, where an employee's expectation of privacy might reasonably be diminished. You must now show that the invasion of privacy is justified because it "substantially furthers" one or more legitimate and important interests outweighing the privacy interest of the employee.

27. *Fraslawsky v. Upper Deck, Inc.* 56 Cal. App. 4th 179 (1997)
28. *International Brotherhood of Teamsters v. Department of Transportation,* 932 F.2d 1292 (9th Cir. 1991)
29. *Loder v. City of Glendale,* 14 Cal. 4th 846 (1997)
30. *Hill v. NCAA, 7 Cal. 4th 1 (1994)*

Denial of Unemployment Benefits

The California Unemployment Insurance (UI) Appeals Board ruled in 1988 that positive drug tests can disqualify discharged workers from receiving unemployment compensation, as long as workers agreed to the tests and the tests are scientifically accurate. The Board said that every employer and employee has a vital interest in its workplace being drug free. The Board added that it is the right of an employer or other employees to create and maintain a workplace free of illegal drugs.

The ruling resulted from a case in which a janitor was fired by Kaiser Permanente after 16 years of employment and filed for UI benefits. The janitor had been placed in a rehabilitation program by Kaiser and had agreed to counseling. A subsequent urine test revealed the presence of methamphetamines. When he applied for UI benefits, he was denied. The Board said that the janitor waived his constitutional right to privacy by agreeing to random testing. The Board added that the janitor showed a disregard of a standard of behavior that the employer had a right to expect. The Board overruled an administrative law judge who decided in the janitor's favor.

In a 1987 decision, the Board ruled that for purposes of the UI law, drug tests were permissible when employers have reasonable suspicion that a worker in an inherently dangerous occupation is impaired.[31]

Denial of Workers' Compensation Benefits

You have no liability under workers' compensation laws for on-the-job injuries sustained in the course of employment by your employees or for the death of any employee if the proximate cause of the injury or death is alcohol intoxication or unlawful use of a controlled substance.[32]

Termination for Violating Testing Agreement

A California Court of Appeal refused an employee's claim that he was wrongfully terminated when he failed to comply with the terms of a drug treatment plan to which he had agreed. After the employee divulged a drug and alcohol problem, the employer paid for treatment at a private clinic, temporarily assigned the employee to a less stressful position at full pay and entered into a rehabilitation/treatment agreement with the employee. The employer terminated the employee when he allowed unsafe work to be performed, appeared at work under the influence of alcohol and/or drugs, missed work on several occasions and failed to attend required therapy sessions.[33]

---

31. *Ables v. Shultz Steel Co.* No. P-B-454 (1987)
32. Lab. Code sec. 3600
33. *Gosvener v. Coastal Corp.,* 59 Cal. Rptr. 2d 339 (1996)

Disability Discrimination and Drug Use

The federal ADA and the California FEHA do not protect individuals who currently use drugs. You may refuse to hire or discipline or terminate any individual who currently uses controlled substances illegally or who is addicted to them, regardless of whether the illegal usage has any effect on job performance, without being in conflict with the discrimination provisions of ADA or FEHA. However, illegal use of drugs does not include the use of drugs taken under the supervision of a licensed health-care professional. To assure that this requirement is met, you should give the employee an opportunity to discuss and explain test results. For more information, see Chapter 29, "Disabilities In the Workplace."

The ADA and FEHA protect persons who formerly abused alcohol or illegal drugs and who successfully rehabilitated themselves either through a supervised rehabilitation program or through their own program, and who no longer uses illegal drugs. This protection extends to individuals participating in a drug or alcohol rehabilitation program.

The Ninth U.S. Circuit Court of Appeals ruled that a blanket prohibition on re-employment of workers terminated for violating company policy may violate the ADA if it excludes recovered drug or alcohol abusers from re-employment. Hughes Missile Systems allowed an employee to resign in lieu of termination after he had a positive drug test and an alcohol problem. He applied for rehire three years later, with evidence attesting to his recovery. After review of his application and the personnel record, he was found ineligible for rehire because of the company's policy prohibiting rehire of terminated employees. The appeals court ruled that the application of the blanket rule resulting in the employee's rejection was unlawful and the policy invalid as applied to recovered drug or alcohol abusers.[34]

You may have an employment policy in accordance with the Drug-free Workplace Act that prohibits employees from being under the influence of drugs or alcohol while in the workplace without running contrary to the ADA or FEHA. You can require your employees who have drug or alcohol dependencies to maintain the same job performance standards as other employees, and you have the right to discipline or terminate employees for lack of job performance, tardiness, excessive absences, workplace accidents, etc.

"Legal" Marijuana User Not Protected

NEW for 2009 Employers have the right to enforce a drug-free policy in their workforce, even though medical marijuana use is permitted under state law. When an employer received the results of a pre-employment drug test, it discharged an employee after eight days of employment for marijuana use. The employee sued for wrongful termination, employment discrimination and breach of contract. He alleged that he was permitted to use marijuana under his doctor's prescription for pain pursuant to the California Compassionate Use Act of 1996.

Gary Ross suffers from chronic back pain. His doctor prescribed marijuana, pursuant to the Compassionate Use Act to obtain relief. Because of his condition, Ross is considered a qualified individual with a disability under the FEHA. After RagingWire Telecommunications, Inc., offered Ross a job as a lead systems administrator, it required him to take a drug test as a condition of employment. Ross tested positive for marijuana. RagingWire reviewed Ross's documentation regarding his marijuana use but fired him because he failed the drug test.

---

34. *Hernandez v. Hughes Missile Systems Company*, 298 F.3d 1030 (9th Cir., 2002)

Ross claimed his disability and use of marijuana to treat pain does not affect his ability to perform the essential functions of the job for which he was hired. Thus, Ross claimed that RagingWire violated FEHA because the company failed to make reasonable accommodation for his disability. RagingWire countered that it terminated Ross based on its policy to deny employment to people who test positive for illegal drugs. Ross was essentially asking RagingWire to accommodate his marijuana use at home by waiving its policy requiring a negative drug test of new employees. Ross claims that his marijuana use is akin to the use of insulin or other prescription medications that are legal under California law.

However, according to the state Supreme Court, the Compassionate Use Act did not give marijuana the same legal status of other legal prescription drugs because marijuana is still an illegal drug under federal law. Further, the Act only specifies that users of marijuana under the Act are only exempted from criminal liability. Indeed, FEHA does not require employers to accommodate the use of illegal drugs nor does the Act address the issue as it impacts California employers. If the Legislature intended the Act to impact employer rights, legislators would have stated as much in the law. The Legislature has not.[35]

Recent Drug and Alcohol Abuse Not Protected

The ADA does not protect workers participating in drug or alcohol rehabilitation programs unless they have refrained from drug or alcohol use for a significant period of time, according to a 2001 decision of the federal 9th Circuit Court of Appeals. For more information about this case, see "Recent Drug and Alcohol Abuse Not Protected" in Chapter 29, page 873.

Drug Use at Work Not Protected Disability

Terminating an employee for engaging in the illegal use of drugs at work is not an ADA violation. A decision of the Ninth Circuit Court of Appeals in 1995 held that such a discharge is based on the employee's misconduct rather than any disability (drug addiction) that would otherwise be protected under the ADA.[36]

The Ninth Circuit case clarifies that the ADA does not protect individuals currently using illegal drugs. You may discharge or deny employment to persons who illegally use drugs. However, employees who have either been rehabilitated successfully or are in the process of completing a rehabilitation program are protected under the ADA. It is highly recommended that you thoroughly investigate any suspected illegal use of drugs before discharging those involved. An individual discharged after erroneously being perceived as a drug addict is likely to have a valid claim under the ADA and FEHA, but performance of a good faith investigation may serve in your defense.

---

35. *Ross v. Ragingwire Telecommunications, Inc.* 42 Cal. 4th 920. (2008)
36. *Collings v. Longview Fibre Co.,* 63 F.3d 828 (9th Cir. 1995), cert. denied, 116 S.Ct. 711 (1996)

Wrongful Discharge and Drug Testing

California courts developed at least three wrongful discharge theories, which employees discharged for refusing to submit to drug testing can employ as a basis for suits.

These are:

- Breach of an explicit or implied-in-fact contract to discharge only for "good cause;"

- Breach of an implied covenant of good faith and fair dealing; and

- Termination in violation of public policy.[37]

In the public policy cases, the public policy at issue was whether the company violated the constitutional right of privacy by terminating an employee who refused to submit to a random drug test. A significant damage award was provided by a jury to an employee who was wrongfully terminated for refusing to submit to a random drug test.[38]

Drug-Free Workplace Policies

Taking into account this chapter's review of case law, you may want to create a drug-free workplace policy, regardless of whether your company comes under the requirements of the Drug-Free Workplace Act. You also may want to add a policy or create a drug-free workplace provision to your employee handbook.

Policy Guidelines

Take the following steps when developing a drug-free workplace policy:

- Thoroughly brief all supervisors about the drug-free workplace program and impress upon them the purpose and seriousness of the policies;

- Train your supervisors to identify signs of drug or alcohol use. Typical signs are frequent absences, chronic tardiness or early departure, excessive use of sick leave, bankruptcy, increased medical claims, decreased productivity, accidents resulting in injury, theft, misrepresentations or lying. Employees who exhibit a relatively sudden personality change are often suspect. Supervisors should keep written records of such problems and review them for patterns;

- Establish a policy banning the use, possession or sale of drugs in the workplace and on company property. The policy should assert that drug use is extremely harmful to workers' health, interferes with productivity and alertness and that a worker under the influence of drugs is a danger to himself/herself and to fellow workers;

- Establish a disciplinary policy for those found using, possessing or selling drugs on company premises. Discipline may range from a warning to immediate termination of employment. Emphasize a counseling and/or a rehabilitation program; any court that hears an employee challenge to an employer's drug-free workplace policy will look favorably on this emphasis;

- Identify areas of high risk (areas that contain hazardous materials, machines requiring high skills, or other potentially dangerous equipment, etc.) and jobs where drug-impaired personnel may place other employees or members of the general public at risk. The security and safety of

---

37. *Luck v. Southern Pacific Transportation Co.*, 218 Cal. App. 3d 1 (1990); *Semore v. Pool*, 217 Cal. App. 3d 1087 (1990)
38. *Semore v. Pool*, 217 Cal. App. 3d 1087 (1990)

employees, property and the company's clientele are your primary goals. Remember, there must be a connection between any job you designate requiring drug testing and a legitimate business need. Subject all violations of the company's drug policy to company disciplinary procedures;

- Ask company supervisors to review the outline of a drug-free workplace policy when completed. Their input is important because they will eventually police employees. The policy should clearly state the supervisors' role. You may choose to ask employees for comment before putting the plan into effect;

- Advise all employees in writing of the program and have them sign a statement acknowledging they have read your policy. This form should be placed in the employee's personnel file. You must make the program clear to all employees, along with an announcement of when the policy becomes effective and, advising all employees of a grace period if one has been adopted;

- Consider financing a rehabilitation plan or giving time off, with or without pay, to permit employees to enroll in a rehabilitation plan. Be careful to establish clear rules concerning those who would qualify for the company's rehabilitation plan. Working under a federal contract requires you to establish an employer assistance program. State law requires California employers to reasonably accommodate employees who wish to enter an alcohol or drug rehabilitation program; and

- Follow-up on the program once it has been installed. One person should have the responsibility for monitoring and coordinating the program. This responsibility should include counseling employees, enforcing drug testing, recommending discipline and rehabilitation programs and working out the termination procedure. Include a serious employee educational program in the drug-free workplace policy.

Drug Testing as Part of Policy

If you decide to make drug testing part of your drug-free workplace policy, you must decide:

- Which jobs require drug testing? Among those you should consider are those that involve job safety or public safety, or company or national security. Remember that a drug testing requirement should always be job-related;

- When do you test an employee: Pre-employment? During employment? Promotion? Transfer? After a workplace crisis? Only in certain workplaces?

- What are the costs of drug testing? Drug testing should be conducted only by a licensed laboratory acting under U.S. Department of Health and Human Services guidelines. Drug tests should not be conducted by a place selected by the employee;

- What penalties should the employee expect if tests are positive and what procedures, if any, should be followed after a drug violation is determined?

- If you have adopted a rehabilitation policy, at what point should you require the employee to enroll in it?

- What is the company policy if an employee refuses to be tested or to enter a rehabilitation program?

 You must retain drug testing records in a private file separate from the employee's personnel file for at least as long as you would retain any other medical record.

Example of Drug-Free Workplace Policy

Consider the example of a *Drug-Free Workplace Policy* when developing a policy. Of course, you should adapt any drug-free workplace policy to meet the particular needs of your company. Do not use the sample policy without careful review.

Drug or Alcohol Rehabilitation

If you have 25 or more employees, you must reasonably accommodate any employee who volunteers to enter an alcohol or drug rehabilitation program, provided the reasonable accommodation does not impose an undue hardship on you.[39] Reasonable accommodation includes, among other actions, time off with or without pay and adjusting of working hours. You do not need to provide time off with pay. The employee may use whatever sick time that he/she is entitled.[40] The employee may file a complaint with the Labor Commissioner's office if he/she believes that he/she has not been reasonably accommodated.[41]

You must take reasonable measures to safeguard the privacy of the employee concerning his/her enrollment in an alcohol or drug rehabilitation program.[42] You or your representative cannot misrepresent the performance record of an employee who voluntarily left, or prevent the employee from getting another job.[43]

Even if you are not required to provide such rehabilitation, you should consider offering this option rather than discharging an employee. Programs designed to assist employees and deter drug use are not only good policy, but they are also more likely to be looked upon favorably by juries in wrongful discharge cases than would be programs aimed at punishing employees with admitted drug or alcohol problems.

Employee Assistance Programs

Many companies developed EAPs in the workplace to provide treatment and counseling for employees' drug- and alcohol-related problems, and to address financial, emotional and other personal problems related to these areas. EAPs enable you to address the issue of drugs in the workplace in a nonthreatening and cost-effective manner. Although you may be reluctant to incur the cost of instituting an EAP, many companies faced with an extensive drug problem are likely already paying a high price in absenteeism, accidents, workers' compensation claims, poor performance and medical costs. Successful treatment under an EAP can considerably reduce these costs. In addition, implementing an EAP can improve employee morale by demonstrating to employees the humane manner in which you address the issue.

The goal of an EAP can be both rehabilitation and prevention. It may be established in-house, by utilizing an outside program or a combination of the two. In addition, an EAP may offer a number of services, ranging from referral to treatment to employee education to an explanation of options for an employee concerned about his/her own use of drugs or alcohol.

Referral to an EAP may occur in several ways. The most widely used approach is constructive confrontation, which generally utilizes a system of progressive discipline to provide employees

39.Lab. Code sec. 1025
40.Lab. Code sec. 1027
41.Lab. Code sec. 1028
42.Lab. Code sec. 1026
43.Lab. Code sec. 1050

feedback on work performance and to modify their behavior. At each such disciplinary step, the employee is offered help through the EAP.

Constructive confrontation serves two purposes:

- Identifying troubled employees; and
- Attempting to motivate them to change their behavior.

To make constructive confrontation successful, supervisors must be well-trained and willing to use the strategy.

Smoking In the Workplace

The public debate over the issue of smoking in public places, and particularly the workplace, has been ongoing over the past several decades. In 1994, this debate came to a zenith with legislation and a statewide initiative directing public attention to this important matter.

California Labor Code section 6404.5, which took effect in 1995, placed a uniform statewide ban on smoking in the workplace, with limited exceptions, and overrode local ordinances on the subject.

The law specifically supersedes any local ordinances regulating smoking in the workplace.

Prohibiting Smoking In Enclosed Spaces

You may not knowingly permit the smoking of tobacco products in an enclosed space at a place of employment. This prohibition includes permitting nonemployees to smoke in an enclosed workplace. The law exempts a number of workplaces from these prohibitions, as discussed in "Exceptions to the Ban on Workplace Smoking" on page 218.

A law passed in 2006 clarifies that the prohibition on knowingly permitting smoking in enclosed spaces in places of employment includes lobbies, lounges, waiting areas, stairwells, elevators and restrooms. It prohibits smoking inside public buildings, except in covered parking lots.[44]

Prevention of Smoking by Nonemployees

When you permit nonemployees access to the workplace on a regular basis, the following steps must be taken to prevent liability for violation of this law when nonemployees smoke on the premises:

- Where smoking is prohibited throughout the building, a sign stating "No Smoking" must be posted at each entrance to the building;
- Where smoking is permitted in designated areas of the building under one of the law's limited exceptions, a sign stating "Smoking is prohibited except in designated areas" must be posted at each entrance to the building; and

---

44. Gov't. Code sec. 7596; Lab. Code sec. 6404.5

- Nonemployees who are smoking must be requested, where "appropriate," to refrain from smoking. The law does not define when it is appropriate to make such a request.

The law specifies that it is not necessary, in complying with the law, to:

- Physically eject a nonemployee from the workplace; or

- Make a request to a nonemployee to refrain from smoking, under circumstances involving a risk of physical harm to your employees.

Exceptions to the Ban on Workplace Smoking

The following places of employment are exempted from the complete ban on smoking in the workplace:

- 65 percent of the guest room accommodations in a hotel, motel or similar transient lodging establishment;

- Areas of the lobby in a hotel, motel or other similar transient lodging establishment designated for smoking by the establishment. Such an establishment may permit smoking in a designated lobby area that does not exceed 25 percent of the total floor area of the lobby or, if the total area of the lobby is 2,000 square feet or less, an area that does not exceed 50 percentof the total floor area of the lobby. "Lobby" means the common public area of such an establishment in which registration and other similar transactions are conducted and in which the establishment's guests and members of the public typically congregate;

- Meeting and banquet rooms in a hotel, motel or other transient lodging establishment similar to a hotel or motel, restaurant or public convention center, except while food or beverage functions are taking place, including set-up, service and clean-up activities, or when the room is being used for exhibit purposes. At times when smoking is not permitted in a meeting or banquet room, the establishment may permit smoking in corridors and pre-function areas adjacent to and serving the meeting or banquet room if no employee is stationed in that corridor or area other than on a passing basis;

- "Private smokers' lounges," defined as any enclosed area in or attached to a retail or wholesale tobacco shop dedicated to the use of tobacco products, including cigars and pipes;

- "Retail or wholesale tobacco shops," defined as any business establishment in which the main purpose is the sale of tobacco products, including cigars, pipe tobacco and smoking accessories;

- Cabs of motor trucks or truck tractors if no nonsmoking employees are present;

- Warehouse facilities with more than 100,000 square feet of total floor space, and 20 or fewer full-time employees working at the facility. Smoking is not permitted in any area within such a facility that is utilized as office space;

- Theatrical production sites, if smoking is an integral part of the story in the theatrical production;

- Medical research or treatment sites, if smoking is integral to the research and treatment being conducted;

- Private residences, except for private residences licensed as family-day care homes, during the hours of operation as family day-care homes and in those areas where children are present;

- Patient smoking areas in long-term health-care facilities; and

- Break rooms you designate for smoking, provided that all of the following conditions are met:

– An exhaust fan must divert air from the smoking room directly to the outside. Air from the smoking room may not be recirculated to other parts of the building;

– You must comply with any ventilation standard or other standard utilizing appropriate technology, including mechanical, electronic and biotechnical systems, adopted by the Occupational Safety and Health Administration (OSHA) or the federal Environmental Protection Agency (EPA);

– The smoking room must be located in a nonwork area where no one, as part of his/her work responsibilities, is required to enter. "Work responsibilities" does not include any custodial or maintenance work carried out in the break room when it is unoccupied; and

– There are sufficient nonsmoking break rooms to accommodate nonsmokers.

Exception for Employers of Five or Fewer Employees

If you have a total of five or fewer full- and part-time employees, you may permit smoking in enclosed areas if all of the following conditions are met:

• The smoking area is not accessible to minors;

• All employees who enter the smoking area consent to permit smoking. No one may be required to work in an area where smoking is permitted. Using coercion to obtain consent or requiring an employee to work in the smoking area subjects an employer to a fine of up to $7,000;

• Air from the smoking area must be exhausted directly to the outside by an exhaust fan. Air from the smoking area may not be recirculated to other parts of the building; and

• The employer must comply with any ventilation standard or other standard utilizing appropriate technology, including mechanical, electronic and biotechnical systems, adopted by OSHA or the federal EPA.

Total Ban Permissible

You retain the right to prohibit smoking in an enclosed place of employment for any reason. Even if you are totally or partially exempted under the law, you may nonetheless choose to prohibit smoking in the workplace entirely.

Fines

Violation of this statewide workplace smoking ban is punishable by a fine up to $100 for the first violation, $200 for the second violation and $500 for the third and subsequent violations in one year.

Chapter 9 Forms

This chapter contains samples of forms associated with this topic. *The forms in this section are for visual reference only; download the most up-to-date forms and checklists in their entirety from CalBizCentral.*

To download either individual forms or your entire Formspack containing all the forms referenced in this book:

1. Visit ***www.calbizcentral.com/support*** and select "Labor Law Digest" from the list of product titles.

2. Have this copy of Labor Law Digest handy — you will need to enter the access code featured on the inside covers of this book.

3. Enter the access code, select the documents you want to download to your computer, then follow the on-screen instructions.

For more detailed instructions, see "Forms Available Online" on page xix.

Drug-Free Workplace Policy

Note: Use this policy only if your company is required to have a drug-free workplace because you are a federal contractor or grantee as defined under the Drug Free Workplace Act.

1. **Purpose:** The purpose of this policy is to furnish disciplinary and rehabilitative guidelines for handling first-time violators of the illegal drug prohibitions set forth in Section 2 of this policy.

2. **Coverage:** This policy covers only regular employees who are first-time violators of any one of the following prohibitions:

   a. Use, possession, offer for sale, or being under the influence of illegal drugs during working hours, including lunch and break periods.

   b. Use, possession, offer for sale, or being under the influence of illegal drugs on

      _____ (the Company) property at any time.

      For purposes of this policy, engaging in any of the activities above shall be considered as a violation of the Company policy.

3. **Alternatives to Discharge:** The guidelines in the policy are alternatives to immediate discharge. The refusal of an employee covered by this policy to comply with the specified guidelines shall result in the immediate discharge of that employee.

4. **Rehabilitation:** An employee covered by this policy shall enroll in and complete an approved rehabilitation treatment program as determined by an outside treatment professional approved by the Company. The employee shall bear the costs of the rehabilitation program and shall be entitled to utilize whatever available vacation, sick, and/or medical leave benefits necessary for program participation. An employee's refusal to enroll in and complete such rehabilitation program shall be grounds for discharge.

5. **After-care:** An employee covered by this policy shall enroll in and complete an approved after-care program as determined by an outside treatment professional approved by the Company. The recommended after-care program must also be approved by the Company. The employee shall bear the cost of the after-care program and shall be entitled to utilize whatever available vacation, sick, and/or medical leave benefits are necessary for program participation. An employee's failure to complete the after-care program shall be grounds for discharge.

6. **Exemption from Rehabilitation and After-care:** At the discretion of the Company, based upon the recommendation of an outside treatment professional, an employee covered by this policy may be exempt from the rehabilitation and after-care provisions of this policy. Such employee, however, may be required to enroll in a substance abuse education or similar program approved by the Company.

7. **Outside Treatment Professionals:** The outside treatment professional referred to in Sections 4, 5, and 6 above shall be selected from an established list of treatment professionals maintained by the Company.

✕ calbizcentral™

© CalChamber   Page 1 of 1

Drug-Free Workforce Policy

Chapter 10

Arbitrating Employment Claims

Resolving employment disputes in court is a costly and often lengthy process. Arbitration is an alternative, which offers the ability to resolve issues more quickly and economically. Arbitration is the final and binding settlement of disputes between parties by a method voluntarily agreed to by the parties themselves, including the selection of the person to serve as arbitrator.

 As this chapter demonstrates, the status of the law relating to mandatory arbitration is always being challenged. Be sure to consult with legal counsel to ensure your agreements are consistent with the current status of the law.

This chapter defines arbitration, provides you with some useful historical background and discusses the advantages and disadvantages of using it as a strategy to resolve disputes. It also discusses state and federal laws which permit you to make arbitration mandatory as a condition of employment, and the pitfalls of an improperly drafted agreement for mandatory arbitration of employment disputes. It explains how to measure the benefits of arbitration, when and how to obtain and implement arbitration agreements with your employees and where to find arbitrators.

Background

Although the common law originally frowned upon agreements to waive access to a judicial forum and to submit the dispute to binding arbitration, the Federal Arbitration Act (FAA) of 1925 made private agreements to arbitrate disputes enforceable when the agreement was contained in a commercial contract and when the dispute arose out of that contract or transaction involving that contract. At the time of the FAA's passage, statutory claims generally were not considered arbitrable.

Arbitration gained popularity after World War II as a method of settling union-management disputes and as an alternative to litigation within the business community. The Supreme Court viewed arbitration extremely favorably as a method of resolving disputes in labor management communities.[1] The most common form found in collective bargaining agreements is referred to as "grievance arbitration." This is an alternative to having the collective bargaining agreement enforced by the courts in which the parties agree to an alternative system of arbitration to resolve their disputes over the meaning and interpretation of that agreement.

---

1. *Textile Workers v. Lincoln Mills*, 353 U.S. 448 (1957)

Advantages Over Litigation

As a practical matter, by using arbitration rather than the court system the employee is simply trading one forum for hearing the dispute (the court system) for another (the arbitrator).

However, there are significant reasons to prefer final and binding arbitration over a judicial forum for wrongful discharge claims and other employment disputes. Among the advantages of arbitration are the expertise of specialized, experienced employment law professionals who understand the applicable law and the realities of the workplace, who have decided similar disputes, and who are relatively insulated from community pressures and attitudes that tend to influence juries. Unlike a jury trial, both arbitration as a private dispute resolution mechanism and the arbitrator's award generally are treated as confidential unless the parties agree otherwise.

Other major advantages include the significant saving of time, expense and trouble. Arbitration can resolve disputes more quickly than litigation. The average time between the filing of a grievance in the collective bargaining context and the ultimate arbitration decision is less than one year, compared to the costly prolonged technical procedures of court where frequent continuances and appeal of judgments can lead to significant additional years and costs of litigation. Without a jury present, the hearing usually is conducted expeditiously, and arbitrators tend to render decisions significantly more quickly than judges burdened by an ever-increasing workload. Moreover, a court may overturn an arbitrator's award only on very narrow grounds, such as where the award was procured by fraud or the arbitrator exceeded his/her jurisdiction by deciding an unsubmitted issue. Thus, unlike in court, where appeals from judgments often are routine, arbitration tends to be final. These advantages also accrue to employees, who may have similar concerns regarding time, expense and hassle.

This principle of limited review of arbitration awards, established to assure the finality of arbitration decisions, prevented review of an award where the arbitrator allegedly misinterpreted state law. The losing party argued that the decision should be set aside because the arbitration agreement instructed the arbitrator to apply California law in reaching his decision. The court was asked to find that by incorrectly applying the law, the arbitrator exceeded his authority, a basis for invalidating the award.

The court ruled that there was no evidence that the arbitrator applied any law other than California's. Thus the parties got what they bargained for, and neither party was entitled to court review of whether he applied it incorrectly.[2]

Although some might claim that the finality of arbitration is a disadvantage to employers, the opposite is true. Arbitrators know that issuance of decisions either extreme in nature or without basis will result in refusal by similarly situated parties to select that arbitrator in the future. Thus, there is institutional pressure for arbitrators to render only reasonable and well-supported decisions.

Disadvantages of Arbitration

Although arbitration is generally less costly than litigation, it occasionally can be more expensive. For example, a judge can dismiss a lawsuit at the summary judgment stage, long before the employer incurred the legal costs of discovery and a trial. Summary judgment is a ruling that there is no material issue of fact to dispute, and one party is entitled to win as a matter of law without a trial. There is no equivalent to summary judgment in arbitration.

2.*Baize v. Eastridge Companies,* 142 Cal. App.4th 293 (2006)

Another potential disadvantage to arbitration is that there is almost no opportunity for appeals. Both parties generally must accept the judgment of the arbitrator as final.

Mandatory Arbitration Agreements

State and federal law permit you to require employees to submit most employment disputes to arbitration, with certain restrictions and safeguards.

California Standards for Mandatory Arbitration

The California Supreme Court confirmed that employers have the right to require employees to sign take-it-or-leave-it arbitration agreements as a condition of employment. The court, however, placed certain restrictions on those agreements, without which the agreements may be unenforceable. The court said it will refuse to enforce an arbitration agreement that is procedurally and substantively "unconscionable." An arbitration agreement is procedurally unconscionable if one party insists on it, and has such bargaining power over the other that the other party can't refuse to accept it. An arbitration agreement is substantively unconscionable if, by its terms, it is so one-sided that it is unfair.[3]

An arbitration agreement will be set aside only if it is both procedurally and substantively unconscionable. Where an agreement is found to be procedurally unconscionable, a sliding scale is applied based upon the degree of substantive unfairness. Thus, an agreement that has been imposed on one party may still be enforceable if the terms of the agreement are not found to be too unfair. [4]

Conditions for Mandatory Arbitration

Under California law, arbitration agreements covering wrongful termination or employment discrimination claims under California's Fair Employment and Housing Act (FEHA) must:[5]

- Provide a neutral arbitrator who sets forth a written arbitration decision. This will allow a court, if necessary, to review the essential findings and conclusions on which an award is based;

- Provide time and access for adequate discovery. This means there must be a fair and simple method for the employee to get information necessary for his or her claim, including access to essential documents and witnesses, as determined by the arbitrator;

- Not limit the employee's potential damages to less than what could be awarded in court. This means an employee must be able to seek all available remedies, including punitive damages and any attorneys' fees;

- Not generally require the employee to pay any type of expense he/she would not be required to pay if he/she were free to bring the action in court. For example, employees cannot be required to pay arbitrators' fees, generally ranging from $200 to $1,000 per day or more, since they would never be required to pay for a judge in court; and

---

3.*Armendariz v. Foundation Health Psychcare Services, Inc.*, 24 Cal.4th 83 (2000)
4.*McManus v. CIBC World Markets Corp.*, 109 Cal App. 4th 76 (2003)
5.*Armendariz v. Foundation Health Psychcare Services, Inc.*, 24 Cal.4th 83 (2000)

- Not be overly harsh or one-sided. An agreement would generally not be enforceable if it requires employees to arbitrate all claims but leaves the employer free to pursue claims against the employee in court.

Arbitration may be used to resolve employment disputes involving wage and hour issues as well. A California Court of Appeal enforced an agreement to arbitrate where several store managers filed a class action lawsuit alleging that their employer improperly classified them as exempt employees and refused to pay overtime compensation. The court granted the employer's motion to compel arbitration, approving arbitration on a class basis, but postponed the arbitration proceeding until the court itself could decide which employees would be in the class whose rights would be determined.[6]

The California Supreme Court ruled that the enforceability standards set forth in its *Armendariz* decision apply equally to arbitration of nonstatutory claims, such as wrongful termination, as they do to claims based upon statutory rights, such as violations of FEHA. The court also approved enforcement of mandatory arbitration where certain portions of the underlying arbitration agreement are contrary to those standards, but can be severed from the agreement. The objectionable provision in that case permitted either party to appeal an award in excess of $50,000 to a second arbitrator. The court ruled that provision unenforceable, but then enforced the rest of the provisions. Finally, the court discussed the fact that the arbitration provision was silent as to the apportionment of arbitration costs, but ruled that rather than set aside the agreement, such silence permitted an inference that the employer pay all costs of arbitration.[7]

No Wrongful Termination for Refusal to Sign Arbitration Agreement

A California Court of Appeal has held that an employer may terminate or refuse to hire an individual who will not sign a predispute arbitration agreement as a condition of employment.[8] In this case, an employer required all employees to sign an agreement requiring that work-related disputes be resolved through binding arbitration. An employee was terminated for refusing to sign the agreement and sued for wrongful termination. He alleged that it was a violation of public policy to terminate an employee for refusal to give up one's constitutional rights to a jury trial and a judicial forum for the resolution of disputes. The court disagreed, finding that "general social policies will be advanced by not allowing a wrongful termination claim. This is so because public policy favors the resolution of disputes through arbitration. To impose liability in a case such as this would thwart that policy."

A California appeals court also compelled arbitration for an executive-level employee, ruling that he cannot avoid contractual arbitration and instead go to court to enforce his right to profit-sharing and severance pay when his employment involved interstate commerce. Federal law preempts California law on the issue of mandatory arbitration when the employee has dealings in more than one state. Further, the employee's claim for multiple millions of dollars does not fall under nonwaivable wage claims under state law. Thus, the arbitration clause in his employment agreement was valid and enforceable under California law.[9]

James Giuliano served as executive vice president and chief financial officer of Inland Empire Personnel, Inc., for two years, during which time he attended meetings, site visits and grand opening visits, and negotiated multimillion-dollar loan agreements in California and other states. Upon hire, he signed binding arbitration agreements with Inland Empire relating to the resolution of disputes under the employee handbook, the bonus plan and in his employment agreement. The

---

6.*Sanders v. Kinko's Inc.*, 99 Cal. App. 4th 1106 (2002)
7.*Little v. Auto Stiegler, Inc.*, 29 Cal. 4th 1064 (2003)
8.*Lagatree v. Luce, Forward, Hamilton & Scripps*, 74 Cal.App.4th 1105 (1999)
9.*Giuliano v. Inland Empire Personnel, Inc.*, 149 Cal. App. 4th 1276 (2007)

bonus plan and employment agreement arbitration clauses included waivers of the parties' right to go to court.

When Giuliano left Inland Empire, he claimed he was owed a $5 million to $8 million profit-sharing bonus and a $500,000 severance agreement under his employment agreement. He claimed the arbitration agreements were unenforceable under California law. The court disagreed because the FAA preempts state arbitration laws. The FAA establishes the strong federal policy of enforcing arbitration of contracts involving interstate commerce. The interstate nature of Giuliano's employment was undisputed.

Giuliano also claimed that his right to court enforcement of his unpaid wage claims was not waivable under California law and public policy. He relied on the *Armendariz* case in which the California Supreme Court explained that the right to enforce claims under the California FEHA or claims closely tied to a fundamental public policy in court cannot be waived. This court emphasized that Giuliano's contract claim for more than $8 million is distinguishable from a case involving unpaid overtime or failure to pay minimum wage.

However, this court did not address the enforceability of the arbitration agreement. The court discussed only the public policy in favor of resolving disputes through arbitration as opposed to going to court.

Arbitration Agreements and Class Action Lawsuits

According to the California Supreme Court, class action waivers in arbitration agreements may or may not be enforced, depending on whether the class arbitration would be a significantly more effective way of vindicating the rights of employees than individual arbitration. If a dispute involves a small amount of damages, and a group of employees with the same dispute, then class arbitration may be the most efficient and least expensive way of enforcing employee rights. Further, if one provision of an arbitration agreement is deemed unenforceable, the entire agreement may still be effective depending on factors such as if the employer had superior bargaining power or the agreement gave employees fewer rights through arbitration that they would have been granted through the courts.[10]

Robert Gentry filed a class action lawsuit against Circuit City Stores, Inc., on behalf of salaried customer service managers who allegedly, were misclassified as exempt employees and were owed unpaid wages for overtime hours worked in excess of eight hours in a day or 40 hours in a week. When hired, Gentry received a packet of information including Circuit City's dispute resolution procedures and options. If employees elected arbitration to resolve employment disputes, they waived all rights to go to court as well as a class action waiver, meaning an arbitrator could only hear individual employee claims and not a group of employee claims in one case.

The Court analyzed the rights of employees to be paid minimum wage and overtime wages and confirmed that these rights cannot be waived and "arbitration cannot be misused to accomplish a *de facto* waiver of these rights." The Court defined minimal requirements for such an arbitration agreement: (1) the arbitration agreement may not limit the amount of money normally available under the statutes employees may receive if their claim is successful; (2) there must be an opportunity for employees to gather evidence sufficient to defend their claim; (3) the arbitrator must issue a written decision and judicial review to ensure the arbitrator followed all legal requirements; and (4) the employer must pay all costs that are unique to

---

10.*Gentry v. Superior Court of Los Angeles County* 42 Cal. 4th 443 (2007)

arbitration. These requirements are "necessary to enable an employee to vindicate un-waivable rights in an arbitration forum."

The Court then looked at what circumstances are appropriate for class action. Class actions enforce overtime laws by giving employees the opportunity to challenge the unlawful practice in a relatively less expensive way. The amount of the potential award in a wage and hour claim is low – the state Department of Labor Standards Enforcement records indicate the average award per employee is about $6,000.00. Further, class actions eliminate repetitious claims and provide redress for claims that would otherwise be too small to warrant individual litigation. The Court noted that individual employees may fear retaliation if they file a claim against the employer, but will feel safer in a group suit. Indeed, because employees must be notified of a class action that may impact them, class suits sometimes make employees aware of rights that they did not know they had.

The Court sent this case back to the lower court to make a determination of whether a class action in this case is appropriate based on (1) the modest size of individual recovery; (2) the potential for employer retaliation against members of the class; (3) the fact that absent members of the class may not be well informed of their rights; and (4) other "real world obstacles" of class members' right to overtime pay through individual arbitration. The Court emphasized that this analysis applies to both class action arbitration and nonarbitration.

Gentry also claimed that the arbitration agreement is not enforceable because it is unconscionable, or so one-sided to his detriment and the employer's benefit. In this case, the explanation of the benefits of arbitration did not include the significant disadvantages to arbitration under Circuit City's agreement, including a one-year statute of limitations compared to three years in court, only one year of back pay as opposed to three years through a court, a limitation on punitive damages, and giving the arbitrator the discretion to award attorneys' fees, whereas if Gentry prevailed in court he would be entitled to reasonable attorneys' fees and costs. The agreement also included a nine page, single-spaced explanatory document that the Court described as one that "only a legally sophisticated party would have understood." Circuit City's argument that it recommended employees seek legal counsel before signing was deemed "unrealistic" by the Court because only "higher echelon employees hire an attorney to review what appears to be a routine personnel document." Further, though the agreement gave employees 30 days to opt out, the materials provided to Gentry made it "unmistakably clear that Circuit City preferred that the employee participate in the arbitration program."

Because the lower court determined that the whole agreement was unenforceable, the Court sent the case back to the lower court to analyze in more detail whether voiding the agreement in its entirety was appropriate.

Federal Courts on Mandatory Arbitration

The U.S. Supreme Court agreed with the California Supreme Court in holding that employers have the right to require and enforce mandatory arbitration agreements against employees. In a 5-4 decision, the U.S. high court held that under the FAA an employer can enforce arbitration agreements that require the employee to take all employment-related disputes to arbitration rather than to court.[11]

In the past, the Ninth U.S. Circuit Court of Appeals and the California Supreme Court reached different conclusions about whether binding arbitration of discrimination claims can be made mandatory.

---

11. *Circuit City Stores v. Adams*, 532 U.S. 105 (2001)

But in 2002, the Ninth Circuit Court enforced a mandatory agreement to arbitrate a discrimination claim brought under FEHA, measuring its enforceability against the standards set by the California Supreme Court in *Armendariz*.[12] In another case, the Ninth Circuit enforced a mandatory arbitration policy where the employee acknowledged receipt of the policy, but did not exercise a chance to "opt-out." The court rejected the argument that the employee should not be bound because he did not explicitly agree to be bound.[13]

In yet another Ninth Circuit case, the court found employers that require their employees to sign "mandatory" arbitration clauses may find those clauses unenforceable. Agreements requiring arbitration of disputes arising out of the employment relationship will not be enforced if the employee has no meaningful opportunity to opt out of the agreement and if the agreement places the employer in a significantly superior legal position.[14]

In a reversal of its earlier position on arbitrating discrimination claims, the Ninth Circuit rejected its earlier decision in *Duffield* and agreed with the California Supreme Court that employers may require binding arbitration of discrimination claims with mandatory arbitration policies.[15]

The Ninth Circuit court, in an *en banc* decision, later affirmed the result of the case, although it overruled the *Duffield* decision for other reasons. Thus, employers do not discriminate when they require individuals to agree to mandatory arbitration. However, while the court ruled out discrimination, it left open the related question for employers having to do with unlawful retaliation. What remains important for employers now is whether they can enforce mandatory arbitration without being accused of unlawful retaliation. The Ninth Circuit noted that, if employers may rightfully require employees to arbitrate all employment claims, it makes no sense to treat enforcement of this right as retaliation. But, the court also said it would permit the Equal Employment Opportunity Commission (EEOC) to present its position on the retaliation question to the lower court.[16]

The Ninth Circuit reviewed two additional cases involving the Circuit City arbitration program. It refused to enforce arbitration in both, finding objectionable terms and that the employees had no meaningful opportunity to "opt out" of the program.[17]

Even where an employer has an enforceable policy requiring employees to arbitrate discrimination claims, the U.S. Supreme Court held that the EEOC may file a lawsuit for damages and other relief, though employees of the company may be unable to do so because of the binding arbitration agreement.[18]

Arbitration Agreements and State Administrative Hearings

Disputes under arbitration agreements requiring all disputes relating to the agreement to be arbitrated must be heard by an arbitrator, regardless of any state law requiring another form of dispute resolution, including administrative hearings. The U.S. Supreme Court found that attacks on an entire contract's validity, distinguished from attacks on the arbitration clause alone, fall under federal law, which dictates that such disputes must be heard by an arbitrator.[19]

---

12. *Circuit City v. Ahmed*, 283 F.3d 1198 (9th Cir., 2002)
13. *Circuit City v. Najd*, 294 F.3d 1104 (9th Cir.,2002)
14. *Davis v. O'Melveny & Myers*, (9th Cir., 2007) 485 F.3d 1066
15. *EEOC v. Luce, Forward, Hamilton & Scripp*s 303, F.3d 994 (9th Cir., 2003)
16. *EEOC v. Luce, Forward, Hamilton & Scripps*, 345 F.3d 742 (9th Cir., 2003)
17. *Ingle v. Circuit City Stores*, 328 F.3d 1165, 9th Cir., 2003; *Circuit City Stores, Inc. v. Mantor* 335 F.3d 1101 (9th Cir. 2003)
18. *EEOC v. Waffle House, Inc.*, 534 U.S. 279, (2002)
19. *Preston v. Ferreer* 128 S. Ct. 978 (2008)

Arbitration Agreement May Be Unenforceable

Despite the state and federal high court decisions upholding mandatory arbitration clauses, a court may deny enforcement of an arbitration agreement on basic contract grounds. Each of the parties has the right to show a legal reason the agreement should be revoked, just as with any other type of contract.[20]

For example, a contract could be revoked if it is or was:

- Unconscionable (extremely unfair or oppressive);

- Formed using fraud or duress;

- Entered into by one or more persons who did not have the legal capacity to do so (someone under the age of 18 or mentally incompetent); or

- Entered into by mistake.

To avoid revocation, always give employees adequate and reasonable notice of the meaning and exact scope of the arbitration agreement and its consequences.[21]

Measuring Benefit of Arbitration

Before adopting a policy requiring arbitration as a substitute for litigation in employment-related areas, determine whether such a policy is appropriate on a cost/benefit basis, and what effect it might have on existing employment relations. Some factors to consider in making this analysis:

- What is the company's history in the area of employment disputes, factoring in the number of disputes, time required and cost?

- What would be the effect on employment relations with the company's employees and on employee morale?

- Will the relatively simpler arbitration proceedings be disadvantageous?

- Will the time and cost of handling potentially more claims offset the savings the company would gain by avoiding judicial litigation of fewer claims?

New Agreements

Once you adopt a policy requiring arbitration for employment disputes, draft an arbitration agreement that defines not only what will be arbitrated, but also how covered disputes will be arbitrated.

Where the law gives some direction on a particular issue, comments appear in italics after the issue is raised. In drafting an arbitration agreement, consider the following:

- What type of disputes will be subject to arbitration? Will claims be limited only to those arising from termination of employment? Or should all employment-related disputes be arbitrated? *In making that determination, consider the method of resolution, the relative time and expense involved in arbitration versus other available proceedings and your economic liability should the employee prevail.*

---

20. Code of Civil Procedure sec. 1281; 9 U.S.C. 2

21. *Graham v. Scissor-Tail, Inc.*, 28 Cal. 3d 807 (1981); *Hope v. Superior Court*, 122 Cal. App. 3d 147, 154 (1981)

In most cases, there will be more at stake in an employment termination situation than in disputes that arise with a current employee;

- Which employees will the policy cover? Only new employees hired after the arbitration policy is in place? Or all employees? Will the policy cover only managers and supervisors only rank-and-file employees or both? *It might be appropriate to select a sampling of employees to provide you with a first experience with arbitration before making it applicable to all employees;*

- During what time limits may an employee bring any claim to arbitration? Should the employee have a shorter time in which to request arbitration than he/she would have in civil actions in court for the same type of claim? *If the agreement provides significantly shorter time than the employee would otherwise have, the employee may challenge it in court as unconscionable;*

- How and to whom does the employee request arbitration? *At a minimum, the request should be in writing to a designated company representative and contain a short statement of the claim;*

- Will the arbitration agreement require the parties to attempt some sort of voluntary dispute settlement mechanism informally before proceeding to arbitration? *It might be advisable for the parties to have a mediation step prior to arbitration, wherein a mutually selected mediator is brought in to attempt to assist the parties in resolving the dispute voluntarily, and failing that, to provide an informal opinion concerning his/her view of the ultimate outcome of the claim;*

- How will the arbitrator be selected? *Under the most common procedure, the party requesting arbitration submits a request for a list of an odd number of experienced professional arbitrators from either the California State Mediation and Conciliation Service, the American Arbitration Association or the Federal Mediation and Conciliation Service. These sources also provide extensive background descriptions of the arbitrators listed. The parties alternately strike names from the list until only one name remains;*

- What procedures will govern the conduct of the arbitration hearing, pre-hearing matters and enforcement of the arbitrator's award? *The more closely you model the arbitration procedures on comprehensive statutes, such as the California Arbitration Act, the more likely they are to be viewed as fair by the court;*

- What restrictions, if any, will apply on the remedies available in arbitration? *The California Supreme Court has said the arbitration agreement may not limit the employee's potential damages to less than could be awarded in court. This means an employee must be able to seek all available remedies, including punitive damages and attorneys' fees;* and

- How will the cost of arbitration, including the arbitrator's fee, be allocated? *The California Supreme Court has said the arbitration agreement generally cannot require employees to pay any type of expense he/she would not be required to pay if he/she were free to bring the action in court.*

Obtaining Agreements

Once you decide to require arbitration for employment disputes, secure the arbitration agreement.

Applicants

If you decide to use arbitration, provide notice of the arbitration requirements to applicants in both the employment application and the offer of employment letter. These documents should clearly provide that employment-related disputes will be subject to binding arbitration and contain a clear reference to a separate document containing the actual arbitration agreement and arbitration procedures.[22] A disclaimer clearly explaining that the applicant foregoes his/her right to pursue legal action on any claim within the scope of the arbitration agreement should preface the arbitration agreement and procedures.

Existing Employees

A more difficult question is whether you can require existing employees to arbitrate any employment-related disputes. Unlike the applicant or newly hired employee — who agrees at the outset of his/her employment relationship to binding arbitration of employment-related disputes — existing employees do not have that expectation. Unilateral imposition of a binding arbitration policy is more likely to be challenged as unconscionable because, arguably, the addition of this policy was beyond the expectations of existing employees and was not separately bargained with each employee, as was the case with the applicant/newly hired employee.

To reduce this risk, request that each employee sign an agreement acknowledging the binding arbitration policy and its provisions, and provide some sort of monetary or related inducement to the employee. Employees who sign such agreements are similarly situated to newly hired employees, and the risk of the courts finding an unconscionable contract may be reduced.

Employee Handbook Policy Change

In 2000, the California Supreme Court granted California employers the right to unilaterally terminate or change policies contained in their employee handbooks without having to be concerned about violating an implied contract of employment. According to the court, a policy may be terminated or changed as long as the employer makes the change after the policy has been in place for a reasonable time, gives employees reasonable notice and does not interfere with employees' vested benefits.[23]

Though the case addressed *terminating* or *changing* existing policies, it could arguably allow you to amend your employee handbook by *adding* a reasonable arbitration agreement to it.

Policy Presentation

Carefully consider how you present your arbitration policy to your employees. Explain the benefits of arbitration to employees before implementing the policy or executing the agreement.

The benefits of arbitration are not one-sided, and are significant for the employee as well. In talking about arbitration to employees, emphasize that employees give up no substantive rights by arbitrating rather than litigating employment disputes, but rather are selecting a different, less expensive and less time-consuming forum for resolving those disputes. In arbitration, the employee also may have legal representation. Arbitration has major benefits for employees as well, in that it is relatively fast and informal and generally simpler than judicial procedures.

The following is a typical clause providing for agreement to arbitration of employment-related disputes:

22.*Chan v. Drexel Burnham Lambert, Inc.*, 178 Cal. App. 3d 632, 641 (1986)
23.*Asmus v. Pacific Bell*, 23 Cal.4th 1 (2000)

Any controversy or claim arising·out of or relating to the employee's employment with the employer, or the termination of that employment, will be settled by binding arbitration. Judgment upon the award rendered by the arbitrator may be entered in any court having jurisdiction over the matter.

Be aware that this sample language constitutes the broadest form of an arbitration agreement and may encompass matters you do not wish to arbitrate. If you wish to restrict arbitration to certain disputes or to disputes related only to an employee's termination from employment, the language of the agreement should reflect that limitation. Consult with legal counsel before implementing an arbitration agreement.

Sources of Arbitrators

The arbitration agreement must designate a neutral body as a source of arbitration. If either party views the designated arbitration tribunal as biased, that party may later be able to have the agreement voided in court.[24]

The American Arbitration Association is a nationwide organization used for alternative dispute resolution in various types of disputes. It has rules governing such matters as the format and scheduling of initial pleadings, filing fees, selection of the arbitrator(s), availability of discovery, hearing procedures and other related matters. Similar related organizations providing arbitration expertise are the Federal Mediation and Conciliation Service and the California State Mediation and Conciliation Service with offices in San Francisco, Los Angeles, San Diego and Fresno.

Other Forms of Alternative Dispute Resolution

In addition to arbitration, you may also use other forms of dispute resolution as an alternative to litigation. The following is a review of some of the more common procedures.

Mediation

Mediation involves a neutral third party who facilitates settlement discussions between the parties. The mediator does not have the authority to render a decision or to decide factual disputes. However, through the mediator's ability to question extreme positions, to flush out hidden agendas and to develop alternative approaches to the same problem, mediation can be greatly successful in voluntarily resolving disputes between employers and employees. When requested, the mediator also may express his/her opinions based upon the parties' discussions. But those opinions are not binding upon the parties.

Early Neutral Evaluation

Early neutral evaluation involves a case evaluation session early in the life of the possible litigation. The evaluation normally is presided over by a mediator or advisory arbitrator. At the session, the parties and their lawyers present their positions, and the evaluator attempts to reduce the scope of the dispute by identifying areas of agreement between the parties, assessing

---

24. *Graham v. Scissor-Tail, Inc.*, 28 Cal. 3d 807 (1981)

the strengths and weaknesses of the case and assisting the parties in developing a plan for sharing information and potentially resolving the case on their own.

Other Alternatives

Other formal programs also exist in the context of litigation, including judicial arbitration, summary jury trials and mini-trials. Each of these procedures becomes progressively more formal and expensive, but you can explore them as a less costly and time-consuming alternative to litigation.

Appealing an Award

An agreement to arbitrate employment disputes that provides for review of a decision by a second arbitrator is valid.

The arbitration arose under an agreement signed by the employee at time of hire. The agreement provided that either the employer or employee could ask a second arbitrator to affirm, modify or reverse the initial arbitrator's decision using procedures and standards that would apply to review of a civil judgment in an appeals court. The first arbitrator ruled in the employee's favor, and the employer appealed to a second arbitrator. The employee asked a judge to confirm the initial reward and find the second-level arbitration unenforceable. The judge rejected the employee's lawsuit and a state appeals court agreed, finding nothing unconscionable about the second-level review, as long as the employer bore the costs and completed it within a reasonable time.[25]

---

25. *Cummings v. Future Nissan,* 128 Cal. App. 4th 321 (Ca. App., 3rd Dist., 2005)

Wage and Hour Laws

California's wage and hour laws rank in the toughest in the nation. When federal law sets a standard, California law often goes beyond that standard, requiring more of employers. With dual sets of regulations, the law easily becomes confusing, making compliance a challenging exercise for California employers.

This chapter comprehensively explains federal and state wage and hour laws. You will learn how federal and state law interrelate and which prevails when provisions conflict. It thoroughly discusses all sources of wage and hours law:

- The federal Fair Labor Standards Act (FLSA);

- The California Labor Code; and

- Wage Orders created by California's Industrial Welfare Commission (IWC).

The chapter also explains:

- The 17 California Wage Orders and determining which apply to your business;

- How the law is enforced;

- Requirements for record keeping; and

- Penalties for non-compliance.

This chapter also contains sections on laws regulating industrial homeworkers, the car wash industry and "sweat shops."

 Download forms referenced in this chapter at **www.calbizcentral.com/support**. Be sure to have your access code from the inside covers of this book ready to enter into the forms download area. Your access code for the forms in the online Formspack is on the inside covers of this book. See "Forms Available Online" on page xix for more information.

State Versus Federal Law: Which Prevails?

As a California employer, you are subject to labor laws and regulations from the state and federal governments and from other jurisdictions that legislate on employment matters. For example, San Francisco adopted its own minimum wage ordinance, see "San Francisco Minimum Wage" on page 35, and many local governments adopted their own "living wage" laws, see "Living Wage Versus Minimum Wage" on page 265. When these laws conflict, there often is no easy answer to the question of which law prevails. In general, the law that is most restrictive to the employer and most generous to the employee must be followed. The *2009 California Labor Law Digest* includes federal and state law, setting forth whichever rule you must follow in a given instance.

In most instances, employers and unions cannot use the collective bargaining process to waive individual employee rights under state employment law even though that process is regulated by federal law. For more information, see "Waiver of State Employment Rights" in Chapter 33, page 949.

California's Wage Orders

California's IWC regulates wages and hours of nonexempt employees by creating documents called Wage Orders. California employers must comply with 17 Wage Orders plus a Minimum Wage Order.

Each of the Wage Orders is specific to the industry or occupations it covers. You can find a description of each of the 17 Wage Orders in "Wage Order Listing" on page 238. Within each Wage Order, you can find regulations on such topics as:

- Hours and days of work;

- Minimum wages;

- Overtime;

- Alternative workweeks;

- Reporting time pay;

- Special licenses for disabled workers;

- Record retention;

- Cash shortage and breakage;

- Uniforms and equipment;

- Meals and lodging;

- Meal periods; and

- Rest periods.

It is important to understand which Wage Order applies to your business to comply with wage and hour laws in California. Once you determine the proper Wage Order, you must post a copy of it in the workplace where it is available for all employees to view.

See the *IWC Wage Order Checklist* for compliance with the IWC orders.

The Most Current Wage Orders

Wage Orders are numbered 1 through 17, with each number followed by the year in which the Wage Order was last amended and reprinted.

Current effective Wage Orders are listed in the *IWC Wage Order Checklist* .

Posting Requirement

All California employers must post:

- At least one of 17 industry-specific Wage Orders;

- A summary of the industry-specific Wage Order (employers under Wage Order 16 do not need to post the summary); and

- California's Minimum Wage Order (MW-2001).

Download copies of these required Wage Orders at no charge from ***https:// www.calbizcentral.com/hrc/lawlibrary/compensation/californiawageandhourlaws/Pages/ CaliforniaWageandHourLaws.aspx***.

Employee Classification

To determine which IWC Wage Order applies to an employee or group of employees, you must first determine whether your business is covered by one of the industry orders. If it is, the industry order applies to all classifications of employees regardless of the kind of work they do, unless they are specifically exempted by the "applicability" section of that order. Industry orders include all but Wage Orders 4, 14, 15 and 17 (which are occupation orders) and the Minimum Wage Order.

Example:

A clerical worker employed by a toymaker works in the manufacturing company covered by Wage Order 1 (manufacturing). A driver who delivers supplies for a chain of beauty shops in the personal service industry is covered by Wage Order 2 (personal service industry). A mechanic who works for a retail chain is covered by Wage Order 7 (mercantile industry).

If your business cannot be covered by an industrywide order because it does not fall within the definition of any covered industry, the employee's occupation must be examined to see which one of the occupation orders applies.

Example:

An employee is a nurse — in what kind of establishment? He/she might be an industrial nurse employed by a manufacturer under Wage Order 1, or be employed by a weight-control establishment under Wage Order 2 or by a hospital under Wage Order 5. If the employer operated a clinic that did not provide overnight beds or meals, it would not be covered by any industry order. But the nurse would be in an occupation covered by Wage Order 4. The same is true of a nurse employed by a registry. When dispatched to a Wage Order 5 hospital, however, that nurse would be subject to the applicable conditions of Wage Order 5, and a joint employment relationship exists.

Wage Order Listing

The following are California's 17 Wage Orders, along with a description of the industries or occupations covered by each. These descriptions are exactly as they appear in the Wage Orders.

Order 1 - Manufacturing Industry

"Manufacturing industry" means any industry, business or establishment operated for the purpose of preparing, producing, making, altering, repairing, finishing, processing, inspecting, handling, assembling, wrapping, bottling or packaging goods, articles or commodities, in whole or in part; except when such activities are covered by orders in the:

- Canning, preserving and freezing industry;

- Industries that handle products after harvest;

- Industries that prepare agricultural products for market, on the farm; or

- Motion picture industry.

Order 2 - Personal Service Industry

"Personal service industry" means any industry, business or establishment operated for the purpose of rendering, directly or indirectly, any service, operation or process used or useful in the care, cleansing or beautification of the body, skin, nails or hair, or in the enhancement of personal appearance or health; including but not limited to, beauty salons, schools of beauty culture offering beauty care to the public for a fee, barber shops, bath and massage parlors, physical conditioning, weight control salons, health clubs and mortuaries.

Order 3 - Canning, Freezing and Preserving Industry

"Canning, freezing and preserving industry" means any industry, business or establishment operated for the purpose of canning soups, or of cooking, canning, curing, freezing, pickling, salting, bottling, preserving or otherwise processing any fruits or vegetables, seafood, meat, poultry or rabbit product, when the purpose of such processing is the preservation of the product and includes all operations.

Order 4 - Professional, Technical, Clerical, Mechanical and Similar Occupations

"Professional, technical, clerical, mechanical and similar occupations" includes professional, semi-professional, managerial, supervisory, laboratory, research, technical, statisticians, clerical, office work and mechanical operations. These occupations include:

- Accountants, agents, appraisers, artists, attendants and audio-visual technicians;

- Bookkeepers, bundlers and billposters;

- Canvassers, carriers, cashiers, checkers, clerks, collectors, communications and sound technicians, compilers, copy holders, copy readers, copy writers and computer programmers/operators;

- Demonstrators/display representatives, dispatchers, distributors, doorkeepers and drafters;

- Elevator operators, estimators and editors;

- Graphic arts and technicians, guards and guides;

- Hosts;

- Inspectors, installers, instructors, interviewers and investigators;

- Librarians and laboratory workers;

- Machine operators, mechanics, mailers, messengers, medical/dental technicians and technologists and models;

- Nurses;

- Packagers, photographers, porters and cleaners, proof readers, process servers, printers, salespersons/sales agents, secretaries, sign erectors, sign painters, social workers, solicitors and stenographers;

- Teachers;

- Telephone, radio, telephone-telegraph and call-out operators;

- Tellers;

- Ticket agents;

- Tracers;

- Typists;

- Vehicle operators;

- X-ray technicians and their assistants; and

- Other related occupations listed as professional, semi-professional, technical, clerical, technical and kindred occupations.

Order 5 - Public Housekeeping Industry

"Public housekeeping industry" means any industry, business or establishment that provides meals, housing or maintenance services whether operated as a primary business or when incidental to other operations in an establishment not covered by an industry order of the commission, and includes:

- Restaurants, night clubs, taverns, bars, cocktail lounges, lunch counters, cafeterias, boarding houses, clubs and all similar establishments where food in either solid or liquid form is prepared and served to be consumed on the premises;

- Catering, banquet, box lunch services and similar establishments that prepare food for consumption on or off the premises;

- Hotels, motels, apartment houses, rooming houses, camps, clubs, trailer parks, office or loft buildings and similar establishments offering rental of living, business or commercial quarters;

- Hospitals, sanitariums, rest homes, child nurseries, child care institutions, homes for the aged and similar establishments offering board or lodging in addition to medical, surgical, nursing, convalescent, aged or child-care services;

- Private schools, colleges or universities and similar establishments that provide board or lodging in addition to educational facilities;

- Establishments contracting for development, maintenance or cleaning of grounds, maintenance or cleaning of facilities and/or quarters of commercial units and living units; and

- Establishments providing veterinary or other animal care services.

Order 6 - Laundry, Linen Supply, Dry Cleaning and Dyeing Industry

"Laundry, linen supply, dry cleaning and dyeing industry" means any industry, business or establishment operated for the purpose of washing, ironing, cleaning, refreshing, restoring, pressing, dyeing, storing, fumigating, mothproofing, waterproofing or any other associated processes, on articles or fabrics of any kind, including clothing, hats, draperies, rugs, curtains, linens, household furnishings, textiles, furs or leather goods; and includes self-service laundries, self-service dry cleaning establishments and similar types of commercial establishments, and the collection, distribution, storage, sale or resale at retail or wholesale of the foregoing services.

Order 7 - Mercantile Industry

"Mercantile industry" means any industry, business or establishment operated for the purpose of purchasing, selling or distributing goods or commodities at wholesale or retail, or for the purpose of renting goods or commodities.

Order 8 - Industries Handling Products after Harvest

"Industries handling products after harvest" means any industry, business or establishment operated for the purpose of grading, sorting, cleaning, drying, cooling, icing, packing, dehydrating, cracking, shelling, candling, separating, slaughtering, picking, plucking, shucking, pasteurizing, fermenting, ripening, molding or otherwise preparing any agricultural, horticultural, egg, poultry, meat, seafood, rabbit or dairy product for distribution, and includes all the associated operations.

Order 9 - Transportation Industry

"Transportation industry" means any industry, business or establishment operated for the purpose of conveying persons or property from one place to another, whether by rail, highway, air or water, and all associated operations and services; and also includes storing or warehousing of goods or property, and the repairing, parking, rental, maintenance or cleaning of vehicles.

Order 10 - Amusement and Recreation Industry

"Amusement and recreation industry" means any industry, business or establishment operated for the purpose of furnishing entertainment or recreation to the public, including amusement parks, athletic fields, theaters, dance halls, bowling alleys, billiard parlors, skating rinks, riding academies, race tracks, swimming pools, gymnasiums, golf courses, tennis courts, carnivals and wired music studios.

Order 11 - Broadcasting Industry

"Broadcasting industry" means any industry, business or establishment operated for the purpose of broadcasting or taping and broadcasting programs through the medium of radio or television.

Order 12 - Motion Picture Industry

"Motion picture industry" means any industry, business or establishment operated for the purpose of motion picture or television film production, or primarily allied with theatrical or television motion picture productions, including motion pictures for entertainment, commercial, religious or educational purposes, whether made by film, tape or otherwise.

Order 13 - Industries Preparing Agricultural Products for Market, on the Farm

"Industries preparing agricultural products for market, on the farm" means any operation performed in a permanently fixed structure or establishment on the farm or on a moving packing plant on the farm for the purpose of preparing agricultural, horticultural, egg, poultry, meat, seafood, rabbit or dairy products for market when such operations are done on the premises owned or operated by the same employer who produced the products referred to herein, and includes all operations incidental thereto.

Order 14 - Agricultural Occupations

This Wage Order covers "agricultural occupations" related to the maintenance of soil, buildings and machinery that constitute the basic farm facilities and to the cultivation and handling of farm commodities up through harvest, including field packing and transportation to the place of first processing or distribution. Employees in these occupations may work for the grower, for a farm labor contractor or for a company providing agricultural services.

"Agricultural occupations" mean any of the following described occupations:

- Preparation, care and treatment of farm land, pipeline or ditches, including leveling for agricultural purposes, plowing, discing and fertilizing soil;

- Sowing and planting any agricultural or horticultural commodity;

- Care of any agricultural or horticultural commodity. "Care" includes cultivation, irrigation, weed control, thinning, heating, pruning or tying, fumigating, spraying and dusting;

- Harvesting any agricultural or horticultural commodity, including picking, cutting, threshing, mowing, knocking off, field chopping, bunching, baling, balling, field packing and placing in field containers or in the vehicle in which the commodity will be hauled, and transportation on the farm or to the place of first processing or distribution;

- Assembly and storage of any agricultural or horticultural commodity, including loading, road siding, banking, stacking, binding and piling;

- Raising, feeding and managing livestock, fur-bearing animals, poultry, fish, mollusks and insects, including herding, housing, hatching, milking, shearing, handling eggs and extracting honey;

- The harvesting of fish, as defined by Section 45 of the Fish and Game Code, for commercial sale; and

- Conserving, improving or maintaining such farm and its tools and equipment.

Farm Employees

Wage Order 14 does not cover all farm employees. If the grower has a packing or processing operation under Wage Order 8 or Wage Order 13 (industry orders that cover handling operations after harvest), all of the support personnel on the farm — clerical workers and drivers, for example — and the packing house workers would fall under the industry order. If there is no Wage Order 8 or 13 operation, the white collar workers usually would fall under Wage Order 4, but there are other possibilities. If, for example, a grower operates a produce store or retail nursery substantial and distinct enough to constitute a separate mercantile business, Wage Order 7 would cover all employees connected with it in any way.

Other Agricultural Occupations

Although farm employers do often engage in various enterprises, the Division of Labor Standards Enforcement suggests that you should make every effort to limit the number of applicable Wage Orders to two, if possible — either the two occupation Wage Orders, 14 and 4, or Wage Order 14 and the industry order that best reflects the main purpose of your nonfarm operations.

Commercial Agricultural Services

Companies providing commercial agricultural services employ some individuals who work on farms in agricultural occupations, such as tractor drivers, etc., who fall under Wage Order 14. If the company is in the business of selling chemicals, irrigation systems, etc., its other employees fall under Wage Order 7 (mercantile). Some firms, however, only contract to provide the service, in which case their support employees are under Wage Order 4.

Order 15 - Household Occupations

Wage Order 15 covers employees who work for private households in various kinds of occupations. "Household occupations" means all services related to the care of persons or maintenance of a private household or its premises by an employee of a private householder. Said occupations shall include the following:

- Butlers;

- Chauffeurs, companions and cooks;

- Day workers;

- Gardeners, graduate nurses and grooms;

- House cleaners;

- Housekeepers;

- Maids;

- Practical nurses;

- Tutors; and

- Valets.

Order 16 - On-Site Construction, Drilling, Logging and Mining Industries

"On-site construction, drilling, logging and mining industries" includes all persons employed in the on-site occupations of construction, including work involving alteration, demolition, building, excavating, renovation, remodeling, maintenance, improvement, repair work and work for which a contractor's license is required by the California Business and Professions Code Division 3, Chapter 9, sections 7025 et seq.; drilling, including all work required to drill, establish, repair and rework wells for the exploration or extraction of oil, gas or water resources; logging work for which a timber operator's license is required pursuant to California Public Resources Code sections 4571 through 4586; and mining (not covered by Labor Code section 750 et seq.), including all work required to mine and/or establish pits, quarries and surface or underground mines for the purposes of exploration or extraction of nonmetallic minerals and ores, coal and building materials such as stone and gravel, whether paid on a time, piece rate, commission or other basis.

Order 17 - Miscellaneous Employees

"Miscellaneous employees" means any industry or occupation not previously covered by, and all employees not specifically exempted in, the IWC's Wage Orders in effect in 1997, or otherwise exempted by law.

Employees Not Covered by Industry Orders

Most employers who are not covered by industry orders are engaged in listed or related occupations covered by Wage Order 4. Several major types of businesses do not have industry-wide orders, and the IWC treats these businesses as Wage Order 4 businesses. Some organizations and businesses that generally employ the classes of occupations covered by Wage Order 4 include banks, newspapers, public utilities, insurance companies and many others indicated in the listing of businesses by order.

Industries and occupations not covered by Wage Orders 1 through 16 may be covered by Wage Order 17, Miscellaneous Employees. This may include newly emerging industries and jobs in high technology and other fields as they develop over time.

Employees of Temporary Agencies

Employees of a temporary agency sent to work for other employers are covered by whichever order applies to the on-site employer where they perform work. An employee of ABC Temp Services sent to work a temporary job at XYZ Manufacturing would work under Wage Order 1, Manufacturing, while working at XYZ. If that same employee were sent later to another temporary job at Limelight Movie Studios, he/she would work under Wage Order 12, Motion

Picture Industry. Wage Order 4 covers employees directly employed by the temporary service (for example, taking job orders, training or assigning work).

 Wages for employees of temporary services employers must be paid weekly, or daily if an employee is assigned to a client on a day-to-day basis, or to a client engaged in a trade dispute. This requirement does not apply to employees who are assigned to a client for more than 90 consecutive calendar days unless the employer pays the employee weekly. Failure to do so can result in civil and criminal penalties.[1]

On-Site Construction Employees

Wage Order 16 covers employees in "construction occupations" defined as all job classifications associated with construction, including, but not limited to, work involving alteration, demolition, building, excavation, renovation, remodeling, maintenance, improvement, and repair work and any other similar, or related occupations or trades.[2]

These employees are entitled to daily and/or weekly overtime.[3]

Wage Order Determination

An industry, business or establishment generally must comply with the Wage Order applicable to the main purpose of the business, except in Order 5 (see "Incidental Housekeeping Activities" on page 245). Most large businesses conduct a variety of operations, but where they all tend to carry out a common business purpose under common general control, they are treated as one business.

Example:

A manufacturer with a production plant in California may have a separate warehouse and a fleet of trucks and separate sales offices to handle distribution of the manufacturer's products. All are part of one business under Wage Order 1.

Separate Units of Multi-Purpose Companies

Distinctly separate units of multi-purpose companies may be classified separately by division or establishment if the units are different, operating for distinctly different business purposes and the operational management is organized separately at all levels.

Example:

A large retail department store chain also owns an insurance company and a savings and loan company whose representatives have office space in the stores. But each company operates separately as separate corporate identities. They are classified separately, but the retail business's fleet of trucks, appliance installers, etc., are part of the mercantile industry under Wage Order 7. If that company owns any of the factories producing items under its brand name, the factories are under Wage Order 1. It may help to ask: Who is the competition? In this case, is the unit in question in competition with banking institutions, insurance companies or other retail stores?

---

1. Lab Code 203 (a) and Lab. Code 210
2. Wage Order 12 (2)(C)
3. Lab. Code sec. 510

Businesses of a Mixed Nature

To avoid classification problems, businesses that engage in multiple activities should define their primary purpose. This does not mean auditing receipts to compare income from sales and services offered, but determining the nature of the business on the basis of simple observation and common sense.

Examples:

- A car wash establishment that really operates for the purpose of cleaning and maintaining vehicles is under Wage Order 9, even if it offers a gas pump or two for convenience and a few items for sale. On the other hand, an establishment with car wash facilities and several rows of pumps is mostly in the business of selling gasoline under Wage Order 7, which would be emphasized by a sign offering a bargain car wash with a fill-up;

- A "bakery" where there are no tables is a retail establishment under Wage Order 7, but if there are tables for patrons' use, it is an Wage Wage Order 5 establishment. The same principle can be applied to stores selling ice cream;

- A gift shop operated as part of the general facilities of a hotel would be under Wage Order 5;

- A publishing company that prints books or magazines is manufacturing products under Wage Order 1. But a newspaper company is disseminating news, a business purpose not covered by an industry order, so Wage Order 4 covers its employees;

- A garage operating for the purpose of repairing cars is in the transportation industry under Wage Order 9. But the service department of a vehicle dealer, whose main purpose is to sell cars, falls under Wage Order 7. Similarly, a garage operated as a secondary activity by a "service station," which mostly is in business for the purpose of selling gas, tires, etc., is a Wage Order 7 garage; and

- A company producing motion pictures or programs on videotape for corporate customers would be under Wage Order 12 even if it made and distributed several copies of a program. But a firm mostly in the business of manufacturing, reproducing tapes for wholesale, would fall under Wage Order 1.

Incidental Housekeeping Activities

Wage Order 5 does not limit coverage to businesses whose main purpose is providing meals, housing or maintenance services. Instead, the Wage Order specifies that if any business provides any of these things to the public, even incidentally, and is not covered by a different industry order, it is part of the public housekeeping industry under Wage Order 5.

Example:

A factory that operates a cafeteria is covered by Wage Order 1 so it is not covered by Wage Order 5. A private school that is not covered by an industry order and which provides dormitories or dining facilities is covered by Wage Order 5. Where a concessionaire contracts to operate lodging or dining facilities, the concessionaire's business is under Wage Order 5, and the rest of the enterprise (school, factory, etc.) is otherwise classified.

Enforcement and Penalties

It is illegal for an employer and an employee to agree to a wage lower than the minimum wage.[4]

Failure to pay the minimum wage subjects you to fines and imprisonment. The state Labor Commissioner can assess a civil penalty of $100 for each underpaid employee for each pay period during which you did not pay the minimum wage. For each subsequent intentional failure to pay the minimum wage, the penalty is $250.[5]

If the Labor Commissioner files charges with the district attorney, you or your representative may be found guilty of a misdemeanor and:

- Can be punished by a fine of not less than $100 or by imprisonment for 30 days or both;[6]

- Liable for the difference between the minimum wage and the wage paid during the period of violation, plus court costs (any employee receiving less than the applicable minimum wage or the legal overtime compensation is entitled to recover in a civil action the difference between the wages paid and those due, including interest, reasonable attorneys' fees and costs of suit);[7] and

- May be ordered by the court to refrain from further violations.[8]

In addition, courts may assess civil penalties against an employer or any other person acting on behalf of an employer where there is a violation of any wage and hour provision of the state Labor Code or any provision in any IWC Wage Order. For the first offense, the fine is $100 per underpaid employee plus 25 percent of the amount of underpaid wages. For the second and subsequent offenses, the fine is $200 per underpaid employee plus 25 percent of the amount of underpaid wages.[9]

Personnel Liable for Fines

The phrase "other person acting on behalf of the employer" means that payroll personnel, other employees who perform payroll functions (human resources staff) and payroll services hired by employers could potentially be liable to pay fines out of their own pockets for miscalculating overtime under the new law. However, the Labor Commissioner states that individual employees will not be fined, unless they formulate policies that lead to nonpayment of required overtime.[10]

Arguably, you might be required to reimburse your penalized employee for these fines under the state Labor Code section requiring an employer to reimburse an employee for all necessary expenses or losses in direct consequence of job performance.[11]

Agreeing with both the trial and appeals courts, the California Supreme Court ruled that corporate agents and managers acting within the scope of their agency are not personally liable for their corporate employer's failure to pay its employees' wages."

---

4. Lab. Code sec. 223
5. Lab. Code sec. 1197.1
6. Lab. Code sec. 225
7. Lab. Code sec. 1194
8. Lab. Code sec. 1194.5
9. Lab. Code sec. 210
10. DLSE Memorandum of December 23, 1999, "Understanding AB 60: An In-Depth Look at the Provisions of the Eight Hour Day Restoration and Workplace Flexibility Act of 1999"
11. Lab. Code sec. 2802

A former manager filed a lawsuit, asking the court to require the individual officers and directors personally to pay for his unpaid wages because of their failure to comply with several California Labor Code sections and the applicable Wage Order. He asserted that the officers and directors were within the definition of "employer" and negligently failed to assure the company's compliance with these laws.

This decision means that individuals can be liable for civil or criminal penalties but not for unpaid wages. Individual officers and directors are not responsible for the corporation's negligent acts just because of their official positions, unless they participated in the negligent acts or authorized or directed them.[12]

Business owners should realize that this decision does not protect those who control unincorporated businesses

In a case involving another attempt to hold individual managers liable for unpaid wages, the federal U.S. Ninth Circuit Court of Appeals recently rejected a lawsuit brought under the federal Racketeer Influenced and Corrupt Organizations (RICO) Act. This law was originally passed to aid prosecution of organized crime. A successful RICO claim would have resulted in managers' personal liability plus recovery of triple damages.

The lawsuit alleged that employees were victims of mail and wire fraud when company managers misrepresented their status as exempt from overtime pay. Each time the employer mailed a paycheck, pay stub, or W-2 Form, the employer engaged in mail fraud. Each time the employer directly deposited payroll funds by wire transfer, the employer engaged in wire fraud. Both these actions allegedly constitute violations of the RICO Act. The complaint further alleged that managers conspired to commit these illegal acts, an additional RICO violation.

The Ninth Circuit ruled that neither the employer nor its managers had engaged in mail fraud or wire fraud, because such claims cannot rest solely on the employee-employer relationship.[13]

Extended Time Period for Claims

The willful failure to pay a terminated or quitting employee in a timely fashion subjects you to a penalty consisting of continuation of the employee's wages on a day-to-day basis until the final paycheck is ready or a maximum of 30 days has elapsed.[14] This rule applies to both exempt and nonexempt employees.[15]

A willful failure to pay need not include a showing of bad faith or evil intent. The waiting time penalty is excused if there is a good faith dispute that no additional wages are due.[16]

In the event of a dispute over wages, you must pay, without condition, all wages you admit are due. You must pay any additional wages determined due by the Labor Commissioner within 10 days after receiving notice from the Labor Commissioner that wages are due. Failure to do so may subject you to a penalty of triple the amount due to the employee.[17]

---

12. *Reynolds v. Bement*, 36 Cal. 4th 1075 (2005)
13. *Miller v. Yokohama Tire Corporation*, 358 F.3d 616 (9th Cir., 2004)
14. Lab. Code sec. 203
15. *Mamika v. Barca*, 68 Cal. App. 4th 487 (1998)
16. 8 CCR sec. 13520
17. Lab. Code sec. 206

In addition, if you violate wage payment provisions when paying employees, you commit a misdemeanor.[18] Either the district attorney or the DLSE can sue to recover statutory penalties.[19]

In any court action brought for the nonpayment of wages, fringe benefits or pension fund contributions, the court must award reasonable attorneys' fees to the prevailing party if requested by the prevailing party. A California Court of Appeal recently held that even the Labor Commissioner may be ordered to pay costs to the prevailing party in litigation.[20]

Insufficient Funds Paycheck

If a paycheck is refused payment because you have no account with the bank or have insufficient funds, you are liable for one day's wages for each day until the amount is paid or until the employee files an action to recover the wages, up to a maximum of 30 days' wages. The employee must have attempted to cash or deposit the paycheck within 30 days of receiving it.[21]

The penalty does not apply if you can establish, to the satisfaction of the Labor Commissioner or court, that the violation was unintentional. The penalty also does not apply if the employee has recovered a returned check service charge under California's Civil Code.

Complaints and Appeals

Employees may file complaints with the Labor Commissioner to recover unpaid wages. The Labor Commissioner has the authority to:[22]

- Investigate these complaints;

- Hold hearings and take action to recover wages; and

- Assess penalties and make demands for compensation.

The Labor Commissioner must notify the parties whether a hearing will be held within 30 days after a complaint has been filed, and must hold that hearing within 90 days of the date that it has been determined a hearing will be held.[23]

When a hearing is set, a copy of the complaint together with a notice of time and place of the hearing is served on all parties, personally or by certified mail, or by leaving a copy at the home or office of the person being served, with a copy mailed to the person at the place where a copy was left. If left at a home, the copy must be received by a person over the age of 18; if left at an office, by a person who appears to be in charge. The complaint must include the amount of compensation requested.[24]

The Labor Commissioner must file an order, decision or award within 15 days after the hearing is concluded and serve notice on the parties. Within 10 days after serving notice, the parties may seek a review of the case by filing an appeal in the municipal or superior court. If the appeal is unsuccessful, the court determines the costs and reasonable attorneys' fees incurred by the winning

---

18. Lab. Code sec. 217
19. Lab. Code secs. 217, 218
20. *Division of Labor Standards Enforcement v. Lee,* 73 Cal. App. 4th 763 (1999)
21. Lab. Code sec. 203.1
22. Lab. Code sec. 98
23. Lab. Code sec. 98(a)
24. Labor Code sec. 98(b)

party and assesses those costs on the party filing the appeal. An employee is successful if the court awards an amount greater than zero.[25]

All awards made by the Labor Commissioner accrue interest on all due and unpaid wages.[26] The interest runs from the date the wages were due and payable until the wages are paid. This interest-bearing period includes the period in which the Labor Commissioner's decision is being appealed.

Time Limits To File a Claim

The California Supreme Court decided a case in 2000 that extends the period of time in which a person can file a claim against an employer for failure to pay wages, including overtime, and allows an individual to file a claim on behalf of him/herself as well as all other similarly situated employees.[27]

Under the state Labor Code,[28] an employee has three years to file a lawsuit for unpaid wages.[29] The California Supreme Court decided a case that extends the period of time in which a person can file a claim against an employer for failure to pay wages, including overtime, and allows an individual to file a claim on behalf of him/herself as well as all other similarly situated employees.[30]

The Supreme Court found that failure to pay earned wages, including overtime, constitutes an unfair business practice in violation of the California Unfair Competition law (UCL). Under the UCL, an employee can file a claim for unpaid wages up to four years after the alleged failure to pay. This means employees can now collect up to four years of back wages under the UCL rather than three under the Labor Code.

In addition to seeking his or her unpaid wages, an employee may also now file a claim under the UCL on behalf of all other similarly situated employees of the employer, without having to file a class action lawsuit. In the case decided by the Supreme Court, the employee filed claims on behalf of herself and 175 other employees.

Private Court Action

An individual aggrieved employee, acting on his or her own behalf and/or on behalf of other current and former employees, may bring a civil action to enforce provisions of the Labor Code if the government has not done so.[31] Lawsuits for most violations of posting, notice, agency reporting or filing requirements are excluded from such private enforcement, except those requirements as they relate to payroll or workplace injury reporting

An aggrieved employee may recover the applicable civil penalty on behalf of himself or herself and other current or former employees against whom one or more of the alleged violations was committed. Claims under the workers' compensation program are excluded.

---

25. Lab. Code sec. 98.2
26. Lab. Code sec. 98.1
27. *Cortez v. Purolator Air Filtration Products Company*, 23 Cal.4th 163 (2000)
28. Lab. Code sec. 1194
29. Code of Civil Procedure sec. 338
30. *Cortez v. Purolator Air Filtration Products Company*, 23 Cal. 4th 163 (2000)
31. Lab. Code sec. 2698-2699

Prior to filing a lawsuit, certain procedural steps must be followed for three broad categories of alleged Labor Code violations. These steps are designed to permit voluntary, early resolution of the employer violation with or without the intervention of a state agency.[32] In all three categories, the employee must first notify the employer and the appropriate state agency of the alleged violation. The notice must include the specific code provisions allegedly violated, and the facts and arguments supporting the violation. All time limits run from the postmark date of this notice.

The first category specifies approximately 150 Labor Code sections that relate to:

- Setting and paying wages and salaries;

- Regulating hours of work, meals and rest breaks;

- Employing minors;

- Employment under state and public works contracts;

- Protection of whistle-blowers; and

- Other specified sections regulating conditions of employment.

An employee who believes that his/her rights under one of these sections have been violated must notify the employer and the Labor and Workforce Development Agency (the Agency). The Agency must notify the employer and employee within 30 calendar days of the postmark date of the notice received from the employee that it does not intend to investigate the alleged violation.

- If the Agency says it will not investigate or no notice is provided within 33 calendar days of the postmark date of the notice given by the employee, the employee may file a lawsuit; or

- If the Agency notifies the employer and employee that it intends to investigate, the Agency can then take up to 120 calendar days to complete its investigation.

The employee may file a lawsuit if:

- The Agency decides not to cite the employer, in which case the Agency must notify the employer and employee within five working days of its decision; or

- The Agency fails to issue a citation against the employer within 158 calendar days.

The second category includes alleged violations of Labor Code Division 5, which regulates occupational health and safety, except sections 6310, 6311 and 6399.7, which are included in the first category. Before filing a lawsuit, an employee must notify the employer, the Division of Occupational Safety and Health (DOSH) and the Agency.

DOSH must then inspect or investigate as required by law and, if it issues a citation, no lawsuit may be filed. DOSH must notify the employer and employee within 14 calendar days of certifying that the violation was corrected.

If DOSH does not issue a citation within its inspection deadline, the employee may challenge that decision in court. If the court directs DOSH to issue a citation, the employee may file no other lawsuit. If DOSH fails to inspect or investigate, the employee may proceed as with other third category claims.

No private lawsuit can be filed where the employer and DOSH are already parties to an agreement for long-term abatement of conditions, or where they have previously entered into a consultation agreement with regard to a condition at a particular work-site. However, a consultation agreement

---

32. Lab. Code secs. 2699.3, 2699.5

entered into after receiving an employee's notice does not prevent this process from continuing.

The third category applies to all other alleged Labor Code violations and the failure of DOSH to inspect or investigate, in which case the following conditions apply:

- The employer has 33 calendar days after the postmark date of the notice to cure the alleged violation and notify the employee and the Agency of the actions taken. To "cure" the violation means to come into compliance and address the concerns of any aggrieved employee;

  - If the employer does not act in a timely manner to cure the alleged violation, the employee may file a lawsuit; and

  - If the employee believes that the employer's actions did not cure the violation, he/she may notify the Agency, which can then take up to 17 days to investigate and grant the employer three additional business days to cure the violation.

- If the Agency determines that the alleged violation has not been cured the employee may file a lawsuit; or

- If the Agency determines that the alleged violation has been cured, but the employee disagrees, the employee may appeal the Agency's decision.

Any employee who prevails in any action is entitled to an award of reasonable attorneys' fees and costs. The employee may also pursue other remedies available under state or federal law either separately or concurrently with this action.

Where a specific provision of the Labor Code does not provide for a penalty, the penalties that can be assessed by the court are:

- If, at the time of the alleged violation, the person does not employ one or more employees, the civil penalty is $500; or

- If, at the time of the alleged violation, the person employs one or more employees, the civil penalty is $100 for each aggrieved employee per pay period for the initial violation, and $200 for each aggrieved employee per pay period for each subsequent violation.

A court must review and approve penalties in connection with any settlement agreement. Courts have discretion to award lesser penalties to avoid unjust results.

Civil penalties recovered by aggrieved employees are divided, giving 75 percent to the Labor and Workforce Development Agency and 25 percent to the aggrieved employees. Where the claim is against a company with no employees, the penalty is paid to the Labor and Workforce Development Agency.

To protect employees from discrimination or retaliation for giving a notice alleging a violation to the Agency or the employer, or filing a lawsuit, the Labor Code provides safeguards against actions involving:

- Employment;

- Discharge or threat of discharge;

- Demotion;

- Suspension;

- Terms and conditions of employment; or

- Training opportunities.

The protection extends to employees who testify, or are about to testify, in connection with a notice or claim. It applies whether the claim is filed on the individual's own behalf or on others' behalf.[33]

Disclosure of Wages or Working Conditions

You may not:

- Prohibit employees from discussing their wages or working conditions;

- Require an employee to sign any document denying the employee the right to disclose the amount of his/her wages or working conditions; or

- Discharge, formally discipline or otherwise discriminate against an employee for disclosing his/her wages or working conditions.[34]

This law is not intended to permit employees to disclose your proprietary information, trade secret information or other legally protected information without your consent.

A California Court of Appeal found that an employer violated the Labor Code when it fired an employee for engaging in a discussion of bonus payments with co-workers. At a meeting with co-workers, she discussed the fact that some received bonuses while others did not. Six days later, she was fired. The termination papers indicated the discharge was for violating company rules. A company investigation concluded that the bonus discussion was one reason for her discharge.

The Court of Appeals said she had the right to a trial on her claim for an unlawful termination. The claim was based directly on California Labor Code section 232, which the court interpreted to include discussion of bonuses as well as wages.[35]

Car Wash Industry

A law extends the repeal date of the car wash industry compliance program from January 1, 2007 to January 1, 2010. All car washing and polishing businesses were required to have been registered no later than July 30, 2006.

Effective January 1, 2007, citations and civil fines of $100 for each calendar day (not to exceed $10,000) will be issued to any unregistered employer. The civil fine will be calculated from the date the employer was required to have been registered, even if prior to July 30, 2006.

Every employer in the car-wash industry must register annually with the Labor Commissioner.[36] Registration may not be completed until all the following conditions are satisfied:

- Proof of compliance with the local government's business licensing or regional regulatory requirements;

- A surety bond issued by a surety company admitted to do business in California is obtained and filed with the Labor Commissioner. The principal sum must be not less than $15,000. The bond must be payable to the people of the state of California for the benefit of any employee

---

33. Lab. Code sec. 98.6.
34. Lab. Code sec. 232
35. *Grant-Burton v. Covenant Care, Inc.*, 99 Cal. App. 4th 1361 (2002)
36. Lab. Code sections 2050-2067

damaged by his or her employer's failure to comply with employment laws and regulations;

- A current workers' compensation insurance policy is in effect and documented; and

- Registration fees of $250 for each branch location are paid. This amount may be adjusted for inflation.

Proof of registration shall be by an official DLSE registration form. Each employer must post the registration form where it may be read by the employees during the workday.

In addition to the registration fee, each employer is assessed an annual fee of $50 for each branch location to be deposited in the Car Wash Worker Restitution Fund.

The application for registration requires extensive information regarding the company's ownership, and financial and legal history.[37]

Every car wash employer must keep accurate records for three years showing all of the following:

- The names and addresses of all employees engaged in rendering actual services for any business of the employer;

- The hours worked daily by each employee, including the times the employee begins and ends each work period;

- All gratuities received daily by the employer, whether received directly from the employee or indirectly by deduction from the wages of the employee, or otherwise;

- The wage and wage rate paid each payroll period;

- The age of all minor employees; and

- Any other conditions of employment.

No registration will be granted or renewed if:

- The employer has not fully satisfied any final judgment for unpaid wages owed to an employee or former employee of a business for which the employer is required to register under this chapter;

- The employer failed to remit the proper amount of contributions required by the Unemployment Insurance Code; or when the Employment Development Department makes an assessment for those unpaid contributions against the employer that has become final and the employer has not fully paid the amount of delinquency for those unpaid contributions; and

- The employer failed to remit the amount of Social Security and Medicare tax contributions required by the Federal Insurance Contributions Act (FICA) to the Internal Revenue Service, and the employer has not fully paid the amount or delinquency for those unpaid contributions.[38]

The penalty for failure to register is $100 for each day of unregistered operation to a maximum of $10,000.[39]

---

37. Lab. Code sec. 2061
38. Lab. Code sec. 2062
39. Lab. Code sec. 2064

A successor to any employer who is engaged in car washing and polishing, and who owed wages and penalties to the predecessor's former employee or employees is liable for those wages and penalties if the successor meets any of the following criteria:

- Uses substantially the same facilities or workforce to offer substantially the same services as the previous employer;

- Shares in the ownership, management, control of the labor relations or interrelations of business operations with the previous employer;

- Employs in a managerial capacity any person who directly or indirectly controlled the wages, hours or working conditions of the affected employees of the previous employer; and

- Is an immediate family member of any owner, partner, officer or director of the previous employer, or any person who has a financial interest in the previous employer.

Sweatfree Code Of Conduct for State Contractors

Except as related to a public works contract, contracts with state agencies providing for procurement or laundering of apparel, garments or corresponding accessories, or the procurement of equipment, materials or supplies, require that a contractor certify that no apparel, garments or corresponding accessories, equipment, materials or supplies furnished to the state under the contract have been laundered or produced in whole or in part by sweatshop labor, forced labor, convict labor, indentured labor under penal sanction, abusive forms of child labor or exploitation of children in sweatshop labor, or with the benefit of sweatshop labor, forced labor, convict labor, indentured labor under penal sanction, abusive forms of child labor or exploitation of children in sweatshop labor.

All of these terms are defined in the state statute.[40] In particular, "sweatshop labor" is defined as all work or service extracted from or performed by any person for an employer, where the employer violates one or more laws governing wages, employee benefits, occupational health, occupational safety, nondiscrimination or freedom of association in the country of manufacture.

A contractor must cooperate fully in providing reasonable access to his/her records, documents, agents or employees, or premises if reasonably required by authorized officials of the contracting agency, or if the Department of Industrial Relations or the Department of Justice determine that the contractor must comply with these requirements. Following notice and a hearing, sanctions for violation of these conditions may include:

- The contract may be voided at the option of the state agency to which the equipment, materials or supplies were provided;

- The contractor may be assessed a penalty equal to the greater of $1,000 or 20 percent of the value of items the state agency demonstrates were produced in violation of the conditions and were supplied to the state agency under the contract; and

- The contractor may be removed from the bidder's list for a period not to exceed 360 days.

Any person who certifies as true any material matter that he or she knows to be false is guilty of a misdemeanor. These provisions apply in addition to any other provisions that authorize the prosecution and enforcement of local labor laws and criminal or civil actions against an individual or business.

---

40. Public Contract Code sec. 6108

Sweatfree Code of Conduct

On February 1, 2004, the Department of Industrial Relations established a contractor responsibility program, including a Sweatfree Code of Conduct, signed by all bidders on state contracts and subcontracts. For every contract entered into by any state agency for the procurement or laundering of apparel, garments or corresponding accessories, or for the procurement of equipment or supplies, it is required that the contractor certify compliance with the Sweatfree Code of Conduct. Contractors must ensure that their subcontractors comply in writing with the Sweatfree Code of Conduct, under penalty of perjury. Sweatfree Code of Conduct procurement policies may be permitted a phase-in period of up to three years.

No state agency may enter into a contract with any contractor unless the contractor meets the following requirements:

- Contractors and subcontractors in California must comply with all appropriate state laws concerning wages, workplace safety, rights to association and assembly, and nondiscrimination standards, and to appropriate federal laws;

- Contractors based in other states within the United States must comply with all appropriate laws of their states and appropriate federal laws;

- Contractors whose locations for manufacture or assembly are outside the United States must ensure that their subcontractors comply with the appropriate laws of countries where the facilities are located;

- No employee may be terminated except for just cause, and employees shall have access to a mediator or to a mediation process to resolve workplace disputes not regulated by the National Labor Relations Board;

- At the minimum, workers must be paid wages and benefits in compliance with applicable local, state and national laws of the jurisdiction in which the labor is performed. The applicable labor standards established by the local jurisdiction apply with regard to the contract or purchase order for which the expenditure is made, unless the applicable local standards conflict with state law, or if state law explicitly preempt the local standards. A state agency may not require, as a condition for the receipt of state funds or assistance, that a local jurisdiction refrain from applying labor standards otherwise applicable to that local jurisdiction;

- All overtime hours shall be worked voluntarily and in compliance with the overtime laws and regulations of the country in which employees are working. Workers must be compensated for overtime at either:

  - The rate of compensation for regular hours of work; or

  - As legally required in the country of manufacture, whichever is greater.

- No person may be employed who is younger than the legal age for children to work in the country in which the facility is located. In no case may children under the age of 15 years be employed in the manufacturing process. Where the age for completing compulsory education is higher than the standard for the minimum age of employment, the age for completing education applies to this section;

- There may be no form of forced labor of any kind, including slave labor, prison labor, indentured labor or bonded labor, including forced overtime hours;

- The work environment must be safe and healthy and, at a minimum, comply with relevant local, state and national laws. If residential facilities are provided to workers, those facilities must also be safe and healthy;

- There may be no discrimination in hiring, salary, benefits, performance evaluation, discipline, promotion, retirement or dismissal on the basis of:
  - Age;
  - Sex;
  - Pregnancy;
  - Maternity leave status;
  - Marital status;
  - Race;
  - Religion;
  - Nationality;
  - Country of origin;
  - Ethnic origin;
  - Disability;
  - Sexual orientation;
  - Gender identity;
  - Political opinion.

- No worker may be subjected to any physical, sexual, psychological or verbal harassment or abuse, including corporal punishment, under any circumstances. This includes retaliation for exercising his or her right to free speech and assembly;

- No worker may be forced to use contraceptives or take pregnancy tests. No worker may be exposed to chemicals, including glues and solvents, that endanger reproductive health; and

- Contractors and bidders must list the names and addresses of each subcontractor used in the performance of the contract, and list each manufacturing, facility or operation of the contractor or subcontractor for performance of the contract. The list, which must be maintained and updated to show any changes in subcontractors during the contract's term, must include company names, owners or officers, addresses, telephone numbers, e-mail addresses and the nature of the business association.

Fair Labor Standards Act

The Fair Labor Standards Act (FLSA) ranks as the most important federal law affecting wages and hours. The FLSA establishes minimum wage, overtime pay, record keeping and child-labor standards affecting more than 113 million full-time and part-time workers in the private sector and in federal, state and local governments.

Though the FLSA sets basic minimum wage and overtime pay standards and regulates the employment of minors, the law does not regulate a number of employment practices. The FLSA does not require:

- Vacation, holiday, severance or sick pay;

- Meal or rest periods;

- Premium pay for weekend or holiday work;

- Pay raises or fringe benefits; and

- A discharge notice, reason for discharge or immediate payment of final wages to terminated employees.

Wage payment or collection procedures for an employee's usual or promised wages or commissions in excess of those required by the FLSA are matters for agreement between the employer and the employees or their authorized representatives, or are covered by state law. All employers subject to the act must comply with its provisions, and with any more stringent California law.

The Wage and Hour Division of the U.S. Department of Labor administers and enforces the FLSA. Special rules apply to state and local government employment involving fire protection and law enforcement activities, volunteer services and compensatory time off in lieu of cash overtime pay.

 Review Chapter 12, "Wages, Salaries and Other Compensation" of this *Digest* to understand how these federal laws interact with California law. In some instances, California employers must comply with more stringent standards.

Who Is Covered By the FLSA?

The FLSA covers a large majority of California businesses. An entire "enterprise" (business) may be covered if it meets certain tests, as explained below and if the FLSA covers an enterprise, it covers all employees of that enterprise. However, even if an enterprise does not meet those tests, some of its employees may fall under the FLSA through "individual" coverage.

When neither enterprise coverage nor individual coverage apply, you are not subject to the provisions of the FLSA and should look to California law only.

Enterprise Coverage

The FLSA covers all employees of enterprises engaged in interstate commerce, producing goods for interstate commerce; or handling, selling or otherwise working on goods or materials moved in or produced for such commerce by any person.

Employees who work for certain businesses or organizations (or "enterprises") are covered by the FLSA. These enterprises, which must have at least two employees, are:

- Those that have an annual dollar volume of sales or business done of at least $500,000; and

- Hospitals, businesses providing medical or nursing care for residents, schools and preschools, and government agencies.

Individual Coverage

- Even when there is no enterprise coverage, employees are protected by the FLSA if their work regularly involves them in commerce between states ("interstate commerce"). The FLSA covers individual workers who are "engaged in commerce or in the production of goods for commerce."

- Examples of employees who are involved in interstate commerce include those who:

- Produce goods (such as a worker assembling components in a factory or a secretary typing letters in an office) that will be sent out of state;

- Regularly make telephone calls to persons located in other states;

- Handle records of interstate transactions;

- Travel to other states on their jobs; and

- Perform janitorial work in buildings where goods are produced for shipment outside California. Domestic service workers, such as day workers, housekeepers, chauffeurs, cooks or full-time baby-sitters fall under the FLSA if they:

  - Receive at least $50 in cash wages in a calendar quarter from their employers; or

  - Work a total of more than eight hours a week for one or more employers.

See the *FLSA Worksheet - Determining Coverage* to assist in determining whether the FLSA covers your business.

Wage and Hour Provisions

The FLSA includes provisions defining minimum wage and permissible subminimum wage levels, maximum hours of work and overtime pay, and restrictions on employment of minors and categories of exempt employees. These issues also fall under California law which, in most cases, contains more favorable conditions for employees. Where both state and federal law govern the same issue, the law most favorable to the employee prevails. The details are covered in the following chapters, which guide you to the law you must comply with in California.

- Minimum wage and other compensation issues are covered in Chapter 12, "Wages, Salaries and Other Compensation;"

- Hours of work are covered in Chapter 13, "Hours of Work and Recording Time Worked;"

- Overtime obligations, computation and payment are covered in Chapter 14, "Overtime;" and

- Classification of employees as exempt or nonexempt from overtime is covered in Chapter 16, "Exempt and Nonexempt."

Keeping Records

The FLSA requires you to keep records on wages, hours and other items as specified in Department of Labor recordkeeping regulations. Most of the information is of the kind generally maintained by employers in ordinary business practice and in compliance with other laws and regulations. You do not have to keep the records in any particular form, and you do not have to use time clocks. With respect to an employee subject to both minimum wage and overtime pay provisions, you must keep the following records:

- Personal information, including employee's name, home address, occupation, sex and birth date (if less than 19 years of age);

- Hour and day when workweek begins;

- Total hours worked each workday and each workweek;

- Total daily or weekly straight-time earnings;

- Regular hourly pay rate for any week when overtime is worked;

- Total overtime pay for the workweek;

- Deductions from or additions to wages;

- Total wages paid each pay period; and

- Date of payment and pay period covered.

Records required for exempt employees differ from those for nonexempt workers, and special information is required for:

- Homeworkers;

- Employees working under uncommon pay arrangements;

- Employees to whom lodging or other facilities are furnished; or

- Employees receiving remedial education.

Enforcement

Investigators stationed across the United States carry out the Wage and Hour Division's enforcement of the FLSA. As the division's authorized representatives, they conduct investigations and gather data on wages, hours and other employment conditions or practices to determine FLSA compliance. Where investigators find violations, the investigators also may recommend changes in employment practices to bring an employer into compliance with the FLSA.

An employer, including individual owners, found guilty of violating the minimum wage and maximum hours provisions may be required to pay the amount due to employees plus an equal amount in liquidated damages.[41]

An employer, including individual owners, found guilty of child labor violations may be subject to a civil penalty not to exceed $10,000 for each employee who was the subject of such a violation. Any person who repeatedly or willfully violates section six or seven may be subject to a civil penalty not to exceed $1,000 for each such violation.[42]

It is a violation of the FLSA to fire or in any manner discriminate against an employee for filing a complaint or participating in a legal proceeding under the FLSA.[43] The law provides for payment of back pay and damages in such cases.[44]

Business owners found guilty of willful violations may be prosecuted criminally and subjected to fines of up to $10,000. A second willful violation may result in up to six months imprisonment.[45]

The FLSA prohibits the shipment of goods in interstate commerce that were produced in violation of the minimum-wage, overtime-pay, child-labor or special minimum wage provisions.[46]

41.29 U.S.C. sec. 216(a)
42.29 U.S.C sec. 216(e)
43.29 U.S.C. sec. 215(a)(3)
44.29 U.S.C. sec. 216(a)
45.29 U.S.C. sec. 216(a)
46.29 U.S.C. sec. 215(a)

Further Information

More information about the FLSA can be found on the U.S. Department of Labor Wage and Hour Division's Web site at *www.dol.gov/esa/whd*. You can find more information on California Wage Orders on the California Industrial Welfare Commission's Web site at *www.dir.ca.gov/iwc/iwc.html*.

Chapter 11 Forms

This chapter contains samples of forms associated with this topic. *The forms in this section are for visual reference only; download the most up-to-date forms and checklists in their entirety from CalBizCentral.*

To download either individual forms or your entire Formspack containing all the forms referenced in this book:

1. Visit **www.calbizcentral.com/support** and select "Labor Law Digest" from the list of product titles.

2. Have this copy of Labor Law Digest handy — you will need to enter the access code featured on the inside covers of this book.

3. Enter the access code, select the documents you want to download to your computer, then follow the on-screen instructions.

For more detailed instructions, see "Forms Available Online" on page xix.

FLSA Worksheet - Determining Coverage

Coverage by the Fair Labor Standards Act (FLSA) can occur in one of two ways. If the "enterprise coverage" test is met, all employees are covered. If not, there may be "individual coverage" of certain employees.

Enterprise Coverage

☐ Are workers engaged in interstate commerce (sales, trading or transportation from one state to another), producing goods for interstate commerce or handling, selling, or otherwise working on goods or materials that have been moved in or produced for interstate commerce by any person? AND

☐ Is the annual gross volume of sales made or business done not less than $500,000 (exclusive of excise taxes at the retail level that are separately stated)? OR

☐ Is the enterprise engaged in the operation of a hospital, an institution primarily engaged in the care of those who are physically or mentally ill or disabled or aged, and who reside on the premises, a school for children who are mentally or physically disabled or gifted, a preschool, an elementary or secondary school, or an institution of higher education (whether operated for profit or not for profit)? OR

☐ Is the enterprise an activity of a federal, state, or local government agency?

Individual Coverage (minimum wage, overtime and child labor provisions only)

☐ Are individual employees engaged in interstate commerce? Some examples are:

- Work in communications or transportation;
- Regularly use the mail, telephone, or telegraph for interstate communication, or keep records of interstate transactions;
- Handle, ship, or receive goods moving in interstate commerce;
- Regularly cross state lines in the course of employment;
- Work for independent employers who contract to do clerical, custodial, maintenance, or other work for firms engaged in interstate commerce or in the production of goods for interstate commerce.

☐ Do you employ domestic service workers (i.e., day workers, housekeepers, chauffeurs, cooks, full-time babysitters) who:

- Receive at least $50 in cash wages in a calendar quarter from their employers; OR
- Work a total of more than 8 hours a week for one or more employers.

IWC Wage Order Checklist

California's Industrial Welfare Commission (IWC) Wage Orders regulate wages and hours of non-exempt employees in California. The following checklist can help avoid violations of the wage and hour laws.

☐ Determine the appropriate Wage Order for your business or employees.

- What is the main purpose of the business?

_____

- If the business does not fall within the definition of a covered industry, consider each employee's occupation to determine which occupation order applies (usually 4 or 5).

☐ Do you have the most currently amended version of your Wage Order? Wage Orders are numbered 1 through 17, with each followed by the year in which it was last amended and reprinted. The orders effective January 1, 2005 are:

- 1-2001 (amended January 1, 2007);
- 2-2001 (amended January 1, 2007);
- 3-2001 (amended January 1, 2007);
- 4-2001 (amended January 1, 2007);
- 5-2001 (amended January 1, 2007);
- 6-2001 (amended January 1, 2007);
- 7-2001 (amended January 1, 2007);
- 8-2001 (amended January 1, 2007);
- 9-2001 (amended January 1, 2007);
- 10-2001 (amended January 1, 2007);
- 11-2001 (amended January 1, 2007);
- 12-2001 (amended January 1, 2007);
- 13-2001 (amended January 1, 2007);
- 14-2001 (amended January 1, 2007);
- 15-2001 (amended January 1, 2007);
- 16-2001 (amended January 1, 2007);
- 17-2001.

☐ Do you have the Wage Order Summary posted in front of the Wage Order?

☐ Are your Wage Order and Summary posted where employees can read them easily?

☐ Have you also posted the Minimum Wage Order, MW-2007?

Note: This listing is current as of the date of publication. Some wage orders are updated periodically. The most current versions can be found using the California Chamber of Commerce's *Wage Order Wizard* at *http://www.hrcalifornia.com/wageorders*.

FLSA Worksheet - Determining Coverage

IWC Wage Order Checklist

Wages, Salaries and Other Compensation

California's wage and wage payment law can confuse even the most seasoned human resources professional. Employers must comply with hundreds of state and federal codes, regulations, court cases and opinion letters. Sometimes state and federal law conflict, making it difficult for California employers to know which one to follow.

This chapter begins with a comprehensive discussion of California's minimum standards for straight time hourly wages, incentive pay and special pay arrangements as required by the Industrial Welfare Commission (IWC) Wage Orders. To avoid confusion with the laws discussed in this chapter, the issue of overtime is discussed in Chapter 14, "Overtime."

Timely payment of wages and the way in which payment is made are equally important to paying the right amount. The chapter deals with these issues, including how and when you must pay terminating employees and when you can and cannot make deductions from employee wages.

Finally, the chapter describes rules regarding tools, uniforms and equipment, work facilities and industry specific wage laws covering domestic services, garment industries and agriculture.

 Download forms referenced in this chapter at ***www.calbizcentral.com/support***. Be sure to have your access code from the inside covers of this book ready to enter into the forms download area. Your access code for the forms in the online Formspack is on the inside covers of this book. See "Forms Available Online" on page xix for more information.

Definitions

The following examples definesome of the key terms used in wage and hour law:

Employee

An employee is any person rendering actual service in any business for an employer, whether gratuitously or for wages.[1] Certain volunteers, independent contractors and participants in a joint enterprise are not considered employees for certain purposes, such as workers' compensation coverage.[2]

1.Lab. Code sec. 350(b)
2.Lab. Code secs. 3351, 3352

Employer

An employer means every person engaged in any business or enterprise in California, who has one or more persons in service.[3] An employer can be a person, association, organization, partnership, business trust, limited liability company or corporation.[4]

Volunteer

Whether a person is properly classified as an "employee" or a "volunteer" is determined by the intent of the parties. If the individual intends to volunteer his/her services for public service, religious or humanitarian objectives, not as an employee and without expecting pay, the individual is not an employee of the religious, charitable or similar nonprofit corporation that receives the services.[5] However, a person who offers to work for nothing, for the purpose of gaining experience, is an employee, not a volunteer. The term "volunteer" cannot be loosely used to evade the requirements of the law.

Student

Students who perform work in the course of their studies as part of the curriculum are not employees if they receive no payment for their work and no credit toward their school fees.[6]

Wages

A wage is money received by an employee for labor performed of every description, whether the amount is fixed or ascertained by the standard of time, task, piece, commission or by other methods of calculation.[7]

Full-Time and Part-Time

Generally, you are free to determine the number of hours required for an employee to be considered full-time versus part-time. Some employers require employees to work 40 hours per week to be considered fulltime, and others designate as full-time those employees who work as little as 24 or 32 hours. As a matter of convenience, you can set the number of work hours required to be a full-time employee as the same number of hours your health insurer requires an employee to work to be eligible for coverage.

You may offer different benefits or levels of benefits to full-time employees than you offer to part-time employees. Providing more benefits to full-time employees does not byitself create liability for illegal discrimination. However, beware that if nearly all of your part-time employees who are *denied* benefits fall into one protected category, and nearly all of your full-time employees *with* benefits do not, you may create the appearance of illegal discrimination.

3.Lab. Code sec. 350(a)

4.Lab. Code sec. 18

5.DLSE Opinion Letter 1988.10.27; DLSE *Enforcement Policies and Interpretations Manual* sec. 43.6.7

6.DLSE *Enforcement Policies and Interpretations Manual* sec. 43.6.8; DLSE Opinion Letters 1993.10.21, 1993.01.07-1, 1993.09.07

7.Lab. Code sec. 200

Example:

All of XYZ Corporation's full-time employees are less than 40 years of age and receive full benefits, but nearly all part-time employees are more than 40 years of age and receive no benefits. XYZ Corporation may not intend to discriminate on the basis of age, but the company should consider that the schedules of its current workforce create that appearance and could invite costly litigation.

Minimum Wage

California's minimum wage increased to $8.00 per hour on January 1, 2008 and is unchanged for 2009. The federal minimum wage is $6.55 per hour, and increased to $7.25 per hour on July 24, 2009. When state and federal law differ, comply with the more restrictive requirement. California state minimum wage is higher so that is the rate that you must pay employees in California.

All work that qualifies for overtime must be paid at $12.00 per hour (time and one-half) or $16.00 per hour (double time). For more information on overtime, see Chapter 14, "Overtime."

If your company policies create special pay rates determined by application of the minimum wage rate, those policies will need attention. For example, travel pay that is paid at minimum wage will require attention. If you pay some nonexempt employees on a salary basis, be sure to take a look at their earnings to assure yourself that the effective hourly rate resulting from that salary meets the new minimum wage. For more information on exempt and nonexempt status, see Chapter 16, "Exempt and Nonexempt."

Living Wage Versus Minimum Wage

You may have to pay more than the minimum wage in some cities and counties as a result of local "living wage" ordinances. Living wage ordinances generally require employers who contract to provide services to a municipality to pay their employees a rate well above the minimum wage. Often the ordinances also require additional contributions toward health benefits.

The following cities and counties adopted some version of a living wage ordinance:

Cities	Counties	Towns
Berkeley	Los Angeles	Fairfax
Hayward	Marin	
Los Angeles	San Francisco	
Oakland	Santa Clara	
Oxnard	Santa Cruz	
Pasadena	Ventura	
Port Hueneme		
Richmond		
Sacramento		

Cities	Counties	Towns
San Diego		
San Fernando		
San Jose		
Santa Cruz		
Santa Monica		
Sebastopol		
Sonoma		
Watsonville		
West Hollywood		

The Port of Oakland also adopted a living wage ordinance.

Minimum Wage "Averaging" Prohibited

California Wage Orders provide that every employee must receive no less than the state minimum wage per hour for all hours worked. In contrast, the federal Fair Labor Standards Act (FLSA) requires payment of minimum wage to employees who work in any workweek. The difference resulted in a substantial award against a California employer for minimum wage violations.

A California Court of Appeal ruled that the differences between California and federal minimum wage prohibits employers from averaging the hourly rate to determine compliance with state minimum wage law. California law provides greater employee protection by mandating that each hour of work be regarded independently to determine if the employer met its obligation to pay the agreed-upon wage.

The plaintiffs in the case were union workers whose collective bargaining agreement provided that employees would be paid wages of $9.08 to $20.00 per hour. The employer, Osmose Inc., categorized work hours as "productive" or "nonproductive" time. Productive time was time spent maintaining utility poles, and the employer paid employees their regular rate of pay. Nonproductive time included travel time, tool repair, vehicle maintenance and paperwork, and the plaintiffs alleged that the employer did not properly pay them for nonproductive time. The employer argued that the average wage for each worker came to more than $6.75 per hour when nonproductive and productive work hours were averaged were averaged into the employees' pay. The court found that this violated California law, even though the FLSA allows minimum wage averaging.[8]

Subminimum Wages

In extremely limited circumstances, you may pay some employees less than the minimum wage. The following summarizes state and federal regulations regarding subminimum wages:

The FLSA allows you to pay a subminimum wage called the "opportunity wage." You may pay employees less than 20 years of age $4.25 per hour for their first 90 consecutive calendar days of

8. *Armenta v. Osmose, Inc.*, 135 Cal. App. 4th 314 (2005)

employment. You may not displace employees, or reduce employees' hours, wages or employment benefits to hire a youth at subminimum wage.[9]

State

The IWC Wage Orders allow you to pay "learners" (workers who have no previous similar or related experience in the occupation) 85 percent of the minimum wage, rounded to the nearest nickel, but not less than $6.80 per hour. You can only pay the learner's rate for the first 160 work hours, after which the minimum wage is due.[10]

Overlap of Federal and State Subminimum Wages

State and federal laws regulating payment of a subminimum wage do differ, but also overlap. If you fall under the FLSA's provisions, the overlapping federal law limits your ability to pay a subminimum wage under state law. (See "Who Is Covered By the FLSA?" in Chapter 11, page 257, for more information about who is subject to the FLSA). You may pay subminimum wages only in the following limited circumstances:[11]

- The federal opportunity rate may be paid only to a learner (one with no previous or similar experience in the occupation);

- The California learner's rate may be paid only if it is the employee's first employment with the employer; and

- The period for payment of subminimum wages to an eligible learner is the first 90 days after the employee first begins work or the first 160 hours of work, whichever comes first. As soon as either eligibility period expires, the employee must be paid the then-current minimum wage.

The subminimum wage is always based on the higher of the state or federal minimum wage rate in effect at the time. Since the federal opportunity wage is only $4.25 per hour, you must pay the higher learners' rate of 85 percent of the state minimum wage, rounded to the nearest nickel, which amounts to $6.80 per hour.

Other Exemptions

Other exceptions to the minimum wage:

- You may obtain licenses from the IWC to pay less than the minimum wage to learners and apprentices, or to persons whose productivity is affected by certain mental or physical disabilities;[12]

- Organized camp counselors, program counselors and student employees are exempt from the minimum wage if they receive a salary of at least 85 percent of the minimum wage for a 40-hour week regardless of the number of hours per week they work at the organized camp. If they work fewer than 40 hours per week, they must be paid at least 85 percent of the minimum wage for each hour worked. The organized camp may, with the employee's written permission, deduct a fair market value of meals and lodging from employee salaries;[13]

---

9. 29 U.S.C. 206(g)
10. IWC Orders sec. 4
11. DLSE Memorandum Issued by State Labor Commissioner, October 9, 1996
12. Lab. Code secs. 1191-93

- Any individual who is a parent, spouse, child or legally adopted child of the employer is not subject to the minimum wage laws;[14]

- Outside salespersons are not subject to the minimum wage law (see "Outside Sales" on page 273 to learn what qualifies as an "outside salesperson");[15] and

- Exempt executive, administrative and professional employees. See Chapter 16, "Exempt and Nonexempt" for more information.

Some Exemptions Eliminated

In 2000, the IWC eliminated the following full and partial exemptions from the minimum wage:

- State and local government employees;

- Full-time carnival ride operators;

- Professional actors;

- Personal attendants in private homes;

- Student nurses; and

- Minors.

Incentive Pay

In some businesses tips and gratuities make up part of employees' pay in addition to wages, as do piece rates, commissions and bonuses in other businesses. The distinction between these forms of pay becomes important when applied to certain wage and hour laws that contain exceptions for commissioned workers (for example, timing of wage payments, final wages and exemptions from overtime), and when determining whether and when payment of these types of wages is due.

Tips and Gratuities

Food servers, valets and others performing services often receive tips or gratuities for such services. These tips and gratuities, which are subject to income tax, are the sole property of the employee to whom they were given. You cannot collect or receive any gratuity left for the employee. You may not credit the employee's tips against his/her wages to satisfy wage requirements.[16]

Though you are prohibited from sharing in or keeping any part of a gratuity left for employees, California law does not specifically prohibit involuntary tip pooling, in which you require employees to pool all or a portion of their tips and then share those tips with other employees.[17]

An agent of an employer is prohibited from collecting, taking or receiving any gratuity given to an employee by a patron. The law defines an agent as every person other than the employer with the authority to hire or discharge any employee or supervise, direct or control the employees' actions.[18]

13. Lab. Code sec. 1182.4
14. IWC Minimum Wage Order
15. IWC Minimum Wage Order
16. Lab. Code sec. 351
17. Decision of Office of Administrative Law, March 24, 1987
18. Lab. Code secs. 351 and 350(d)

In a California Court of Appeal case, a restaurant was found to have imposed a mandatory tip sharing policy on its servers in violation of state law. A floor manager interviewed an applicant for a job as a server, offered her the position and she accepted. Servers were required to give 10 percent of their tips to the floor manager, whose job was to supervise servers, greet and seat patrons, set up reservations and assist in serving tables.

The court acknowledged that floor managers were involved in serving customers and were therefore entitled to share the tips. The court said that the law does not require the floor manager's duties to be exclusively, or even primarily, hiring, discharging or supervising employees. The fact that floor managers provided some direct customer service did not alter their status as "agents" under the law.[19]

If you permit patrons to pay tips by credit card, employees must receive their tip amounts no later than the next regular payday following the date the patron authorized the credit card payment. You must keep accurate records of tips received, including those received by employees through a customer's credit card.[20] You cannot offset the cost of credit card charges you incur against tips paid by the customer on a credit card. Because you chose to use the services of the credit-card company, you, not the employee, must bear the cost of using that service.[21]

Any amounts paid directly by a patron to a dancer subject to Wage Orders 5 or 10 are considered a gratuity.

Piece Rates

A piece rate is based on a figure paid for completing a particular task or making a particular piece of goods.[22] You might pay piece rates based on the number of appointments set by an employee or the number of service calls completed.

Calculation

A piece rate basis is a method of payment based on units of production, and it is an accepted method of paying wages. Many employers pay piece rate to establish an incentive system. However, all requirements that apply to hourly employees alsoapply to piece rate employees.

At the end of the payroll period, the employee must receive at least minimum wage for all hours worked, despite slow production hours or slow production days.[23]

Repeated Work

You can require employees to "re-do" their work if necessary without paying them additional piece rate, as long as you pay the minimum wage for all hours worked in the payroll period. For example, when a beautician is required to "re-do" a perm, he/she is not entitled to a second piece rate. However, minimum wage is guaranteed for the total hours worked in the payroll

---

19. *Jameson v. Five Feet Restaurant, Inc.*, 107 Cal. App 4th 138 (2003).
20. Lab. Code sec. 353
21. *Hudgins v. Neiman Marcus,* 34 Cal. App. 4th 1109 (1995); Lab. Code sec. 351
22. DLSE *Enforcement Policies and Interpretations Manual* sec. 2.5.1
23. DLSE *Enforcement Policies and Interpretations Manual* sec. 47.7

period, including the time spent on the "re-do." The same principles apply to flat rate mechanics and to other piece-rate employees.

Overtime Calculation

Piece-rate employees are entitled to premium pay for overtime hours, though the calculation is different than for hourly employees.[24]

Example:

A factory production worker (Wage Order 1) is paid on a piece rate basis of $10.00 for each unit of production completed. This employee is paid weekly (on Friday) for the previous week ending Saturday. During the work week (which coincides with the payroll period), the employee worked eight hours per day, Monday through Friday, and worked four hours overtime on Saturday. This employee completed 60 units of production during the work week/payroll week, earning $600 in straight time wages. The premium pay due is calculated by dividing $600 by 44 (total hours worked), equaling $13.64. This is the regular rate of pay, and the employee is now due extra half-time of $6.82 per hour for four hours, equaling $27.27. The total wages due this employee is $627.27.

To calculate the "regular rate" for piece workers, straight-time wages are divided by actual hours worked, even if more than 40 hours. This differs from the "regular rate" calculation for salaried or hourly employees, for which the regular rate is determined by dividing by the actual hours worked **but never more than 40.**

Bonuses

A bonus is money you give to an employee in addition to the salary or hourly rate usually due as compensation. Bonuses may be in the form of a gratuity where there is no promise for payment (for example, you decide at the end of the year to reward employees for a job well done), or when you promise a bonus in return for a specific result (i.e., you promise a specific or percentage bonus if the company adds 50 new clients).[25]

Legal Considerations of Bonus programs

An employee incentive compensation plan (ICP) based on the employer's profits, calculated by subtracting operating expenses from revenues, is not an unlawful wage deduction according to the California Supreme Court. An employer that offers supplementary compensation, in addition to regular wages, designed to reward employees if and when their collective efforts result in higher profits for the company is not a violation of California wage protection laws. [26]

Eddy Prachasaisoradej worked as a produce manager for Ralphs Grocery, which offered an ICP to provide certain employees additional compensation depending on the profits of each store. The formula used to determine the supplementary monies under the ICP subtracted each store's operating expenses from store revenues. Prachasaisoradej claimed the formula violated California law because Ralphs shifted its costs of running its business to the employees by withholding, deducting or recouping from them wages belonging to the employees. California law prohibits wage deductions except in very limited circumstances.

24.DLSE *Enforcement Policies and Interpretations Manual* sec. 49.2.1.5

25.DLSE *Enforcement Policies and Interpretations Manual* sec. 2.5.4

26.*Prachasaisoradej v. Ralphs Grocery Company, Inc.* 42 Cal 4th 217 (2007)

The Court of Appeal found the ICP invalid because the store considered workers' compensation costs when calculating the store's profit, and invalid as applied to nonexempt employees because the ICP factored cash shortages and merchandise damage and loss into the profit calculation. In essence, according to the Court of Appeal, Ralphs charged back a portion of its costs to employees through deductions from their wages.

The California Supreme Court disagreed. The ICP did not create an entitlement or expectation for a specific wage and then deduct from it to reimburse Ralphs for its business costs. All employees earned the rate of pay they were promised for the hours they worked, regardless of how profitable the store was. The ICP was in addition to the regular wage, and plan participants understood that their entitlement to ICP money and the amount received resulted from a formula that compared the store's actual ICP-defined profit with the company's pre-defined target figures. Once the employee's ICP compensation was calculated using this formula, Ralphs did not reduce it by taking unauthorized deductions from any employee wages. According to the court, "After fully absorbing the expenses at issue, Ralphs simply determined what remained as profits to share with its eligible employees in addition to their normal wages." As such, no violation of law occurred.

Commissions

Compensation can be considered a true commission only if it is based on a proportional amount of sales of the employer's property or services.[27] The worker receiving the commission must be involved principally in selling the goods or services on which the commission is measured. Employees who receive payments based on performance of services really receive a piece rate. Employees who share in a percentage of the profits of a store do not receive a commission, but a hybrid hourly plan based on profits.[28]

Commission wage compensation plans offer some of the most difficult problems for employers. Each plan presents some unique feature that must be interpreted and applied to establish the rights and liabilities of the parties.

A California Court of Appeal defined the term "commission wages" with two requirements:

- The employees must be involved principally in selling a product or service, not making the product or rendering the service; and

- The amount of their compensation must be a percent of the price of the product or service they sell.[29]

Simply devising a plan that relies on a "percentage" of some sum, such as the cost of the goods or services rendered, does not constitute a "commission wage." The worker also must be "principally" involved in selling the goods or services.

Many plans that simply equate "commission" with "percentage" are nothing more than piece rate plans. Other plans that call for the employees to share in a percentage of the gross (or net) profits of the employer usually are a hybrid hourly pay plan. Under a hybrid plan, the hourly rate is based on a percentage of the profit and may, for that reason, vary from week to week. These pay plans, based on percentages, do not usually violate the law. But they are not "commission wages" in California.

---

27. Lab. Code sec. 204.1; *Keyes Motors, Inc. v. DLSE*, 197 Cal. App. 3d 557 (1988)
28. DLSE *Enforcement Policies and Interpretations Manual* sec. 2.5.4
29. *Keyes Motors, Inc. v. DLSE*, 197 Cal. App. 3d 557 (1988)

Bonuses also get confused with commission wages. Usually, bonuses are not based on the price of a particular product or service, which distinguishes them from commission wages. Another difference is that a bonus is often paid to individuals not engaged in sales at all.

Commission Pool Arrangements

In some situations, the commission payable to the worker is based upon a "pool" arrangement. Under this arrangement, a group of employees, all of whom must be engaged principally in selling the products or services on which the commission percentage is based, share in the "pool." Such an arrangement does constitute a commission scheme if all other requirements of the law are met.

Draw Against Commissions

If an employee receives a draw against commissions to be earned at a future time, the "draw" must be equal at least to the minimum wage and overtime due the employee for each pay period (unless the employee is exempt, such as an outside salesperson). The draw is the basic wage and is due for each period the employee works even though commissions do not equal or exceed the amount of the draw (unless there is a specific agreement to the contrary).[30] Reconcile draws against commissions with earned commission at regular intervals dependent on the frequency with which commissions are earned, and the amounts involved. Do this at least once a year.

Forfeitures

Each commission payment plan is unique and you must base the commission wage computation on the plan. Many commission plans state that certain conditions must be met before the commissions are payable, creating "forfeitures.' A distinction must be drawn between compliance with the conditions and forfeitures.

As a general rule, the employee must complete the condition to be entitled to recover the commission wage. Unless the employer prevented the employee from completing the condition (for example, by discharging the worker before the commission is earned) or the condition is impossible to complete as a result of conditions beyond the expectations of the parties, the employee's failure to complete the condition will result in no commission being owed.

However, courts do not favor forfeitures. Unless the language regarding the forfeiture is clear and unambiguous, the courts will not enforce the language if any logical reading of the contract would avoid the forfeiture. But if the forfeiture is clearly provided in the language of the contract or the agreement of the parties is within the expectations of the parties and violates no public policy, the forfeiture is valid and enforceable.

A California Court of Appeal ruled that an employer may lawfully deduct unearned commissions from future compensation advances without violating the California Labor Code. The case involved a commission plan for a newspaper's telephone sales people that created commissions based on sales from the preceding pay period. An employee training manual described the plan, as did a written agreement signed by the employees. This agreement provided that the commission was not earned until the sale was approved by the employer and the customer maintained the subscription for at least 28 days. The employee agreement gave the employer the right to deduct chargebacks from subsequent pay.

30.*Agnew v. Cameron*, 247 Cal. App. 2d 619 (1967)

A group of employees sued, alleging that chargebacks of commissions for cancelled subscriptions constituted illegal deductions from pay. The court agreed that an employer may chargeback unearned commission advances paid prior to completion of all conditions that were to be satisfied before the commissions are due. The commission was not actually earned until the conditions were satisfied.[31]

A different result occurred in another case, again involving newspaper telemarketing employees questioning their employer's charging them back for canceled subscriptions. The employer's policy said that any subscription canceled within 16 weeks would result in the full point value of the commission being charged back to the salesperson. The court found the policy to be unclear whether the employees earn full commission after the 16-week mark or if the commission is earned at the time of the sale. If the commission is indeed earned at the time of the sale, the company policy would amount to an unlawful chargeback.[32]

Outside Sales

Outside commissioned salespersons are exempt from minimum wage and overtime requirements in some circumstances. An outside salesperson is one who regularly spends more than half his/her working time outside the company offices selling or obtaining orders for a product or service. You must pay sales commissions earned by outside salespersons no later than when you receive the money for the sale from the buyer. This rule prevails after the outside salesperson leaves the company.[33] Employees classified as "outside sales" may not always be exempt under a recent California Supreme Court decision. See "Outside Salesperson Exemption" in Chapter 16, page 400.

Inside Sales

An inside salesperson sells merchandise in a store or sales lot or sells a product or service via a company telephone. Inside salespeople are nonexempt, and therefore minimum wage and overtime requirements apply. An inside salesperson who is paid by commissions is entitled to a minimum wage pay each week if his/her commissions during the 40 hours of the workweek add up to less than the total of 40 hours multiplied by the minimum wage. You cannot recover this money even if the inside salesperson goes on to have a string of unsuccessful sales weeks and then leaves the job having earned less in sales than he/she was paid in minimum wage.[34] You must pay sales commissions by inside salespersons no later than when the money for the sale is received from the buyer, even if the salesperson leaves the company. You must pay commission wages to vehicle salespeople at least once per month.[35]

Overtime Exemption

Employees working under Wage Orders 4 and 7 are not entitled to overtime under California law if their earnings exceed one and one-half times the minimum wage and more than half of the employee's compensation represents commissions.[36] Of course, the employee also must meet one of the federal exemptions (see "Outside Salesperson Exemption" in Chapter 16, page 400) to be exempt from federal overtime requirements.

---

31. *Steinhebel v. Los Angeles Times Communications*, 126 Cal. App. 4th 696 (2005)
32. *Harris v. Investor's Business Daily, Inc.* 138 Cal. App. 4th 28 (2006)
33. *Prudential Insurance Co. v. Fromberg*, 240 Cal. App. 2d 185 (1966)
34. *Leighton v. Old Heidelberg Limited*, 219 Cal. App. 3d 1062 (1990)
35. Lab. Code sec. 204.1
36. IWC Wage Orders 4 and 7, sec. 3

Because this overtime exemption is conditioned, in part, on the amount of earnings attributable to commissions, it is critical that those earnings satisfy the definition of "commission." The California Labor Code defines commission as compensation paid for services rendered in the sale of property or services based proportionately on the amount or value of the sale.[37]

An employer relying on the sales exemption from overtime (see "Outside Salesperson Exemption" in Chapter 16, page 400, and "Commissioned Inside Sales Employee Exemption" in Chapter 16, page 401) whose compensation plan did not meet this requirement lost the overtime exemption for its sales force. In that plan, employees selling newspaper subscriptions received varying point levels based on the subscription's duration and other sales activities. The commission was based on the number of points earned, but the point values were not tied to the value of the subscription sold. As an employee earned more points, the dollar value of the points increased. The Court of Appeal found these payments were not a "commission" and could not be considered in compliance with the exemption requirements. The employees did not meet the exemption test.[38]

Vacation Benefits

There is no specified way under state law for employers who offer vacation benefits to commissioned employees to compute the dollar value of accrued vacation leave. You can base vacation pay on an average earnings figure over a reasonable time period or pay a set hourly amount regardless of actual normal earnings. To avoid disputes in this area, include the method of determining vacation pay in company policy or a contract with commissioned salespeople.

Employers Outside California

If you have no fixed place of business in California and your payments to employees involve commissions, you must have a written employment contract setting forth the method of computation and payment. Failure to do so may leave you vulnerable to the employee in a civil action for triple damages.[39]

Miscellaneous Pay Practices

Miscellaneous pay practices include special pay arrangements created to compensate for atypical hours of work. Rules applicable to these payments require careful attention to determining when they apply and how much is earned.

Split Shift Pay

A split shift is any two distinct work periods separated by more than a one-hour meal period. If there is more than one hour between shifts, the employee must receive at least one hour's pay at no less than the minimum wage rate for the time between shifts.[40] You can use any hourly amount the employee earns above minimum wage to offset the split shift requirement. In addition, you need not count the compensation for the time between split shifts for overtime purposes since it is not compensation for hours actually worked.

---

37. Lab. Code sec. 204.1
38. *Harris v. Investor's Business Daily, Inc.* 138 Cal. App.4th 28 (2006)
39. Lab. Code secs. 2751, 2752
40. IWC Wage Orders sec. 4(C)

The dollar amounts in the following examples are based on the state minimum wage of $8.00 per hour.

Example 1: One Hour Split Shift Due

The following example typifies a restaurant employee earning minimum wage working the lunch and dinner shifts:

Hourly wage:	$8.00
Hours worked:	11:00-2:00 and 4:00-9:00 (total of eight hours)
Split shift wage:	One hour at $8.00
Wages Due:	Eight hours worked ($64) plus one split shift hour ($8.00) = $72.00.

Though the employee was paid for nine hours, no overtime is owed because only eight hours were actually worked in the day.

If the employee in the above example received a higher hourly wage, the split shift requirement would be either fully or partially offset:

Example 2: Split Shift Partially Offset by Hourly Wage

Hourly wage:	$8.15 (15 cents higher than minimum wage)
Hours worked:	11:00-2:00 and 4:00-9:00 (total of eight hours)
Split shift wage:	One hour at $8.00
Offset:	15 cents x 8 hours = $1.20 (split shift partially offset: $8.00 - $1.20 = $6.80)
Wages due:	Eight hours worked ($65.20) plus partially offset split shift hour ($6.80) = $72.00

Shift Differential Pay

Though many employers *choose* to pay a small premium (called a "shift differential") to employees who work swing, graveyard or other less desirable shifts, no law *requires* you to pay a shift differential.

Reporting Time Pay

Reporting time pay is designed to discourage employers from having employees report to a job unless there is work to be done. It must be paid in a number of circumstances:

Reporting time pay is owed when an employee reports to work at his/her regularly scheduled time but is not put to work or is given less than half the usual or scheduled day's work. In this case, you must pay the employee for at least half of the hours he/she was scheduled to work, but never less than two hours pay and never more than four hours pay:

Scheduled Hours	Reporting Time Pay Owed
10	4
9	4
8	4
7	3.5
6	3
5	2.5
4	2
3	2
2	2

Reporting time pay is also owed if an employee is required to report to work a second time in any one workday and is given less than two hours work on the second reporting. In this case, the employee must receive at least two hours pay for the second appearance.[41] These provisions do not apply to workers:

- On a paid standby status, called to work at times other than their usual shift;

- When operations cannot begin due to threats to the employer or property or when recommended by civil authority;

- When public utilities fail, such as water, gas, electricity or sewer; and

- When work is interrupted by an act of God or other causes not within the employer's control.

Reporting time pay must be paid if an employee reports to work at an assigned time and is told that there is no work but to report back later. The employee would be entitled to pay for one-half his regular shift (not less than two hours) even though he may report back later and work a full shift. If, at the subsequent reporting time, the employee is not provided with at least two hours of work, he is entitled to at least two hours pay.[42]

The Division of Labor Standards Enforcement (DLSE) provided new advice concerning reporting time pay relating to required attendance at meetings. Where an employee is required to attend a meeting on a day he or she is not scheduled to work, reporting time pay must be paid as shown in the table above. If the meeting takes place on an employee's regularly scheduled work day but the employee must return sometime after the end of his or her shift to attend the meeting, two hours of reporting time pay must be paid.[43]

---

41. IWC Wage Orders sec. 5
42. *DLSE Enforcement Policies and Interpretations Manual*, sec. 45.1.2
43. *DLSE Enforcement Policies and Interpretations Manual*, sec. 45.1.4

Call-in Pay

When an employee is called in to work on a day other than his/her normal work schedule (when there is no specified number of hours the employee is scheduled to work), that employee receives at least two hours pay at the then-applicable rate based on the reporting time pay requirement.[44]

On-Call/Standby Pay

Requiring an employee to stay at home or at work on an "on-call" (also known as "standby") status may qualify that time as hours worked. "On-call" time is not compensable if the employee can use the time spent on-call primarily for his/her own benefit. In determining whether on-call time is work time, consider:

- Geographic restrictions on the employee's movements;
- Required response time;
- The employment relationship and industry practice; and
- Any other limitation on the employee's ability to use the time for his/her own benefit.[45]

Agreements between you and your employee that the on-call time is noncompensable do not hold up against state requirements.

Carrying a beeper or similar paging device normally does not constitute hours worked, provided the employee is free to come and go as he/she pleases. You must give the employee sufficient time to report (generally at least 20 to 30 minutes, depending on geographic population density) so that he/she can be free to use the nonduty time to his/her own benefit.

All time spent on call-backs during a standby period is counted as time worked. This includes a reasonable time for travel both to and from the work site from the point at which the employee is summoned to return to work. Use good judgment and reasonableness in determining travel time. For example, consider an employee who lives three miles from the jobsite but is at the beach 20 miles away when reached at 12:00 p.m. to return to work. The employee returns and works until 9:00 p.m. In this case, it is reasonable that the travel time would be calculated from the beach to the jobsite and back to the employee's home.

Call-back or controlled standby time is paid the same as regular hours worked, and the regular or agreed wage for this period as well as applicable overtime must be paid.

Assigned Job Duties

On-call resident employees under Wage Order 5, such as resident managers, need only be paid for time spent performing their assigned job duties. Employers are not required to pay on-call resident employees for the time the employees spend on-call if the employees may freely engage in personal activities, regardless of any geographic restrictions imposed by the employer on such activities.[46]

---

44. IWC Wage Orders sec. 5

45. *Berry v. County of Sonoma,* 763 F. Supp 1055 (1990); *Madera Police Officers Assoc. v City of Madera,* 36 Cal. 3d 403 (1984)

46. *Isner v. Falkenberg/Gilliam Associates,* 160 Cal. App. 4th 1393 (2008)

Power Outage Pay

California's 2001 power crisis raised the issue of how to pay employees during rolling blackouts or power failures.

Sending Employees Home

You may send employees home. Pay requirements differ for exempt and nonexempt employees who are sent home.

Normally rules may require "reporting time pay" when a nonexempt employee is sent home before the end of a scheduled shift. However, reporting time pay requirements do not apply when public utilities fail to supply electricity, water or gas, or there is a failure in the public utilities or sewer system. You would only pay a nonexempt employee sent home because of a power outage for the time actually worked that day.

If an exempt employee worked any part of the day, he or she is entitled to a full day's pay if sent home due to a power outage. You may not make a deduction for the portion of the day not worked.

Calling Employees Back to Work

If power is restored, you have the option of calling employees back to work to finish the rest of their shift. The normal "call-back pay" requirement, a minimum of two hours of pay for the second reporting in a single day, does not apply when public utilities fail to supply electricity, water or gas, or there is a failure in the public utilities or sewer system.

Requiring Employees to Remain at Work

You may require employees to remain in the workplace to wait for power to return. However, even if employees do not perform any work they must receive pay for the time while waiting for power to be restored because they remain under your control.

If the power goes out near a scheduled meal period, you may still take employees off the clock for a meal break for up to one hour. If power is still out when the break is over, you can require employees to wait it out in the workplace or send them home for the day.

Deductions from Wages

You may not collect previously paid wages from an employee.[47] This prevents the fraud usually associated with kickbacks in these situations.[48] It also is unlawful for you to withhold any part of a collectively bargained wage with intent to defraud an employee, a competitor or any other person.[49] This prevents unlawful private agreements from nullifying collective bargaining contracts.[50]

The law also prohibits charging an employee for medical examinations required for employment or necessitated by law.[51] You also may not make a deduction of any type unless authorized by law or by

---

47.Lab. Code sec. 221
48.*Sublett v. Harry's Tork & Taylor Lunch,* 21 Cal. 2d 273 (1942)
49.Lab. Code sec. 222
50.*Breitman v. Brady,* 113 Cal. App. 2d 642 (1952)

the employee's written consent to cover medical plans or insurance.[52] No deduction can occur if it represents an attempt to evade minimum wage laws or a valid collective bargaining agreement.[53] Secret payments from employees back to you also violate the Labor Code.[54]

Overpayment of Wages

If an employee fails to turn in a timecard and you pay his/her wages for the normal work period as required by law, inform him/her that the paycheck may include some overpayment, since you cannot determine whether the employee actually worked his/her full normal work period. If the employee was in fact overpaid, you could then ask him/her to repay that amount, or to sign an agreement to have that amount deducted from the next paycheck. You may not make any deduction from the next paycheck without the employee's consent.

Note that the Labor Commissioner published an Interpretive Bulletin in 1985 that clearly allowed a deduction from the next paycheck if the employee was aware or reasonably should have been aware of the overpayment.[55] However, the Labor Commissioner's Interpretive Bulletins were invalidated,[56] and no similar provision exists in the Labor Commissioner's *Enforcement Policies and Interpretations Manual*, which replaced the Interpretive Bulletins.

If you overpay wages and catch the error immediately, the Labor Commissioner generally allows you to make a deduction from the next payment. Indeed, an employer may make deductions from wages to reflect predictable and expected wage overpayments made in the immediately prior paycheck that resulted from the employer's payroll system, if the employee provides voluntary, written authorization.[57] The problem arises if the "overpayment" continues over a period of time, resulting in the accumulation of a substantial amount. Such a circumstance may cast serious doubt as to whether there was an "error" or whether the employer increased the employee's wages. Payroll deductions made to correct such an error may be seen by the Labor Commissioner as not recoverable and not allowed.

One of the reasons for the state's diligence on this problem is to prevent kickbacks from employee to employer that would avoid payment of minimum or prevailing wages or other wages due, such as overtime pay. In any case involving improper deductions, courts will consider the overall legislative purpose of preventing kickbacks.

Employee Tardiness

If an employee is tardy, you may not deduct from the employee's wages any amount in excess of the wage that would have been earned during the time actually lost. However, if the loss of time is less than 30 minutes, you may deduct one-half hour of wages.[58] If such a deduction is made, you may not put the employee to work during that half-hour period.

---

51. Lab. Code sec. 222.5
52. Lab. Code sec. 224
53. Lab. Code sec. 222
54. Lab. Code sec. 223
55. DLSE Interpretive Bulletin 85-3
56. *Tidewater Marine v. Bradshaw*, 14 Cal. 4th 557 (1996)
57. DLSE Opinion Letter 2008.11.25.1
58. Lab. Code sec. 2928

Employee Debts

California law severely limits the circumstances in which you may deduct damages or debts owed by an employee from his/her wages.[59] The Labor Commissioner is guided by the following:[60]

- **Simple negligence:** You may not deduct from the employee's wage any amount to compensate yourself for loss or damage caused by the employee's simple negligence.[61] You must bear the burden of losses which result from an employee's ordinary negligence or incompetency;

- **A debt:** You may not deduct from an employee's final check any amount representing the unpaid balance of a debt owed by the employee even though the indebtedness is contained in a written agreement to pay the full amount of the debt on demand, at termination or otherwise;[62] and

- **Gross negligence, willful misconduct or dishonesty:** You may deduct from the employee's wages amounts to compensate for loss or damage resulting from any such conduct and may make the deduction from the employee's wages during employment and/or from the final check.

If you deduct from an employee's paycheck any amount believed to be the result of gross negligence, willful misconduct or dishonesty, the burden of proof is on you to justify the withholding. If you fail to meet the burden of proof, you will likely be subject to waiting time penalties.[63] Any doubt as to your ability to prove misconduct is probably best resolved in a small claims or other court proceeding against the employee, rather than a deduction from wages owed that employee.

Illegal Deduction Penalties

A California Court of Appeal ruled that a casual employee who was not called back to work after he objected to an illegal deduction from his paycheck had a claim for wrongful termination. The Court found it a violation of public policy for an employer to withhold money from an employee's paycheck unless authorized by the employee or a state or federal law.[64]

Balloon Payments Not Allowed

An employee may pay debts periodically if, by written agreement, he/she authorizes deductions from his/her wages, including the regular deduction on the final paycheck. However, you may not deduct the balance of the obligation from the final paycheck (a "balloon payment") without a separate written agreement executed at the time of the final paycheck and signed by the employee.[65] Otherwise, the loan agreement extends beyond the employment period and should continue to be paid on a regular basis. If a former employee defaults on the loan, you can seek repayment of the full amount in court.

---

59. *Barnhill v. Robert Saunders & Co.*, 125 Cal. App. 3d 1 (1981); *Kerr's Catering Service v. Dept. of Industrial Relations*, 57 Cal. 2d 319 (1962); DLSE *Enforcement Policies and Interpretations Manual* sec. 11.2.3

60. DLSE *Enforcement Policies and Interpretations Manual* sec. 11.2

61. *Kerr's Catering Service v. Dept. of Industrial Relations*, 57 Cal. 2d 319 (1962); DLSE *Enforcement Policies and Interpretations Manual* sec. 11.2.3

62. *Barnhill v. Robert Saunders & Co.*, 125 Cal. App. 3d 1 (1981)

63. Lab. Code sec. 203

64. *Phillips v. Gemini Moving Specialists*, 63 Cal. App. 4th 563 (1998)

65. DLSE *Enforcement Policies and Interpretations Manual* sec. 11.2.5; *Barnhill v. Robert Saunders & Co.*, 125 Cal. App. 3d 1 (1981)

Unreturned Tools and Uniforms

The IWC Wage Orders provide that, in lieu of posting a bond, an employee may agree to a deduction from his/her last paycheck to cover the cost of tools, uniforms or other items you furnished which he/she did not return to you.[66] However, based on decisions of the California Supreme Court and a California appellate court, you may not make such deductions without proving theft or culpable negligence, even where the employee signed an agreement authorizing the deduction.[67]

Cash Bonds and Deposits

You may not demand cash bonds from an employee, unless he/she is entrusted with property of an equivalent value or the bond is in an amount equivalent to the value of goods, wares or merchandise periodically advanced to the employee.[68] You must return any money put up as a bond or deposit to the employee with accrued interest immediately upon return of the property.[69] Property put up as a bond may not be commingled with your property; this is viewed as theft under the Penal Code.[70]

Meals and Lodging

You can credit meals and lodging supplied as part of an employee's compensation against state minimum wage obligations. Meals must provide a variety of nutritious foods, and lodging must meet customary standards of adequacy and sanitation. You cannot deduct from the minimum wage for meals and lodging unless the employee authorized such a deduction in writing and the meals and lodging are used. You cannot require employees to share beds.

If, as a condition of employment, the employee must live at the place of employment or occupy quarters you own or under your control, then you may not charge rent in excess of the values listed in the following table.

The minimum wage order limits the extent to which meals and lodging can be credited against the minimum wage. The meal and lodging credits increased in 2008 and are unchanged for 2009.

Lodging	Effective January 1, 2008
Room occupied alone	$37.63 per week
Room shared	$31.06 per week
Apartment — two-thirds of the ordinary rental value, and in no event more than	$451.89 per month

---

66. IWC Wage Orders sec. 9(c)

67. *Barnhill v. Robert Saunders & Co.*, 125 Cal. App. 3d 1 (1981); *Kerr's Catering Service v. Dept. of Industrial Relations*, 57 Cal. 2d 319 (1962); DLSE *Enforcement Policies and Interpretations Manual* sec. 11.2

68. Lab. Code sec. 402

69. Lab. Code sec. 404

70. Lab. Code sec. 405

Lodging	Effective January 1, 2008
Where a couple are both employed by the employer, two-thirds of the ordinary rental value, and in no event more than	$668.46 per month

Meals	Effective January 1, 2008
Breakfast	$2.90
Lunch	$3.97
Dinner	$5.34

Despite the IWC's dollar limit on rent, the law allows you to charge a resident manager of an apartment house up to two-thirds of the fair market rental value of the apartment supplied pursuant to a voluntary written agreement. You may not use credit for the apartment to meet your minimum wage obligation to the manager.[71]

Garnishment Against Wages

Employers occasionally receive court orders garnishing an employee's paycheck for payment of child support or other debts. The law places limits on the percentage of wages that may be withheld, depending on the type of garnishment. You may deduct $1.50 from the employee's earnings for each payment made in accordance with any garnishment order.[72]

Guidelines

Follow these general guidelines if you receive a garnishment order:

- Advise the employee of the court order and the date the first deduction will be made;

- Do not garnish a paycheck for more than 25 percent of its total, or 50 percent for child support. However, the courts enforce that limitation, not you;

- Do not discharge the employee because his/her wages are garnished for the payment of one judgment.[73] A judgment against an employee is a single debt, regardless of the number of garnishments based on it. Employers may discharge employees for garnishments for multiple judgments other than child support;

- Pay child support payments first if an employee is subject to multiple garnishments (see "Child Support" on page 283); and

- Keep a copy of the court orders in the employee's personnel file as the legal basis for making the payroll deduction.

---

71. Lab. Code sec. 1182.8
72. Code of Civil Procedure sec. 706.034
73. Lab. Code sec. 2929

Child Support

Your obligation to withhold child support owed by an employee pursuant to an appropriate order is even more extensive than the requirements concerning other garnishments. The law makes you responsible for your employees' child-support obligations. You face severe penalties for noncompliance in some cases, and you may become liable for the full amount of child-support claim filed against the employee plus interest, cost and penalties.[74] The law requires each state to establish standard award guidelines and make child-support payments as certain as tax payments through automatic wage deductions.

Be aware of the following general provisions of this law:

- You may deduct and retain $1.50 from the earnings of the employee for each payment made pursuant to a Wage and Earnings Assignment Order for child support. This fee is in addition to the amount ordered to be withheld on the Wage and Earnings Assignment Order.[75] You may not make retroactive deductions;

- The law prohibits job discrimination based upon automatic child-support withholding. You may open yourself to state and federal penalties if an applicant claims discrimination based upon pre-employment inquiries about child support obligations. An increase in payroll costs due to child-support withholding is not a valid reason for rejecting an applicant;

- State and federal law prohibit terminating an employee for child-support withholding, garnishment or threatened garnishment;

- The law requires that you provide, in writing, the employee's last known address and new employer's name and address, if known. You also must keep the order on file and honor its provisions if the employee returns to work;

- Although notifying the employee of the withholding notice is not required, it is a sound practice. Advise the employee of the date the notice is received, the date withholding begins, the amount to be withheld and the requirement that you must comply with the order;

- You must comply with the child support withholding order as written until directed otherwise by the issuing agency or the court, even if the employee insists the withholding order is incorrect. Refer the employee to the local child-support enforcement office to correct any inaccuracies;

- Child-support claims take precedence over all other claims, except taxes. If the total amount to be withheld exceeds the 50 percent rule, contact the state support enforcement agency for guidance;

- You must pay multiple child-support garnishments in *pro rata* shares, with current support payments taking priority over past due support still owed. If the total amount exceeds the limit that state and federal laws exempt from a portion of the employee's wages, or if out-of-state orders are involved, ask the local child-support office for guidance. If you are a multistate employer, an order delivered to your representative in the issuing state but applicable to an employee working in another state binds you to the issuing state's laws;

- When you receive the child support order, mark the date received on the notice and retain the envelope with its postmark in case timely compliance becomes an issue. Federal law requires that withholding begin no later than the first pay period occurring after the

---

74. Family Support Act of 1988
75. Family Code sec. 5235(d)

mailing date of the notice. The wage withholding order requires delivery of the withheld child support within 10 days; and

- You may stop child-support withholding only upon order from the state's child-support enforcement agency or the court. You must inform the appropriate agency if an employee subject to wage withholding leaves, and you must resume withholding immediately upon the employee's rehire.

Establish a standard procedure for processing child-support withholding and garnishment orders, apply it consistently and include any confidentiality guidelines. In addition, given the emotional nature of such orders in some situations, train your payroll coordinator not only on law and compliance procedures, but also on company policy for handling distressed employees.

For more information about child-support wage garnishments, call the state Department of Child Support Servicesat (866) 249–0773.

Penalty for Failure to Comply With Child-support Order

A court may order a child-support garnishment to be paid by electronic transfer from the employer's bank account if the employer willfully fails to comply with the garnishment.[76] An electronic transfer also may be ordered when the employer fails to comply with the garnishment on three separate occasions within a 12-month period, regardless of whether the failures were willful.

In addition, you may be subject to a civil penalty of up to 50 percent of the support amount not received, plus interest on the unpaid support.

A law passed in 2006 imposes liability upon any person or business entity that knowingly assists a person who has an unpaid child support obligation to escape, evade or avoid current payment of those unpaid child-support obligations. The penalty is three times the value of the assistance to have been provided, up to the total amount of the entire child-support obligation due. The penalty will not apply if the unpaid obligation is satisfied. When an individual or entity knows of or should have known of the child-support obligation, prohibited actions include:

- Hiring or employing a person who owes child support without timely reporting to the EDD's New Employee Registry;

- Retaining an independent contractor who owes child support and failing to file a timely report of such engagement with the EDD; or

- Paying wages or other forms of compensation (including cash, barter or trade) not reported to the EDD.

Employment and Income Information for District Attorney

Under state law, district attorneys enforce parents' obligations to support their children, and you must provide information to assist with the enforcement process.[77] The law provides protection from liability for employers who provide such information (for more information, see "District Attorney" in Chapter 8, page 158).

---

76. Family Code sec. 5241
77. Family Code sec. 5283; Welfare and Institutions Code sec. 11478.7

An employer who fails to provide relevant employment information to the district attorney within 30 days of receiving such a request may be assessed a civil penalty of a maximum of $1,000, plus attorneys' fees and costs.

Timely Payment

In addition to paying the correct amount of compensation to employees, you are expected to pay it on time and in the manner required by law. Different rules apply to the routine payment of wages on regular paydays and the payment of wages when an employee resigns or is laid off or terminated. Adhere to these rules to avoid stiff penalties.

Regular Paydays

The California Labor Code is quite specific about the timing of wage payments and regularity of paydays. Striking employees' earned wages become payable in full on the next regularly scheduled payday.[78]

Paydays for Nonexempt Employees

All wages for the normal work period for nonexempt employees come due and are payable at least twice each calendar month on days designated in advance by the employer (see Chapter 16, "Exempt and Nonexempt" for an explanation of exempt and nonexempt status).[79] You must post a notice informing employees of paydays.[80]

You also may choose to pay employees weekly, bi-weekly or semi-monthly with payment within seven days of the end of the pay period.[81] Paydays on a twice-monthly schedule must be as follows:[82]

Work performed between:	Payment must be made by:
1st and 15th days of the month	26th day of the same month
16th and last day of the month	10th day of the next month

For employees who work in an industry involving work for several employers in the same industry interchangeably, the employers may establish a plan for the payment of wages in a central place and at a single time.[83]

Paydays for Exempt Employees

Salaries of executive, administrative and professional employees of employers covered under the FLSA may be paid once a month on or before the 26th day of the month. This paycheck must

---

78. Lab. Code sec. 209
79. Lab. Code sec. 204
80. Lab. Code sec. 207
81. Lab. Code secs. 204, 204(b)
82. Lab. Code sec. 204
83. Lab. Code sec. 204(a)

include the as yet unearned portion between the date of payment and the last day of the month.[84]

Payday Notice

The day, time and place of the regular payday must be posted.[85] As a convenience, the state provides a small form for this purpose. However, it is satisfactory to post this information in any understandable form. The payday notice is included as part of CalBizCentral's *Employer Notices Poster.*

No specific law requires a particular amount of advance notice to employees if you change your payday schedule. However, to avoid potential violations of payday laws, notify employees of the planned change at least one full payroll cycle in advance of the new schedule.

Overtime Wages

Payment of overtime wages earned in one pay period may be delayed until no later than the payday for the next pay period. Only the payment of *overtime* wages may be delayed to the following pay period. *Straight-time* wages must be paid within the times set forth above.[86]

Since January 1, 2007, if you delay payment of overtime wages to the following pay period, you may itemize the hours as corrections on the pay stub for the period in which they are paid, provided you identify the date of the pay period to which they are attributable.

Employer Closed on Payday

If you are closed on a payday that falls on a Sunday or a holiday listed in the state Government Code, you may pay wages on the next business day.[87]

Holidays listed in the Government Code:

- January 1 — New Year's Day;
- Third Monday in January — Martin Luther King Jr. Day;
- February 12 — Lincoln's Birthday;
- Third Monday in February — Washington's Birthday (*observed*);
- Last Monday in May — Memorial Day;
- July 4 — Independence Day;
- First Monday in September — Labor Day;
- Second Monday in October — Columbus Day;
- November 11 — Veterans Day;
- Fourth Thursday in November — Thanksgiving Day;
- Day after Thanksgiving;

---

84. Lab. Code sec. 204
85. Lab. Code sec. 207
86. Lab. Code sec. 204
87. DLSE *Enforcement Policies and Interpretations Manual* sec. 7.6

- December 25 — Christmas; and

- Other days appointed by the governor for a public fast, thanksgiving or holiday.

If a listed day falls on a Sunday, the following Monday is considered to be the holiday. If November 11 falls on a Saturday, the preceding Friday is the holiday.[88]

It should be noted that state law does not require private employers to provide holidays, and the payday exception will apply only if the business is closed.[89]

Employee Failure to Complete Timecard

Even when an employee fails to turn in a record of time worked, you remain legally obligated to pay the employee on the established payday. There is no exception in the law allowing you to require the employee to wait until the next payday or until the timecard is turned in to receive those wages.

But with no time record, how should employers comply with this law? Pay all wages due for the employee's normal work period (for example, 40 hours for a full-time employee) and defer payment of any overtime worked until the next regular payday.[90]

Though you may not withhold wages as a penalty for failing to turn in a timecard, you may discipline the employee in other ways. You may treat failure to turn in a timecard as a violation of a work rule and penalize the employee with suspension, demotion or termination. Of course, you should follow your own established disciplinary procedures.

Some employers use positive methods to remind employees to turn in timecards, such as a small bonus or party if all department members turn in their timecards on time for a calendar quarter.

Expense Reimbursements

You must reimburse employees for all monies that they necessarily expend or lose directly relating to the performance of their duties or following your directions.[91]

Common examples include mileage, travel and dining expenses. In extreme cases, this also includes compensating employees sued by third persons for conduct within the scope of employment.[92]

Effective January 1, 2009, the standard IRS mileage rate is 55 cents per mile. This is a decrease from the 58.5 cents per mile rate in effect from July 1, 2008 through December 31, 2008. The mileage rate is based on study of vehicle operating cost conducted annually for the IRS, and is considered the most reasonable reimbursement rate by California state agencies.

Wage laws, such as those regulating the time and place of payment, do not apply to expense reimbursements. You may make expense reimbursements on any reasonable schedule.

88.Govt. Code sec. 19853(a)

89.DLSE *Enforcement Policies and Interpretations Manual* sec. 7.6.2

90.Lab. Code sec. 204

91.Lab. Code sec. 2802

92.*Douglas v. Los Angeles Herald Examiner,* 50 Cal. App. 3d 449 (1975)

Final Pay

The time requirement for a final paycheck depends on whether the employee quit without notice, quit with at least 72 hours' notice or was terminated or laid off. Certain industries are granted exceptions to the final paycheck requirements.

Termination and Layoff

If you terminate an employee or lay him/her off with no specific return date within the normal pay period, all wages and accrued vacation earned but unpaid are due and payable immediately.[93] It is not acceptable to ask or require an employee to wait until the next regular payday for his/her final wages.

You may not withhold a final paycheck. It is illegal to withhold a final paycheck to induce the former employee to:

- Return tools, uniforms, pagers, laptop computers, keys or any other items belonging to the employer;

- Pay back money that may be owed to the employer; and

- Turn in expense reimbursement forms.

If there is a layoff with a return to work date within the pay period and the employee is scheduled to return to work, you may pay the wages at the next regular payday.[94]

The California Labor Code requires that employees receive all earned and unpaid wages at the time of discharge from employment. If not, the employer may be assessed waiting time penalties. The California Supreme Court ruled that neither length of employment nor reason for termination changes this requirement. An employee's service to an employer is completed either by completion of the hired-for task or at termination by the employer. Both constitute a discharge as defined by law. The "discharge" does not require an involuntary termination from an ongoing employment relationship. An employee hired to perform one day of service must be paid at the end of that day.[95]

Suspension

Some employers routinely suspend employees before termination to have time to prepare a final paycheck or to receive one from a payroll service or the employer's out-of-state headquarters. You may be penalized for a willful failure to pay final wages on time, unless there is a good faith dispute that any wages are due.[96] An employee who could show that his/her suspension was a way merely to extend the time for final payment of wages, rather than legitimate time for your investigation, probably would be awarded waiting time penalties due to the lack of any good faith dispute.

---

93. Lab. Code sec. 201; *Campos v. EDD,* 132 Cal. App. 3d 961 (1982)
94. DLSE *Enforcement Policies and Interpretations Manual* sec. 3.2.2
95. *Smith v. The Superior Court of Los Angeles County* 39 Cal. 4th 77 (2006)
96. 8 CCR sec. 13520

Voluntary Quit: More Than 72 Hours' Notice

All wages and accrued vacation earned but unpaid for an employee who quits with more than 72 hours' notice to his/her employer are due and payable on the last day of work.[97]

Voluntary Quit: Less Than 72 Hours' Notice

All wages and accrued vacation earned but unpaid for an employee who quits with less than 72 hours' notice to his/her employer are due and payable not later than 72 hours after notice is given. An employee who gives less than 72 hours' notice is entitled to receive his/her final wage payment by mail if he/she so requests and designates a mailing address. The date of mailing is considered the date of payment for purposes of the 72 hour requirement.[98]

You are not obligated to mail or otherwise deliver a paycheck, unless an employee who quits with less than 72 hours' notice requests payment by mail and provides a mailing address.[99] The DLSE clarifies that quitting employees must return to the office or agency of the employer in the county where the work was performed to recover wages after quitting except where the worker gave 72 hours' notice or requested payment by mail and provided an address. [100]

Place of Final Payment

Quitting employees normally must return to the office or agency of the employer in the county where work was performed to pick up their final paycheck.[101] Unless the employee specifically requests payment by mail, you may simply hold the employee's final paycheck until it is picked up. Mailing the final paycheck without a request to do so could subject you to waiting time penalties, since the employee could show up to pick up the check after it has been mailed but before it is delivered to him or her. Unless you are willing to cut a duplicate check and stop payment on the original, the employee will be forced to wait for his or her wages beyond the legal deadline.

Every employee who quits shall be paid at the office or agency of the employer in the county where the employee performed labor.[102] Discharged employees must be paid at the place of discharge.[103] The place of discharge is the employee's location, not yours. If you discharge an employee who is not at your place of business, such as an employee who works remotely, you must be prepared to deliver the final paycheck at the moment you say, "You are terminated." Otherwise, you must pay the employee up until the date that they will actually receive their final pay.

Final wages earned and unpaid at the time an employee is discharged or quits may be paid by direct deposit to the employee's account — if the employee authorized you to do so. The time limits for making final pay available to the terminating employee must still be observed.[104]

---

97. Lab. Code sec. 202
98. Lab. Code sec. 202
99. Lab. Code sec. 202
100. DLSE *Enforcement Policies and Manual* section 3.7
101. Lab. Code sec. 208
102. Lab. Code sec. 208 and DLSE *Enforcement Policies and Manual* section 7.4
103. DLSE *Enforcement Policies and Manual* section 7.4.2
104. Lab. Code sec. 213(d)

Payment By Mail

Labor Code section 202 provides that an employee may elect to receive termination wages by mail. In those cases, the date of the mailing constitutes the date of payment. In the event that the employer contends that the employee elected to receive termination wages by mail, it is necessary that the employer prove that:

- The employee chose this method of delivery; and
- The check was received by the employee.[105]

Expense Reimbursements

The payment deadlines for final wages do not apply to reimbursement of expenses the employee may have incurred on your behalf. Those reimbursements may be made at the normal time for payment.[106]

Wrongful Termination Based on Improper Wage Payment

A 1995 case held that prompt payment of wages is a fundamental public policy of California, and that terminating an employee to avoid paying due wages subjects an employer to the claim of "wrongful termination in violation of public policy." Be aware that terminating an employee who recently alleged improper payment of wages to himself/herself or others can create a huge liability unless the reason for the termination clearly is unrelated to the wage allegations and is thoroughly documented.[107]

Employees In the Theatrical and Concert Industries

Unionized employees in the live theatrical and concert industries, who are dispatched routinely from hiring halls to jobs at theaters or concerts, may negotiate time limits for final payment of wages through collective bargaining.

Severance Pay

Severance pay is not required by law. Be cautious when giving severance pay to a discharged employee because it may set a precedent for future terminations. After paying one employee severance pay, failure to do so for another employee could invite legal claims that the subsequent denial of severance pay was discriminatory.

Severance pay generally will not be considered "wages" by the EDD for purposes of determining eligibility for and benefit levels related to unemployment insurance.

---

105. DLSE *Enforcement Policies and Manual* section 7.3.2
106. DLSE *Enforcement Policies and Interpretations Manual* sec. 4.3.4
107. *Gould v. Maryland Sound Industries, Inc.*, 31 Cal. App. 4th 1137 (1995)

Final Commission Payments

Commissions are considered wages, subject to the normal rules regarding timing of wage payments. However, commissions present special issues regarding the timing of final wages. Many commission plans delay payment of commissions until payment for a sale is received from a customer. Therefore, receipt of a customer's payment on a sale may occur after a commissioned employee quits or is terminated from employment. The Labor Commissioner recognizes that it is impossible to calculate commissions on customer payments not yet received and exempts these wages from the normal final wage payment deadlines. You may continue to pay out commissions to a former employee after the employment relationship ends. The law is unclear as to whether you must send the former employee a check each time a customer pays for a sale that he/she had made, or whether you may continue to pay him/her on the normal pay schedule for all customer payments made within that period. You may wish to consult legal counsel about this issue.

Temporary Employees

 Wages for employees of temporary services employers must be paid weekly, or daily if an employee is assigned to a client on a day-to-day basis or to a client engaged in a trade dispute. This requirement does not apply to employees assigned to a client for more than 90 consecutive calendar days unless the employer pays the employee weekly. Failure to do so can result in civil and criminal penalties.

Labor Code 201.3 was amended to provide that:

- Employee's wages are due and payable no less frequently than weekly, regardless of when the assignment ends, and wages for work performed during any calendar week shall be due and payable not later than the regular payday of the following calendar week.

- If an employee of a temporary services employer is assigned to work for a client on a day-to-day basis, that employee's wages are due and payable at the end of each day.

Both requirements apply unless the worker is assigned for more than 90 days.

Form of Payment of Wages

All paychecks must be payable in cash, on demand and without discount at some established place of business in the state, the name and address of which must appear on the paycheck. At the time the paycheck is issued and for at least 30 days after, sufficient funds or credit in the payroll account must exist for the paycheck's payment.[108]

Paying any wage with a check backed by insufficient funds is unlawful, and the dishonored check constitutes evidence that youviolated the law.[109]

The law does not prohibit you from using an electronic transfer system (direct deposit) to transfer wages to a bank, savings and loan or credit union pursuant to an employee's voluntary choice and authorization. You may not force employees to use a direct deposit system.[110]

---

108. Lab. Code sec. 212
109. Lab. Code sec. 212
110. Lab. Code sec. 213

The DLSE issued two opinion letters stating the use of payroll debit cards and money network checks does not violate the Labor Code so long as:

- The receipt of payment in this manner is voluntary;

- Employees have other payroll payment options;

- There is no fee to use this form of payment at least once per pay period at a banking institution in California;

- The employee has immediate access to the funds; and

- The employee has specifically authorized such form of payment.

Be sure to consult with legal counsel before implementing a payroll program using either of these payment methods.[111]

The Legislature did not intend absolute criminal liability for all cases of issuing paychecks with insufficient funds. In cases where insufficiency results from unforeseen or unpreventable circumstances, violation of the statute becomes excusable.[112]

Public employers, including California and all local governments, do not fall under provisions that establish time and form of payment.[113]

Statement of Wage Deductions Required

At the time wages are paid, you must provide each employee an itemized statement, in writing, that contains the following information:

- Gross wages earned;

- Total hours worked (except salaried exempt employees);

- Piece rate units and rate, if applicable;

- All deductions, including taxes, disability insurance and health and welfare payments (deductions ordered by the employee may be aggregated and shown as one item);

- Net wages earned;

- The inclusive dates of the pay period;

- Name of the employee and Social Security number (SSN), except that, since January 1, 2008, all employers may print no more than the last four digits of an employee's Social Security number on check stubs or similar documents, or can substitute some other identifying number;

- Name and address of employer (legal entity);

- All applicable hourly rates in effect during the pay period and the corresponding number of hours worked at each hourly rate by the employee; and

- Piece rate units and applicable piece rate, if the employee is paid on a piece rate basis.[114]

---

111. DLSE Opinion Letters 2008.07.07 and 2008.07.07.2
112. *People v. Hampton*, 236 Cal. App. 2d 795 (1965)
113. Lab. Code sec. 220
114. Lab. Code sec. 226

In addition, farm labor contractors, agricultural employers and agricultural associations that employ migrant or seasonal agricultural workers must include the employer's identification number assigned by the IRS.[115]

Intentional failure to provide this paycheck information entitles the employee to recover all actual damages, or up to $50 for the initial pay period in which a violation occurs and $100 per employee for each violation in a subsequent pay period, up to a total of $4,000, plus costs and reasonable attorneys' fees.[116]

If you do not provide the required statements to the employee in writing or fail to keep the above records for the required three years, you are subject to civil penalties of $250 per employee per violation for the first violation and $1,000 per employee for each subsequent violation.[117]

If you make a clerical error or inadvertent mistake on the first violation, the Labor Commissioner has discretionary power not to penalize you.[118]

In situations involving cash wage payments, you must keep an indelible record of these payments for at least three years at the place of employment. You must make these records available for inspection by the employee upon reasonable request to allow the employee to inspect and/or copy them.[119]

Execution of Release

The governor signed a bill amending Labor Code 206.5 which makes null and void the execution of any release on account of wages due. Employers who violate this law are guilty of a misdemeanor. The new law, effective January 1, 2009, adds the following language:

For purposes of this section, "execution of a release" includes requiring an employee to sign a statement of the hours he or she worked during a pay period, which the employer knows to be false, as a condition of being paid.

This new law muddies the water a bit. Most importantly, follow the law, keep accurate time records, do not force employees to work off the clock or miss meal and rest breaks, and pay employees on time.

Tools, Uniforms and Equipment

If you require uniforms of the employee as a condition of employment, you must provide and usually maintain them, regardless of how much the employee is paid. You may not make deductions for normal wear and tear. A uniform is defined as wearing apparel and accessories of distinctive design or color. Clothing which is standard in the industry and can be worn from one job to the next is not considered a uniform. For example, white nurses uniforms and black-and-white uniforms for food servers need not be supplied by the employer since these uniforms are standard in their industries and can be used from one job to the next.[120]

---

115. 29 CFR 500.80(d), Migrant and Seasonal Worker Protection Act
116. Lab. Code sec. 226
117. Lab. Code sec. 226.3
118. Lab. Code sec. 226.3
119. Lab. Code sec. 226
120. IWC Wage Orders sec. 9

You must pay for and maintain a uniform if it is not standard in the industry, even if it could be worn off the job as street apparel. For example, a tropical-themed restaurant might ask servers to wear khaki shorts and any Hawaiian shirt. Although this might be appropriate street apparel, since it is not standard apparel for servers throughout the restaurant industry it would be considered a uniform.

Under Cal/OSHA regulations, you must provide all necessary safety equipment for employees, such as gloves and safety shoes.[121] Specific regulations require some employers to provide eye and face protection.[122]

When you require tools or equipment necessary to perform the job, you must provide and maintain them. Employees whose wages are at least two times the minimum wage may be required to provide and maintain hand tools and equipment customarily required by the trade or craft in which he/she works.[123]

Work Facilities

If the job requires changing clothing, you must provide employees with:

- Rooms to permit clothing changes in reasonable privacy;

- Lockers, closets or equivalent space for safekeeping of employees' clothing; and

- Change areas and lockers separated from toilet rooms.[124]

If work allows the employee to sit, you must provide suitable seats. If the work does not allow for sitting, you must provide seats close to the work area and permit workers to use them.[125]

You also must maintain temperature levels consistent with industry standards for process and work. If the process involves high heat or humidity, take all reasonable steps to reduce this hazard. If it produces extreme cold, prevailing temperatures less than 60 degrees, you must furnish a room heated to at least 68 degrees where employees can retire for warmth. Changing federal and state energy guidelines will prevail over these requirements.[126]

Specific Industries

The following exceptions to wage and hour laws exist for specific industries.

Government Contractors

If you do business with government entities, you fall underadditional state and federal requirements in many matters. Wages and benefits are prominent among them and are often heavily influenced by collectively bargained rates.

---

121. Lab. Code sec. 6401
122. CCR Title 8, Div.1, sec. 3382
123. IWC Wage Orders sec. 9; DLSE *Enforcement Policies and Interpretations Manual* sec. 30
124. IWC Wage Orders sec. 13
125. IWC Wage Orders sec. 14
126. IWC Wage Orders sec. 15

Higher Wages

The prevailing wage obligation is imposed when you:

- Contract to provide materials, services or construction work under contracts with federal or state governments;

- Provide services or construction work for public entities; or

- Participate in certain federally funded programs.

A prevailing wage obligation is virtually synonymous with the minimum wage obligation, although the amount you must pay as prevailing wages is generally significantly higher than the minimum wage. The principal difference is that prevailing wage legislation frequently requires the provision of both local prevailing wages and fringe benefits, or payment of the costs of such benefits.

The Walsh-Healey Act covers employers with federal government contracts that manufacture or supply articles with a value of more than $10,000. Under this law, government contractors must pay prevailing wage rates in addition to conforming to the FLSA's requirements.[127] The Act requires such employers to pay the locally prevailing minimum wage as determined by the Secretary of Labor, but does not require payment of locally prevailing fringe benefits.

The Walsh-Healey Act is enforced by the U.S. Department of Labor. The relief available for violations includes liquidated damages to claimants and the possibility of being excluded from government work.

 California employers with lawful alternative workweek schedules who work on federal contracts covered by this law should carefully review the contracts for applicable overtime requirements.

Required Benefits

The Davis-Bacon Act requires all laborers and mechanics engaged in the construction, alteration or repair of public work pursuant to a contract with the federal government in excess of $2,000 to be paid an amount equal to the total of the locally prevailing minimum wage and fringe benefits as determined by the Secretary of Labor.[128] The Davis-Bacon Act applies to the principal contractor and all subcontractors who work for the principal contractor.

State Prevailing Wage Laws

California imposes prevailing wage obligations upon employers who provide services or construction work for public entities under contract and in excess of $1,000.[129] You must maintain certified payrolls for public work performed and provide copies to the DLSE or the entity that awarded the contract within 10 days of written request,[130] including names of employees and hours worked by day and week. You must also keep records open at reasonable hours for inspection by DLSE or the entity that awarded the contract.[131]

---

127. 41 U.S.C. 35 et seq.
128. 40 U.S.C. 276(a)
129. Lab. Code sec. 1774
130. Lab. Code sec. 1812
131. Lab. Code sec. 1812

In many cases, the prevailing wage and benefits required by California public works projects are higher than those required by federal law. For example, California requires overtime after eight hours of work in a day and 40 hours of work in a week on state public works projects.[132]

Work that is performed by a volunteer, a volunteer coordinator, by members of the California Conservation Corps or members of a certified Community Conservation Corps are exempt from the prevailing wage requirement. This exemption applies retroactively to otherwise covered work concluded on or after January 1, 2002, and remains in effect until January 1, 2009, unless modified by further legislative action.

A penalty per day per employee can be imposed for failing to pay prevailing wages or overtime on state jobs in California.[133] The penalty starts at $10 per day per employee unless it is the result of a good faith mistake that is promptly and voluntarily corrected. The minimum penalty increases to $20 per day per employee if the contractor has been subject to a penalty within the previous three years, and to $30 per day per employee if the Labor Commissioner determines that a willful violation occurred. When any amount is collected from a contractor, the amount will be applied first to satisfy any outstanding wage claim before applied to the penalty.

In addition, the Labor Commissioner publishes a list of contractors and subcontractors that have committed willful violations or against which a final compliance order was issued. The list is to include the date of each assessment, the amount of wages and penalties assessed and the amount collected. The list is updated quarterly, and a name remains on the list until the date the assessment is satisfied or three years, whichever is later.

Committee Access to Payroll

California law permits a federally recognized joint labor-management committee to obtain a copy of a certified payroll from a contractor on a public works project, with names and SSNs deleted.[134] If the committee discovers unpaid prevailing wages or fringe benefits due and related penalties, the committee may file a civil action to collect them. Courts may award restitution to employees and attorneys' fees and costs to the committee.[135]

Confidentiality for Employees Reporting Violations

The DLSE is authorized to conduct investigations to determine if state prevailing wage laws have been violated. During such an investigation, the DLSE must keep confidential the name of any employee who reports a violation of prevailing wage laws, and any other information that may identify the employee.[136]

Public Employer

Employees directly employed by the state or any county, incorporated city or town or other municipal corporation do not fall under provisions that establish time and form of payment.[137]

---

132. Lab. Code sec. 1815
133. Lab. Code secs. 1775, 1813
134. Lab. Code sec. 1776
135. Lab. Code sec. 1771.2
136. Lab. Code sec. 1736
137. Lab. Code sec. 220

Seasonal Labor Outside of California

Seasonal laborers hired in California to work outside the state receive full protection of laws regulating the form and timing of payment that apply to persons working in California. "Seasonal laborers" under California law include those hired to work outside of California for more than one month, excluding seamen and others covered by federal law.[138] For such seasonal labor, the Labor Commissioner resolves all disputes concerning payment of wages, though the courts may review such determinations.[139]

Camps

Student employees of organized camps are not subject to the minimum wage for a 40-hour week, regardless of the number of hours the employee might work at the organized camp. If the employee works less than a 40-hour week, the employee must receive at least 85 percent of the minimum hourly wage for each hour worked. The organized camp may deduct the value of meals and lodging from the salary of such student employees, pursutant to the appropriate IWC Wage Orders.[140]

"Organized camp" means a site with program and facilities established for the primary purposes of providing an outdoor group living experience with social, spiritual, educational or recreational objectives for five days or more during one or more seasons of the year. It does not include a motel, tourist camp, trailer park, resort, hunting camp, auto court, labor camp or penal or correctional camp; nor does it include a child care institution or home-finding agency.[141]

Ski Industry

The IWC amended Wage Order 10 in 2000, shortening the allowable regularly scheduled workweek and establishing a daily overtime requirement for the ski industry. For more information, see "Ski Industry" in Chapter 14, page 356.

Labor Contractors

A contract or agreement for labor or services with a construction, farm labor, garment, janitorial or security guard contractor violates the law if the contracting party "knows" or "should know" that the terms provide insufficient funds to allow the contractor to comply with all applicable local, state and federal laws or regulations governing the labor or services to be provided. This includes a contract or agreement with any person, licensed or not, who acts in the capacity of a construction, farm labor, garment, janitorial or security guard contractor.

A contracting party "knows" that terms are insufficient if the party has the knowledge, arising from familiarity with the normal facts and circumstances of the business activity, that the contract or agreement does not include funds sufficient to allow the contractor to comply with applicable laws. A contracting party "should know" that terms are insufficient if the party has

---

138. Lab. Code secs. 253, 255
139. Lab. Code secs. 253, 255
140. Lab. Code sec. 1184.4
141. Health and Safety Code sec. 18897

knowledge of any additional facts or information that would make a reasonably prudent person question whether the contract or agreement contains sufficient funds to allow the contractor to comply with applicable laws. A failure to request or obtain any information from the contractor that is required by any applicable statute or by the contract or agreement constitutes knowledge of that information for purposes of this section.

Labor Code Section 2810

The law presumes that a contract or agreement meets these requirements if the contract is a single written document that includes:

- The name, address and telephone number of the person or entity and the construction, farm labor, garment, janitorial or security guard contractor through whom the labor or services are to be provided;

- A description of the labor or services to be provided and a statement of when those services are to be commenced and completed;

- The employer identification number for state tax purposes of the construction, farm labor, garment, janitorial or security guard contractor;

- The workers' compensation insurance policy number and the name, address and telephone number of the insurance carrier of the construction, farm labor, garment, janitorial or security guard contractor;

- The vehicle identification number of any vehicle owned by the construction, farm labor, garment, janitorial or security guard contractor and used for transportation in connection with any service provided pursuant to the contract or agreement; the number of the vehicle liability insurance policy that covers the vehicle; and the name, address and telephone number of the insurance carrier;

- The address of any real property to be used to house workers in connection with the contract or agreement;

- The total number of workers to be employed under the contract or agreement, the total amount of all wages to be paid and the date or dates when those wages are to be paid;

- The amount of the commission or other payment made to the construction, farm labor, garment, janitorial or security guard contractor for services under the contract or agreement;

- The total number of persons who will be utilized under the contract or agreement as independent contractors, along with a list of the current local, state and federal contractor license identification numbers that the independent contractors must possess under local, state or federal laws or regulations;

- The signatures of all parties and the date the contract or agreement was signed; and

- Any other provisions that may be required by regulations adopted by the Labor Commissioner.

If the information required by paragraph (7) or (9) is unknown at the time the contract or agreement is executed, the best estimate available at that time is sufficient. If an estimate is used, there is a continuing duty to determine the information and put it in writing once that information becomes known. A material change to the terms and conditions of a contract or agreement must be in writing in a single document and contain all of the provisions affected by the change.

A copy of any such contract or agreement must be retained for not less than four years following the termination of the contract or agreement.

This does not apply to a person or entity who executes a collective bargaining agreement covering the workers employed under the contract or agreement, or to a contract or agreement for labor or services to be performed in a residence provided that a family member of the contracting party resides in the residence or residences for which the labor or services are to be performed for at least a part of the year.

An employee affected by a violation may bring an action for injunctive relief and file for damages to recover the greater of:

- All of his or her actual damages;

- $250 per employee per violation for an initial violation; or

- $1,000 per employee for each subsequent violation.

The employee, upon prevailing, may recover costs and reasonable attorneys' fees. The employee must prove that he/she was adversely affected as a result of a violation of a labor law or regulation in connection with the performance of the contract or agreement.

Garment Industry

Garment manufacturers must register with the Labor Commissioner and take an examination covering the laws and regulations that protect workers in the industry.[142] Garment manufacturers must certify that they have a current workers' compensation insurance policy in force for all employees.[143] The name of the business, address and registration number must be displayed at the entrance of the premises.[144] Those who manufacture garments by themselves, tailors solely engaged in alterations and employees who have wages as sole compensation are exempted from these garment manufacturing laws.[145]

The initial registration fee is $250, with the Labor Commissioner authorized to increase future fees, including renewal fees, based on the manufacturer's annual volume, not to exceed $2,500. The amount of special wage account fees (to make whole aggrieved employees) is $75. Garment manufacturers who do not register are guilty of a misdemeanor.[146]

Any garment manufacturer who contracts with any other garment manufacturer not registered with the Labor Commissioner is deemed the employer and jointly liable with the contracting person for any violations of workers' compensation requirements.[147] The Labor Commissioner may revoke the registration of any garment manufacturer that fails to pay wages awarded to an employee by the commissioner.[148]

All garment manufacturers are liable for the guaranteed wages, including civil penalties, of the entity with whom they have contracted to make garments. A wage guarantee may be limited on a proportional share basis when the work of two or more persons is performed at the same worksite.[149]

Employees can file a lawsuit to recover wages and overtime payments due from a manufacturer who has contracted with an unregistered manufacturer, with reasonable attorneys' fees and

---

142. Lab. Code sec. 2675
143. Lab. Code sec. 2675(a)(4)
144. Lab. Code sec. 2676.5
145. Lab. Code sec. 2671
146. Lab. Code sec. 2676
147. Lab. Code sec. 2677
148. Lab. Code sec. 2673.1(m)
149. Lab. Code sec. 2673.1

costs being awarded.[150] The Labor Commissioner is authorized to confiscate garments if all wages due and owed have not been paid to employees performing the garment manufacturing during a period of 180 days prior to an investigation by DLSE.[151] The Labor Commissioner also is authorized to confiscate manufacturing equipment (sewing machines, for example) of those manufacturers who violated labor laws after having their manufactured apparel confiscated by the Labor Commissioner in the previous five years due to labor violations.

Every employer engaged in the business of garment manufacturing must keep accurate records for three years which show all of the following:

- Names and addresses of all garment workers directly employed by the employer;

- Hours worked daily by employees, including the times the employees begin and end each work period;

- Daily production sheets, including piece rates;

- Wages and wage rates paid each payroll period;

- Contract worksheets indicating the price per unit agreed to between the contractor and manufacturer;

- Ages of all minor employees; and

- Any other conditions of employment.[152]

Failing to maintain wage and hour records on employees will result in a civil penalty of $100 for each affected employee on the first violation and $200 for subsequent violations.[153]

Farm Labor Contractors

Farm labor contractors must be licensed by the state Labor Commissioner and must post a wage surety bond based on annual payroll as follows:

- A payroll up to a $500,000 requires a $25,000 bond;

- A payroll from $500,000 to $2 million requires a $50,000 bond; and

- A payroll of $2 million or more requires a $75,000 bond.

Farm labor contractors must pay annual license fees of $500. A $50 deposit to the Farmworker Remedial Account (FRA) is required for disbursal to farmworkers not paid because a surety bond was depleted or employment by an unlicensed contractor.

Farm labor contractors must provide growers a detailed payroll record of all wages and hours worked by farmworkers employed by the contractor.[154]

The bond and FRA funds may be used as compensation for a farm worker whose employer violates any provision of the Labor Code.[155] Examples of Labor Code violations include:

- Issuance of bad checks;

---

150. Lab. Code sec. 2677(b)
151. Lab. Code sec. 2680(a)
152. Lab. Code sec. 2673
153. Lab. Code sec. 2678
154. Lab. Code secs. 1682.8, 1684, 1695.55, and 1698.1
155. Lab. Code sec. 1684

- Failure to provide meal or rest periods;

- Failure to provide itemized wage statements; and

- Discriminating against an employee for filing a health and safety complaint.

Employees of a farm labor contractor must be paid each week. Agricultural workers and domestics can receive monthly pay if lodged and boarded by their employers. Wages of workers employed by a farm labor contractor must be paid on payroll breaks at least once every week on a business day designated in advance by the contractor. Payment on that payday must include all wages earned up to and including the fourth day before the payday.[156]

Fishing Crews

Crew members on a licensed commercial passenger fishing boat became subject to the minimum wage in 2001.[157] The minimum wage obligation may, at the employer's option, be satisfied by paying employees according to the following formula:

- A "one-half day trip" (maximum of six hours of work) = no less than six times the hourly minimum wage;

- A "three-quarter day trip" (maximum of 10 hours of work) = no less than 10 times the hourly minimum wage;

- A "full-day trip" (maximum of 12 hours of work) = no less than 12 times the hourly minimum wage; and

- An "overnight trip" (maximum of 12 hours worked within no less than 24 hours) = no less than 12 times the hourly minimum wage.

Hours worked in excess of this formula must be recorded on the employee's pay record as additional hours worked.

A crew member on a commercial passenger fishing boat on an overnight trip must receive no less than eight hours of work during each 24 hour period.

See "Commercial Passenger Fishing Boats" in Chapter 14, page 357, for information about overtime requirements for this industry.

Sheepherders

The minimum wage for sheepherders is $1,200.00 per month. Wages paid to sheepherders may not be offset by meals or lodging provided by the employer.[158]

Additional changes were made to California's employment laws relating to sheepherders' wages, hours, breaks, housing, tools and working conditions.[159] Those changes are contained in Wage Order 14, available on **www.hrcalifornia.com** in the Law Library's Posters and Notices section.

---

156. Lab. Code sec. 205
157. IWC Order 10
158. Wage Order 14-2001 sec. 4(E)
159. Lab. Code secs. 2695.1-2695.2

Motion Pictures

An employer who lays off an employee engaged in the production of motion pictures, whose unusual or uncertain terms of employment require special computation to determine the amount due, may pay that employee's final wages on the next regular payday following the layoff. A "layoff" means the employee retains eligibility for employment with that employer. If an employee is discharged, payment of wages must be made within 24 hours after discharge, excluding Saturdays, Sundays and holidays. "Discharge" means the unconditional termination of employment of the employee. Payment may be mailed, and the date of mailing is considered the date of payment.[160]

Curing, Canning or Preservation of Fruits, Fish or Vegetables

An employer who lays off a group of employees because of seasonal employment in the curing, canning or preservation of fruits, fish or vegetables must pay all earned but unpaid wages within 72 hours. Payment may be made by mail to employees who make such a request and who provide a mailing address.[161]

Under the terms of this limited exception, payment will be timely if the wages are mailed within 72 hours of the termination, regardless of when they are received.[162]

Oil Drilling

An employer in the business of oil drilling who lays off an employee or group of employees is given 24 hours after discharge to pay all wages and accrued vacation due, excluding Saturdays, Sundays and holidays. If the payment is mailed, the date of mailing is considered the date of payment.[163]

Mining, Logging and Refining

The mining industry in California must make a deposit of cash or negotiable securities equal to the wages coming due on the next payday.[164] This applies to logging camps and all mining and refining industries unless they have a free and unencumbered title to real property in California with a value at least equal to wages coming due.[165] Logging industries and sawmill operators can meet this requirement by posting a bond from a surety company in California. Cash or securities used to meet wage requirements cannot be mingled with other assets or used to meet other obligations. The petroleum industry is not governed by this law.

Sales

Enterprises employing telephone or door-to-door salespersons and having no fixed place of business in California must give security for wage obligations of one payday or one four-week period,

---

160. Lab. Code sec. 201.5

161. Lab. Code sec. 201

162. DLSE *Enforcement Policies and Interpretations Manual* sec. 3.2.1; Code of Civil Procedure sec. 1012(a)

163. Lab. Code sec. 201.7

164. Lab. Code sec. 270

165. Lab. Code sec. 270.5

whichever is longer.[166] This may be a deposit of cash or securities that can be easily sold. It also may take the form of a certificate of deposit payable to the Labor Commissioner or a bond issued by a licensed California surety company.

Theater, Radio and Television

Theaters, radio and television enterprises must deposit cash or readily marketable securities sufficient to meet obligations on a single payday. This applies to most business in which persons receive payments for performing.[167]

All deposits must be placed in a bank or trust company located in the county where employment takes place. Failure to make the deposit or otherwise post required security for wages constitutes a misdemeanor.[168] Employers also must conspicuously post notice of the place where required deposits have been made.[169] Failure to post such a notice is sufficient evidence that an employer has not made required deposits.

Domestic Service

This section addresses obligations of the employer of household employees under both federal and state law.

Employee or Independent Contractor?

First, a home employer must determine whether the worker at issue is categorized as an employee or an independent contractor. If the work involved is legitimately that of an independent contractor, the home employer likely will not have obligations under the laws discussed below. Examples of independent contractors are persons who take care of a lawn using their own tools, hire helpers as necessary and care for a number of other lawns. See "Independent Contractors" in Chapter 5, page 93, formore information on determining whether a worker is an employee or an independent contractor.

If the homeowner exercises control as to what is done and how it is done, the worker will likely be an employee. Common examples of household employees are maids, housekeepers, cooks, babysitters, butlers, caretakers and drivers. If a home employer hires employees, the employer must comply with the following labor laws.

Wages and Hours

Non-live-in domestic service employees are covered both by state and federal minimum wage and overtime laws, absent an exception discussed below. Domestic service employment includes services of a household nature performed by an employee in or about a private home of the person by whom he/she is employed, such as cooks, waiters, butlers, valets, maids, housekeepers, governesses, nurses, janitors, laundresses, caretakers, chauffeurs and babysitters

---

166.Lab. Code sec. 170.6
167.Lab. Code sec. 271
168.Lab. Code secs. 270, 271
169.Lab. Code sec. 270.6

employed on other than a casual basis.[170] Such domestic service employees are covered by minimum wage and overtime requirements if they:

- Earn $50 or more in a calendar quarter; or

- Work in one or more homes for more than eight hours in a workweek.

Babysitting services provided on a casual basis are exempt from both minimum wage and overtime requirements.[171] "Babysitting services" refers to the casual care and protection of infants or children in or about the private home in which the infants or young children reside and which takes place during any part of a 24-hour day.[172] The term "casual basis" refers to work performed on an irregular or intermittent basis and not performed by an individual whose vocation is babysitting.[173] Casual babysitting may include performing incidental work not related to child care, as long as such work does not exceed 20 percent of the total hours worked on a particular babysitting assignment.[174]

Individuals providing companionship services for the aged or infirm similarly are exempted from the federal overtime and minimum wage requirements.[175] "Companionship services" refers to the provision of fellowship, care and protection for a person who, because of advanced age or physical or mental infirmity, cannot care for his/her own needs. Such services may include housework related to that care, as long as such work does not exceed 20 percent of the employee's work time.[176] The companionship services exemption does not apply to trained personnel, such as nurses, who provide care to the aged and infirmed.

Employees who reside in their employer's household generally are exempt from overtime requirements but not minimum wage requirements.[177] Employees who reside on the employer's premises for at least 120 hours in a week or spend five consecutive days or nights residing on the employer's premises qualify for the exemption.

Under state law, however, live-in employees under Wage Order 15 must have 12 consecutive hours free of duty each day, with an additional three or more hours free during each 12-hour work span. Live-in employees required to work during such free hours are entitled to one and one-half times the regular wage. Moreover, live-in employees may not be required to work more than five consecutive days without a 24-hour off-duty period, except in emergencies, unless overtime is paid at the rate of one and one-half times the regular rate for the first eight hours worked on the sixth day and two times the regular rate for all work in excess of eight hours on that sixth day in the workweek.[178]

Domestic employees must be paid at least the minimum wage for all their hours of work unless the employer falls into one of the above exemptions. For purposes of satisfying the minimum wage requirement, an employer may take credit for meals and lodging provided to the domestic employee, as long as the employee voluntarily authorizes such a deduction in writing. See "Deductions from Wages" on page 278 for amounts which may be credited against the minimum wage.

170. 29 CFR 552.3
171. 29 U.S.C. 213(a)(15)
172. 29 CFR 552(4)
173. 29 CFR 552(5)
174. 29 CFR 552.104(c)
175. 29 U.S.C. 213(a)(15)
176. 29 CFR 552.6
177. 29 U.S.C. 213(b)(21); IWC Wage Orders 15-80
178. IWC Wage Order 15, sec. 3

Tax Requirements

Home employers must comply with federal and state tax laws that govern an employer-employee relationship if the employee is paid wages of a sufficient amount. For important information about tax requirements, please consult IRS publication 926, available at your local IRS office, by calling (800) 829-3676 or on the IRS Web site at *www.irs.gov*. Also, see "Domestic Service Employer Filing" in Chapter 18, page 429, for information about filing wage reports by telephone.

Workers' Compensation

Domestic service employees generally are covered by California workers' compensation laws, unless those employees are casual workers employed less than 52 hours and earning less than $100 during a 90-day calendar period before the injury that is allegedly subject to workers' compensation.[179] For more information, see Chapter 26, "Workers' Compensation."

Immigration

Household employees also may be subject to the Immigration Reform and Control Act (IRCA), which makes it unlawful for a person to hire an individual who is not lawfully admitted to work in the United States and who fails to comply with the employment verification procedures set forth in that law.[180] For further important information concerning employer requirements under this law, consult Chapter 4, "Verifying Eligibility to Work."

Ambulance Companies

An employee working as an ambulance driver or attendant on a 24-hour shift may enter into an agreement with the employer to exclude up to three, one-hour duty-free meal periods and up to eight hours of uninterrupted sleep time from "hours worked," provided adequate sleeping facilities are provided by the employer.[181] Wage Orders 5 and 7 require employers to provide adequate dormitory and kitchen facilities in such circumstances.[182]

Dormitory and Kitchen Facilities Required for Ambulance Drivers

Wage Order 5 and Wage Order 7 require employers to provide adequate dormitory and kitchen facilities for ambulance drivers and attendants scheduled for 24-hour shifts. This requirement applies when drivers or attendants have agreed in writing to exclude from daily time worked not more than three meal periods of not more than one hour each and a regularly scheduled, uninterrupted sleeping period consisting of not more than eight hours.

---

179. Lab. Code secs. 50.8.8
180. 8 U.S.C. 1324a et seq.
181. DLSE *Enforcement Policies and Interpretations Manual* sec. 45.2; *Monzon v. Schaefer Ambulance Service,* 224 Cal. App. 3d 16 (1990); DLSE Opinion Letter 1998.05.29
182. IWC Wage Orders 5 and 7

Further Information

The following resourses contain details regarding the Labor Code, cost of living, and consumer price index information.

California Labor Code Online

The California Labor Code, as well as the other state codes regulating wage and hour law, are available online on the Web site of California's Legislative Counsel at ***www.leginfo.ca.gov/ calaw.html***. The state's Department of Industrial Relations (DIR), which interprets labor laws, makes information available for employers online at ***www.dir.ca.gov***.

Cost of Living/Consumer Price Index Information

Employers often base raises on the "cost of living" or Consumer Price Index (CPI). Information about the CPI in California can be obtained through the state's DIR at:

Department of Industrial Relations
Division of Labor Statistics and Research
P.O. Box 420603
San Francisco, CA 94142-0603
(415) 972-8620

The information also is available on the DIR Web site at ***www.dir.ca.gov/dlsr/ statistics_research.html***.

The federal Bureau of Labor Statistics (BLS) also releases CPI information by region. You may contact the federal BLS for recorded CPI information 24 hours a day at (415) 975-4406 or view CPI data by region on the BLS Web site at ***http://stats.bls.gov/ro9/#news.htm***.

Chapter 12 Forms

This chapter contains samples of forms associated with this topic. *The forms in this section are for visual reference only; download the most up-to-date forms and checklists in their entirety from CalBizCentral.*

To download either individual forms or your entire Formspack containing all the forms referenced in this book:

1. Visit **www.calbizcentral.com/support** and select "Labor Law Digest" from the list of product titles.

2. Have this copy of Labor Law Digest handy — you will need to enter the access code featured on the inside covers of this book.

3. Enter the access code, select the documents you want to download to your computer, then follow the on-screen instructions.

For more detailed instructions, see "Forms Available Online" on page xix.

Labor Commissioner's Office

Labor Commissioner's Office	
Bakersfield: 5555 California Avenue, #200 Bakersfield, CA 93309 (661) 395-2710	**San Diego:** 7575 Metropolitan Drive, #210 San Diego, CA 92108 (619) 220-5451
Eureka: 619 Second Street, #109 Eureka, CA 95501 (707) 445-6613	**San Francisco:** 455 Golden Gate Avenue, 8th Fl. East San Francisco, CA 94102 (415) 703-5300
Fresno: 770 E. Shaw Avenue, #315 Fresno, CA 93710 (559) 244-5340	**San Francisco—Headquarters:** 455 Golden Gate Avenue, 9th Fl. East San Francisco, CA 94102 (415) 703-4810
Long Beach: 300 Oceangate Boulevard, #302 Long Beach, CA 90802 (562) 590-5048	**San Jose:** 100 Paseo de San Antonio, #120 San Jose, CA 95113 (408) 277-1266
Los Angeles: 320 W. 4th Street, #450 Los Angeles, CA 90013 (213) 620-6330	**Santa Ana:** 28 Civic Center Plaza, Room 625 Santa Ana, CA 92701 (714) 558-4910
Oakland: 1515 Clay Street, Suite 801 Oakland, CA 94612 (510) 622-3273	**Santa Barbara:** 411 E. Canon Perdido Street, #3 Santa Barbara, CA 93101 (805) 568-1222
Redding: 2115 Civic Center Drive, Room 17 Redding, CA 96001 (530) 225-2655	**Santa Rosa:** 50 D Street, #360 Santa Rosa, CA 95404 (707) 576-2362
Sacramento: 2031 Howe Avenue, #100 Sacramento, CA 95825 (916) 263-1811	**Stockton:** 31 E. Channel Street, #317 Stockton, CA 95202 (209) 948-7770
Salinas: 1870 Main Street, #150 Salinas, CA 93906 (831) 443-3041	**Van Nuys:** 6150 Van Nuys Boulevard, #206 Van Nuys, CA 91401 (818) 901-5315
San Bernardino: 464 W. 4th Street, #348 San Bernardino, CA 92401 (909) 383-4334	

Labor Commissioner's Offices

Final Paycheck Worksheet

Employee Name _____ SSN _____

Prepared By _____ Date _____

Company _____

Employee paid previously through: Date _____ Unpaid hours begin on: Date _____

Final date of employment: Date _____ *Time _____ a.m./p.m. * If termination is involuntary, estimate time employee will be terminated.

☐ The separation is a voluntary termination (employee-initiated: resignation, retirement) the final paycheck must be issued within 72 hours of the final date of employment or by _____.

☐ The separation is an involuntary termination (employer-initiated: discharge or layoff with no date of rehire) all wages and accrued vacation earned but unpaid are due and payable on the last day of work.

Determine Regular Rate $ _____ Regular Rate

Calculate Time

Dates:	Mon	Tue	Wed	Thurs	Fri	Sat	Sun	Total
Hours Worked:								
Regular Time:	0	0	0	0	0	0	0	0
Overtime Hours:	0	0	0	0	0	0	0	0
Double Time:	0	0	0	0	0	0	0	0
Total Hours:	0	0	0	0	0	0	0	0

Dates:	Mon	Tue	Wed	Thurs	Fri	Sat	Sun	Total
Hours Worked:								
Regular Time:	0	0	0	0	0	0	0	0
Overtime Hours:	0	0	0	0	0	0	0	0
Double Time:	0	0	0	0	0	0	0	0
Total Hours:	0	0	0	0	0	0	0	0

Dates:	Mon	Tue	Wed	Thurs	Fri	Sat	Sun	Total
Hours Worked:								
Regular Time:	0	0	0	0	0	0	0	0
Overtime Hours:	0	0	0	0	0	0	0	0
Double Time:	0	0	0	0	0	0	0	0
Total Hours:	0	0	0	0	0	0	0	0

Totals: 0 Regular time   0 Overtime   0 Double time

Final Paycheck Worksheet (Page 1 of 2)

Final Paycheck Worksheet

Calculate Gross Wages

$ ____ Hourly Rate

# of Hours	Rate of Pay Description		Hourly Rate		Wages to be Paid
____	Regular time = 1.0	x	$ ____	=	$ ____
____	Overtime = 1.5	x	$ ____	=	$ ____
____	Double time = 2.0	x	$ ____	=	$ ____

Total wages to be paid $ ____

Calculate Vacation Payable

If the employee is eligible to accrue vacation, you must calculate vacation pay due the employee. Refer to your company policy regarding the rate of accrual.

Rate of Accrual		Length of Accrual Period		Accrued Vacation	minus	Used Vacation		Accrued, Unused Vacation Payable
____	x	____	=	____		____	=	$ ____

Payment must be made for other items the employer owes to the employee or which are due by policy (i.e., accrued and payable sick leave, severance pay, expenses advanced by the employee on behalf of the employer, etc.).

Calculate Final Paycheck

Total Wages to be Paid

		Withholding	
Regular Hours	$ ____	Federal Income Tax	$ ____
Overtime Hours	$ ____	Social Security	$ ____
Double time Hours	$ ____	Medicare Tax	$ ____
Vacation Payable	$ ____	State Income Tax	$ ____
Other	$ ____	UI/SDI	$ ____
Total	$ ____	Parking	$ ____
		Life Insurance	$ ____
Subtract Advanced Vacation *	$ ____	Health Insurance	$ ____
Other	$ ____	Long-term Disability	$ ____
Total	$ ____	Advances *	$ ____
		Other	$ ____

Total Deductions $ ____

Final Check # ____

Footnotes:
* Only with prior written authorization, unless advanced within final pay period.

Final Paycheck Acknowledgment

I, the undersigned recipient, have received my final paycheck from:

Company ____

The total amount of the paycheck is: $ ____

Paycheck amount represents:

Wages	$ ____
Accrued Vacation Pay	$ ____
Other	$ ____
Deductions	$ ____
	$ ____
	$ ____
	$ ____

To the best of my knowledge, there is no additional money owed to me by the employer at the present time.

Name of Recipient ____

Signature of Recipient ____ Date ____

Signature of Person Issuing Final Paycheck ____ Date ____

Final Paycheck Worksheet (Page 2 of 2)

Final Paycheck Acknowledgement - English

Final Paycheck Acknowledgment

Yo, el beneficiario que firma al pie, recibí mi último cheque del sueldo de:

Compañía _____

El monto total del cheque es: $ _____

El monto total del cheque representa:

Sueldos _____ $ _____

Pago por vacaciones devengadas _____ $ _____

Otros _____ $ _____

_____ $ _____

_____ $ _____

Deducciones _____ $ _____

_____ $ _____

_____ $ _____

_____ $ _____

_____ $ _____

A mi leal saber y entender, mi empleador no me adeuda ninguna suma de dinero a la fecha.

_____   _____
Nombre del beneficiario

_____   _____
Firma del beneficiario   Fecha

_____   _____
Firma de la persona que emite el último cheque del sueldo   Fecha

Final Paycheck Acknowledgement - Spanish

Employer Proof of Identity and Disbursement of Final Pay

Complete this form upon receipt of the *Affidavit to Collect Compensation of Deceased—Not To Exceed $5000 Net*. The Affiant must provide reasonable proof of identity in conjunction with the Affidavit. If the Affiant is claiming to be a guardian or conservator of the estate, a letter from the surviving spouse or registered domestic partner indicating such appointment is sufficient. Place a copy of this completed form in the Decedent's file and provide a copy to the Affiant.

Proof of Identity Obtained (of spouse, registered domestic partner, or guardian/conservator)
Check one:

☐ Driver's License Number _____

☐ Passport Number _____

☐ Government Issued Identification Card

Name of Identification Card _____

Identification Number _____

If the person presenting the affidavit or declaration is the person claiming to be the guardian or conservator of the estate of the surviving spouse or registered domestic partner, be provided with reasonable proof, satisfactory to _____ (the Company), of the appointment of the person to act as guardian or conservator of the estate of the surviving spouse or registered domestic partner. (Attach copy of proof to this form.)

I, _____ (Affiant) have received a check (number _____) in the amount of $ _____ .

I am satisfied that this is the total amount of compensation owed from _____ (Decedent), (the Company) regarding _____ .

_____   _____
Signature of Affiant   Date

I, _____ (authorized Company official), in good faith have relied upon the statements in the attached Affidavit and that the statements contained therein are true.

_____   _____
Signature of Authorized Company Official   Date

Employer Proof of Identity and Disbursement of Final Pay

Responding to a Wage Claim

Employees and former employees are entitled to file claims for unpaid wages with the state's Division of Labor Standards Enforcement, commonly known as the Labor Commissioner or Labor Board. This checklist is designed to help an employer respond to a wage claim.

Step 1: When the wage claim is received:

☐ Check the wage claim notice ("Notice of Claim Filed and Conference") to be sure the claimant was/is employed by you, and that the dates on the claim match the dates of the claimant's employment.

☐ Determine whether the claimant is seeking final wages. Failure to pay final wages may entitle the claimant to "waiting time penalties." These penalties are one day's wages for each day the employee's final wages are delayed, up to 30 days. In some cases you may wish to settle a claim rather than risk additional waiting time penalties.

☐ Collect any written evidence you may have regarding the payment of wages to the claimant. Some examples include payroll records, timecards, schedules, and termination or resignation letters (to verify the date final wages were due).

☐ Consider whether there are any witnesses who can provide evidence for your case. This may include employees, supervisors, managers, human resources personnel, or others.

Step 2: Determine whether to settle the claim rather than attend the conference:

☐ Is the amount of the claim worth your time preparing for and attending the conference?

☐ Do you have clear evidence to show the claim has no merit?

☐ Are you involved in any other dispute with this employee (i.e. unemployment insurance, workers' compensation, discrimination complaint, civil lawsuit)? If so, consider consulting with your legal counsel to ensure you do not provide the employee with "ammunition" for the other dispute at the conference.

Step 3: Preparing for the conference:

☐ Be sure you are available to attend the conference on the scheduled date, and mark it on your calendar.

☐ Organize all evidence disputing the claim.

☐ Prepare two extra copies of your evidence, one for the claimant and one for the Deputy Labor Commissioner conducting the conference. Number the pages and highlight any information (on all copies) that is particularly relevant to proving your case. This will avoid the confusion of passing papers around the room as you discuss them, and allow you to focus everyone's attention on the relevant information.

☐ Consider whether you need legal counsel at the conference. While it is not necessary to have legal counsel attend, it may be helpful for large or complex claims.

☐ Determine whether you are willing to offer a settlement at the conference, and if so, how much you are willing to offer.

☐ Speak with any witnesses you may need in the event the conference does not result in a settlement and a hearing is scheduled. The witnesses do not need to attend the conference. However, their willingness to testify if necessary at the hearing, and the content of their testimony or written statements, can help you determine the strength of your case.

Step 4: Attending the conference:

☐ Show up to the conference on time with all relevant evidence.

☐ Allow the Deputy Labor Commissioner to conduct the conference without undue interruption of argument.

☐ Stick to the matter at hand (the dispute over wages), avoiding the temptation to delve into other problems you may have had with this employee.

✕ calbizcentral™

Responding to a Wage Claim

Affidavit to Collect Compensation of Deceased – Not to Exceed $5000 Net

(To be completed by the surviving spouse, registered domestic partner, guardian or conservator of an estate.)

To collect salary or other compensation of a deceased spouse or registered domestic partner ("Decedent"), a surviving spouse, registered domestic partner, guardian or conservator of an estate must complete this Affidavit under penalty of perjury under the laws of the State of California.

I, _____ (name), declare:

1. On _____ (date), _____ (Decedent), hereinafter referred to as "Decedent", died in _____ County, California.

2. Check the applicable statement:

   ☐ I, _____, am the surviving spouse or registered domestic partner of the Decedent, hereinafter "Affiant."

   Or

   ☐ I, _____ am the guardian or conservator of the estate of the surviving spouse or registered domestic partner of the Decedent, hereinafter "Affiant."

3. The Affiant is entitled to the Decedent's earnings under the Decedent's will or by intestate succession and no one else has a superior right to the earnings.

4. No proceeding is now being, or has been, conducted in California for administration of the Decedent's estate.

5. California Probate Code sections 13600 to 13605 require that the earnings of the Decedent, including compensation for unused vacation, not in excess of $5000.00 net, be paid promptly to the Affiant.

6. The net total of $5000.00 may be increased based on cost of living adjustments (COLA) made after January 1 of _____ (year) year preceding the Decedent's death: _____ % (COLA percentage). The *Consumer Price Index for all Urban Consumers*, as published by the United States Bureau of Labor Statistics (http://www.bls.gov/), shall be used as the basis for determining the changes in the cost of living. The cost-of-living increase shall equal, or exceed, 1 percent before any adjustment is made. The net amount payable may not be decreased as a result of the cost-of-living adjustment.

7. Neither the surviving spouse/registered domestic partner, nor anyone acting on behalf of the surviving spouse/registered domestic partner, has a pending request to collect compensation owed by another employer for personal services of the Decedent, pursuant to California Probate Code sections 13600 to 13605.

8. Neither the surviving spouse/registered domestic partner, has collected any compensation owed by an employer for personal services of the Decedent, nor anyone acting on behalf of the surviving spouse/registered domestic partner, pursuant to California Probate Code sections 13600 to 13605, except the sum of _____ dollars ($_____), which was collected from _____.

9. The Affiant requests that he or she be paid the salary or other compensation owed by _____ (the Company) for personal services of the Decedent, including compensation for unused vacation or paid time off, not to exceed $5000.00, less the amount of _____ dollars ($_____), which was previously collected.

I, _____ affirm under the penalty of perjury under the laws of the State of California that the foregoing is true and correct.

_____   _____
Signature of Affiant   Date

Affidavit to Collect Compensation of Deceased

Absence Request

Employee Name _____ Date _____

To: Payroll

☐ I *shall* be absent from the office   ☐ I *have been* absent from the office

Date/s: _____   Date/s: _____

Number of days: _____   Number of days: _____

Number of hours: _____   Number of hours: _____

☐ Illness   ☐ Kin Care

☐ Employee believes this absence may qualify for Family Medical Leave (FMLA)

☐ Vacation/PTO

_____
Number of negative vacation hours requested

☐ Jury Duty (attach summons)   ☐ Bereavement

_____
Relationship to deceased

☐ Other (explain): _____

Employee's Signature _____ Date _____

Supervisor's Approval _____ Date _____

Absence Request - English

Absence Request

Nombre del empleado _____ Fecha _____

Para: Nómina

☐ Me *ausentaré* de la oficina   ☐ Me *ausenté* de la oficina

Fecha/s: _____   Fecha/s: _____

Cantidad de días: _____   Cantidad de días: _____

Cantidad de horas: _____   Cantidad de horas: _____

☐ Enfermedad   ☐ Cuidado de un familiar

☐ El empleado considera que esta ausencia puede calificar como Licencia por Enfermedad o por Motivos Familiares (FMLA, por su sigla en inglés)

☐ Vacaciones/Días libres con goce de sueldo (PTO, por su sigla en inglés)

_____
Cantidad de horas de vacaciones solicitadas

☐ Servicio como jurado (adjuntar citación)   ☐ Duelo

_____
Relación con el fallecido

☐ Otro motivo (explíquelo): _____

Firma del empleado _____ Fecha _____

Autorización del supervisor _____ Fecha _____

Absence Request - Spanish

Direct Deposit Authorization

To:

Employee _____

From:

Company Name _____

A full or partial deposit of your wages may be made to up to _____ different banks or credit unions. You may specify the amount to be deposited to any account. deposits be directed to any account.

For the Account #1, select the account type and specify the dollar amount or check the box indicating that you want the total amount deposited to that account. For the remaining accounts, select the account type and specify the dollar amount or select the check box indicating that you want the remaining balance deposited to that account.

NOTE: When filling in the "9 Digit Routing Number" and "Account Number" information, please *be sure to verify them* with your bank or credit union before submitting this form.

Account #1	Select Account Type: ☐ Checking *(attach voided check)*		☐ Savings
Bank Name:			
Bank Address:	City:	Phone:	
9 Digit Routing Number:	Account Number:		
Requested amount per pay period for this account:	$		☐ Remaining balance

Account #2	Select Account Type: ☐ Checking *(attach voided check)*		☐ Savings
Bank Name:			
Bank Address:	City:	Phone:	
9 Digit Routing Number:	Account Number:		
Requested amount per pay period for this account:	$		☐ Remaining balance

Account #3	Select Account Type: ☐ Checking *(attach voided check)*		☐ Savings
Bank Name:			
Bank Address:	City:	Phone:	
9 Digit Routing Number:	Account Number:		
Requested amount per pay period for this account:	$		☐ Remaining balance

Account #4	Select Account Type: ☐ Checking *(attach voided check)*		☐ Savings
Bank Name:			
Bank Address:	City:	Phone:	
9 Digit Routing Number:	Account Number:		
Requested amount per pay period for this account:	$		☐ Remaining balance

I hereby authorize _____ (the Company) to deposit my paycheck as specified above. This authorization shall be effective as quickly as the Company and the designated bank(s) or credit union(s) can act upon it. This authorization is to remain in effect until I notify the Company in writing to terminate this authorization or replace it with a substitute authorization and the Company and the designated bank(s) or credit union(s) have sufficient time to act on it. I understand that the Company may cancel this agreement upon notice to me, and that, at the discretion of the Company, this authorization may not apply to any payment due at termination of employment.

Signature _____   Date _____

Direct Deposit Authorization - English

Direct Deposit Authorization

Para:

Empleado _____

De:

Nombre de la compañía _____

Se puede depositar el total o parte de su salario en hasta _____ cuentas de cheques o de ahorro, en un máximo de _____ bancos o cooperativas de crédito distintos. Usted puede indicar el monto que desea que se deposite o indicar que el saldo restante luego de los depósitos anteriores se destine a una determinada cuenta.

Para la Cuenta #1, seleccione el tipo de cuenta e indique el monto en dólares, o marque la casilla que indica que desea que le depositen el total de su salario en esa cuenta. Para las cuentas restantes, seleccione el tipo de cuenta e indique el monto en dólares, o seleccione la casilla que indica que desea que el saldo restante se deposite en dicha cuenta.

NOTA: Al llenar el "Número bancario de 9 dígitos" y el "Número de cuenta", *asegúrese de corroborarlos* con su banco o cooperativa de crédito antes de presentar este formulario.

Cuenta #1	Seleccione tipo de cuenta: ☐ De cheques *(adjuntar cheque anulado)*		☐ De ahorro
Nombre del banco:			
Domicilio del banco:	Ciudad:	Teléfono:	
Número bancario de 9 dígitos:	Número de cuenta:		
Monto a ser depositado en esta cuenta en cada periodo de pago:	$		☐ Saldo restante

Cuenta #2	Seleccione tipo de cuenta: ☐ De cheques *(adjuntar cheque anulado)*		☐ De ahorro
Nombre del banco:			
Domicilio del banco:	Ciudad:	Teléfono:	
Número bancario de 9 dígitos:	Número de cuenta:		
Monto a ser depositado en esta cuenta en cada periodo de pago:	$		☐ Saldo restante

Cuenta #3	Seleccione tipo de cuenta: ☐ De cheques *(adjuntar cheque anulado)*		☐ De ahorro
Nombre del banco:			
Domicilio del banco:	Ciudad:	Teléfono:	
Número bancario de 9 dígitos:	Número de cuenta:		
Monto a ser depositado en esta cuenta en cada periodo de pago:	$		☐ Saldo restante

Cuenta #4	Seleccione tipo de cuenta: ☐ De cheques *(adjuntar cheque anulado)*		☐ De ahorro
Nombre del banco:			
Domicilio del banco:	Ciudad:	Teléfono:	
Número bancario de 9 dígitos:	Número de cuenta:		
Monto a ser depositado en esta cuenta en cada periodo de pago:	$		☐ Saldo restante

Por el presente autorizo a _____ (la Compañía) a depositar mi cheque del sueldo según se indica anteriormente. Esta autorización entrará en vigencia en el momento en el que la Compañía y los bancos o cooperativas de crédito designados estén en condiciones de realizar dicho depósito. Esta autorización continuará vigente hasta que yo notifique a la Compañía por escrito que deseo cancelar esta autorización o remplazarla por otra, y la Compañía y los bancos o cooperativas de crédito tengan suficiente tiempo para cumplir con dicha indicación. Entiendo que la Compañía puede cancelar este acuerdo enviándome una notificación y que, a criterio de la Compañía, quizá esta autorización no se aplique a ningún pago adeudado en el momento del cese.

Firma _____   Fecha _____

Direct Deposit Authorization - Spanish

Hours of Work and Recording Time Worked

Though Chapter 12, "Wages, Salaries and Other Compensation," discussed wage law, this chapter discusses another important element when paying employees — hours worked. Laws governing hours of work derive from three sources: the federal Fair Labor Standards Act (FLSA), the California Labor Code and Industrial Wage Orders.

This chapter explains various federal and state requirements regarding limitations on work hours and how to determine which to follow when federal and state laws conflict. Topics include:

- Meal and rest periods;

- Time off between shifts and days off;

- Exceptions; and

- Work hours for specific occupations.

A section dedicated to time keeping and recording guidelines is included to help protect you from penalties.

This chapter should be read in conjunction with applicable sections of Chapter 14, "Overtime" and Chapter 16, "Exempt and Nonexempt," because both contain important information on payment for hours worked in excess of the "regular work week." In addition, Chapter 15, "Alternative Workweek Scheduling," contains guidance on how to modify the effect of maximum hours laws discussed in this chapter.

 Download forms referenced in this chapter at ***www.calbizcentral.com/support***. Be sure to have your access code from the inside covers of this book ready to enter into the forms download area. Your access code for the forms in the online Formspack is on the inside covers of this book. See "Forms Available Online" on page xix for more information.

Hours

California law and Wage Orders contain many provisions that govern how you schedule hours that may be worked by your employees and the time carved out of those hours for use by your employees, either on a paid or unpaid basis. Penalties may result from an employer's failure to comply with those rules, in some cases increasing your compensation costs for nonexempt employees by as much as 20 percent.

Maximum Hours of Work

Employees who work under Wage Orders 4 (Professional, Technical and Clerical), 8 (Industries Handling Products After Harvest), or 13 (Industries Preparing Agricultural Products for

Marketing, On the Farm) generally cannot be required to work more than 72 hours per week. The other Wage Orders contain no limitation on working hours.

There are other limits placed on weekly hours of work for certain types of employees, such as minors (see "Working Hours" in Chapter 7, page 135), truck drivers (see "Transportation" in Chapter 14, page 355) and health-care employees (see "Health Care" in Chapter 15, page 377). Limitations exist for pharmacy personnel, railroad personnel and some mining-related occupations and underground workings. These limitations are described in "Exceptions for Specific Industries" on page 327.

Minimum Hours of Work

No existing law specifies a minimum number of hours for which an employee must be *regularly* scheduled each shift, unless employees have voted in an alternative workweek agreement. (See "Minimum Shift Length" in Chapter 15, page 378, for more information about minimum shift requirements in alternative workweek schedules.) You may schedule an employee for a recurring one-hour shift to attend a training meeting or to provide additional coverage during the "lunch-rush" at a restaurant. In these circumstances, the employee would be entitled to just one hour's pay. However, the reporting time pay provisions of the Wage Orders' section five require pay for specified minimum hours if an employee:

- Reports to work on a regularly scheduled day and is allowed to work less than half his/her scheduled or normal shift;

- Is called in on a nonscheduled day to attend a meeting or other duties; or

- Is recalled back to work after completing a shift. For more information, see "Reporting Time Pay" in Chapter 12, page 275, and "Call-in Pay" in Chapter 12, page 277.

Mandatory Days Off

Generally, every employee is entitled to at least one day off in a seven-day workweek.[1] However, an employee may accumulate rest days when the nature of employment requires him/her to work seven or more consecutive days. The employee must receive rest days equivalent to one day in seven during each calendar month.[2] This requirement does not apply to emergencies, agricultural work, work performed in the protection of life or property from loss or destruction[3] or when hours worked do not exceed 30 in any workweek or six in any workday.[4]

Minimum Time between Shifts

No existing law specifies a minimum time between an employee's shifts, with a few safety-related exceptions noted elsewhere in this *Digest* (train crews and drivers regulated by the Department of Transportation, for example). It is legal to schedule an employee for a "double," where a second shift immediately follows the end of an employee's first shift, but you should carefully consider the impact of requiring such long hours on the health and safety of that employee and all others.

1.Lab. Code secs. 551, 552
2.Lab. Code sec. 554
3.Lab. Code sec. 554
4.Lab. Code sec. 556

If more than one hour passes between shifts in a workday, other than a bona fide meal break, you may have to pay a split shift premium. For more information, see "Split Shift Pay" in Chapter 12, page 274.

Travel Time

Time spent in home-to-work travel by an employee in an employer-provided vehicle is not "hours worked" and does not have to be paid. The same is true of activities performed by an employee incidental to the use of the vehicle for commuting, such as filling the fuel tank. These provisions apply only if:

- The travel is within the normal commuting area for the employer's business; and

- The use of the vehicle is subject to an agreement between the employer and the employee (or the employee's representative).

See "Mandatory Mode of Transportation" on page 318 for an important exception to this rule created by the California Supreme Court in 2000.

With the exception of travel from home to work and back,[5] most travel time is considered work time. Because traveling does not require the employee to employ his/her skills, pay for travel time may be at a rate of pay less than the employee's normal rate of pay. The employer may pay the employee as little as the minimum wage for travel pay, subject to the following conditions. Travel time is counted as work time, and overtime pay may be due for travel. See "Calculating" in Chapter 14, page 344, for more information on calculating the overtime rate when two or more rates of pay apply.

Travel time pay, if less than the employee's normal earnings, must be clearly outlined to all employees in advance, preferably as part of your personnel policy. You must reimburse the employee for all out-of-pocket travel expenses.

The following examples demonstrate how nonexempt employees required to travel in the course of conducting their work would be paid:

- If an employee reports to the regular workplace and is then required to travel to another site to work for the day, travel time to the assigned workplace must be paid;[6]

- When an employee is required to report to a work site other than the regular site and goes directly to that site without first going to the regular site, the employer must pay the employee travel time for any time in excess of the employee's normal commute time to and from the regular site;[7] and

- Employees required to travel to a distant work place. For example, an employee works eight hours at his/her regular work place in Sacramento, then goes to the airport to hop a flight to Los Angeles. The employee stays at a hotel, works six hours at the assigned work place in Los Angeles the next day, finishes his/her work assignment after six hours of work and then returns to Sacramento. Under these circumstances, the employee gets his/her regular pay for the first eight-hour period. Travel pay begins when he/she leaves the work place to go to the airport. It ends when the employee arrives at the Los Angeles hotel. The employee receives his/her regular six hours of pay while at the work place in Los Angeles.

---

5. 29 CFR 785.35
6. 29 CFR 785.38
7. 29 CFR 785.37

When the employee leaves the Los Angeles work place for the airport, travel pay begins. It ends when he/she arrives at the Sacramento airport to go home.

If travel time in either direction or travel time and work time exceeds eight hours in a workday, the employee must receive travel pay at one and one-half times the weighted average of his/her regular pay rate and the travel time rate, if any.[8] See "Basic Overtime Requirements" in Chapter 14, page 339, for more details.

Time spent in home-to-work travel by an employee in an employer-provided vehicle or on activities performed by an employee incidental to the use of the vehicle for commuting does not count as "hours worked" and does not have to be paid. This provision applies only if the travel is within the normal commuting area for the employer's business and the use of the vehicle is subject to an agreement between the employer and the employee or the employee's representative.[9]

Accurate recordkeeping is imperative in such scenarios. Employers should communicate with nonexempt employees regarding these obligations, particularly when traveling. When employees travel to a different time zone, require them to track all hours based on California time it will make the math a lot easier and your payroll people will sincerely appreciate it. Consistent communication by e-mail or phone can also cut down on later disputes regarding hours actually worked.

Mandatory Mode of Transportation

The California Supreme Court ruled in 2000 that time workers spend traveling to and from work on an employer-provided bus must be paid because the employees fall under the control of an employer during this time, even though they are not working.[10] The case involved a group of agricultural workers required to meet for work each day at certain parking lots or other assembly areas. After the workers met at these departure points, the employer transported them to the fields where they actually worked in buses that the employer provided and paid for. At the end of each day, the employer transported the workers back to the departure points on the buses. The time spent waiting for and traveling in the buses was unpaid. The employer's work rules prohibited employees from using their own transportation to get to and from the fields.

The Supreme Court's decision could impact many other employment circumstances, such as cases in which an employee must wear a pager and be able to report to work within a very limited time after being paged. The employee could argue that the limits on his or her ability to engage in personal activities put the employee under the employer's control, even if the employee is not actively performing work. Employees required to live on the employer's premises, such as apartment managers or maintenance personnel, could also claim to be under the employer's control at all times based on this decision.

Optional Employer Provided Transportation

Employers may provide optional free transportation to employees without having to pay them for their travel time if the employers do not require employees to use this transportation.

In one such case, an employee sought pay for commuting time on a tram provided by the Walt Disney Company to take employees from a remote parking area to the park entrance. The employee complained that new construction prevented him and other employees from parking close to the

---

8. 29 CFR 785.39
9. 29 U.S.C. 254(a)
10. *Morillion v. Royal Packing Co.*, 22 Cal. 4th 575 (2000)

entrance, and the employees were "required" to ride the tram to work — time for which the employees should have been compensated.

The court disagreed, ruling that employees were free to use a variety of methods to arrive at work, including public transportation, van pools, being dropped off by family or friends, walking or riding bicycles from the lot in question, or arriving early enough to park at other parking areas. Therefore, using the employer-provided tram was not required, nor were the employees under the control of the employer during their commute.[11]

Preparation Time

Time spent in uniform-changing and washing-up activities must be counted as hours worked if the employee must do so at work. However, time spent changing into a simple uniform may not be considered work time even if it is done on the employer's premises and wearing of uniforms is required by the employer if the time is too short to be counted as a practical matter.[12]

Education and Training Time

Employees who spend time at lectures, work courses, employer-sponsored training programs or employee meetings must count that time as hours worked for pay purposes unless:

- Time is outside of normal working hours;

- Course work is unrelated to the employee's regular job (such as learning the requirement of a new or higher-rated job);

- Attendance is strictly voluntary (except for continuing education training); and

- No production work is performed.[13]

Attendance at employee meetings, employer-sponsored training programs, lectures, work courses or meetings is not deemed voluntary if required by the employer or if the employee is led to believe that his/her nonattendance would adversely affect his/her current working conditions or continued employment. Training is directly related to the employee's job if it aids him/her in performing the present job more effectively, as distinguished from training for another labor skill.[14] However, training is not considered directly related to an employee's job if the intention of such training is to prepare him/her for advancement to a higher skill.

Mandatory meetings that require an employee to report to work on days off or return to work following the end of a workday will incur reporting time pay. For more information, see "Reporting Time Pay" in Chapter 12, page 275.

Time spent by employees in a state-mandated training program is not compensable hours worked if the training is not required by the employer and is not tailored to meet the individual needs of employers.[15] For example, it has been held that a job training program whereby mechanics and skilled laborers voluntarily and on their own time enrolled in courses on advanced electrical circuitry did not result in compensable time because the training was not

---

11. *Overton v. Walt Disney Company* 136 Cal. App.4th 263 (2006)
12. DLSE *Enforcement Policies and Interpretations Manual* sec. 46.6.5
13. 29 U.S.C. 201 et seq.; DLSE *Enforcement Policies and Interpretations Manual* sec. 46.6.4
14. 29 CFR 785.27-31
15. 29 CFR 553.226 (b)(1)

designed to enable the employees to perform their present jobs more efficiently.[16] An employer is not required to pay overtime compensation for time spent completing courses at home if enrollment in the course was voluntary and the employer did not require the course as a prerequisite to continued employment in the employee's current position.[17]

Attendance outside regular working hours at specialized or follow-up training that is required by law for certification of public and private sector employees within a particular governmental jurisdiction does not constitute compensable hours of work for public employees within that and subordinate jurisdictions.[18]

Time voluntarily spent by employees to maintain their physical fitness is not considered working time even though fitness is a job requirement. On the other hand, the time will be considered working time if the employee is required to participate in a remedial physical fitness program as a condition of continued employment.[19]

Meal and Rest Breaks

Nonexempt employees (employees not exempt under the Fair Labor Standards Act and the California Wage Orders from overtime and meal and rest break requirements) must be given an opportunity to take a 10 minute paid rest break for every four hours worked (or significant portion thereof — usually about 3 hours) and a 30 minute unpaid meal break if their shift cannot be completed in six hours or less. The meal break must begin no later than four hours and 59 minutes into the employee's shift. If either rest break is not given, the employer owes the employee one hour of pay, which you must include in the next pay check — same goes if the employee is unable to take a meal break.

It is imperative that you understand these complex requirements, and do everything you can to communicate the legal requirements to employees and give them an opportunity to take the requisite breaks.

Rest Breaks

Provide rest breaks at the rate of not less than 10 consecutive minutes for each four hours worked (or major portion thereof), occurring as near as possible to the middle of the work period.

 The wage orders require a duration of "net" 10 minutes, which the DLSE interprets as requiring not less than 10 minutes in a rest area away from the work station if the employee so desires. If the rest area is at a distance from the workplace, the time required for the rest break may be more than 10 minutes.

You may not combine rest breaks or add them to meal breaks even at the employee's request, and they may not be used to allow an employee to come in 10 minutes late or leave 10 minutes early. You control rest breaks, and you must pay break time as time worked. You may require employees to remain on the premises during the rest break.

16. Wage and Hour Opinion Letter No. 1174 (4/28/71)
17. *Price v. Tampa Electric Co.*, 806 F.2d 1151 (11th Cir. 1987)
18. 29 CFR 553.226 (b)(1)
19. Wage and Hour Opinion Letter No. 1589 (9/12/85)

The Industrial Welfare Commission (IWC) may create an exception to these rest period rules for governmental employees who operate commercial motor vehicles as defined in Vehicle Code section 15210, provided they are covered by a collective bargaining agreement.[20]

Provide 10-minute rest breaks as follows for the work hours involved:

Hours of Work	Rest Breaks
0 - 3.5	0
3.5 - 6.0	1
6.0 - 10.0	2
10.0 - 14.0	3
14.0 - 18.0	4

Failure to Provide Rest Breaks

Following the *Murphy v. Kenneth Cole* case (see "Statute of Limitations on "Additional Hour of Pay"" on page 325), for each workday you fail to "authorize and permit" an employee to take a required rest break, you owe the employee one additional hour of pay at the employee's regular rate no later than the next paycheck.[21]

Unlike meal periods, during which the employer must ensure that workers are actually relieved of all duty, not performing any work and free to leave the worksite; the employer is merely required to "authorize and permit all employees to take rest periods." An employer will probably not face any sort of premium pay obligation if an employee, who was truly authorized and allowed to take a rest break, *freely chooses without any coercion or encouragement* to forego or waive a rest period.[22] Keep in mind that this area of the law is controversial in light of *Murphy* and may not be fully resolved until the Legislature responds.

Extended Rest Breaks for Breastfeeding Mothers

California law requires you to provide a reasonable amount of break time and a private place for employees to express breast milk.[23] See "Employees Expressing Breast Milk at Work" in Chapter 22, page 574, for more information about this law.

Meal Breaks

Provide a meal break of at least one half-hour for every work period of more than five hours. If six hours of work complete the day's work, the employee may voluntarily choose not to take the meal break. Meal breaks may be unpaid only if:

- They last at least 30 minutes;

- The employee is relieved of all duty; and

---

20. Lab. Code sec. 512.5
21. Lab. Code sec. 226.7
22. Legal Opinion Letter of California Labor Commissioner, September 17, 2001
23. Lab. Code secs. 1030-103

- The employee is free to leave the premises.[24]

Meal breaks may be longer than a half-hour at your discretion. Anything longer than a one-hour meal break may raise issues related to a split shift. See "Split Shift Pay" in Chapter 12, page 274, for more information.

Provide a second meal break of no fewer than 30 minutes for all workdays on which an employee works more than 10 hours.

The Labor Commissioner no longer has the discretion to grant an employer an exemption from the meal break requirements.[25]

Wage Order 1 provides that the parties to a valid collective bargaining agreement may agree to a meal period that commences after no more than six hours of work for employees covered by that collective bargaining agreement.

The IWC may create an exception to these meal period rules for governmental employees who operate commercial motor vehicles, as defined in Vehicle Code section 15210, provided the employees fall under a collective bargaining agreement.[26]

Failure to Provide a Meal Break

For each workday you fail to provide an employee a meal break as required, you owe the employee one additional hour of pay at the employee's regular rate.[27]

With respect to meal breaks following *Murphy v. Kenneth Cole* (see "Statute of Limitations on "Additional Hour of Pay"" on page 325), the employer must ensure that workers are actually relieved of all duty, not performing any work, and free to leave the worksite.[28]

Based on this opinion, you must ensure that employees actually take meal breaks.

Second Meal Break Waiver

An employee may waive the second meal break only if:

- The total hours worked on that workday do not total more than 12;

- The employer and employee mutually consent; and

- The first meal break of the workday was not waived.[29]

These requirements do not apply to Wage Order 12 (Motion Picture Industry). See "Motion Pictures" on page 331.

---

24. Lab. Code sec. 512; *Bono v. Labor Commissioner*, 32 Cal. App. 4th 968 (1995)
25. IWC Wage Orders, sec. 17
26. Lab. Code sec. 512.5
27. IWC Wage Orders sec. 11, Lab. Code sec. 226.7
28. Legal Opinion Letter of California Labor Commissioner, September 17, 2001
29. Lab. Code sec. 512

On-duty Meal Breaks

Employees may take on-duty meal breaks in certain circumstances. An on-duty meal break:

- Is permitted only when the nature of the work prevents an employee from being relieved of all duty;

- Must be agreed to in writing by the employee and employer;

- Must be paid; and

- May be revoked at any time in writing by the employee (except under Wage Order 14).

A California Court of Appeal clarified that an "on-duty meal break" is a type of meal break that employees take, and that it must be paid. Contrast this with considering the "on-duty meal break" as a waiver of an employee's meal break. This is particularly important if employees work between 10 and 12 hour shifts. Employees cannot waive the second meal break, which is required by law, if they waived the first meal break. If employees take an "on-duty meal break," they can still waive their second meal break and employers will not be liable for the additional hour of pay for a missed meal break.[30]

Designated Eating Place

If employees must eat on the premises, you must designate a suitable place for that purpose.[31]

Wages Required if Employees May Not Leave

A California Court of Appeal ruled that if an employer requires employees to remain on the premises for a meal break, the employer denies that employee the use of the time for his/her own purposes. Since the employee remains under the employer's control, the meal break must be paid.[32]

The courts and Labor Commissioner are likely to rule in most situations that wages are owed any time the employee is under your control. This applies not only to meal breaks but also to education and training sessions, travel time required (other than an employee's normal commute), preparation (changing and clean-up time) and other similar time that you might not consider time worked.

Meeting or Training during Lunch Break

Employers often hold meetings or training for employees during lunch or other meal breaks. Even if a meal is provided by the employer, this is still considered working time for which an employee must be paid. In addition to paying for the time spent in the meeting or training, the employer will owe an additional one hour's pay for each nonexempt employee denied a meal break. See "Failure to Provide a Meal Break" on page 322 for more information about this penalty.

30.*McFarland v. Guardsmark, LLC* 538 F. Supp. 2d 1209 (2008)
31.IWC Wage Orders sec. 11
32.*Bono v. Bradshaw*, 32 Cal. App. 4th 968 (1995)

You may avoid the penalty if you hold a meeting during the normal lunch break time by allowing employees an off-duty meal break of at least one half-hour before or after the meeting. Providing food during the meeting is optional.

Court Invalidates Meal Period Provision in Wage Order 16

A California Court of Appeal ruled that a provision in Wage Order 16 covering the construction, drilling, logging and mining industries that exempts employees working under the terms of a collective bargaining agreement from meal period requirements is invalid. The employer relied on the Wage Order, which the court found to be contrary to the Labor Code's meal period provision.

The Court found that the Wage Order unlawfully expanded the requirements of the statute. It was left to the trial court to decide whether the Court of Appeal's determination will apply retroactively, thereby imposing significant penalties on the employer. This case serves as a reminder that though regulations and Wage Orders provide useful guidance to employers, statutory requirements will prevail.[33]

Meal and Rest Compliance Unresolved

 Compliance with California's meal- and rest-period requirements — mainly the question of whether employers must ensure breaks are taken or just simply provide them — has been a source of significant litigation in both federal and state courts. In early 2008, class certification for a meal- and rest-period lawsuit was denied by a federal district court, which found that nothing in California law required the employer to ensure that employees took their meal breaks, but rather the employer need only supply or make such time available to employees.[34] However, because this is a federal court ruling it did not change the law in California that employers must ensure employees stop working during their meal breaks. As such, merely providing meal breaks to nonexempt employees is insufficient.

Then, in July 2008, a California court of appeal denied class certification for almost 60,000 restaurant employees because the lower court did not properly consider the elements of the employees' claims in determining if they were susceptible to class treatment. Specifically, the court found that:

- Though employers cannot impede, discourage or dissuade employees from taking rest periods, they need only provide, not ensure, rest periods are taken;

- Employers need only authorize and permit rest periods every four hours or major fraction thereof and they need not, where impracticable, be in the middle of each work period;

- Employers are not required to provide a meal period for every five consecutive hours worked;

- Though employers cannot impede, discourage or dissuade employees from taking meal periods, they need only provide them and not ensure they are taken; and

- Though employers cannot coerce, require or compel employees to work off the clock, they can only be held liable for employees working off the clock if they knew or should have known they were doing so.

Because rest and meal breaks need only be made available and not ensured, the court also found that individual issues predominate and, based upon the evidence presented to the trial court, these individual issues do not lend themselves to class treatment. Further, the off-the-clock claims do not

33.*Bearden v. U.S. Borax Inc.*, 138 Cal. App. 4th 429 (2006)
34.*Brown v. Federal Express Corporation* 249 F.R.D. 580 (2008)

lend themselves to class treatment because individual issues predominate on the issues of whether employees were forced to work off the clock, whether the employer changed time records and whether the employer knew or should have known employees were working off the clock.[35]

This case was appealed to the California Supreme Court, which on October 22, 2008, agreed to hear the case. Until the California Supreme Court issues its ruling, this case cannot currently be relied upon and should not be followed. Contact legal counsel to ensure that your policies reflect the most prudent practices relating to meal and rest breaks and tracking of employee time; always track all hours worked and not worked of all your nonexempt employees; and make sure supervisors and managers consistently enforce your policies and procedures, in particular, as they relate to meal and rest breaks for nonexempt employees.

Statute of Limitations on "Additional Hour of Pay"

The California Supreme Court ruled that a three-year statute of limitations, not one year, applies to the "one additional hour of pay" employers must pay employees when meal and/or rest breaks are not provided. The court also found that employees and employers can add wage claims not presented in an administrative hearing when a trial court hears the case.

John Paul Murphy worked as a store manager for Kenneth Cole Productions for two years, classified as an exempt employee. He was paid a weekly salary and generally worked 10-hour days without an opportunity to break for lunch or even to go to the restroom when the store was busy. His primary job functions were making sales, processing markdowns, cleaning and working in the stock room. After Murphy resigned, a friend told Murphy that he was not paid correctly because he was wrongly classified as an exempt employee. Murphy then filed a claim with the Labor Commissioner for unpaid overtime because he should have been classified as a nonexempt employee. Murphy won his case with the Labor Commissioner. The employer appealed the case to the courts, and the case eventually made it to the California Supreme Court.

California law requires employers to provide nonexempt employees 10-minute paid rest breaks for every four hours worked; a 30-minute unpaid meal break for every five hours worked; and premium or overtime pay for hours worked in excess of eight in a day or 40 in a week. Because Kenneth Cole wrongly classified Murphy as exempt, the company did not pay him overtime and did not provide meal and rest breaks. If meal and/or rest breaks are not provided, employers must pay employees one additional hour of pay at the employees' regular rate of compensation. Kenneth Cole presented two questions to the California Supreme Court.

First, the court was asked to determine whether the one hour of pay is a penalty against the employer or an additional wage payable to the employee. If a penalty, employees' claims would be limited to one year of the unpaid compensation. If a wage, employees could claim up to three years. Second, Kenneth Cole argued that because the meal and rest period claim was not made before the Labor Commissioner (Murphy was unaware at that time that he could make such a claim), the claim could not be presented for the first time when the employer appealed the Labor Commissioner's decision.

After extensive review of the history behind the missed meal and rest breaks pay requirement, the Court clarified that wages are benefits that an employee is entitled to as part of compensation, including money, vacation pay, room and board, and sick pay. California law entitles nonexempt employees to an unpaid 30-minute, duty-free meal period upon their fifth

---

35.*Brinker v. Superior Court* 165 Cal. App. 4th 25 (2008)

hour of work if their shift is longer than six hours, and a paid 10-minute rest break per four hours of work. Employees who must forgo the meal and rest breaks give the employer "free" work and lose a benefit to which they are entitled. In other words, they lost wages they were owed. The hour of additional pay is not only an incentive for employers to comply with the law but, foremost, a premium wage that compensates employees.

The Court also found that when a trial court hears a Labor Commissioner case, the court hears the case without regard to the case as heard by the Labor Commissioner; in essence, the case starts over as if a court had never heard the case. In the interest of efficiency, it is at the trial court's discretion to decide whether it hears claims in addition to those originally posed to the Labor Commissioner, provided that the claims legally and factually flow from the same underlying wage dispute. By the same token, the employer may abandon, change or add defenses not brought before the Labor Commissioner.[36]

Timekeeping and Recording Guidelines

You must maintain an accurate record of employees' hours of work and compensation. Failure to do so may force you to disprove what an employee claims to have been his/her actual work hours. The basic recordkeeping obligation includes the employee's:

- Name;
- Home address;
- Date of birth (if less than18 years of age);
- Occupation in which employed;
- The clock time when each work period and off-duty meal period begins and ends;
- Total wages and other compensation paid during each payroll period;
- Total hours worked in each payroll period and applicable rates of pay; and
- The number of piece-rate units earned and any applicable piece rate paid.

Section 7 of each IWC Wage Order contains recordkeeping requirements. You must keep accurate time records showing when the employee begins and ends each work period, including in and out time records for meal breaks. When a piece rate or incentive system is in operation, the number of piece rate units earned must be part of the payroll records.[37]

Implications of Failing to Maintain Records

The chief danger in failing to maintain adequate or accurate work records is that, in a dispute, a government agency or a court will credit the employees' testimony as to their hours worked in the absence of accurate records of such work. The courts and agencies administering wage/hour laws believe you can hardly complain about this consequence because it easily could have been avoided by accurate recordkeeping.

For information on other recordkeeping requirements, see Chapter 8, "Personnel Records and Privacy."

36.*Murphy v. Kenneth Cole Productions, Inc.* 40 Cal. 4th 1094 (2007)
37.Lab. Code sec. 1174

Rounding Practices

The state Labor Commissioner uses the U.S. Department of Labor practice of rounding employees' hours to the nearest five minutes when calculating the number of hours worked.[38] However, for enforcement purposes, the Labor Commissioner will accept the practice of computing working time by rounding to the nearest five minutes, or one-tenth or one-quarter of an hour, provided that it is used in such a manner that it will not result in failure to compensate the employees properly for all the time they actually worked over a period of time.

According to the Labor Commissioner, "When auditing payroll records, Division personnel will ascertain the facts regarding the time keeping requirements" (e.g., the true work patterns of the workers and whether the time records accurately reflect these patterns).[39] In recording working time, you may disregard insubstantial or insignificant periods of time beyond the scheduled working hours, which cannot be precisely recorded for payroll purposes as a practical administrative matter.[40]

Clock Records Versus Actual Hours Worked

If you use time clocks, you do not have to pay employees who voluntarily come in before their regular starting time or remain after their shift ends for these periods of time as long as they do not engage in any work. You may disregard their early or late clock punching. You cannot always avoid minor differences between the clock records and actual hours worked, but you should discourage major discrepancies since they cast doubt on the accuracy of the records of the hours actually worked.[41]

Exceptions for Specific Industries

The operational needs of certain industries require variations in the way hours of work are recorded, how records are maintained and how certain types of hours are treated for pay purposes. The following industry groups should review the material in this section:

- Public works — contractors and subcontractors;
- Pharmacy;
- Railroad;
- Smelters;
- Agriculture and agricultural processing;
- Construction, drilling, logging and mining;
- Residential care;
- Health care; and
- Motion picture.

---

38. DLSE *Enforcement Policies and Interpretations Manual* sec. 47.1 and 47.2
39. DLSE *Enforcement Policies and Interpretations Manual* sec. 47.2.2.2; 29 CFR sec. 785.48(b)
40. DLSE *Enforcement Policies and Interpretations Manual* sec. 47.2.1 and 47.2.1.1
41. DLSE *Enforcement Policies and Interpretations Manual* sec. 47.2.2 and 47.2.2.1

Public Works — Contractors and Subcontractors

Each contractor and subcontractor engaged in public works is required to keep accurate payroll records that show the worker's name, address, SSN, work classification and straight time and overtime hours worked each day and each week.[42] Such records should also show the actual per diem wages paid to each journeyman, apprentice, worker or other employee by the contractor or subcontractor in connection with any public works project. The payroll must be certified and available for inspection at all reasonable hours at the employer's principal office. If the contractor willfully fails to comply with disclosure requirements, he/she will be denied the right to bid on any public works contracts for one year and will forfeit $100 for each calendar day of noncompliance.[43] The public does not have access to records at the principal office of the contractor, but rather through the body awarding the contract, the Division of Apprenticeship Standards. The individual worker's name, address and SSN are not available to the general public.

Pharmacies

Persons employed to sell retail drugs and medicines or to compound physicians' prescriptions may not work at the store, pharmacy, dispensary or laboratory more than an average of nine hours per day, more than 108 hours in any two consecutive weeks or more than 12 days in any two consecutive weeks.[44]

Pharmacists are not exempt from overtime, unless they individually meet the tests for either the executive or administrative exemptions.[45]

Railroads

No train crew member may work more than 12 continuous hours, after which he/she is required to be off duty for at least 10 consecutive hours.[46] Any train crew member who has been on duty for 12 hours in the aggregate within a 24-hour period is required to take off eight consecutive hours before returning to duty.[47] Exceptions to these limits include emergencies which could not have been foreseen.[48]

Smelters

Employment period for smelters and underground workings may not exceed eight hours within any 24-hour period, excluding meals.[49] However, you may allow your employees to vote to exceed eight hours in a 24-hour period. This vote requires a two-thirds majority, a secret ballot, certain advance notice to employees and informational meetings.[50]

---

42. Lab. Code sec. 1776
43. Lab. Code sec. 1777.7
44. Lab. Code sec. 850
45. Lab. Code sec. 1186
46. Lab. Code secs. 601, 602
47. Lab. Code sec. 603
48. Lab. Code sec. 607
49. Lab. Code sec. 750
50. Lab. Code sec. 750.5(b)

If an employer and a labor organization representing employees have entered into a valid collective bargaining agreement pertaining to wages and work hours, employees in these industries may work up to 12 hours in any 24-hour period.[51]

Agriculture

Individuals employed in an agricultural occupation covered by Wage Order 14 are not subject to the requirement of one day's rest in seven.[52]

Agricultural Processing

Wage Orders 3 (Canning, Freezing and Preserving), 8 (Industries Handling Products After Harvest) and 13 (Industries Preparing Agricultural Products for Market, On the Farm) allow you to exclude from "hours worked" recess periods occurring during the workday, provided the following conditions are met:

- The recess must last at least 30 minutes;

- You must notify the employee of the time to report back to work;

- The employee must be allowed to leave the premises;

- No more than two work recesses can occur on a single shift; and

- The total recess time must be less than two hours long.[53]

Construction, Drilling, Logging and Mining

Wage Order 16 (On-Site Construction, Drilling, Logging and Mining) provides more rest break flexibility than is available under the other Wage Orders. In addition, the Labor Commissioner issued a legal opinion in 2001 allowing even greater flexibility than provided in the wording of Wage Order 16.

Wage Order 16 applies to employees in the on-site occupations of construction, drilling, logging and mining. It is important to note that employees in these industries who are not "on-site" workers, such as clerical employees, generally work under Wage Order 4 and do not fall under the exceptions discussed here.

For employees working under Wage Order 16, you may:

- Stagger rest breaks to avoid interruption in the flow of work and to maintain continuous operations;

- Schedule rest breaks to coincide with breaks in the flow of work that occur in the course of the workday;

- Require employees to take their rest breaks in the employees' immediate work area;[54] and/or

---

51. Lab. Code sec. 750.5(a)
52. Lab. Code sec. 554
53. DLSE *Enforcement Policies and Interpretations Manual* sec. 47.3
54. Wage Order 16, sec. 11

- Where two rest breaks are required in a workday, combine the second rest break with the meal break as long as the first rest break was provided within the first four hours of work.[55]

Under Wage Order 16, you do not need to provide rest breaks in limited circumstances when the disruption of continuous operations would jeopardize the product or process of the work. However, you must make up the missed rest break within the same workday or compensate the employee for the missed 10 minutes of rest time at the regular rate of pay.

Residential Care

The IWC created an exemption from rest break[56] and meal break[57] requirements for certain residential-care employees effective January 1, 2002. These exemptions apply to:

- Employees of 24-hour residential-care facilities for the elderly, blind or developmentally disabled individuals; and

- Employees with direct responsibility for children receiving 24-hour residential care, when those children are:

  - Less than 18 years of age; or

  - Not emancipated from the foster-care system.

You may require these residential-care employees to remain on the premises and maintain general supervision of residents during rest periods if they are in sole charge of residents. You must allow another rest period if an employee is required to interrupt a break to respond to the needs of residents.

Similarly, you may require these residential care employees to work on-duty meal periods when necessary to meet regulatory or approved program standards and one of the following two conditions is met:

- The residential care employees eat with residents during residents' meals, and you provide the same meal at no charge to the employee; or

- The employee is in sole charge of the resident(s) and, on the day shift, you provide a meal at no charge to the employee.

These employees, except for the night shift, may have an off-duty meal period if they give you 30 days' notice for each instance where an off-duty meal is desired. However, there may be no more than one off-duty meal period every two weeks.

Health Care

Employees in the health-care industry who work shifts in excess of eight hours total in a workday may voluntarily waive their right to one of their two meal breaks. To be valid, the waiver must be documented in a written agreement voluntarily signed by both you and your employee. The employee may revoke the waiver at any time by providing you with at least one day's written notice. The employee must be fully compensated for all working time, including an on-the-job meal break, while the waiver is in effect.[58]

---

55. Legal Opinion of California Labor Commissioner, September 17, 2001
56. Wage Order 5-2002, sec. 12
57. Wage Order 5-2002, sec. 11

Motion Pictures

In the motion picture industry (Wage Order 12), no employee may work more than six hours without a meal break of no fewer than 30 minutes nor more than one hour. You must call subsequent meal breaks for all employees sooner than six hours after the end of the earlier meal break.

Unless the employee is relieved of all duty during a 30-minute meal break, the meal break is considered an "on-duty" meal break and counted as time worked. An "on-duty" meal break is permitted only when the nature of the work prevents an employee from being relieved of all duty and with a written agreement between you and your employee.

If an employee in the motion picture industry is covered by a collective bargaining agreement that provides for meal periods and a monetary remedy if a meal period required by the agreement is missed, the provisions of the agreement supersede the meal period penalty provisions in the Labor Code[59] and Wage Order 11.

Where employees must eat on the premises, you must designate a suitable place for that purpose.

Broadcast Industry

If an employee in the broadcasting industry is covered by a collective bargaining agreement that provides for meal periods and a monetary remedy if a meal period required by the agreement is missed, the provisions of the agreement supersede the meal period penalty provisions in the Labor Code[60] and Wage Order 12.

Where employees must eat on the premises, you must designate a suitable place for that purpose.

Wholesale Baking Industry

A wholesale baking company that has a collective bargaining agreement providing for a 35-hour workweek (five seven-hour days, and pays one and one-half times the regular hourly rate for hours in excess of seven per day) is exempt from the meal period rules, provided it gives covered employees a rest period of not less than 10 minutes every two hours.[61]

Further Information

The DLSE *Enforcement Policies and Interpretations Manual* is available at ***www.dir.ca.gov/DLSE/manual-instructions.htm***.

58. IWC Wage Orders 4 and 5
59. Lab. Code sec. 227(a)
60. Lab. Code sec. 227(a)
61. Lab. Code sec. 512(c)

Chapter 13 Forms

This chapter contains samples of forms associated with this topic. *The forms in this section are for visual reference only; download the most up-to-date forms and checklists in their entirety from CalBizCentral.*

To download either individual forms or your entire Formspack containing all the forms referenced in this book:

1. Visit **www.calbizcentral.com/support** and select "Labor Law Digest" from the list of product titles.

2. Have this copy of Labor Law Digest handy — you will need to enter the access code featured on the inside covers of this book.

3. Enter the access code, select the documents you want to download to your computer, then follow the on-screen instructions.

For more detailed instructions, see "Forms Available Online" on page xix.

Makeup Time Request

Employee Name _____ Employee Number _____

I am requesting time off as a result of a personal obligation on:

Day of the week _____ Date _____

From the hours of _____ a.m./p.m. (circle one) to _____ a.m./p.m. (circle one).

I will make up the time within the same workweek as follows: *(Fill in the dates and hours you plan to work to make up the missed time.)* **Employees may not work more than 11 hours in a day or 40 hours in a workweek as a result of making up time that was or will be lost due to a personal obligation.**

_____

_____

I understand that:

1. Any makeup time I work will not be paid at an overtime rate;
2. A separate written request is required for each occasion that I request makeup time;
3. My makeup time request must be approved in writing before I take the requested time off or work makeup time, whichever is first;
4. If I take time off and am unable to work the scheduled makeup time for any reason, the hours missed will normally be unpaid;
5. If I work makeup time before the time I plan to take off, I must take that time off, even if I no longer need the time off for any reason;
6. The company does not encourage, discourage, or solicit the use of makeup time.

Employee Signature _____ Date Submitted _____

For Employer Use Only:

Check One:

☐ Your makeup time request has been approved and submitted.

☐ You may take the time off requested, but must work the following makeup time hours rather than those submitted in your request:

_____

_____

_____

☐ Your makeup time request has been denied.

Signature _____ Date _____

Please Print Name _____ Title _____

Company _____

calbizcentral This form brought to you by www.calbizcentral.com. © California Chamber of Commerce Page 1 of 1

Makeup Time Request - English

Makeup Time Request

Nombre del empleado _____ Número de empleado _____

Solicito permiso para ausentarme con motivo de un compromiso personal el:

Día de la semana _____ Fecha _____

Desde las _____ a.m./p.m. (seleccionar lo que corresponda) hasta las _____ a.m./p.m. (seleccionar lo que corresponda).

Repondré el tiempo en la misma semana de trabajo, de la siguiente manera: *(Indique las fechas y horas en que planea trabajar para reponer el tiempo de ausencia.)* **Los empleados no pueden trabajar más de 11 horas por día, ni más de 40 horas por semana laboral, para reponer el tiempo de ausencia con motivo de un compromiso personal.**

_____

_____

Entiendo que:

1. El tiempo de reposición que trabaje no se pagará a la tarifa de horas extras;
2. Debe presentarse una solicitud por escrito diferente por cada ocasión en la que solicite tiempo de reposición;
3. La solicitud de tiempo de reposición debe ser autorizada por escrito antes de que me ausente o de que trabaje el tiempo de reposición, lo que ocurra primero;
4. Si me ausento y por algún motivo no puedo trabajar el tiempo de reposición programado, por lo general, las horas de la ausencia no se pagarán;
5. Si trabajo el tiempo de reposición antes de ausentarme, debo ausentarme según lo programado aunque ya no necesite ausentarme por ningún motivo;
6. La compañía no alienta, desalienta ni solicita el uso del tiempo de reposición.

Firma del empleado _____ Fecha de presentación _____

Para uso exclusivo del empleador:

Marque una casilla:

☐ Se autorizó y se presentó su solicitud de tiempo de reposición.

☐ Puede tomarse el tiempo libre solicitado, pero debe trabajar las siguientes horas de reposición en lugar de las que usted indicó en su solicitud:

_____

_____

_____

☐ No se autorizó su solicitud de tiempo de reposición.

Firma _____ Fecha _____

Nombre en letra de molde _____ Cargo _____

Compañía _____

Makeup Time Request - Spanish

Makeup Time Policy

_____ (the Company) allows the use of makeup time when non-exempt employees need time off to tend to personal obligations. **Makeup time worked will not be paid at an overtime rate.**

Employees may take time off and then make up the time later in the same workweek, or may work extra hours earlier in the workweek to make up for time that will be taken off later in the workweek.

Makeup time requests must be submitted in writing to your supervisor, with your signature, on the Company-provided form. Requests will be considered for approval based on the legitimate business needs of the Company at the time the request is submitted. A separate written request is required for each occasion that the employee requests makeup time.

If you request time off that you intend to make up later in the week, you must submit your request at least 24 hours in advance of the desired time off. If you request to work makeup time first in order to take time off later in the week, you must submit your request at least 24 hours before working the makeup time. **Your makeup time request must be approved in writing before you take the requested time off or work makeup time, whichever is first.**

All makeup time must be worked in the same workweek as the time taken off. The company's seven day workweek is

(Seven-day workweek, such as Sunday through Saturday.)

Employees may not work more than 11 hours in a day or 40 hours in a workweek as a result of making up time that was or would be lost due to a personal reason.

If you take time off and are unable to work the scheduled makeup time for any reason, the hours missed will normally will be unpaid. However, your supervisor may arrange with you another day to make up the time, if possible, based on scheduling needs. If you work makeup time in advance of time you plan to take off, you must take that time off, even if you no longer need the time off for any reason.

An employee's use of makeup time is completely voluntary. The company does not encourage, discourage, or solicit the use of makeup time.

wu 1/06

Makeup Time Checklist

If you are considering a makeup time policy for your employees, use this checklist before implementing the policy to make sure you are covering all the key issues.

Step 1: **Determine whether your employees can use makeup time:**
☐ Not automatically applicable to employees with collective bargaining agreements
☐ Not to be used for exempt employees

Step 2: **Prepare a Makeup Time Policy**
☐ Review the sample *Makeup Time Policy* available on **www.hrcalifornia.com.**
☐ Review the information on legal requirements regarding makeup time.
☐ Items to consider:

- Will your response to makeup time requests be in writing, or will an oral approval by a supervisor suffice?
- To whom will copies of makeup time requests be forwarded for filing?
- How much advance notice will you require for makeup time requests?
- How will you handle the situation where an employee takes time off, intending to make it up later in the week, but then is unable to make up the time for whatever reason (i.e. illness, machinery breakdown)? Will the time be unpaid? Will the employee be able to use sick or vacation time to cover the time already taken off?
- How is your Company's seven-day workweek defined? If you do not otherwise define it, the state labor commissioner will presume it is Sunday through Saturday.
- How often will employees be allowed makeup time?

Step 3: **Prepare a Makeup Time Request Form**
☐ Review the *Makeup Time Request* form available on **www.hrcalifornia.com.**
☐ Make changes to it based on the policy your Company decides to adopt (or create your own form)

Step 4: **Set Up a System to Track and Manage Makeup Time Requests**
☐ Will requests be tracked by an employee's immediate supervisor, a department manager, or human resources personnel?
☐ How will incidents of makeup time be reported to the payroll department or payroll service so no overtime is paid?
☐ Consider whether your timecards or time clock allow an employee to show what time is "overtime" and what time is "makeup time" for which no overtime pay is due.

Step 5: **Train Supervisors**
☐ Inform all supervisors that makeup time may never be "encouraged or solicited".
☐ Provide them with *Makeup Time Request* forms and your Company's *Makeup Time Policy* and answer any questions they may have about the new procedure.
☐ Explain that they must provide the employee a copy of the approved or denied request form.
☐ If the request form must be forwarded within the Company after it is approved or denied, be sure supervisors know to whom they should forward it (such as, HR, office manager, president).
☐ Explain the concept of "workweek" and your Company's own workweek so they understand when work may be made up without overtime pay.
☐ Consider requiring supervisors to attach copies of approved makeup time requests to each employee's timecard, so your payroll department or payroll service can accurately calculate wages.

v101507

Meal and Rest Periods Policy

Meal and Rest Periods Policy

It is the policy of _____ (the Company) to ensure all non-exempt employees are provided with meal and rest periods.

No employee shall work for a period of more than five (5) hours without an unpaid meal period of at least 30 minutes. A 10-minute, paid rest period must be taken approximately halfway through any work period of 3 and ½ hours or more.

When a work period of not more than six (6) hours will complete the day's work, the meal period may be waived by mutual consent of the employer and the employee.

Under no circumstances shall a meal period be missed without a valid and approved written waiver. Questions regarding meal period waivers may be directed to _____ (title).

If employees choose to stay on the premises during their meal period, the following locations are available to ensure they are relieved of all work during their 30-minute meal period:

_____

_____

_____

Meal Break Waiver – On Duty

Meal Break Waiver - On Duty

Employee Name _____   Employee Number _____

I am scheduled to work:

Date(s) _____

From the hours of _____ a.m./p.m. (circle one) to _____ a.m./p.m. (circle one).

My job duties on this date _____ are as follows: _____

The nature of these job duties prevents me from being relieved of all duty because of the following objective criteria, which both _____ (Employee) and _____ (Employer) agree upon: _____

I understand that:

1. I may waive my 30-minute unpaid meal break only when my work, based on objective criteria listed above, prevents me from being relieved of all duty.
2. An on-duty meal period is not valid merely because it is desired or helpful.
3. Even if all of the circumstances exist to allow an on-duty meal period, I must still be provided with the opportunity to eat my meal while performing the duties required.
4. In order for this waiver to be valid, an authorized company official must also authorize the waiver in writing by signing below.
5. I may revoke this agreement to waive, in writing, my meal break at any time by signing this form as indicated below unless I work under Wage Order 14.

Employee Signature _____   Date Submitted _____

REVOCATION: I hereby revoke this waiver.

Employee Signature _____   Date _____

Check One:

☐ Your meal break request has been approved and submitted.

☐ Your meal break request has been denied.

For Employer Use Only:

Signature _____   Date _____

Please Print Name _____

Company _____   Title _____

Meal Break Waiver

Employee Name _____

Employee Number _____

I am scheduled to work a shift of 6 hours or less on:

Date(s) _____

From the hours of _____ a.m./p.m. (circle one) to _____ a.m./p.m. (circle one).

I understand that:

1. I may waive my 30-minute unpaid meal break only when my work and/or scheduled shift will be completed in 6 hours or less in one workday.

2. In order for this waiver to be valid, an authorized company official must also authorize the waiver in writing by signing below;

3. I may revoke this agreement to waive, in writing, my meal break at any time by signing this form as indicated below.

Employee Signature _____

Date _____

REVOCATION: I hereby revoke this waiver.

Employee Signature _____

Date Submitted _____

For Employer Use Only:

Check One:

☐ Your meal break waiver request has been approved and submitted.

☐ Your meal break waiver request has been denied.

Signature _____

Date _____

Please Print Name _____

Title _____

Company _____

Meal Break Waiver - English

Meal Break Waiver

Nombre del empleado _____

Número de empleado _____

Debo trabajar un turno de 6 horas o menos el:

Fecha(s) _____

Desde las _____ a.m./p.m. (seleccionar lo que corresponda) hasta las _____ a.m./p.m. (seleccionar lo que corresponda).

Entiendo que:

1. Puedo renunciar a mi receso de 30 minutos para comer, no remunerado, sólo si mi turno de trabajo programado y mis tareas concluirán en 6 horas o menos en una jornada laboral.

2. Para que esta renuncia sea válida, debe estar firmada por un ejecutivo de la compañía que la autorice.

3. Firmando este formulario, como se indica más abajo, puedo revocar en cualquier momento este acuerdo de renuncia a mi receso para comer.

Firma del empleado _____

Fecha _____

REVOCACIÓN: Por el presente, revoco esta renuncia.

Firma del empleado _____

Fecha _____

Para uso exclusivo del empleador:

Marque una casilla:

☐ Se autorizó y se presentó su solicitud de renuncia al receso para comer.

☐ No se autorizó su solicitud de renuncia al receso para comer.

Firma _____

Fecha _____

Nombre en letra de molde _____

Cargo _____

Compañía _____

Meal Break Waiver - Spanish

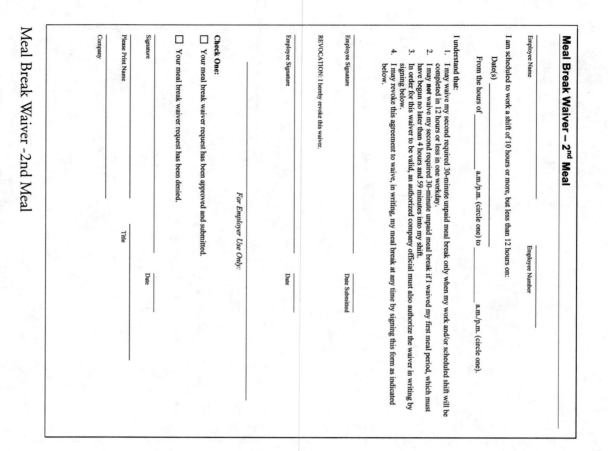

Meal Break Waiver – 2nd Meal

Employee Name _____   Employee Number _____

I am scheduled to work a shift of 10 hours or more, but less than 12 hours on:

Date(s) _____

From the hours of _____ a.m./p.m. (circle one) to _____ a.m./p.m. (circle one),

I understand that:

1. I may waive my second required 30-minute unpaid meal break only when my work and/or scheduled shift will be completed in 12 hours or less in one workday.
2. I may **not** waive my second required 30-minute unpaid meal break if I waived my first meal period, which must have begun no later than 4 hours and 59 minutes into my shift.
3. In order for this waiver to be valid, an authorized company official must also authorize the waiver in writing by signing below.
4. I may revoke this agreement to waive, in writing, my meal break at any time by signing this form as indicated below.

Employee Signature _____   Date Submitted _____

REVOCATION: I hereby revoke this waiver.

Employee Signature _____   Date _____

For Employer Use Only:

Check One:

☐ Your meal break waiver request has been approved and submitted.

☐ Your meal break waiver request has been denied.

Signature _____   Date _____

Please Print Name _____   Title _____

Company _____

Meal Break Waiver -2nd Meal

Overtime

This chapter provides a detailed explanation of the rules and exceptions for paying overtime in California, which favor employees more than federal rules and exceptions. Topics discussed include:

- Basic overtime requirements, including the California daily overtime law;

- Workday/workweek definitions and why it is important to properly define and understand them;

- Overtime calculation, including complex examples;

- Mandatory overtime, when it can and cannot be required;

- Make up time — unique provisions in California to provide flexibility to employees and save you overtime costs;

- Compensatory time off, who can and cannot have it; and

- Exceptions for specific industries.

Alternative workweek options to avoid daily overtime (to some degree), are explained in detail in Chapter 15, "Alternative Workweek Scheduling."

 Download forms referenced in this chapter at **www.calbizcentral.com/support**. Be sure to have your access code from the inside covers of this book ready to enter into the forms download area. Your access code for the forms in the online Formspack is on the inside covers of this book. See "Forms Available Online" on page xix for more information.

Posting Requirements

You must place certain posters regarding overtime where all employees can see them. See "Posters" in Chapter 2, page 5, for more information about overtime and other posting requirements.

Basic Overtime Requirements

For almost all nonexempt private-sector California employees not covered by collective bargaining agreements, overtime pay is based primarily on the number of hours worked in a day. You must also account for weekly totals when calculating overtime. See Chapter 16, "Exempt and Nonexempt" for information on which employees are exempted from overtime pay.

Daily Overtime — California Law

A basic summary of California and federal overtime pay requirements follows, with industry-specific exceptions discussed at the end of this chapter.

- You must provide time-and-one-half the employee's regular rate of pay for:

  - All hours worked beyond eight in a single workday; and

  - The first eight hours worked on the seventh consecutive day worked in a single workweek.

- You must pay double the employee's regular rate of pay for:

  - All hours worked beyond 12 in a single workday; and

  - The hours worked beyond eight on the seventh consecutive day worked in a single workweek.

For definitions on what constitutes a workday or workweek, see "Workday Defined" on page 340 and "Workweek Defined" on page 341.

 Regarding minors and daily overtime, it is a misdemeanor to require a minor to work more than eight hours in any one workday, regardless of whether you pay overtime for the hours over eight.[1] See *Chapter 7, "Employing Minors,"* for more information about restrictions on a minor's hours of work.

Weekly Overtime — California and Federal Law

Multiply the employee's regular rate of pay times one and one-half for all hours worked beyond 40 straight-time hours in a "workweek" (see below for legal definitions of "workweek" and "straight-time hours").

Defining Workdays and Workweeks

Defining your workday and workweek is important because these definitions will impact overtime obligations owed to employees. For example, an employee may work 10 eight-hour days straight, but if five of those days fall in one workweek and five days fall in the next workweek, the employee receives no overtime pay. In this example, the employer defined a workweek of Monday through Sunday. The employee works 10 days straight, from Wednesday of the first workweek to Friday of the next workweek. The employee worked Wednesday through Sunday the first workweek (five days), and then Monday through Friday in the second workweek (five days), never exceeding 40 hours in a single workweek. Therefore, the employee never is paid more than his/her straight hourly wage. Of course, any hours worked in excess of eight per day would be compensated at an overtime rate.

Workday Defined

A workday is not simply the hours an employee normally works (for example, 8:00 a.m. to 5:00 p.m., Monday through Friday). A workday means any consecutive 24-hour period starting at the same time each calendar day.[2] The workday may begin at any hour of the day. Unless you specifically designate another starting time (for example, 4:00 p.m. each afternoon), the Labor Commissioner

---

1. Lab. Code sec. 1392
2. DLSE *Enforcement Policies and Interpretations Manual* sec. 55.8

will presume a workday of 12:01 a.m. to midnight. You may define different workdays for different groups of employees. Once you define a workday, it must stay consistent and unchanged for that employee until there is a legitimate business reason for a change (for example, the employee is promoted to a different location that has a different workday defined for that group of employees). Daily overtime is based on the number of hours worked in a single workday. An employee on a traditional 12:01 a.m. to midnight workday could work 16 hours straight without being paid overtime, if he/she worked 3:30 p.m. until midnight and then continued working from midnight to 8:30 a.m. (assuming a one-half hour unpaid meal period in each "workday").

Workweek Defined

A workweek is not simply the scheduled days an employee normally works (for example, Monday through Friday). A workweek means any seven consecutive 24-hour periods starting on the same calendar day each week.[3] Unless you specifically designate another workweek, the Labor Commissioner will presume a workweek of Sunday through Saturday. Like the workday, the workweek can be different for different groups of employees, but should remain consistent and unchanged unless you have a legitimate business reason. The definition of workweek becomes extremely important when calculating overtime under the "seventh-day" rule, because this rule applies only on the last day of your defined workweek, not simply any time an employee works seven days in a row.

For example, in a Sunday through Saturday workweek, the seventh day rule applies only on Saturdays. If an employee works Wednesday through Tuesday, Tuesday would not count as the seventh consecutive day in that "workweek."

Seventh Day of the Workweek

The seventh consecutive day worked in a workweek is paid differently than the first six (see "Workweek Defined" on page 341). On the seventh consecutive day worked in a single workweek you must pay an employee:

- Time-and-one-half the regular rate of pay for the first eight hours worked; and

- Double the regular rate for all hours worked beyond eight.

Example:

- An employee on a Sunday through Saturday workweek works four hours each day Sunday through Friday, and then works 10 hours on Saturday. Since Saturday is the seventh consecutive day worked in the workweek, the employee would receive eight hours at time-and-one-half and two hours at double-time.

	Sun	Mon	Tues	Wed	Thur	Fri	Sat	Total
Hours	9 a.m.-1 p.m.	9 a.m.-1 p.m.	9 a.m.-1 p.m.	9 a.m.-1 p.m.	9 a.m.-1 p.m.	9 a.m.-1 p.m.	9 a.m.-7 p.m.	
Total	4	4	4	4	4	4	10	34

---

3. DLSE *Enforcement Policies and Interpretations Manual* sec. 55.8

	Sun	Mon	Tues	Wed	Thur	Fri	Sat	Total
Wages Due								
1.0x	4	4	4	4	4	4	0	24
1.5x	0	0	0	0	0	0	8	8
2.0x	0	0	0	0	0	0	2	2

Seventh Day Stays Consistent

Once a workweek is defined (for example, Sunday through Saturday), the seventh day rule applies only on the seventh day of that specifically defined workweek. For a Sunday through Saturday workweek, the seventh day rule will apply only on Saturdays. An employee who works seven consecutive days spread throughout two workweeks (for example, Thursday through Wednesday) will not receive seventh day pay on Wednesday, since it is not the seventh consecutive day of the employee's Sunday through Saturday workweek.

Straight-time Hours Defined

Only hours worked at straight-time apply to the weekly 40-hour limit. This prevents "pyramiding" of overtime, where an employee earns overtime on top of overtime already paid. Once an employee has been paid overtime for hours over eight in a day, those overtime hours do not count toward the weekly 40-hour limit.

Example:

- An employee works 10 hours each day Monday through Thursday, and is owed eight hours of straight-time and two hours of overtime pay for each of those days. When that employee comes in on Friday morning, although he/she actually worked 40 hours already in the workweek, he/she has worked only 32 hours of straight-time and does not begin earning weekly overtime until he/she works eight more hours.

Hours Paid but not Actually Worked

Hours paid for vacations, holidays, sick leave, etc., not actually worked by the employee are not considered for calculating overtime.[4] Therefore, an employee who is paid eight hours for the Thanksgiving holiday (Thursday) and works eight-hour days on Monday, Tuesday, Wednesday, Friday and Saturday that same week, will be paid 48 straight-time hours for the week. Base overtime strictly on hours worked, not hours paid.

Regular Rate of Pay Defined

The employee's regular rate of pay is the basis for calculating overtime. The regular rate is not simply an employee's normal hourly amount. *Regular rate* means the employee's actual rate of pay, including all hourly earnings plus many other types of compensation. The regular rate must include nearly all forms of pay received by that employee, including commissions, production bonuses,

---

4. *DLSE Enforcement Policies and Interpretations Manual* sec. 49.1.2.4

piece work earnings and value of meals and lodging. Base overtime on the employee's regular rate of pay including all the above forms of payment.[5]

Amounts *not* included in the regular rate of pay include:

- Gifts (such as those received for holidays or birthdays or as a reward for service, the amounts of which are not based on hours worked, production or efficiency);

- Hours paid but not worked (such as vacation, holidays and sick leave, reporting time and split-shift pay);

- Reimbursement of expenses;

- Discretionary bonuses (typically awarded in recognition of services performed during a given period, these bonuses occur at your sole discretion, and you decide the amount of the bonus and the timing of the bonus payment);

- Profit-sharing plans (payments made in recognition of services performed during a given period to a profit-sharing plan or trust or bona fide thrift or savings plan, without regard to hours of work, production or efficiency);

- Employment Retirement Income Security Act (ERISA) plan payments (irrevocable contributions for old age; retirement; life, accident or health insurance; or similar employee benefits); and

- Overtime pay.[6]

For an employee's compensation based wholly or partly on bonuses, commissions or multiple hourly rates, you must calculate the regular rate of pay each workweek. Determining an employee's regular rate of pay each workweek is important because the employee's overtime rate each week must be based on the regular rate of pay, not just the normal hourly rate of pay.[7]

Calculating the regular rate of pay requires that all compensation received for the week (including multiple hourly rates, bonuses, commissions, etc.) must be divided by the total number of hours worked.[8]

Calculate a full-time (40-hour) salaried nonexempt employee's regular rate by dividing the weekly total regular compensation (salary) by 40.[9] For piece or commission workers, compute the regular rate of pay using either of two methods:

- When using the piece or commission rate as the regular rate and paying one and one-half times this rate for production during overtime hours, in no case may the regular rate be below the applicable minimum wage.[10] Compute the regular rate by dividing the total earnings for the week, including the overtime hours, by the total hours worked during the week, including overtime hours. For each overtime hour worked, the employee is entitled to an additional one-half the regular rate for hours requiring time and one-half and to an additional full rate for hours requiring double-time; or

- A group rate for piece workers is an acceptable method of computing the regular rate of pay. In this method the total number of pieces the group produces is divided by the number of persons in the group, and each person is paid accordingly. Determine the

---

5.*DLSE Enforcement Policies and Interpretations Manual* sec. 49.1.2.4

6.*DLSE Enforcement Policies and Interpretations Manual* sec. 49.1.2.3

7.*DLSE Enforcement Policies and Interpretations Manual* sec. 49.1

8.*DLSE Enforcement Policies and Interpretations Manual* sec. 49.2.1.2

9.Lab. Code sec. 515(d)

10.*DLSE Enforcement Policies and Interpretations Manual* sec. 49.2.1.8

regular rate for each worker by dividing the pay received by the number of hours worked. The regular rate cannot be less than the minimum wage.[11]

Regular Rate for More than One Rate of Pay

Different rates may be paid for different jobs, as long as the work involved is objectively different. In addition, you may pay for nonproductive time, such as time spent traveling, at a different rate (see "Travel Time" in Chapter 13, page 317). Employees must have previous notice of the lower rate.[12]

When an employee with more than one rate of pay works overtime, you must calculate the employee's regular rate of pay to determine the overtime rate.[13] See "Regular Rate of Pay Defined" on page 342, and "Calculating" on page 344.

Calculating

The trickiest part of payroll administration is calculating overtime. It is best approached on a step-by-step basis, first identifying those hours that must be paid on an overtime basis, deciding what overtime rate must be applied then determining the regular rate to which overtime must be applied. This *Digest* provides an *Overtime Calculation Worksheet* and numerous examples of overtime in this chapter to assist you in working through some of the more common situations you may face.

Hourly Employees

The overtime rate must be based on the employee's regular rate of pay, described in "Regular Rate of Pay Defined" on page 342. When an employee works overtime and earns time-and-one-half, he/she receives the hourly rate plus one-half of the regular rate of pay. When the employee earns double-time, he/she receives the hourly rate plus the full regular rate of pay.

Example of paying overtime to an employee with two rates of pay:

An employee normally earns $10 per hour working at trade shows for his/her employer and $8.75 per hour for travel time. In one week, the employee works 40 hours at a trade show and spends 10 hours traveling.

> $10/hour x 40 hours = $400
>
> $8.75/hour x 10 hours = $87.50
>
> $400 + $87.50 = $487.50 (total weekly compensation before adding in overtime premiums)
>
> $487.50 divided by 50 hours (total hours) = $9.75 (regular rate of pay)
>
> $9.75 divided by 2 = $4.88 (overtime premium for time-and-one-half)

Based on the above calculations, you would pay an employee entitled to daily overtime (worked and traveled in the same day) as follows:

- Time-and-one-half: If the employee travels while time-and-one-half is due (for example, the ninth hour of a day), he/she would receive $13.63 per hour. This is the $8.75 travel rate plus the $4.88 overtime premium.

---

11. *DLSE Enforcement Policies and Interpretations Manual* sec. 49.1.8
12. DLSE Opinion Letter 1994.02.03-3
13. DLSE Opinion Letter 1994.02.03-3

- If the employee performs his/her regular duties while time-and-one-half is due, he/she would receive $14.88 per hour. This is the $10 rate he/she normally earns, plus the $4.88 overtime premium.

• Double-time: If the employee travels while double-time is due (for example, the 13th hour of a day), he/she would receive $18.50 per hour. This is the $8.75 travel rate plus the $9.75 regular rate of pay.

- If the employee performs his/her regular duties while double-time is due, he/she would receive $19.75 per hour. This is the $10 rate he/she normally earns, plus the $9.75 regular rate of pay.

This formula presumes only two rates of pay. When more than two rates apply, simply multiply the additional rates by the number of hours worked at those rates and include them in the total weekly compensation. If other forms of compensation apply, such as bonuses or commissions, these must be included in the total weekly compensation as well.[14]

Salaried Nonexempt Employees

Nonexempt employees may be paid a "salary" rather than an hourly or piece rate wage. However, placing a nonexempt employee on salary in no way excuses you from paying that employee overtime, reflecting the hours worked and applicable rates on the pay stub or ensuring that the employee receives mandatory rest and meal breaks. Therefore, salaried nonexempt employees must be required to record their daily hours, which allows you to pay for required overtime and protects you from claims concerning missed meal periods.

A full-time (40-hour), salaried nonexempt employee's regular hourly rate is 1/40th of the employee's weekly salary. The regular hourly rate then is used to calculate an employee's regular rate of pay. The employee's overtime rate then is based on the regular rate of pay, which would include the regular hourly rate plus most commissions, bonuses or other compensation. (See "Regular Rate of Pay Defined" on page 342 for more information.) By placing a nonexempt employee on salary, you must go through three different calculations in each workweek in which the employee works any overtime.

The law does not specify how to calculate the hourly rate when a salaried nonexempt employee regularly or occasionally works fewer than 40 hours. It also does not tell you how to calculate the weekly salary when the employee's agreed-upon salary is a monthly or yearly amount.

The definition of "full-time" as 40 hours per week applies only to this particular pay calculation. You retain the option to define "full-time" as fewer than 40 hours for all other purposes, such as eligibility for employee benefits.

Overtime Examples

Calculating daily and weekly overtime can be quite confusing, especially with the many recent changes to California's overtime laws. The following examples show the proper overtime calculations in six common situations.

---

14. DLSE Opinion Letter 1992.05.14

For ease of calculation, these examples do not take into account legally required meal breaks. Remember that a one-half hour unpaid meal break generally is required for shifts of more than five hours. See "Meal and Rest Breaks" in Chapter 13, page 320, for more information.

Sample 1: Edith E. Employee

Edith worked Monday through Friday, with overtime on three of those days. She earns eight hours of straight time each day, with overtime at time-and-one-half for two hours on Tuesday, one hour on Wednesday and three hours on Thursday. The overtime hours on Tuesday, Wednesday and Thursday do not count toward the weekly (40-hour) overtime requirement, because they were already paid at an overtime rate. Thus, her employer does not have to "pyramid" weekly overtime on top of daily overtime that already has been paid.

	Sun	Mon	Tues	Wed	Thur	Fri	Sat	Total
Hours	off	8 a.m. - 4 p.m.	8 a.m.- 6 p.m.	8 a.m.- 5 p.m.	7 a.m. - 6 p.m.	8 a.m.- 4 p.m.	off	
Total	0	8	10	9	11	8	0	46
Wages Due								
1.0x	0	8	8	8	8	8	0	40
1.5x	0	0	2	1	3	0	0	6
2.0x	0	0	0	0	0	0	0	0

Sample 2: Donny D. Donutmaker

Donny works six days this week, with overtime due for all days but Sunday and Wednesday. On Tuesday Donny works more than 12 hours, and so earns time-and-one-half for hours 9 through 12 and double-time for the 13th hour. When Donny comes in on Friday morning, he already completed 40 hours of straight-time in the workweek so he earns time-and-one-half for his first 12 hours on Friday and double-time for the 13th hour. The overtime paid for Sunday through Thursday does not count toward the weekly (40-hour) overtime requirement, because it has already been paid at an overtime rate. Thus, his employer does not have to "pyramid" weekly overtime on top of daily overtime that already has been paid.

	Sun	Mon	Tues	Wed	Thur	Fri	Sat	Total
Hours	3 p.m. - 11 p.m.	3 a.m. - 2 p.m.	3 a.m. - 4 p.m.	3 p.m. - 11 p.m.	3 a.m. - 2 p.m.	3 a.m. - 4 p.m.	off	
Total	**8**	**11**	**13**	**8**	**11**	**13**	**0**	**64**
Wages Due								
1.0x	8	8	8	8	8	0	0	40
1.5x	0	3	4	0	3	12	0	22
2.0x	0	0	1	0	0	1	0	2

Sample 3: Sarah S. Swingshift

Sarah works the swing shift, usually starting work at 8:00 p.m. each evening and working into the morning of the next calendar day. Thus, each shift is partially in one workday and partially in another. On Sunday, even though Sarah works a nine-hour shift, only four of those hours are on the first workday (Sunday). The hours from 12:00 a.m. until she goes home at 5:00 a.m. count toward the second workday (Monday), as do the hours she works when she returns to work from 8:00 p.m. until midnight on Monday. This entitles Sarah to overtime at time-and-one-half on Monday, Tuesday and Wednesday. On Friday, even though Sarah comes in and works a 10-hour shift, she earns no overtime on that shift. This is because four hours of the shift fall on the sixth workday (Friday) and six hours of the shift fall on the seventh workday (Saturday). To avoid the confusion caused by working on two workdays each shift, her employer might change the definition of the workday and workweek for employees on the swing shift, perhaps making their workday run from 7:00 p.m. to 6:59 p.m., each day, with a workweek starting at 7:00 p.m. on Sunday.

	Sun	Mon	Tues	Wed	Thur	Fri	Sat	Total
Hours	8 p.m. - 12 a.m.	12 a.m. - 5 a.m. 8 p.m. - 12 a.m.	12 a.m. - 5 a.m. 8 p.m. - 12 a.m.	12 a.m. - 6 a.m. 8 p.m. - 12 a.m.	off	8 p.m. - 12 a.m.	12 a.m. - 6 a.m.	
Total	**4**	**9**	**9**	**10**	**0**	**4**	**6**	**42**
Wages Due								
1.0x	4	8	8	8	0	4	6	38
1.5x	0	1	1	2	0	0	0	4
2.0x	0	0	0	0	0	0	0	0

Sample 4: Wally W. Workaholic

Wally works all seven days this week. Although the law requires one day's rest in seven, an employee may take the day off at some other point in the calendar month if the nature of the work reasonably requires that the employee work seven or more consecutive days. Wally is entitled to daily overtime on Sunday through Thursday, with time-and-one-half for hours nine through 12 each day and double-time for the 13th hour and beyond. On Friday when Wally comes into work, he already completed 40 hours of straight-time in the workweek so he earns time-and-one-half for the first 12 hours on Friday and double-time for the 13th hour. Since Wally works seven consecutive days in this workweek, his employer pays his first eight hours on Saturday at time-and-one-half, and hours nine and beyond at double-time. The overtime paid for Sunday through Thursday does not count toward the weekly (40-hour) overtime requirement because it has already been paid at an overtime rate. Thus, his employer does not have to "pyramid" weekly overtime on top of daily overtime, which has already been paid.

	Sun	Mon	Tues	Wed	Thur	Fri	Sat	Total
Hours	6 a.m. - 5 p.m.	6 a.m. - 9 p.m.	6 a.m. - 10 p.m.	6 a.m. - 4 p.m.	6 a.m. - 7 p.m.	6 a.m. - 7 p.m.	6 a.m. - 7 p.m.	
Total	**11**	**15**	**16**	**10**	**13**	**13**	**13**	**91**

	Sun	Mon	Tues	Wed	Thur	Fri	Sat	Total
Wages Due								
1.0x	8	8	8	8	8	0	0	40
1.5x	3	4	4	2	4	12	8	37
2.0x	0	3	4	0	1	1	5	14

Sample 5: Patty P. Part-Timer

Patty works all seven days in this workweek, between two and four hours each day, for a total of 16 hours. Since Patty worked seven consecutive days in the workweek, the "seventh-day" rule (requiring time-and-one-half for the first eight hours on the seventh consecutive day worked in a workweek) applies.

	Sun	Mon	Tues	Wed	Thur	Fri	Sat	Total
Hours	1 p.m. - 3 p.m.	1 p.m. - 3 p.m.	1 p.m. - 4 p.m.	1 p.m. - 5 p.m.	1 p.m. - 3 p.m.	1 p.m. - 5 p.m.	1 p.m. - 4 p.m.	
Total	**2**	**2**	**3**	**4**	**2**	**4**	**3**	**20**
Wages Due								
1.0x	2	2	3	4	2	4	0	17
1.5x	0	0	0	0	0	0	3	3
2.0x	0	0	0	0	0	0	0	0

Sample 6: Victor V. Vacationman

Victor works five days in this workweek, eight hours per day, and takes Thursday as a paid vacation day. He is paid 48 straight-time hours in this workweek. Overtime is applied only to hours actually worked. Although Victor was paid for 48 hours in the workweek, he actually worked only 40 hours, so he earned no overtime.

	Sun	Mon	Tues	Wed	Thur	Fri	Sat	Total
Hours	off	9 a.m.- 5 p.m.	9 a.m. - 5 p.m.	9 a.m. - 5 p.m.	Vacation (8)	9 a.m. - 5 p.m.	9 a.m. - 5 p.m.	
Total	**0**	**8**	**8**	**8**	**(8)**	**8**	**8**	**40**
Wages Due								
1.0x	0	8	8	8	8	8	8	48
1.5x	0	0	0	0	0	0	0	0
2.0x	0	0	0	0	0	0	0	0

Mandatory Overtime

With the exception of limitations under certain specific wage orders, a company policy or union contract addressing the subject, employees have no statutory or regulatory basis upon which they may refuse your request that they work overtime. When faced with overtime needs, you should first request volunteers among qualified employees, and require overtime only in the absence of volunteers. If an employee refuses your overtime request, you can take disciplinary action.

The following limitations are included in wage orders:

- Wage Order 3 - An employee may work up to a maximum of 72 hours in seven consecutive days after which the employee shall have a 24-hour period off duty.

- Wage Order 4 - No employee shall be terminated or otherwise disciplined for refusing to work more than 72 hours in any workweek, except in an emergency.

- Wage Order 8 - An employee may work up to a maximum of 72 hours in any workweek after which the employee shall have a 24-hour period off duty, except that:

    (a) In the grape and tree fruit industry the following key personnel, receivers, loaders, fork lift operators, shipping clerks and maintenance workers, may be exempt from the mandatory day off requirement; and

    (b) In the cotton ginning industry and in the tree nut hulling and shelling industry, all employees shall have the voluntary right to be exempt from the mandatory day off provision in this order. Any employee desiring to exempt himself/herself from the mandatory day off provision may exercise that exemption by notifying the employer in writing. Any employee who wishes to withdraw that exemption may do so by notifying the employer in writing at least five (5) days in advance of the desired day off (this notice provision is not intended to be applicable to instances of illness or emergencies); and

    (c) In the exercise of any exemption from the mandatory day off provided above or by action of the Labor Commissioner, (administrative exemptions from the mandatory day off are permitted by Lab. Code section 1198.3 under certain conditions) no employer shall discriminate against any employee who desires to take 24 hours off after 72 hours worked in a workweek; and

    (d) All employers who permit any employees to work more than 72 hours in a workweek must give each employee a copy of the applicable provision for exemption, including subparagraph (c) above in English and in Spanish, and post it at all times in a prominently visible place.

- Wage Order 13 - Any work by an employee in excess of seventy-two (72) hours in any one workweek shall be on a voluntary basis. No employee shall be discharged or in any other manner discriminated against for refusing to work in excess of seventy-two (72) hours in any one workweek.

- Wage Order 16 - No employee shall be terminated, disciplined or otherwise discriminated against for refusing to work more than 72 hours in any workweek, except in an emergency.

Makeup Time

You are not obligated to, but you may, upon an employee's request, allow makeup time under certain conditions. Makeup time allows an employee to request time off for a personal obligation and make up the time without receiving overtime pay.

Makeup Time Guidelines

If you choose to allow makeup time, you must comply with the following:

- While you may inform an employee of the makeup time option, you may not encourage or otherwise solicit an employee to request approval for makeup time;

- An employee may work no more than 11 hours on another workday, and no more than 40 hours in a workweek, to make up the time off;

- The time must be made up within the same workweek; and

- The employee must provide you with a signed, written request for each occasion that he/she desires makeup time.
  Exception:
  If an employee knows in advance that he/she will be requesting makeup time for a personal obligation that will recur at a fixed time over a succession of weeks, the employee may request to make up work time for up to four weeks in advance. The makeup work must be performed in the same workweek that the work time was lost. For example, an employee who wants to leave an hour early every Monday and Wednesday afternoon for a college course may turn in one makeup time request every four weeks, rather than two requests per week.

If an employee requests time off for a personal obligation, but does not submit a written request which would be required for makeup time, you may inform the employee of the makeup time option. However, since you are prohibited from "encouraging or otherwise soliciting" an employee to request makeup time, you may not condition granting the employee's request on his/her agreement to submit a written request for making up the time. If the employee does not wish to make up the time, you may grant or deny the request based on company policy and business needs.

On occasion, after working make up time to take time off later in the week, an employee may decide not to take the time off after all. You are not liable for daily overtime pay for the makeup time that was worked as long as the employee did not end up working more than 40 hours that workweek, nor more than 11 hours in any workday.[15]

Time Records for Makeup Time

When using makeup time, it is extremely important to maintain a time-record system (for example, timeclock, cardsweep or manual timesheet) that shows which hours you pay at an overtime rate and which hours you pay at straight-time as makeup time. One suggestion is to require that the employee attach a copy of the signed makeup time requests for that pay period to his/her timecard when he/she turns it in at the end of the period.

---

15. DLSE Memorandum of December 23, 1999, "Understanding AB 60: An In Depth Look at the Provisions of the Eight Hour Day Restoration and Workplace Flexibility Act of 1999"

Not a Substitute for Alternative Workweek

If you require or encourage employees to submit makeup time requests each week to create an alternative workweek schedule (without complying with the legal requirements for such a schedule), you are in violation of the law.

On the other hand, nothing exists in the law or Industrial Welfare Commission (IWC) Wage Orders limiting the number or frequency of makeup time requests allowed from each employee. An employee could submit a request each week and, with employer approval, therefore work more than eight hours a day on a regular basis without receiving overtime pay.

Makeup Time Example

An employee might request three hours off on Monday to go to a doctor's appointment. The employee might then make up the time by working:

- 11 hours on Tuesday (or any other day during that workweek); or

- One extra hour each day on Tuesday, Wednesday and Thursday (or any combination of days during that workweek).

The employee is limited to 11 hours per day and 40 hours per week when working makeup time.

Checklist, Policy, and Request Form

This **Digest** includes a sample *Makeup Time Policy*. A *Makeup Time Checklist* and a *Makeup Time Request - English* are also included.

Compensatory Time Off

A private employer in California is not permitted to offer compensatory time off (CTO) to nonexempt employees in lieu of paying overtime, unless the employer is one of the rare few exempt from the federal Fair Labor Standards Act. Therefore, if you are subject to the FLSA, you are prohibited from offering employees CTO in lieu of overtime (see "Who Is Covered By the FLSA?" in Chapter 11, page 257, for more information about FLSA coverage).

Non-Exempt Employees under Certain Wage Orders

Under a circumstance that only applies to the rare few California employers that are not covered by the FLSA, (see "Who Is Covered By the FLSA?" in Chapter 11, page 257) you may offer CTO only if you can take advantage of an extremely limited exemption contained in Wage Orders 2, 4, 6, 7, 9, 11, 12 or 15. If you meet these criteria, you may offer CTO at applicable overtime rates subject to four conditions:

- The CTO is provided pursuant either to a collective bargaining agreement or, in the absence of such agreement, to a written agreement entered into between you and your employee before performance of the work;

- The employee has not accrued more than 240 hours of CTO;

- The employee requests, in writing, CTO in lieu of overtime compensation; and

- You regularly schedule the employee to work no fewer than 40 hours in a workweek.[16]

You must permit the employee to use the accrued time within a reasonable period after making the request, as long as such use does not unduly disrupt your operations.[17]

16.Lab. Code secs. 204.3(a) and (b)
17.Lab. Code sec. 204.3(e)(1)

The following factors are relevant to determine whether you have granted a request to use CTO within a reasonable period:

- The normal schedule of work;

- Anticipated peak work loads based upon experience;

- Emergency requirements for staff and services; and

- The availability of qualified substitute staff.[18]

You must pay overtime to employees who accrued 240 hours of CTO for any additional overtime work hours.[19] Keep accurate records reflecting CTO earned and used.

You must pay CTO at the regular rate earned by the employee at the time the employee receives payment[20] except that upon termination of employment, the payment rate for unused CTO may be either the final regular rate or the average regular rate received by the employee during the last three years of employment, whichever is higher.[21]

At the employee's request, you must pay overtime in cash in lieu of earned CTO for at least two pay periods.[22]

Limits on Use of CTO by Public Employees

Public employers may require employees to use accrued CTO, according to a decision of the United States Supreme Court made in 2000. The case stemmed from a policy adopted by the sheriff's department in Harris County, Texas, which required employees to begin taking scheduled CTO to reduce the amount of time that had been accrued.

The policy was implemented because Harris County feared having to pay out large amounts of CTO when employees were terminated, retired or reached a pre-determined cap. A group of deputy sheriffs sued, claiming the federal FLSA does not permit an employer to force an employee to use CTO unless there is an agreement permitting the employer to do so. The U.S. Supreme Court held that nothing in the FLSA or its implementing regulations prohibits public employers from forcing employees to use accrued CTO.[23]

Compensatory Time Off and the Exempt Employee

CTO regulations do not apply to exempt employees (see Chapter 16, "Exempt and Nonexempt," for more information about exempt versus nonexempt employees). Providing an exempt employee with formal CTO (hour-for-hour, or day-for-day) likely would destroy that employee's exempt status.

---

18. Lab. Code sec. 204.3 (e)(3)
19. Lab. Code sec. 204.3 (c)(1)
20. Lab. Code sec. 204.3 (c)(2)
21. Lab. Code sec. 204.3(d)
22. Lab. Code sec. 204.3(e)(2)
23. *Christensen, et al. v. Harris County, et al.* 529 US 576 (2000)

Exceptions for Specific Industries

The IWC's Wage Orders for specific industries contain certain exceptions to the general rules for calculating overtime and premium pay. If you are in one of those industries, familiarity with those exceptions can help you avoid penalties and sometimes even save you money.

Private School Teachers

 California provides a state overtime exemption for teachers at private elementary or secondary academic institutions meeting the following requirements:

- The employee must be primarily engaged in the duty of teaching, instructing or lecturing in the activity of imparting knowledge to students;

- The employee must earn a monthly salary equivalent to not less than two times the state minimum wage;

- The employee must customarily and regularly exercise discretion and independent judgment in performing the duties of a teacher; and

The employee must have attained either:

- A Baccalaureate or higher degree from an accredited institution of higher learning; or

- Current compliance with the requirements set forth by the California Commission on Teacher Credentialing or the equivalent certification authority in another state for obtaining a preliminary or alternative teaching credential.

Hospitals

Hospitals and other institutions primarily engaged in the care of the sick, the aged or the mentally ill who reside on the premises may agree with employees to create a work period of 14 consecutive days instead of a 7 day workweek. If they reach such an agreement, employees are entitled to time-and-one-half their regular rate for all work beyond 80 hours in the 14-day work period.[24]

Employees of licensed hospitals are subject to daily overtime. However, these employees may vote to implement an alternative workweek that allows up to 12 hours of work per day without daily overtime pay. Alternative workweeks for all other industries allow no more than 10 hours of work per day without daily overtime pay. See "Health Care" in Chapter 15, page 377.

On-Site Construction, Drilling and Logging

In 2000, the Labor Commissioner and the IWC clarified that on-site construction, drilling and logging employees are subject to California's daily overtime laws as a result of AB 60. These employees formerly were exempted from daily overtime because they were not covered under the IWC's Wage Orders, which regulate wages and hours of nonexempt employees in California.

---

24. IWC Wage Order 5, sec. 3

Wage Order 16 covers on-site construction, drilling, logging and mining employees. See "Order 16 - On-Site Construction, Drilling, Logging and Mining Industries" in Chapter 11, page 243.

On-site workers often have long commute times to various worksites. An employee's commute time from home to the worksite generally is not paid time and therefore not subject to overtime. However, see "Travel Time" in Chapter 13, page 317.

On-site mining, which also was previously not covered by the IWC orders, is subject to daily overtime and limitations on hours through separate provisions of the state Labor Code.[25]

Agriculture

Different overtime rules apply to employees working in agriculture.[26] Agricultural laborers earn overtime pay after working 10 hours per day or on the seventh consecutive day in a workweek. Overtime pay is at the rate of one and one-half times straight pay after 10 hours per day and for the first eight hours on the seventh consecutive workday in a workweek, and two times straight pay after eight hours on the seventh day. The "one day of rest in seven" requirement does not apply.[27]

Employees whose primary duties are those of an irrigator are not entitled to overtime.[28]

You must pay at least the minimum wage to all agricultural workers, even those who work piece-work jobs.

Transportation

Most long-haul truck drivers are exempted from standard overtime requirements, as are taxicab drivers and certain airline employees.[29] The provisions of the FLSA covering hours and days of work do not apply to drivers of commercial vehicles regulated by the U.S. Department of Transportation (DOT).[30] In essence, DOT regulations do not provide for overtime for covered drivers. They do, however, limit allowable driving time.

Drivers of commercial motor vehicles not regulated by DOT, whether or not they engage in interstate commerce, may be covered by state law.[31] However, state law also exempts drivers of the following vehicles from overtime otherwise mandated by state law:

- Motor trucks with more than two axles, truck tractors and all trailers, semi-trailers and auxiliary, logging, pole or pipe dollies used in combination with them;

- Two-axle motor trucks (excluding pickups) when coupled in any combination of vehicles exceeding 40 feet in length; and

- Buses, school buses, school pupil activity buses and farm labor vehicles.[32]

25.Lab. Code sec. 751.8
26.IWC Wage Order 14
27.IWC Wage Order 14
28.IWC Wage Order 14 sec. 3
29.IWC Wage Orders sec. 3
30.29 U.S.C. 213(b)
31.DLSE *Enforcement Policies and Interpretations Manual* sec. 50.8
32.13 CCR sec. 1200

Collective Bargaining Agreements

Employees are exempted from statutory overtime requirements if they are covered by a collective bargaining agreement which:

- Explicitly provides for the wages, hours and working conditions of the employees;

- Pays premium rates for overtime hours; and

- Pays at least 30 percent more than the state minimum wage.

Residential Care

The IWC created an overtime exemption effective January 1, 2002, for certain residential care employees.[33] The exemption applies to employees with direct responsibility for children receiving 24-hour residential care when those children are:

- Under 18 years of age; or

- Not emancipated from the foster care system.

These residential care employees may be paid overtime as follows:

- One-and-one-half times the employee's regular rate of pay for all hours over 40 in the workweek;

- Double the employee's regular rate of pay for all hours over 48 in the workweek; and

- Double the employee's regular rate of pay for all hours over 16 in a workday.

The employee may not work more than 24 consecutive hours until the employee receives at least eight consecutive hours off-duty immediately following the 24 consecutive hours of work. Time spent sleeping is not considered hours worked.

There are also new meal and rest period exemptions effective January 1, 2002, for these residential care employees. See "Residential Care" in Chapter 13, page 330, for more information.

Ski Industry

A ski establishment may institute a regularly scheduled workweek of not more than 48 hours during any month of the year when Alpine or Nordic skiing activities, including snowmaking and grooming activities, are actually being conducted by the ski establishment. You must compensate employees at not less than one-and-one-half times the employee's regular rate of pay for any hours worked in excess of 10 hours in a day or 48 hours in a workweek.

A "ski establishment" means an integrated, geographically limited recreational industry, comprising basic skiing facilities together with all related operations and facilities.[34]

---

33. IWC Wage Order 5-2002, sec. 3
34. IWC Wage Order 10

Commercial Passenger Fishing Boats

Employees of commercial passenger fishing boats are exempt from overtime pay when they perform duties as licensed crewmembers. Other employees in the industry, such as clerical and maintenance personnel, are entitled to overtime pay.

See "Fishing Crews" in Chapter 12, page 301, for information about minimum wage and off-duty period requirements for this industry.

Mechanics

Auto mechanics paid a flat rate for each assigned job are *not* exempt from overtime pay. They are not considered to be working for a commission. A California Court of Appeal ruled that commissions are:

- Paid to any person for services rendered in the sale of an employer's property or services, and not in making the product or service; and

- The amount of an employee's compensation is based upon a percentage of the price of the product or service.[35]

The court ruled that the mechanics were engaged in rendering a service, not selling it. The mechanic performs labor, not sales. Thus the mechanic's pay does not fit the definition of "commission" that is exempt from overtime rules.[36] Typically, the mechanic takes the customer's order, makes the repair and examines the auto for further problems. The mechanic has little or no contact with the customer. Therefore, the courts ruled that the mechanic was not a salesperson but a mechanic repairing an auto for a fee.

Calculate overtime payments to flat rate mechanics by adding together all of the mechanic's flat rate earnings and dividing them by the total hours worked, even if that number is more than 40. The result is the hourly wage of the mechanic for that week. Divide the hourly wage in half to determine the overtime premium. The mathematical result is the overtime pay (time-and-one-half) for the mechanic. For example, if a mechanic earns $600 for 48 hours of work under the flat rate system, he/she earns $12.50 per hour ($600 divided by 48 hours). Premium pay amounts to extra half-time of $6.25 per hour — a sum of $50 for eight hours of overtime. The total due this employee is $650.

Further Information

The California Labor Code, as well as the other state codes regulating wage and hour law, are available online on the website of California's Legislative Counsel at ***www.leginfo.ca.gov/ calaw.html***. Additional information, including the Industry Wage Orders, is available for employers online at ***www.dir.ca.gov/IWC/iwc.html***.

---

35. *Keyes Motors, Inc. v. DLSE*, 197 Cal. App. 3d 557 (1987)
36. IWC Wage Order 7

Chapter 14 Forms

This chapter contains samples of forms associated with this topic. *The forms in this section are for visual reference only; download the most up-to-date forms and checklists in their entirety from CalBizCentral.*

To download either individual forms or your entire Formspack containing all the forms referenced in this book:

1. Visit **www.calbizcentral.com/support** and select "Labor Law Digest" from the list of product titles.

2. Have this copy of Labor Law Digest handy — you will need to enter the access code featured on the inside covers of this book.

3. Enter the access code, select the documents you want to download to your computer, then follow the on-screen instructions.

For more detailed instructions, see "Forms Available Online" on page xix.

Overtime Calculation Worksheet

This overtime calculation worksheet is designed for employers who are subject to California's daily overtime requirements.

It is important to fill in the days at the top of the chart in accordance with your seven-day workweek. The Labor Commissioner will presume a workweek of Sunday through Saturday unless your company has designated otherwise (i.e., Monday through Sunday).

Employee Name _____

Company _____

Fill in seven-day work week.

								Hours Paid		
Total Hours Worked	0	0	0	0	0	0	0	0	**Wage Rate**	**Wages Paid**
Straight Time x 1.0 [A]	0	0	0	0	0	0	0	0		
Overtime x 1.5 [B]	0	0	0	0	0	0	0	0		
Doubletime x 2.0 [C]	0	0	0	0	0	0	0	0		
								Wages Paid for Workweek		

Notes:

[A] All hours worked in a single workday up to and including eight, to a maximum of 40 in a workweek.

[B] Hours nine through twelve in a workday; and all hours up to and including eight on the seventh consecutive day of work in a workweek; and all hours beyond 40 straight-time hours in a workweek.

[C] Hours 13 through 24 in a workday; and; hours 9 through 24 on the 7th consecutive day of work in a workweek.

Overtime Calculation Worksheet

Overtime Request

Employee Name _____   Employee Number _____

I am requesting additional work hours on:

Day of the week _____   Date _____

From the hours of _____ a.m./p.m. (circle one) to _____ a.m./p.m. (circle one).

I need to work these additional hours for the following reason(s): (*Fill in the project you are working on and why additional hours beyond your scheduled workday are necessary*).

_____

I understand that:

1. I will only be paid at an overtime rate if I work more than 8 hours in one workday or more than 40 hours in one workweek;

2. A separate written request is required for each occasion that I request overtime;

3. My over time request must be approved in writing before I work the additional hours.

Employee Signature _____   Date Submitted _____

For Employer Use Only:

Check One:

☐ Your overtime request has been approved and submitted.

☐ Your overtime request has been denied.

Signature _____   Date _____

Please Print Name _____   Title _____

Company _____

Overtime Request - English

Overtime Request

Nombre del empleado _____

Número de empleado _____

Solicito horas adicionales de trabajo el:

Día de la semana _____   Fecha _____

Desde las _____ a.m./p.m. (seleccionar lo que corresponda) hasta las _____ a.m./p.m. (seleccionar lo que corresponda).

Necesito trabajar estas horas adicionales por el siguiente motivo o motivos: (Indique en qué proyecto está trabajando y por qué es necesario que trabaje horas adicionales a su jornada laboral programada).

_____

_____

_____

Entiendo que:

1. Sólo me pagarán la tarifa de horas extras si trabajo más de 8 horas en una jornada laboral o más de 40 horas en una semana laboral;

2. Debe presentarse una solicitud por escrito diferente por cada ocasión en la que solicite horas extras;

3. Mi solicitud de horas extras deberá ser autorizada por escrito antes de que yo trabaje las horas adicionales.

Firma del empleado _____   Fecha de presentación _____

Para uso exclusivo del empleador:

Marque una casilla:

☐ Se autorizó y se presentó su solicitud de horas extras.

☐ No se autorizó su solicitud de horas extras.

Firma _____   Fecha _____

Nombre en letra de molde _____   Cargo _____

Compañía _____

Overtime Request - Spanish

Alternative Workweek Scheduling

Alternative workweek scheduling is a feature unique to California. It allows nonexempt employees to work more than eight hours per day without requiring daily overtime payment. Such a schedule may be implemented following a vote of all employees in a work unit following proper disclosure and procedures set forth in law and the Industrial Wage Orders. Safeguards are provided for employees in the affected work unit who cannot or will not work the alternative workweek schedule. This chapter provides a thorough explanation of alternative workweeks, including:

- The legal basis for alternative workweeks;

- Types of alternative schedules;

- Formal procedures required to implement them;

- Rights of individual employees in the work unit;

- Paying for overtime in alternative workweek situations;

- Terminating alternative workweek arrangements; and

- Exceptions to scheduling provisions as allowed by law.

Alternative workweek scheduling eliminates most aspects of the scheduling flexibility employers enjoyed with a traditional workweek. Scheduling flexibility is greatly limited by the requirement that you must implement a regular work schedule and, generally, you must pay all hours worked outside that regularly scheduled workweek at an overtime rate.

It is critical to follow the correct procedure when implementing an alternative workweek schedule. Failure to comply with even one requirement could cause the alternative workweek schedule to be invalidated by the state Labor Commissioner, resulting in awards of three to four years of back overtime to employees who worked the invalid alternative schedule.[1]

If considering alternative workweek scheduling, seek the advice of a competent employment law attorney who can assist you in developing and implementing the plan.

Download forms referenced in this chapter at **www.calbizcentral.com/support**. Be sure to have your access code from the inside covers of this book ready to enter into the forms download area. Your access code for the forms in the online Formspack is on the inside covers of this book. See "Forms Available Online" on page xix for more information.

---

1. Code of Civil Procedure 338(a); Lab. Code sec. 1194; *Cortez v. Purolator Air Filtration Products Company*, 23 Cal.4th 163 (2000)

Alternative Workweek Defined

An alternative workweek is defined as "any regularly scheduled workweek requiring an employee to work more than eight hours in a 24-hour period."[2] An alternative workweek may be a single schedule or a menu of schedules an employee can choose from. See "Propose a Schedule" on page 365 for more information about the menu option.

Creating a Schedule

Creating an alternative workweek schedule requires careful planning and excellent recordkeeping. The following step-by-step guide shows you how to create an alternative workweek schedule under California law.[3] See "Health Care" on page 377 for special rules that apply only to that industry.

Determine the Affected "Work Unit"

Alternative workweek schedules are not meant for the handful of employees within a department who want flexibility. With limited exceptions, everyone in the work unit must work the alternative workweek schedule.

A work unit may be a:

- Division;

- Department;

- Job classification;

- Shift;

- Separate physical location; or

- Recognized subdivision of any such work unit.

A work unit may consist of an individual employee if he/she is the only person in the division, department, job classification, shift, separate physical location or recognized subdivision of any such work unit.

Wage Order 16 provides, the scope of the term "affected employees" is narrowed for workers employed in occupations covered by Order 16-2001. The definition of the term "work unit" (Order 16-2001, Section 2(U)) for Order 16 purposes only, means affected employees will only include "all nonexempt employees of a single employer within a given craft who share a common work site." Thus, not all carpenters employed by a single employer may be eligible to vote on an alternative workweek arrangement. The workers must not only share a craft, but also a work site. Order 16 further provides that "A work unit may consist of an individual employee as long as the criteria for an identifiable work unit in this subsection is met."[4]

Further, those workers employed in occupations covered by Wage Order 16 who are otherwise eligible and who are not on the job site on the day of the election must be notified and allowed to vote in any election for an alternative workweek if such worker has been employed in the affected work unit within 30 calendar days immediately preceding the election.[5]

---

2. Lab. Code sec. 500(c)
3. IWC Wage Orders sec. 3
4. DLSE Enforcement Policies and Procedures Manual sec. 56.8.4 & 56.8.5

Propose a Schedule

You must present a written proposal for an alternative workweek schedule to employees in the affected work unit. Employees cannot create an alternative workweek without your proposal or approval.

The proposed agreement must designate a regularly scheduled alternative workweek in which the specified number of workdays and work hours regularly repeat. The actual days worked within that alternative workweek schedule do not need to be specified. The schedule must provide no fewer than two consecutive days off within each workweek, except employees working an alternative workweek in Wage Orders 4, 5, 9, 10, 15 and 16.[6]

Examples:

- You propose a workweek of Sunday through Saturday. Employees will work four 10-hour shifts each workweek (4/10 schedule); and

- You propose a workweek beginning at noon Friday and ending at noon the following Friday. Employees will work four nine-hour shifts and one four-hour shift each workweek (9/80 schedule).

Propose a Single Schedule or Menu

You may propose a single work schedule that would become the standard schedule for all workers in the work unit, or a menu of work schedule options from which each employee in the work unit would be entitled to choose.

Section 3(C)(1) of the Wage Orders allows the employer to propose a menu of options which will suit the employer's business needs so long as the proposal clearly provides a specified number of regularly recurring work days and the number of hours in the work shift. The Wage Orders do not require a proposal to designate the starting and ending time of the shifts which will be available during the alternative workweek.

Two examples of acceptable regularly scheduled alternative workweeks:

- A 3/12 and 1/4 workweek; and

- A 4/10 workweek.[7]

The menu options cannot offer a regular 8- hour day since that is not an alternative workweek. (Labor Code § 500(c)). However, accommodation of any employee who is unable to work the alternative schedule is an option after the vote.[8]

The DLSE recommends to employers allowing the employees to freely choose the shift they will work, to advise employees of the fact that each shift is limited as to the number who may choose that shift and, further, be made aware of the "nondiscriminatory" method to be utilized in assigning the employees to a particular shift.[9]

5.DLSE Enforcement Policies and Procedures Manual sec. 56.8.5
6.DLSE Enforcement Policies and Procedures Manual sec. 56.5
7.DLSE Enforcement Policies and Procedures Manual sec. 57.7.2
8.DLSE Enforcement Policies and Procedures Manual sec. 56.7.2.2
9.DLSE Enforcement Policies and Procedures Manual sec. 56.7.2.3.1

Determine the Maximum/Minimum Hours Allowable

An alternative workweek schedule may be any combination of hours up to twelve hours per day within a workweek as long as the overtime premium is paid for all hours over ten in a day and over forty in a workweek.[10]

The alternative workweek arrangements adopted pursuant to Wage Orders 1-3, 6-13 and 16 (and all employees subject to Orders 4-2001 or 5-2001 except those employed in the Health-Care Industry) must provide that all work in excess of the schedule established by the agreement and up to twelve hours a day or beyond forth hours per week shall be paid at one and one-half times the employee's regular rate of pay. All work performed in excess of twelve hours per day and any work in excess of eight hours on those days worked beyond the regularly scheduled number of workdays established by the alternative workweek shall be paid at double the employee's regular rate of pay.

A regular schedule of three 12-hour days is not permitted, except in the health-care industry, and for some employees working under Wage Order 16.[11] For more information, see "Health-care Employer/Employee Defined" on page 377.

Distribute a Written Disclosure

When proposing an alternative workweek schedule, you must provide a written disclosure of the effects of the proposed schedule on the employees' wages, hours and benefits. Failure to comply with this requirement invalidates the alternative workweek schedule election.

The written disclosure must be in a non-English language as well in English if at least five percent of the affected employees primarily speak that non-English language.

Employees who did not attend the meeting to discuss the alternative workweek must receive a mailed copy of the written disclosure.

Hold at Least One Meeting

You must hold a meeting at least 14 days prior to voting for the specific purpose of discussing the effects of the alternative workweek schedule. Give employees advance notice of the meeting date and time. You may need to hold more than one meeting if it is not practical or possible for all affected employees to attend at the same time.

Do Not Coerce Employee Support

You may express your position concerning the alternative workweek to the affected employees. However, you may not intimidate or coerce employees to vote either in favor of or against a proposed alternative workweek. You cannot discharge or discriminate against employees for expressing opinions concerning the alternative workweek election or for opposing or supporting its adoption or repeal.

10.*Mitchell v. Yoplait* 122 Cal.App.4th Supp 8 (2004)
11.Wage Order 16 sec. 3(B)(1)(h)

Hold a Secret Ballot Election

All affected employees in the work unit are entitled a vote to approve or reject the proposed schedule in a secret ballot election. A two-thirds vote is required for the schedule to become effective. Do not require employees to put their name or other identifying information on their ballots. Both the statute and the Wage Orders clearly require that the number of votes in favor of adoption must be two-thirds of the affected workers. Thus, it is not two-thirds of the affected workers who voted that will determine the result. A worker not voting, in effect, votes no.[12]

You must hold the election during regular working hours at the worksite of the affected employees, and you must pay all the costs. The vote must take place before the employees begin working the alternative workweek schedule. A retroactive vote is not effective.

Only those employees affected by the alternative workweek schedule may vote. Exempt employees in the unit do not vote.

Upon receiving a complaint by an affected employee, the Labor Commissioner must investigate and may require you to select a neutral third party to conduct the election.

Wage Order 16

For purposes of enforcing the provisions providing for an election for alternative workweeks under Wage Order 16-2001, the DLSE requires the employer to, in good faith and at least 14 days prior to the scheduled election, notify (at their last known address) all workers who would be eligible to vote under the criteria set out in the Wage Order (i.e., employed on the job site by the employer within 30 calendar days immediately preceding the election) of the date, time and place of the election and furnish all such employees with a ballot to be brought to the election site on the date and at the time set for the election.

The employer bears the burden of proof that good faith efforts have been utilized to effect the notice and the delivery of ballots. Failure to show that good faith efforts have been utilized in informing all eligible workers will void the election.[13]

The Wage Orders provide that "[t]he election shall be held during regular working hours at the employees' work site." Recognizing that some employees of a single employer in the on-site occupations covered by Order 16 may be eligible to vote on one particular job site while currently assigned to another job site, DLSE has concluded that each employee currently employed by the employer and eligible to vote must have the opportunity to vote without loss of pay. If necessary, the employer must provide any current employee of the employer transportation to the work site where the election is held and must pay for the time reasonably lost by the employee in voting during working hours.[14]

 Do not require employees to work the alternative workweek schedule for at least 30 days after announcing the final election results.

---

12. DLSE Enforcement Policies and Procedures Manual sec. 56.8.3
13. DLSE Enforcement Policies and Procedures Manual sec. 56.8.5.4
14. DLSE Enforcement Policies and Procedures Manual sec. 56.9

File Election Results with the Division of Labor Statistics and Research

File the results of the election with the Division of Labor Statistics and Research (DLSR) within 30 days of the final election. After, the results become a public document.

Do not send the actual ballots. Election results must be sent to:

> Division of Labor Statistics and Research
> Attention: Alternative Workweek Election Results
> P. O. Box 420603
> San Francisco, CA 94142

The information listed below should be included in memo format:

- Company name, phone number, address and contact person;

- Date of the election;

- Statement of passage or failure of the election;

- Election results (e.g., "...50 out of 60 voting employees voted in favor of the alternative workweek schedule...");

- Description of the actual alternative workweek schedule that is the subject of the election;

- *If more than one person voted*: a statement that the vote was a written, secret ballot and that it passed by at least two-thirds of the vote; and

- *If only one person voted*: a statement that the vote was a written ballot and that the one person voting voted in favor of the alternative workweek schedule.

Retain Complete Records

It is important to keep complete records of the alternative workweek election, as well as documentation showing how the schedule is being followed, including:

- The proposal submitted to employees;

- The written disclosure distributed to employees;

- Minutes from the meeting(s) held to discuss the proposed schedule;

- Records of the election procedure;

- Election results;

- A copy of the memorandum regarding the election results submitted to DLSR;

- Documentation indicating the results were properly filed with DLSR;

- Any documentation regarding employees who cannot or will not work the alternative workweek schedule, and who are being accommodated with a different schedule;

- Actual alternative workweek schedules or calendars;

- Documentation of occasional changes to the schedule and notice given to employees about such changes;

- Overtime records;

- Meal period waivers;

- Requests by employees to substitute their regularly scheduled working days;

- Make up time requests; and

- Petitions to repeal the alternative workweek schedule.

Nonexempts Only

Alternative workweeks apply only to nonexempt employees. Employees properly classified as exempt do not earn overtime, and so do not need alternative workweeks. See Chapter 16, "Exempt and Nonexempt" for more information about exempt and nonexempt status.

Flexible Schedule Versus Alternative Workweek

People often confuse flexible work schedules with alternative workweek schedules. A flexible schedule is a workweek schedule of eight hours per day where some employees begin the shift early in the day and others begin work later in the day. Some employees may come in at 7:00 a.m. and others at 9:00 a.m., but all regularly work no more than an eight-hour day. Flexible scheduling does not eliminate the legal requirement of paying daily overtime for all work in excess of eight hours in each workday. Unlike the alternative workweek schedules discussed in this chapter, you may institute flexible scheduling at any time. Employees may not change their own schedules for such flexibility without your approval.

The 9/80 Schedule

Subject to the limitations discussed in this chapter, you may implement a 9/80 schedule, also referred to as the 5-4/9 flexible schedule. The 9/80 schedule usually translates into a total of nine days of work in an 80-hour period — five days one calendar week and four days the following calendar week. Eight of the shifts are nine hours and one shift is eight hours. Employees on this schedule would receive one extra day off per 80-hour pay period.

"Workdays" traditionally extend from midnight to midnight; likewise, "workweeks" extend from midnight on a certain workday until midnight one week (seven days) later. Under these traditional parameters, a 9/80 schedule requires an employee to work 36 hours ($4 \times 9 = 36$) one week and 44 ($[4 \times 9] + 8 = 44$) the next, for a total of 80 hours ($36 + 44 = 80$) over a two-week period.

Avoiding the necessity for overtime payments in this situation requires a nontraditional method of defining workdays and workweeks. Under the 9/80 schedule, you must begin the workweek for day shift employees between the fourth and fifth hours of work on any day of the week. This means the employee would work some hours of the shift on one workday, and the remaining hours of that shift on the next workday. In addition, you would define the workweek so that employees will not be required to work more than 40 hours (for example, start the workweek at noon Friday and end at noon the following Friday) in that workweek. In this example, employees could work nine hours each day, except on alternate Thursdays employees work eight hours and on alternate Fridays employees do not work. This allows some of the Friday hours to be worked in one workweek, and some in the next workweek.

Examples of 9/80 Workweeks

See the following sample 9/80 schedules as examples of how the 9/80 system functions. In both examples, the workweek and workday begin at noon on Friday and end at noon on the following Friday. The workday begins at noon on any given day and continues until noon the following day. This 9/80 alternative workweek schedule is consistent and repeatable over every two-week period.

Example 1:

	Fri	Sat	Sun	Mon	Tues	Wed	Thur	Fri	Total
Workweek 1 "---"=noon	--- 4	off --- off	off --- off	5 --- 4	5 --- 4	5 --- 4	5 --- 4	off ---	40 hrs
Workweek 2 "---"=noon	--- off	off --- off	off --- off	5 --- 4	5 --- 4	5 --- 4	5 --- 4	4 ---	40 hrs
Workweek 3 "---"=noon	--- 4	off --- off	off --- off	5 --- 4	5 --- 4	5 --- 4	5 --- 4	off ---	40 hrs
Workweek 4 "---"=noon	--- off	off --- off	off --- off	5 --- 4	5 --- 4	5 --- 4	5 --- 4	4 ---	40 hrs

Example 2:

	Fri	Sat	Sun	Mon	Tues	Wed	Thur	Fri	Total
Workweek 1 "---"=noon	--- 5	off --- off	off --- off	4 --- 5	4 --- 5	4 --- 5	4 --- 4	off ---	40 hrs
Workweek 2 "---"=noon	--- off	off --- off	off --- off	4 --- 5	4 --- 5	4 --- 5	4 --- 5	4 ---	40 hrs
Workweek 3 "---"=noon	--- 5	off --- off	off --- off	4 --- 5	4 --- 5	4 --- 5	4 --- 4	off ---	40 hrs
Workweek 4 "---"=noon	--- off	off --- off	off --- off	4 --- 5	4 --- 5	4 --- 5	4 --- 5	4 ---	40 hrs

Pre-1999 Schedules

Under Wage Orders 1, 4, 5, 7 and 9, a limited provision exists for employees who were voluntarily working alternative workweek schedules before July 1, 1999. You may continue such an alternative workweek schedule if:

- It was an individual agreement made after January 1, 1998, between the employee and employer;

- It provides for a workday of not more than 10 hours; and

- On or before May 30, 2000, the employee submitted a written request to continue the schedule, which you approved.

An employee may revoke this voluntary authorization to continue the schedule with 30 days written notice to you.

Maintaining the Schedule

Once a two-thirds vote approves the alternative workweek schedule (see "Hold a Secret Ballot Election" on page 367), you must comply with the following to properly maintain the schedule.

Create the Schedule

You do not need to specify the actual days worked within the alternative workweek schedule before employees vote. In advance of beginning to work the schedule, you must schedule the actual workdays and the starting and ending time of the shifts.

Occasional changes to the schedule are acceptable if you provide employees with reasonable notice. The DLSE will consider a one-week notice to be reasonable notice.[15]

However, you may not create a system of "on-call" employment, in which the days and hours of work are subject to continual changes, depriving employees of a predictable work schedule.

Accommodate Employees Who Cannot or Will Not Work the Schedule

You have three different obligations to accommodate employees who cannot or will not work an alternative workweek schedule:

- **Accommodation of employee's religion.** You must explore any available reasonable alternative means of accommodating an affected employee's religious belief or observance that conflicts with an adopted alternative workweek schedule. See "Religion" in Chapter 27, page 752, about an employer's general obligation to reasonably accommodate an employee's religious beliefs;

- **Employees who were eligible to vote in the election.** You must make a reasonable effort to find a work schedule of no more than eight hours in a workday to accommodate any affected employee who was eligible to vote in the election and who is unable to work the alternative workweek schedule hours. You must make a reasonable effort to accommodate the employee regardless of whether that employee actually voted in the election as long as the employee was eligible to vote. The regulations do not define what it means to be "unable" to work an alternative workweek schedule. It seems fairly certain that an employee would be unable to work the long hours of an alternative workweek schedule based on a medical restriction. But less clear would be a situation where an employee's child day-care situation or college schedule makes it difficult for him/her to work longer hours; and

---

15. DLSE Enforcement Policies and Procedures Manual sec. 56.23.2

- **Employees hired after the election.** You are permitted to provide a work schedule of no more than eight hours in a workday to accommodate any employee hired after the election and who is unable to work the alternative schedule established as the result of that election. Again, the regulations do not define what it means to be "unable" to work an alternative workweek schedule.

Ensure Meal and Rest Periods

Employees on alternative workweek schedules are generally entitled to the same meal and rest periods as employees on traditional schedules. See "Travel Time" in Chapter 13, page 317 and "Meal and Rest Breaks" in Chapter 13, page 320. An employee who works ten hours or more in a shift is normally entitled to two half-hour meal periods. You and your employee may waive the second with mutual consent if the first meal period was not waived.

Ensure One Day's Rest in Seven

Generally, every employee is entitled to at least one day off in a seven-day workweek.[16] However, an employee may accumulate rest days when the nature of employment reasonably requires that he/she work seven or more consecutive days, as long as he/she receives days of rest equivalent to one day's rest in seven during each calendar month.

This requirement for one day off in seven does not apply to emergencies, agricultural work, work performed in the protection of life or property from loss or destruction or when hours worked do not exceed 30 in any workweek, or six in any workday.[17]

Paying Overtime

You can require employees on an alternative workweek to work overtime. This summary discusses your overtime obligations for employees on an alternative workweek schedule. For additional information on overtime, see Chapter 14, "Overtime."

Basic Overtime Obligation

On an alternative workweek schedule, overtime is paid as follows:

- Time-and-one-half:
  - All work performed in any workday beyond the schedule established by the alternative workweek agreement, up to 12 hours a day; and
  - All work performed beyond 40 hours per week.
- Double-time:
  - All work performed in excess of 12 hours per day; and

---

16. Lab. Code secs. 551, 552
17. Lab. Code secs. 554, 556

– Any work in excess of eight hours on days other than those regularly scheduled by the alternative workweek agreement.

However, exceptions exist to these requirements for makeup time (see "Makeup Time" in Chapter 14, page 350), and for occasions when you approve an employee's request for a substitution of workdays.

Exception: Substituting Work Days

Normally, any work performed by an employee outside of his or her regular schedule is paid at an overtime rate. However, you may substitute one day of work for another day to meet the *personal needs of the employee*, without having to pay overtime for the otherwise "unscheduled" day.

Such substitutions must be:

- On an occasional basis;

- At the employee's request; and

- A shift of the same length.

Example:

An employee on an alternative workweek is scheduled for four 10-hour shifts each week, Monday through Thursday. The employee asks to take Monday off and work Friday instead. If you approve the request, there would be no overtime obligation on Friday if the employee worked 10 hours.

No "Pyramiding" of Overtime Required

Only hours worked at straight time apply to the weekly 40-hour limit. This prevents "pyramiding" of overtime, where an employee earns overtime on top of overtime already paid. Once an employee is paid daily overtime for hours over those scheduled in the alternative workweek agreement, those overtime hours do not count toward the weekly 40-hour limit. See "Overtime Examples" in Chapter 14, page 345.

Regularly Scheduled Overtime Work Allowed

You may require employees to work beyond the number of hours established by the alternative workweek agreement even if the overtime hours are worked on a recurring basis as long as appropriate overtime compensation is paid.[18]

Overtime Due for Shortened Shift

If you require an employee to work less than the agreed-upon hours in a shift, the employee is entitled to time-and-one-half for hours in excess of eight and double-time for hours in excess of

---

18. Industrial Welfare Commission Statement as to the Basis for Wage Orders 1-2001 to 15-2001, sec. 3

12 on that day. This is true only if you require the employee to work less hours than scheduled. If the employee asks to leave early, this penalty does not apply.

Example:

An employee scheduled for a 10-hour shift is sent home after nine and one-half hours because of a mechanical breakdown. The employee is entitled to eight hours at straight time and one and-one-half hours at time-and-one-half for that day.

Overtime Examples

The following examples show various overtime situations involving employees working on an alternative workweek schedule. The employee in each example earns $10 per hour.

Example 1: 4/10 Workweek

The employee is scheduled for four 10-hour days, Monday through Thursday. On Monday, the employee earns two hours overtime at time-and-one-half. On Wednesday, the employee works four hours overtime, for which the employee is paid time and one-half for the first two hours and double-time for the last two hours. The employee is paid time and one-half for the first eight hours worked on Friday, and two hours at double-time, since work hours in excess of eight on the unscheduled fifth day in the 4/10 workweek must be paid at the double-time rate.

	Mon	Tues	Wed	Thur	Fri	Sat	Sun	Hours Paid	Wage Rate	Wages Paid
Total Hours Worked	12	10	14	10	10	0	0	56		
Straight Time (x 1.0)	10	10	10	10	0	0	0	40	$10	$400
Overtime (x 1.5)	2	0	2	0	8	0	0	12	$15	$180
Double-time (x 2.0)	0	0	2	0	2	0	0	4	$20	$80
Wages Paid for Workweek										$660

Example 2: 4/10 Schedule with Makeup Time

The employee is scheduled for four 10-hour workdays, Wednesday through Saturday. However, the employee requests in writing two hours off to attend his son's birthday party on Saturday. Following the employer's makeup time policy, the employee makes up the two hours lost on Sunday. Because the makeup time policy was followed, the employee is owed no overtime for the week. If the two hours were worked outside the regularly scheduled workweek without following the makeup time requirements, the employee would have been owed 38 hours at straight time and two hours at time-and-one-half.

	Mon	Tues	Wed	Thur	Fri	Sat	Sun	Hours Paid	Wage Rate	Wages Paid
Total Hours Worked	0	0	10	10	10	8	2	40		
Straight Time (x 1.0)	0	0	10	10	10	8	2	40	$10	$400
Overtime (x 1.5)	0	0	0	0	0	0	0	0	$15	0
Double-time (x 2.0)	0	0	0	0	0	0	0	0	$20	0
Wages Paid for Workweek										$400

Repealing the Schedule

You may terminate an alternative workweek schedule unilaterally without holding a repeal election, but only after providing reasonable advance notice to your employees.[19] Employees may repeal an alternative workweek schedule by holding another secret ballot vote. The procedure is as follows:

- Employees must petition to repeal the schedule. One-third of the affected employees must sign the petition to require you to conduct a repeal vote; and

- You must hold a new secret ballot election to decide whether to repeal the schedule. A two-thirds vote of the affected employees is required to reverse the alternative workweek schedule. The election must take place during regular working hours at the employees' work site.

Hold the election to repeal the alternative workweek schedule not more than 30 days after the petition is submitted to you, except that the election shall not be held less than 12 months (six months under Order 16-2001) after the date that the same group of employees voted in an election held to adopt or repeal an alternative workweek schedule.[20]

However, you cannot be forced to hold an election to repeal the schedule if less than 12 months elapsed since that same group of employees:

- Voted to adopt the alternative workweek schedule; or

- Held an election to repeal an alternative workweek schedule.

---

19. December 23, 1999, Memorandum "Understanding AB 60: An In Depth Look at the Provisions of the 'Eight Hour Day Restoration and Workplace Flexibility Act of 1999,'" written by chief counsel for the California Labor Commissioner
20. Industrial Welfare Commission Orders, sec. 3(C)(5)

Exception:

For alternative workweek schedules adopted under Wage Orders 4 and 5 between October 1, 1999, and October 1, 2000, a new secret ballot election to repeal that alternative workweek schedule is not subject to the above limitation of 12 month intervals between elections.

You must comply within 60 days if the alternative workweek schedule is revoked. The Labor Commissioner may grant an extension if you can show that revoking the schedule within 60 days would cause undue hardship on normal business operations.

 You may not reduce an employee's regular rate of hourly pay as a result of the adoption, repeal or nullification of an alternative workweek schedule.

Invalidating Alternative Workweeks

The Labor Commissioner invalidates alternative workweeks for many reasons. Some of the most common:

- The alternative workweek schedule was improperly implemented:
  - No secret ballot election was conducted;
  - Too many hours scheduled per day;
  - The schedule was not reported to DLSR; or
  - Not all employees in work unit are on alternative workweek schedules.
- You did not pay overtime properly for the alternative workweek schedule;
- The people on the alternative workweek schedule no longer belonged the original work unit;
- Employees consistently work outside the regular schedule;
- The alternative workweek schedule was changed without the required procedures (vote, etc.). For example, you might ask employees on a 4/10 schedule to work a 4/9 schedule during off-peak months; and
- A collective bargaining agreement containing an alternative workweek schedule expires.

Exceptions to the Alternative Workweek

The alternative workweek scheduling provisions of the law do not cover employees on public works projects and agriculture, although Wage Order 14 permits agricultural employees to work beyond eight hours per day without overtime in limited circumstances.

Employees working under a collective bargaining agreement fall under the agreement's terms as long as the agreement provides premium pay for overtime hours and at least 30 percent higher wages than the state minimum wage.

The most notable variations in the alternative workweek scheduling provisions relate to the health-care industry, where significant differences were created to allow for operational and customary practices.

Health Care

Certain employees in the health-care industry may work shifts longer than 10 hours on an alternative workweek schedule. The alternative workweek schedule regulations with respect to these employees differ in other ways as well. The following explains which employees fall under the exceptions and details pertinent regulations.

Health-care Employer/Employee Defined

The term "health-care industry" is defined as:

- Hospitals;

- Skilled-nursing facilities;

- Intermediate care and residential-care facilities;

- Convalescent-care institutions;

- Home health agencies;

- Clinics operating 24 hours per day; and

- Clinics performing surgery, urgent care, radiology, anesthesiology, pathology, neurology or dialysis.

Employees in the health-care industry who fall under the alternative workweek schedule exceptions are those who:

- Provide patient care (or care to residents in a residential care facility);

- Work in a clinical or medical department, including pharmacists dispensing prescriptions in any practice setting;

- Work primarily or regularly as a member of a patient care delivery team; or

- Work as licensed veterinarians, registered veterinary technicians and unregistered animal-health technicians providing patient care.

Those workers not considered health-care employees and therefore not subject to the health-care employee exemptions are those staff primarily engaged in the following duties or combination of duties:

- Providing meals;

- Performing maintenance or cleaning services; or

- Performing business office or other clerical functions.

12-Hour Shifts Permissible

Employees in the health-care industry may vote to implement a regularly scheduled alternative workweek schedule that includes workdays of up to 12 hours within a 40-hour workweek. (See "Health Care" on page 377 for important information about which employees are eligible for these alternative workweek schedules.)

You may permit longer shifts under certain limited circumstances described in the sections "Longer Shifts for Health-care Emergencies" on page 378 and "Relief For Employee No-Show" on page 379.

Minimum Shift Length

An alternative workweek schedule in the health-care industry may not provide fewer than four hours of work in any shift.

Health-Care Emergency

Health Care Industry employees assigned to work twelve (12) hour shifts may not be required to work more than 12 hours in a 24-hour period unless there is a "health care emergency."[21]

A "health-care emergency" may be declared only by the Chief Nursing Officer or authorized executive of the hospital staff.[22] There must be an objective showing that:

1. All reasonable steps have been taken to provide required staffing, and

2. Considering overall operations status needs, continued overtime is necessary to provide required staffing as defined at Section 2(I) of Orders 4-2001 and 5-2001.

Overtime Pay Obligations

Employees in the health-care industry on alternative workweek schedules are owed overtime at the following rates:

- Double the employee's regular rate of pay for all hours worked in excess of 12 in a workday; and

- One and one-half times the employee's regular rate of pay for all hours worked in excess of 40 in a workweek.

These overtime obligations also apply to employees temporarily assigned to a health-care employer's alternative workweek schedule.

A California appeals court has confirmed that health-care workers on a 3/12 schedule need not be paid time and one-half for the 37th through 40th hour in the regularly scheduled workweek.[23]

Longer Shifts for Health-care Emergencies

You may require an employee assigned to a 12-hour shift to work more hours in narrowly defined "health-care emergencies." A health-care emergency consists of an unpredictable or unavoidable occurrence at unscheduled intervals relating to health-care delivery, requiring immediate action.

A health-care emergency occurs when the Chief Nursing Officer or authorized executive declares that:

- A "health-care emergency" exists;

---

21. DLSE Enforcement Policies and Procedures Manual sec. 56.23.3.2
22. Industrial Welfare Commission Wage Orders 4-2001, 5-2001 sec. 3(B)(9)
23. *Singh v. Superior Court*, 140 Cal. App.4th 387 (2006)

- All reasonable steps have been taken to provide the required staffing; and

- Considering overall operational status needs, continued overtime is necessary to provide required staffing.

Even in a health-care emergency, an employee may work no more than 16 hours unless there is a voluntary mutual agreement between you and the employee.

Relief For Employee No-Show

An employee scheduled for a 12-hour shift may work up to 13 hours if the employee scheduled for the next shift does not report for duty and does not inform you more than two hours in advance that he/she will not be reporting.

Meal Period Waiver

Employees in the health-care industry who work shifts in excess of eight hours total in a workday may voluntarily waive their right to one of their two meal periods. To be valid, the waiver must be documented in a written agreement voluntarily signed by both you and your employee. The employee may revoke the waiver at any time by providing you with at least one day's written notice. You must fully compensate the employee for all working time, including an on-the-job meal period, while the waiver is in effect.

Employees Unable to Work the Schedule

You must make a reasonable effort to find another work assignment for any employee who participated in a valid election prior to 1998 under Wage Orders 4 or 5 and who is unable to work the alternative workweek schedule established.

If you are engaged in the operation of a licensed hospital that institutes a valid 3/12 schedule (three 12-hour workdays) or provide personnel for such an operation, you must make a reasonable effort to find another work assignment for any employee who participated in the vote and is unable to work the 12-hour shifts. You are not required to offer a different work assignment to an employee if such a work assignment is not available or if the employee was hired after the adoption of the 3/12 alternative workweek schedule.

Pre-1998 Schedules

Arrangements adopted in a secret ballot election prior to 1998, or under the rules in effect prior to 1998 and before the performance of the work, remain valid if the results of the election were properly reported to the DLSR by January 1, 2001.

Further Information

The text of AB 60 is available online at *www.dir.ca.gov/iwc/ab60.html*.

Chapter 15 Forms

This chapter contains samples of forms associated with this topic. *The forms in this section are for visual reference only; download the most up-to-date forms and checklists in their entirety from CalBizCentral.*

To download either individual forms or your entire Formspack containing all the forms referenced in this book:

1. Visit **www.calbizcentral.com/support** and select "Labor Law Digest" from the list of product titles.

2. Have this copy of Labor Law Digest handy — you will need to enter the access code featured on the inside covers of this book.

3. Enter the access code, select the documents you want to download to your computer, then follow the on-screen instructions.

For more detailed instructions, see "Forms Available Online" on page xvii.

Alternative Workweek Calendar - Sample

November

Sunday	Monday	Tuesday	Wednesday	Thursday	Friday	Saturday
1 A Shift 6:30am-5:00pm	2 A Shift 6:30am-5:00pm	3 A Shift 6:30am-5:00pm	4 A Shift 6:30am-5:00pm	5 B Shift 5:00pm-3:30am	6 B Shift 5:00pm-3:30am	7
8 A Shift 6:30am-5:00pm	9 Company Holiday (Veteran's Day)	10 A Shift 6:30am-5:00pm B Shift 5:00pm-3:30am	11 A Shift 6:30am-5:00pm B Shift 5:00pm-3:30am	12 A Shift 6:30am-5:00pm B Shift 5:00pm-3:30am	13 B Shift 5:00pm-3:30am	14
15 A Shift 6:30am-5:00pm	16 A Shift 6:30am-5:00pm	17 A Shift 6:30am-5:00pm B Shift 5:00pm-3:30am	18 A Shift 6:30am-5:00pm B Shift 5:00pm-3:30am	19 A Shift 6:30am-5:00pm B Shift 5:00pm-3:30am	20 B Shift 5:00pm-3:30am	21
22 A Shift 6:30am-5:00pm B Shift 5:00pm-3:30am	23 A Shift 6:30am-5:00pm B Shift 5:00pm-3:30am	24 A Shift 6:30am-5:00pm B Shift 5:00pm-3:30am	25 A Shift 6:30am-5:00pm B Shift 5:00pm-3:30am	26 Company Holiday (Thanksgiving)	27 Company Holiday (Friday After Thanksgiving)	28
29 A Shift 6:30am-5:00pm	30 A Shift 6:30am-5:00pm					

In this example, Ace Widget Company has two shifts working alternative workweeks. Ace Widget Company's workweek is Sunday through Saturday. Each shift works four 10-hour days per week, and takes one unpaid half-hour lunch break each day. "A" Shift normally works Sunday through Wednesday. "B" Shift normally works Tuesday through Friday.

Workday Adjustments: Ace Widget requires full production in November to keep up with holiday season orders, and some overtime may be required as well. Because of the Veteran's Day and Thanksgiving holidays that fall in November, the schedule has been adjusted in advance to allow each shift to work a full 40 hours each week. As long as the schedule adjustment is made with reasonable notice, no overtime pay is required for the work performed on the days each shift normally would be off. On the other hand, if an equipment breakdown at Ace required the plant to shut down, causing Ace to make last minute scheduling adjustments to make up the lost time, overtime would be required for the work performed on the days each shift would normally be off.

Holiday Pay: Whether employees will receive holiday pay is a matter of company policy. In this case, Ace does provide holiday pay of 10 hours to its employees, even when a holiday is observed on a day not within the employee's normal workweek. So, during the second week of November, each employee would receive 50 hours of pay (their normal wages for 40 hours of work, plus 10 hours of holiday pay according to company policy). No overtime pay is required in this example because the employees worked only 40 of the 50 hours paid, and overtime pay is required only for time actually worked. Note that holiday pay is not required by law.

Alternative Workweek Calendar

Alternative Workweek Policy

_____ (the Company) has implemented an alternative workweek schedule for

the following work unit(s):

_____

_____

Work Schedule

The work schedule consists of four, 10-hour days.

_____ (the Company) will notify new employees at the time of hire of the days they will work. For current employees, this work schedule is the work schedule presented at the meeting on _____ and approved by a vote of at least 2/3 of the affected work unit(s) by secret ballot on _____.

The workday will begin at _____ [e.g., 6:30 a.m.] and end at _____ [e.g., 5:00 p.m.] A lunch break of 30 minutes, unpaid, will be taken from _____ [e.g., 11:30 a.m.] until _____ [e.g., noon] Two 10-minute paid breaks will be taken during the day and your supervisor will notify you of the time you should take your break. Workweeks are defined as _____ [e.g., Monday through Thursday] or _____ [e.g., Tuesday through Friday]

Holiday Time

When a Company-paid holiday falls on a Monday, all employees will work Tuesday through Friday for that week. When a holiday falls on a Friday, all employees will work Monday through Thursday for that week. Paid holidays will be paid at the rate of _____ [e.g., 10 hours per day]

Overtime

Overtime worked on any regularly scheduled workday will be paid at the rate of:

- Time-and-one-half for all hours over 10 and less than 12, which were not regularly scheduled
- Double time for hours after 12 in one day

Overtime will be paid for hours worked on a day that is not a regularly scheduled workday in any workweek, including any seventh consecutive workday, at the rate of:

- Time-and-one-half for the first eight hours in a day
- Double time after eight hours in a day

Sick and Vacation Time

Sick and vacation time for employees on an alternative workweek schedule will accrue at the rate of _____ [e.g., 10 hours per day] If an employee is absent for a full day, accrued sick or vacation time will be deducted in 10-hour increments. Otherwise, sick and vacation time may be taken in 30-minute increments.

Alternative Workweek Policy

Alternative Workweek Policy Checklist

Follow the steps below to create and implement an alternative workweek policy for your company.

Step 1: Locate and Display the Appropriate Wage Order

- Before implementing an alternative workweek policy, identify and read the Wage Order that covers your company. You can access CalBizCentral's *Wage Order Wizard* for help at: *http://www.calchamber.com/HRC/BusinessResources/Tools/WageOrder/WizardSplash.htm*
- Post the Wage Order applicable to your business in a prominent spot in your workplace, such as a break room or other place employees frequent.

Step 2: Determine the Employees Affected by the Wage Order

- Define the work unit, which may include one or more nonexempt employees in a:
  o Division
  o Department
  o Job classification
  o Shift
  o Separate physical location
  o Recognized subdivision of any such work unit

Step 3: Develop and Propose a Written Alternative Workweek Schedule to Employees in the Affected Work Unit

- Designate a regularly scheduled alternative workweek in which the specified number of workdays and work hours are regularly recurring.
- Prepare a written disclosure of the effects of the proposed schedule on the employees' wages, hours and benefits. For example, specify:
  o The specific days those employees will work, if you are proposing only one schedule.
  o The amount of time that will be charged to an employee's vacation or sick time if they miss a day. For example, if the workday is 10 hours, will you charge 8 hours or 10 hours?
  o What impact the alternate workweek plan will have on sick, vacation or PTO accruals. Will employees accrue the same amount of sick, vacation or PTO, but at an accelerated rate—e.g., for every day worked? There are 260 days in a work year (52 weeks x 5 days), but there would be only 208 days in an alternative workweek of 4 days a week (52 weeks x 4 days).
  o What days will employees work when there is a company holiday during the week? Will the holiday be unpaid or paid, and if paid, for how many hours—8 or 10?
  o If you observe company holidays, do the employees get paid only if the holiday falls on a day that is in their alternative workweek schedule?
  Note: The written disclosure must be in a non-English language, as well as in English, if *at least five percent* of the affected employees primarily speak that non-English language.
- Present a written proposal, including all disclosures, for the alternative workweek schedule to employees in the affected work unit.

Step 4: Hold a Meeting to Inform Employees of the Upcoming Alternative Workweek Election

Note: All employees affected by the proposed alternative workweek schedule are entitled to vote.

- Hold at least one meeting to inform employees of an upcoming election at least 14 days prior to the election. Date(s) meeting held: _____
- Mail a copy of the written disclosure to employees who did not attend the meeting.
- Attach a list of attendees with dates of attendance to this checklist for your records.

Alternative Workweek Policy Checklist

Step 5: Schedule a Secret Ballot Election on an Appropriate Date

Note: All affected employees in the work unit are entitled a vote to approve or reject the proposed schedule in a secret ballot election. A two-thirds vote is required for the schedule to become effective.

- Hold the election during the regular working hours at the worksite of the affected employees. Date of vote: _____

Step 6: If the Vote is Passed, Set an Appropriate Alternative Workweek Start Date

Note: You cannot require employees to work the alternative workweek schedule for at least 30 days after announcing the final election results.

- If the vote passes, set an appropriate alternative workweek start date: First day of alternative workweek: _____

Step 7: File the Election Results and Required Information with the Department of Industrial Relations, Division of Labor Statistics and Research

- File the results of the election, along with the required information, with the Department of Industrial Relations, Division of Labor Statistics and Research (DLSR) within 30 days of the final election. You can use CalBizCentral's sample letter, *Department of Industrial Relations Letter - Notice of Alternative Workweek Adoption*. Date letter sent: _____

Step 8: Maintain the Appropriate Records

- Maintain the following records:
  o The proposal submitted to employees
  o The written disclosure distributed to employees
  o Minutes from the meeting(s) held to discuss the proposed schedule
  o Records of the election procedure
  o Election results
  o A copy of the *Department of Industrial Relations Letter - Notice of Alternative Workweek Adoption* submitted to the Division of Labor Statistics and Research (DLSR) regarding the election results
  o Documentation indicating the results were properly filed with DLSR
  o Any documentation regarding employees who cannot or will not work the alternative workweek schedule, and who are being accommodated with a different schedule
  o Actual alternative workweek schedules or calendars
  o Documentation of occasional changes to the schedule and notice given to employees about such changes
  o Overtime records
  o Meal period waivers
  o Requests by employees to substitute their regularly scheduled working days
  o Makeup time requests
  o Petitions to repeal the alternative workweek schedule

Department of Industrial Relations Letter – Notice of Alternative Workweek Adoption

Use this sample letter to file the results of an alternative workweek election, along with the proposed and adopted alternative workweek schedule, with the Department of Industrial Relations, Division of Labor Statistics and Research (DLSR) within 30 days of the final election.

Keep a copy of this letter, along with the other required records listed in CalBizCentral's *Alternative Workweek Policy Checklist*, as documentation of your compliance with alternative workweek requirements.

Department of Industrial Relations - Notice of Alternative Workweek Adoption (Page 1 of 2)

Department of Industrial Relations
Division of Labor Statistics and Research
P.O. Box 420603
San Francisco, CA 94142-0603

To Whom It May Concern:

This letter is to notify you of an alternative workweek adoption by our employee(s) in

_____ (name of Department or Division of employees) on

_____ (date of election, at most 30 days before date of letter).

The election in favor of an alternative workweek passed by a vote of _____ (# in support) to _____ (# against).

☐ [For elections with more than one employee.] The ballot was a written, secret ballot, and it passed by at least two-thirds of the vote.

☐ [For elections with only one employee.] The vote was a written ballot and the one person voting voted in favor of the alternative workweek schedule.

The alternative workweek schedule that was provided to employees in advance of the election, and was the subject of the election, is as follows: (Fill in or attach schedule.)

_____

_____

_____

If you should have any questions regarding this alternative workweek schedule, please contact:

Company Name _____

Contact Person _____

Address _____

Telephone (___) ___ - ___

Sincerely,

_____

Authorized Company Official

Department of Industrial Relations - Notice of Alternative Workweek Adoption (Page 2 of 2)

DWC-AD 10133.53 NOTICE OF OFFER OF MODIFIED OR ALTERNATIVE WORK
For injuries occurring on or after 1/1/04

THIS SECTION COMPLETED BY CLAIMS ADMINISTRATOR:

Employer (name of firm) _____ is offering you the position of a

(name of job) _____

You may contact _____ concerning this offer. Phone No.: _____

Date of offer: _____ Date job starts: _____

Claims Administrator: _____ Claim Number: _____

NOTICE TO EMPLOYEE Name of employee: _____

Date of injury: _____ Date offer received: _____

You have 30 calendar days from receipt to accept or reject this offer, the remainder of your permanent disability payments may be decreased by 15%. However, if you fail to respond in 30 days or reject this job offer, you will not be entitled to the supplemental job displacement benefit unless:

Regardless of whether you accept or reject this offer, the attached offer of modified or alternative work.

Modified Work ☐ or **Alternative Work** ☐

A. You cannot perform the essential functions of the job; or
B. The job is not a regular position lasting at least 12 months; or
C. Wages and compensation offered are less than 85% paid at the time of injury; or
D. The job is beyond a reasonable commuting distance from residence at time of injury.

THIS SECTION TO BE COMPLETED BY EMPLOYEE

___ I accept this offer of Modified or Alternative work.

___ I reject this offer of Modified or Alternative work and understand that I am not entitled to the Supplemental Job Displacement Benefit.

I understand that if I voluntarily quit prior to working in this position for 12 months, I may not be entitled to the Supplemental Job Displacement Benefit.

_____   _____
Signature   Date

I feel I cannot accept this offer because:

NOTICE TO THE PARTIES

If the offer is not accepted or rejected within 30 days of the offer, the offer is deemed to be rejected by the employee.

The employer or claims administrator must forward a completed copy of this agreement to the Administrative Director within 30 days of acceptance or rejection. (A.D., "SJDB", Division of Workers' Compensation, P.O. Box 420603, S.F., CA 94142-0603). If a dispute occurs regarding the above offer or agreement, either party may request the Administrative Director to resolve the dispute by filing a Request for Dispute Resolution (Form DWC-AD 10133.55) with the Administrative Director.

Form DWC-AD 10133.53 (August 18, 2006)   MANDATORY FORM (Page 1 of 3)
                                                  STATE OF CALIFORNIA
                                                  (08/06)

DWC-AD 10133.53 NOTICE OF OFFER OF MODIFIED OR ALTERNATIVE WORK
For injuries occurring on or after 1/1/04

POSITION REQUIREMENTS

Actual job title: _____

Wages: $ _____ per ___ Hour ___ Week ___ Month

Is salary of modified/alternative work the same as pre-injury job? Yes ___ No ___

Is salary of modified/alternative work at least 85% of pre-injury job? Yes ___ No ___

Will job last at least 12 months? Yes ___ No ___

Is the job a regular position required by the employer's business? Yes ___ No ___

Work location: _____

Duties required of the position:

Description of activities to be performed (if not stated in job description):

Physical requirements for performing work activities (include modifications to usual and customary job):

Name of doctor who approved job restrictions (optional): _____ Date of report: _____

Date of last payment of Temporary Total Disability:

Preparer's Name:

Preparer's Signature: _____ Date

Form DWC-AD 10133.53 (August 18, 2006)   MANDATORY FORM (Page 2 of 3)
                                                  STATE OF CALIFORNIA
                                                  (08/06)

DWC-AD 10133.53 NOTICE OF OFFER OF MODIFIED OR ALTERNATIVE WORK
For injuries occurring on or after 1/1/04

Proof of Service By Mail

I am a citizen of the United States and a resident of the County of _____. I am over the age of eighteen years and not a party to the within matter.

My business address is:

On _____, I served the **Notice of Offer of Modified or Alternative Work** on the parties listed below by placing a true copy thereof enclosed in a sealed envelope with postage fully prepaid, and thereafter deposited in the U. S. Mail at the place so addressed.

I declare under penalty of perjury under the laws of the State of California that the foregoing is true and correct.

Executed at _____ on _____

Signature: _____

Copies Served On: _____

Form DWC-AD 10133.53 (August 18, 2006)

MANDATORY FORM (Page 3 of 3)
STATE OF CALIFORNIA
(08/06)

Notice of Offer of Modified or Alternative Work - DWC-AD 10133.53 (Page 3 of 3)

Exempt and Nonexempt

Federal and state laws exempt certain employees from wage and hour requirements, especially overtime pay. If you have a problem distinguishing between exempt and nonexempt personnel in your company, you are not alone. Some of the largest multimillion-dollar awards of back pay to plaintiffs by the courts stem from employers' misclassification of nonexempt employees as exempt from overtime. The subject is particularly thorny for California employers because our state's exemption requirements create more restrictions than does federal law. As defined in our Industrial Wage Orders, California's requirements exceed even the new federal standards adopted by the U.S. Department of Labor in 2004, making those federal standards generally ineffective for California employees.

This chapter discusses the exempt and nonexempt classifications with particular reference to California standards for minimum salary and job responsibilities. It thoroughly explains requirements for each exempt classification:

- Executive;

- Administrative;

- Professional;

- Computer professional;

- Outside sales; and

- Commissioned inside sales and others.

This chapter also discusses the "salary test" and includes information about allowed salary deductions and those deductions that violate the salary test — thus invalidating the employee's exempt status.

 Download forms referenced in this chapter at **www.calbizcentral.com/support**. Be sure to have your access code from the inside covers of this book ready to enter into the forms download area. Your access code for the forms in the online Formspack is on the inside covers of this book. See "Forms Available Online" on page xix for more information.

Employee Classification

An exempt employee is normally an executive, administrative or professional employee. Other exempt employee types include some inside salespeople and outside salespeople. All other employees generally fall under the nonexempt category. All nonexempt employees are subject to the wage and hour laws of the state and federal government. To avoid the payment of overtime premiums, an employee must be exempt from the overtime requirements of both state and federal law.

Job Title Irrelevant

Job titles do not designate an employee as exempt or nonexempt. An employee with an impressive job title may not qualify as an exempt employee if his/her actual duties do not qualify for an exemption. An employee who performs routine bookkeeping tasks does not become an exempt employee when given the title "controller" rather than "bookkeeper." Giving an employee the title of "store manager" does not make him/her exempt if he/she simply opens or closes the store alone, serves customers, maintains merchandise displays and performs the work of a retail clerk. Calling an employee a "computer systems analyst" or "software engineer" does not make that employee exempt unless the employee meets all the exemption tests. (See "Computer Professional Exemption Tests" on page 400.)

Salary

Exempt employees generally must earn a minimum monthly salary of no less than two times the state minimum wage for full-time employment. However, placing an employee on a salary does not exempt that employee from wage-and-hour laws. A nonexempt employee placed on a "salary" earns overtime the same as hourly wage earners.

The following topics describe some of the more important issues you should consider regarding an exempt employee's salary.[1]

Minimum Salary Level Increased in 2008

The minimum salary level for most exempt executive, administrative and professional employees each month is no less than two times the state minimum wage for full-time employment.

When the state minimum wage rose from $7.50 per hour to $8 per hour on January 1, 2008, the minimum salary level for exempt employees also rose to $2,773 per month. Calculate this amount by multiplying the state minimum wage of $8.00 by 2,080 hours, multiplying by two and dividing by 12 months ($8.00 x 2,080 = 16,640 x 2 = 33,280 ÷ 12 = $2,773.33). These amounts are unchanged for 2009.

Salary is limited to cash wages. It may not include payments "in kind," such as the value of meals and lodging.

General Salary Requirements

The exempt employee generally must receive a predetermined amount constituting all or part of his/her compensation for each pay period. The amount cannot be subject to reduction because of variations in the quality or quantity of the work performed.

As a general rule, you need not pay an exempt employee for any workweek in which he/she performs no work.

Subject to the exceptions provided in this chapter, the employee must receive his/her full salary for any week in which he/she performs any work without regard to the number of days or hours worked.

---

1. DLSE *Enforcement Policies and Interpretations Manual* sec. 51.1, Lab. Code sec. 515, 29 CFR sec. 541.118

Temporary Assignments

An employee who does not perform exempt duties on a regular basis is not exempt on a temporary assignment unless he/she works the exempt job and meets the duties and salary tests for at least one month. An exception exists for the motion-picture industry, which allows a short-term "equivalent" to the monthly amount. An exempt employee in the motion-picture industry may be paid for a period as short as one week if the amount is proportionate to the required monthly minimum ($2,340.00 x 12 = 28,080.00 ÷ 52 = $540.00).[2]

Payment on an Hourly Basis

Employees compensated on an hourly basis generally do not meet the salary test required for exempt employees.[3] Exceptions exist for certain computer professionals and doctors paid on an hourly basis. See "Computer Professional Exemption" on page 399 and "Exemption for Physicians Paid on Hourly Basis" on page 398.

You may pay an exempt employee on an hourly basis for hours in excess of the standard 40 hour workweek, in addition to his/her regular salary. If the standard workweek in a particular industry is less than 40 hours, the Labor Commissioner allows an hourly rate for all hours beyond the industry standard. In addition, any hourly rate paid to otherwise exempt employees for work in excess of eight hours in any one day will not affect the exempt employee's status.[4]

Labor Commissioner's Determination

To determine whether the employee primarily engages in exempt work, the Labor Commissioner examines the work performed by the employee during the workweek. The amount of time the employee spends on exempt work, together with your realistic expectations and the realistic requirements of the job, also receive consideration in determining whether the employee is exempt.

Discretion and Independent Judgment

Most exemptions detailed in this chapter require the employee to customarily and regularly exercise discretion and independent judgment. Discretion and independent judgment involve comparing and evaluating possible courses of conduct, and acting or making a decision after considering various possibilities. An employee with discretion and independent judgment must either:

- Have the power to make independent choices free from immediate supervision and pertaining to matters of significance; or

- Be able to make a recommendation for action subject to the final authority of a superior, as long as the employee possesses sufficient authority for the recommendations to affect matters of consequence to the business or its customers.

2.IWC Wage Order 12
3.*DLSE Enforcement Policies and Interpretations Manual* sec. 51.6.1
4.DLSE Opinion Letter 1997.09.03

To "customarily and regularly" exercise discretion and independent judgment is to do so frequently in the course of day-to-day activities. This phrase signifies a frequency that is more than occasional but may be less than constant.

An employee who merely applies his/her knowledge in following prescribed procedures or in determining which procedures to follow, or determines whether specified standards are met or whether an object falls into one or another grade or class, does not exercise discretion and judgment of the independent sort associated with exempt status. Inspectors and graders, for example, may have some leeway regarding the application of knowledge to a particular situation, but only within closely prescribed limits.

Almost every employee must make decisions requiring discretion. This exemption requires that the decisions must involve matters of consequence of real and substantial significance to the policies or general operations of your business or customers. The tasks may be related directly to only a particular business segment, but still must substantially effect the whole business.

Exercising discretion and independent judgment on matters of consequence is different than making decisions that can lead to serious loss through the choice of wrong techniques, improper application of skills, neglect or failure to follow instructions. Further, employees in training for an exempt position are not exempt employees because they do not exercise discretion and independent judgment during the training process.

Federal Salary Basis Rules

Though the revised federal exemption regulations have no impact in California due to the state's more rigorous standards, the salary basis regulations[5] warrant some attention. The Division of Labor Standards Enforcement indicated that though differences do exist between the state and federal exemption standards, the federal regulations may serve as a guide where there is no conflict.[6] Also, an increasing number of class action lawsuits now get filed under the Fair Labor Standards Act alleging exemption violations.

The federal regulations include a "safe harbor provision" that provides some protection from liability under federal law and that a state court could consider if an employer is sued under state law. Under this provision, an employer may avoid total loss of an exemption as a result of making improper deductions from salary provided:

- It has a clearly communicated policy that prohibits improper deductions;

- It reimburses any adversely affected employees for losses resulting from such deductions; and

- It ceases making such prohibited deductions when learning that they were made.[7]

A copy of the new rules are included on the form, *Federal Salary Basis Rules*.

---

5. 29 CFR 541.602
6. DLSE Manual Enforcement Policies and Interpretations Manual sections 51.6.5, 51.6.6
7. 29 CFR 541.603(d)

Executive Exemption

The executive exemption usually applies to managerial employees. However, managers often do not meet the executive exemption and must be classified as nonexempt.

To determine whether an employee is exempt, consider the duties he/she performs as well as salary. An executive employee is exempt from overtime pay if he/she meets the following requirements:

- Has duties and responsibilities involving the management of the enterprise in which he/she is employed or of a customarily recognized department or subdivision;

- Directs the work of two or more other employees customarily and regularly;

- Has the authority to hire or fire other employees, or make meaningful suggestions and recommendations relating to the hiring or firing and advancement and promotion or any other change of status of other employees;

- Exercises discretionary powers customarily and regularly (see "Discretion and Independent Judgment" on page 389);

- Is "primarily engaged" in duties which meet the above tests (see ""Primarily Engaged In" Defined" on page 391); and

- Earns a monthly salary equivalent to no less than two times the state minimum wage for full-time employment. Full-time employment is defined for this purpose as 40 hours per week.[8] See "Minimum Salary Level Increased in 2008" on page 388.

These tests must be met even if the employee is in "sole charge" of an establishment. See *Exempt Analysis Worksheet - Executive Managerial Exemption.*

"Primarily Engaged In" Defined

"Primarily engaged in" means that more than one-half of the employee's work time is spent engaged in exempt work. An exempt employee must spend more than 50 percent of his/her time doing:

- Exempt duties;

- Work directly and closely related to exempt work; or

- Work properly viewed as a means for carrying out exempt functions.

8.Lab. Code sec. 515(c)

Examples include:

- A manager prepares a management policy memo on his/her computer and faxes it to another manager at a branch office. The typically nonexempt duties of typing and faxing would likely be considered exempt duties because they are directly and closely related to the exempt function of creating the policy and communicating it to another manager; or

- During a busy time at a retail store, a customer knocks several glass jars off a shelf. Normally a clerk would be assigned to clean up the mess. But on seeing all the clerks busy with other customers, a manager grabs a broom and sweeps away the mess so no one steps on broken glass and gets hurt. Although sweeping broken glass is typically a nonexempt duty, in this case it could be properly viewed as directly and closely related to carrying out the manager's exempt function of providing for the safety of the employees, customers and property.

Examples of Exempt Duties for an Executive

Exempt duties must be directly and clearly related to managerial work, such as:

- Interviewing, selecting and training employees;
- Setting, adjusting or recommending pay rates and work hours or recommend same;
- Directing work;
- Keeping production records of subordinates for use in supervision;
- Evaluating employees' efficiency and productivity;
- Handling employees' complaints;
- Disciplining employees;
- Planning work;
- Determining work;
- Distributing work;
- Deciding on types of merchandise, materials, supplies, machinery or tools;
- Controlling flow and distribution of merchandise, materials and supplies; and
- Providing for safety of employees and property.

Examples of Nonexempt Duties for an Executive

Examples of nonexempt duties a manager might perform include:

- Performing the same type of work as subordinates;
- Performing any production work not part of a supervisory function, though not like the work performed by subordinate employees;
- Making sales, replenishing stock or returning stock to shelves, except for supervisory training or demonstration;
- Performing routine clerical duties such as bookkeeping, cashiering, billing, filing or operating business machines;

- Checking and inspecting goods as a production operation rather than as a supervisory function; and

- Performing maintenance work.

However, some otherwise nonexempt duties occasionally could be considered exempt if they relate directly and closely to exempt work and can be viewed as a means for carrying out exempt functions.

Working Managers

"Working manager" refers to an employee with managerial responsibilities and a managerial title but is primarily engaged in nonexempt duties such as, cooking, selling on the floor, cashiering, pumping gas, keeping records, taking care of patients or acting as a desk clerk. Working managers often get misclassified as exempt.

Some examples of working managers usually classified as nonexempt include those in:

- Service stations;

- Restaurants;

- Rest homes;

- Branch retail stores; and

- Motels.

Assistant managers and trainees usually are nonexempt. They do not customarily and regularly direct the work of other employees but share the responsibility instead. They focus on learn the position and do not perform the duties of the exempt position on a regular basis.

Apartment managers usually fall into the nonexempt classification. If the facility and staff are large enough, an apartment manager may meet the duties test for an exempt executive.

Administrative Exemption

The administrative exemption applies to a wide variety of employees. However, many employees whose jobs involve administrative work do not meet the administrative exemption and must be classified as nonexempt.

To determine whether an employee is exempt, consider the duties he/she performs as well as salary. An administrative employee is exempt from overtime pay if the employee meets the following requirements:

- Has duties and responsibilities involving:

  - Office or nonmanual work directly related to management policies or general business operations of the employer or the employer's customers; or

  - The administrative functions of a school system or educational establishment, or one of its departments or subdivisions engaging in work directly related to its academic instruction or training.

- Customarily and regularly exercises discretion and independent judgment;

- Employment involving:

    – Assisting a proprietor or an employee in a bona fide executive or administrative capacity on a regular basis (as such terms are defined for purposes of this section); or

    – Performance under only general supervision of work along specialized or technical lines requiring special training, experience or knowledge; or

    – Execution under only general supervision of special assignments and tasks.

- Being "primarily engaged" in duties that meet the above tests (see ""Primarily Engaged In" Defined" on page 391); and

- Earning a monthly salary equivalent to no less than two times the state minimum wage for full-time employment. Full-time employment is defined for this purpose only as 40 hours per week.[9]

See *Exempt Analysis Worksheet - Administrative Exemption*.

Challenge of Administrative Exemption

A California Court of Appeal case highlights the difficulty of an employee meeting the administrative exemption from overtime. An employer who misclassifies an employee as exempt owes the employee unpaid overtime, interest and attorneys' fees. If the employer does not track the employee's hours (which the employer would not do if the employer considered the employee exempt) a court will rely on the employee's evidence as to how many hours of unpaid overtime are owed.[10]

Michael Eicher worked for Advance Business Integrators, Inc. (ABI) as a "senior consultant" installing a software program created by ABI for its various customers. He spent about half of his time in the office and the other half at customer sites. Most of his time was spent providing customer service and training clients to use the software. Eicher was not a computer professional; his background was in sociology. ABI paid him an annual salary based on Eicher's classification as an exempt administrative professional. It closely monitored, but did not document, his hours for client billing purposes and to ensure he worked at least 40 hours per week. ABI also deducted partial-day absences from Eicher's salary if he did not have accrued paid time off. He frequently worked more than eight hours per day and 40 hours per week.

California regulations provide a five-part test to determine if an employee falls under the administrative exemption. The employee must meet all five parts of the test, including earning a salary equal to twice the state's minimum wage, to be exempt from overtime. Both federal and California law note a clear difference between employees performing work directly related to company policies or business operations (exempt), and employees whose work constitutes the company's core business, or production workers (nonexempt). The court found Eicher's primary duties directly related to ABI's day-to-day business – implementing the software and supporting customers. Eicher did not participate in policy making or have any impact on the business's operation. Eicher was a production worker who did what he was told by his supervisors. Therefore, Eicher did not meet eligibility for the administrative exemption.

In determining how much unpaid overtime Eicher was owed, the court relied on Eicher's testimony and other evidence of his work hours. The court clarified that though it is the employee's burden to prove that he worked the hours he claimed he was owed, it should not be an impossible hurdle for

---

9. Lab. Code sec. 515(c)
10. *Eicher v. Advanced Business Integrators, Inc.* 151 Cal. App. 4th 1363 (2007)

the employee. If the employer's records are inadequate or nonexistent, the employee should not lose his right to the compensation. ABI did not keep track of Eicher's hours because the company thought he was exempt so the court relied on Eicher's evidence. The court also found that the law supports holding ABI responsible for Eicher's attorneys' fees because the law encourages employees to enforce their right to unpaid overtime. In this case, the overtime award totaled more than $46,000, but Eicher incurred more than $40,000 in attorneys' fees – resulting in only a 14 percent recovery if he was not awarded attorneys' fees. If attorneys' fees were not available, employees may be discouraged from filing these claims.

"Primarily Engaged In" Defined

For purposes of the administrative exemption, "primarily engaged in" means that more than one-half of the employee's work time is spent engaged in exempt work. This means an exempt employee spends more than 50 percent of his/her time performing:

- Exempt duties (see "Examples of Exempt Duties For an Administrator" on page 395);

- Work directly and closely related to exempt work; or

- Work properly viewed as a means for carrying out exempt functions.

Examples of Exempt Duties For an Administrator

Exempt duties must relate directly and clearly to administrative work.

Examples include:

- Advising management;
- Planning;
- Negotiating;
- Representing the company;
- Purchasing materials and supplies;
- Promoting sales;
- Researching business opportunities;
- Analyzing business data; and
- Determining company/personnel policies.

Administrative Exemption Upheld

 A California company avoided costly penalties of alleged unpaid overtime and meal and rest breaks after a California Court of Appeal upheld an administrative exemption for a high-level IT position.

The employee who filed the claim was responsible for maintaining a broadband Internet provider's network "well-being." Employees who direct network operations, do project management, purchasing, forecasting and oversight of day-to-day operations, among other job duties, more than 50 percent of the time and earn at least two times the minimum wage can be exempt from overtime and meal and rest break requirements.[11]

Examples of Nonexempt Duties For an Administrator

Examples of nonexempt duties an administrator might perform include:

- Performing routine clerical duties;

- Making deliveries;

- Operating equipment;

- Inspecting products; and

- Tabulating data.

The 9th Circuit Court of Appeals discussed applying the administrative exemption to a job commonly called "field service engineer" or "customer service engineer."

An employee worked mainly at the location of a large customer but reported to his employer's offices several times a week to do paperwork, receive training and meet with supervisors. The employer contended that the employee was an account manager working independently at the client's location to supervise installation, repair and maintenance of equipment, solve problems and make recommendations to better serve the customer. The employer classified him as an exempt administrative employee, excluding him from overtime.

The employee claimed that his job consisted of installing, troubleshooting and maintaining equipment at the customer's location and that he did not exercise independent discretion or judgment.

The court said that to qualify for administrative exemption, the employee must have been engaged in running the employer's business or determining the overall course of its policies. The court said the employee functioned essentially as a highly skilled repair man responsible for installing equipment, diagnosing problems, formulating a work or repair plan and advising his employer of proposed repair procedures and improvements. Such work could not be considered of substantial importance to the general management policies or business operations of his employer or customer, or require the exercise of independent discretion or judgment.

11.*Combs v. Skyriver Communications, Inc. 159* Cal. App. 4th 1242 (2008)

Professional Exemption

Though an employee commonly may be considered a "professional," specific legal requirements exist that must be met to qualify for the professional exemption.

A professional employee is exempt from overtime pay if the employee meets the following requirements:

- Is licensed or certified by California and primarily engaged in the practice of one of the following recognized professions: law, medicine, dentistry, optometry, architecture, engineering, teaching or accounting (see "Licensing Requirements" on page 397); or

- Is primarily engaged in an occupation commonly recognized as a learned or artistic profession. "Learned or artistic profession" means an employee who is primarily engaged in the performance of:

  - Work requiring advanced knowledge in a science or learning field customarily acquired by a prolonged course of specialized intellectual instruction and study, as opposed to a general academic education or an apprenticeship, and from training in the performance of routine mental, manual or physical processes or work that is an essential part of any of the above work;

  - Work that is original and creative in character in a recognized field of artistic endeavor (as opposed to work which can be produced by a person endowed with general manual or intellectual ability and training), and the result of which depends primarily on the invention, imagination or talent of the employee, or work that is an essential part of any of the above work; or

  - Work that is predominantly intellectual and varied in character (as opposed to routine mental, manual, mechanical or physical work) and the output produced or the result accomplished cannot be standardized in relation to a given period of time.

- Exercises discretion and independent judgment in the performance of the duties previously described (see "Discretion and Independent Judgment" on page 389); and

- Earns a monthly salary equivalent to no less than two times the state minimum wage for full-time employment. Full-time employment is defined for this purpose only as 40 hours per week.[12] See "Minimum Salary Level Increased in 2008" on page 388. A new exception to the salary requirement exists for certain doctors paid at least an hourly rate set by the state. You can find the current rate in the *Exempt Analysis Worksheet - Professional Exemption*.

Licensing Requirements

With regard to the licensing requirement for professional employees, the Labor Commissioner determined that:

- The medical profession exemption includes physicians but not nurses;

- Attorneys are exempt but paralegals are not;

- Certified public accountants are exempt but uncertified accountants are not; and

- Licensed civil, mechanical and electrical engineers are exempt but junior drafters or engineers are not.

---

12. Lab. Code sec. 515(c)

Specific Listing of Nonexempt Professional Employees

California's Wage Order 4 classifies as nonexempt many occupations commonly considered artistic or learned professions, including artists, copy writers, editors, librarians, nurses, photographers, social workers, statisticians, teachers (other than state certified) and many others. Unless an employee in one of these positions clearly meets one of the other exemptions discussed in this chapter, based on the duties of the job, the employee must be classified as nonexempt.

Private School Exemption

Teachers at private elementary and secondary schools are exempt from overtime and meal and rest break requirements.[13]

Exemption for Physicians Paid on Hourly Basis

 A licensed physician or surgeon primarily engaged in performing duties for which licensure is required is exempt from overtime if he/she is paid at least the minimum hourly rate set annually by the state.

Effective January 1, 2009, the minimum hourly rate is $69.13.

This exemption does not apply to employees in medical internships or resident programs, physician employees covered by collective bargaining agreements or veterinarians.

Pharmacists

California's Wage Orders specify that pharmacists employed to engage in the practice of pharmacy do not meet the test for professional exemption.

However, a pharmacist may be exempt if he/she individually meets the criteria established for exemption as an executive or administrative employee.

Nurses

Registered nurses employed to engage in the practice of nursing do not meet the test for professional exemption.[14]

Certified nurse midwives, certified nurse anesthetists and certified nurse practitioners may be exempted from overtime if they primarily engage in performing duties for which state certification is required. These employees must meet the other requirements established for executive, administrative and professional employee exemptions (the salary test and use of discretion and independent judgment).[15]

---

13. Lab. Code sec. 515.8
14. Lab. Code sec. 515(f)(1)
15. Lab. Code sec. 515(f)(2)

Physician Assistants

An opinion letter issued by the Department of Labor Standards Enforcement (DLSE) on August 14, 2002, declared that physician assistants, occupational therapists and physical therapists, as a class, typically do not meet eligibility for exemption as "professional employees" because they are not required to possess advanced degrees. The status of particular positions of this kind must be reviewed on a case-by-case basis.

Computer Professional Exemption

 Effective January 1, 2009, Labor Code 515.5 was amended to allow payment to computer professionals as a monthly or annual salary. Before this change, computer professionals had to earn a minimum hourly rate, set by the Division of Labor Statistics and Research (DLSR) annually. The change sets a minimum monthly and annual amount for computer professionals who are paid on a salaried basis and who are exempt from overtime.

The change sets a minimum monthly and annual amount for computer professionals who are paid on a salaried basis and who are exempt from overtime. The hourly rate for 2009 is increased from $36.00 to $37.94. For 2009, the minimum monthly salary exemption is $6,587.50, and the minimum annual salary exemption is $79,050.00. The state Division of Labor Statistics and Research (DLSR) determined this increase based on the California Consumer Price Index.

> Computer professionals who meet the exemption tests are only exempt from overtime. They are not exempt from meal and rest break requirements (see "Meal and Rest Breaks" in Chapter 13, page 320).

Exemption Does Not Apply to Certain Employees

An employee is not exempt as a computer professional if any of the following apply:

- The employee is a trainee or involved in an entry-level position and learning to become proficient in the theoretical and practical application of highly specialized information to computer systems analysis, programming and software engineering;

- The employee works in a computer-related occupation but has not attained the level of skill and expertise necessary to work independently and without close supervision;

- The employee engages in the operation of computers or in the manufacture, repair or maintenance of computer hardware and related equipment;

- The employee is an engineer, drafter, machinist or other professional whose work is highly dependent on or facilitated by the use of computers and computer software programs, and who is skilled in computer-aided design software, including CAD/CAM, but who is not in a computer systems analysis or programming occupation;

- The employee is a writer engaged in writing material, including box labels, product descriptions, documentation, promotional material, setup and installation instructions and other similar written information either for print or for onscreen media, or who writes or provides content material intended to be read by customers, subscribers or visitors to computer-related media such as the World Wide Web or CD-ROMs; or

- The employee creates imagery for effects used in the motion picture, television or theatrical industry.

No Degree or Licensing Requirement

Though employees exempt as computer professionals may possess a bachelor's degree or higher, no particular academic degree is required for this exemption, nor do requirements exist for licensure or certification.

Computer Professional Exemption Tests

An employee is an exempt computer professional if he/she:

- Is primarily engaged in work that is intellectual or creative;

- Is primarily engaged in work that requires the exercise of discretion and independent judgment;

- Is primarily engaged in duties that consist of one or more of the following:

  - Applying systems-analysis techniques and procedures, including consulting with users, to determine hardware, software or system-functional specifications;

  - Designing, developing, documenting, analyzing, creating, testing or modifying computer systems or programs, including prototypes, based on and related to user or system-design specifications; or

  - Documenting, testing, creating or modifying computer programs related to the design of software or hardware for computer operating systems.

- Is highly skilled and proficient in the theoretical and practical application of highly specialized information to computer systems analysis, programming and software engineering; and

- Is paid at least $37.94 per hour (an increase from the 2008 rate).

An employee's pay may be expressed as the annualized full-time equivalent of the applicable minimum hourly rate, provided that all other exemption requirements are met and the employee receives not less than the minimum hourly rate per hour for all hours worked.

Outside Salesperson Exemption

Outside salespersons are exempt from overtime pay if they:

- Are 18 years of age or older; and

- Spend more than 50 percent of their working time away from the employer's place of business selling tangible or intangible items or obtaining orders or contracts for products, services or use of facilities.

Outside salespersons do not have to meet the minimum salary requirement that applies to the executive, administrative and professional exemptions.

Unlike federal law, California law does not allow work performed incidental to and in conjunction with the employee's own outside sales or solicitations, including incidental deliveries and collections, to be considered exempt work. This distinction is particularly important for route salespeople and others who perform many functions other than sales during an average day, such as delivery, repair and maintenance. The California Supreme Court's 1999 decision in the case of *Ramirez v. Yosemite Water*[16] clarified that to be exempt, outside salespeople in California must spend at least 50 percent of their time performing exempt duties, which do not include work such as delivery, repair and maintenance. Work performed incidental to and in conjunction with the employee's outside sales is not considered exempt work in California, and cannot exceed 50 percent of an employee's working time.

See *Exempt Analysis Worksheet - Salesperson Exemption*.

Commissioned Inside Sales Employee Exemption

Employees working under Wage Orders 4 and 7 qualify as exempt from overtime if their earnings exceed one-and-one-half times the minimum wage and more than one-half the employee's compensation represents commissions.[17] This exemption applies to overtime only, not all other wage and hour laws.

If a guaranteed draw against commissions exists, the Labor Commissioner may consider that the earnings do not qualify as commissions but as a salary instead, and this exemption may therefore not apply.

Similarly, the U.S. 9th Circuit Court of Appeals ruled that finance and insurance managers employed by automobile dealerships qualify as exempt from overtime under federal law when commissions on goods or services make up more than half of their pay and their regular rate of pay exceeds one and one-half times the applicable minimum wage. The court found that these managers qualify under the section of the FLSA that exempts commission-based employees of retail or service establishments.

After the car is sold by dealer sales personnel, finance officers verify the sales contract and sell financing agreements, extended warranties, insurance contracts and additional accessories and services. Finance officers receive commissions on these transactions but not from the sale of the vehicle itself. The court applied the exemption although finance officers did not strictly sell retail goods and services. The employees were properly treated as exempt as long as their work was an integral part of the retail operation as a whole.[18]

The California Labor Code defines "commissions" in the retail vehicle sales industry as compensation paid to any person for services rendered in the sale of property or services and based proportionately upon the amount or value thereof.[19] The applicability of this federal court decision to the California vehicle sales industry is not certain so request advice from your employment law counsel.[20]

Artist Exemption

Relatively few individuals qualify for exemption as members of artistic professions in California since most of those who exert sufficient control over the nature of their own work and their work hours are self-employed. Academic degrees are not required, but a specialized course of study of at least four years is generally one element involved in establishing a professional standing in the fine arts. By itself, this is not enough. A composer or vocal or instrumental soloist may be exempted because of the individual's wide-ranging discretionary powers,

---

16.*Ramirez v. Yosemite Water,* 20 Cal.4th 785 (1999)

17.IWC Wage Orders 4 and 7 sec. 3; Fair Labor Standards Act

18.*Gieg v. DRR Inc.,* d/b/a/ Courtesy Ford, 407 F.3d 1038 (9th Cir., 2005)

19.Lab. Code Sec. 204.1

20.*Keyes Motors, Inc. v. Division of Labor Standards Enforcement,* 197 Cal. App. 3d 557 (Ca. App., 2nd Dist.,1987)

including control over his/her working conditions. But a member of the orchestra will not be, no matter how professional a musician he/she may be. A few writers employed in the motion picture or broadcast industries possess sufficient discretionary powers to be considered exempt, but most do not even when they work at home because of time limits, restricting outlines or other constraints on the creative aspects of their work. A newspaper columnist required to furnish only five columns per week, regardless of subject, time of preparation, etc., could be exempted from Wage Order 4, Professional, Technical, Clerical, Mechanical and Similar Occupations. But reporters, editors and advertising copy writers could not. Any individual exempted by virtue of the creative and discretionary nature of the work in an artistic profession also must meet the salary test.

National Service Program Participant Exemption

Participants in national service programs, such as AmeriCorps, are exempted from state employment laws relating to wages, hours and working conditions. Nonprofits and other entities using the AmeriCorps volunteer services must inform participants of any overtime requirements prior to the beginning of service and offer participants the chance to opt out of the program. Participants may not be discriminated against or be denied continued participation in the program for refusing to work overtime for a legitimate reason.[21]

Under federal law, participants in national service programs are considered volunteers and qualify as exempt from federal wage and hour laws.[22]

Deductions From Salary of an Exempt Employee

The "salary test" required to validate overtime exemptions provides that full weekly salary be paid for any week in which any work is performed. As a result, the salary of an exempt employee is subject to very limited deductions.

Impermissible Deductions from Salary

Quality or quantity of work — Do not make deductions from the salary of an exempt employee for variations in the quantity or quality of work performed.

Unavailability of work — Do not make deductions when work is unavailable because of the operational requirements of the business, provided exempt employees are ready, willing and able to work. If July 4th falls on a Tuesday and the business shuts down for that day and the balance of the week, exempt employees who worked on Monday of that week are entitled to a full week's pay.

Disciplinary reasons — Though federal regulations and court decisions permit deductions from exempt employees' salary for limited disciplinary reasons, the Labor Commissioner issued a legal opinion stating that such deductions are incompatible with California law and will not be permitted.[23]

Jury/witness/military duty — California follows the federal law with regard to deductions from the salary of an exempt employee who serves on jury duty, as a witness or is on military leave. Deductions may not be made from an exempt employee's salary for periods of less than a full

---

21. Lab. Code sec. 1171
22. Federal National and Community Service Act of 1993
23. DLSE Opinion Letter 97.04.28

workweek. If the exempt employee performs no work within the week, you may deduct from their salary for the week.[24]

Limited Deductions from Salary

Vacations, personal leave and religious observances — You may make deductions from an exempt employee's salary for absences of a full day or more for personal reasons such as vacation, personal leave and religious holidays. However, treat the religious observances of all exempt employees alike.

Under limited circumstances, you may also deduct accrued vacation from an exempt employee for partial day absences. For more information, see "DLSE Clarifies Position on Partial Day Vacations for Exempt Employees" in Chapter 17, page 418.

A conflict exists between the Labor Commissioner's interpretation of the law and that of an appellate level court. You should consult with your own employment counsel before making such deductions.

Sickness or disability — Where the company maintains a bona fide sick-leave plan (a plan, policy or practice that replaces compensation lost due to sickness or disability), a corresponding deduction may be made from salary. If such a plan exists, you may make a deduction from salary before the exempt employee qualified for the sick /disability pay, and after the employee exhausted benefits under the plan.

Workers' compensation leave — You may make deductions if the exempt employee is compensated for loss of salary in accordance with the state workers' compensation law or a self-insured workers' compensation plan. The employer must have a plan, policy or practice that replaces compensation lost due to nonindustrial sickness or disability.

Initial/final weeks of work — You may prorate an employee's salary in full-day increments for the initial and final weeks of work. However, this does not mean that an employee is on a salary basis within the meaning of the regulations if he/she is employed occasionally for a few days and is paid a proportionate part of the weekly salary when so employed. Even the full weekly salary payment under such circumstances would not meet the requirement, since casual or occasional employment for a few days at a time is inconsistent with employment on a salary basis.

Family/Medical Leave — Leave under the federal Family and Medical Leave Act (FMLA) and California Family Rights Act (CFRA) by an exempt employee will not affect the exempt employee's status. You may make deductions from the exempt employee's salary and/or benefits (such as paid sick leave) for hours taken as intermittent or reduced FMLA/CFRA leave without affecting the employee's exempt status.

Pregnancy leave — State pregnancy-disability-leave regulations allow you to require an employee to use available accrued sick leave for partial day absences. The same regulations specify that an employee may elect, at her option, to use any vacation time or other accrued time off for partial-day absences. However, unlike the federal family leave regulations, the pregnancy-disability-leave regulations do not address whether making such partial day deductions from salary (even when replaced by sick/vacation pay) will affect exempt status. If you are considering partial-day deductions for exempt employees disabled by pregnancy, consult with legal counsel.

---

24. *DLSE Policies and Interpretations Manual* sec. 51.6.21 and 51.6.21.1

Chapter 16 Forms

This chapter contains samples of forms associated with this topic. *The forms in this section are for visual reference only; download the most up-to-date forms and checklists in their entirety from CalBizCentral.*

To download either individual forms or your entire Formspack containing all the forms referenced in this book:

1. Visit **www.calbizcentral.com/support** and select "Labor Law Digest" from the list of product titles.

2. Have this copy of Labor Law Digest handy — you will need to enter the access code featured on the inside covers of this book.

3. Enter the access code, select the documents you want to download to your computer, then follow the on-screen instructions.

For more detailed instructions, see "Forms Available Online" on page xix.

Federal Salary Basis Rules

Section 541.602 Salary basis.

(a) General rule. An employee will be considered to be paid on a "salary basis" within the meaning of these regulations if the employee regularly receives each pay period on a weekly, or less frequent basis, a predetermined amount constituting all or part of the employee's compensation, which amount is not subject to reduction because of variations in the quality or quantity of the work performed. Subject to the exceptions provided in paragraph (b) of this section, an exempt employee must receive the full salary for any week in which the employee performs any work without regard to the number of days or hours worked. Exempt employees need not be paid for any workweek in which they perform no work. An employee is not paid on a salary basis if deductions from the employee's predetermined compensation are made for absences occasioned by the employer or by the operating requirements of the business. If the employee is ready, willing and able to work, deductions may not be made for time when work is not available.

(b) Exceptions. The prohibition against deductions from pay in the salary basis requirement is subject to the following exceptions:

(1) Deductions from pay may be made when an exempt employee is absent from work for one or more full days for personal reasons, other than sickness or disability. Thus, if an employee is absent for two full days to handle personal affairs, the employee's salaried status will not be affected if deductions are made from the salary for two full-day absences. However, if an exempt employee is absent for one and a half days for personal reasons, the employer can deduct only for the one full-day absence.

(2) Deductions from pay may be made for absences of one or more full days occasioned by sickness or disability (including work-related accidents) if the deduction is made in accordance with a bona fide plan, policy or practice of providing compensation for loss of salary occasioned by such sickness or disability. The employer is not required to pay any portion of the employee's salary for full-day absences for which the employee receives compensation under the plan, policy or practice. Deductions for such full-day absences also may be made before the employee has qualified under the plan, policy or practice, and after the employee has exhausted the leave allowance thereunder. Thus, for example, if an employer maintains a short-term disability insurance plan providing salary replacement for 12 weeks starting on the fourth day of absence, the employer may make deductions from pay for the three days of absence before the employee qualifies for benefits under the plan; for the twelve weeks in which the employee receives salary replacement benefits under the plan; and for absences after the employee has exhausted the 12 weeks of salary replacement benefits. Similarly, an employer may make deductions from pay for absences of one or more full days if salary replacement benefits are provided under a State disability insurance law or under a State workers' compensation law.

(3) While an employer cannot make deductions from pay for absences of an exempt employee occasioned by jury duty, attendance as a witness or temporary military leave, the employer can offset any amounts received by an employee as jury fees, witness fees or military pay for a particular week against the salary due for that particular week without loss of the exemption.

(4) Deductions from pay of exempt employees may be made for penalties imposed in good faith for infractions of safety rules of major significance. Safety rules of major significance include those relating to the prevention of serious danger in the workplace or to other employees, such as rules prohibiting smoking in explosive plants, oil refineries and coal mines.

(5) Deductions from pay of exempt employees may be made for unpaid disciplinary suspensions of one or more full days imposed in good faith for infractions of workplace conduct rules. Such suspensions must be imposed pursuant to a written policy applicable to all employees. Thus, for example, an employer may suspend an exempt employee without pay for three days for violating a generally applicable written

policy prohibiting sexual harassment. Similarly, an employer may suspend an exempt employee without pay for twelve days for violating a generally applicable written policy prohibiting workplace violence.

(6) An employer is not required to pay the full salary in the initial or terminal week of employment. Rather, an employer may pay a proportionate part of an employee's full salary for the time actually worked in the first and last week of employment. In such weeks, the payment of an hourly or daily equivalent of the employee's full salary for the time actually worked will meet the requirement. However, employees are not paid on a salary basis within the meaning of these regulations if they are employed occasionally for a few days, and the employer pays them a proportionate part of the weekly salary when so employed.

(7) An employer is not required to pay the full salary for weeks in which an exempt employee takes unpaid leave under the Family and Medical Leave Act. Rather, when an exempt employee takes unpaid leave under the Family and Medical Leave Act, an employer may pay a proportionate part of the full salary for time actually worked. For example, if an employee who normally works 40 hours per week uses four hours of unpaid leave under the Family and Medical Leave Act, the employer could deduct 10 percent of the employee's normal salary that week.

(c) When calculating the amount of a deduction from pay allowed under paragraph (b) of this section, the employer may use the hourly or daily equivalent of the employee's full weekly salary or any other amount proportional to the time actually missed by the employee. A deduction from pay as a penalty for violations of major safety rules under paragraph (b)(4) of this section may be made in any amount.

Section 541.603 Effect of improper deductions from salary.

(a) An employer who makes improper deductions from salary shall lose the exemption if the facts demonstrate that the employer did not intend to pay employees on a salary basis. An actual practice of making improper deductions demonstrates that the employer did not intend to pay employees on a salary basis. The factors to consider when determining whether an employer has an actual practice of making improper deductions include, but are not limited to: the number of improper deductions, particularly as compared to the number of employee infractions warranting discipline; the time period during which the employer made improper deductions; the number and geographic location of employees whose salary was improperly reduced; the number and geographic location of managers responsible for taking the improper deductions; and whether the employer has a clearly communicated policy permitting or prohibiting improper deductions.

(b) If the facts demonstrate that the employer has an actual practice of making improper deductions, the exemption is lost during the time period in which the improper deductions were made for employees in the same job classification working for the same managers responsible for the actual improper deductions. Employees in different job classifications or who work for different managers do not lose their status as exempt employees. Thus, for example, if a manager at a company facility routinely docks the pay of engineers at that facility for partial-day personal absences, then all engineers at that facility whose pay could have been improperly docked by the manager would lose the exemption; engineers at other facilities or working for other managers, however, would remain exempt.

(c) Improper deductions that are either isolated or inadvertent will not result in loss of the exemption for any employees subject to such improper deductions, if the employer reimburses the employees for such improper deductions.

(d) If an employer has a clearly communicated policy that prohibits the improper pay deductions specified in § 541.602(a) and includes a complaint mechanism, reimburses employees for any improper deductions and makes a good faith commitment to comply in the future, such employer will not lose the exemption for any employees unless the employer willfully violates the policy by continuing to make improper deductions after receiving employee complaints. If an employer fails to reimburse employees for any improper deductions or continues to make improper deductions after receiving employee complaints, the exemption is lost during the time period in which the improper deductions were made for employees in the same job classification working for the same managers responsible for the actual improper deductions.

The best evidence of a clearly communicated policy is a written policy that was distributed to employees prior to the improper pay deductions by, for example, providing a copy of the policy to employees at the time of hire, publishing the policy in an employee handbook or publishing the policy on the employer's Intranet.

(e) This section shall not be construed in an unduly technical manner so as to defeat the exemption.

Section 541.604 Minimum guarantee plus extras.

(a) An employer may provide an exempt employee with additional compensation without losing the exemption or violating the salary basis requirement, if the employment arrangement also includes a guarantee of at least the minimum weekly-required amount paid on a salary basis. Thus, for example, an exempt employee guaranteed at least $ 455 each week paid on a salary basis may also receive additional compensation of a one percent commission on sales. An exempt employee also may receive a percentage of the sales or profits of the employer if the employment arrangement also includes a guarantee of at least $ 455 each week paid on a salary basis. Similarly, the exemption is not lost if an exempt employee who is guaranteed at least $ 455 each week paid on a salary basis also receives additional compensation based on hours worked for work beyond the normal workweek. Such additional compensation may be paid on any basis (e.g., flat sum, bonus payment, straight-time hourly amount, time and one-half or any other basis), and may include paid time off.

(b) An exempt employee's earnings may be computed on an hourly, a daily or a shift basis, without losing the exemption or violating the salary basis requirement, if the employment arrangement also includes a guarantee of at least the minimum weekly required amount paid on a salary basis regardless of the number of hours, days or shifts worked, and a reasonable relationship exists between the guaranteed amount and the amount actually earned. The reasonable relationship test will be met if the weekly guarantee is roughly equivalent to the employee's usual earnings at the assigned hourly, daily or shift rate for the employee's normal scheduled workweek. Thus, for example, an exempt employee guaranteed compensation of at least $ 500 for any week in which the employee performs any work, and who normally works four or five shifts each week, may be paid $ 150 per shift without violating the salary basis requirement. The reasonable relationship requirement applies only if the employee's pay is computed on an hourly, daily or shift basis. It does not apply, for example, to an exempt store manager paid a guaranteed salary of $ 650 per week who also receives a commission of one-half percent of all sales in the store or five percent of the store's profits, which in some weeks may total as much as, or even more than, the guaranteed salary.

Section 541.605 Fee basis.

(a) Administrative and professional employees may be paid on a fee basis, rather than on a salary basis. An employee will be considered to be paid on a "fee basis" within the meaning of these regulations if the employee is paid an agreed sum for a single job regardless of the time required for its completion. These payments resemble piecework payments with the important distinction that generally a "fee" is paid for the kind of job that is unique rather than for a series of jobs repeated an indefinite number of times and for which payment on an identical basis is made over and over again. Payments based on the number of hours or days worked and not on the accomplishment of a given single task are not considered payments on a fee basis.

(b) To determine whether the fee payment meets the minimum amount of salary required for exemption under these regulations, the amount paid to the employee will be tested by determining the time worked on the job and whether the fee payment is at a rate that would amount to at least $ 455 per week if the employee worked 40 hours. Thus, an artist paid $ 250 for a picture that took 20 hours to complete meets the minimum salary requirement for exemption since earnings at this rate would yield the artist $ 500 if 40 hours were worked.

Exempt Analysis Worksheet - Administrative Exemption

This worksheet is to be used only as a guideline to determine exempt or non-exempt status. The completion of this worksheet does not imply or guarantee that the analysis of the position as exempt will be recognized as accurate by the Division of Labor Standards Enforcement.

Position

Current Employee

Department

Supervisor and Title

Date of Evaluation

Evaluator

Many types of employees might qualify under the administrative exemption. An exempt administrator's job duties and salary must meet all of the following five tests:

1. Duties and responsibilities involve either:

   (a) The performance of office or non-manual work directly related to management policies or general business operations of the employer or the employer's customers, or

   (b) The performance of functions in the administration of a school system, or educational establishment or institution, or of one of its departments or subdivisions, in work directly related to its academic instruction or training.

   Describe office or non-manual work directly related to management policies or general business operations of the employer or the employer's customers:

   Or, describe functions in the administration of a school system, or educational establishment or institution, or of one of its departments or subdivisions, in work directly related to its academic instruction or training:

   and

2. Customarily and regularly exercises discretion and independent judgment.
   Describe the ways in which the employee customarily and regularly uses discretion and independent judgment.

   and

Exempt Analysis Worksheet - Administrative Exemption

3. Must be one who:

(a) regularly and directly assists a proprietor, or an employee employed in a bona fide executive or administrative capacity;

(b) performs under only general supervision work along specialized or technical lines requiring special training, experience, or knowledge; or

(c) executes under only general supervision special assignments and tasks.

Describe the tasks assigned to the employee that meet one or more of the above tests:

_____

_____

_____

and

4. Is "primarily engaged" in duties that meet the above tests. "Primarily engaged in" means that more than one-half of the employee's work time must be spent engaged in exempt work, or work that is directly and closely related to exempt work and work which is properly viewed as a means for carrying out exempt functions.

List the employee's duties and the percentage of time required for each:

Exempt duties (or directly/closely related)	% of time	Nonexempt duties	% of time
_____	____	_____	____
_____	____	_____	____
_____	____	_____	____
_____	____	_____	____
_____	____	_____	____
_____	____	_____	____

and

5. Earns a monthly salary equivalent to no less than two times the state minimum wage for full-time employment. Based on the state minimum wage of $7.50 per hour, an exempt employee must be paid no less than $2,600 per month ($7.50 x 2080 = 15,600, times two = 31,200, divided by 12 = $2,600.00).

Monthly Salary: $ _____

Exempt Analysis Worksheet - Administrative Exemption
(Page 2 of 2)

Exempt Analysis Worksheet - Computer Professional Exemption

This worksheet is to be used only as a guideline to determine exempt or non-exempt status. The completion of this worksheet does not imply or guarantee that the analysis of the position as exempt will be recognized as accurate by the Division of Labor Standards Enforcement.

Position _____

Current Employee _____

Department _____

Supervisor and Title _____

Date of Evaluation _____

Evaluator _____

A professional employee in the computer field is exempt from overtime pay if the employee meets all the following tests:

1. Primarily engaged in work that is intellectual or creative.

Describe the employee's intellectual or creative work.

_____

_____

2. Primarily engaged in work that requires the exercise of discretion and independent judgement.

Describe the ways in which the employee customarily and regularly uses discretion and independent judgment.

_____

_____

3. Primarily engaged in duties that consist of one or more of the following:

• The application of systems analysis techniques and procedures, including consulting with users, to determine hardware, software, or system functional specifications.

• The design, development, documentation, analysis, creation, testing, or modification of computer systems or programs, including prototypes, based on and related to, user or system design specifications.

• The documentation, testing, creation, or modification of computer programs related to the design of software or hardware for computer operating systems.

Describe the employee's duties.

_____

_____

Exempt Analysis Worksheet - Computer Professional Exemption
(Page 1 of 2)

Exempt Analysis Worksheet - Computer Professional Exemption

v102106

4. Highly skilled and proficient in the theoretical and practical application of highly specialized information to computer systems analysis, programming, and software engineering.

Describe the employee's skills and proficiencies in these areas.

_____

_____

5. Paid at least $37.94 per hour, effective January 1, 2009.

Employee's hourly rate: $ _____ /hour

OR

Paid $6587.50 at least once monthly, and at least $79,050 paid annually if employee is paid on a salaried basis, effective January 1, 2009.

Employee's monthly salary: $ _____

Employee's monthly salary: $ _____ / annual salary: $ _____

Caution: Certain Employees Categorized as Nonexempt By Law

An employee is not exempt as a computer professional if any of the following apply:

• The employee is a trainee or employee in an entry-level position who is learning to become proficient in the theoretical and practical application of highly specialized information to computer systems analysis, programming, and software engineering.

• The employee is in a computer-related occupation but has not attained the level of skill and expertise necessary to work independently and without close supervision.

• The employee is engaged in the operation of computers or in the manufacture, repair, or maintenance of computer hardware and related equipment.

• The employee is an engineer, drafter, machinist, or other professional whose work is highly dependent upon or facilitated by the use of computers and computer software programs and who is skilled in computer-aided design software, including CAD/CAM, but who is not in a computer systems analysis or programming occupation.

• The employee is a writer engaged in writing material, including box labels, product descriptions, documentation, promotional material, setup and installation instructions, and other similar written information, either for print or for onscreen media or who writes or provides content material intended to be read by customers, subscribers, or visitors to computer-related media such as the World Wide Web or CD-ROMs.

• The employee is creating imagery for effects used in the motion picture, television, or theatrical industry.

Exempt Analysis Worksheet - Executive/Managerial Exemption

This worksheet is to be used only as a guideline to determine exempt or non-exempt status. The completion of this worksheet does not imply or guarantee that the analysis of the position as exempt will be recognized as accurate by the Division of Labor Standards Enforcement.

Position _____

Current Employee _____

Department _____

Supervisor and Title _____

Date of Evaluation _____

Evaluator _____

An executive is one who is in charge of a unit with permanent status and function and who ordinarily supervises the activities of others. In order for an employee to be exempt as an executive, **all** six of the following tests must be met:

1. Has duties and responsibilities involving the management of the enterprise in which he/she is employed or of a customarily recognized department or subdivision;

Describe duties and responsibilities involving the management of the enterprise or of a customarily recognized department or subdivision.

_____

and

2. Customarily and regularly directs the work of two or more other employees.

List the employees who are customarily and regularly supervised by this employee, and their titles.

_____

and

3. Has the authority to hire or fire other employees or make suggestions and recommendations, which will be given particular weight, as to the hiring or firing and as to the advancement and promotion or any other change of status of other employees.

Does the employee have such authority? _____

If the employee does not have such authority, how much weight is given to his/her suggestions and recommendations as to hiring, firing, advancement, promotion or other change of status?

_____

and

Exempt Analysis Worksheet - Executive/Managerial Exemption

4. Customarily and regularly exercises discretionary powers in the performance of his/her duties.

   Give examples of decision-making responsibilities and the consequences of such decisions to the business or its customers.

   and

5. Earns a monthly salary equivalent to no less than two times the state minimum wage for full-time employment. Based on the state minimum wage $7.50 per hour, an exempt employee must be paid no less than $2,600 per month ($7.50 x 2080 = 15,600, times two = 31,200, divided by 12 = $2,600.00).

   Monthly Salary: $ _____

   and

6. Is "primarily engaged" in duties that meet tests 1 through 4 above. "Primarily engaged in" means that more than one-half of the employee's work time must be spent engaged in exempt work, or work that is directly and closely related to exempt work and work which is properly viewed as a means for carrying out exempt functions.

List the employee's duties and the number of hours required for each:

Exempt Duties (or closely related)	Number of hours each week	Non-Exempt Duties	Number of hours each week
Interviewing employees	—	Performing same kind of work as subordinates	—
Selecting employees	—	Performing any production work which is not part of a supervisory function	—
Training employees	—	Making sales	—
Setting and adjusting pay rates and work hours or recommending same	—	Replenishing stock	—
Directing work	—	Returning stock to shelves (except for supervisory training or demonstration purposes)	—
Keeping production records of subordinates for use in supervision	—	Performing routine clerical duties, such as bookkeeping, cashiering, billing and/or filing, operating business machines	—
Evaluating employees' efficiency and productivity	—	Checking and inspecting goods as a production operation, rather than as a supervisor function	—
Handling employees' complaints	—	Performing maintenance work	—
Disciplining employees	—	Other:	—
Planning work	—		—

Exempt Analysis Worksheet - Executive/Managerial Exemption

Exempt Duties (or closely related)	Number of hours each week	Non-Exempt Duties	Number of hours each week
Determining work	—		—
Distributing work	—		—
Deciding on types of merchandise, materials, supplies, machinery or tools	—		—
Controlling flow and distribution of merchandise, materials and supplies	—		—
Providing for safety of employees and property	—		—
Other:	—		—

Hours Summary:

1. Total number of weekly hours worked _____

2. Total number of weekly exempt hours worked _____

3. Exempt hours as a percentage of the total hours (Divide total exempt hours by total hours worked) _____%

The analyzed position will be **non-exempt** when **any one of the following** occurs:

1. The percentage of exempt duties is less than 50 percent;

2. The monthly compensation is less than two times the state minimum wage for full time employment; **or**

3. The employee does not meet tests 1-6 on this Worksheet.

Exempt Analysis Worksheet - Professional Exemption

This worksheet is to be used only as a guideline to determine exempt or non-exempt status. The completion of this worksheet does not imply or guarantee that the analysis of the position as exempt will be recognized as accurate by the Division of Labor Standards Enforcement.

Position _____

Current Employee _____

Department _____

Supervisor and Title _____

Date of Evaluation _____

Evaluator _____

In order to be exempt as a professional, the employee must meet tests 1 through 3 below:

1. The employee must either be:

   a. Licensed or certified by the state of California and primarily engaged in the practice of one of the following recognized professions:

   ☐ Law
   (does **not** include paralegals)

   ☐ Medical
   (does **not** include nurses; may include physician assistants)

   ☐ Accounting
   (Certified Public Accountants, not uncertified accountants)

   ☐ Teaching

   ☐ Optometry

   ☐ Architecture

   ☐ Engineering
   (includes licensed civil, mechanical, and electrical engineers, but not junior engineers or drafters)

   ☐ Dentistry
   (does **not** include dental hygienists except in very limited circumstances)

   or

   b. Primarily engaged in an occupation commonly recognized as a learned or artistic profession. "Learned or artistic profession" means an employee who is primarily engaged in the performance of:

   • Work requiring knowledge of an advanced type in a field or science or learning customarily acquired by a prolonged course of specialized intellectual instruction and study, as distinguished from a general academic education and from training in the performance of routine mental, manual, or physical processes or work that is an essential part of or necessarily incident to any of the above work; or

   • Work that is original and creative in character in a recognized field of artistic endeavor (as opposed to work which can be produced by a person endowed with general manual or intellectual ability and training), and the result of which depends primarily on the invention, imagination, or talent of the employee or work that is an essential part of or necessarily incident to any of the above work; and

   • Work that is predominantly intellectual and varied in character (as opposed to routine mental, manual, mechanical, or physical work) and is of such character that the output produced or the result accomplished cannot be standardized in relation to a given period of time.

Exempt Analysis Worksheet - Professional Exemption

Describe occupation that meets the preceding criteria:

_____

_____

and

2. Customarily and regularly exercises discretion and independent judgment in the performance of his/her duties.

Give examples of decision-making responsibilities and the consequences of such decisions to the business or its customers:

_____

_____

and

3. Earns a monthly salary equivalent to no less than two times the state minimum wage for full-time employment. Based on the state minimum wage of $7.50 per hour, an exempt employee must be paid no less than $2,600 per month ($7.50 x 2080 = 15,600, times two = 31,200, divided by 12 = $2,600.00). For doctors paid on an hourly rate, the minimum rate is $64.18 effective January 1, 2007.

Monthly Salary: $ _____

Exempt Analysis Worksheet - Salesperson Exemption

This worksheet is to be used only as a guideline to determine exempt or non-exempt status. The completion of this worksheet does not imply or guarantee that the analysis of the position as exempt will be recognized as accurate by the Division of Labor Standards Enforcement.

Position _____

Current Employee _____

Department _____

Supervisor and Title _____

Date of Evaluation _____

Evaluator _____

OUTSIDE SALES:

An outside salesperson is exempt from overtime requirements if he/she meets both tests below:

1. Eighteen years of age or older.

    Is employee 18 years of age or older? ☐ Yes ☐ No

2. Spends more than 50% of his/her working time away from the employer's place of business, selling tangible or intangible items, or obtaining orders or contracts for products, services or use of facilities. Work performed incidental to and in conjunction with the employee's own outside sales or solicitations, including incidental deliveries and collections, is not considered exempt work (i.e. delivery, repair and maintenance).

    List the employee's duties and the percentage of time required for each:

    Duties   Percentage of time

    _____   _____

    _____   _____

    _____   _____

    _____   _____

Note: Outside salespersons are not required to meet the minimum salary requirement that applies to the executive, administrative and executive exemptions.

INSIDE SALES:

An inside salesperson is one who sells merchandise in a store or sales lot (for example, car or RV sales lot) or one who sells a product or service via a company telephone. Certain inside sales employees working under Wage Orders 4 and 7 are exempt from overtime. This exemption applies to overtime only, not all other wage and hour laws.

Exempt Analysis Worksheet - Salesperson Exemption

An inside salesperson may be exempt from overtime if both of the following tests are met:

1. The employee's earnings exceed one-and-one-half times the minimum wage.

    Employee's earnings: $ _____

2. More than half the employee's compensation represents commissions.

    Percentage of compensation representing commissions: _____ %

Note: If there is a guaranteed draw against commissions, the labor commissioner may consider that the earnings are not in fact commissions but rather a salary, and this exemption may therefore not apply.

Exempt Analysis Worksheet - Salesperson Exemption
(Page 1 of 2)

Exempt Analysis Worksheet - Salesperson Exemption
(Page 2 of 2)

Vacations, Holidays and Paid Time Off

Vacations, holidays and paid time off (PTO) makeup the most common types of paid benefits granted to employees. The law does not require you to offer vacation, holidays or PTO, but if you do offer these benefits, California created unique rules regulating these benefits. This chapter explains the appropriate administration of these benefits and explains regulations and prohibitions in areas that can get you into trouble or cost you money

 Download forms referenced in this chapter at **www.calbizcentral.com/support**. Be sure to have your access code from the inside covers of this book ready to enter into the forms download area. Your access code for the forms in the online Formspack is on the inside covers of this book. See "Forms Available Online" on page xix for more information.

Vacations

If you choose to offer paid vacations to employees, you must follow the Labor Commissioner's rules concerning vacation benefits.

Vacation Is a Contract between Employer and Employee

You have the right to set the amount of vacation employees will earn each year, or if they will earn any at all.[1] You also have the right to determine when employees take vacations, and for how long. It is critical that your vacation policies clearly express how much vacation you offer, the rate of accrual and whether accrual begins immediately or after some period of time. You may create a policy under which employees do not begin earning vacation immediately upon hire.[2]

Vacation Rights Vest on a Daily Basis

Vacations constitute a form of wages.[3] The right to vacation vests as the employee renders services so employees earn a portion of the annual vacation each day.[4] If employees receive two weeks of vacation per year (80 hours), vacation accrues at a rate of approximately 0.30 hours daily. If employees receive one week of vacation per year (40 hours), vacation accrues at a rate of approximately 0.15 hours daily.

---

1. DLSE *Enforcement Policies and Interpretations Manual* sec. 15.1.2
2. DLSE *Enforcement Policies and Interpretations Manual* sec. 15.1.3
3. *People v. Bishopp*, 56 Cal. App. 3d Supp. 8, 11 (1976); *In re Wil-Low Cafeterias*, 111 F.2d 429, 432 (2nd Cir. 1940); *Suastez v. Plastic Dress-Up Co.*, 31 Cal. 3d 777, 781 (1982)
4. *Suastez v. Plastic Dress-Up Co.*, 31 Cal. 3d 777, 782-784 (1982)

No Use-it-or-Lose-it Policies Allowed

Once an employee earns vacation, treat it like money in the bank for that employee never to be taken away. California courts and the Labor Code prohibit a "use-it-or-lose-it" policy, in which employees lose earned vacation not taken by a specific time.[5] You may not require employees to forfeit accrued vacation for any reason. The Labor Commissioner approved reasonable caps on vacation and cash-out policies as alternatives to "use-it-or-lose-it" policies. These alternatives will be discussed below.

An exception to this rule exists for employees under a collective bargaining agreement. If a collective bargaining agreement forms the basis for earned vacation, the Labor Commissioner will not prohibit "use-it-or-lose-it" provisions.[6] If you eventually pay the vacation time, the Labor Commissioner may impose waiting time penalties on late payment.[7]

Reasonable Cap on Accrual Allowed

Under a reasonable cap plan, once a certain level of accrued vacation is earned but not taken, vacation no longer accrues until some of the previously accrued vacation is taken.[8] Once some vacation is taken, vacation again begins to accrue at the usual rate. You are not required to retroactively grant the employee the amount he/she would have earned during the time the vacation was at the cap. The cap should be reasonable, based on factors such as the amount of vacation offered, the opportunity for employees to take vacation during the year and the type of business or industry involved. Caps often used by employers are one-and-one-half or two times the annual accrual rate (for example, 60 or 80 hours for an employer granting 40 hours of vacation per year). An employee must have a reasonable amount of time after the accrual of vacation to take the vacation time before a cap is effective.

The following is an example of a plan with a low cap. Such a plan may not be valid unless the employee is free to use vacation as earned.

Examples:

- XYZ Company offers 40 hours of vacation per year and created a 60-hour cap on vacation accrual. Eddie Employee started working for XYZ on January 1, 2009, and began accruing vacation immediately. Eddie did not take any vacation in 2009, and finally took a week off from October 1 through October 7 in 2010. Eddie accrued 40 hours of vacation in 2009. Eddie continued accruing vacation in 2010 until June 30, when he hit the 60-hour cap. Eddie did not accrue any vacation in July, August or September, and did not begin accruing vacation again until October 1, 2010, when he began his first vacation. XYZ was not required to retroactively give Eddie the vacation he otherwise would have earned in July, August and September. Eddie simply lost the opportunity to earn vacation during those months because he already reached the cap. However, at no time did XYZ violate the rule against "use-it-or-lose-it" policies.

- ABC Company offers 40 hours of vacation per year and created an 80-hour cap on vacation accrual. Wilma Worker started working for ABC on January 1, 2009, and began accruing vacation immediately. Wilma was ineligible to take any vacation in 2009, as she had not completed a year of service. She finally took a week off from October 1 through October 7, 2010. Wilma accrued 40 hours of vacation in 2009 and continued accruing vacation in 2010, never reaching the 80-hour cap.

5.*Suastez v. Plastic Dress-Up Co.*, 31 Cal. 3d 777, 782-784 (1982); Lab. Code sec. 227.3; *Boothby v. Atlas Mechanical*, 6 Cal. App. 4th 1595, 1601 (1992)

6.Lab. Code sec. 227.3; *Livadas v. Bradshaw*, 512 U.S. 107, 114 S.Ct. 2068 (1994)

7.DLSE *Enforcement Policies and Interpretations Manual* sec. 15.1.1

8.DLSE *Enforcement Policies and Interpretations Manual* sec. 15.1.4

Cash-Out Policies

You may choose to offer your employees the option to cash out their vacation benefits. You can offer this option on an "as needed" basis or allow it only once a month or once a year. You may require employees to accept pay each year for vacations that they accrued but did not take.[9]

Vacation Taken Before Earned

Because of schedules and employee wishes, you may allow employees to take vacation before they actually accrue it.

Because vacation is a form of wages, this practice is, in effect, a loan against future wages. The law does not permit balloon payments at the time of termination.

Of course, nothing precludes you from permitting employees to take vacation only when they have already earned or accrued it.

Taking Vacation Day Without Advance Notice

If an employee fails to report to work and then declares the missed day as a vacation day and if company policy requires employees to give notice before taking vacation days, you do not need to pay the employee for the claimed vacation day. You are entitled to discipline the employee for failure to report to work in accordance with your policies.

Payment of Accrued Vacation at Termination

Since accrued vacation is considered wages, you must pay out all accrued but unused vacation at the termination of the employment relationship.[10] This is true even for an employee who had accrued vacation that he/she was not yet eligible to take. Though you may base your vacation-earning policy on the week, pay period or other time period, you must base computation of vested vacation benefits for a terminated employee on the employee's daily accrual or vesting, including the final day of work.

You must pay out accrued but unused vacation at the employee's final rate of pay, regardless of the rate of pay at which it was earned.[11] An employee who earned 10 hours of vacation while making $8 per hour and who is then terminated or quits while making $10 per hour, will receive $100 in vacation wages with his/her final paycheck. Similarly, an employee who receives a cut in pay will receive his/her vacation pay at the lower rate at termination. Be aware that the Labor Commissioner will likely not tolerate the artificial lowering of an employee's rate of pay just before termination to avoid paying a fair amount of earned vacation.

---

9. DLSE Opinion Letter 1994.03.08
10. Lab. Code sec. 227.3; *Suastez v. Plastic Dress-Up Co.*, 31 Cal. 3d 777, 782-784 (1982)
11. Lab. Code sec. 227.3

Four-Year Limit on Payment

According to the Division of Labor Standards Enforcement's *Enforcement Policies and Interpretations Manual*, the statute of limitations on vacation pay due at termination would be four years of accruals in the case of a written employment contract, or two years of accruals in the case of an oral employment contract. A state appeals court rejected the DLSE interpretation and applied the literal wording of Labor Code section 227.3 as requiring the payment of all vested vacation to a terminating employee. If an at-will employee terminates after three years of employment never having use any of his annually accruing two weeks of vacation, he will be entitled at termination to six weeks of vacation pay at his then-current rate.[12]

ERISA Pre-emption and Vacation Plans

If your vacation plan is covered by the Employee Retirement Income Security Act (ERISA), the federal law concerning employee pension and welfare plans, the Labor Commissioner will not agree to consider employee claims relating to those plans.[13] Generally, ERISA covers a plan if the vacation pay does not come out of the employer's general assets. The Labor Commissioner will, however, take an employee's claim to investigate whether the vacation plan is in fact covered by ERISA.[14]

Advance Notice of Vacation During Plant Shutdown

In 2005, the California Labor Commissioner revoked an Opinion Letter No. 2002-08-30. The letter previously required employers to provide at least nine month's notice to exempt employees if they would be required to use vacation or PTO time during a plant shutdown. The Labor Commissioner's revised position is that reasonable notice should be given as far in advance as possible but generally no less than one fiscal quarter or ninety days, whichever is greater.

No such requirement applies to nonexempt employees unless required by a collective bargaining agreement.

Holidays

You are not required to offer employees time off for holidays, nor are you required to pay for time for holidays granted. Exempt employees who perform any work during the workweek in which a holiday occurs must be paid their full weekly salary, whether they work on the holiday. Note that accommodation of religious holidays is required in certain circumstances, discussed further under "Religion" in Chapter 27, page 752. It is wise to set forth at the beginning of each year which, if any, holidays you will grant and whether you will pay for the time.

The most commonly granted holidays in California:

New Year's Day
Presidents' Day
Memorial Day
Fourth of July

---

12. *Church v. Jamison*, 2006 Cal.App. Lexis 1652 (Cal. App. 5th Dist., 2006)

13. *California Hospital Assn. v. Henning*, (9th Cir. 1985) 770 F.2d 856, modified 783 F.2d 946, cert. den. 477 U.S. 904

14. DLSE *Enforcement Policies and Interpretations Manual* sec. 15.1.7; *Millan v. Restaurant Enterprises Group, Inc.*, 14 Cal. App. 4th 477 (1993), rev. den. 5/19/93

Labor Day
Thanksgiving
Friday after Thanksgiving
Christmas

You should set forth in your holiday policy an explanation of what will happen if an employee is required to work on a day you designate as a paid holiday. Since the courts interpret the policy of giving a paid day off as a contract to do so, you must make up the lost benefit to the employee in some manner. The normal procedure is to:

- Grant another day off with pay; or

- Pay holiday wages, plus all hours worked on the day designated as a holiday.

Establish a policy for the situation where a holiday falls on a day that is the employee's usual day off. If it is your policy to give that holiday as a paid day and you pay all other employees for that holiday, then also pay the employee in question for the holiday unless your policy clearly specifies otherwise.

When an employee quits or is terminated, no entitlement exists to pay for future holidays.

Personal Days and/or Floating Holidays

The way your policy defines personal days or floating holidays is critical to whether you must pay out unused days at the end of the employment relationship. Treat time off that is tied to a specific event, such as a birthday or employee anniversary date, as a holiday. Treat time off that is not tied to a specific event (time off that an employee may take at any time for any reason — even if previous notification to the employer is required) as vacation time.[15] A personal day or holiday taken only upon the occurrence of a specific event need not be paid out at termination.

You may place a reasonable cap on the accrual of personal days or floating holidays, just like vacation accrual. You must give the employee a reasonable opportunity to take personal days or floating holidays so that he/she may stay below the cap.

Paid Time Off

Some employers choose to lump together various combinations of vacation, sick leave, holidays and personal days and/or floating holidays into a benefit called "paid time off" (PTO). This allows employees a certain number of days off per year to use for illness, vacation, holidays and personal needs.

Though PTO is an acceptable benefit, be aware that the Labor Commissioner considers the entire sum of PTO as vacation since it is not tied to a specific event and may be taken at whatever time the employee chooses.[16] Therefore, you must pay out the entire amount of accrued but unused PTO at the termination of the employment relationship.

As discussed in Chapter 21, "Voluntary Sick Leave," employees may use one-half of their annual sick leave accrual for care of a child, parent, spouse, registered domestic partner or registered domestic partner's child (known as "kin care"). Since PTO is generally available when an employee is sick, the new law apparently entitles employees to use one-half of their annual PTO

---

15. DLSE *Enforcement Policies and Interpretations Manual* sec. 15.1.12
16. DLSE *Enforcement Policies and Interpretations Manual* sec. 15.1.12

accrual for kin care. Though this conflicts with the Labor Commissioner's position that PTO is considered vacation (unless tied to a specific event), it is prudent to apply the new law to PTO until the Labor Commissioner clarifies what constitutes "sick leave" for purposes of kin care entitlement.

Partial Day Deductions for Exempt Employees

Exempt employees may wish to take a one-half day of vacation or may leave work early due to illness. An exempt employee's salary may be replaced from vacation or sick leave banks in some circumstances.

DLSE Clarifies Position on Partial Day Vacations for Exempt Employees

An amendment to the DLSE's *Enforcement Policies and Interpretations Manual* authorizes employers to charge an exempt employee's accrued vacation/PTO bank for partial day absences of four hours or more, but only if the employee has such accrued time available.[17]

This reflects the DLSE's adoption of a ruling from a California Court of Appeal case decided in July of 2005. The court decided that an employer's policy of making deductions from exempt employees' vacation leave banks for partial-day absences did not constitute either a reduction in salary based on the quantity of work or a forfeiture of vested benefits. Instead, it is a valid policy related to the scheduling of time off, requiring exempt employees to use it when they want to be absent from work for four or more hours in a single workday.[18]

Different rules apply to partial day absences due to illness. Deductions may be made from an exempt employee's available sick leave bank without requiring that the absence be for four hours or more.

---

17. DLSE *Enforcement Policies and Interpretations Manual* sections 51.6.and 15.6.15
18. *Conley v. Pacific Gas & Electric Co.*, 131 Cal. App. 4th 260 (Ca. App. 1st Dist., 2005)

Chapter 17 Forms

This chapter contains samples of forms associated with this topic. *The forms in this section are for visual reference only; download the most up-to-date forms and checklists in their entirety from CalBizCentral.*

To download either individual forms or your entire Formspack containing all the forms referenced in this book:

1. Visit **www.calbizcentral.com/support** and select "Labor Law Digest" from the list of product titles.

2. Have this copy of Labor Law Digest handy — you will need to enter the access code featured on the inside covers of this book.

3. Enter the access code, select the documents you want to download to your computer, then follow the on-screen instructions.

For more detailed instructions, see "Forms Available Online" on page xix.

Vacation Policy

Remove the option(s) that does/do not apply to your Company.

Option: Vacation Accrual from First Day

Employees are entitled to accrue (choose the option that applies to your accrual system and remove the other):

_____ weeks (_____ days) vacation for each year of active service, to a maximum of _____ weeks (_____ days).

_____ hours vacation for each month worked, to a maximum of _____ hours.

Active service commences with an employee's first day of work and continues thereafter unless broken by an absence without pay, a leave of absence, or termination of employment. Temporary and part-time employees do not accrue paid vacation.

Vacation can accrue up to a maximum of six paid weeks. Once this cap is reached, the employee will have nine months to take accrued vacation. If no vacation is taken during that nine month time period, no further vacation will accrue until some vacation is used.

Employees become eligible to take accrued vacation after six months of active service as work schedules permit. Vacation schedules must be coordinated and cleared with your supervisor. Company schedules determine permissible vacation periods, which employees may need to defer or otherwise adjust _____ (the Company) accordingly.

Exempt employees must take vacation in four-hour increments. Employees absent for four hours or more will have the corresponding amount of time deducted from their accrued vacation.

An employee whose employment terminates will be paid for accrued unused vacation days on a pro rata basis.

Option: Vacation Accrual after Six Months

Regular full-time employees accrue paid vacations in accordance with the following policy:

0-6 months	no accrual
6 months-1 year	5 days
2-4 years	10 days per year
5-14 years	15 days per year
15 years and thereafter	20 days per year

Temporary and part-time employees do not accrue paid vacation time. Regular full-time employees do not accrue vacation time during the first six months of employment. No vacation time may be taken until after completion of the first year of employment.

After completion of the initial six months of continuous employment, full-time employees begin to accrue vacation time at the rate of .0385 hours per hour worked. An employee who is scheduled to and does work 40 hours per week will normally accrue five working days or 40 hours of vacation in the second six months of continuous employment.

In the second, third, and fourth years of continuous employment, full-time employees will accrue vacation time at the rate of .0385 hours per hour worked. An employee who is scheduled to and does work 40 hours per week will normally accrue 10 working days or _____ hours vacation time in the second, third, and fourth years of employment.

Beginning with the fifth year of continuous employment, full-time employees begin to accrue vacation time at the rate of .0575 hours per hour worked. An employee who is scheduled to and does work an average of 40 hours per week will normally accrue 15 working days or 120 hours of vacation beginning in the fifth year of employment.

calbizcentral™   © CalChamber   Page 1 of 2

Vacation Policy

Holiday Policy

For the _____ calendar year, _____ (the Company) observes the following paid holidays:

• January 1 - New Year's Day
• Martin Luther King Jr.'s Birthday
• Presidents' Day
• Memorial Day
• July 4th - Independence Day
• Labor Day
• Thanksgiving Day and the Friday after
• Christmas Eve
• Christmas Day
•
•
•
•

When a holiday falls on a Saturday or Sunday, it is usually observed on the preceding Friday or the following Monday. However, the Company may grant another day off in lieu of closing. Holiday observance will be announced in advance.

Each non-exempt employee's eligibility for holiday pay begins after completion of his or her trial period. To be eligible for holiday pay, you must be regularly scheduled to work on the day on which the holiday is observed and must work your regularly scheduled working days immediately preceding and immediately following the holiday, unless an absence on either day is approved in advance by your supervisor. If you are required to work on a paid scheduled holiday you will receive _____ (straight time pay, double time pay).

calbizcentral™   © CalChamber   Page 1 of 1

Holiday Policy

CalBizCentral

Index

Cameras for electronic monitoring of employees, 166–167

Cameron, Agnew v., 272

Camp counselors, subminimum wages for, 137, 267, 297

Campbell v. Board of Trustees, 176

Campbell, State Farm Mutual Automobile Ins. Co. v., 782

Campos v. Employment Development Department, 288

Canning industry
    seasonal employees in, wages for, 302
    wage order for, 238

Capital Public Radio, Inc., Starzynski v., 901

Cardiopulmonary resuscitation (CPR), employees trained in, 680

Carnival ride operators, minimum wages for, 268

Carpal tunnel syndrome, 855

Carpenters District Council v. Dillard Department Stores, 923

Carriage Carpet Co., Dunlap v., 147

Carroll v. Federal Express Corporation, 207

Cash bonds from employees, 281

Cash wage payments
    availability of, 291
    records of, 293

Cassista v. Community Foods Inc., 770, 853

Casual labor, excluded from unemployment insurance, 427

Cedarapids, Meade v., 909

Cell phone use, employee handbook on, 121

Cerros v. Steel Technologies, Inc., 757

Certificate of Group Health Plan Coverage, 495

Certification petition, 939, 941

Certification to Consumer Credit Reporting Agency, 162

Certified nurse assistants (CNAs)
    temporary, 91–92
    verification for, 91–92

CH2M Hill, Inc., Richards v., 776, 818

Chacon v. Ochs, 752

Chan v. Drexel Burnham Lambert, Inc., 232

Chapman University, Schmoll v., 776

Checkoff authorization, 955

Cherosky et.al. v. Henderson, 859

Chevron U.S.A. v. Echazabal, 862, 863

Chevron U.S.A., Inc., Bhatia v., 753

Chicago Transit Authority, Kerr v., 485

Child labor laws, 129–137

Child Labor Laws Pamphlet 2000, information on, 139

Child support
    penalty for failure to comply, 284
    wage garnishment for, 283–284

Children of employees
    and school activities leave, 609
    definition of, 554

    family care to care for, 533
    kin care to care for, 554
    medical certificate for, 539

Childress v. Darby Lumber, Inc., 924

Christensen, et al. v. Harris County, et al., 353

Chrysler Credit Corporation, Adcock v., 773

CIBC World Markets Corp., McManus v., 225

Circuit City Stores, Inc. v. Adams, 228

Circuit City Stores, Inc. v. Ahmed, 229

Circuit City Stores, Inc. v. Mantor, 229

Circuit City Stores, Inc. v. Najd, 229

Circuit City Stores, Inc., Ingle v., 229

CIT Technology Financing Services, Inc., Alexander v., 757

Citizenship
    as condition of employment, 68
    discrimination based on, laws prohibiting, 67, 764

City of Glendale, Loder v., 160, 207, 210

City Of Moorpark v. Superior Court, 724

City of Palm Bay v. Bauman, 209

City of San Mateo, Brooks v., 809

City of Tucson, Brown v., 876

City/county taxes, of telecommuters, 82

Civil liability
    for violations of Cal/OSHA standards, 635

Civil Rights Act
    of 1866
        on discrimination by race, 752
    of 1964, Title VII of
        on discrimination, 760
            by national origin, 67, 757
            by race, 752
            by sexual orientation, 150
            claims under, 772
            remedies under, 772
        on sexual harassment, 800
            in hostile work environment, 808
    of 1991
        on discrimination, 761
            compensatory and punitive damages under, 780–781
            front pay under, 781

Civil Rights Act of 1866
    on discrimination, 760

Clackamas Gastroenterology Associates, P.C. v. Wells, 3

Claims
    disability harassment, 875
    privacy, 146
    sexual harassment, 817–818
    time limits for filing, 818

Clark, Hardeman v., 35

Cleary v. American Airlines, Inc., 899

Clerical occupations
    minors employed in, 137
    wage order for, 238–239

Expedited representation elections, **947**
    picketing and, **965**
Expenses, reimbursements for
    after final payday, **290**
    timing of, **287**, **290**
Experience modification, **619**
Extended disability leave, **611**
Exxon Company U.S.A., Bins v., **499**

F

F. Korbel & Bros., Inc., Paris v., **476**
Fair Credit Reporting Act (FCRA)
    failure to comply with, **149**
    harassment investigations under, **171**, **757**, **820**
    on credit reports, **161**, **164**
    rights under, **162**, **163**, **164**
Fair Employment and Housing Act (FEHA) (1980)
    disability defined by, **852**
    obtaining pregnancy disability leave regulations from, **585**
    on "major life activities", **855**
    on applications and job tests, **875**
    on arbitration agreements covering wrongful termination or discrimination, **225–226**
    on benefits for employees with disabilities, **874**
    on correctable impairments, **854**
    on direct threat to health or safety to others, **862**
    on direct threat to health or safety to self, **862**
    on disability discrimination, **850**
        posters on, **877**, **880**
        remedies under, **877**
    on disability-related inquiries and medical examinations, **867**, **869**, **870**
    on discrimination, **758–759**
        age, **743**
        awards under, **780**
        by race, **752**
        claims under, **773**
        marital status, **749**
        perceptions and associations in, **743**
        protection from retaliation in, **768**
        remedies under, **779**
        weight, **770**
    on drug and alcohol abuse, **212–213**, **872**
    on harassment
        of independent contractors, **103**, **776**
    on medical records, **149**
    on non-work related disability, **611**
    on physical examinations, **159**
    on pre-employment physical examination, **207**
    on private membership clubs, **877**
    on reasonable accommodations, **857**, **859**, **874**
    on repetitive strain injury, **855**

    on sexual harassment, **801–804**
        of independent contractors, **802**
        posters on, **803**
        professional relationships, **803**
        romantic relationships, **802**
    on undue hardship, **861**
Fair Employment and Housing Commission (FEHC), sexual harassment defined by, **801**
Fair Labor Standards Act (FLSA) (1938)
    enforcement of, **259**
    enterprise coverage under, **257**
    Equal Pay Act in, **763**
    individual coverage under, **257**, **257–258**
    on child labor, **129**, **130**, **132**
    on compensatory time off, **352**, **353**
    on employees of organized camps, **137**
    on hours of work, **315**
    on record keeping, **258–259**
    on subminimum wage, **266**
    wage and hour provisions of, **258**
"Faltering company" exception to 60-day notice requirement, **923**
Family and Medical Leave Act (FMLA) (1993)
    and HIPAA privacy rules, **186**
    counting part-time employees toward threshold for, **89**
    on exempt employees, **403**
    on family leave, **478**, **527**, **528**, **529**, **530**, **531**, **538**, **541**, **542**, **544**, **552**
    on pregnancy disability leave, **529**, **574–576**
    on right of employer to change sick leave policies, **128**
Family care leave, **533**
    and medical certificate, **539**
    intermittent, **536–537**
Family Medical Leave Policy, information on, **532**
Family/medical leave, **478**, **528–552**
    abuse of, **550**
    calculation of, **120**, **537–539**
    combining with pregnancy disability leave, **574–576**, **581**, **583**
    common ailments and, **541**
    company policy on, **552**
    deductions from exempt employee's salary for, **403**
    duration of, **535–553**
    eligibility for, **532**
    employee handbook on, **120**, **542**, **553**
    employee request for, **543**
    health insurance during, **530**, **531**
        recovery of cost of, **547**
    holidays during, **538**
    intermittent, **536–537**
        temporary transfer during, **537**
    medical certification of, **539–540**
    notice requirements for, **542–544**
    pay and benefits during, **545–548**

G

H

Sweatshop labor
    definition of, **254**
Swing shift, **347**
Swinton v. Potomac Corp., **773**

T

Tampa Electric Co., Prive v., **320**
Tardiness, wage deduction for, **279**
Targeted Inspection and Consultation Program (TICP), **634**
Tattoos, **770**
Tax(es)
    city/county, of telecommuters, **82**
    evading payment of, penalties for, **431**
    federal, of independent contractors, **97–99**
    for domestic servants, **305**
    on unemployment insurance benefits, **435**
    replacement income, **692**
Taylor v. O'Grady, **209**
TBG Insurance Services Corporation v. Superior Court of Los Angeles County, **170**
Technical occupations, wage order for, **238–239**
Telecommuters
    at meetings, **79**
    city/county taxes and licenses of, **82**
    communicating with customers/clients, **79**
    company policies for, **80**
    computers for, **81**
    equipment maintenance for, **81**
    office equipment and supplies for, **80–82**
        maintenance of, **81**
    posters and notices for, **82**
    relocation of, **85**
    reporting to the main office, **78**
    safe and healthy workplace for, **84–85**
    selection of, **78**
    supervision and evaluation of, **79**
    support staff of, **79**
    termination of, **85**
    turning in work/picking up projects, **79**
    wage of, **82–84**
    workers' compensation for, **84**
    working hours of, **82–83**
Telecommuters, *See also* Work from home
Telephone
    for telecommuters, **81–82**
    monitoring use of, **168–170**
Television industry, security for wage obligations in, **303**
Temperature levels, **294**
Temporary employees
    benefits for, **90, 92**
    disability discrimination of, **874**
    discussion of, **88–89**
    employee handbook on, **124**
    final pay for, **291**
    in unions, **93**

wage order for, **243–244**
Temporary resident alien status, **69**
Temporary restraining order, obtaining, **682**
Termination
    abuse of family leave, **550**
    activities protected from, **894–895**
    after positive drug test, **206**
    based on salaries, as age discrimination, **746**
    because of "whistleblowing", **892**
    constructive discharge, **813–814, 907**
    employee handbook on, **117–118, 123**
    final paycheck after, **897**
    for dishonesty, **166**
    for drug abuse, **206, 214**
    for good cause, **821**
    for refusal to sign arbitration agreement, **226**
    for sexual harassment, **906**
    for violating drug treatment agreement, **211**
    good faith standard, **906**
    notice of, **8, 430, 897, 897–898**
    of at-will employees, **889**
    of janitors and building maintenance personnel, **896–897**
    of strikers, **937**
    of telecommuters, **85**
    payment of accrued vacation at, **415**
    preparing for, **904–906**
    restrictions and regulations on, **890–897**
    retaliation for filing charges and, **956**
    severance pay after, **290**
    statement of reasons for, **898**
    warnings before, **902**
    wrongful
        and award of damages to undocumented aliens, **68**
        arbitration agreements covering, **225–226**
        avoiding suits of, **904–909**
        based on improper wage payment, **290**
        drug testing and, **214**
        in violation of public policy, **907–908**
        liability for, **909**
        limiting time to file lawsuits of, **906–907**
Termination of industrial and commercial operations, **917**
Testing
    applicants and employees, **159–161**
    disability discrimination laws on, **875**
    lie detector, **160**
    psychological, **161**
    reasonable accommodation during, **875**
    written honesty, **161**
Textile Workers v. Lincoln Mills, **223**
Theater industry, security for wage obligations in, **303**
Thomas v. Pearle Vision, **551**
Three-twelve (3/12) schedule, **379**
Tidewater, **279**